Saints on Stage

An Anthology of Mormon Drama

INTRODUCED AND EDITED BY

Mahonri Stewart

PROVO, UTAH

© 2013 by Mahonri Stewart. Individual plays included by permission of their copyright holders. For rights information, see page 658.

ISBN 978-0-9883233-1-5

Cover and interior design by Ben Crowder.

Printed in the U.S.A.

Published by:
Zarahemla Books
869 East 2680 North
Provo, UT 84604
info@zarahemlabooks.com
ZarahemlaBooks.com

Table of Contents

iv	*Acknowledgments*
vi	*Restoration in the Spotlight: An Introduction to Mormon Drama* Mahonri Stewart
1	*Fires of the Mind* Robert Elliott
57	*Huebener* Thomas F. Rogers
117	*J. Golden* James Arrington
153	*Burdens of Earth* Susan Elizabeth Howe
213	*Matters of the Heart* Thom Duncan
259	*Gadianton* Eric Samuelsen
341	*Hancock County* Tim Slover
411	*Stones* J. Scott Bronson
451	*Farewell to Eden* Mahonri Mackay Stewart
541	*Martyrs' Crossing* Melissa Leilani Larson
601	*I Am Jane* Margaret Blair Young
658	*Performance rights*

Acknowledgments

This project has taken the better half of a decade in getting published, so I have accumulated a number of debts of gratitude towards those who have helped this anthology on its way. First off, I must thank the publisher at Zarahemla Books, Chris Bigelow. He has believed in this project ever since I first pitched it to him, and he has stuck to it through delay after delay, complication after complication, obstacle after obstacle. I hope all of you feel as he and I do, that bringing the texts of these marvelous plays into a single volume (some of them published for the first time) was worth the toil and patience involved. It is due to Chris and his continued faith that this volume has been possible.

I'd also especially like to thank Lavina Fielding Anderson who, after my first several revisions and editing of the plays, was kind enough to go through and do the final edits of the text. Chris and I offered a co-editing credit to her, but she humbly deferred, feeling like I should hog all the glory. Without her, however, many a technical mistake would have been made, as I was only an English major rather briefly in college. Rather, I got my BA in Theatre and am getting my MFA in Dramatic Writing (the a-lot-less-technical skills of playwriting and screenwriting). So, my lack of technical fine tuning being what it is, Lavina's expert presence was vital in the finishing stages of this project and I warmly and willingly give a great deal of that credit directly to her. I thank her from the uttermost depths of my heart. Whether officially or unofficially, she has been an amazing co-editor on this project and I have appreciated every contribution she has made.

Ben Crowder, once again, has been on hand to do a magnificent layout. It's a skill I have come to value greatly the past several years, as Ben has been involved in a number of projects of mine and others' that I have greatly appreciated (including his brainchild the *Mormon Artist* magazine, which is one of the resources that is liberally quoted in the anthology's essays and commentaries). Ben also did some very useful proofreading of the text during the layout process, as well as taking an image that Chris Bigelow and I loved and implementing it into the beautiful cover design. I consider Ben a friend and a reliable craftsman who, once again, has done a great work in the name of Mormon Letters.

We had a number of proofreaders volunteer to help vet the text as well, and I would like to warmly thank all of them that I'm aware of: DeWayne Hafen, Shirley Johnson, Inari Porkka, Linda Shelton, Johnny Townsend, Beatrix Whitehall. I am so grateful to those who so charitably gave of their time and talents.

Then, of course, deep thanks goes to all the playwrights who allowed their work to be included in this historical collection.

My wife Anne Marie Stewart has been Wonder Woman throughout our marriage, and regarding this project she has been very patient with the time and continual effort it has required to sort out the various issues/complications to do it right. Once again she has been one of my best resources and a true helpmeet and friend.

One last special thanks goes to all the theatre companies, universities, etc. who first put on these plays. As Eric Samuelsen said, every Mormon Shakespeare needs a Mormon Globe. Without organizations like BYU, UVU, The Nauvoo Theatrical Society,

New Play Project, Zion Theatre Company, and every other theatre group willing to do Mormon drama, these plays would have never been performed and would still be sitting next to a dusty typewriter or in the aging databases of an outdated computer.

I'd like to dedicate this volume to James Arrington, who was the philosopher's stone that jump started my trajectory as dramatic writer over a decade ago. He changed the iron of desire into the gold of reality. That's the kind of alchemic transformation that has been truly a wonder to experience.

—Mahonri Stewart

Restoration in the Spotlight: An Introduction to Mormon Drama

Mahonri Stewart

"Upon the Stage of a Theater": A Historical Support

In the religious planting ground of nineteenth-century America, theatre was generally seen as a noxious weed. Religious leaders two centuries ago often condemned theatre as a house of vice, a place of libertines and moral outcasts. However, from the outset, The Church of Jesus Christ of Latter-day Saints, popularly known as the Mormons, cultivated theatre as part of its religious and artistic heritage. In one of nineteenth-century Mormonism's most prominent gathering places, Nauvoo, Illinois, theatre was encouraged by the church's Prophet and founder, Joseph Smith Jr. In fact, the anti-Mormon newspaper *The Nauvoo Expositor* brought up this tolerance and enjoyment of the theatre as one of its many grievances against the prophet: "We discountenance and disapprobate the houses of reveling and dancing; dram shops and theaters; verily believing they have a tendency to lead from paths of virtue and holiness, to those of vice and debauchery."[1]

The encouragement of theatre in Mormonism received an additional boost when professional actor Thomas Lyne was converted in Philadelphia and moved to Nauvoo to produce a handful of plays there. The city's Masonic Lodge hosted plays, among other social events and amusements. One such play was Richard Brinsley Sheridan's *Pizarro*. Thomas Lyne and George Adams were both active in directing the play, in which prominent Church leaders performed as actors. Future Church president Brigham Young played the role of the Incan high priest.[2] Helen Mar Kimball Whitney (who was a plural wife of Joseph Smith and whose husband Horace Whitney would later become an actor in Utah) said of *Pizarro* and other Nauvoo productions:

> [George Adams] was a very good actor, and J. Hatch, a young lawyer . . . was also good as well as Amasa Lyman and W. H. Folsom and others. But no part in "Pizarro" was better played than was the priest by Brigham Young. There was some good acting done—some so life-like that at times nearly the whole audience would be affected to tears. Joseph [Smith] did not try to hide his feelings, but was seen to weep a number of times. Among our best comedians was Hiram B. Clawson, who I think was the youngest of the boys.

---

1   "Resolutions," *Nauvoo Expositor* 1, no. 1 (June 7, 1844): 2.
2   Ronald W. Walker and D. Michael Quinn, "'Virtuous, Lovely or of Good Report': How the Church Has Fostered the Arts," *Ensign*, July 1977, 81.

That was forty years ago, and the scenes have been changing until but few are now left who took part in the first dramatic entertainments held in our beautiful city.³

Whitney also mentions a time when George Adams's wife, whom Whitney described as "quite a distinguished looking woman" who "made a fine appearance on stage," was cast as the countess in a production of *The Orphan of Geneva* at the Masonic Hall. However, when Adams discovered that she was actually recognized despite all the costumes and makeup, she was mortified. Adams consequently dropped the show after the first performance, and someone had to be found to replace her. Helen Mar Whitney continued:

> I was just at the age to enjoy such amusements, which made time pass very agreeably . . . [Adams or Lyne] proposed my taking the part . . . and the women and all set in flattering and teasing me to take it. But I was a timid girl of fifteen and frightfully bashful, and the idea of taking so dignified a part was to my mind utterly absurd, having only been upon the stage in two plays, first as one of the virgins in "Pizarro," and another simple part, but all my excuses were useless and I was fairly pressed into service.
>
> Adams said encouragingly, "I'll help you out," and as Lyne was leaving he said, "Now study the part over good tonight and then retire and sleep on it, and you'll nearly know it in the morning," which direction I followed, and having a quick memory was able to repeat every word at the rehearsal, but when before an audience I was so frightened that I remembered very little. My wits nearly deserted me, but Adams was true to his promise and by his readiness assisted me to recover from my confusion. Though he was never up in his own part, he was never at a loss for a substitute in every emergency, but which was anything but pleasing to those who depended upon him for their cue.⁴

After Joseph Smith's martyrdom and the Latter-day Saint migration to Utah, Brigham Young continued to encourage theatre among the Saints, even when other competing factions of Mormonism discouraged it, such as the later group called the Reorganized Church of Jesus Christ of Latter Day Saints (now Community of Christ). Joseph Smith's youngest son, David Hyrum Smith, once sneaked into a theater and hid in the balcony. He was afraid that his brother, RLDS Church President Joseph Smith III, would disapprove,⁵ which illustrates how effectively religious climates discouraged theatrical participation.

---

3 Helen Mar Kimball Whitney, "Life Incidents," *http://www.boap.org/LDS/Early-Saints/HWhitney.html* (accessed May 10, 2012).
4 Ibid.
5 Valeen Tippetts Avery, *From Mission to Madness: Last Son of the Mormon Prophet* (Urbana: University of Illinois Press, 1998), 154–55.

Brigham Young, however, instead of seeing a place of debauchery and vice, saw theatre as a possibility to express the gospel, conjure the Spirit of God, and build up the kingdom of God. At the dedication of the Salt Lake Theater, Young said:

> [There are Christians] who are against all amusements because of the evils attendant at public places. Now it is for the saints to neither follow the traditions of the one, nor fall into the errors of the other.... Upon the stage of a theater can be represented in character, evil and its consequences, good and its happy results and rewards; the weakness and the follies of man, the magnanimity of virtue and the greatness of truth. The stage can be made to aid the pulpit in impressing upon the minds of a community an enlightened sense of a virtuous life, also a proper horror of the enormity of sin and a just dread of its consequences. The path of sin with its thorns and pitfalls, its gins and snares can be revealed, and how to shun it.... [T]he Lord understands the good and the evil. Why should not we likewise understand them? We should. Why? To know how to choose the good and refuse the evil; which we cannot do unless we understand the evil as well as the good.[6]

Beyond its ability to teach, Young considered that the theatre also had a certain civilizing effect. He once stated that if placed upon a cannibal island in charge of civilizing its inhabitants, he would construct a theater.[7] This clear support from Church leaders bore some good fruit for the Saints as they slowly developed a solid reputation for drama.

Within the first week of the Mormons' arrival in Utah in 1847, Young had members of the Mormon Battalion construct a bowery for a place of worship and social gatherings. A second bowery was constructed the following spring and then a third in 1849. This third bowery, the most roomy and comfortable, was the place of genesis of theatre in the American desert. It was this structure that housed the first performance of a play in Utah and was the first home of the Deseret Musical and Dramatic Society.[8]

The Deseret Musical and Dramatic Society was organized on October 6, 1849, under Brigham Young's direction. Because of its distance from any other major town or city in the East, the society experienced difficulties in obtaining playbooks and paper for copying, much less material for costumes and sets. Some of the society's first theatrical performances in 1850 included *Robert Macaire, or the Two Murderers*, some dancing, and a farce called *Dead Shot*.[9] The society went on to produce a number of

---

6   Ila Fisher Maughan, *Pioneer Theatre in the Desert* (Salt Lake City: Deseret Book, 1961), 84; and Leonard J. Arrington, *Brigham Young: American Moses* (Urbana: University of Illinois Press, by arrangement with Alfred A. Knopf, 1985), 289.
7   Walker and Quinn, "'Virtuous, Lovely or of Good Report,'" 81.
8   Maughan, *Pioneer Theatre in the Desert*, 12, 16–17. See also Arrington, *Brigham Young*, 288.
9   Ann W. Engar, "Theater in Utah," *Utah History to Go*, historytogo.utah.gov/utah_chapters/utah_today/theaterinutah.html (accessed December 8, 2011); also see Edward W. Tullidge,

popular plays of its day, including *The Triumph of Innocence, The Stranger, Don Caesar de Bazan,* and *Hector Timid*.[10]

In 1851 Brigham Young instructed William Clayton[11] to organize a more theatre-specific organization to replace the Deseret Musical and Dramatic Society. On February 20, 1852, the Deseret Dramatic Association was formed. As its first offerings, the association produced two plays that were already in the Saints' repertoire: a play called *Money* and a revival of the first Mormon theatrical success story, William Sheridan's *Pizarro*. The association subsequently produced a steady stream of plays, ranging from Shakespeare's *Othello* to popular farces.

Although plans were made to create a fourth bowery, Brigham Young decided that the popularity and beneficial elements of the theater and other social/artistic activities in Utah were sufficient to construct a building solely dedicated to such purposes. Thus the Social Hall was constructed, and the building was inaugurated on New Year's Day, 1853. The Social Hall was designed by Church architect Truman O. Angell, who, incidentally, was also the architect for the Salt Lake Temple. The very man who conceived the Mormons' most holy building was used also to create a second place of enacted ritual. The Social Hall was the first official theater in the western United States.

About the Social Hall and the Deseret Dramatic Association, the *Deseret News* wrote: "We have often heard the performances and scenery highly spoken of, and gentlemen who have been accustomed to theatricals in Europe and America say they have seldom seen our stage equaled in any country; and this is more surprising as all our actors procure their living by constant daily labor, while their evening labor is for amusement rather than lucrative income."[12]

The contention between the Saints and the U.S. government, which has now come to be known as the Utah War (1857–58), slowed the progress of theatre in Utah for a number of years. Yet Mormon drama came back strongly with the establishment of a more intimate, privately run theater called the Bowring Theater, whose first performance was attended by Utah's most loyal theatrical patron, Brigham Young. Soon other community theaters and groups started to spread throughout Mormon settlements.

However, it was the dedication of the Salt Lake Theater on March 8, 1862, that became the next big benchmark in Mormon drama. The Mormon temple endowment was originally delivered via a theatrical enactment of scriptural stories and principles. These days, it is a film presentation, except in a couple of temples, such as the Salt Lake Temple, that continue the theatrical medium. Thus, in its own way, the temple ceremony itself can be considered a part of the Mormon theatrical tradition. This fact is

---

"Dramatic Reminisces: With Biographical Sketches of Our Actors," *Tullidge's Quarterly Magazine* 2 (April 1882): 567. Tullidge records the actors in *Robert Macaire* as John Kay, Hiram B. Clawson, Phillip Margetts, Miss Orum, and M. Judd.

10 Maughan, *Pioneer Theatre in the Desert*, 19.
11 Clayton is most famous for penning the words to "Come, Come, Ye Saints," one of the LDS Church's most beloved and poignant hymns.
12 Maughan, *Pioneer Theater in the Desert*, 34.

significant considering that Western theatre had its roots in religious rituals and festivals. Just as the classics of Greek drama cannot be separated from their connection to the religious observation of the Festival of Dionysus, so is it impossible to divorce Mormon drama from its theatrically religious environment. One can easily see why a people who were comfortable delivering divine truths through a theatrical medium had no difficulty in continuing that exploration upon the stage of a community's theater.

Ironically, it was the occupation of the U. S. Army in Utah that provided the Mormons with the capital to build the Salt Lake Theater. Maintaining an army so far from the eastern states was an expensive enterprise for the U. S. government, and the Saints reaped the rewards by providing the army with their necessities. When the army had to leave hastily at the onset of the Civil War, Brigham Young shrewdly instructed Hiram B. Clawson to buy up the materials that the army was selling at ridiculously low prices due to the speed with which they needed to leave. Brigham Young would later say, "Thank God for the United States Army. I made $200,000 from them."[13] The army that had come to crush the Saints ended up enriching them.

With some of these funds, the Salt Lake Theater was built. Designed by the new LDS Church architect William H. Folsom and consciously modeled after the Drury Lane Theater in London, it could accommodate 7,500 people. It had a parquet, a dress circle, and three balconies. By far the most ambitious theatrical building in the West, it was also one of the largest buildings in Utah at the time.[14] Author, journalist, and explorer Fitz Hugh Ludlow was greatly impressed with the Salt Lake Theater:

> I was greatly astonished to find in the desert heart of the Continent a place of public amusement which, regarding comfort, capacity, and beauty, has but two or three superiors in the United States.... My greatest surprise was excited by the remarkable artistic beauty of the gilt and painted decorations of the great arch over the stage, the cornices, and the moulding about the proscenium boxes. President Young assured me that every particle was done by indigenous and Saintly hands.
>
> "But you don't know yet," he added, "how independent we are of you at the East. Where do you think we got that chandelier, and how d'ye suppose we paid for it?"
>
> It was a piece of work that would have been creditable to any New York firm, apparently a richly carven circle, twined with gilt vines, leaves and tendrils, blossoming all over with flaming wax lights, and suspended by a massive chain of golden lustre. So I replied that he probably paid a thousand dollars for it in New York. "Capital!" exclaimed Brigham; "I made it myself! That circle is . . . the wheel of one of our common Utah ox-carts. I had it waxed and gilded it with my own hands. It hangs by a pair of ox chains which I also gilded; and the gilt ornaments of the candlesticks were cut after my patterns of sheet tin.[15]

---

13   Ibid., 76–77.
14   Ibid., 76; Arrington, *Brigham Young*, 288.
15   Arrington, *Brigham Young*, 288.

One non-Mormon theater manager wrote of the state of theatre in Salt Lake in nearly ecstatic tones: "Sweeping as the statement may seem, I do not believe the theatre has ever rested upon a higher plane, both as to its purpose and its offerings, than at Salt Lake City, the capital of Mormondom."[16] The Salt Lake Theater was the first, and often hailed as the best, professional playhouse west of the Mississippi.

Although Young has been recorded as criticizing "tragedy" in drama, Mormon historian Leonard Arrington postulated that by this he meant graphic violence rather than tragedy in the classical sense. Young had often censored violence from plays, including Nancy's brutal murder in an adaptation of Charles Dickens's *Oliver Twist* and a graphic hanging in a play called *Neck and Neck*.

However, Shakespearean tragedies were often performed in Brigham Young's theater. In fact, "Brother Brigham" had a discerning taste in theatre, including his robust appreciation for the Bard:

> During the years Brigham was the producer, really the manager-producer, the theater ran old and new plays. Brigham's favorites were said to have been *The Lady of Lyons*, a romantic comedy by Edward Bulwer-Lytton; *The School for Scandal*, by Richard Sheridan; and Shakespeare and Boucicault. During Brigham's life, the theater produced *Hamlet* nineteen times; *Macbeth*, eighteen; *Richard III*, fourteen; *Romeo and Juliet*, fourteen; *Othello*, ten; *Merchant of Venice*, nine; and many others. Brigham also produced two plays by [local Mormon playwright] Edward Tullidge and three by local writer Edward L. Sloan. And he instructed missionaries in English-speaking nations to be on the alert to purchase playbooks for acceptable productions.[17]

It is encouraging that both of Mormonism's most towering figures, Joseph Smith and Brigham Young, were enthusiastic supporters of the dramatic arts in Mormonism. Brigham Young, especially, was the vital force behind nearly every major theatrical development in early Mormonism, from his heralded performance in *Pizarro*; to his financial, organizational, and moral support of Utah's early theaters; to encouraging his own family, including ten daughters and son-in-law Hiram B. Clawson, in participating in the theatrical arts as actresses and a theater manager.[18] Brigham Young was an incredibly visible figure proclaiming to the Saints that they had nothing to fear from the dramatic arts, if the Saints kept their hearts clean and were pure vessels in their dramatic performances.

Although much of the nineteenth century's religious culture condemned the theatre as a haven for vice, Young took an opposing view. He sealed together theatre and religion, so that prayers could be offered before comedies and Shakespeare could be housed in a church. As a result, support for the dramatic arts rained down upon the

---

16   Walker and Quinn, "'Virtuous, Lovely or of Good Report,'" 85.
17   Arrington, *Brigham Young*, 293.
18   Engar, "Theater in Utah."

rank and file of the Latter-day Saints, many of whom went on to create their own community groups and productions.

This encouraging attitude toward theatre allowed future apostles like Orson F. Whitney to dream, as a young man, of moving to New York to pursue his acting interests. Although he eventually chose a different route and stayed in Salt Lake City, he never abandoned his literary and theatrical tastes. It also allowed the inclusion of luminous LDS figures like Brigham Young and Helen Mar Kimball Whitney to be numbered among the cast lists on the playbills. An environment was cultivated where Mormons would not only be able to invite the larger theatrical world among themselves, but in which eventually the Saints would develop their own distinctive Mormon voices to create a distinct branch of drama. Never content to be only actors in another person's play, the Mormons would eventually become creators themselves.

"If We Strive for Perfection": Nineteenth-Century Pioneers in Mormon Playwriting

Even most Mormon dramatists are not aware that there were LDS playwrights as far back as the nineteenth century. Ranging from staunch Mormon apostles to disaffected cultural Mormons, the early breadth of Mormon dramatists had a surprising variety compared to what has been previously mentioned in many Mormon dramatic histories.

One of the first theatrical segments written by a Mormon was authored by the Parley P. Pratt, one of the original Quorum of the Twelve Apostles, an early and popular figure in Mormon cultural history. The fact has been much neglected that Pratt authored one of the first Mormon plays, *The Mormon Prisoners*. This play was recently rediscovered by Mormon literary commentator and publisher Kent S. Larsen II, and it is a jewel of a historical find.[19] Although the play was unfinished,[20] the short work is very significant to Mormon theatrical history. Not only is *The Mormon Prisoners* perhaps the first play to be written *by* a Mormon playwright, but it is also perhaps the first play to be written *about* the Mormon experience, using Mormon characters to tell a Mormon story. This alone makes it a significant piece of Mormon history.

The Mormon Prisoners draws from Pratt's own experiences as a prisoner in Missouri after the depredations against the Mormons following Governor Lilburn Boggs's infamous extermination order. The play begins with a satirical scene between a Missouri judge and a lawyer, their dialogue highlighting the Missouri justice system's hypocrisies. Then follows a scene showing the Mormon prisoners (including Pratt and Joseph Smith) in a dungeon, enduring their foul-mouthed guards' boasts of murdering,

---

19   I am very much in debt to Kent S. Larsen II for this very important piece of information, as I was not aware of it previously, nor have I encountered any references to it in any of my research. Larsen plans to publish this important text in the relatively near future.

20   The text of the play finishes with "End Act 1st," thus implying further acts.

looting, and raping their Mormon victims. Joseph subsequently stands and rebukes the guards, a scene made famous by Pratt's recording it in his autobiography.[21] The first act ends with another scene showing the prisoners on trial, once again dramatizing the illegal injustices heaped upon the Mormons during the Missouri persecutions.

Although the play contains the kind of hyperbole and overt agenda one might expect from a nineteenth-century Mormon text, *The Mormon Prisoners* has some surprising complexities and shows a certain sophistication and skill. Pratt weaves the interaction of the characters with the biting satire typical of his other literary work. The exaggeration is intentional, with Pratt emphasizing the tragic ridiculousness of their situation. The dialogue that Pratt uses for the prison guards reflects an authentic kind of syntax, colloquialism, and accent, all of which indicates a Twain-like ear for patterns of speech.

Pratt also doesn't downplay the portrayal of the unpleasant. His guards swear, are crude, and are surprisingly graphic for Pratt's time. In the prison scene, the guards boast of their murders and rapes. Rather than adhering to polite etiquette and sensitive censorship, this Mormon apostle put into practice what Brigham Young preached about representing evil in theatre. Pratt does not shy away from representing "evil and its consequences."

But perhaps what is most notable about *The Mormon Prisoners* is that Parley Pratt is not merely writing detached historical fiction. Rather he is writing from *memory*. It is a Mormon historical play written by one of Mormon history's early participants. The playwright is also one of the characters. This melding of playwriting and Mormon historical autobiography is a startling but fascinating combination.

The Mormon Prisoners also puts four of Pratt's other creative works into a different light. Pratt's "A Dialogue between Joseph Smith and the Devil" and the mostly unknown "Heaven: A Dialogue," "A Dialogue between a Latter-day Saint and an Enquirer After Truth," and "A Dialogue between Tradition, Reason and Scripture" are not written like prose or short stories. They are written like plays, complete with character indications, action lines, theatrical dialogue, and even exits/entrances.

Considering how they are written, it is entirely plausible that these short works were written to be performed rather than just read. This theatrical formatting of the "dialogues" makes Pratt's contribution to Mormon drama wider than just his incomplete *The Mormon Prisoners*. It is likely that these works can be considered the first Mormon-themed plays. And since they were written before Mormonism's other early plays, it appears that Parley P. Pratt is Mormonism's first playwright.

But Pratt was not alone in being a nineteenth-century Mormon playwright. Edward Tullidge, whose historical dramas earned him considerable praise from his contemporaries, is a significant early Mormon playwright in his own right. In addition to being a playwright, Tullidge was a man of letters and arts—a historian, biographer,

---

21 Parley P. Pratt, *Autobiography of Parley Parker Pratt, One of the Twelve Apostles of the Church of Jesus Christ of Latter-day Saints*, edited by Parley P. Pratt Jr., 1874; (Salt Lake City: Deseret Book, 1975), 179–80.

scholar, editor, writer, journalist, theater critic, and publisher. It is in large part due to Tullidge that we know as much as we do about the early days of the Social Hall and early Mormon drama.[22]

Tullidge was a British convert who joined the LDS Church and immigrated to Utah. Once in Utah, he was a shoemaker by trade, but a man of arts and letters in his heart. However, Tullidge's faithfulness to Mormonism was in constant flux. He at times joined in atheistic (and later deistic) musings; followed the Godbeite rebellion against Brigham Young's economic strictures in the 1860s, advocating a pro-capitalist position against the communal path that the United Order represented. At one point in the 1870s, Tullidge even joined the RLDS Church, headed by Joseph Smith III and headquartered in the Midwest—only to travel back to Utah again at the end of his life. It is difficult to gauge what his personal beliefs about the official LDS Church had become at that point. However, in those twilight years, at the very least he considered himself a cultural Mormon and maintained his belief in the Joseph Smith story and his high regard for Brigham Young, about both of whom he had written successful biographies.[23]

In 1865 Tullidge wrote *Eleanor DeVere* specifically for the celebrated actress Julia Dean.[24] Dean was a professional actress who, at the age of sixteen, became a sensation in New York and then went west to perform in California, then in Oregon and Idaho. She eventually ended up in Utah.[25] Pleased by the love, respect, and attention she received from the Mormons, as well as impressed with the state of theatre in Utah, Dean decided to remain in Utah for a time.

After completing her agreement with Potter's stock company, she signed on with Brigham Young's Salt Lake Theater and the Deseret Dramatic Association in 1865.[26] She was a much-loved figure among the Mormons for many years, and she loved them in

---

22 Maughan, *Pioneer Theatre in the Desert*, 141.
23 For an excellent overview of Tullidge's life, see Ronald W. Walker's "Edward Tullidge: Historian of the Mormon Commonwealth," *Journal of Mormon History* 3 (1976): 55–72.
24 Julia Dean married Arthur Hayne, but the two divorced in 1865, due to his drunkenness, cruelty, and physical abuse. The strict laws in the United States would not have allowed this divorce; but the Territory of Utah had much more flexible divorce laws. Thus, Utah became the site of this "celebrity" divorce. Julia Dean Hayne Papers, *http://db3-sql.staff.library.utah.edu/lucene/Manuscripts/null/Ms0293.xml/complete* (accessed December 17, 2011).
25 By a twist of fate, when Julia Dean was touring as part of John S. Potter's stock company from British Columbia into Oregon and then Idaho, the stock company's seasonal contract with the new Forrest Theatre in Idaho City encountered a sudden complication when the theater burned down. Thus, Potter thought to bring his group to Utah, where he knew the Salt Lake Theater was thriving. See Maughan, *Pioneer Theatre in the Desert*, 130.
26 The San Francisco *Golden Era* said: "At President Young's great Salt Lake Theater Mrs. Julia Dean Hayne has created the greatest dramatic sensation ever known in the city of the saints. The immense theater is filled to overflowing every night.... Mrs. Hayne is today the finest actress on the American or English stage and the people and the press of Utah's capital honor themselves in honoring her." *Ibid.*, 131. For a more detailed treatment of Dean's story, see Maughan's *Pioneer Theatre in the Desert*, chap. 20.

return, with specific praise for the kindness and courtesies of Brigham Young.[27] *Eleanor DeVere* added to Tullidge's and Dean's reputations and was a great success at the Salt Lake Theater.

Eleanor DeVere was a historical piece that dealt with the house of the Earls of Oxford in the Elizabethan era of England:

> One scene set in the chapel of the DeVere estate was midnight mass for Count Phillip Devere lying there in state surrounded by family, servants, Lords and Ladies of the Court, guards, novitiate nuns, and a group of choral voices in the background. It was tenderly and reverently done and as legitimately as though an artist had painted it. Thomas A. Lyne declared the play to be a great drama and likened the midnight mass to the musical scene in *Pizarro*, declaring it to be fully as well done.[28]

Impressed with Tullidge's writing, as well as with his grasp of British history, Dean commissioned Tullidge to write another play for her in which she would star as Queen Elizabeth. Tullidge fulfilled the commission, completing *Elizabeth of England*, and Thomas Lyne once again called Tullidge's script "a truly great play."[29]

Dean had high hopes of performing the play in New York. However, an Italian actress had performed a similar play about Queen Elizabeth in Europe, and it was brought to America, where it became very successful. So, the dream of a Mormon playwright's first foray into Broadway theaters, headlined by a famous actress, was disappointingly left unaccomplished in the nineteenth century.[30]

However, this setback did not end Tullidge's playwriting. Tullidge went on to write several other historical plays, some of which were published. He subsequently wrote *Oliver Cromwell*; *Ben Israel: Or, From under the Curse*; and *Napoleon*. Tullidge also wrote many influential historical books and biographies. Tullidge had a keen interest in history and this fascination extended to the epic heroes of history and influential elites.[31] Tullidge wanted to be the writer of "great" men and planned his dramas with an epic sweep.

---

27 In a farewell speech given at her last performance after the curtain, Julia Dean said: "To President Brigham Young for many courtesies to a stranger alone and unprotected, I return thanks which are hallowed by their earnestness. I trust that he will permit me in the name of my art to speak my high appreciation of the order and beauty that reigns throughout this house. I would that the same purity prevailed in every temple of the drama's teachings. Then, indeed, the grand object would be achieved, and it would become a school, 'To wake the soul by tender strokes of art, To raise the genius, and to mend the heart.'" Ibid., 135.

28 Ibid., 134–35.

29 Ibid., 135.

30 Ibid.

31 Walker, "Edward Tullidge," 68.

In addition to Pratt and Tullidge, another early pioneer playwright was Edward Sloan, who wrote several farces, including *Advertising for a Wife* and *The Indescribable*. A third play was the "intensely sensational melodrama," *Nick of the Wood*. Less well known but of the same period is J. S. Lindsay, who wrote and starred in *The Rath Boys of Kilkenny*.[32]

Despite these promising beginnings in Mormon playwriting, Parley P. Pratt seems to have been the only one among these early Mormon playwrights to attempt to create a play dealing specifically with the Mormon experience. Except for Pratt's work, there were no other plays detailing the dramatic stories of Joseph Smith. Brigham Young, Emma Smith, and Eliza R. Snow were not honored in dramatic form during the nineteenth century. There were no plays based on Mormon scripture. There were no comedies or dramas that dealt with the day-to-day lives of rank-and-file Latter-day Saints. After Pratt's *The Mormon Prisoners*, it would not be until almost the twentieth century that such Mormon-centric plays would appear again.

Mentions of two plays in the late nineteenth century that count as among the earliest in Mormon drama have been rediscovered by Kent Larsen. In 1886 George A. Hicks wrote a five-act play called *Celestial Marriage*. In 1897 there was a week of performances of a play (without a known title) about the life of Joseph Smith. Neither of these plays has survived in its written form, but the *Salt Lake Herald* commented on the play about Joseph Smith[33]:

> A curious gathering which filled about one-half of the Lyceum auditorium came out to see what sort of a play the author had succeeded in making out of the life of Joseph Smith. Probably there was more surprise than anything else felt after it was all over, for despite the great length of piece, its decided preachiness and some ludicrous mishaps, one in the first representation and the smallness of the stage, there was still a great deal in the play to commend and to entitle it to a respectful hearing. It is written entirely from the Mormon standpoint and Joseph Smith, who is on the stage almost constantly, is little short of deified, while all who oppose him are made vipers and fiends of a description that caused the shudders to run down the auditors' backs.
>
> The play is nothing but a series of the dramatic episodes of the Mormon prophet's career; the prologue shows his visit from the angel Moroni; the next act shows him in the hands of a mob which starts to tar and feather him, heaven's lightning interposes and baffles them; the next shows him as a

---

32   Maughan, *Pioneer Theatre in the Desert*, 142.
33   Kent Larsen, "Another Early Mormon Drama," *A Motley Vision*, http://www.motleyvision.org/2011/another-early-mormon-drama/ (accessed October 30, 2012). Kent Larsen has truly been a fountain of information when it comes to discovering obscure references to Mormon literature and drama. In addition to his discovery of Parley P. Pratt's *The Mormon Prisoners*, Larsen has done valuable work in unearthing and documenting hidden manifestations of Mormon literature.

general, and in an act too long, the actor delivers almost verbatim the celebrated speech Joseph Smith rendered just before his assassination; the last act shows the death of the two brothers and the wounding of John Taylor.

The play is set in heroic, almost grandiloquent cast, and the actors rendered it in a style tragic to a degree. Many of the sentiments, and much of language, was undeniably striking, and the actors were all above the average seen in cheap houses.... We shall not be surprised if the play attracts a great deal of curious attention before the week is out.[34]

Beyond these two lost works, another Mormon play surfaced more famously at the turn of the century. In 1902, the Salt Lake Theater premiered *Corianton*, authored by Orestes Utah Bean. Based on the Book of Mormon character Corianton, son of Alma the Younger—and plagiarized shamelessly from two novels by B. H. Roberts—the play was a success among Mormon audiences and even had a short New York run, where it was derided by critics. Nevertheless, the ever-confident Bean went on to produce a feature-film version of the story. A copy of the film, once thought lost, has been rediscovered. It is now in safekeeping in the Harold B. Lee Library at Brigham Young University and has had received subsequent screenings.[35]

Then followed another significant gap. The next major Mormon play did not appear until 1947 when the LDS Church commissioned the play *Promised Valley*, as a part of the centennial celebrating the Mormon trek to the West. Written by non-Mormon Broadway playwright Arnold Sundgaard, with music by Mormon composer Crawford Gates, the play follows the story of a Mormon married couple, Jed and Celia, and the epic journey west to their Rocky Mountain home in Utah.[36]

In the 1960s, Mormon poet and BYU professor Clinton F. Larson contributed a number of historically and scripturally themed dramas, including *The Mantle of the Prophet*, *Coriantumr and Moroni*, *The Brother of Jared*, *Mary of Nazareth*, *Saul of Tarsus*, and *Third Nephi*.

Yet, despite these important contributions from various pioneers in Mormon drama, it was not until the 1970s that Mormon drama could truly be considered a substantial movement and a genre within its own right. But by then the trail had been blazed so that a more modern era of Mormon drama could follow.

---

34 Ibid.

35 See Ardis E. Parshall, "Corianton, Genealogy of a Mormon Phenomenon," Times and Seasons, June 8, 2007, *http://timesandseasons.org/index.php/2007/06/corianton-genealogy-of-a-mormon-phenomenon/* (accessed May 9, 2012).

36 *http://www.simivalleystake.org/promisedvalley/synopsis.htm* (accessed May 9, 2012).

"Shakespeares of Our Own":
The Modern Mormon Playwrights

The support of Brigham Young University's theatre program was crucial in the development of Mormon drama as a genre. It owes much to the mentorship and direction provided by Charles Whitman and Max Golightly, whom many playwrights from that period still proudly credit as their literary parents. Under their encouragement and sponsorship, a number of plays were produced that have since become classics in Mormon drama. Martin Kelly's *They Shall Be Gathered,* Robert Elliott's *Fires of the Mind,* Orson Scott Card's *The Apostate* (about Alma the Younger from the Book of Mormon), Card's comedy *Across Five Summers,* and Thomas F. Rogers's *Huebener* were all plays produced at BYU by student playwrights or faculty during this period. They were complex dramas, skillfully written, and focused on realistic characters. They were also plays where conflict in its extremes could be played out, without resorting to trite sentimentalism or didacticism, while never disparaging the divine gospel of Jesus Christ. BYU's Margetts Experimental Theater in the basement of the Harris Fine Arts Center was a setting in which Mormon drama was finally coming of age.

And although the likes of Rogers, Kelly, and Elliott ended up being the heavy hitters for this period, artistically speaking, other talented Mormon playwrights made themselves known. Charles Whitman chose *No Greater Crown* by Martin C. Malder as the first original play performed by BYU. Thom Duncan had two plays produced at BYU early in the decade: *A Sword, A Scepter, and a Scented Rose* (a Book of Mormon play about King Lamoni and Ammon produced in 1972) and *Prophet* (a musical about Joseph Smith, with music by Jerry Jackman, 1973). There was also Ed Walker's *The Dove* (1974); Beverly Warner's *Shepherd of the Lord* (1973, a New Testament play about Peter); Louise Hanson's *Tragedy of Korihor* and *Covenant in Gold*[37]; Robert Stoddard's *Giraffe Story;* Gerald Pearson's *The Naked Veil;* and Fran Smeath's Nauvoo-era *The Returning.*[38]

Just as significant as the volume and quality of straight dramas cropping up during this period was another phenomenon: the Mormon musical. Orson Scott Card (who would later become a science-fiction author and one of Mormonism's most famous writers) premiered his plays *Father, Mother, Mother, and Mom,* dealing with the subject of Mormon polygamy; *Stone Tables,* based on the biblical tale of Moses; and *Liberty Jail,* based on Joseph Smith's imprisonment in Missouri, all of which became successful, influential, and well-respected additions to the Mormon musical. Poet and playwright Carol Lynn Pearson was making a name for herself with her musicals *The*

---

37 Orson Scott Card categorized these plays as belonging to the tradition of "miracle" and "hero" plays, an important analysis of Mormon drama up to that time. Frederick Bliss and P. Q. Gump (pseud. of Card), "Mormon Shakespeares: A Study of Contemporary Mormon Theatre," *Sunstone Magazine,* Issue No. 2, Spring 1976.

38 For information on some of these more obscure plays, I am indebted once again to Card, "Mormon Shakespeares: A Study of Contemporary Mormon Theatre."

Order Is Love (with music by Lex De Azevedo), *The Dance*,[39] and the popular theatrical presentation of the plan of salvation in *My Turn on Earth*. Another contribution of the 1970s was *Brigham,* by Arnold Sungaard and Newell Dayley, a celebratory musical about Brigham Young. In the same vein as *Brigham* was the musical *A Right Honorable Saint*, about Karl G. Maeser. *Nineveh* was a musical by Connie Walker and R. C. Christiansen. And, of course, as previously mentioned, there was Thom Duncan's musical about Joseph Smith, *Prophet*.

However, the most popular and best-known musical in this period (and probably the best-known piece of Mormon theatre, period) was Doug Stewart's *Saturday's Warrior*. Its pro-family message against the "zero population" philosophy, its speculative theology, building upon the Mormon doctrine of the preexistence, combined with seventies pop ballads by Lex De Azevedo, resonated strongly with Mormon audiences.

Before writing *Saturday's Warrior*, Stewart was a senior at BYU when Charles Whitman encouraged him to take his playwriting class. Stewart had not considered himself to be a playwright and almost quit the class when he discovered they were supposed to write a *full-length* play. In the class, Stewart wrote his Book of Mormon musical about Jesus Christ's visit to the Americas *A Day, A Night, and a Day*, which played to full houses and several extensions. Stewart then went to work as a screenwriter for the LDS Church's Motion Picture Studio until penning *Saturday's Warrior*.[40]

The subsequent success of *Saturday's Warrior* was first performed as a class project at BYU in 1973. Its subsequent success is now is now legendary to Mormons who lived during that period. Enthusiastic sell-out audiences in California and Utah and subsequent touring groups (not to mention a version on video made in the 1980s), made the play a phenomenon unlike any of its predecessors. Although many Mormon plays have been highly successful during their runs, few have ever approached *Saturday's Warrior* "event" status and lasting influence.

In part because of this popularity, *Saturday's Warrior* was a worry to some Mormon dramatists. Despite the show's unexpected success, some have expressed concern about the play's effect on (and reflection of) Mormon culture. There were also those who saw its popularity as a problem—as theatre it didn't match up to the more sophisticated version of Mormon drama they would have liked to see. One of Stewart's mentors even took him aside and harshly criticized the work to his face. This experience left an unfortunate cloud on the new playwright's confidence but he was determined to produce more work that he felt would be spiritually uplifting and that was overwhelmingly supported by his surrounding community.[41]

---

39 This play was remade as a non-musical film, also titled *The Dance*. I attended a showing of the film at the 2007 LDS Film Festival, at which the director, McKay Daines, quoted Pearson as saying that she thought that the film didn't resemble her play a great deal.

40 Cori and Doug Connors, "Doug Stewart and Mary: A Tribute to Doug Stewart," Mormon Artist's Foundation Website, October 2011.

41 Comments by Doug Stewart in his keynote address at the April 2006 Mormon Artists' Foundation Retreat at the Little America Hotel, at which I was present. Notes in my possession.

This critical attitude against Stewart's play by academics could be seen as a kind of theatrical elitism which is out of touch with the more populist sensibilities of its community—and is, perhaps, tinged with a degree of jealousy. Or it can be seen as a valid concern for the welfare and quality of Mormon drama. Whatever the case may be, *Saturday's Warrior* showed that a Mormon theatrical endeavor could be successful—highly successful—if it spoke to its target audience in a way that they could relate. Orson Scott Card perhaps said it best:

> *Saturday's Warrior*'s contribution to Mormon theatre is not so much artistic as commercial. Stewart and D'Azevedo produced a slick, tight work that reached Mormons who had never known that a play could make them laugh and cry and feel wonderful about being Mormons. While literary writers screamed "foul," Stewart brought hundreds of thousands of people into theaters in Utah Valley, Salt Lake City, Los Angeles, and elsewhere. Most of them had never been to a live play before. People who are not ready for the intense realism of Elliot or Card, or who are bored by Kelly's gentle writing, have been introduced to Mormon theatre through *Saturday's Warrior*, and the literati who complain about it may eventually benefit as much as Stewart. . . .
>
> No Broadway show in Utah has ever made so much money, and the lessons are clear; a large Mormon audience does exist, and there is a paying market for strictly Mormon entertainment. It would be unfortunate if . . . writers . . . let sour grapes keep them from writing for the largest theater audience in Utah; for as long as that audience sees no better, they will remain content with milk and never get the meat.[42]

Mormon drama owes a great debt to Doug Stewart, who went onto to produce several more musicals, including *Star Child*, *Threads of Glory*, *Almost Perfect*, and *White Star*.

Saturday's Warrior drew a line in the sand for many Mormon artists, making them feel that there were two kinds of Mormon drama—either sentimental, populist plays (very often musicals) which celebrate Mormonism in unabashed song; or challenging, intellectually aggressive plays that may not attract the same numbers in terms of audience, but which receive glowing reviews from critics and academics. Yet it is most likely the case that these distinctions are too narrow, reductive, and shallow to encompass the multifaceted and multivoiced colorations that are provided by the now wide range of Mormon plays and playwrights.

Ironically, two of the most influential playwrights of the 1970s were known less for their plays than for their students. As mentioned above, Charles Whitman[43] and

---

42 Card, "Mormon Shakespeares."
43 Whitman's plays include *Phantom Empire, Play the Drum So It Is Heard Again, Tema, Patches of Oz, Montpelier Farewell*, and a stage adaptation of John D. Fitzgerald's novel *Papa Married a Mormon*.

Max Golightly,[44] both BYU professors, were the instructors of the majority of the most successful playwrights of the decade. Orson Scott Card, Robert Elliott, Doug Stewart, Martin Kelly, and Scott Bronson all trace their dramatic and artistic genealogy to Whitman; while Eric Samuelsen, Thom Duncan, and even film-maker Richard Dutcher, who resigned his membership in a somewhat spectacular public gesture, have all cited Golightly as a major inspiration. Card went so far to label Whitman as "The Father of Mormon Theatre":

> Other directors have put on Mormon plays, of course, but as head of the playwriting program at BYU, Whitman has been in a unique position of influence. The growth of Mormon playwriting has been his dream, and his encouragement has been the impetus for many a playwright. His excellent directing ability has made many original plays better than the scripts warranted, and if there is a large audience for Mormon plays, it is partly because Whitman has taught them [that] when they come to an original play they will not be disappointed. He has a unique ability to draw out of actors, and the casts of such plays as *Stone Tables*; *Shepherd of the Lord*; *A Day, A Night and A Day*; and *Fires of the Mind* find themselves fulfilled, not only artistically, but spiritually.[45]

After the "boom" period of Mormon drama in the 1970s, the genre may very well have plateaued in the 1980s, if it were not for the work of a handful of gifted playwrights. Although not as numerous (and perhaps not as influential) as the playwrights of the 1970s, these gifted dramatists added significant contributions to a now-established genre.

One notable star was James Arrington, whose popular one-man shows *Farley Family Reunion, Here's Brother Brigham*, and *J. Golden* were not only by turns thoughtful and hilarious, but also had a sharp edge of intelligent satire.

Also of particular note were Thom Duncan's *Matters of the Heart*; Susan Elizabeth Howe's *Burdens of Earth*; Reed McColm's *Together Again, for The First Time*, and *Holding Patterns*; Rob Lauer's *Digger*; and the plays of J. Scott Bronson including *Heartlight, Arthur's Place,* and *City of Peace* (with music by Arlen Card). These were significant, quality contributions during this second wave of Mormon plays, and they carried the torch proudly through yet another decade.

In the 1990s and the beginning of the twenty-first century, Mormon drama received a significant boost from the contributions of playwrights like Eric Samuelsen, Margaret Blair Young, Elizabeth Hansen, and Tim Slover, along with continuing contributions from now-established playwrights like James Arrington, Reed McColm, and J. Scott Bronson. This period seemed especially fruitful, as former students of previous decades were now becoming the professors. The skills they had learned from previous pioneers

---

44 Golightly's plays include *The Wisdom Tree, The Forge and the Fire,* and *Turn the Gas Back On.*
45 Card, "Mormon Shakespeares."

were being implemented and taught to a new generation. This period was marked by a higher volume of quality Mormon plays and a more consistent output from individual playwrights. More playwrights also stuck to their theatrical craft, rather than petering out after one success, or switching to another medium of writing. Playwrights like James Arrington and J. Scott Bronson continued to build their successes of the previous decade.

Of specific note in the 1990s was the rise of Eric Samuelsen. Talented and prolific, BYU playwriting professor Samuelsen's *Accommodations, The Seating of Senator Smoot*, and *Gadianton* were only the beginning of a large volume of excellent and socially conscious Mormon plays that Samuelsen was on course to produce at BYU and other venues.[46] Not only through volume, but also in quality, Samuelsen became perhaps the most influential playwright of the 1990s and into the 2000s, especially since his position as the playwriting professor at BYU let him influence a whole new generation of Mormon playwrights, reaching even beyond his students at BYU. His recent retirement from BYU's Theatre and Media Arts program due to illness was a surprise to many, but he left behind an age of progressive and powerful playwrights, making an indelible mark on Mormon drama. Longtime faculty member George Nelson has now taken up the playwriting position in Samuelsen's stead.

Elizabeth Hansen also came to prominence. While not having the same output as Samuelsen, she refined a few very solid works. Hansen's one-woman show, *A High and Glorious Place* about Mormon icon Eliza R. Snow, was a powerful addition, which was made into a video retitled *Eliza and I*. This film gave fledgling director Richard Dutcher one of his first film credits. Hansen's play, *A String of Pearls,* was showcased at BYU and also had a run in New York.

Tim Slover made big strides with his plays *The Dreambuilder* and *A March Tale*, but he then became a bona fide success when his *Joyful Noise* (about Handel) went on to play in San Diego, New York, and several other cities in the United States and Canada. BYU then produced another of his plays *Hancock County*, which was later released on DVD.[47] Slover, who had started as a playwriting professor at BYU, now teaches playwriting at the University of Utah.

---

46 Samuelsen's plays include *Letter from a Prophet* (co-written with Charles Metten), *A Girl Who Blushes* (one act), *Playing the Game, Emma* (opera libretto, music by Murray Boren), *Sex and the New York Yankees* (one act), *Accommodations, The Seating of Senator Smoot, Gadianton, Without Romance, The Christmas Box* (adapted from the runaway popular novel by Richard Paul Evans), *Three Women* (three one-act plays on Mormon women), *What Really Happened, The Way We're Wired, Magnificence* (translated/adapted from Middle English), *Peculiarities* (several one acts, produced in several iterations), *A Love Affair with Electrons, Family, Miasma* (first done as a ten-minute play for Plan-B SLAM Festival as *The Butcher, The Beggar, and the Bed-time Buddy*) *Blood Pudding* (a ten-minute play), *Behind the Blue Door* (a ten-minute play), *Burning Desire* (ten-minute play), *Perfect Circle* (ten-minute play), *Inversion, Intersection, Amerigo,* and *Borderlands*.

47 Slover continues to teach at the University of Utah, and his plays continue to premiere and be performed around the country. Other plays by Slover include *Cassidy: The True Story of Butch Cassidy and the Wild Bunch; Lightning Rod* (about Benjamin Franklin), and *Treasure* (about the controversies surrounding Alexander Hamilton).

Carol Lynn Pearson, who had made such an impact in the 1970s and 1980s, debuted a significant, one-woman play in 1992 titled *Mother Wove the Morning*, which she toured. A powerful, feminist piece, *Mother Wove the Morning* ties together the stories of several different women who were searching for the Divine Feminine throughout history. The play obviously closely relates to the Mormon idea of a Heavenly Mother (including a segment about Emma Smith, the first Mormon Relief Society president and wife of Joseph Smith) and advocates a closer relationship to Her.

Margaret Blair Young's *Dear Stone*, a challenging, heart-wrenching story about a family's struggle with their wife/mother's debilitating affliction with multiple sclerosis; and her powerful *I Am Jane*, telling the story of Jane Manning James and Elijah Abel, nineteenth-century African-American Mormon pioneers; were both welcome additions to the genre. *I Am Jane* in particular has been a monumental work and a giant step that attempts to help heal the wounds caused by the Church's former policy (since corrected) of excluding men of African heritage from the LDS priesthood.

Marvin Payne, Steven Kapp Perry, and James Arrington also contributed another significant Mormon musical with their telling of the Mormon pioneer trek *Trail of Dreams* at Utah Valley University and other theaters, coinciding with the Church's sesquicentennial celebration of the event. Perry contributed another musical, *Polly: A One Woman Musical*, a touching pioneer piece performed by his talented wife, Johanne Frichette Perry. Steven Kapp Perry and Marvin Payne reunited on another musical in 2007, *Take the Mountain Down*, a blue-grass retelling of the story of the prodigal son.

Pam Blackwell's *Parley P. Pratt's Great Escape*, which premiered during BYU's Education Week in 2005, was another notable musical during this period. The play told the tale of Parley P. Pratt's time in Richmond Jail, bolstered with music composed by Kelly Eisenhour, ranging from jazz to African American spirituals.

BYU has continued to show a strong commitment in producing Mormon drama, not only by established Mormon playwrights like Eric Samuelsen, Elizabeth Hansen, and Tim Slover, but also new works by current and former students. The quality playwrights BYU has turned out have been invaluable. Plays from this group of dramatists include *Prodigals* by Adam Boulter (BYU's Margetts Theatre, November 9–26); *Prisoner* by James Bell;[48] *Blind Dates* by Adam Blackwell (Margetts Theatre, May 17–June 3, 1995); *Free at Last* by Scott Livingston (Margetts Theatre, 1996); *Joyce Baking* by Josh Brady (Pardoe Theatre, September 1998); four by Melissa Leilani Larson: *Lady in Waiting* (August 1, 2001); *Wake Me When It's Over* (BYU's Nelke Theatre, July 17–20, 2002); *Angels Unaware* (retitled *Martyrs' Crossing*; Margetts Theatre, March 8–25, 2006); an adaptation of *Persuasion* (Pardoe Theatre, March 16–April 1, 2011); *Archipelago* (Pardoe Theatre, March 26–April 12, 2003; won the 2004 KC/ACTF Mark Cohen Playwriting Award), and *Yellow China Bell* (Margetts Theatre, 2002) by LeeAnne Hill Adams; *Soft*

---

48 Performed in BYU's Margetts Theatre, November 18–December 4, 1994. Special note should be made of this Vietnam War drama, as it won the Kennedy Center American College Theater Festival's National Playwriting Award and was performed in the Kennedy Center at its national festival in Washington, D.C.

Shoe, with book and lyrics by George Nelson (faculty) and music by Daniel Larson (student; Pardoe Theatre, October 2–19, 2002); *Smart Single Guys* by Tony Gunn (Margetts Theatre, November 7–22, 2003); *Three Mormon Women: Three One Act Plays* by Morag Plaice Shepherd, Leslie Hart Gunn, and Linda Colloton (Margetts Theatre, May 11–28, 2005); *Stuck on the Edge* by Elizabeth Leavitt (Margetts Theatre, March 7–24, 2007); *Roofsliding* by Morag Plaice Shepherd (Pardoe Theatre, March 21–April 4, 2008); and *Houseboat Honeymoon* by Joel Bree (Pardoe Theatre, November 12–December 6, 2008). Most recently, BYU produced Ariel Mitchell's significant *A Second Birth* (Sept. 25–28, 2012) in the Margetts Theatre. The play received the Kennedy Center American College Theater Festival's Harold and Mimi Steinberg National Student Playwriting Award. Mitchell was recently accepted into NYU's Musical Theatre Writing program.

BYU's other branches, BYU–Idaho and BYU–Hawaii, have also performed a number of works by Mormon playwrights including James Arrington's *The Prophet* (BYU–I); Susan Elizabeth Howe's *Burdens of Earth* (BYU–H and BYU–I); Reed McColm's 9/11 drama *Fires in the Sky* (BYU–I); and J. Omar Hansen's *Pioneer Song*, as well as his *Biezely and Gottfried: A Modern Morality Play* (BYU–I).

Another university has recently proven to be a welcoming institution for Utah playwrights. In the past several years, Utah Valley University (formerly Utah Valley State College) has produced several plays by Mormon dramatists. Plays from UVU's current and former faculty include revivals of James Arrington's plays *The Farley Family Christmas* (which has become a holiday tradition in its Ragan Theater), *The Farley Family Reunion, Trail of Dreams* (co-written with Marvin Payne and Steven Kapp Perry), and *J. Golden*; Elizabeth Hansen's musical adaptation of Elizabeth von Arnim's *Enchanted April* (April 13–22, 2006, UVU's Blackbox Theater); as well as Christopher Clark's *A Marrying Man* (November 21–December 3, 2005, UVU's Blackbox Theater).

UVU has also produced plays by other veteran Mormon playwrights with *Polly: A One Woman Musical* by Stephen Kapp Perry; *Almost Perfect* (premiered November 2002, UVU's Blackbox Theater) by Doug Stewart; a run of Tim Slover's *Joyful Noise*; and *SFX5*, a collection of short science fiction plays by James Arrington, Scott Bronson, Thom Duncan, and Isaac Walters.

In its mentoring efforts for new playwrights, UVU has been led by James Arrington. Under Arrington's tutelage, UVU has proven its commitment to invest in future playwrights by producing student work in its Blackbox Theater. Student-written productions at UVU include Paul Walstead and Christopher J. Frankhauser's[49] *People Become Real* (the first UVU production to be invited to the KC/ACTF festival, performed at the festival February 11, 1998) and three of Mahonri Stewart's plays: *Farewell to Eden* (November 13–22, 2003), *Legends of Sleepy Hollow* (October 18–22, 2004), and *Rings of the Tree* (September 6–8, 2007). Stewart and Arrington also collaborated on *March*

---

49 Paul Walstead was the chief playwright in this piece, although Frankhauser had written some poetry that was included in the play. Tragically, Frankhauser drowned while the cast of *People Become Real* was at the KC/ACTF Festival in California. Jeffrey P. Henry, "Drama Student at UVSC Drowns at California Beach," *Deseret News*, February 18, 1998.

of the Salt Soldiers which had been commissioned to celebrate the sesquicentennial of the Utah War.⁵⁰ Stewart's *Farewell to Eden* became a kind of watershed play for UVU's Theatre Department. The play was invited to the regional competition of the Kennedy Center American College Theater Festival, and then Stewart went on to the national competition in Washington, D.C. There he received second place for the KC/ACTF National Playwriting Award, as well as a National Selection Team Fellowship Award.

By the early twenty-first century, it has become clear that Mormon drama is not only still alive, but destined to stay, as the number of Mormon plays and playwrights has increased steadily since the 1970s. Yet at present, it has reached a plateau. Schools like BYU's campuses and UVU are willing to produce Mormon plays on the university and college levels. But beyond that initial threshold, it seems unlikely that the professional world of theatre is close to embracing Mormon drama as part of its regular repertoire. Theatre hubs like New York and London have yet to welcome the genre.

However, a couple of recent attempts seem promising in breaking the Broadway barrier. Michael McLean, well known in the Mormon community for his religious pop music, recently opened off-Broadway with his musical, *The Ark,* about the biblical Noah's family. Lambasted by the critics, it closed after thirty-six previews and only eight regular performances.

BYU alumni Erik Orton also had limited success with the New York showcase premiere of his musical about the Berlin air lifts, *Berlin,* but it also has had no luck in being picked up by Broadway producers. It was later performed by BYU and broadcast on television.

Significantly, Mormon playwright Matthew P. Greene recently had his drama, *#MormonInChief,* play at the New York International Fringe Festival. The play has a Mormon presidential candidate (a fictionalized, but thinly veiled version of Mitt Romney), who says some inflammatory things at a Church meeting which are then tweeted by a young Mormon who is present. It creates a firestorm in the media and blogosphere. The play has received mixed reviews, but *#MormonInChief* is a significant accomplishment for Greene and a step forward for Mormon drama, which has had too few Mormon playwrights telling their own story before a broader audience, especially in places like New York, the cultural heart of the American theatrical community.

For a time, Neil LaBute, a convert to the Church and a BYU graduate, appeared to be the most likely candidate to break the success roadblock for Mormons. His increasing international reputation as a playwright encouraged many Mormon dramatists to consider the possibility of making a success in the playwriting business.⁵¹ However, his *Bash:*

---

50 Premiered September 10–19, 2008, in both UVU's Centre Stage and Ragan Theaters, as well as performances in the Salt Lake City Library on September 12, 2008, and the Caine Lyric Theater in Logan, Utah, on October 11, 2008.

51 Pat Jordan, "Neil LaBute Has a Thing about Beauty," *New York Times,* March 25, 2009; see also http://en.wikipedia.org/wiki/Neil_LaBute (accessed November 9, 2011), and the *Theatre Blog's* recent take on LaBute's departure as the MCC Theater's playwright in residence, http://www.guardian.co.uk/stage/theatreblog/2009/jun/18/reasons-to-be-pretty-

Latter-day Plays drew negative attention and discipline from the Church. It appears that LaBute's relationship with the Church was both complex and deeply private, as he rarely shared details about why he joined the Church. The *New York Times* reported:

> After high school, LaBute attended BYU on a scholarship. It was there that he converted to the Church of Jesus Christ of Latter-day Saints, although he wouldn't tell me why, except to say that his conversion was about "faith." But he added, "Americans have so many misconceptions about the church." . . . .
>
> It may seem an odd fit, the creator of so many misanthropic characters and a religion of "fellowship," but the relationship survived for a few years. LaBute even won an award from the Association for Mormon Letters for his play "In the Company of Men," which is about two businessmen who seduce a deaf woman as a cruel joke, then dump her. But when LaBute wrote a devastating series of three one-act monologues, "Bash: Latter-Day Plays," in which Mormon characters are portrayed as murderers, the church "disfellowshipped" him, essentially putting him into a state of limbo from which he never quite returned. Today, he told me, he is no longer a Mormon.[52]

LaBute certainly was a much darker version of the "Mormon Shakespeare"[53] than many Latter-day Saint artists and writers often hoped for. Those who were looking for a bright, flawless beacon to portray a squeaky clean representation of the Church's artists have not found their hopes represented in the current LaBute oeuvre . However, despite LaBute's frank subject matter, salty language, and seeming pessimism about humanity, many of his plays present dark morality tales that oddly *do* connect to Mormonism, with subtle and not so subtle religious and moral undertones. In a Church whose keystone scripture, the Book of Mormon, has its own tragic and self-destructive ending, perhaps LaBute's themes are not so far out of step as they may appear at first glance. Whatever the cause of his separation from the Church, losing such a prized talent as LaBute's was a sad casualty to the Mormon theatrical community.

LaBute's plays include *Filthy Talk for Filthy Times, In the Company of Men, Bash: Latter-Day Plays, The Shape of Things, The Distance from Here, The Mercy Seat, Autobahn, Fat Pig, This Is How It Goes, Some Girl(s), Wrecks, In a Dark House, Reasons to Be Pretty, Helter Skelter/Land of the Dead, The Break of Noon,* "The New Testament," and *Some White Chick.*

LaBute isn't the only successful playwright to have connections to Mormonism, whether in subject matter or personal history. Ex-Mormon Julie Jensen was born LDS

---

neil-labute-mcc-theatre (accessed July 1, 2011).

52 Jordan, "Neil LaBute Has a Thing about Beauty."

53 LDS Apostle Orson F. Whitney, who aspired to become a professional actor at one point, encouraged the production of "home literature" by and about Mormons; he predicted that Mormons "will yet have Miltons and Shakespeares of our own." "Home Literature," June 3, 1888, *http://mldb.byu.edu/homelit.htm* (accessed November 7, 2011).

in Beaver, Utah, but personally asked the Church to excommunicate her "a few decades ago," when her identity as a lesbian and her personal politics were too opposed to the Church's positions.[54]

Jensen has had many successes, including awards from a host of different organizations, including the Kennedy Center's American College Theater Festival. Her plays have performed in many cities across the United States and abroad, including London, New York, Hamburg, and at the Edinburgh Fringe. Jensen taught playwriting at the University of Nevada, Las Vegas, and is now the resident playwright at Salt Lake Acting Company.

Two of Jensen's successful plays deal specifically with Mormonism: *Two-Headed*, about two pioneer women in southern Utah who struggle against issues as broad as same-gender attraction and as specific as the Mountain Meadows Massacre; and *Dust Eaters*, that tells the complicated family histories of two families who live near each other, one Goshute, the other white Mormon.

Other plays, such as non-Mormon Tony Kushner's Pulitzer Prize winning *Angels in America* and former Mormon Stephen Fale's one-man show *Confessions of a Mormon Boy*, were both productions with Mormon characters that played successfully in New York and nationally. *Angels in America* has been hailed as a modern classic.[55] And they were plays that followed the increasing trend of putting the Church in the hot seat for its strong stand against LGBTQ issues.

Addressing the tension between the Mormon and homosexual communities, devout Mormon playwrights such as Carol Lynn Pearson and Melissa Leilani Larson have taken a brave and compassionate approach in their plays concerning homosexuality, while also maintaining a stance of faithfulness toward the Church. Addressing the heart-wrenching experiences LGBTQ individuals experience in the Mormon community, both Pearson's play *Facing East* (which has performed in Salt Lake City, San Francisco, and New York) and Larson's play *Little Happy Secrets* have created an exquisite balance between faith and compassion.

But on the national stage, that is not the story being told. Nuanced and balanced portrayals of Mormons are difficult to find, and nowhere is that more evident than the recent success of the multiple Tony Award-winning Broadway hit musical *The Book of Mormon*. Matt Stone and Trey Parker (the creators of the intentionally shocking and raunchy animated series *South Park*) as well as their collaborator Robert Lopez (one of the Tony Award-winning creators of *Avenue Q*) recently put out the highest-profile play dealing with Mormonism since *Angels in America*. With their satirical *The Book*

---

54 Adminwp, "Julie Jensen: Two Headed Playwright," http://gaysaltlake.com/2009/10/09/julie-jensen-two-headed-playwright/ (accessed September 10, 2012).

55 *Angels in America* has received a lot of criticism from Mormon writers and critics, not necessarily for its support of the LGBTQ community, but because of its shallow representation of the Mormon community. Although Kushner's Mormon characters have a lot of depth and are fully realized characters, Kushner shows very little understanding of how they should have reflected Mormon culture.

of Mormon musical, Stone, Parker and Lopez have earned a torrent of accolades from critics with their musical about two modern Mormon missionaries who serve in a traumatized Uganda.

Jon Stewart gushed over Stone and Parker in his interview with them on *The Daily Show*, climaxing with the hyperbolic statement about the musical, "There is a song in this that I think . . . when the aliens come thousands of years from now, it may exist as the only memory of Earth, and I gotta say, I'm happy to go down with it."[56]

Meanwhile the *New York Times* exclaimed, "This is to all the doubters and deniers out there, the ones who say that heaven on Broadway does not exist. . . . I am here to report that a newborn, old-fashioned, pleasure-giving musical has arrived at the Eugene O'Neill Theater, the kind our grandparents told us left them walking on air if not on water. So hie thee hence, nonbelievers (and believers too), to *The Book of Mormon*, and feast upon its sweetness."[57]

But amid all the exclamatory responses among secular critics for *The Book of Mormon*, the Mormon response has been decidedly divided. Ironically, much like their occasional takes on Mormons in *South Park*, Parker and Stone are generally positive about Mormon members in their interviews and in the show, even though they personally believe that the Mormon religion is utter nonsense and sketch a less than flattering (and at times factually inaccurate) portrait of Joseph Smith. But through it all, they seem to genuinely *like* Mormons themselves. Stone said in an interview, "Do goofy stories make people nice? What if, in their goofiness, these stories somehow inspire that in the right way. Is that a social good?"[58] The word "affectionate," "sweet," and "warm" regularly appear in many reviews of the show, describing how the musical portrays Mormons.

However, as much as the creators of *The Book of Mormon* may like Mormons, they have not disguised their skepticism about the religion. Further, they have also shoveled in a large amount of material that many have deemed excessive and offensive, from coarse language to minstrel show-like Mormon and African stereotypes. One New York Mormon artist and critic made this assessment of the audience's reaction:

> *The Book of Mormon: The Musical* is mostly what everybody says it is. Its tone is sweet and its delivery calculatedly offensive. I sat by an African-American woman who winced throughout the show when Ugandans were stereotypically portrayed. An older man in the row in front of me was clearly offended by the language and the onstage sex acts. He didn't applaud for those songs, I noticed. And I sat on my hands for a couple of numbers too. When

---

56 Mandi Bierly, "Jon Stewart Is Probably Somewhere STILL Raving about the Book of Mormon Musical," *EW.Com, Entertainment Weekly*, March 11, 2011.

57 Ben Brantley, "Missionary Men with Confidence in Sunshine," *New York Times*, March 24, 2011 (accessed March 13, 2011).

58 Dave Itzkoff, "A Sweet Show, with Blasphemy and Cussing," *New York Times*, February 16, 2011.

the character of Jesus is portrayed in pretty ugly ways in the song about his upcoming crucifixion in the song, "Man Up," some people in the audience cheered and a few others sat, battered and shell-shocked. I would say the vast majority let it all roll off of them though, and they just had a good time.[59]

The portrayal of the Mormon characters *is* two dimensional and broad, regardless of also being "warm" or "sweet." With perhaps the exception of Elder Price, these are not sophisticated, nuanced characters. That result can partly be attributed to the fact that the show is meant to be a broad satire and that Trey and Parker are well known to be "equal opportunity offenders," meaning that they enjoy skewering all groups. Yet if the characters had been Jewish, or Muslim, or Catholic, would the show have had the same popularity, or rather would there have been more cries of "bigotry!" or "stereotype!" in response to the broad strokes it takes. The accolades the show has received brings up the question of whether anti-Mormonism is the most fashionable prejudice of the early twenty-first century. Whether the show is seen as good-natured, even affectionate, satire or as a startling Mormon minstrel show, many Mormons do not recognize themselves in the misadventures of Elders Price and Cunningham, despite its clever, affectionate, even at times compassionate delivery.

Thus, Mormonism *is* receiving strong attention from the national theatre community, but much of it is coming in ways that many Mormons do not appreciate. With the increasing attention that plays such as *Angels in America* and *The Book of Mormon* have received, it may be helpful to look back to how Eric Samuelsen defined the need for having a Mormon drama that is created by those within the faith, not just outsiders and ex-Mormons who have an ax to grind about the Church, or those who are affectionate but condescending about our beliefs and practices: "To me, the distortions and blasphemies of *Angels in America* profoundly illustrate our need for a drama that offers a counter vision, a more culturally accurate frame of reference for audiences and playwrights both. But that drama should also have a richness and subtlety to match or even surpass the talented work of the Kushners of today. It should be a drama of genuine insight, a drama that looks with clear eyes at the world while occasionally seeing beyond to celestial glory."[60]

But with Mormon plays rarely extending further than the occasional university or community production, does Mormon drama have the ability to sustain itself on a regular basis? Will a Mormon dramatist arise who can live comfortably off his or her creative work? What real hope does it have to go further than where it has already reached?

---

59   Glen Nelson, "Elders on Broadway: My Thoughts on *The Book of Mormon: The Musical*," themormonartistsgroup.com, April 2011.
60   Eric Samuelsen, "Whither Mormon Drama? Look First to a Theater," *BYU Studies* 35, no. 1 (1995): 91.

"Yet to Reveal Themselves": The Future of Mormon Drama

As a recent playwriting professor at the LDS Church-sponsored Brigham Young University, Eric Samuelsen, more than anyone else, has had the chance to see the future of Mormon drama in working with his students. He liked what he saw:

> I love the next generation of Mormon playwrights, and I'm exceedingly optimistic about the future. I love teaching at BYU. Ibsen once said that he loved being around young people, because they kept his mind from growing old. . . . The biggest challenge they face is the lack of venue for their work. But I can't wait to see what Melissa Larson or Mahonri Stewart or Elizabeth Leavitt or Morag Plaice or Leslie Gunn are going to write over the next twenty years. I think we have some brilliant young writers coming up. And the best of them are not paying much attention to the cultural baggage I had to spend half my life discarding. . . . Leslie Gunn is from Nova Scotia; Morag Plaice is from Scotland; Elizabeth Leavitt, okay, she's from Sacramento, but the poor side of town. Their experience of Mormonism is from outside Utah, with everything that implies. What I hope and pray is that there's a completely brilliant Mormon playwright I've never heard of doing amazing work in Brazil or Ghana or Korea. Wouldn't that be awesome?[61]

But what does it matter when talent is cultivated, if there is nowhere to perform these works? Samuelsen has referred to venues as the "biggest challenge" future Mormon playwrights must face:

> What such playwrights need is a theater. The great eras of the world's dramatic literature have tended to come after the establishment of theaters and theater companies sufficiently robust to support them. Further, those theaters have always been subsidized to some degree—either financially underwritten or politically supported—and the reality is that the need for such subsidies is greater now more than ever. In short, we will never develop a satisfying Mormon drama until we have established and supported a theater from which such a drama might emerge. The Mormon Shakespeare needs a Mormon Globe.[62]

Such a "Mormon Globe" had a short-lived history that began in September of 2005, under the name of the Nauvoo Theatrical Society. Founded in Orem, Utah, by Mormon

---

61 Mahonri Stewart, "Eric Samuelsen," interview, A Motley Vision, May 2, 2006, *http://www.motleyvision.org/2006/an-interview-with-eric-samuelsen/* (accessed November 13, 2011).
62 Samuelsen; "Whither Mormon Drama?" 93–94.

playwrights and dramatists Thom Duncan and J. Scott Bronson, it seemed for a moment that it could be the bright light that would illuminate and call into reality the visions of Mormon playwrights. It was hoped to be a permanent home for Mormon drama.

The Nauvoo Theatrical Society had its beginnings during the meeting of the Playwrights' Circle, a group of Mormon playwrights who came together to read and support each other's work. Rather like a Mormon equivalent of the Bloomsbury Group or the Inklings, members of the group were many of the veteran playwrights of Mormon drama, including Eric Samuelsen, James Arrington, Tim Slover, Elizabeth Hansen, Marvin Payne, and others:

> [Scott] Bronson and [Thom] Duncan, friends since the mid-80s, were members of that group, which sought to foster plays by LDS authors. "We saw that we were going to have a hard time producing anything anywhere, even at (Brigham Young University)," Duncan said. "Their (new plays) are usually by students and teachers." Duncan's experience in producing a show he co-wrote, *Prophet*, at the SCERA in 1999 further inspired him.[63]

The theater went up in 2002 with a season of several plays by Mormon playwrights, including Carol Lynn Pearson's *My Turn on Earth*; Tim Slover's *Joyful Noise*; Eric Samuelsen's *The Way We're Wired*, and Scott Bronson's *Stones*. In regards to their artistry, the plays were of a high quality, despite their limited resources. However, due to issues involving city ordinances, building codes, insufficient advertising, a lack of fund-raising and other disputed issues, the theater was forced to close. Along with the close of the Nauvoo Theatrical Society came the closure of another hope for Mormon drama.

Other groups are beginning to take up where the Nauvoo Theatrical Society left off. One of the most promising is the New Play Project, a non-profit group based in Provo, Utah. Founded in 2006 by James Goldberg, Arisael Rivera, Julie Saunders, and Jennefer Franklin, the New Play Project is committed to plays that are both intelligent and infused with moral value. They started performing on BYU campus, then moved to the Provo City Library, and then at the Provo Theatre. With the building's recent closure and poetic transformation into a Christian church, New Play Project is once again back to scouting out a regular venue. Despite having to adapt their work to whatever space is available, they are creating a limited, but very loyal audience, an audience that is growing far beyond their original expectations, and growing fast.

Consisting largely of BYU and UVU students, they have been prolific in the amount of material they put out, focusing on regular festivals of short, low-budget plays, including bi-annual productions of religious works in this format. Ranging from ten to thirty minutes, each play in an individual festival follows a pre-determined theme. The festivals have produced some surprisingly excellent theatre, especially coming from authors so young.

---

63 Eric Snider; "New Theater Showcasing LDS Plays," *Provo Daily Herald*, September 25, 2002.

Most notable in this shorthand form of Mormon drama is the body of work produced by James Goldberg. As one of the driving forces behind the creation of the New Play Project, Goldberg and his short plays (especially his one-act *Prodigal Son*, which won the 2008 Association for Mormon Letters prize in drama) continue to make notable strides for the organization. Goldberg's lyrical, even wordy, style is paradoxically balanced with his vocal dedication to short plays. This combination causes his poetic outbursts and beautiful monologues to rush at a deadline even as they are taking breaks to revel in heightened language and poetic philosophy. It's an effective contradiction and a memorable style.

Young Mormon playwrights like Katherine Gee, Matthew Greene, Adam Stallard, Arisael Rivera, Ben Crowder, Davey and Bianca Dillard-Morrison, Stephen Gashler, and Melissa Leilani Larson, to name just a few, have also made quality contributions to these short-play festivals. The New Play Project's increasing quality of work has attracted even seasoned playwrights like Eric Samuelsen to submit short work, which has been warmly received at the festivals.

New Play Project has also produced full-length works by a number of Mormon playwrights. New Play Project's first full-length contribution was Arisael Rivera's *Really Cool and Smart and Better Than You*.

Katherine Gee's examination of politics and religion, *God for President*, took an untraditional route, as it was a "devised" work of theatre, meaning that it was improvised and developed by the actors and Gee in rehearsals.

New Play Project produced a few of Mahonri Stewart's plays. These plays include *Swallow the Sun* (May 16, 2008, Provo Theatre Company), about C. S. Lewis's early life and Christian conversion; *The Fading Flower* (May 29, 2009, Provo Theatre Company), about Joseph and Emma Smith's children's adult lives; and his "anti-absurdist comedy" *Uneaten Cantaloupe* (November 7, 2008, Provo Theatre Company). Stewart's plays with NPP received strong attendance and significant critical attention, with *The Fading Flower* being hailed by one critic as "an important, historical achievement."[64]

Melissa Leilani Larson's magnificent and heartbreaking play *Little Happy Secrets* (March 19, 2009, Provo Theatre Company), about a young Mormon woman who struggles with same-gender attraction but remains in the Church, has been New Play Project's most important production to date. *Little Happy Secrets* was praised by critics and audiences alike and won the Association for Mormon Letters 2009 prize for best drama.

Stephen Gashler's musical comedic-fantasy *The Bent Sword* (November 2010), Eric Samuelsen's young adult comedy *He and She Fighting* (February 2011), and Anna Lewis's *WWJD* (March–April 2011), about Jesus hanging out with a group of modern college students and assisting them in sometimes humorous, sometimes moving ways, were New Play Project's most recent plays.

---

64 Nan McCulloch, "The New Play Project: *Fading Flower* (drama)," May 30, 2009, Association for Mormon Letters, *http://www.aml-online.org/Reviews/Review.aspx?id=4565* (accessed November 20, 2012).

Since that last group of plays, however, their output has been minimal, causing some to wonder if they, like the Nauvoo Theatrical Society before them, are about to peter out. Hopefully, that will not be the case, for the New Play Project is a worthy group, though a young one. New Play Project's ever-evolving, volunteer staff has often left the group's future in doubt as its founders move off to different pastures and the group sometimes struggles to find enough dedicated people to fill the void.

The majority of NPP's playwrights, actors, and directors are between eighteen and thirty years old. Many of them represent the rising generation of Mormon playwrights and perhaps are an indication of Mormon drama's future. They are faithful Latter-day Saints who show no indication of becoming another "lost generation" of Mormon artists, who stereotypically lose their faith in consequence of their art. Yet they also do not reduce their works to propaganda or sentimentality. They have made their dedication to the faith clear, even with their most culturally critical works. As a kind of "new Mormon faithful," their powerful balance of loyalty to the faith and intelligent cultural analysis will be a significant boon to Mormon drama in the years to come.

In addition to its artistic and spiritual integrity, New Play Project is a significant group because of its independence from academic or institutional ties. It will take groups like New Play Project to bring Mormon drama out of the insular realms of schools and universities where it has remained for several decades and secure for it a permanent place in the larger domain of the private and nonprofit sectors.

Other groups such as Bluelight Stage Company, Leilani Productions, the BYU Experimental Theatre Company, and Zion Theatre Company have also cropped up in the past decade following similar values-driven trajectories as those mapped out by the New Play Project. Many of these groups were founded by former collaborators with the New Play Project, such as Melissa Leilaini Larson's Leilani Productions, and Mahonri Stewart's Zion Theatre Company.

Zion Theatre Company especially had an intense output from 2010 through 2012. It has focused on Stewart's plays, including premieres of his *The Opposing Wheel* and *A Roof Overhead*, as well as remounts of his previous work in addition to showcasing work from other Mormon playwrights and nationally recognized plays.

Also, although not specifically tied to any faith-based mission, the Utah Theatre Bloggers Association has also been an influential group of theatre critics that have helped to refine the theatre community in Utah. Other online groups such as Front Row Reviewers Utah have followed their example and are establishing a network of critics to help energize and develop Utah's theatrical community.

Eric Samuelsen's comment that a "Mormon Shakespeare needs a Mormon Globe" hangs over the Mormon theatre community like a prophecy, but it will take more than academic papers, discussions, or wishful thinking to establish that reality. Marketing, creativity, fine-tuned storytelling, organization, practical business sense, understanding of one's audience, artistry, intelligence, critical analysis, and tenacious grit will all be factors, if Mormon drama is to break out of the limited place it has carved in the Mormon educational sphere and from there reach new achievements.

Mormon drama has had its shares of figurative Joseph Smiths, who outline the future and produce the powerful literature. Now it needs the Brigham Youngs, those who will give those creative visions a structure to breathe and live in, where the pragmatic can join the esoteric. It is then that Mormonism's theatrical desert will blossom like the rose.

Even more than any of the previously listed qualities, Mormon drama can't forget from which fountain it has drawn its inspiration. Its artists need a deep-seated spirituality and a commitment to the restored gospel. Many of the Church's great artists have, after tasting a little success, abandoned the Church for what they considered to be more promising horizons. So the need for the Church to retain its artists, while still putting out monumental work, has been felt by many of its leaders and spokespeople. LDS President and Prophet Spencer W. Kimball declared:

> For years I have been waiting for someone to do justice in recording in song and story and painting and sculpture the story of the Restoration, the reestablishment of the kingdom of God on earth, the struggles and frustrations; the apostasies and inner revolutions and counter-revolutions of those first decades; of the exodus; of the counter-reactions; of the transitions; of the persecution days; of the miracle man, Joseph Smith, of whom we sing "Oh, what rapture filled his bosom, For he saw the living God" . . . ; and of the giant colonizer and builder, Brigham Young. . . . We are proud of the artistic heritage that the Church has brought to us from its earliest beginnings, but the full story of Mormonism has never yet been written nor painted nor sculpted nor spoken. It remains for inspired hearts and talented fingers *yet* to reveal themselves. They must be faithful, inspired, active Church members to give life and feeling and true perspective to a subject so worthy. Such masterpieces should run for months in every movie center, cover every part of the globe in the tongues of the people, written by great artists, purified by the best critics.[65]

Off in the future is perhaps the long-hoped for resurrection of The Nauvoo Theatrical Society,[66] the continued progress of the New Play Project, or perhaps another similarly themed group's rise that will bring Mormon drama to new heights. There also might be an already established playwright or a new, promising, faithful Mormon playwright who reaches national or international prominence. Perhaps this playwright's

---

65 Spencer W. Kimball, "The Gospel Vision of the Arts," *Ensign*, July 1977, 3.
66 In 2007, the Nauvoo Theatrical Society teamed up with the Covey Center for the Arts in Provo to produce Scott Bronson's play *Dial Tones*, November 29–December 22, 2007. Bronson has continued as the artistic director of the Center's Little Theater, continuing to highlight Mormon playwrights every so often, including productions of his *Stones* and *The Brothers*; Tim Slover's *Joyful Noise*; Steven Kapp Perry and Marvin Payne's *Wedlocked*; Perry's *Polly*; and a collection of short plays by various playwrights called *An Anthology of Love*.

work may contain Mormon characters and/or themes. Perhaps this playwright's works will run in playhouses in New York, across the nation, perhaps even the world. It is in hope of such an event or a similar one that we publish this anthology of Mormon drama, that it may contribute and pay honor to the proud heritages already created by so many creative pioneers who have established the foundations upon which future works of art, intimacy, and grandeur can be built.

Fires of the Mind

Robert Elliott

About the Playwright

In 1986, Mormon critic, scholar, and essayist Eugene England wrote, "*Fires of the Mind*, by Robert Elliott, is the best single play written about the Mormon experience."[1] Although the play may not be recognized by younger audiences who weren't around in 1974 when it was first produced, it is certainly the case that it was one of the driving forces that jump-started Mormon drama's maturation towards more searching subject matter. *Fires of the Mind*'s ferociously intelligent, achingly honest, and strongly spiritual dimensions boded well for Mormon drama during a pivotal period in its history as a movement.

Elliott was born into a "part-member" family in the Susquehanna River town of Sidney, New York, very near where Joseph Smith was married. Recruited by BYU on a Presidential Scholarship in 1967, he was very active at BYU as a sophomore class officer and as head of Brotherhood Week, an attempt to bring prominent African American speakers to the BYU campus and generally help BYU students prepare for and deal with the accusations of racism being leveled against them at that time. This was before the 1978 revelation to President Spencer W. Kimball, which opened up the LDS priesthood to worthy men of all races, destroying the ban that had been placed upon ordaining men of African descent.[2]

Between his years of study at BYU, Elliott was called on an LDS proselyting mission from 1969 to 1971 in Taiwan, where the central action of *Fires of the Mind* takes place. When asked whether the play is autobiographical, Elliott responded:

> My mission experience paralleled Johnson's in some ways; I agonized frequently over the issues that torment him. None of the other characters, though, are drawn directly from former companions or other missionaries I knew. They are composites, created for dramatic purposes. Some who knew me on my mission might recognize more of me in Lucas than in Johnson. Act Three and the epilog, especially, are pure invention.[3]

---

1   Eugene England, Review of Thomas F. Rogers, "*God's Fools*: Plays of Mitigated Conscience." *BYU Studies* 26, no. 3 (Summer 1986): 114–18.
2   This factor is especially significant since *Fires of the Mind* does touch upon some attitudes and issues concerning race among some Latter-day Saints before this vitally important revelation. Pre-dating the revelation, it shows tremendous understanding and cognizance from a Latter-day Saint on the issue.
3   Robert Elliott, email to Mahonri Stewart, January 13, 2008.

After his mission, Elliott returned to BYU where he pursued a B. A. in English. As part of a group that went to study abroad in London, he was drawn toward dramatic literature as a subject of study while watching the performances of plays there. "I came back to Provo determined to write, as my honors project, a play about missionary life that would shake up Mormon drama in the same way that Ibsen shook up nineteenth-century continental and Victorian drama. It took me longer than I planned."[4]

Elliott graduated from BYU and then returned for an M. A. in English; these credits were eventually transferred to the University of Utah to better manage his business affairs in Salt Lake City. It was during this period of his life that he wrote *Fires of the Mind*. It premiered October 31, 1974, in the Margetts Arena Theatre and sold out both its initial run and the subsequent extension. Reactions to the play's inaugural run were very positive.[5] The BYU student newspaper, *The Daily Universe*, ran a glowing review that included this vignette: "*Fires of the Mind* is not only a play, it is an experience.... The play is filled with high tension. Dramatic scenes between the elders touched many people, including those who had not been on missions. Between acts on Saturday, a cast member found two girls crying and asked, 'Is the play upsetting you?' One of the girls responded, 'Isn't it supposed to?'"[6]

Elliott went on to earn his English M. A. from the University of Utah and a Ph.D. from Cornell University in dramatic literature. Even more importantly, he married Dorice Williams, a fellow academic and, eventually, educator.

Eight years later, *Fires of the Mind* received a second performance at BYU, but this run was marked with much more controversy than the initial euphoric premiere. BYU theatre professor Robert Nelson directed *Fires of the Mind* as part of the 1982 Mormon Festival of Arts Celebration on the Pardoe main stage at BYU.

Although on opening night the show was produced as written, an extremely negative review from *The Deseret News* caused concern among BYU's administrators. The review claimed that the show portrayed missionaries as "turkeys" and either "cliché-spouting boobs" or "testimony-less trouble makers." It also leveled accusations of (ironically) racism, sermonizing, and "taking liberties with sacred things," called the play "too esoteric to be believable," and concluded that it amounted to "two hours of discouragement."[7]

This complete misreading of the text caused BYU professor Eugene England to respond indignantly in a letter to the editor to the *Deseret News*.

> Joseph Walker's misinformed and flippant review of "Fires of the Mind," the fine drama based in LDS missionary experience . . . was a disservice to the actors, the director, the author, and to the hope for better Mormon drama. . . .

---

4   Robert Elliott, Autobiography, January 13, 2008, in my possession..
5   *Fires of the Mind* was picked up by Elliott's fellow graduate student at the University of Utah, Peggy Fletcher, and published in the inaugural issue of the Mormon intellectual periodical *Sunstone Magazine*, Winter 1975.
6   Barry Lynn Rishton, "'Fires' Portrays Modern Tragedy," *BYU Daily Universe,* Tuesday, November 5, 1974.
7   Joseph Walker, The Deseret News, March 24, 1982, section, 7.

In fact, this production provides one of the most challenging and moving dramatic experiences I have ever had in this region....

If there is to be a significant Mormon drama it must present the conflicts of good and evil (and of opposed ideas) that are part of our real world and thus give us understanding and strength for our own real struggles. "Fires of the Mind" does this, but Mr. Walker completely missed such things as the deeply moving power of the second act, one of the most daring in its range and in its execution I have seen anywhere.[8]

Other reviews agreed with England. Theron Luke at the *Provo Daily Herald* called *Fires of the Mind* "a powerful play, a thinking play, a gripping play,"[9] while Lee Nelson at the *Central Utah Journal* wrote: "*Fires of the Mind* does not end like most Mormon productions, Elder Johnson hugging his companions and bearing testimony. It isn't a raving, rah-rah audience that leaves the theater, but rather a thoughtful, sober one.... Probing the depths of testimony is serious business."[10]

Yet the extremely positive press and powerful nature of the play was not enough to calm the anxieties of certain decision-makers at BYU caused by *The Deseret News* and similar complaints from other individuals. Even though Elliott had expressly told Nelson that the play was to be performed as written or not at all and a contract was made to that effect,[11] BYU administrators ordered that the content be edited. Elliott recalled:

Returning to Provo for the final performance, I was greeted by Tim Slover [who was playing the role of Elder Lucas], who asked me what I thought about all the script changes. When I professed ignorance, he wryly noted that I was in for some surprises. I found Bob Nelson, who invited me to the Green Room. He explained that, toward the middle of the run, he had, in essence, been ordered by higher administration to make changes in the script. Accordingly, he had eliminated the stage prayers, modified certain word choices and phrasings, and softened the ending. He had also been asked to remove all references to missionaries without a testimony. When he pointed out that making this last change would force the closure of the play, the administration backed off, apparently fearing bad press.... After considerable soul-searching, I did not take legal action against BYU [for breach of contract].[12]

---

8   Eugene England, "'Play Review a Disservice,' He Says," *Deseret News*, Letters to the Editor, March 1982.
9   Theron H. Luke. "'Fires of the Mind' Draws Critical Acclaim," *Provo Daily Herald*, March 1982.
10 Lee Nelson. "*Fires of the Mind*—One of the Most Controversial Plays Ever Performed by BYU, Certainly a Timely Performance," *Central Utah Journal*, March 24, 1982.
11 Elliott, Autobiography.
12 *Ibid.*

The condemnation of intellectual pride and the championing of genuine spirituality which the text clearly presents seems to make this initial concern over the play's honest nature more than a bit reactionary. Elliott made his intentions perfectly clear in a published preface to the play:

> I believe that contemporary LDS society is prepared to accept penetrating self analysis which, without resorting to outrage or negativism, attempts to deal honestly with the human problems and weaknesses which plague it. *Fires of the Mind* does not intend, in any way, to disparage the divine doctrines and principles on which our religion is founded. It is a human drama reflecting the imperfect thoughts and actions of several imperfect but good young men, each struggling in his own way to become better.[13]

In 1976 Orson Scott Card reviewed what he considered several significant, "watershed" Mormon plays, and he declared that *Fires of the Mind* was "the best of them all":

> The play is sometimes moving, often humorous, always gripping. Elliott has captured missionary language perfectly, and his characters are unbearably real. *Fires* would be important for this alone, but Elliott has advanced Mormon theatre in another respect: in *Fires of the Mind* the bad guys are as Mormon as the good guys. This kind of frankness could have degenerated into wholesale debunking, but Elliott very carefully balanced every argument presented. Johnson may accuse Markham and Matthews of lacking testimonies, but Lucas is always there to insist that he is wrong, and when Johnson is under attack as a bad missionary, a few who understand him are able to give a kinder view. And yet, in spite of his complete fairness, Elliott gives the play a moral, though not moralistic, conclusion: Unless an audience member is determined to side with Johnson, he will see Johnson's decision at the end as a mistake, however understandable it is.[14]

Since the 1982 production of *Fires of the Mind*, Elliott has not produced another play.[15] He has written an unfinished full-length family drama called *Primogeniture*, a draft of which won Cornell University's Forbes–McCalmon Playwriting Competition in 1978. A one-act farce, *From Ribs to Riches*, which pre-dates *Fires*, won an honorable mention in the same contest, but neither of those plays has had much exposure in the public realm.

In answering why he hasn't written more dramatic material after such a successful start, Elliott stated:

---

13   Robert Elliott, Author's Preface, *Fires of the Mind, Sunstone Magazine*, 1 (Winter 975).
14   Card, "Mormon Shakespeares."
15   Orson Scott Card directed *Ribs* in the mid-70s for BYU's Mask Club in the Nelke Experimental Theatre.

I've always been hesitant to ascribe my lack of productivity to writer's block, but I suppose the term applies. I have attempted to jump-start my playwriting numerous times since 1975, most recently and fully in 1996 when I devoted myself to it for two years after selling my business and before I began work at the University of Kansas. I have only fragments and false starts to show for it. . . . Sometimes I wonder if I've been smitten with a "stupor of thought." Those infuriated by *Fires* would gleefully endorse that explanation. Sometime in the 1980s, Tom Rogers told me I would eventually find my voice again. Perhaps I will.[16]

---

16   Elliott, email to Stewart, January 13, 2008.

About *Fires of the Mind*

Fires of the Mind premiered at Brigham Young University from October 31–November 15, 1974, with the following cast and crew:

CAST

Elder Barney Johnson: Rodger McDonald
Elder Keith Poll: Kent Smith
Elder Mark Markham: Steve Mackay
Elder Stephen Lucas: Keith Stepp
Elder Joseph Matthews: Max Mulliner
Brother Tang Li Sun [Uncle Sam]: Paul Jan
Sister Chou Li Ts-Wun [Holly]: Nadine Saito
Brother Ch'en Yun Ta: Frank Maxwell

CREW

Director: Charles Whitman
Assistant to the Director: John Williams
Stage Manager: Henry Irving
Lighting and Set Designer: Brent Lefavor

Brigham Young University then produced the revival from March 18–April 2, 1982, with the following cast and crew:

CAST

Elder Barney Johnson: Scott Eckern
Elder Keith Poll: Mark Parmley
Elder Mark Markham: Kirk Strickland
Elder Stephen Lucas: Tim Slover
Elder Joseph Matthews: David Val Christiansen
Brother Tang Li Sun [Uncle Sam]: Ronald Gima
Sister Chou Li Ts-Wun [Holly]: Kaoru Yamamoto
Brother Ch'en Yun Ta: Ji You Meng

CREW

Director: Robert Nelson
Assistant Director: Paula Eckern

Stage Manager: James Van Leishout
Set Designer: Charles A. Henson
Costume Designer: Mary Jane Hegyessy
Lighting Designer: Robert Saxon
Technical Director: Paul Nibley
Costumer: Sandra Gray

CHARACTERS

ELDER BARNEY JOHNSON, 22, a Latter-day Saint missionary in Nationalist China (Taiwan).

ELDER KEITH POLL, 21, Johnson's third senior companion.

ELDER MARK MARKHAM, 20, Johnson's fourth senior companion.

ELDER JOSEPH MATTHEWS, 21, Johnson's zone leader.

ELDER STEPHEN LUCAS, 19, Matthews's junior companion, the ZLC.

BROTHER T'ANG LI SUN (UNCLE SAM), 45, their Chinese houseboy.

SISTER CHOU LI TS'WUN (HOLLY), 20, a Chinese college student.

BROTHER CH'EN YUN TA, 32, a Chinese college professor.

SYNOPSIS OF SCENES

The action occurs over a three-week period in the summer of 1970 in Taipei, capital city of the Republic of China (Taiwan), and one of its suburbs, Lung Nan.

ACT ONE: A missionary apartment in Lung Nan. Late afternoon.

ACT TWO: A chapel classroom in Taipei two weeks later. Early evening.

ACT THREE: The missionary apartment one week later. Early morning.

EPILOGUE: The same. That night.

SETTING

Although the play might best be performed in the round, with a less cluttered set, I have provided proscenium directions for convenience in visualization. The missionary apartment, though it is situated on the third floor of a medium-rent Chinese apartment building, might easily be mistaken for a cheap flat in mid-town Kansas City. It contains a front room and a kitchen, both uncarpeted, visible to the audience. A door backstage left leads to a bedroom and bath facilities. Backstage right is the entrance from the apartment balcony and staircase. The front room contains a small dinner table, a coffee table, several hard-back chairs, two armchairs, a sofa, a coat rack, a bookcase, and nefarious other articles strewn about haphazardly. Only a few curious items—a Chinese painting, a coolie hat hanging from the coat rack, a Chinese newspaper—suggest that the apartment's inhabitants are 10,000 miles from home. The kitchen is nondescript, stripped to essentials, containing only a stove, a sink, a refrigerator, and some drawer or cabinet space. The chapel classroom is of white cement, very small and windowless. It contains only a small table or desk and a number of fold-up metal chairs. The entrance from the corridor is backstage right.

DRESS

Except for ACT THREE, the missionaries wear standard white shirts and ties, with reasonably dressy pants, but without coats. Due to the weather, the shirts may be short-sleeved, or the characters may roll their sleeves up. Jeans, T-shirts, and tennis shoes are perfectly appropriate for the playday. UNCLE SAM wears rough working clothes, sporting a besmeared apron in the kitchen. HOLLY dresses in fashionable Western styles, preferably classy pants outfits. BROTHER CH'EN wears an uninspired business suit, of any color, a white shirt, and a thin dark tie.

*"If assurance is a burning in the bosom,
doubts are the fires of the mind."*

Act One

The missionary apartment. Late afternoon. POLL *and* JOHNSON *are seated in the front room at the dinner table, drinking Chi Shui. The lights come up on* JOHNSON *first, then spread to* POLL *and the entire scene.*

JOHNSON. *(Lightly)* Well, how do you feel, Elder Poll?

POLL. I don't know. It's a little like dying.

JOHNSON. Come on.

POLL. No, really. I'm scared. *(Pause.)* It's not just going home. You see this ring?

JOHNSON. Your class ring?

POLL. No, *not* my class ring. *A* class ring.

JOHNSON. I thought it was yours.

POLL. So has everyone my whole mission. Well it's not.

  Pause.

JOHNSON. *(Curious now.)* Whose is it?

POLL. Her name is Jenny Peterson.

JOHNSON. Jenny Pe— J. P.! I thought that was your mother writing you all those letters!

POLL. Pretty close.

JOHNSON. Oh, man.

  JOHNSON *starts laughing.*

POLL. She's waiting, and she thinks we'll be married in two months.

  This is even more hilarious. JOHNSON *laughs harder.*

POLL. I'm up the creek; I mean what can I say? Two years and the only guy she's been out with is her cousin. Jeez. *(Pause.)* What's so doggone funny?

JOHNSON. *(Grandly, with a grin.)* Romeo Poll.

POLL. *(Unamused.)* Yeah.

JOHNSON. *(Still chuckling.)* Hey, take it easy, it'll work out.

POLL. Yeah, well . . . well, it's just that things are so different.

JOHNSON. Maybe, maybe not. Missions are screwy. They warp people. And not only about girls. Jeez, I've never been so neurotic. Everything's so . . . unnatural.

POLL. *(Needling good-naturedly.)* The natural man is an enemy to God.

JOHNSON. *(Studying his half-full glass.)* I wonder if anyone's ever been baptized in soda pop.

POLL. *(Grabbing the bottle.)* Stay where you are, Johnson, or so help me, I'll soak you.

They both get up and circle the table warily. JOHNSON *stops.*

JOHNSON. To Keith and Jenny Poll. Cheers.

POLL *laughs and they drink. A terrible barking breaks out outside the door. There are bumping noises and* MARKHAM *appears, haggard and winded.*

MARKHAM. Garbage!

POLL *and* JOHNSON *laugh.* MARKHAM *grins.*

MARKHAM. What was that?

JOHNSON. We call him Cerberus. Can we help you?

MARKHAM. No, I've got it.

He bumps in, puts down bags.

MARKHAM. Whew! That's a hard climb with a foot locker.

POLL. Welcome to the Lung Nan Arms Celestial Suite.

Laughter.

MARKHAM. Is that what you guys call this place? *(Looks around.)* Well, it is pretty nice. You should see the places in the south.

POLL. I've been there, you young whipper. Hey, you guys haven't met, have you?

JOHNSON. No.

POLL. Elder Barney Johnson, Elder Mark Markham.

MARKHAM. Hi.

JOHNSON. How are you?

They shake hands.

POLL. Hey, how about some Chi Shui?

MARKHAM. All right! *(Laughter.)* Oh, I've still got some stuff in the cab. Save me a glass, okay?

Goes out; barking. POLL *and* JOHNSON *retire to the table, both are meditative.*

JOHNSON. Seems like a nice guy.

POLL. Yeah, you'll get along great.

JOHNSON. You think so?

POLL. Yeah.

Pause.

JOHNSON. Listen, will you talk to him? I'm tired of going through it.

POLL. You want me to?

JOHNSON. Yeah—I get so tired.

POLL. I'm sure he knows some of it already.

JOHNSON groans irritably.

POLL. Well, you let the cat out of the bag at conference.

JOHNSON. What else could I do? Jeez! Bearing testimonies like it was a game of dominoes. One guy plops down, the next guy stands up, everyone trying to outdo the guy before. No way out. I just sat there and watched it coming. Man, I had to be honest! Pressure testimony. Social testimony. Jeez, that irks me!

POLL. Come on.

JOHNSON. *(Burned.)* Well...

POLL. Listen, you know most of those guys mean what they say.

JOHNSON. Yeah, but they just say what everybody wants to hear. It's not the whole truth. It's propaganda. It's a big psyche-up session.

POLL. Sure it is. The Communists do the same thing over on the mainland. Political parties do it. Businesses do it. It's positive thinking. Everybody's got doubts, but they only discuss them in private. Everybody wants to be riding a winner, so they try to convince themselves they are. Except for us. We know we've got the truth.

JOHNSON. Some of us do.

Bumping, barking; they lapse into silence. MARKHAM *reappears.*

MARKHAM. Should it cost 50 kwai to get here from the train station?

POLL. That's about right.

MARKHAM. Huh, I gave the guy a hard time for nothing. *(He grins.)* Oh well.

POLL. You want that Chi Shui?

MARKHAM. You bet! It's not as hot here, but it sure is muggy.

POLL. Elder Johnson, why don't you store Elder Markham's stuff in the bedroom. I'll fill him in on our investigators. And work on that fifth discussion, Okay?

JOHNSON. Aye, aye, cap'n. Hey—let me know before you leave.

POLL. I will.

JOHNSON goes into the bedroom.

MARKHAM. *(Drinking.)* Boy, that tastes good. You remember Tate? Marlowe says that Tate's working out a plan to import this stuff to the States. He'll make a fortune.

POLL. It'll never fly. Tate's all mouth.

MARKHAM. Yeah, well, probably so—say, how's the work going here?

POLL. A little slow, right now. We've got one good man coming along, and one of those eternal girls, and two students and a housewife on firsts. But summers are awful, you know. Everybody falls out, or goes on vacation, or some other doggone thing. We're frustrated.

MARKHAM. *(Casually checks bedroom door, which* JOHNSON *has closed.)* How's Johnson?

POLL. What?

MARKHAM. I wondered—well, you know—since the conference—and Larsen moved in with us after he left here. He told us there'd been some—problems.

POLL. Larsen talks too much.

MARKHAM. Well, we all talk.

POLL. Yeah, you're right. We all talk—too much! Listen, I don't know what Larsen told you, or what conclusions you drew from that little incident at conference, but you've got one heckuva good companion on your hands. Johnson's a good man—he's a good man. *(Pause.)* Hey, I'm sorry. I know you're probably nervous about this assignment. Well, it's not easy. But don't lose faith in Johnson. He's got all the tools.

MARKHAM. Except one.

POLL. *(Agreeing reluctantly.)* Yeah.

MARKHAM. What's his problem?

POLL. Well, he's hung up on this "real communication" thing. He knows the Church rests basically on revelation and individual testimony, and he's not satisfied with what he's got.

MARKHAM. *(Snorts.)* Well, who is?

POLL. Yeah, but he looks at it different. He doesn't want a sign, but he figures the "warm feelings" everybody talks about aren't enough to base your life on. He wants something more, and until he gets it, he has to reserve judgment. And he's honest, painfully honest. I mean he can't just accept the fact that he hasn't completely arrived, and work at it slowly. He's always thinking about it and tormenting himself, and sometimes he has to let loose. I guess that's what happened at conference. He's too intellectual, I suppose. He is smart. Sometimes he goes through all his arguments and counter-arguments with me. Most of the time I don't know what he's talking about. I just tell him to be patient and stop worrying. Yeah, he is intelligent.

MARKHAM. The glory of God is intelligence.

POLL. Huh?

MARKHAM. The glory of God is intelligence; the wisdom of men is foolishness and it profiteth them not. That's Second Nephi.

POLL. Yeah, I know where it's from. Jeez, Elder, don't throw that at him. He'd go into a shell for weeks.

MARKHAM. *(Worried and indignant.)* Well, why's he here if he doesn't have a testimony? How'd he get through his interviews?

POLL. Ahh, you know how it is. Half the guys out here didn't have a testimony when they left. I didn't. I didn't know enough. Blind faith pulled me through, and I'm glad, but I'm sure I wasn't very impressive when I was interviewed. All they really look for is desire, and Johnson's got plenty of that. He says his stake president just smiled when he told him all his doubts and said, "You scoundrel, you'll be the best missionary of them all." And, well, that is the important thing, Elder Markham. Johnson wants to know the truth and he wants to share. School was getting him nowhere. He figured a mission would force some answers. So he came.

MARKHAM. How can I help him?

POLL. Be patient. President Jones drops him a line about once a week, and they talk whenever he comes in from Hong Kong. That's why they've kept him here in the capital—for easy access. It's kind of a shame, though. Johnson's always been a leader, and here he is, stuck in the same city after ten months, still a junior companion, while all his LTM group are senior companions or branch presidents. He gets depressed.

MARKHAM. I can imagine.

POLL. Well, listen, if you'll do the work, he'll follow you and help you. He's no slacker. Just stay with him, and I think it'll come.

Barking; enter MATTHEWS *and* LUCAS.

LUCAS. Scramble, baby. The great white bird awaits.

POLL. Lucas, I only regret that I'm leaving this beautiful island to the likes of you.

Laughter.

LUCAS. Come on, graybeard. I promised Osborne I'd have you back at the chapel inside of twenty minutes.

POLL Osborne? Man, it's been a long time since I saw him!

LUCAS. He and Anderson are terrorizing the greenies. You know how thin Anderson is. Well, he convinced one kid that he weighed 220 when he came on the island. And I heard Osborne warning two kids going to Kaohsiung about blood leeches and poisonous spiders.

Laughter.

POLL. Wow, I'd better get down there. I don't want to miss all the action. *(Looks around.)* Well...

MATTHEWS. Are your bags in the bedroom?

POLL. Yeah. Hey, send Johnson out.

MATTHEWS and LUCAS go into the bedroom.

MARKHAM. Good luck, Elder Poll.

POLL. Same to you, Elder. And be patient.

JOHNSON. *(Coming out.)* Time?

POLL. Yeah.

He hesitates; MATTHEWS *and* LUCAS *come out heavily laden.*

MARKHAM. *(To* LUCAS.*)* Here, give me one of those.

LUCAS. With pleasure.

Gives him the heaviest, laughing; they go out; barking.

JOHNSON. Thanks, Elder Poll. You've been like a brother.

POLL. It's been good, Barney. Take care. Look me up.

JOHNSON. You and the Mrs.?

POLL. If Markham came back and found you dead, they'd never catch me. *(They laugh.)* I—love you, Elder.

JOHNSON. Me too.

They hesitantly embrace, arm on shoulder.

LUCAS. *(Outside.)* Quick, Poll! We're being attacked by Red commandos!

POLL. Ha. I'm glad the ZLs are moving in here. I don't like Matthews much, but Lucas is gonna be one of the best. Talk to him.

JOHNSON. Okay. Seriously, good luck with the lady. And write.

POLL. Thanks, I will . . . Dzai Jyan.

JOHNSON. Dzai Jyan.

Barking: POLL *is gone.* JOHNSON *goes out on the balcony, waits a few seconds, is seen waving; comes back in, pours out a glass of Chi Shui, wanders, opens a scripture, closes it, ponders; barking; enter* MARKHAM.

MARKHAM. Brother, that dog is something! I'm sure glad they've got him chained up. What'd you say you called him?

JOHNSON. Cerberus.

JOHNSON. What's that? Sounds like some kind of mass transportation.

JOHNSON. Heh, no. It's from the Greek myths. Cerberus was the three-headed dog that guarded the gates of Hell. He kept the dead in and the living out.

MARKHAM. *(Going along lightly.)* And which is Hell—in here or out there?

JOHNSON. *(Coldly.)* It depends. Wherever I am, Hell follows. I better study.

He walks quickly into the bedroom; MARKHAM *looks deflated and bewildered.*

JOHNSON. *(Returning.)* Hey, I'm sorry, Elder. I guess I just like to shock people or something. I figure if they already think I'm a louse, I can't disappoint them with the real me. Really, I'm sorry. Can we talk about it later?

MARKHAM. Sure. *(Pause.)* Where you from?

JOHNSON. Mesa. You?

MARKHAM. Salt Lake. *(Pause.)* You go to the Y?

JOHNSON. Yeah, you?

MARKHAM. No, U. of U. One year?

JOHNSON. Three.

MARKHAM. How old are you?

JOHNSON. 22.

MARKHAM. Hmm.

JOHNSON. What are you studying?

MARKHAM. Oh, I haven't really decided. I'd like to be a doctor.

JOHNSON. Competition's rough.

MARKHAM. Yeah. How 'bout you?

JOHNSON. Oh, I've bounced around a lot. Social science, humanities, history. I don't know.

   Pause.

MARKHAM. Uh, you always been a member?

JOHNSON. Well, I was baptized when I was eight, if that's what you mean. Yeah, I'm a lifer.

MARKHAM. Your folks active?

JOHNSON. *(Looks up irritably, then smiles.)* Yeah. Look, I guess I better explain some things. Elder Poll didn't have much time. I come from a good Mormon family. My dad's been in bishoprics half his life, and my mom's a stalwart Mormon homemaker. My brother was an AP in England and my little sister's a seminary officer. *(Mildly sarcastic.)* Everybody in our ward thinks we're wonderful.

MARKHAM. What's wrong with that?

JOHNSON. *(Sizing him up.)* Let's talk about it another time.

MARKHAM. No, wait, now if we're gonna be companions we've got to know each other. I want to know what makes you tick. What's wrong with being respected?

JOHNSON. Well, my family's got problems like anybody else. My dad works too long and too hard, my mom's got an awful temper. You know. But it's not their fault. It's the lifestyle. Upper middle-class. Split-level home. Two cars, a camper, a garden, sprinklers, dishwasher, workshop. I don't know. It's so domestic, and lifeless—bloodless. The boredom grates on everybody, even if they don't realize it. And the Church goes right along with it. Everything's geared to the family—which is fine—except all the families are geared to money, success, drudging work, and boring leisure. For me, the gospel and the Church don't jibe. It's hard to explain. It seems like there should be more.

Pause.

MARKHAM. More what?

JOHNSON. I don't know. Excitement, maybe. Well, not really. Real active happiness. Joy. Life.

MARKHAM. The Church brings me joy.

JOHNSON. Really? It brings most people peace. Then they sleep through life satisfied. They're content, not joyful. They fall into a pattern and spend the rest of their lives following a program. And they think they're happy.

MARKHAM. *(Mildly defiant.)* Maybe they are.

JOHNSON. Hey, I'm not aiming this at you or anybody. It's just that, well, the gospel tells us not to be of the world, and we interpret that as meaning to avoid sex and drugs and alcohol. But what about materialism, the whole middle-class mentality? That's twice as insidious! *(He hits the table. Pause.)* I think it's funny that they call good Mormons "active." It oughta be "passive." *(Silence.)* You shouldn't have started me.

MARKHAM. No, that's fine.

JOHNSON. Look, I believe in the gospel. The principles strike me really right. The New Testament is beautiful, though there was a time I wondered about all that self-denial. Anyway, it's the doctrines that worry me—and some of the things the Church does to people. But I could swallow the whole ball of wax if I knew it was true. I just want that assurance, and then I'll work within the system to make it all meaningful. The Lord promises individual revelation. That's what I want. Then I could surrender myself. But not before. *(Shrugs.)* That's why I'm here. They said in order to know the gospel you have to live it and share it. I mean it is good. It brings people out of total confusion and gives them self-respect. It just seems like it should do more. I want more. What do you think?

MARKHAM. Mmm, Elder, I feel like I should bear my . . .

Barking; outside a booming voice.

VOICE. Sup-per! Sup-per!

JOHNSON. Uncle Sam!

MARKHAM. The servant?

JOHNSON. Oh, man, don't call him that. *(Going to door.)* Say hey, Uncle!

UNCLE SAM. Hey! Arizona still here! Good! Tonight, bacon, lettuce, and tomato, heh, heh, heh.

JOHNSON. Where'd you get it?

UNCLE SAM. Black market, heh, heh, heh.

JOHNSON. You old rascal. *(They both laugh. To MARKHAM.)* When he cooked for the army, they always called him the "old rascal." He stole them blind, but they loved him.

UNCLE SAM. *(To MARKHAM.)* Don't worry, I've reformed, heh, heh, heh. The Mormons came and told me about John Smith. . . .

JOHNSON. Joseph Smith.

UNCLE SAM. Joseph Smith and the Book of Moroni.

JOHNSON. Mormon.

UNCLE SAM. Mormon, heh, heh, heh. They perverted me.

JOHNSON. Converted, you old rascal.

UNCLE SAM. Heh, heh, heh.

JOHNSON. His English is better than mine. Don't let him put you on. He's a hopeless ham and his favorite role is the funny-dumb Chinaman. He picked it up from American TV shows. You remember Hop Sing from *Bonanza*?

UNCLE SAM. *(Mugs and kowtows a bit; then, to JOHNSON.)* Who's the new tenant?

JOHNSON. Elder Mark Markham—Salt Lake.

UNCLE SAM. Utah 22.

MARKHAM. What?

JOHNSON. You're the twenty-second Utah elder that's lived here since he started work. I'm Arizona 5. Poll was Idaho 16. Uncle Sam, a treat! A Canadian!

UNCLE SAM. Oh, my very first, heh, heh, heh. What else?

JOHNSON. Where's Matthews from?

MARKHAM. California.

UNCLE SAM. *(Wrinkles his nose.)* Ooh.

JOHNSON. He doesn't like Californians. *(To SAM.)* How's your family?

UNCLE SAM. The same. Ai Mei is still sick, and my wife is very tired. She works too hard.

MARKHAM. Where does she work?

JOHNSON. The Zenith plant. *(To SAM.)* Hey, Uncle, maybe this'll help.

Pulls pouch off coffee table.

UNCLE SAM. What is it?

JOHNSON. It's Idaho's Chinese money. He figured it wouldn't do him much good in Boise.

UNCLE SAM. Idaho was a good elder. *(Pause)* Well, sup-per!

JOHNSON. Okay, Uncle. If you need any help holler.

UNCLE SAM. *(Roaring)* I am the master of my kitchen, Arizona! You learn Chinese!

JOHNSON. *(Laughing.)* Okay. *(To* MARKHAM.*)* The guy's a riot.

MARKHAM. How long has he worked here?

JOHNSON. Three years.

MARKHAM. Any trouble?

JOHNSON. *(Scoffing.)* No; he's a counselor in the MIA. And he loves the elders, even though he's down on Americans. The army raked him over good.

MARKHAM. Sounds like it was mutual.

JOHNSON. Dog eat dog, brother. That's one thing I like about the gospel. At least it puts a stop to a lot of cutthroating.

> *Barking.* MATTHEWS *and* LUCAS *are heard singing "God Be with You." They come in, finishing the hymn together, self-consciously, very low and out of key. Laughter.*

LUCAS. Man, that was beautiful. You should've seen it. The whole place was going nuts when we got there. Osborne and Anderson and Jeffries were doing a cancan on the lawn and Moffitt had some fireworks. Then Poll did his Nixon imitation and waved peace signs at everybody. I thought I was gonna split.

MATTHEWS. It's not so funny for us, Canadian.

LUCAS. Well, if you can do a Trudeau imitation, I promise to laugh just as hard.

UNCLE SAM. *(From the kitchen door.)* I am Pierre Trudeau, the most beautiful prime minister in the world. Mah, mah, mah, mah!!!

> *He does kissing imitations. Laughter.*

LUCAS. *(Delighted.)* Is that the houseboy?

JOHNSON. Uncle Sam.

LUCAS. You don't really expect me to call him that, do you? What's his last name?

JOHNSON. T'ang.

LUCAS. *(Taking* SAM's *wooden serving spoon, taps him on both shoulders.)* Brother T'ang, I dub you Pierre.

UNCLE SAM. *(Takes back the spoon.)* What does "dub" mean?

LUCAS. It means I've given you a title.

Sam raps LUCAS *once, lightly, on the head.*

UNCLE SAM. I dub you Canada 1.

He retires. Laughter.

LUCAS. Anyway, Gordon finally stopped the festivities and led a prayer. Then we all sang "God Be with You." It was really something—the old heads, and the greenies, and the office staff, and the chapel elders. Some of the members came down, too. *(Pause.)* Man, I've gotta be careful or I'll start crying again. *(Pause.)* Yea, even the great Stoneface did shed a tear.

He points to MATTHEWS, *who grins sheepishly.*

MATTHEWS. It reminded me of leaving the LTM. A mission's too short.

Pause; then, authoritatively, but apprehensively:

MATTHEWS. Elder Johnson? We need to set you some new language goals. Your old ones are out of date.

JOHNSON. Oh, great!

MATTHEWS. Let's go in the bedroom.

JOHNSON. *(Heaving a sigh.)* Like a lamb to the slaughter.

Walking into the bedroom.

JOHNSON. How many times have we been through this?

MATTHEWS *closes the door.*

MARKHAM. He hasn't even got the sixth yet?

LUCAS. Not yet.

MARKHAM. How's his conversation?

LUCAS. Really good; he speaks as well as anybody, and he's got the gist of all the lessons. It's just the memorizing that bogs him down. He's sort of . . . got other things on his mind.

MARKHAM. Yeah, we talked a little already.

LUCAS. He's probably got more talent for the language than any elder I've met.

MARKHAM. Hmm! Well, he couldn't have any more talent than you. They tell me you learned all six in the LTM. Down south they call you Wonder Boy.

LUCAS. *(Quietly)* You know, I'm a little ashamed about that.

MARKHAM. *(Astonished)* Are you kidding?

LUCAS. No, really. Oh, I'm glad I learned the lessons, all right. It's been a big help. But I sure had a bad attitude in the LTM.

MARKHAM. How so?

LUCAS. I come from a little hick town in Alberta. When I got my mission call, I made up my mind that no big-city Heart of Zion boys were ever gonna show me up. I was determined to beat 'em all. You see what I mean? I went into the LTM red hot, and I burned the place up. But it wasn't for the Lord. I worked really hard, but only to prove that I was the best. All that work was an ego trip. I felt competitive. You know, I not only felt good when I succeeded on a conclusion or a discussion—I felt good when my companions failed! I'm surprised the Lord didn't humble me—hit me with a stupor of thought or something.

MARKHAM. I don't see anything wrong with wanting to be the best. That's what the gospel's all about—reaching exaltation. And only a few'll make it.

LUCAS. Sure, I want to be my best. And I wanna make exaltation. But it's not a contest. We're supposed to love and help each other. You can't kick and elbow your way to glory—it's just not Christlike. I don't know how this "better" and "best" thing got started, anyway; it's the same stuff that ruined the Nephites. Everywhere, everybody wants to be the best. The best roadshow, the best Sunday School, the best mission. It's not enough just to live righteously and do the Lord's work. People expect all kinds of praise and recognition for it.

MARKHAM. Praise reinforces people. It helps them.

LUCAS. Sometimes; but people are too praise-oriented, you know? They all want a reward. Rewards are a Law of Moses concept. Do we obey the commandments just to gain a reward—a blessing? I hope not. Christ said, "If ye love me, keep my commandments." That's the ticket. We obey out of love for God, not because we know what He can do for us.

MARKHAM. *(Blankly.)* Yeah.

LUCAS. It's funny the way rewards sort of creep up on us. You're from Salt Lake; you ever notice how many people consider leadership positions rewards for living the best lives? No, really, think about it. Don't you set up a ranking system in your mind about which Church positions are the most prestigious? And don't you judge people by the positions they're called to? And don't you look at the supposedly more prestigious jobs as rewards? It's hard not to; I have an awful time. But that's the worldly perspective. The world is completely reward-oriented. The gospel is based on love.

MARKHAM. *(Fairly snowed.)* That's pretty heavy stuff, Elder Lucas. You come on like a philosophy prof.

LUCAS. *(Laughs.)* Yeah, well, it's been my pet subject ever since I realized what a bum I was in the LTM. I didn't mean to talk your ear off.

MARKHAM. No, it's interesting. I'll have to think about it. *(Pause.)* I guess I've been thinking a little about it already—rewards, I mean. I've been out almost a year and things just haven't been like I expected.

LUCAS. The mission field, you mean?

MARKHAM. Yeah, I don't know. I've worked hard since I came out, and sometimes I wonder if it's been worth it. A few people that I've taught have come into the Church, but three of them are inactive already, and I don't think the rest really know what they're doing. Every time somebody really feels the gospel and comes in, somebody else loses it and goes out. I hit the doors, and check all the referrals, and fast and pray and study, and I beat my brains out at night trying to think of creative new approaches, new introductions. If I could have baptized one family, or just one good man...

LUCAS. You'd like to see some results.

MARKHAM. *(Pursuing this rapidly.)* Well, I've seen some good come from my work; but it sure seems insignificant compared to the scriptures, or Church history, or even some of the things I used to hear in sacrament meetings. It seems like there should be something here, too—something I could put my finger on and say, "That was a success."

LUCAS. Yeah, I know how you feel. Usually there is; but really if we have faith and work hard, the Holy Ghost will tell us we've done well. Besides, tangible success is just another reward—an outward sign. Rewards are a lot like signs. They're artificial. Take Johnson—now he's a sign-seeker even though he's pretty subtle about it. He wants some glorious inner manifestation. But he still wants it to come from an external source. He won't accept anything his own spirit tells him, even when he's been touched by the Holy Ghost. He calls it emotion and goes on waiting for something supernatural. Reward-seekers aren't that complex. They just want some outer confirmation that they've done well—material comforts and blessings, praise, or a position. But it amounts to the same thing. Reward-seekers and sign-seekers are both looking for proof that they're worthy. They're both insecure, and they want the Lord to compensate them for it. Sometimes He will, but sometimes He won't. I guess that's the trial of faith, or at least one of them. *(Synthesizing.)* Yeah. Reward-seeking equals sign-seeking. *(Brightly.)* I like that.

Pause.

MARKHAM. It sounds good. But, you know, it seems like half the scriptures talk about life and the commandments in terms of rewards. Obey, and receive a blessing, obey and inherit the earth, obey and receive exaltation.

LUCAS. That's terrestrial stuff. It's milk, not meat.

MARKHAM. Maybe so. *(Pause.)* You know, you just hit on something else I didn't expect out here. I was ready for bad food, sickness, crummy apartments, doors slammed in my face, even persecution, and I haven't had problems with any of 'em. The food and the apartments are pretty good and the people are really pretty nice. But I wasn't ready for a companion without a testimony. I thought even if we didn't get along personally, we'd at least have common goals. What can I do about Johnson?

LUCAS. Listen, his bark is worse than his bite. He's been a fine missionary these last three months. Give him a chance. His spirit's coming around, and it's telling him good things, even if his head doesn't know it yet.

MARKHAM. I hope so. *(Earnestly.)* I want to do the work here, and we've got to do it together. *(Pause.)* I just want to be a good missionary, you know?

LUCAS. We all do.

> MATTHEWS *and* JOHNSON *come out of the bedroom.* MATTHEWS *is visibly rattled and perturbed.* JOHNSON *is bland and whimsical, his eyes twinkling.*

MATTHEWS. Elder Markham. Sorry I didn't talk to you right away. I wanted to get those goals set with Elder Johnson while we had a chance. Welcome to Lung Nan.

> *Handshake.*

MARKHAM. Thanks, Elder Matthews.

> *There is some obvious hero worship here.*

LUCAS. Whew, I'm bushed. How long till supper?

UNCLE SAM. *(Roaring from kitchen.)* Twenty minutes! Any complaints, Canada?!

LUCAS. Mais, non, Pierre. Pardonnez-moi. *(Laughter.* LUCAS *staggers in mock agony.)* Uhh! It's got me!

MARKHAM. What?

LUCAS. *(Moving toward bedroom as though being sucked into a vacuum.)* The Force, it's irresistible. *(He clutches the door frame as though being blown by gale force winds; hoarsely.)* Mattress gravity. I'm a goner, boys. Wake me for dinner.

> *He vanishes. There is a plop and a long sigh.* MARKHAM, MATTHEWS, *and* JOHNSON *laugh.*

MATTHEWS. Crazy kid.

MARKHAM. Well, how's the work here in the North?

MATTHEWS. Oh, it's coming; the Lord is blessing us daily. The harvest is at hand if we'll just thrust in our sickles and reap. If the Lord is with us, we can't fail.

MARKHAM. The gospel's so beautiful. I've never been so happy.

MATTHEWS. Yes, these are the best two years of our lives.

MARKHAM. It's so wonderful to be serving these people. They're so humble and beautiful. I work my tail off and I love every minute of it. It makes me feel so good. I wish I could just do this forever.

MATTHEWS. How long have you been out?

MARKHAM. 11½ months tomorrow.

> JOHNSON *has been relaxing with his Chi Shui, listening in quiet disbelief. This cracks him up.* MATTHEWS *and* MARKHAM *glance over.* JOHNSON *stops laughing. They continue.*

MATTHEWS. Well, the worth of souls is great in the eyes of the Lord. It gives me a warm feeling all over to see the gospel spreading here.

MARKHAM. Like a rock cut from a mountain without hands.

MATTHEWS. Huh?

JOHNSON puts an open Bible over his face to hide his laughter.

MARKHAM. Daniel's prophecy.

MATTHEWS. Oh. *(Pause.)* Yes, these are the best two years of our lives.

MARKHAM. Yup. *(Nods his head; pause.)* I've never been so happy.

Pause; JOHNSON *is obviously laughing again. They look at him.*

MATTHEWS. *(Nettled)* Something funny, Elder Johnson?

JOHNSON. *(Barely under control.)* No, no. I'd better go study.

He goes into the bedroom shaking with silent mirth.

MARKHAM. Say, when does Gordon leave?

MATTHEWS. The AP? Oh, three weeks or so. President Jones wanted him to supervise the move and make sure everybody's settled okay.

MARKHAM. When he goes, who'll take his place?

MATTHEWS. Oh, I don't know.

MARKHAM. I'll bet it's you. You're surely qualified.

MATTHEWS. Thanks. Well, the Lord will call whoever's best for the job. Besides I've only got three months left.

MARKHAM. That's plenty of time. Gordon's only been in nine weeks. I'm sure it'll be you.

MATTHEWS. Maybe so.

MARKHAM. Wow!

MATTHEWS. What?

MARKHAM. That'd be some job. *(Brief pause.)* I mean think of the responsibility. With President Jones only here once a month, the AP has to handle everything. Gee! I don't think I could *ever* prepare for anything like that.

MATTHEWS. Oh, in these positions you learn to trust the Lord. He never lets you down. No one ever feels prepared for a calling, but the Lord makes weak vessels strong.

MARKHAM. I'll remember that.

MATTHEWS. We've heard good things about you up here, Elder Markham. You and Elder Morris baptized six people in the last two months, didn't you?

MARKHAM. Yes.

MATTHEWS. And you averaged seventy hours a week. That's moving.

MARKHAM. Well, there's no time to waste, you know.

MATTHEWS. And seventeen investigators! How many will make it?

MARKHAM. Oh, hard to say. They're all on early lessons.

MATTHEWS. Any families?

MARKHAM. No, we've been trying to start a couple, but none yet.

MATTHEWS. Good men?

MARKHAM. Well, mostly high school kids really. You know how it is in the South.

MATTHEWS. It's the same here.

Pause.

MARKHAM. Say, if you do go AP, who'll be the new zone leader here?

MATTHEWS. Oh, President Jones really likes Lucas but he's only been out eight months, so I imagine he and Jensen would go co-ZL.

MARKHAM. Jensen's the district leader now here, isn't he? *(MATTHEWS nods.)* Hmm, who'll take his place?

MATTHEWS. Well, it's up for grabs. Wouldn't surprise me if it was you, though.

MARKHAM. Me!

MATTHEWS. Your reports have looked very good.

MARKHAM. Wow!

MATTHEWS. It's not a sure thing.

MARKHAM. Oh, of course not. Wow, I. . . .

MATTHEWS. See what you and Elder Johnson can do here in Lung Nan. I'll be talking to Elder Gordon and President Jones in a couple of weeks.

MARKHAM. I'll do my best. *(Pause; MARKHAM sighs.)* Brother. . . .

MATTHEWS. You worried about Johnson?

MARKHAM. Yeah.

MATTHEWS. *(Talking lower.)* Well, you got a right. He's a pain in the butt. I've talked to him twice, and it didn't do any good. He thinks he's twice as smart as anybody. And he just mopes around. He hasn't even learned the lessons yet. Says he can't concentrate. The guy's a loafer and a goldbrick. He drags down everybody. Don't let him get to you.

MARKHAM. He's already started telling me some of the junk he thinks about. It's incredible.

MATTHEWS. I haven't seen many guys I thought were worthless out here, but Johnson's one. He makes things miserable.

MARKHAM. What can I do?

MATTHEWS. Well, the big thing is don't baby him. Poll let him have his way, and it messed them both up. Their hours went way down. It killed the zone average. They were always talking. Or at least Johnson was. Poll'd pick his toenails or his nose or something *(MARKHAM laughs)* and Johnson'd just rattle on. Poll didn't have the guts to lay on him. You know how he was. He never even made DL. Straight senior for fifteen months. No leadership. I don't know how many hours they wasted.

MARKHAM. What about their contacts?

MATTHEWS. Well, that was funny. They did really well. They baptized two people a month all three months they were together. I don't know where they found 'em. And they've got one great guy now, too. Brother Ch'en. Gee, don't lose him. He's a potential branch president.

MARKHAM. How'd they find him?

MATTHEWS. Johnson met him on a bus. He's good at that. He just starts talking to people. Like Lucas. Yeah, Johnson's okay sometimes.

MARKHAM. But mostly he's a pain.

MATTHEWS. You wouldn't believe. He makes everybody nervous. You've got to get him moving. Stay on him. Work his tail off. And don't take any crap. If he starts to fizzle, remind him who he is and what he's here for.

MARKHAM. I'll try. What about their other investigators? Poll mentioned an "eternal girl"?

MATTHEWS. Holly Chou. Yeah, she's a foxy college chick that just walked into the chapel one day and started talking to Poll. Her English is pretty good, and I think she just wanted some practice. Poll got her into English class, and a week later they started teaching her the lessons. She was a fire-eater right up until they started seriously talking baptism. Then they found out she had some family problems. Her dad's a traditionalist and doesn't want her to join. I think he's pretty mean to her. She comes out to church and all the members love her. I think she's got a testimony, but it's hard to tell with girls, you know. They've been teaching her an extra lesson now and then, and Poll wanted to talk to her father, but she wouldn't let him. There's potential there. Stay with her. Careful, though, she's a knockout.

MARKHAM. Don't worry. I've had it with little girls. I want a good man or two.

MATTHEWS. Don't we all. *(Pause.)* Well, Johnson can tell you about the others. *(Earnestly.)* But listen, Elder Markham, you've gotta have some ready by the end of July. The zone's running low. Even Hong Kong beat us last month.

MARKHAM. We'll have some. Hey, how's the food here?

MATTHEWS. I've heard it's the best. Brother T'ang alternates Chinese and American food. Oh, and that's another thing. Most of the elders like Brother T'ang. But frankly, he bugs me. I don't trust these slant-eye houseboys even if they are members. And this one's too savvy. You know? He. . . .

UNCLE SAM. *(From kitchen.)* Arizona!

JOHNSON. *(From bedroom.)* Yo!

UNCLE SAM. Set the table!

JOHNSON. Aye aye, Uncle— *(Comes out; looks at* MARKHAM *and* MATTHEWS; *chuckles.)* Well, you guys got all our problems solved?

MATTHEWS. I forgot to tell you he's a wise guy, too. I don't envy you, Elder Markham. Remember, don't take any crap.

END ACT ONE

Act Two

The chapel classroom. Early evening. Two weeks later. JOHNSON *is seated at the table, studying. The lights come up on him, then spread.* MARKHAM *is pacing impatiently.*

MARKHAM. He's fifteen minutes late already.

JOHNSON. He'll be here.

MARKHAM. Is he always late?

JOHNSON. Always.

MARKHAM. Boy, I hope we haven't lost him. *(Pause.)* How's that fifth coming?

JOHNSON. Awful. I can't concentrate.

MARKHAM. Well, you'd better get on it. Matthews wants you to have all six by the move next week. He's holding me responsible. How long have you been out anyway? *(Silence.)* Come on, let's hear the first three conclusions.

JOHNSON. I'm not ready.

MARKHAM. *(Rebuking him, but without malice.)* Johnson, when are you gonna get smart? You've been dogging it ever since we started working together. You don't study in the mornings. You just sit there and read, or write in your journal, or stare off into space. That won't get you anywhere. You dog it on your bike. You dog it when we're tracting. I always have to wait for you. You even dog it in meetings. I might as well be alone most of the time. *(Pause.)* You better shape up. *(Pause.)* Understand?

JOHNSON. I ought to. I hear it daily.

MARKHAM. And you'll hear it until you do something about it! My patience is wearing thin. So is Elder Matthews's and President Jones's.

JOHNSON. President Jones understands.

MARKHAM. Wanna bet?

JOHNSON. You haven't talked to him.

MARKHAM. He wrote me a letter before the move.

JOHNSON. *(Interested.)* What'd he say?

MARKHAM. He said, Johnson, that you're his biggest headache right now and that he doesn't know what to do with you.

JOHNSON. He did not.

MARKHAM. He did. And he said he was sorry to put me into such a tricky situation, but somebody had to babysit, and he wanted someone responsible.

JOHNSON. He didn't say "babysit."

MARKHAM. *(Slightly abashed, then kindly advising.)* Well, that's what he meant. So shape up. You say you don't want to be the "problem missionary." Don't be. Get on the ball, Elder. Come on, let's hear that first conclusion.

He waits; pause.

JOHNSON. *(In a serious tone.)* Have you ever wondered what it'd be like to be Satan or Cain? I was reading today how Cain became Master Mahan. That's powerful stuff.

MARKHAM. Don't talk about it.

JOHNSON. *(Enjoying this.)* I look in the mirror sometimes and wonder what it'd be like to be possessed. I kind of let my eyes gleam and flash, and screw up my cheekbones and squint. Then I tighten every muscle in my body, and think about war or murder or sex. Once I started to shiver.

MARKHAM. You're talking evil, Elder Johnson. I don't want to hear it. That kind of talk brings on darkness. You've heard the stories. Drop it and, for your own sake, don't even think about it.

JOHNSON. Stories. I wouldn't mind seeing a devil. At least I'd know.

MARKHAM. *(Loudly.)* Will you shut up? *(Pause.)* Look, please give me the first conclusion.

JOHNSON. Don't worry, Elder. Sometimes I think I'd be better at wickedness than I am at righteousness. I have all kinds of ingenious ideas for evil. I bet I could be really creative. But it scares me as much as it does you.

MARKHAM. If it did, you wouldn't talk about it.

JOHNSON. Huh, maybe you're right. *(Gets up.)* No, I want to be righteous. I want the gospel to be true. Hmm! It's funny. I don't know if there are devils any more than I know there's a God. But they're a lot easier to talk about.

MARKHAM. Haven't you ever felt like you've had an answer to prayer?

JOHNSON. Sure, for a day or so. Even before my mission I'd get so uptight about truth that I'd go for a week or so not really thinking about anything else. Then I'd pray my guts out, and cry, and yell, and plead with God to hear me and answer me. Once or twice, when I was really into it, I'd suddenly feel good and all the tension and bitterness would leave me.

MARKHAM. That sounds like an answer.

JOHNSON. I thought so too until I cooled off and began to think objectively. Then I realized I'd been under a great emotional strain. Pressure does strange things to people. They'll do anything to relieve it—even lie to themselves. Every time I'd begin to feel good, I'd start wondering if I'd convinced myself I'd had an answer. Then all my doubts would come flooding back and I'd start over. *(Pause.)* Well, I don't know why I'm using the past tense. It's exactly the same now. *(Pause.)* You know, if the Church isn't true, whoever thought up this personal revelation trip was a genius. I mean there's no way out. You can't prove the gospel is false. No way. They'll always tell you you weren't worthy, or you asked wrong, or God's reserving his answers. But you want it to be true. So you keep on plugging. The Mormon God is a one-armed bandit and I'm a compulsive gambler. I feed him coins of my time and I keep on losing. A month, a year, now two years for this mission. And I always say I'll quit if I don't get an answer. But, everyone says, "Try, just once more, try. You've tried so hard and so long. Don't quit now. Maybe it'll come this time." And it never does. A taste, sometimes—a feeling, a thought—but it's only a tease. They never last. Never. *(Pause.)* I'm sick and tired of the whole routine.

MARKHAM. Elder Johnson, all I can say is I know the gospel is true.

JOHNSON. *(Starts to retort, then:)* Yeah.

MARKHAM. I know it's true because it makes me happy.

JOHNSON. Ahh. There! That's where we see things differently. When I was fifteen, I decided that a man could seek truth or happiness, but one had to take priority. I decided I couldn't really be happy without truth. Truth had to come first. You see? I could never say something's true because it makes me happy. For me, it's got to be the other way around. It makes me happy because it's true.

MARKHAM. *(Shakes his head.)* Wow! All I know is the gospel can give us both.

JOHNSON. I'd like to think so.

MARKHAM. I wish Brother Ch'en would get here. *(Pause.)* You know, I've been out almost a year and this is the first really older man I've had a chance to teach. I'm so sick of little girls. But they're the only ones that seem to hang in there.

JOHNSON. Male chauvinist.

MARKHAM. *(Smiles.)* President Jones says this island needs priesthood. Girls are all right, but they're no good to us.

JOHNSON. *(Teasing again.)* That's a pretty brutal thing to say.

MARKHAM. *(Laughs.)* Jeez, I'm a nervous wreck. I'm gonna go wait out front. Will you work on that fifth?

> JOHNSON *nods.* MARKHAM *smiles and goes out.* JOHNSON *sits thinking for a minute, then begins to study. The door opens;* LUCAS *pops his head in.*

LUCAS. Hey, what's happening?

JOHNSON. Hi, Elder Lucas. We're waiting for Brother Ch'en. What are you doing here?

LUCAS. Elder Matthews had to talk to Elder Gordon and President Jones about the mini-move next week. They're on the horn to Hong Kong right now. Hey, I've got a letter for you.

JOHNSON. My folks?

LUCAS. Nope, it's from Boise.

JOHNSON. Poll! All right! Lemme see that! *(Ripping it open.)* Probably a doggone wedding announcement.

> *Reads, laughs, reads, laughs again.*

LUCAS. What's he say?

JOHNSON. You remember that girl I told you about?

> LUCAS *nods.*

JOHNSON. Catch this. "Dear Barney, *(Exaggeratedly.)* Well, it wasn't so bad after all."

> *They both laugh.*

JOHNSON. "Don't worry. I'm not making any rash decisions. How could I after knowing you?" *(Grins, then goes on, again exaggerating slightly.)* "She sure is beautiful, though."

> *They laugh. He skims on down the page, goes on to the next one.*

JOHNSON. *(Admiringly.)* Listen to this: "Give my best to all the people we baptized together. I've included a note for each of them." *(Looks in envelope.)* Sure enough. "Also one for Holly and Brother Ch'en. How are they doing? If you lose either one, I'll wring your neck. How's it going with Markham? And how are you?" Umm, then he philosophizes. What a good guy!

LUCAS. He was a great missionary. Take his advice.

JOHNSON. That's what he said about you.

> LUCAS *laughs.*

LUCAS. Hasn't Brother Ch'en already heard all six?

JOHNSON. Yeah, but he's still wavering. We had him read through Third Nephi, and we're gonna try to answer his questions today.

LUCAS. He's a good man. What does he teach?

JOHNSON. He's an economics professor at Tai Ta.

LUCAS. I wonder if he could teach me how to live on eighty bucks a month.

JOHNSON. Is that all you get?

LUCAS. Well, my folks don't have much. They're not too jazzed about my mission anyway. Our seventies quorum is helping out.

JOHNSON. Aren't your folks members?

LUCAS. Well, sort of. They've been inactive most of my life. My dad runs a ranch and he's always busy. And when he does get a break, he prefers fishing to Sunday School. My mom does whatever he wants to do. The neighbors always took us to church—my little sister and me.

JOHNSON. They're not against the Church then.

LUCAS. Oh, no; my mom and dad are good people. They wanted us to grow up right. I guess somewhere in early married life they just got their values crossed up. You know how middle-aged people are. They think they've lost all their illusions. They consider themselves hard-bitten veterans in the war of life. I keep working on 'em, though. My sisters tell me that my letters really help. They've started having family home evenings. There's hope.

JOHNSON. It must've taken a lot for you to go to Church without your parents.

LUCAS. Are you kidding! I'd do anything to get out of chores! *(Laughter)* No, I suppose I could've stayed home if I'd wanted. My dad couldn't have put up too much of a fuss. But it always seemed right for me to go. I thought about quitting when I was sixteen or so, but I had some good teachers that worked with me and . . . I gained a real testimony.

JOHNSON. How?

LUCAS. Well, at first it was intellectual, I guess—at least as intellectual as you can get at sixteen. It all seemed so logical, given certain premises. It wasn't until later I began to wonder about the premises. I remember sitting in a geometry class one day and the teacher saying, "Now, this theorem works out perfectly assuming parallel lines will never meet in a given plane. We always make assumptions. We take certain absolutes for granted in order to move ahead pragmatically." Then some joker asked what "pragmatic" meant and the whole discussion fell apart. But I remember thinking "Hmm, I assume God, don't I? I take him for granted. And Joseph Smith, too." I mean I'd thought about there not being a God before, or about Joseph Smith being a crank, but it didn't mean anything. I never internalized it. That's when I began to understand all that about the Book of Mormon being the "keystone of our religion."

So I began studying the scriptures on my own. And I tried really praying.

JOHNSON. What happened?

LUCAS. Well, I never had any angels come flapping down into my bedroom, but I sure felt good a few times. And as I got more active in our branch work and really saw the way the Church could help people, it reinforced me. Since then there've been times the Spirit's just seemed to wash over me. I guess mostly I've just felt myself growing in what seems to be the right direction. And the gospel's at the heart of it. Sometimes I have doubts. I'll be gunning along full blast in some doctrinal discussion and my mind'll say, "Whoa, do you really believe that?" Then I have to ponder it out and hit the knees; but I've always come away accepting it. I know the gospel's true.

JOHNSON. How can you ever have doubts if you know?

LUCAS. Semantics. "Know" is just a word we use that means "beyond belief." Hey, there's semantics again! Not "beyond belief," I mean "more than belief." When I say "I know" it means I "more than believe." I haven't had any Second Comforter.

JOHNSON. If that's the case, why don't people say what they mean?

LUCAS. Most people aren't semanticists. They don't give a rat about ambiguity. They just talk. I'm that way. It's only when I get with a linguist like you that I get inspired. Which reminds me, how's that fifth coming?

JOHNSON. Oh, jeez!

Pause.

LUCAS. Look, I'm just studying written characters in the mornings now, and they aren't that much use to me. I mean can you see me in Asian studies? I'm going into business and get rich! So, why don't you and I start slipping out front after gospel study and before breakfast, and you can teach me a few lessons. I'll throw you every goofy answer I've ever heard; we'll have a real good time. What d'ya say?

JOHNSON. Would Elder Matthews mind?

LUCAS. Elder Matthews is paranoid about my being in the bedroom anyway. He's got a guilty conscience because he spends his study time setting up a filing system for those ten thousand slides of his. Well, it does bug me a little. If we don't need to study, we oughta be out on the street. But he's the boss. And once we're out, he runs me ragged doing the work and helping the elders. He really works hard.

JOHNSON. I hear the elders in Ping Tung used to call him pea-brain.

LUCAS. Hey, no backbiting, fella. Elder Matthews is okay.

JOHNSON. Right, I'm sorry.

The door opens. HOLLY *stands there grinning.*

HOLLY. Hol-lee Hello!

JOHNSON. Hol-lee Hello! Come in! Elder Lucas, this is Holly Chou.

LUCAS. Chou jye mei, ni hau ma?

HOLLY. Hau, sye sye ni.

They shake hands.

JOHNSON. Holly has the best English of any Chinese student I've heard. What are you doing here?

HOLLY. We just finished with English class. *(She giggles, stands upright, says seriously.)* I am your soul sister. Will you be my soul brother? *(LUCAS and JOHNSON laugh.)* I didn't say it right?

JOHNSON. No, you said it right.

HOLLY. Give me five.

She sticks out her hand, palm up.

JOHNSON. Right on, sister. *(He slaps her hand, turns his palm up; she slaps it.)* Groovy. Did you learn this in English class?

HOLLY. Yes, Elder Ferguson says that's how the niggers talk in America.

Brief silence.

JOHNSON. Did he teach you that word?

HOLLY. Which word?

JOHNSON. "Niggers."

HOLLY. Yes. Is something wrong?

JOHNSON *looks at* LUCAS.

LUCAS. I'll talk to him.

JOHNSON. *(To* HOLLY.*)* It's not a nice word. It's like calling somebody a "shagwa" in Chinese.

HOLLY. *(Unpleasantly surprised.)* Ooh!

MATTHEWS's *voice is heard bellowing outside: "Lucas!"*

LUCAS. Whoops! The ZL cometh. Sister Chou, it was nice to meet you. *(To* JOHNSON.*)* Good luck with Brother Ch'en. See ya tonight.

He goes out.

JOHNSON. *(Sits down at table.)* How's school, Holly?

HOLLY. Pretty good. My number two boyfriend got drafted.

JOHNSON. And that's good?

HOLLY. He was starting to get serious. Now the army has saved me. How do you say? The cavalry to the rescue?

JOHNSON. *(Laughs.)* Right. What about your number one boyfriend?

HOLLY. He's safe. I am his number four girlfriend.

She giggles.

JOHNSON. Holly, you're delightful. If you represent the Western influence on Chinese youth, I guess it can't be all bad.

HOLLY. *(Serious now.)* My father thinks it is all bad. He says Chinese culture is being destroyed by the Americans. He says Taiwan will be like Vietnam. First spheres of influence, then wars, then big power domination.

JOHNSON. I hope he's wrong. I don't think the fact that Chinese students want to grow long hair and wear bell-bottom pants is America's fault. Kids everywhere are beginning to question their cultures, their lifestyles. There's a world-wide awakening. France, Greece, Thailand, the U. S., Japan—it's the same there. Students are dissenting, looking for a better way. I just hope they'll preserve what's good as well as overturn what's bad. Your father has a right to be proud of the Chinese culture. Many of your traditions are very beautiful.

HOLLY. My father says Western missionaries do the most damage of anyone. He says they turn our people away from honoring their ancestors and teach them to worship white gods.

JOHNSON. Well, some of them do. I hope we've convinced you, though, that our Church is universal. We believe in honoring our ancestors and do something about it too. You remember what we taught you about temple work?

HOLLY. Gynecology?

They both laugh.

JOHNSON. No, genealogy. Where'd you learn that other word?

HOLLY. Biochemistry.

Giggling.

JOHNSON. *(Shaking his head, laughing.)* Holly, you're amazing. *(Pause.)* Have you finished the Book of Mormon yet?

HOLLY. No, I just started reading the book of Ether last night.

JOHNSON. How do you feel?

HOLLY. I believe it is true. I believe all that you have taught me is true. My life is better since I met you. I have done well in school . . . and had many friends, but I have never been happy for very long. Everything seemed so . . . fleeting. So temporary. The Mormon Church has helped me understand eternal things. You have helped me. I will be baptized as soon as my father agrees. And if he does not agree, I will be baptized as soon as I am old enough to decide for myself. Okay, Joe?

JOHNSON. I'm glad. *(Pause.)* How do you like the book of Ether?

HOLLY. Oh, so much war! It is like a . . . a gudai pyan.

JOHNSON. A what?

HOLLY. How do you say . . . an ancient Chinese sword movie.

JOHNSON. A sword flick! Oh, man, I guess so.

HOLLY. Have you seen such movies?

JOHNSON. About once a month we go to one. All the missionaries love them.

HOLLY. We must see one together. When is your day off?

JOHNSON. *(Taken aback, but amused.)* No, I can't do that.

HOLLY. It is not allowed?

JOHNSON. No, it is *not* allowed.

HOLLY. Too bad; well you must go see *Blood Mountain* with your friends. It is the best I have ever seen.

JOHNSON. I saw that one last week. The one with David Chiang?

HOLLY. Chiang Da Wei. Yes. Oh, did you like it?

JOHNSON. It was great! I loved that final scene. *(He jumps up, pulls out his comb and pen, puts one in each hand, and begins to circle the table slowly, menacingly.)* Your doomsday has come, Black Wang. Release the Princess Lyou.

HOLLY giggles, pulls out two pens from her bookbag, gets up and circles opposite him.

HOLLY. Never, Tiger Chang. You will never see her alive again.

Pause; they continue, breathing heavily, growling, and squinting ferociously.

JOHNSON and HOLLY. Swwaaaya!

They both leap in their places, doing a full twist, gesticulating wildly, then go back to circling. JOHNSON skips nimbly across a row of chairs to HOLLY's delight.

JOHNSON. *(Himself.)* Just practicing.

HOLLY. *(Protesting.)* That wasn't in the script!

They laugh.

JOHNSON. *(Reverting to his role.)* Prepare yourself, Wang. Your life is spent.

HOLLY. Bold words, Tiger Chang. They carry no truth.

JOHNSON. We shall see, devil-man. *(He flies into a frenzy; leaps onto a chair.)* Now! My trustworthy sword shall drink your blood!

HOLLY stops below him, lowers her arms.

HOLLY. *(In mock terror-anger.)* No!

JOHNSON. *(Leaps off the chair in a full twist, gesticulating wildly again.)* Ayeeee! *(Lands at her feet and stabs her with the comb.)* Ha!

   She does not fall, however, because she has been distracted by BROTHER CH'EN *and* ELDER MARKHAM *who are standing at the door dumbfounded.*

MARKHAM. *(Very uncomfortably with a hint of anger, poorly disguised by a smile, and that what-are-you-doing-with-her-here-alone look.)* Elder Johnson, what's going on here?

JOHNSON. Well . . . uh . . . we were acting out the final fight scene from *Blood Mountain*. I was playing Tiger Chang. (HOLLY *has begun to giggle. She sits down and puts her hand over her mouth.)* She was Black Wang.

   This is too much for HOLLY. *She breaks out laughing again.*

MARKHAM. That hardly seems the thing to be doing—does it?

JOHNSON. No, I guess not.

CH'EN. *(To* JOHNSON.*)* It was, however, very accurate. Except your friend is a bit too attractive to play Wang.

MARKHAM. *(Much relieved, laughing.)* Oh, you saw the movie, too?

CH'EN. Yes, last week.

MARKHAM. Well. . . . Oh, Brother Ch'en Yun Ta, this is Sister Chou Li Ts'wun. Sister Chou is another one of our investigators.

HOLLY. Hello.

   They shake hands.

CH'EN. I am very pleased to meet you.

MARKHAM. Well. . . .

   He looks at HOLLY, *nodding his head slightly toward the door.*

HOLLY. *(Remembering she should leave)* Oh! . . . Well, I will see you Sunday. Goodbye. *(She turns to* JOHNSON *and gives two kung fu thrusts.)* Sa! Sa! We will have a rematch.

   She goes out laughing.

CH'EN. A lovely girl.

MARKHAM. Yes. . . . Elder Johnson, Brother Ch'en only has a few minutes. We should get started.

CH'EN. *(To* JOHNSON.*)* I am sorry to be so late. We had an unexpected meeting at the university.

JOHNSON. I understand.

MARKHAM. Brother Ch'en, would you give us an opening prayer?

CH'EN. *(Nods head; heads bow.)* Father in Heaven, I am grateful to be here today to learn from these elders of Thy Church. I am grateful that they have come here to Taiwan to teach the Chinese people more about Thee. Help me to understand what they say, so that I may draw closer to Thee. I say this in Jesus's name. Amen.

MARKHAM. That was a beautiful prayer, Brother Ch'en. Have you been praying twice every day?

CH'EN. Yes.

MARKHAM. Has it helped you?

CH'EN. Yes . . . I think so.

MARKHAM. Did you read Third Nephi in the Book of Mormon since we last met?

CH'EN. Yes.

MARKHAM. Did you enjoy it?

CH'EN. It moved me greatly.

MARKHAM. Good. Will you continue to read the Book of Mormon every day?

CH'EN. Yes.

MARKHAM. We didn't see you in church on Sunday.

CH'EN. Yes, my parents asked me to go on a picnic with them in the country. I am sorry I could not come.

MARKHAM. *(A bit unnerved.)* I see. . . . Well, of course it's good to be close to your family, but church meetings are also very important.

CH'EN. I understand.

MARKHAM. Will you be able to attend both Sunday School and sacrament meeting this Sunday?

CH'EN. No, I am sorry. Because of a shortage of teachers at the university for the next quarter, I have been asked to take my vacation beginning this week rather than in August. I will be visiting my brother and his family in Hua Lien and then return in three weeks to begin teaching immediately. Perhaps I can attend meetings there.

MARKHAM. *(Really jolted.)* Yes, we do have a small branch there. I'm sure they would be happy to have you visit. I will contact the elders there and tell them to expect you.

CH'EN. Of course, I don't know what my brother will have planned.

JOHNSON. Perhaps your brother and his family would be interested in attending church with you.

CH'EN. Perhaps.

An awkward silence. JOHNSON *and* MARKHAM *look at each other.*

MARKHAM. Well, it looks as though we will have to postpone your baptismal date. Do you remember when you were to be baptized?

CH'EN. I believe it was this Saturday, July 1. Yes, I am afraid that will have to be postponed.

Pause.

MARKHAM. Well, let me check my calendar. *(Digs it out.)* Shall we set a new goal date of . . . say . . . July 30?

CH'EN. It is very difficult to know exactly what I will be doing when I return. Perhaps we could establish a new date after I get back.

MARKHAM. *(Reluctantly.)* All right. We will contact you at the university sometime around the 20th. Will you be back by then?

CH'EN. Yes, that would be fine.

JOHNSON and MARKHAM look at each other again.

JOHNSON. Brother Ch'en, are you beginning to feel as though you would rather not be baptized?

MARKHAM looks at JOHNSON angrily.

CH'EN. Why. . . .

JOHNSON. Let's talk about it. What is it that's worrying you?

CH'EN. I should have known you would come straight to the point, Elder Johnson. I am very impressed with your Church. I like your members. I enjoy the Book of Mormon and your meetings. Everything you have told me seems right to me. Yet I worry because I feel I have not received the personal witness which I need to be baptized. I have not felt the Holy Ghost as I sense He ought to be felt.

MARKHAM. How do you feel when you pray, Brother Ch'en?

CH'EN. I feel peaceful at first, and sometimes after I have prayed a short while, I feel warm and very good.

MARKHAM. That's it, Brother Ch'en!

JOHNSON. Yes, that's a beginning, Brother Ch'en. But it's only what we told you to expect. (MARKHAM *glares at* JOHNSON.) If you *really do* feel that, it is a beginning. But only you can recognize God's real answer to you. We can tell you what we feel, but you must seek your answer yourself. If you are not satisfied, you must continue to try. Only you can judge what is enough for you.

MARKHAM. But you must not expect too much. Once you are baptized, you will receive the gift of the Holy Ghost. Then you will have the right to have the Spirit with you at all times. Also, as your knowledge about the Church increases, your faith will grow stronger. And as your faith grows, your ability to communicate with our Father in Heaven will grow also.

JOHNSON. Still, that doesn't mean you're not entitled to a very strong answer now. The scripture in Moroni, which we showed you, is the Lord's promise to individuals truly and humbly searching for the truth. And He is bound to fulfill his promise if we approach him properly. No one is allowed to be baptized who has not had this personal confirmation of the gospel's truthfulness by the Holy Ghost. Isn't that so, Elder Markham?

MARKHAM. Yes; at the same time, though, we don't want you to think you will receive a vision or any sort of overwhelming manifestation. Don't get me wrong. Visions and powerful witnesses are possible, but they generally come to prophets or other Church leaders who have proven their willingness to serve and their unshakeable faith. I don't know any of the elders here, for instance, who have received such a powerful witness.

JOHNSON. Our religion is a very personal affair, Brother Ch'en. Each man must establish his own relationship with God. We cannot really tell you what to look for or how to go about looking. We can only give you broad patterns which can help to streamline your efforts.

MARKHAM. Remember, Brother Ch'en, all testimonies are not gained strictly through prayer. Your good feelings about our members, and our meetings, and about the various principles we have taught you, are just as important as any feelings you might gain through prayer.

JOHNSON. Yes, but these feelings alone are not enough. You must establish a personal communication with God, as well as respond to his work here on earth.

CH'EN. There seems to be a very fine balance in what is required for a true testimony. Apparently revelation, as you call it, has a broad interpretation.

JOHNSON. As broad as the whole earth, and as varied as each individual.

CH'EN. Elder Johnson, you are very ... eloquent. But let me ask you again. What is the proper way to prepare oneself to receive such a ... witness?

MARKHAM. The best guidelines are still in Moroni 10:4–5. First you must think carefully about all you know of the gospel, and especially of the Book of Mormon. Do you do that, Brother Ch'en?

CH'EN. I have thought of little else for some time.

MARKHAM. Good. Now, the scripture says you must also have a sincere heart, real intent, and faith in Jesus Christ. I interpret that as meaning, first, you must be humble and willing to accept what the Lord sees fit to give you. Second, you must really *want* to know if these things are true. If you secretly feel that your life is already sufficient, God will not respond. Finally, faith. Do you believe God has the power to hear and answer prayers?

> JOHNSON *has turned away from the discussion during this speech. He is thoughtful and a bit irritated.*

CH'EN. I have always believed in some supreme power. I have always hoped that I could discover It or Him or Her. *(Smiles.)* Yes, I believe this power, this God, should be able to speak to me. Elder Markham, you have helped me considerably. I feel that I have perhaps not been humble enough in my prayers. I have had a tendency to kneel down and analyze all that I was doing and saying, even while I was praying, and to base my judgments on certain mental criteria I had established. I will try to be more humble. Also, there are times when I feel very satisfied with my life. I become complacent . . . how do the Americans say . . . a fat cat?

CH'EN *and* MARKHAM *smile.*

MARKHAM. Yes.

CH'EN. Although it seems I have been seriously searching for the truth for many years, it is only at moments like these that I feel the need to really know. It is easy to become completely immersed in day-to-day affairs.

MARKHAM. Yes. *(Brief pause.)* Well, I suppose you need to be going, Brother Ch'en.

JOHNSON. *(Out of nowhere.)* May I make one final comment? I would like to add that while you are working on humility and real intent, do not ever sacrifice your honesty or your self-respect. You are a son of God, if God exists; and therefore He will not require you to relinquish these qualities even for Him.

MARKHAM *is restless.*

CH'EN. I am not sure I understand, but I will try to remember.

JOHNSON. Good. Brother Ch'en. I'm very happy I met you on that bus two months ago. I've come to appreciate your intelligence and your sensitivity very much. I want you to know that I think you are a very fine man, and I believe that you can gain a testimony of this gospel. Perhaps during this vacation you will have a chance to relax from your regular routine and concentrate on what we have taught you. I wish you . . . the very best.

CH'EN. Thank you, Elder Johnson.

MARKHAM. *(Honestly, plainly, and deeply felt.)* Brother Ch'en. I'd like to bear you my testimony. I know this gospel and this Church are true. I was brought up in the Church, and I've seen the wonderful effect it has had on the lives of people I've known. I have prayed to know the truth of many things, and God has never failed me. He has answered my prayers; and He will answer yours, if you will fulfill your commitments to us and to Him. I know He wants you to gain a testimony and be baptized. I know He will do everything He can to help you find a better and more meaningful life. I know that Jesus Christ lives and that Joseph Smith was a prophet. I know that we have a living prophet that guides this Church today. I know the Book of Mormon is true. The promise of Moroni is true. I feel I can promise you that, if you will pray humbly and sincerely to God, you will receive an answer and you can come to know as I know. I bear you my testimony in the name of Jesus Christ. Amen.

MARKHAM *gazes straight into* CH'EN'S *eyes.* CH'EN *is moved.*

CH'EN. Thank you.

MARKHAM. Elder Johnson, would you offer the closing prayer?

JOHNSON. Sure. *(Bowed heads.)* Father in Heaven, we're thankful that we have been able to meet with Brother Ch'en this evening. We pray that Thy Spirit will be with him as he leaves now, that he may return home in safety. We also pray that he will receive the answer he needs concerning this gospel. *(Uncomfortable pause.)* Help us all to continually come to know Thee better. We are thankful for all that we have. And we say this in the name of Jesus Christ. Amen.

MARKHAM. Thank you, Elder Johnson. Brother Ch'en? *(They shake hands.)* We'll look you up around the 20th. Have a nice vacation. Try to make it to church in Hua Lien if you can.

CH'EN. I will.

JOHNSON. Good luck, Brother Ch'en.

CH'EN. Thank you. Good night.

He goes out.

MARKHAM. *(Looking after him.)* He's a good man.

JOHNSON. Elder Markham? *(MARKHAM turns.)* I think we pounded out an effective compromise there. Nice job.

Sticks out his hand.

MARKHAM. *(Smiles, takes his hand.)* You, too, Elder Johnson. *(He looks at JOHNSON just as he looked at CH'EN.)* I . . . I just wish you could really bear witness. It'd be so much better. *(He turns to get his things, JOHNSON looks down, grimacing.)* Well, let's go. We have to be at Sister Chang's by eight o'clock.

JOHNSON slams his scriptures onto the floor; MARKHAM looks at him in exasperation; BROTHER CH'EN reappears at the door.

CH'EN. Elder Markham, would it be all right if I read some scriptures here before I leave?

MARKHAM. Well, yes, of course. I thought you had an appointment.

CH'EN. It is not so important. I would like to read for just a few minutes.

MARKHAM. Of course; uh, Elder Johnson and I need to go to another meeting.

CH'EN. Fine, I will only stay a short time.

MARKHAM. Fine. Well, good night again, Brother Ch'en. *(To JOHNSON, who is still looking down, in a concerned and quiet tone.)* Elder Johnson? We need to hurry.

MARKHAM goes out.

JOHNSON. Good night, Brother Ch'en.

JOHNSON follows MARKHAM out. CH'EN closes door, goes and sits down for a moment and opens the Book of Mormon to the end. Then he kneels by the table, the lights dim—silence briefly, then he says, with head bowed:

CH'EN. God? *(Silence again, a bit longer; a spotlight comes in on him very dimly; he looks up; quietly.)* Yes . . . God . . . Yes.

The spotlight comes up on him, brighter.

END ACT TWO

Act Three

The missionary apartment. A week later. It is July 4, a playday. Early morning. Music is heard—The Doobie Brothers, "Jesus Is Just All Right with Me" coming from a cassette tape recorder. Curtain. The spotlight comes up on JOHNSON, *who is dressed very casually, as are all the characters in this act. He has been writing in his journal; he gets up here, however, and begins to dance around the apartment with the music. Barking.*

UNCLE SAM. *(From outside.)* Break-fast!

JOHNSON. Get in here, Uncle. Let's see you shake.

UNCLE SAM. Eh? Heh, heh, heh.

JOHNSON. Come on. Rock out. Relax a little.

UNCLE SAM. Foreign devil music.

They laugh.

JOHNSON. Here, I'll show you. 1–2–3 hey! 1–2–3 hey!

They do a three step and a kick. Both are enjoying themselves immensely. The bedroom door flies open.

MARKHAM. *(Sharply.)* Johnson, turn that music down.

JOHNSON. What?

MARKHAM. Turn that music down.

JOHNSON. Could he be talking to us? (MARKHAM *snaps off the recorder.*) The man has no soul, Uncle. Join me later. I'll teach you to boogaloo.

UNCLE SAM. Be a good boy, Arizona.

JOHNSON. Cook my breakfast, you pagan.

He turns the music on again softly. Begins to write. MARKHAM *reappears.*

MARKHAM. Johnson, I don't think that kind of music, especially that song, is appropriate here.

JOHNSON. *(Casually.)* I do.

MARKHAM. Well, I don't. *(JOHNSON keeps writing.)* Johnson, turn it off.

> JOHNSON *begins humming as he writes,* MARKHAM *retreats to the bedroom. Pause.* MATTHEWS *comes out.*

MATTHEWS. Elder Johnson, please turn that off. I'm trying to read scriptures.

JOHNSON. Fat chance. You're filing slides.

> MATTHEWS *is furious. He pulls the plug out of the wall.*

JOHNSON. Temper, temper!

MATTHEWS. So help me, Johnson, if you push me any further, I'll punch your lights out.

JOHNSON. Fighting's against the rules, Elder Matthews.

MATTHEWS. I don't care.

JOHNSON. *(Oratorically.)* "Then the high priest rent his clothes saying: He hath spoken blasphemy. What further need have we of witnesses? Behold, now we have heard his blasphemy. *(*MATTHEWS *slams the door as he goes back to the bedroom.)* What think ye? They answered and said, He is guilty of death."

UNCLE SAM. Arizona?!

JOHNSON. Who speaks to Caiaphas, the high priest?

UNCLE SAM. Come here. *(JOHNSON goes into kitchen.)* Wise up.

JOHNSON. What do you mean?

UNCLE SAM. There have been others like you. I know my elders. Wise up.

JOHNSON. What do you know about me?

UNCLE SAM. You don't have a testimony.

JOHNSON. *(Deflated.)* Jeez. You're pretty blunt. Is it that obvious?

UNCLE SAM. You see those hotcakes, Arizona. If I don't take them off the fire soon, they'll burn up. But they tell me when they're ready. They rise and bubble and turn brown. Then I know they're ready. I take them off before they scorch. Every one of you elders is in the fire, on the griddle. And you've all got personal problems that make things tough. But almost all of you go through the motions, make the signs, do what's expected. It's called faith. If you don't make the signs, the fire gets hotter. You came out here to make a change. Make it! Have faith. Otherwise you'll go up in smoke. I've seen it happen to one elder and I've heard about others. Wise up. If you didn't have a basic belief, you wouldn't be here. Don't fight it; use it. And don't let those others shape your battle. They're fighting, too, even if they don't know it. Your battle just attracts a little more attention. Wise up.

JOHNSON. I can't be a hypocrite, Sam.

UNCLE SAM. Hypocrite to what? What's your alternative? The world? Do you owe your allegiance to the world?

JOHNSON. I owe allegiance to myself. I can't be a hypocrite to myself. If I don't have faith, I don't.

UNCLE SAM. You can be what you want to be. I know you're afraid you'll talk yourself into something that's false, because you want it so much. Well, you can talk yourself into evil, too. What are you basically—good or evil? Answer that for yourself. There's the gospel or there's nothing, Arizona. Which do you believe in? Which do you want? If you feel like a hypocrite doing good, then you're basically evil. Some people get away because they think it's all relative, but you don't feel that way, do you?

JOHNSON. No.

UNCLE SAM. No, you recognize good and evil. You know they exist. Choose good. Be what you want to be. *(Pause.)* Now, set the table, will you? *(Shouting.)* Break-fast!

JOHNSON *begins to set the table. The others come out warily, except* LUCAS, *who is bouncing.*

LUCAS. What do you think of the Fourth of July, Uncle Sam?

UNCLE SAM. Pierre to you, Canada.

LUCAS. Forgive me, mon petit. *(Aghast.)* Sam, you burned the hotcakes.

SAM *and* JOHNSON *laugh.*

JOHNSON. Inside joke. Listen, I'm sorry about the music.

MATTHEWS. Yeah, forget it. You take the blessing?

JOHNSON. Sure. *(Bowed heads.)* Father in Heaven, we're grateful this morning for all our blessings. We're grateful for this calling which we have to spread the gospel here in this land. Forgive us of our shortcomings and strengthen our faith. We're grateful for this food and pray that it will be blessed to give us nourishment and energy. This we say in the name of Jesus Christ. Amen.

LUCAS. *(To* MARKHAM.*)* Have you ever been to this beach we're going to?

MARKHAM. No.

LUCAS. Oh, it's beautiful. Our district had a playday there right after I came on island. It was fantastic. And we just had watermelon then. Today we cook steaks! It's gonna be great! Elder Johnson, do you play football?

JOHNSON. A little.

LUCAS. I love it. We'll have to be careful, though. The beach is a real temptation. Last time, I remember I was supposed to hit Jensen on a down and in pattern. He ran down and out. I led him right into the ocean. Jackson and the waves both hit him at the same time. He went all the way under and came up laughing like a fool. Then he and Osborne threw Jackson in. It was a free-for-all. After that everybody went in but the sisters, and the only thing that saved them was Sister Jordan's reputation as a holy terror.

MARKHAM. I hear she used to wrestle for the Y.

Laughter.

LUCAS. Anderson dunked me. I asked him before I went under if he thought this was out of line. He said, "Maybe, but I'll bet God's laughing as hard as we are."

Laughter.

MATTHEWS. Well, it won't happen today. We're not going near the water.

LUCAS. Then why go to the beach? I mean we can at least wade.

MATTHEWS. We'll see. Elder Markham, how was that second last night?

MARKHAM. *(A bit flustered.)* Oh, well, not bad. We may not get past a third, though. The guy has ashtrays all over, and they're all full.

JOHNSON. *(Smiling.)* Elder Markham really doesn't know how the second went last night.

MARKHAM. Come on, Johnson.

JOHNSON. Oh, they know how it is, Elder. *(To MATTHEWS.)* We rode our bikes all over the city yesterday and by the time we got to Brother Li's house, we were exhausted. He gave us a cold drink, and I started the second. All of a sudden we heard snores. Elder Markham was completely zonked in the armchair. I thought Brother Li would die laughing.

Laughter.

MARKHAM. I was not completely asleep, and I was not snoring.

The other three shake their heads, humoring him satirically.

JOHNSON, LUCAS and MATTHEWS. No. Of course not. Oh, no.

MARKHAM *is furious.*

MARKHAM. *(To MATTHEWS.)* You know how slowly Johnson gives his lessons. He can't even get through the first without flubbing it all up. *(To JOHNSON.)* It's torture listening to you.

JOHNSON. *(Having a ball.)* I know. Well, you sure didn't get tortured last night. I've never seen anybody look so at peace. *(Laughter.* MARKHAM *leaves the table)* After we finished, Brother Li wanted to put a blanket on him while he and I played chess, but I figured that was a little much.

MARKHAM. *(Icily.)* I'll tell you what's too much, Johnson. You challenged him to baptism, you committed him to read the Book of Mormon, but you didn't bear your testimony to him, did you?

JOHNSON. No.

    MATTHEWS *and* LUCAS *murmur a protest.* MARKHAM *ignores them.*

MARKHAM. Testimony is the heart of the gospel, Johnson. Why didn't you bear your testimony to Brother Li?

JOHNSON. You know why.

MARKHAM. Yes, and I know we may lose Brother Li because of you, just like we lost Sister Chang. What are you doing out here without a testimony, huh? How do you expect to do anything at all? You don't do the Lord's work, Johnson; you hold it up!

    JOHNSON *drops his fork and walks out; barking; Pause.*

LUCAS. *(To* MARKHAM.*)* You knucklehead.

MATTHEWS. Shut up, Lucas. He had it coming. Maybe this'll wake him up.

LUCAS. Sounds like Markham could use some waking up, too.

MARKHAM. Look at what that guy's done to this apartment. We're supposed to be companions! How can we work in a spirit like this? I wish he'd just go home. Anything to get him off my hands.

LUCAS. Off your back, you mean. You don't know how to handle him, and it bugs you. It makes you realize you're not perfect.

MARKHAM. Could you handle him?

LUCAS. I don't know. Poll did all right.

MATTHEWS. Poll babied him. You don't know what you're talking about.

LUCAS. I know they were happy and baptizing. But maybe you're right. He's got to face it sometime.

    JOHNSON *reenters, trembling.*

JOHNSON. Elder Markham, do something for me.

MARKHAM. *(Flat.)* What?

JOHNSON. Come here.

MARKHAM. *(Goes.)* Yeah?

JOHNSON. I want you to use your priesthood.

MARKHAM. How?

JOHNSON. Lift that breakfast table by your faith.

MARKHAM. Get off it, Johnson.

    MARKHAM *starts to walk away.*

JOHNSON. *(Grabbing his arm.)* Noooo, wait a minute, senior companion. You're afraid you couldn't do it. You don't really believe you could do it. Come on. Faith as a mustard seed, Markham. Give us a little show.

MATTHEWS. All right, Johnson, cool off.

JOHNSON. Shut up, pea-brain.

He turns back to MARKHAM.

MATTHEWS. Johnson—

Walks over. Touches JOHNSON *on the shoulder.* JOHNSON *shoves him away.* MATTHEWS *loses his temper. They grapple for an instant.*

UNCLE SAM. *(Grabs* MATTHEWS.*)* Let them get it all out, California.

MATTHEWS. You dirty chink!

UNCLE SAM. Go to your room, little boy!

UNCLE SAM *shoves* MATTHEWS *into the bedroom, closes and holds the door.*

JOHNSON. Come on, Markham.

MARKHAM. You're seeking a sign, Johnson.

JOHNSON. That's right. I'm a priest of Baal, Markham. I'm a Korihor. Are you an Alma? Huh? *(Gives him a little shove.)* Come on; fire from heaven, bright boy, strike me dumb!

MARKHAM. Lucas?

UNCLE SAM. Don't, Canada. It's gotta come.

JOHNSON. Markham, you don't have any more faith than I do. You don't have a testimony either. You and Matthews don't really *believe* or *live* the gospel. You use it to help you plan your petty lives and make you feel important. Maybe the gospel's true and maybe it's not, but you're not the one to tell me or show me anything about it. So keep your trap shut about my testimony. And don't worry; I'm not gonna touch you.

MARKHAM *glowers and heads for the bedroom;* SAM *lets him go in.*

LUCAS. Elder Johnson, sit down.

JOHNSON. I...

LUCAS. Sit down and be quiet. Look, man, I don't care if you're three years older or not. I want to tell you something.

JOHNSON. *(Pugnaciously, but sitting.)* Okay.

LUCAS. You're as screwed up as they are. First of all, Markham does have a testimony. So does Matthews, and so do I. We're not very strong in it because we haven't had it long. We know a little about the priesthood, but not much. It takes a lifetime to build faith. Maybe your little speech will help Markham. He's just a starstruck kid who was brought up in the Church and not in the gospel. Yeah, I know the distinction, too. Markham wants to be a mission leader and baptize a million people because he thinks that's what the gospel's all about. Of course, he'd never admit it. But look, he's basically doing the right thing. He wants to serve the Lord; and even if his adolescent egotism gets in the way, he's on the right track. And at least he likes these people and really wants to help them. Don't be unjust to him.

JOHNSON. What about Matthews?

LUCAS. Matthews is schizophrenic. The world got him by the throat by the time he was twelve. Athletics, keg parties, fashion fads. He's been conditioned to the world. When he thinks about the Church and its principles, he's a great guy. You should've seen him at that send-off. He really feels it. But get him back to temporal affairs, even temporal mission affairs, and he's right back in the world—all its thoughts and all its reactions. I don't know if he'll ever get over it. But listen, Elder Johnson. I don't care how bright you are or how clearly you think you see things. You're the one with real trouble *right now*.

JOHNSON. Why?

LUCAS. Those guys will fight their problems within the Church framework. They'll have bishops and wives to help them overcome themselves all through life. Not to mention that the Lord blesses all of us for doing what we can. They'll probably both become bishops and at least one of them will be good. But you, baby, you're on your way out right now. And its not God's fault, it's yours.

JOHNSON. Why doesn't He answer my prayers?

LUCAS. You won't let him. I'm sure He tries. Look, two things. How long have you been on this agnostic thing?

JOHNSON. Since I was a sophomore in high school.

LUCAS. And you've nourished and cared for it ever since.

JOHNSON. No, I—

LUCAS. Come on, Johnson. Nobody lives in uncertainty. You may think you do and torment yourself with arguments to keep yourself satisfied, but agnosticism has become your creed. You're proud of it. It's made you an individual. You've found your niche. The good but dissenting Mormon, who lives the principles but questions the doctrines. The man above. Pride, Johnson, and a pattern for life every bit as tight, if not so common, as the bourgeois Mormon lifestyle that bugs you so much. You've told us all what a puppet your father is. Well, the world pulls your strings too, buddy. And you jump.

JOHNSON. I've thought of all this before. I've considered it. I've seen the pattern. Maybe you think all my efforts to break out are just red herrings to myself. But I know they're not. I've felt the pain. I've scraped my brain on every wall of this stinking box I live in, and there are no answers! Shouldn't the Lord come to me when I can't do any more?

LUCAS. You think you've thought of everything. How 'bout this, Johnson? Quote. "I can't have the faith to get an answer, until I get an answer." Unquote. . . .

JOHNSON. That's the vicious cycle that drives me insane.

LUCAS. I know it is, for cryin' out loud. Will you lemme finish? That cycle, in your case, is hogwash. You believe in God, through His principles, at least part of the time, and the rest of the time you hope. True?

JOHNSON. Yes.

LUCAS. That should be plenty for God to work with. Alma says desire is enough of a seed to bring a response.

JOHNSON. Yes, but all of Alma 32 is geared to convincing oneself that the gospel is true rather than. . . .

LUCAS. Oh, Johnson. What are you, a computer? How many times have you started that line when somebody brings up Alma's seed? Can you hold off on the stock answers for just a minute? *(JOHNSON looks down.)* What I'm saying is this. You don't lack faith in God. Your belief is sufficient. Your doubts center on yourself. Do you understand me? You doubt yourself. You doubt your ability to receive what other people have received. You look at the Markhams and sneer because they're naive. And so you accuse them of not really knowing the gospel is true. But the Markhams scare you, because they really seem to have had an answer. And, oh, you could pass off the Markhams. They're your age and not so smart. But what about those brilliant Church leaders you've known? And the General Authorities? Are they naive and stupid? Yet they know. They've received answers. Johnson, you're afraid. That's your problem. You're afraid that for all your brains you're not the real, worthwhile, teachable, feeling person that others are. You're afraid you wouldn't receive an answer because you haven't got what it takes. Your agnosticism is one big front of fear.

Long silence.

JOHNSON. No, you're wrong.

LUCAS. Sure I am. Everybody's wrong but you. You're always right. Look where it's got you. *(Pause.)* Pierre, have you got some milk? I talk too much.

SAM *goes to the kitchen.* LUCAS *begins to clear the table. Pause.*

JOHNSON. Elder Lucas. Thanks. I'll think about it.

LUCAS. *Feel* it, Elder. That's what you need.

LUCAS *follows* SAM *into the kitchen with the dishes.* JOHNSON *is in deep thought.*

SAM. Good job, Canada.

LUCAS. I hope it works, Sam. He's a good man. He's bright. He cares about people. In a lot of ways he's very realistic. And he's got a sense of humor. That in itself is worth a lot. I really like him.

SAM. So do I. I think he'll come around.

LUCAS. I don't know. I know what Johnson's going through. I've seen it before, and I've read about it in Church history. Oliver Cowdery, David Whitmer, Thomas Marsh. Some very good and some very brilliant people get hung up on a single point of the gospel, and they can't seem to break loose and catch the whole perspective again. Sometimes it's a major doctrinal question, like Johnson has with revelation, or like others have had with Church government or polygamy. Sometimes it's a much littler thing, like evolution or birth control or the black question. But big or small, it nails 'em just the same. Their question becomes a subtle obsession, a fire in the mind. It's like a whirlpool, and it drags them down to an intellectual pit. They're still good people. They want to see the whole picture. They want to break out. But at the same time they build the walls around them even higher. They've made such a big thing of their question either to themselves or others that it becomes a matter of pride for them to resolve it. So they struggle on, attacking their question one day, reinforcing it the next, until they're so exhausted fighting themselves that they collapse. Then, after a while, they get up and start over again. But their minds are locked in, and the obsession grows stronger. And it becomes a way of life. It's not at all pleasant, but it's individual, or at least they think it is. In their own tormented way they're satisfied. Then Satan slowly feeds on their pain, and takes advantage of their distorted view of the gospel, and they begin to view the whole Church from the standpoint of their terribly personal battle. Suddenly *all* the doctrines and principles are on trial. And the human follies of Church members, like aspiration, or materialism, or apathy seem unbearably wicked and reflect on the gospel rather than on the individual. Then they become bitter and indifferent, and pretty soon, out of pride and frustration, they begin to sin. They're still good people; but after that, they no longer care, or they have to justify themselves by continuing to rebel. It's not long before they're gone.

Pause.

UNCLE SAM. Elder Johnson's only twenty-two.

LUCAS. But he's already been fighting himself for seven years. If he doesn't recognize what he's into now, he never will. He'll just dig deeper and deeper into his hole and then it'll just be a matter of time. I hope I made him see. *(Pause.)* He's a good man. *(Pause.)* Hey! Playday. Bus in twenty minutes. We've gotta roll.

MATTHEWS *and* MARKHAM *come out sullenly.*

JOHNSON. I'd like to stay home, if I could. Sam'll be here.

MATTHEWS. Brother T'ang is through. He's finished. I'm firing him.

LUCAS. Hey, let's hit the playday first. We'll think about it again tonight.

JOHNSON. Would you mind if I stayed here, Elder Markham?

MARKHAM. Fine with me.

MATTHEWS *shrugs.*

LUCAS. Let's go then. See you later, Elder Johnson. We'll bring you back a steak.

JOHNSON. Elder Lucas? *(The others go out.)* You've got all of us pegged. Just out of curiosity, what's *your* problem?

LUCAS. *(Smiles.)* I can't keep my mind off women. Adios, Pierre! Au revoir!

He goes out; barking.

UNCLE SAM. I need to go do some shopping.

JOHNSON. Fine, I want to be alone. I won't run off.

UNCLE SAM. Bacon, lettuce, and tomato tonight, heh, heh, heh.

JOHNSON. That'd be great.

SAM *goes out,* JOHNSON *sits down and writes furiously in his journal for an instant. Stops. Slams it shut, goes to the door and looks out. Comes back. Pulls out a chair. Kneels.*

JOHNSON. Oh, God. *(Lights fade, spotlight on* JOHNSON.*)* God?

Voices are heard.

MARKHAM. Isn't the gospel beautiful? It makes me happy all the time.

MATTHEWS. It makes me feel love. God is love. Love is what it's all about.

MARKHAM. Love and happiness—and truth. That's what makes it so beautiful. It's true, absolutely true, and it'll last forever. Love and happiness and truth, for eternity.

JOHNSON. What do you know about truth?

LUCAS. He knows, Elder Johnson. I know too. Join us.

MARKHAM. Yes, Elder Johnson. Come.

MATTHEWS. You can know too, Johnson. Come.

POLL. It is true, Barney, I know it is.

UNCLE SAM. Wise up, Arizona.

JOHNSON. No. No. There's got to be more. You're just men.

LUCAS. God sends his answers through men. *I* didn't speak to you; it was the Holy Ghost. You felt it. You know.

JOHNSON. No.

LUCAS. What did you feel?

JOHNSON. It made me think.

POLL. What did you *feel*, Barney?

JOHNSON. Nothing.

UNCLE SAM. You felt it, Arizona. Don't be afraid.

JOHNSON. I only felt a little. That's all I ever feel. I . . .

JOHNSON's *own voice is heard.*

JOHNSON'S VOICE. Don't be a fool, Johnson. Was what you felt an answer from God? Be honest, Johnson. Think!

LUCAS. That's your pride talking, Elder. That's your fear. Don't listen to it.

JOHNSON'S VOICE. What does he know about what you've felt, what you've experienced? You know this isn't enough. Don't sell yourself out.

JOHNSON. I want to know.

JOHNSON'S VOICE. Truth or happiness, you can't have both.

MARKHAM. Love and truth and happiness—forever.

JOHNSON'S VOICE. Baloney. Johnson, be honest!

LUCAS. Johnson, you're talking to yourself.

JOHNSON'S VOICE. No.

LUCAS. It's what you've always feared. But the opposite.

JOHNSON'S VOICE. No.

LUCAS. Don't talk yourself *out* of the truth.

JOHNSON'S VOICE. Don't let them talk you into a lie. Truth, Johnson. Honesty!

JOHNSON. Yes.

POLL. No, Barney.

JOHNSON. Yes. There must be more!

UNCLE SAM. No, Arizona. More comes later. We grow!

JOHNSON'S VOICE. Listen to them qualify, Johnson. They're backing down.

LUCAS. He's lying, Johnson. You're answering yourself. Don't make yourself your god.

JOHNSON'S VOICE. Shut up!

LUCAS. Don't make pride and fear your gods. Open up! Break away!

JOHNSON. Yes, I must.

JOHNSON'S VOICE. No! What if they're wrong? How could you live with yourself if they're wrong? Your life would be a joke. All your suffering a joke!

MARKHAM. You'll never know if you're wrong.

JOHNSON'S VOICE. That's right, you'll never know. Never, never, never, know!

POLL. God will add to your light.

JOHNSON'S VOICE. Never!

JOHNSON. Never.

MATTHEWS. Love, Johnson.

MARKHAM. Truth and happiness.

JOHNSON'S VOICE. Never!

LUCAS. It's true, Johnson.

JOHNSON'S VOICE. Honesty.

UNCLE SAM. Faith.

JOHNSON. Honesty!

JOHNSON'S VOICE. Yes!

LUCAS. No! Faith *and* honesty; your pride is *dis*honest! Your fear is *dis*honest! Feel it, Johnson. You know, you know. . . .

All of them join in, in a crescendo. JOHNSON *is racked.*

JOHNSON'S VOICE. *(Terribly loud.)* No!!!

JOHNSON. *(Blending with his own voice.)* No!!!

He stands upright, picks up the chair and stares into the blinding light.

JOHNSON. God!! I . . . No!!!!

He smashes the chair across the table, falls, and lies face upward, sobbing. The spotlight on him slowly fades into nothingness.

END ACT THREE

Epilogue

The missionary apartment. That night. Enter MARKHAM *and* JOHNSON. JOHNSON *is in a black, careless humor.* MARKHAM *is frustrated.* JOHNSON *flops in an armchair,* MARKHAM *at the table.*

MARKHAM. All right, what's on your mind, Elder Johnson?

JOHNSON. My mind? Nothing.

MARKHAM. Come on, you've been down all night. Something's on your mind.

JOHNSON. No. I'm not thinking any more. I'm just feeling. Lucas suggested it.

MARKHAM. Well, you must feel rotten then.

JOHNSON. Yes.

Pause.

MARKHAM. Lucas wants us all to try to forget this morning. At least the personal feelings. I'm willing. What do you say?

JOHNSON. You're willing because you came off a jackass. (MARKHAM *starts to retort angrily.*) But don't worry. I'm not remembering. Memory is a process of mind, and I'm not thinking. I'm just feeling.

MARKHAM. Can't we do anything, Elder? Won't you try?

JOHNSON. My mind is a blank. Are you speaking to me? Beep beep beep.

MARKHAM. *(Bangs his hand down on the table.)* Jeez!

JOHNSON. Golly gumdrops!

He laughs. Pause.

MARKHAM. Oh, wow! The transfer sheet. Come on, we've got to go back to the post office.

JOHNSON. We?

MARKHAM. *We,* Johnson. Let's go.

JOHNSON. Oui, a French word signifying the affirmative. My mind is coming back.

MARKHAM. I said, let's go.

JOHNSON. Yes, my mind! But it's all so hazy. Did you hear a jackass bray?

MARKHAM. Garbage.

Barking.

JOHNSON. Hark, Cerberus! Who comes? Goldilocks, Lucas, and the Pea-brain?

Laughs.

MARKHAM. No, it's too early.

HOLLY *appears; knocks.*

JOHNSON. *(Snaps out)* Hol-lee Hello!

MARKHAM. How'd she know where we live?

JOHNSON. We taught her here once. Come in, Holly. What is it?

HOLLY. Oh, I must talk to you.

MARKHAM. We have to get that transfer sheet. Gordon goes home tomorrow.

JOHNSON. Look, you go ahead. I'll talk to her. It's only five minutes to the post office. I think she wants to talk to me anyway. She knows me better.

MARKHAM. Shoot, it's against the rules.

JOHNSON. Well, but we've got to know about the transfer, don't we?

MARKHAM. All right. *(To* HOLLY.*)* Sister Chou, we have some other business to take care of, but we want to help you, too. You talk to Elder Johnson; I'll be right back.

HOLLY. Thank you. *(He goes out; barking.)* Oh, Elder Johnson.

She is crying.

JOHNSON. Here, sit down.

They sit at the table, corner to corner.

HOLLY. My father, he is so angry with me.

JOHNSON. Why?

HOLLY. I told him I wanted to go to . . . American college . . . to study.

JOHNSON. What's wrong with that?

HOLLY. He says . . . I will stay there . . . and live . . . and forget China. Ohh. *(Sobbing, she takes his hand.)* Forgive me, I am so silly.

JOHNSON. No, no. *(He strokes her hand.)* Holly, you won't forget China. Your father must know that deep down. And it would do you good to study in America. You already have beautiful English, but you could improve it in the States. And anyone who speaks English has a better chance at a job with all the American business here. And those are the people who get better pay. Have your teacher talk to him. Do you have a favorite teacher who would help you?

HOLLY. Yes, I had not thought of that. And he wants me to go very much. I am his prize student.

JOHNSON. There you go. It'll work out.

He strokes her hand again.

HOLLY. Oh, you make me so happy!

She jumps up.

JOHNSON. Good.

Pause.

HOLLY. But *you* are not happy. You have not been happy since Elder Poll left. Is it this Elder Markham?

JOHNSON. No, it's just a lot of things.

HOLLY. Your family?

JOHNSON. No, it's all in my mind.

HOLLY. Tell me. I am your friend. Come, we will go out on the balcony and talk. The night air sets minds free. *(She stops, looks at him a moment, then leans down and kisses him on the cheek.)* This is how American girls show concern, is it not?

JOHNSON. *(Stands up.)* Holly.

HOLLY. It is not allowed?

JOHNSON. *(Looks at her a moment, then leans over slowly and kisses her cheek.)* Yes, it is allowed.

HOLLY. You are wonderful! You make me so happy. How can I make you happy?

Laughs.

JOHNSON. *(Seriously, gently.)* Just talk to me. You're very beautiful.

HOLLY. *(Taking command.)* Come, we will go downtown. I will show you my favorite noodle shop. They serve the best beef noodles in the capital. And gigantic bottles of Chi Shui! Come! It will make you happy again.

JOHNSON. No.

HOLLY. Why not?

JOHNSON. No, I. . . .

HOLLY. It *is* this Elder Markham. He is the reason you are unhappy. I will kick his shins for you.

JOHNSON. No, it's not Elder Markham.

HOLLY. Then why not?

JOHNSON. Well, I'd look ridiculous wearing a tie.

HOLLY. *(Laughs.)* Take it off. You are more silly than me.

JOHNSON. *(Takes off the tie slowly, drapes it over the chair; softly.)* All right, I want to. I just want to talk to you.

Barking.

HOLLY. *(Hand on mouth.)* Elder Markham! He would never let you go. Quick, the back way!

She is giggling. This is great innocent fun. She crosses into the kitchen, waves him to come on. He follows rather dumbly. She opens the back door, beckons him to be quiet. MARKHAM *storms in in roaring good spirits, carrying a big bottle of Chi Shui.* JOHNSON *motions* HOLLY *to go ahead. She beckons him to come, goes out. He stands and listens.*

MARKHAM. Johnson, you won't believe it. *(Sees the tie, addresses the bedroom.)* Come here and have a glass of Chi Shui. *(Pours out* JOHNSON's *drink, then his own.)* Get this Johnson: Matthews—busted to straight senior. I can't believe it! Jensen—AP; Markham—district leader. You get that? Markham—district leader; all right, huh? Lucas—zone leader, and co-senior with Johnson! You get that? Lucas, your buddy, is your companion—and you're co-senior! How's that make you feel? You made it, Johnson! We both made it! And, oh yeah! Here's the best part. A letter from Brother Ch'en. He got his answer. He wants to be baptized in two weeks. Whaddya say, Johnson? *(Pause;* JOHNSON *looks down again.* MARKHAM *shakes his head, begins to read the letter over)* Finally, a good man. *(*JOHNSON *turns and goes out. The lights fade to* *a spotlight on the table*) He's such a good man. (MARKHAM *drinks; a door is heard closing; the lights go off* MARKHAM; *only the empty chair and glass, and the tie can be seen*) A good man.

THE END

Huebener

Thomas F. Rogers

About the Playwright

As stated earlier in this anthology, Eugene England wrote in 1986 that Robert Elliot's *Fires of the Mind* was Mormon drama's "single best play." Yet following that statement he also wrote, "But the best Mormon playwright, on the evidence of cumulative, consistent achievement, is Tom Rogers."[1] Rogers certainly can be rightly considered one of the important pioneers in Mormon drama, one of its founding fathers during one of its most important periods.

Rogers graduated from the University of Utah, after which he attended Yale and Stanford where he received his Ph.D. in Russian literature. He has taught at Howard University, the University of Utah, and Brigham Young University.

Rogers has penned several plays including *Journey to Golgotha, Reunion, Gentle Barbarian, Frere Lawrence, Charades,* and *The Anointed* (with music by C. Michael Perry). However, it is his plays *Fire in the Bones* (about John D. Lee and the Mountain Meadows Massacre), and more especially *Huebener,* that have had the strongest impact upon not only Mormon drama as a genre, but also on the whole of Mormon literary and social culture. Their themes of conscience versus authority have had ethical repercussions that can still be felt to this day within many Mormon circles.

Huebener is about Helmuth Huebener, a young Mormon, who resists not only Hitler and the Third Reich, but also a Nazi branch president from his own faith. Considered one of the great classics of Mormon drama, it is based on a historical episode that Rogers first encountered while he was serving his first mission for the LDS Church:

> My first mission was in Northern Germany, with headquarters in Berlin. Hamburg, Huebener's hometown and the site of his clandestine activity, was one of our cities. I recall a fellow missionary there mentioning Huebener's story, which he had heard from a local member. This was fairly unusual, since our members and investigators were rather tight-lipped about their personal experience during World War II, which had ended just a decade earlier. I was only dimly aware that a number of those we worked with then had been members of the Nazi Party.
>
> After my mission, I put the whole thing out of my mind. It was almost two decades later, as I served on the BYU faculty, that my colleague Alan

---

[1] Eugene England, "Review: *God's Fools: Plays of Mitigated Conscience,*" BYU Studies, 26:3 (Summer 1986), 114.

Keele gave a presentation to our college faculty about Huebener's impact on important post-war German officers, notably Nobel Prize winners Heinrich Boell and Gunther Grass. Knowing of my interest in writing plays, Alan singled me out and challenged me to write a play on the subject. Alan and history professor Douglas Tobler were about to publish a book about it and generously shared with me their research, which became the play's principal source. Until that moment I had almost forgotten I'd ever written plays.[2]

Rogers wrote *Huebener*, which premiered in 1976 at the BYU Margetts Theatre. It was extended several times, played to capacity audiences, and was viewed by an estimated 5,000 audience members. Revival productions, such as the one BYU produced in 2001, have also sold well and received enthusiastic responses.[3]

Margaret Blair Young, who played Huebener's mother in the original production, described the spirit that pervaded the theater after performances: "When the play was over each night, there was a lingering reality that I hadn't often felt in the theatre department. Huebener's ghost was ubiquitous." Part of this powerful feeling was due to the fact that many LDS members who had emigrated from Germany to America after World War II were in the audience, and many of them had known Helmuth Huebener personally. Furthermore, some of the people in the audience were the actual people being played by actors on the stage. Both the real Karl-Heinz Schnibbe and Ruddi Wobbe, prominent characters in the play, were in the audience, and would personally talk to the actors afterwards. Although Karl-Heinz Schnibbe was healthy and handsome when he met the cast, he disclosed that he had been sent to a Siberian prison camp and had weighed only ninety-eight pounds when the Red Cross rescued him. Rare moments occurred when history and drama were meeting and shaking each other warmly by the hand. Margaret Young recalled: "[Karl-Heinz] Schnibbe spoke to me in German after the first show he attended. I told him it was just the accent I had worked on; I couldn't understand the real thing. The other two nights he came, he embraced me after the show and called me 'Mother Huebener.'" Young continued: "And other nameless Germans compared our acting to the truth they had known. 'Yes, the judges were like that—but scarier. They wore red robes. Oh, I will never forget. Blood-red robes.' 'Ach, dat us yust how he was, dat Helmuth. But he cocked his head to the side all de time, like dis. During Sunday School, he vud do dis all de time.' 'Oh, yes, he looked so much like my Helmuth, but my Helmuth was smaller really.' We had scratched at the truth, and we felt it."[4]

---

2   Todd Compton, "A Playwright with a Passion for Unvarnished Depictions: An Interview with Tom Rogers," *Dialogue: A Journal of Mormon Thought* 41, no. 1 (Spring 2008): 70–71.
3   Thomas F. Rogers, "Preface," *Huebener and Other Plays*, (Poor Robert's Publications, Utah, 1992), 5.
4   Margaret Blair Young; "Doing Huebener," *Dialogue: A Journal of Mormon Thought* 21, no. 4 (Winter 1988): 130.

With these still-living figures whom the actors were portraying in their midst, the production utilized the presence of these freedom fighters to create a dramatic scenario that emphasized just how close to the truth this play was coming:

> For both the premiere performance and the anniversary of Helmuth's execution, about a month later, we had intentionally rigged what proved to be an extremely dramatic "postscript." After the initial applause, a line of three equally placed spotlights again lit the stage. In the first stood the real Karl-Heinz Schnibbe, in the third the real Ruddi Wobbe—Huebener's two principal teenage LDS co-conspirators. The middle spot remained empty, commemorating Huebener's own unavoidable absence. The effect was to bring events portrayed through artistic representation vividly into the audience's awareness—almost into their laps in the tiny Margetts Arena Theatre. Two others who had known Huebener—the sister who had been his Sunday School teacher and to whom he had written one of his last letters, which we quote in the play, and the brother who had replaced him as the Church's district clerk—were also present and introduced to the audience, together with Lotte and Siegfried Guertler, professional thespians who, before their own post-war emigration, had as local Church members in Hamburg also known the young Huebener and the other principals. (Karl-Heinz and I had both played roles together on the stage of the Guertlers' Deutsches Theater, Salt Lake City.) The effect was stunning, and word quickly spread.[5]

This spiritual and emotional feast didn't deter controversy from rearing its inevitable head. Leaders of the Church in Salt Lake City raised some concerns as to how the play could affect the progress being made behind Iron Curtain countries and other Communist strongholds because of its representation of a Latter-day Saint opposing an oppressive government. However, BYU President Dallin H. Oaks, who would later become an LDS apostle, commended the play to a patron of the university. He called the play "excellent" and insisted: It "dealt with a subject that tugs at our hearts and reminds us of the complexities of the life we live."[6]

At first, however, Rogers was unaware of the storms stirring on higher levels about his play. He wasn't attempting to be a firebrand and hadn't even worried that the play might be seen as controversial:

> All along I presumed that the play would receive a positive reception, which for the most part it in fact did. My bishop was in fact one of its most enthusiastic viewers. . . . [T]here was no sense in those halcyon days that,

---

5   *Ibid.*
6   Dallin H. Oaks, quoted in Gary James Bergera and Ronald Priddis, *Brigham Young University: A House of Faith* (Salt Lake City: Signature Books, 1985); http://www.signaturebooklibrary.org/byu/chapter8.htm (accessed October 30, 2010).

in our explorations, we were at all dissident. In their *Story of the Latter-day Saints* [James B.] Allen and [Glen M.] Leonard constantly reassure the reader of faith and fundamental commitment to the Church. In the same spirit, I wrote my plays. That was enough to enjoy all the good will and trust one could ever ask for.[7]

Despite the best and most faithful of intentions, Church leaders requested that the play not be performed again. Juggling the many concerns that press upon the leadership of a worldwide, missionary-oriented Church, there were bound to be concerns about a play that dealt with issues that were still so potently in effect in the wider world:

> Our then university president, Dallin Oaks, conveyed the request. . . . It had come from members of the Board of Trustees responsible for Church affairs in Europe, including East Germany, which was still under Russian occupation. We also had a number of members in Allende's Chile, which was at that point a socialist nation. It seemed possible, if unlikely, that one or more well intended members in those societies might be inclined, if it came to their attention, to emulate Huebener vis-a-vis their own regimes, with dire consequences for the Church. I and others have speculated about other possible reasons. Suffice it to say, after the fall of the Iron Curtain, a BYU main stage revival of the play proceeded without any official complaint or censure—as have other productions of the play since then.[8]

Along with the disappearance of any discomfort which the LDS Church may have had with *Huebener*, it is clear that Church leaders have held no ill feelings toward Rogers himself, as he was called to serve as president of the Russia St. Petersburg Mission (1993–96), a very difficult and responsible assignment.[9] This gesture from the Church is a strong signifier of the trust and appreciation its leaders repose in Rogers and his work.

Huebener was not the end of Rogers's playwriting, as more of his plays continued to be produced. A student production of Rogers's *Reunion* played at BYU, and a petition circulated to produce Rogers's play about John D. Lee and the Mountain Meadows Massacre, *Fire in the Bones*. Yet again the inevitable controversy associated with the subject matter of the Mountain Meadows Massacre and its pointed references to polygamy prevented *Fire in the Bones* from playing at BYU. Rogers recalled: "In a two-hour discussion, [Academic Vice President Robert K. Thomas], who had keen instincts about political correctness, explained to the four of us why it would be imprudent to perform this play at BYU. At the time, even allusions to historical polygamy, which prominently figures in the play, proved taboo. *Fire in the Bones* was subsequently

---

7   Compton, "A Playwright with a Passion for Unvarnished Depictions," 72.
8   Ibid., 77.
9   Rogers wrote a memoir about his experiences in Russia: "A Call to Russia: Glimpses of Missionary Life," *BYU Studies* (book, not periodical).

produced in the Salt Lake Valley by the short-lived Greenbriar Theater, made up of former BYU student thespians. I was out of the country at the time and never saw it."[10]

Yet despite Rogers's many excellent plays, time and again, it is his universal tale of Helmuth Heubener that proves to have had the most lasting influence. Helmuth Huebener, in real life, was excommunicated by his branch president, only to have his membership reinstated by the highest leaders of the Church when the injustice came to their attention. The same seems to have occured to Huebener as a character within Rogers's play. He, too, was first silenced, then celebrated. Helmuth Huebener since then has been the subject of several books and a documentary. Plans are seemingly still afoot of Huebener's story being made into a motion picture produced by Kaleidoscope Pictures called *Truth and Treason*.

If Rogers's only contribution was his assistance in courageously unearthing this faithful Mormon's tale, he would have given Mormon drama and the Church itself an invaluable gift. However, as a playwright, as a literature professor at BYU, as a mission president, and as a husband and father, his contributions to his faith, his country, and his family have been many and lasting.

---

10   Ibid., 72–73.

About *Huebener*

Huebener premiered at the BYU Margetts Arena Theatre in the months of October and November of 1976:

CAST

Karl-Heinz Schnibbe: Corey Sprague
Hugo Huebener: Paul Nibley
Emma Huebener: Maggie Blair (later Margaret Blair Young)
Gerhard Kunkel: Robert Godwin
Johannes Sudrow: Mike Evenden
Annaliese Sudrow: Miriam Bean (later Miriam Evenden)
Helmuth Huebener: Russ Card
Rudi Wobbe: J. M. Stoddard
Arnold Zoellner: M. Scott Wilkinson
Jonni Duewer: R. Michael Bird
Werner Kranz: Steve Powers
Second Counselor: Terry Fowler
Sandman: E. J. Patterson
First Officer: Tom Nibley
Chief Justices: Rick Hatch
William Darley
Samuel Dibello
Defense Counselor: Randy King
Prosecutor: J. David Sterago
Soldiers & Others: Don Bowen
Tim Stettler
Robert Liddiard
Christian Petersen
Robin Martell
Hausfrauen: Lissa Woodbury
Christie Nuttall
Pat Smith
Voice of BBC Announcer: Derek Spriggs
Voice of Winston Churchill: Arthur Henry King

CREW

Director: Ivan Crosland

Huebener has been produced in a number of other venues throughout the years, including at Dixie College and in the Bountiful/Davis Fine Arts; Rogers himself directed the latter performance. Brigham Young University produced the play again in the Pardoe Theatre March 26–April 11, 1992, with the following cast and crew:

CAST

Karl-Heinz Schnibbe: Benjamin Hoppe
Hugo Huebener: Dean K. M. Jones
Gerhard Kunkel: Greg S. Whitely
Johannes Sudrow: Tom Rogers
Anneliese Sudro: Hester Devenport
Emma Huebener: Betty Joe Smith
Arnold Zoellner: Corey A. Ewan
Helmuth Huebener: Joseph Riddle
Rudi Wobbe: Dennis M. Wright
Jonni Duewer: Jon L. Jensen
Housewife: Rachel Mabey
Husband, State Police, Second Justice: Eric Robertson
Aide, Investigator, Defense Counselor: Larry Ganson
First Clerk, Sandman, Third Justice: Nathan R. Miles
Second Clerk, Second Counselor, Prosecutor: Aaron Eckhart
Soldiers: Laramie D. Taylor
Michael McKeon
Hausfraus: Kiva Jump
Melanie Ankney
Young Men: Matt C. Crosland
Scott Greg Roberts
Spencer M. Walker
Werner Kranz: J. D. Anderson
Interrogator: Blaine Sundrud

CREW

Director: Ivan Crosland

Act One

SCENE 1

October 1941. Hamburg, Germany. As the curtain parts, the cadence of four heavy boots striking cobblestone or pavement is amplified through the auditorium. The stage is completely dark. Then lights slowly rise on the outlines of an apartment building, focusing on the interior of a second-story sleeping room, where a pajama-clad seventeen-year-old boy, KARL-HEINZ Schnibbe, lies inertly in bed. The cadence of boots becomes ever louder, then abruptly stops, followed by loud banging on a nearby door.

VOICE. *(Shouting.)* In the name of the State police!

WOMAN'S VOICE. *(Whispering.)* The Gestapo!

VOICE. Open your door! *(KARL-HEINZ moves to the wall in the direction of the voices and listens.)* Martin Schultz! In the name of the Fuehrer's Secret State Police we demand the custody of your wife, the Jewess Mirella Rosenthal Schultz.

WOMAN'S VOICE. *(Screaming.)* Martin! No!

MAN'S VOICE. Please!

A door is heard being unlatched.

VOICE. Come!

WOMAN'S VOICE. No!

SECOND VOICE. You will come at once!

WOMAN'S VOICE. Martin! Help me!

MAN'S VOICE. It's no use.

FIRST VOICE. That's right. Come along and you'll have less trouble.

WOMAN'S VOICE. No, I won't!

Sounds of a struggle.

MAN'S VOICE. Please! Please! *(More struggle.)* Please! Please! Mirella, forgive me!

The clatter of boots and a woman's shoes are heard on the stairway. KARL-HEINZ *rushes out to the front of his room, as if staring from a window at the street below. Sounds now come from that direction, suggesting more scuffle—cries, body blows, a woman's subdued whimpering. After the sounds disappear,*

KARL-HEINZ *turns away, throws himself on his bed, and weeps as the lights fade.*

SCENE 2

The same time. A modest living room in the apartment of JOHANNES *and* ANNELIESE *Sudrow. A youth in the uniform of a German army corporal,* GERHARD *Kunkel, dramatically gesticulates as* JOHANNES *Sudrow and* HUGO *Huebener sit nearby and sit attentively looking on.*

JOHANNES. Is it really true? They gave no resistance?

GERHARD. It's there for anyone to see. Across the horizon. Facing east. We hardly fired a shell before they gave up and we overran it.

HUGO. The impenetrable Maginot Line. Imagine. Well, if the Fuehrer managed to take the French with so little effort, it shouldn't be much longer before we cross the Channel and conquer all of England.

JOHANNES' *wife,* ANNELIESE, *enters from another room.*

JOHANNES. That remains to be seen. You Nazis are eternally optimistic.

HUGO. So are you Mormons. We all live by our particular brand of faith.

ANNELIESE. I've been in that cellar for nearly twenty minutes and still can't find the cranberry juice.

GERHARD. That's all right, Grandma. Besides, the others aren't here yet.

ANNELIESE. Where can your mother be, Gerhard? She visits us so seldom these days. But she knew you were coming, didn't she, Hugo? I sent her your letter with a neighbor, I assure you.

HUGO. Of course you did, my dear. I saw it myself. That's why I'm here. And Emma knows. She'll come, too.

JOHANNES. Don't fret, Mother. There's still plenty of time. Besides, I think I know where we put those bottles. We moved a lot of things after the last air raid, remember. To keep them from the rats. I'll go down in a while and look around. Hugo can help me.

HUGO. Sure.

ANNELIESE. Well, all right. Just so no one has taken any. We've only got two or three bottles left—when was it that Emma and I put them up?

JOHANNES. Three years ago. That was the last time you could find any berries in the countryside.

ANNELIESE. And we saved one of them for just this occasion—your furlough.

GERHARD. Isn't cranberry Helmuth's favorite?

ANNELIESE. That's why he insisted we save it until you could be with us.

HUGO. Tell us some more about France, Gerhard. Is it still peopled by lazy peasants who have never seen a train or car?

GERHARD. That's not true, Herr Huebener.

JOHANNES. Father!

GERHARD. Father . . . It's just Doktor Goebbels' propaganda.

ANNELIESE. Gerhard, please! You mustn't say such things.

HUGO. Oh, I don't mind. I sometimes joke about Doktor Goebbels myself—in the right company.

ANNELIESE. But someone may be listening. The neighbors are still awake.

GERHARD. I don't care. They can't be more loyal than I am, can they? They haven't risked their lives at the front! And besides, Doktor Goebbels doesn't always write the truth. . . . Oh, maybe the French aren't as well organized as we are and haven't as efficient a war machine. After all, *we* attacked them, didn't we?

ANNELIESE. *(In a subdued voice.)* Gerhard! Not so loud!

GERHARD. But technologically France is just as advanced as Germany. Take that radio I sent you.

HUGO. It's a fine one, all right. But we have them in Germany.

GERHARD. Not for what I paid for it in France—and not with shortwave and fine-tuning.

HUGO. We're not supposed to know about that anyway.

ANNELIESE. Helmuth often listens to it with one of his friends—after we've gone to bed.

HUGO. He'd better keep it tuned to the right stations. Listening to the enemy's a criminal offense.

ANNELIESE. Oh, Helmuth knows that, I'm sure. And he's such a good boy. He wouldn't do anything illegal.

GERHARD. Just so he doesn't tune in to the BBC. They have the heaviest Allied propaganda. . . . How's Helmuth doing these days anyway?

JOHANNES. You know Helmuth—the eternal scholar, always with his nose in some history book. Or in a map—following the course of the war. I sometimes think he knows more about it than the Fuehrer himself.

GERHARD. That's probably true.

ANNELIESE. Hush! Don't say such things.

GERHARD. They praised him enough on his graduation essay, didn't they? What was it on?

JOHANNES. Corruption in the Western democracies—he called it "The War of the Plutocrats."

GERHARD. Is he still as active in the Hitler Youth?

JOHANNES. *(Eyeing* HUGO*)* I'm . . . not sure.

HUGO. Of course you're sure. And the answer is "no." He hasn't gone near them in a couple of months. I've even been reprimanded for it.

GERHARD. It must not make you look very good—as a Party member.

HUGO. How active Helmuth is is his own business. But I wish he would stop reminding people that we have already taken credit for sinking the same British aircraft carrier at least nine different times.

GERHARD. *(Laughing.)* The *Ark Royal*? See, Grandma, Doktor Goebbels does have trouble keeping his facts straight.

JOHANNES. *(Counting on his fingers.)* All he needs is a decent adding machine.

The men laugh.

ANNELIESE. Shhh!

HUGO. That's right. Not so loud. Or I'll have to turn you all in.

GERHARD. Father . . . you wouldn't!

HUGO. No. *I* wouldn't, but some others might. Some of your good members, for instance. Even Arnold.

JOHANNES. Arnold Zoellner?

ANNELIESE. Hugo! What are you saying?

GERHARD. Not the branch president?

HUGO. Why not? He's joined the Party. Or didn't you know?

JOHANNES. But why?

HUGO. I suppose, Johannes, because he's a man of such great faith. He has that much left over.

GERHARD. But that . . . that's double minded.

HUGO. What did you say, Gerhard? You mean, I couldn't, if I cared to, join your church—the way you've all been after me to these many years—and be a National Socialist, too? You mean one is right and the other wrong—that it's strictly black and white?

JOHANNES. No, he doesn't mean that, Hugo. And if he does, he just doesn't know better. I've no doubt that if Arnold Zoellner has joined the Nazi Party, he did so because it would help the Church. That's the same reason why, when the Fuehrer broadcasts during Sunday meetings, Arnold brings a transmitter and makes us all listen.

HUGO. According to Emma, he even locks the doors so that you have no choice in the matter. That's what I call dutiful.

GERHARD. So it's come to this!

JOHANNES. Come to what, Gerhard? Didn't Joseph Smith himself say that we should be subject to whoever governs us, that we should "obey, honor, and sustain the law"?

HUGO. A shrewd man, Joseph Smith. And you spoke up none too soon, I hear someone outside. They may have been listening.

They all become deathly still. An outer door is heard opening. Then, as EMMA *Huebener comes into the room, the others immediately relax.*

EMMA. *(Seeing* GERHARD *and rushing into his arms.)* My darling son.

GERHARD. Mama.

EMMA. How long it's been. How I've worried about you.

GERHARD. It's been fine, Mama. Since we took France there's been no fighting. So long as I stay in the West...

EMMA. I pray you always will.

GERHARD. But where's Helmuth? I thought he'd be coming with you.

EMMA. I was held over at the hospital. They're terribly short of nurses these days.

ANNELIESE. On account of the air raids.

EMMA. And Helmuth planned to work late tonight, didn't he, Mother? (ANNELIESE *nods.*) But I thought that he would be here by now.

HUGO. Just like him to stop by the library and lose himself in some book.

EMMA. Bruder Zoellner was hoping to come by this evening, too, and leave some records for him.

GERHARD. Records?

ANNELIESE. Helmuth is a branch clerk these days—and Bruder Zoellner's right hand man.

GERHARD. How do they get along?

JOHANNES. Well enough.

EMMA. Helmuth is so helpful that Bruder Zoellner manages to swallow his pride and overlook Helmuth's—

GERHARD. Honesty.

HUGO. Impudence.

JOHANNES. Freshness.

ANNELIESE. Impulsiveness.

EMMA. *(Staring the others down.)* His *youthful innocence* . . . his *sincerity* . . . and his *generosity*. . . . Which reminds me, we were going to toast your return with—

ANNELIESE. The cranberry juice! Johannes, you promised to find it for me.

JOHANNES. Yes, my treasure. But I'll need Hugo's help.

HUGO. By all means.

JOHANNES. There are some heavy crates down there. We'll have to move them.

The two men exit.

GERHARD. And how have you been, Mama—besides overworked?

ANNELIESE. She worries. About Helmuth.

GERHARD. The *Ark Royal*, you mean?

EMMA. You've heard. Well, ja, it's true. That—and his general attitude. You heard what the others just called him just now—"impudent" and "impulsive." Even his grandfather, who loves him so, says he is "fresh" toward the branch president.

GERHARD. Helmuth was always forthright—and spunky.

EMMA. I know. And I love him for it. I don't see it the way the others do. But times have changed. We can't just say whatever comes to mind anymore. And lately Helmuth has gotten so critical of the government and—well, everyone in authority. He doesn't make jokes anymore like he used to. He stares past you and doesn't answer. He is always so preoccupied. He's not the same carefree, life-loving Helmuth, and somebody, I believe, is having their way with him. But who . . . could it be?

GERHARD. Grandma, do you ever hear him talking with friends?

ANNELIESE. They rarely come to the house until after ten o' clock, my dear, and you know that Johannes and I retire early. We couldn't stay up after that hour if we wanted to.

EMMA. If Hugo and I had regular shifts and didn't work such long hours—and if we had as much space as your grandparents—you boys could have lived with us this last while, and we'd have looked out for you.

GERHARD. You know I came here because I didn't get along with . . . your husband, and Helmuth came to keep me company.

EMMA. But you were much younger then and Hugo likes you both. He's very proud of you, even if he never tells you so.

ANNELIESE. Emma, don't you worry. Helmuth is still a good boy. He's just not very cautious. Maybe he trusts people a little too much and expects that they will see things the way he does if he can just once talk to them—that's why he's always wanted to be a missionary. He's still a good boy. And so are his friends.

EMMA. Well, I hope so.

ANNELIESE. I'm sure of it. Why, they're almost all of them Latter-day Saints, like Karl-Heinz Schnibbe and Rudi Wobbe.

JOHANNES *and* HUGO *return from the cellar.*

JOHANNES. We found it!

HUGO. And if I'm to have any, we'll need to toast right away. My shift begins in an hour.

GERHARD. Someone's coming.

ANNELIESE. It must be Helmuth.

EMMA. *(Opening the bottle.)* Then I'll pour the glasses. *(A knock is heard.)* Oh, dear. Helmuth wouldn't bother knocking.

JOHANNES *opens the door, admitting Arnold* ZOELLNER, *middle-aged and typically bourgeois in appearance. He carries a sheaf of papers.*

ZOELLNER. *(Cheerfully.)* Good evening, brothers and sisters.

THE MEN. Evening, Arnold.

ZOELLNER. I see the Huebeners are with you this evening, Johannes. You must be celebrating. I'm intruding?

EMMA. *(As she pours:)* Not at all, Bruder Zoellner. Here's an extra glass—just for you.

ZOELLNER. *(Looking around the room.)* Are you sure it wasn't meant for Helmuth?

JOHANNES. *(Handing him a glass.)* He's not home yet, and we can't wait any longer. You're more than welcome.

ZOELLNER. And the occasion?

HUGO. He's standing right there.

ZOELLNER. Why, it can't be—is it really Gerhard? *(Shaking* GERHARD's *hand.)* And how are they treating you, my boy?

GERHARD. Very well, thank you.

ZOELLNER. We think of you all the time and pray for your safekeeping—and that of all the other noble youth who are defending the Vaterland.

HUGO. *(Suddenly standing and saluting, with mock seriousness.)* Heil, Hitler!

ZOELLNER. Uh . . . er . . . *(Following suit.)* Heil, Hitler! *(All look at* GERHARD, *who silently moves to a chair across the room, sits down, and studies his hands.)* Well, I only came because Helmuth will need to fill out these forms by tomorrow evening. I'm on a double shift again and won't see him tomorrow at the branch house. Your son is a great help to the Church, Sister Huebener. He's as indispensable to the Lord as men like Gerhard are to the Fuehrer. Each serves in his own way. And what counts in the long run, don't you agree, is that, like these young men, whatever our stewardship, we prove reliable—loyal and reliable. That's where, to my mind, the two come together.

JOHANNES. The two?

ZOELLNER. Yes. National Socialism and the gospel. The Lord puts a high priority on loyalty. So does the Fuehrer. . . . And so do I. . . . And how are you tonight, friend Hugo?

HUGO. I'm content, Arnold. And how is the branch president?

ZOELLNER. I only wish that I *were* your branch president, Hugo. How many more years can you make us wait?

HUGO. I'll keep you guessing a while longer, Arnold. It's more fun that way. But I promise to be baptized before the Millennium.

ZOELLNER. The Millennium? But no man knows the hour or the day—

HUGO. Exactly. You see, I'm only trying to follow his example.

ZOELLNER. His?

HUGO. The Lord's. I try to keep you guessing.

The men laugh.

EMMA. Please have some more juice, Bruder Zoellner.

JOHANNES. Go ahead, Arnold.

ZOELLNER. Danke.

HUGO. *(Smiling.)* It's not the least bit fermented, I'm sorry to say.

ZOELLNER. So that's what's holding you up these days.

EMMA. I allow him only an occasional glass of wine.

HUGO. It's too expensive.

EMMA. Just as well. You promised the mission president just before he returned to America—that was how many years ago now?

ANNELIESE. Five at least!

GERHARD. —that you'd quit your drinking and join the Church. Remember?

HUGO. But then I thought the missionaries would be coming back right away. I didn't think we would be fighting them instead. I don't know—to join the Church now seems so unpatriotic.

JOHANNES. That's not so, Hugo. The Church is greater than political movements or even nationalities. I joined myself when I was a soldier in the Great War, in occupied France. It was a family of members in Bordeaux—the DeVigniers—who cared for me and dressed my wounds when I was left behind the lines. I will never forget them. I wonder how they are and if our soldiers are treating them well. You didn't get to see them, did you, Gerhard?

GERHARD. No, Grandfather, my unit never got to the south, but maybe next time. . . .

ZOELLNER. Well, I must be going. Please remind Helmuth that the reports are due the day after tomorrow.

JOHANNES. Don't worry, Arnold, Helmuth will have them for you.

ZOELLNER. Yes, I'm sure he will. And I'm grateful. . . . Well, good night.

THE OTHERS. Good night.

ZOELLNER. Fight bravely, Gerhard. We're proud of you. And thank you for the delicious juice, Sister Huebener.

EMMA. *(Accompanying him to the door.)* You should thank Helmuth. He asked that we save it for Gerhard's return. We still have another bottle. You come back and share it with us when we have another celebration—say, at the end of the war.

ZOELLNER. I'll gladly drink to the Fuehrer's final victory. . . .

HUGO. Heil, Hitler! *(He leaves.)*

GERHARD. He seems fond enough of Helmuth.

HUGO. What he is fond of is Helmuth's brains.

JOHANNES. And he knows that deep down Helmuth's a devout Latter-day Saint.

GERHARD. Just doesn't appreciate Helmuth's wild ideas, is that it?

ANNELIESE. Every other week he says to us: "Can't you make your grandson stay with simple truths? These aren't times for theories and speculation. We should work more—work to end this war—and talk less." And I agree with him.

JOHANNES. And each time I tell him: "Arnold, he is after all a boy still. Only turned seventeen. You know he was an excellent scholar in public school—a regular bookworm. Always got top marks. And a marvel in English. He'll do all right. I'm proud of him." And now that Arnold has to work double shifts at the munitions plant, Helmuth has become his indispensable helper.

EMMA. It's true. Helmuth practically runs the Church in Hamburg—at least the office part. There are still over a thousand of us in the city, so it's a big job.

JOHANNES. We'd have a lot more members if the missionaries could have stayed and there hadn't been a war.

ANNELIESE. Or if in the old days so many converts hadn't left for America. Imagine them and President Reese and all those wonderful young missionaries with their guns trained on us. It's more than I can understand.

HUGO. My feelings exactly, Mutti.

GERHARD. You mustn't blame the Americans. Look, I'm the one they're most likely to shoot at, if they ever get this far.

HUGO. Most of the bombers that come this way—and many of the pilots—are from America. They're not just British. And don't deny it.

GERHARD. I don't deny it, but don't blame them either. After all, they didn't really start it. First the Polish Corridor, then France, and now Russia.

ANNELIESE. Gerhard! Please!

EMMA. That's enough, Gerhard. You might be one of the Fuehrer's best storm troopers, and what you say might all be true, but your grandmother and Bruder Zoellner are right: the less we talk about it the better.

HUGO. Let him talk. He just doesn't have the whole picture. You see, Gerhard, the Fuehrer's strategy is the only way we can right the wrongs that have been such a burden to everyone since they founded this good-for-nothing League of Nations.

GERHARD. Sounds like more Goebbels to me!

EMMA. Gerhard!

GERHARD. What do you think, Grandfather?

JOHANNES. Me? I don't know. I just don't know. Probably none of us has what Hugo calls the "whole picture." I am sure of only one thing anymore—that God has spoken again in these latter days and called forth prophets, not here but in the land we now oppose. Let us be glad that we still have the Church and our testimonies, or it would be easy enough to believe the Fuehrer, or anyone else who is so certain of himself, has all the right answers.

GERHARD. Even so, that doesn't explain why my younger brother isn't here to meet me this evening.

ANNELIESE. Your letter didn't reach us till this morning—till after he left for work. Otherwise, nothing would have kept him away so long—except an air raid.

GERHARD. How is he as a public servant?

HUGO. They like him.

JOHANNES. They like him a lot.

EMMA. *(To* GERHARD.*)* If he just doesn't say the wrong thing at the wrong time, like you.

GERHARD. Don't worry, Mother. Helmuth's too smart to say what he shouldn't.

JOHANNES. Unless he wants to, and then he will—

> HELMUTH *enters. He is blonde, rather stocky and nondescript in appearance with boyish features—hardly the stereotype adventure hero.*

HELMUTH. Cranberry juice? What's the occasion? It must be— *(Then noticing* GERHARD.*)* Gerhard! *(They embrace, then* HELMUTH *abruptly turns to* JOHANNES.*)* What will he do, Grampa? Tell us all.

JOHANNES. He will always speak the truth.

HELMUTH. That he will. . . . By the way, who is this model of integrity?

JOHANNES. My grandson.

HELMUTH. Why, of course. Of course. I should have realized. But be careful, Gerhard. Your commanding officers don't want you to speak the whole truth—just certain half truths.

GERHARD. *(Playfully roughing him up)* He was talking about you, little brother.

HELMUTH. Oh?

GERHARD. And what you just now said to me is your own best medicine.

HELMUTH. I see. Well, ja, my advice . . . my medicine is good for whatever ails one. And I'm no exception.

EMMA. I'm glad to hear you say that, Helmuth. . . .

HELMUTH. But let's talk about Gerhard. How is France? Is Paris as romantic as they say—a pair of lovers on every park bench?

GERHARD. You don't often see such things in an occupying army.

HELMUTH. You mean lovers are gun shy and stay out of view?

GERHARD. Probably.

HELMUTH. Can't say that I blame them.

GERHARD. Nor I. . . . But how do you like the radio I sent you?

HELMUTH. *Mensch*, it's a beauty. It's got wonderful fidelity. You can get anything on it.

GERHARD. *Anything?*

HELMUTH. *(Winking.)* All kinds of *music*, that is—fast rhythm and also classical.

GERHARD. Even foreign?

HELMUTH. Even some foreign.

GERHARD. Be careful, Helmuth—about who you listen with.

HELMUTH. I . . . I am.

A doorbell rings.

EMMA. Who could that be?

She exits.

HUGO. A strange hour for callers.

EMMA *returns to the room, followed by another young man carrying a book and similar in build to* HELMUTH *though somewhat taller and about* HELMUTH's *age.*

EMMA. It's Rudi Wobbe.

RUDI. Good evening.

HUGO. Evening.

JOHANNES. Good evening, Bruder Wobbe.

RUDI. *(To* HELMUTH.*)* Is this your brother Gerhard?

HELMUTH. The same.

> RUDI *and* GERHARD *shake hands.*

RUDI. You look so . . . in that uniform you look so . . .

EMMA. Chic?

GERHARD. Fierce?

HELMUTH. Formidable.

RUDI. Something like that. . . . Excuse me for disturbing you, but I had to ask Helmuth if . . . Helmuth, could you teach my next Sunday School lesson?

HELMUTH. If you can't, I'll be glad to.

RUDI. My Hitler Youth patrol's going for a few days to Goslar.

ANNELIESE. Goslar? The mountains should be lovely now—with the leaves turning—

RUDI. For special training—maneuvers.

HELMUTH. When do you leave?

RUDI. Not until 10:30 Sunday morning. I'll see you at priesthood meeting, but I'll have to leave before Sunday School.

HELMUTH. I see. While I serve God, you will serve the war machine.

RUDI. Of course, I'd rather not, but—

JOHANNES. If you were more like the Schnibbe boy, you wouldn't have to.

GERHARD. Who's that?

HELMUTH. Karl-Heinz. You remember him, don't you? My age? He's been coming to our branch since about the time you were drafted. . . . Well, they expelled him from Hitler Youth.

GERHARD. What did he do?

JOHANNES. Just refused to goose step. So they sent him home and told him not to come back.

> *They all laugh.*

RUDI. He may be sorry. It may keep him from being promoted.

JOHANNES. As a house painter?

HELMUTH. Karl-Heinz will do all right. He's spunkier than most of us. . . . What's the lesson, Rudi?

RUDI. *(Showing him the book.)* It's on the prophet Joseph Smith—and the way he was persecuted after he told people his first vision.

HELMUTH. *(Reading:)* "... how very strange it was that an obscure boy, of a little over fourteen years of age, should be thought ... of sufficient importance to attract the attention of the great ones ... and ... to create in them a spirit of most bitter persecution and reviling. . . . I was led to say in my heart: Why persecute me for telling the truth? Why does the world think to make me deny what I have actually seen?" I'd like to teach that one. And if there are any investigators, I'll compare the prophet to Martin Luther.

EMMA. Luther?

HELMUTH. Where, facing excommunication, he stood before the Inquisition at Worms and declared: "Here I stand, God help me, I can do no other."

HUGO. Martin Luther was a very great man, and a German, too. Don't you Mormons forget that!

GERHARD. We know that. We acknowledge him as a great reformer.

RUDI. But he wasn't a prophet.

HUGO. The theses he nailed on the cathedral door at Wittenberg contain more good sense than you are apt to have if you live to be a hundred. Why, they brought us out of the Middle Ages!

HELMUTH. Of course they did, Father. We also believe that Luther was ... well, inspired. In fact, without Martin Luther and men like him, there probably wouldn't have been a Joseph Smith or a Restoration.

HUGO. So there!

HELMUTH. But ... well, you'll understand the differences someday. Meanwhile, we shouldn't trouble you about it.

GERHARD. Good old Helmuth, always the diplomat!

RUDI. Well, I'll leave you now. . . . Helmuth, may I speak to you for a moment about . . . the lesson?

HELMUTH. Of course, what is it?

RUDI. Let's go outdoors a minute so we don't disturb your family's celebration.

HELMUTH. All right. . . . I'll be right back, Gerhard.

RUDI. Good night.

> HELMUTH *and* RUDI *leave the room, and then reappear on the apron, as if outdoors. As they speak, the lights dim on the scene indoors.*

RUDI. *(First looking about to be sure they cannot be overheard.)* I really didn't want to talk about my Sunday School class.

HELMUTH. I could tell.

RUDI. It's . . . that radio we've been listening to.

HELMUTH. I'm sorry, Rudi, but I won't have time this evening—not with Gerhard here.

RUDI. I didn't mean that.

HELMUTH. But if you'd like to take it, I'll trust you. I could give you the branch house key. You'd be perfectly safe listening to it there.

RUDI. Thanks, Helmuth, but it's not that . . . I . . . I just don't think we should listen to it anymore.

HELMUTH. I see.

RUDI. After all, it's against the law.

HELMUTH. I know.

RUDI. And it's dangerous.

HELMUTH. I know that too. Rudi, it frightens me as much as you. But . . . you know I've been transcribing some of those BBC broadcasts. I've written them down—here, they're in my vest pocket.

RUDI. No. Don't show them to me. Not here. And don't pass them around. It's too dangerous.

HELMUTH. I won't. I'll burn them, I guess, after I've studied them some more. But I've also compared them with our news broadcasts, and that's what really bothers me.

RUDI. What does?

HELMUTH. The detail.

RUDI. Detail?

HELMUTH. Ja. The BBC has so much more detail. It gives the exact times and locations of bombing raids.

RUDI. They could still be lies.

HELMUTH. Not what they say about Hamburg. It's exactly as we've seen it here. With no exaggeration.

RUDI. That's because they've done so much damage. Naturally they'd take credit for it.

HELMUTH. But they also give the statistics on our bombings over London, and their losses are just as heavy.

RUDI. Which means we're not doing so badly after all.

HELMUTH. It's not that. It's just that our broadcasts never admit to any defeat. In ours we're always victorious. It's all too one-sided. I wouldn't have noticed it so much except for the contrast. The British version is always more balanced, more objective, more truthful, while ours . . . ours . . .

RUDI. Not truthful?

HELMUTH. Worse . . . full of lies. Deliberate lies, I'm afraid.

RUDI. But, Helmuth, what can *you* do about it? A junior grade clerk in the State Welfare Office? What good can you do, even if you shout it from the rooftops? No one will dare listen. And before you can say two words, they'll crush you.

HELMUTH. I know.

RUDI. So don't be stubborn. Don't be stupid. It won't do any good.

HELMUTH. I know. . . .

SCENE 3

Early the following Sunday. A cramped office in the meeting house of Hamburg-St. Georg LDS Branch. HELMUTH *is running a duplicating machine, while* KARL-HEINZ *Schnibbe, the boy from Scene 1, watches.*

KARL-HEINZ. I tell you, Helmuth, I haven't been able to sleep since that night. That poor woman. And her husband—he hasn't left their apartment since they took her away, not in four days.

HELMUTH. You say she was a Jew?

KARL-HEINZ. Ja. Besides that she hadn't done a thing. And you remember Bruder Worps and that camp they sent him to last year? He just returned—I talked to him this morning. He's a broken man, Helmuth. He can't live much longer.

HELMUTH. What did they do to him?

KARL-HEINZ. Something they call water treatment. They mostly use it in the winter. They put you in stocks, then drip freezing water onto your hands. It forms large mittens of ice, which the guards knock off a while later with a piece of rubber hose. They joke about it and say it's to keep your hands warm. . . . Bruder Worps wept as he told me about it.

HELMUTH. Why did they send him here? I don't remember.

KARL-HEINZ. He made some remark about Reichsmarschall Goering and all his medals.

HELMUTH. What are we coming to?

KARL-HEINZ. I'd rather not think about it.

ZOELLNER *enters.*

ZOELLNER. Helmuth, are those rosters run off? We'll need to distribute them this morning in the priesthood meeting—in just ten minutes.

HELMUTH. They'll be ready, Bruder Zoellner.

ZOELLNER. Fine. And how are you today, Karl-Heinz? It's good to see you.

KARL-HEINZ. I'm all right, thank you.

ZOELLNER. How is your branch teaching coming? It's nearly the end of the month. Did you get it out yet?

KARL-HEINZ. I . . . I intended to last night. But I just didn't feel like talking to anybody.

HELMUTH. There was a pogrom last week. In Karl-Heinz's neighborhood. He was there when they came for the Jews.

ZOELLNER. Oh? Well, that's too bad. But we mustn't let one or two isolated pogroms upset us too much, Karl-Heinz, particularly when we can't control them. And we must be most careful not to be critical. Not to complain.

KARL-HEINZ. But are such things right?

ZOELLNER. Right or wrong, we are in no position to change them. . . . Well, are we? And then, if we complain too much, they might persecute *us*. The *Church*. Don't forget that we are a very small minority and have strong ties with the Allies. The authorities know that and can exploit it against us if we ever give them a reason. Besides, things will change again for the better. . . . Remember the Savior's admonition: "Render unto Caesar's what is Caesar's." And don't forget the Twelfth Article of Faith. . . . Well, then, everything's in order, isn't it? Karl-Heinz?

KARL-HEINZ. I . . . I guess.

ZOELLNER. Good. I'll see you both shortly.

He leaves.

KARL-HEINZ. What do you think, Helmuth?

HELMUTH. I don't *think*. . . . I *know*.

KARL-HEINZ. What?

HELMUTH. That there are more than one or two isolated pogroms, bad as they are.

KARL-HEINZ. What do you mean?

RUDI *bursts into the room, dressed in the brown shirt of a Hitler Youth.*

RUDI. Did you see him?

KARL-HEINZ. Old Bruder Schwartz!

HELMUTH. Solomon Schwartz?

RUDI. And the sign?

HELMUTH. What sign?

RUDI. On the branch house door? Someone must have just put it up.

KARL-HEINZ. "Entrance is forbidden to Jews!"

HELMUTH. To the Lord's true church? Who put it there?

RUDI. I don't know. . . . He was just standing there when I went in.

HELMUTH. Who was?

RUDI. Old Solomon. Just standing there staring at the sign. I called to him. I said, "Bruder Schwartz. Good morning. May I help you?" But he didn't even hear me, and I . . . I was too ashamed to say anymore, so I came right here. I wish I could take this shirt off and never wear it again, or see another one like it.

HELMUTH. Solomon Schwartz. Seventy-six years old. Why, he's been a member for over sixty years. His parents were converted by John Taylor. He's more Mormon than you or I or the rest of us. . . . I'm going to bring him in here this morning if it is the last thing I do!

HELMUTH rushes out.

RUDI. I'm afraid Rudi Wobbe's just going to be sick today and won't be able to make the trip to Goslar.

KARL-HEINZ. Good for you, Rudi. I've been waiting for you to join my club.

RUDI. What club?

KARL-HEINZ. *(With a mocking strut.)* The ex-goose steppers!

They smile. HELMUTH returns.

HELMUTH. He's gone.

KARL-HEINZ. Damn!

RUDI. Maybe it's just as well. Stirring things up might get him in worse trouble.

HELMUTH. Trouble? We're all in plenty of trouble. And the more we avoid it, the worse it gets. It's not just Solomon Schwartz. What's happening to him is our fault. We're letting it happen. We've got blinders on. And we won't take them off until it's too late—until it's happening to all of us.

KARL-HEINZ. What do you mean?

HELMUTH. You remember that radio that Gerhard sent me?

KARL-HEINZ. Sure.

HELMUTH. Well, Rudi and I . . .

RUDI. Helmuth!

HELMUTH. Rudi and I have been listening to it for some time now.

KARL-HEINZ. Ja?

RUDI. *(Looking furtively toward the door and windows.)* Helmuth, be careful!

HELMUTH. We've been listening to the BBC Deutsche News Service.

KARL-HEINZ. You mean it?

RUDI. Ja, but I quit. I repented.

KARL-HEINZ. What do they say?

RUDI. Don't ask!

HELMUTH. Do you really want to know?

KARL-HEINZ. Sure.

HELMUTH. Why?

KARL-HEINZ. Because I want to know *what's what.* That's why.

HELMUTH. Even if it contradicts what you're supposed to think about things?

KARL-HEINZ. In that case, more than ever!

HELMUTH. *(Impulsively embracing* KARL-HEINZ.*)* You're one of us!

RUDI. What's that supposed to mean?

HELMUTH. And you too, Rudi. You know you can't live with a lie. You can't sing a song that's written off key and feel good about it.

RUDI. Maybe not. But I don't have to sing at all if I don't want to.

HELMUTH. Are you sure you don't want to?

RUDI. Maybe I want to, but it's not worth the risk. I also ran into Sister Hase this morning in the foyer.

KARL-HEINZ. Sister Hase?

RUDI. She'd come early—to practice the organ. She was just leaving, and pale as a ghost. She had one of those leaflets in her hand they've been dropping from British planes. Bruder Zoellner had just gone up to her. He told her to give it to him and never again bring anything like that into the church or—and these were his words, I swear—he would personally make sure she was sent to one of those camps.

KARL-HEINZ. Is this the Lord's church? I can't believe it. Listen, Rudi—I don't care what the risks are—you're really not alive if you can't sing when you feel like it.

RUDI. Then I'm not alive. None of us is alive. But what can we do about it?

HELMUTH *eyes the duplicating machine.*

HELMUTH. I wonder. . . . *(He walks about the room, weighing his thoughts.)* Let me ask you both if you'd be willing . . . if, Rudi, you'd be willing to listen just one more time, and Karl-Heinz, you with us . . . if you'd be willing to listen and look at my transcripts and compare them to those of the State Information Service, and then just tell me who *you* think is telling the truth . . . and what you think we should do about it.

KARL-HEINZ. You say *when*, Helmuth.

HELMUTH. All right. As soon as Rudi comes back from Goslar. . . .

RUDI. I'm not going.

HELMUTH. Not going? Why?

RUDI. Never mind.

HELMUTH. All right then. Tonight. After my grandparents have gone to bed.

KARL-HEINZ. *(Giving* HELMUTH *his hand.)* Agreed.

RUDI. *(Following suit.)* I'm with you.

    ZOELLNER *enters.*

ZOELLNER. Time for priesthood, brethren. Got the rosters, Helmuth?

HELMUTH. *(Handing him the rosters.)* Here . . . *(*ZOELLNER *reaches for the rosters, but, on an impulse,* HELMUTH *holds onto them.)* Before we start, Bruder Zoellner, do you know about the sign?

ZOELLNER. Sign?

HELMUTH. Outside the door. About Jews.

ZOELLNER. Oh . . . Well, yes. Yes, I do.

HELMUTH. Did you put up that sign, Bruder Zoellner?

    With an effort ZOELLNER *dislodges the roster from* HELMUTH'*s grip.*

ZOELLNER. Yes, brethren . . . yes, I did. I'm sorry. Truly sorry. Believe me, I didn't want to, but I . . . felt I had to do it. For the sake of the Church. . . . Come on. It's time for the meeting.

    He leaves for the meeting.

HELMUTH. Just a minute . . .

    HELMUTH *exits to outdoors. A pause. The other two look at each other, puzzled.*

KARL-HEINZ. This is some Sunday!

RUDI. Yeah!

    Another pause. HELMUTH *returns with a makeshift cardboard sign whose legend reads: "Den Juden ist der Eintritt verboten!" He tears it up and tosses it in a wastebasket.*

HELMUTH. Now I can go to priesthood meeting. How about you?

    RUDI *nods.*

KARL-HEINZ. Let's go!

    They exit.

SCENE 4

Later that evening. HELMUTH, KARL-HEINZ, *and* RUDI *are seen in silhouette, gathered around a table and listening to* HELMUTH's *radio. Intermittent whistles and cracklings suggest a short wave transmission. At the outset of their speeches the voices of the announcer and Churchill merge with those of the translators—in German, French, and Russian.*

VOICE. *(In a clipped British accent:)* As for England, do not be deceived about the resistance your soldiers would encounter in attempting to invade the British home isles. In fact, your Reichmarschall Goering's attempt at an air invasion has—contrary to what you are told—already failed, while your fire bombs, though flagrantly and indiscriminately destructive of many innocent British lives, only strengthen the British resolve to resist and fight back to the last man. Do not forget, moreover, that the military and technological might of that sleeping giant, the United States, which is just now awakening and rising to our need, will henceforth be with us and also reinforce our numbers. . . . Listen now to the indignation and the dreadful wrath of Britain's tough and stalwart helmsman, the Prime Minister, Sir Winston Churchill.

CHURCHILL'S VOICE. *(After each sentence an interpreter's voice is also heard with the German equivalent. Later in the same speech the voices of their interpreters are heard as well, speaking in French and Russian:)* My fellow Britons! These are days that test the mettle and the fortitude of the best of England's sons and daughters. We have drawn in our belts and learned austerity. We have keenly felt the loss of dear ones who have fallen to the deluded Axis foe. And this has made us all the more determined. What has happened in France and Russia and in air raids here at home makes no difference to our actions and our purpose. In this hour of need we became for a while the sole champion in arms to defend the world cause, and we shall do our best to be worthy of this high honor. If necessary for years, if necessary alone, we shall defend our island home, and with the British Empire we shall fight on, unconquerable, until the curse of Hitler is lifted from the brow of mankind—cost us what it may in blood, sweat, and tears. We will never parlay, we will never negotiate with Hitler. We shall fight him by land, we shall fight him by sea, we shall fight him in the air, until, with God's help, we have rid the earth of his shadow and liberated its peoples from his yoke. Any man or state who fights against Nazidom will have our aid. Any man or state who marches with Hitler is our foe. That is our policy and that is our declaration.

VOICE. This is the BBC Deutsche News Service.

HELMUTH. *(Turning off the radio.)* Well, what do you think?

RUDI. I think Churchill means business!

KARL-HEINZ. I think the Fuehrer had better build a bunker, if he hasn't already, in the middle of Berlin-Pankhow. And dig it deep!

SCENE 5

A few evenings later. The office of the Hamburg-St. Georg LDS Branch, as in Scene 3. HELMUTH *sits at a table behind a sheaf of papers,* KARL-HEINZ *and* RUDI *at his side.*

KARL-HEINZ. Is it time?

HELMUTH. Not yet. Have some patience. I told you we must wait until Bruder Zoellner comes by for this report.

RUDI. You finished it an hour ago.

HELMUTH. I have to look like I'm still making it out, don't I? Or why would we still be here?

An outer door is heard opening, then closing.

HELMUTH. That must be him now.

ZOELLNER *appears in the doorway.*

ZOELLNER. Well, Helmuth, I see you've had plenty of help with this month's report. How did the branch teaching go?

HELMUTH. A little better, Bruder Zoellner. With so many men away, each teacher has a lot of families to contact. And with the double shifts they're often hard to reach, but almost 40 percent were visited.

ZOELLNER. And did you get all your families, Karl-Heinz?

KARL-HEINZ. Yes, I did, Bruder Zoellner.

ZOELLNER. You are all very faithful. Given the times, we have many faithful priesthood holders. You are all an inspiration to me. I am grateful, and the Lord, I am sure, is equally pleased with all you do for us—you especially, Helmuth. Just watch what you say these days. Be careful of your words.

RUDI. We will, Bruder Zoellner.

ZOELLNER. Be sure you do. Good night.

THE OTHERS. Good night.

ZOELLNER *leaves.*

KARL-HEINZ. I feel bad. . . . I feel. . . .

HELMUTH. Guilty?

KARL-HEINZ. A little.

HELMUTH. How about you, Rudi?

RUDI. I do, too, but . . .

HELMUTH. We've none of us forgotten what he already told us, I'm sure of that. I've thought of nothing else ever since. And so far we've heeded him, haven't we? Have either of you said anything to anyone else about the broadcasts?

KARL-HEINZ. No.

RUDI. I was too scared.

HELMUTH. Well, then, we've followed his advice so far, haven't we—to the letter?

KARL-HEINZ. Sure.

RUDI. I guess so.

HELMUTH. And if we're still careful, like he just now suggested—careful with our words—then we can still say we're doing what he advised us.

RUDI. Only with a vengeance.

HELMUTH. Agreed?

KARL-HEINZ. Sounds fair to me.

HELMUTH. As, in our hearts, we see fit to do our duty. And that no one else can fully dictate. Only the burning of the Spirit within.

KARL-HEINZ. That's right.

RUDI. I . . . I agree.

HELMUTH. And don't forget what the Lord told the prophet Joseph: "It is not meet that I should command in all things. . . . For he that is compelled in all things, the same is a slothful and not a wise servant."

A muffled tapping is heard.

KARL-HEINZ. Someone's signaling.

HELMUTH. That will be Duewer. Let him in, will you, Rudi?

RUDI. *(Exiting.)* Sure.

KARL-HEINZ. Duewer?

HELMUTH. Jonni Duewer. The fellow I told you about. He's an apprentice at the State Welfare Office. Lives in Altona.

KARL-HEINZ. A nonmember?

HELMUTH. Yes, but as committed as any of us.

KARL-HEINZ. Are you sure?

HELMUTH. Sure, I'm sure. You'll like him a lot. (RUDI *returns with* JONNI *Duewer, who is approximately their same age.*) Thanks for coming, Jonni. This is Karl-Heinz.

KARL-HEINZ. Hello.

JONNI *and* KARL-HEINZ *shake hands.*

HELMUTH. You and Rudi already know each other.

RUDI. Sure, we're old friends.

HELMUTH. Well, this is our little group, and that *(pointing to the duplicating machine)* is our secret weapon. Before we begin, though, I need to know—are you still with me or do you have any reservations? You mustn't feel constrained. . . . I take it then we're all of one mind. Why don't we make a pact then, and shake on it? Agreed?

KARL-HEINZ. Fine.

JONNI. Agreed.

HELMUTH *raises his arm. The others, in turn, clasp his hand.*

HELMUTH. Before God and witnessing each other.

THE OTHERS. Before God and witnessing each other.

HELMUTH. Now to work: here are the first fliers. *(Reaching into his briefcase and producing mimeographed papers.)* I already did the stencils and ran them off.

KARL-HEINZ. Holy Goethe! Read this: "Down with Hitler—the people's scourge, the people's destroyer, the people's betrayer—down with Hitler!" Say, Helmuth, you're almost a poet.

JONNI. "Due to almost unlimited air war, hundreds of thousands of defenseless civilians have lost their lives! Hitler alone is guilty!"

RUDI. "Are you a friend of the truth? The broadcasts of the British Overseas Radio Network, which can be received at the hours and on the shortwave bands listed below, will enlighten you."

KARL-HEINZ. And catch this one: "Where is Rudolph Hess? Where is Hitler's deputy Minister, who was last seen in public in May of this year? It can now be revealed! Despairing over the course of his Fuehrer's foreign policy, Hitler's chief counselor flew by private plane to Great Britain, hoping to plead for England's capitulation and a halt to the Allied offensive, but to no avail. He is now a prisoner of war and will shortly address us on the British overseas network, recanting Nazi heresy and apologizing to the deluded German nation and the innocent victims of the war both here and abroad. If you don't believe this, then ask the Fuehrer to produce his Minister. But he won't be able to!" I didn't know that. Is that true, Helmuth?

HELMUTH. It's true. But we'd better organize and move out. Let's each take a different section of the city. For tonight just drop these into random mailboxes or paste them on billboards. *(He produces several small bottles from his briefcase.)* Here's a bottle of paste for each of you. *(Handing out the leaflets.)* Later we'll get these in the hands of the Hitler Youth and even mail them to the front. Jonni—will you take Hammerbrook?

JONNI. Of course.

HELMUTH. Karl-Heinz, you take yours to Hammer Deich, beginning at Louisenweg and Suederstrasse. And, Rudi, you go to Rothenburgsort, and later to Harburg and Wilhemsburg—you'll find a lot of sympathy there among the laborers; some of them are Communists—and I'll cover the center of town and Eppendorf. Are we ready?

JONNI. Ready!

RUDI. At your service!

KARL-HEINZ. *(Saluting.)* Jawohl, mein Fuehrer!

HELMUTH. All right, we're off. But be careful. Remember, don't distribute anything if anyone is in sight. Take your time. One well-placed flyer is worth a whole night's work. Success and . . . and God go with you.

KARL-HEINZ. You too, Helmuth.

RUDI. Good night, Helmuth.

JONNI. Night, Helmuth.

HELMUTH. Till tomorrow.

> *The others leave.* HELMUTH *stares after him, then, turning out the light, moves slowly to the center of the room, where he kneels in an attitude of prayer, then slowly raises his head upward. The lights dim.*

SCENE 6

> *In the following, one brief tableau rapidly follows the next. The stage itself is dark, except for a spotlight which falls on each successive vignette.*

WIFE. *(Holding a flyer.)* Heinrich! Heinrich! What's this?

HUSBAND. *(In laboring garb.)* How do I know? I'm late for work. I'll look at it later.

WIFE. But you haven't eaten.

HUSBAND. It doesn't matter. There's nothing to eat.

WIFE. I think you'd better look at this right now.

> *She hands him the flyer.*

HUSBAND. Why? Where did it come from?

WIFE. It was in the mailbox when I went out to see if they'd had a delivery of potatoes at the store.

HUSBAND. Well, had they?

WIFE. No. They haven't had potatoes or any other vegetables for almost three months.

HUSBAND. *(Reading:)* "Exploited German workers! Awake and protest! In order to finance their unholy war, the Nazis are forcing you to 'save' from thirteen to twenty-six Reich Marks out of every paycheck. You can be sure that you will never see that money again. Meanwhile, when you think of what your money could buy if there was no war, remember to blame not the Allies, but those who started it, those who stroll along *Unter den Linden* in beautiful gray uniforms and glossy patent leather boots and have strudel every afternoon with plenty of whipped cream."

WIFE. What should we do with it?

HUSBAND. Better burn it! No, on second thought, I'll take it to work. This might interest Otto and some of the boys.

WIFE. But hurry!

HUSBAND. Who cares? There's no whipped cream in it for you or me, is there?

~

GENERAL. *(Assisted by an* AIDE *as he dons a heavy trench coat with epaulettes)* That was an important staff meeting. Highly confidential. There must be no more security leaks. Understand?

AIDE. Jawohl, Herr General!

GENERAL. Were the guards posted?

AIDE. Jawohl, Herr General!

GENERAL. All unauthorized persons kept away?

AIDE. Jawohl, Herr General!

GENERAL. Good . . . *(Feeling in his pocket)* What? *(Removing a flier)* What's this? *(Reading)* "Comrade soldiers! The Goebbels propaganda which promises you victory in North Africa and against the Soviet Union has been exposed. No one knows this better than you yourselves." . . . How did this get here? I thought you said no unauthorized person had been admitted.

AIDE. None, Herr General!

GENERAL. Then how did they reach this cloak room?

AIDE. They couldn't have, Herr General. But may I suggest. . . .

GENERAL. Out with it—suggest!

AIDE. Maybe last night—while you were at the Opera. . . .

GENERAL. What? How dare they? In the future, double my bodyguard, and especially when I'm at the opera, do you hear?

AIDE. Jawohl, Herr General.

~

FIRST CLERK. *(Displaying a flier)* Fritz, look at this, will you? "Where is Rudolf Hess?" What can that mean?

SECOND CLERK. I don't know. It can't be an official publication. It looks suspicious to me.

FIRST CLERK. I'd better throw it away.

SECOND CLERK. We'd better show it to the boss.

FIRST CLERK. That's right. . . . But maybe he'll think that we . . .

SECOND CLERK. Yes, it might implicate us. Better throw it away. . . . *(The FIRST CLERK crumples the flier, then throws it in the wastebasket)* Not in *my* waste basket!

FIRST CLERK. *(Retrieving the flier)* Where then?

SECOND CLERK. Take it home and burn it.

FIRST CLERK. You won't tell?

SECOND CLERK. Why should I tell? . . . I won't tell, if you won't.

FIRST CLERK. *(Extending his hand)* Let's shake. *(They do so)* In the name of the Fuerher.

SECOND CLERK. *(Saluting)* Heil Hitler!

FIRST CLERK. *(Returning the salute)* Heil Hitler! *(The SECOND CLERK leaves. The FIRST CLERK looks about him, then cautiously unfolds the flier.)* "Where is Rudolph Hess?" Where is Rudolph Hess?

> He crumples the flier again, considers, then throws it in the SECOND CLERK's wastebasket.

~

FIRST SOLDIER. *(In a soiled, disheveled uniform)* Ernst, look what I just found, stamped with a swastika!

SECOND SOLDIER. *(Reading)* "Comrade soldiers! The Fuehrer has promised you that 1942 will be the decisive year and that this time he will spare no means to keep his promise. He will send you into the fire by the thousands in order to try to end the terrible blood-letting which he himself instigated." Strange! How long has this been here?

FIRST SOLDIER. Who knows? Here's another one I just found in the latrine: *(Reading)* "There is snow and ice everywhere, and the final German assault has still not taken place. Meanwhile the Russians have mounted a counteroffensive and retaken strategic terrain. The German army is defeated!"

SECOND SOLDIER. When are you pulling out?

FIRST SOLDIER. Tonight around midnight. When I have watch.

SECOND SOLDIER. Misery loves company. I'll join you.

~

FIRST HAUSFRAU. *(Brandishing a flier)* Hilde, what is this? "German people, you are deceived. Do not support your perfidious leaders!" Where did this come from?

SECOND HAUSFRAU. I don't know, but I find it disgusting, don't you?

FIRST HAUSFRAU. Certainly, disgusting! I will show it to Ulrich as soon as he flies back from Berlin.

SECOND HAUSFRAU. Praise the Fuhrer, it seems he's in Berlin every other week.

FIRST HAUSFRAU. He's signing another contract with the War Ministry.

SECOND HAUSFRAU. How lucky for you that your Ulrich directs a munitions firm.

FIRST HAUSFRAU. And you, that your Ernst makes tanks. By the way, Hilde, I'm going shopping the afternoon—to replenish my spring wardrobe. I think the new contract will allow for that. Lots of nice Belgian "imports" have just come in, I understand. Expensive, but nice. Can you come with me?

SECOND HAUSFRAU. *Mit* pleasure, darling. *Mit* pleasure.

~

FIRST YOUNG MAN. *(In a Hitler Youth uniform and wielding a shovel, with another flier)* Hey, Dieter, what do you make of this? *(Reading)* "This is a chain letter. Please pass it on. German Youth! For the slightest infraction of regulations you are now liable to a weekend's solitary confinement. You are told that the Fuehrer's program of iron discipline will turn you all into Supermen. But the truth is that it is meant to break your will and turn you into sheep and robots. Recognize your native land for what it is—land without freedom, a land of tyranny and terror. This is Deutschland indeed—Hitlerdeutschland!"

SECOND YOUNG MAN. Hey, let me have that. It will make a good bookmark when I read *Mein Kampf*.

THIRD YOUNG MAN. You'd better keep digging this trench.

SECOND YOUNG MAN. Not so fast. There will be another when we're through with this one. *(Spitting)* Some iron discipline!

FIRST YOUNG MAN. To the glory of the *Vaterland*!

THIRD YOUNG MAN. Heil, Hitler!

THIRD YOUNG MAN *spits.*

~

Over the loudspeaker or from a wide variety of points on the stage:

"Where is Rudolf Hess?"

"Hitler the Murderer: About the mysterious deaths of General von Schroeder, Generalfeldmarschall von Reichenau, Generaloberst Udat and Von Oberst Moelders!"

"Who is the Real Aggressor? Our Japanese friends have launched a cowardly surprise attack upon the U. S. Fleet at Pearl Harbor!"

"Where is Rudolph Hess?"

"Who is lying? The Incredible Reports of the Nationalist Socialist Propaganda Ministry!"

"One and a Half Million: You still haven't been told the true number of casualties the Fuehrer sustained during the invasion of the Soviet Union!"

"Perfidious Rome: The struggle in North Africa and the Italian policy of colonial exploitation!"

"The Riddle about Rudolf Hess!"

"Germany's Scarcity of Petroleum!"

"Fuehrer Talk: Hitler's implausible pronouncements about the progress of the War!"

"An Appeal to End the War by Liquidating Adolf Hitler!"

"Arrogant Aggression, Prelude to Total Destruction and Defeat: On the Japanese military leadership and the War in the Pacific!"

"1942—Year of Decision: A demand for the overthrow of the National Socialist Regime!"

"Where is Rudolf Hess?"

SCENE 7

February, 1942. The State Welfare Office in Hamburg's Beberhaus. It is after working hours. HELMUTH *and* JONNI *sit together on a desk, conversing in confidential tones.*

HELMUTH. How did it go last night, Jonni?

JONNI. Just great. I planted one in every menu in two of the biggest downtown restaurants.

HELMUTH. That must have gagged their Nazi guests.

JONNI. A waiter almost caught me.

HELMUTH. Be careful. I've got another batch for tonight. And there's one group we have completely overlooked. The French.

JONNI. The French?

HELMUTH. The prisoners-of-war. In the munitions factories and war industries. They'd be perfect saboteurs. If we could just plant the idea and help them organize.

JONNI. That's true. The French are notoriously bad organizers. If only some Germans were, too.

HELMUTH. Trouble is, we can't influence them with our propaganda—not without a translator. None of us knows French that well. So I've been wondering—is there someone who's studied French that could join us?

JONNI. Well . . . There's Kranz.

HELMUTH. Werner? That's a coincidence. I've thought of him, too. He's also working late tonight, did you know?

JONNI. Yes, I think he's still here.

HELMUTH. Well, what do you think?

JONNI. I feel right about him. We're on good terms. He jokes a lot about the Nazis and has a lot of complaints.

HELMUTH. All right. Call him over. I've got extra copies of the last several batches. He could start on them tonight.

JONNI. *(Calling into a back office.)* Werner!

VOICE. Who is it?

JONNI. Come here, will you?

VOICE. Coming.

WERNER *Kranz, a pleasant young man of approximately their age, approaches them.*

JONNI. Werner, Helmuth and I have a favor to ask.

WERNER. Sure thing. What can I do for you?

HELMUTH. First tell us, Werner, how you really feel about the Fuehrer.

WERNER. The Fuehrer? That jackass? He belongs in an institution—the crackpot!

HELMUTH. You mean it?

WERNER. Sure, I mean it.

HELMUTH. In that case *(reaching into his briefcase and producing several fliers)*, we'd like you to assist us in a little project—just help us with some translations, into French.

WERNER. *(Taking the fliers, but giving them scant notice.)* Sure. Why not?

HELMUTH. But you've got to be careful.

WERNER gives HELMUTH a slightly quizzical look, then shrugs his shoulders, signaling his halfhearted consent.

SCENE 8

The offices of the Hamburg branch house. President ZOELLNER sits at a desk, staring pensively into space. After several seconds, HELMUTH enters.

HELMUTH. Why, Bruder Zoellner, shouldn't you be at work?

ZOELLNER. Yes, but I wanted to talk to you. Sit down, Helmuth. . . . Tell me, Helmuth, what the Church really means to you.

HELMUTH. A great deal, Bruder Zoellner.

ZOELLNER. But does it mean everything, Helmuth? Are you totally dedicated?

HELMUTH. Everything? Why, ja, almost everything.

ZOELLNER. Almost? But not entirely?

HELMUTH. I suppose I have one reservation.

ZOELLNER. And what is that?

HELMUTH. As I see it, Bruder Zoellner, the important thing in life, well, is life itself. Didn't the Savior himself say that His purpose was to help us achieve "immortality and eternal life"? And that "the Sabbath was made for man and not man for the Sabbath"?

ZOELLNER. Ja, that is true.

HELMUTH. I have to put that, I'm afraid, before the Church, although I am confident that we cannot attain exaltation without the Church either.

ZOELLNER. Good. Then you agree that we must not contend against the Church and its leaders and that to be disloyal to those in authority is a very serious matter?

HELMUTH. Ja. Normally that is so.

ZOELLNER. "Normally"? . . . but who is to decide what is "normal"—you or your leaders?

HELMUTH. Well, the leaders, at least at first—

ZOELLNER. What do you mean, at first?

HELMUTH. I reserve the right to receive a personal witness about what they tell me.

ZOELLNER. I see. But how can you be sure that your so-called "personal witness" isn't just a rationalization—your wanting something you shouldn't have?

HELMUTH. If I can't be sure of that, then I can't be sure of anything—not even my testimony. I guess . . . I guess it depends upon my own personal righteousness.

ZOELLNER. Exactly. And how righteous are you, Bruder Huebener?

HELMUTH. I . . . I don't know. I'm sure I'm not perfect.

ZOELLNER. Indeed you are not. You have been deliberately dishonest.

HELMUTH. Dishonest?

ZOELLNER. You have deceived me.

HELMUTH. What do you mean?

ZOELLNER. *(Taking one of* HELMUTH's *pamphlets from his vest pocket.)* Here . . . what about this? Someone carelessly left it last night in this duplicator—the last I imagine of many copies. . . . Do you deny that you are that someone?

HELMUTH. First may I ask you a question?

ZOELLNER. You may.

HELMUTH. Will you, as my priesthood leader, respect the confidentiality of what I tell you? Will you guarantee me that you that you will not tell another person?

ZOELLNER. I will. The Lord requires it.

HELMUTH. Then I will not deny that I am that someone.

ZOELLNER. You have used Church equipment to run off these inciting statements—I have seen others, they're all around town, and I recognize the type font; they were typed on this very machine. Do you deny it?

HELMUTH. No, Bruder Zoellner.

ZOELLNER. You have done all of this and kept it from me. Why?

HELMUTH. Because . . . in conscience . . . in conscience I have to declare what I know to be the truth—to tell others.

ZOELLNER. Helmuth . . . Helmuth, I don't deny that, politically, our nation, some of our leaders may be going too far. But it isn't for us to judge what is ultimately right or wrong in the affairs of men. There is no complete justice on either side. There never was. That is why the prophet Joseph told us that we must "believe in being subject to kings, presidents, rulers, and magistrates, in obeying, honoring, and sustaining the law." We must keep them and our religion apart. That is also why, as your branch president, I can keep your confession to myself, where, as a loyal German citizen, I would otherwise be obligated to denounce you.

HELMUTH. But aren't we also obligated to uphold the Ten Commandments?

ZOELLNER. Why, of course.

HELMUTH. Without compromising, without qualification?

ZOELLNER. I think so.

HELMUTH. And didn't Moses—didn't the Lord himself—tell us in His fifth commandment: "Honor thy Father and mother"?

ZOELLNER. Ja.

HELMUTH. Do we honor our parents by submitting to a system that encourages young children to spy on and denounce their parents? Well?

ZOELLNER. You don't have to be a spy, yourself. You can still respect your own parents.

HELMUTH. But if I don't speak out against such practices, who else will? Will you? Will the Church?

ZOELLNER. Ja. Normally.

HELMUTH. But right now things aren't so "normal," is that it?

ZOELLNER. Ja, that is so. But there is something else. Where the Church is concerned, I am in authority here—not you, Helmuth. And so I tell you this: if you persist in this most unwise and totally fruitless course of action—one or even a half dozen of you can make no difference—you will place the Church itself in great jeopardy. . . .

HELMUTH. Even if I go elsewhere to print them?

ZOELLNER. Even then. You yourself are an officer of the Church. They will identify the Church with you and apprehend you and they will eventually trace this sort of thing *(gesturing with the pamphlet)* back to us. Helmuth, you may be responsible for destroying the Church—and its members—in all of Germany, in all of occupied Europe and—if the Fuehrer emerges victorious and the Third Reich truly lasts a thousand years—perhaps in the entire world. Think about it.

HELMUTH. Bruder Zoellner, what will the Church be worth, if everywhere we have to sacrifice our Solomon Schwartzes, if we can only hold meetings and say things the Fuehrer approves of? . . . I oppose violent overthrow; I oppose all forms of violence, including assassination—with perhaps one exception. But to educate, to warn people as best I can about the facts as I see them—I must do this. . . .

ZOELLNER. Don't you realize how dangerous this is—for you alone?

HELMUTH. I do. And I'm very frightened.

ZOELLNER. And are you sure you are justified in opposing the Church in this way? Because that is what you are doing!

HELMUTH. Bruder Zoellner, it is the gospel itself that impels me to do these things.

ZOELLNER. Are you sure?

HELMUTH. Quite sure.

ZOELLNER. Even when I warn you that, should you persist and should you be apprehended, I will have no choice but to take action that will completely disassociate you from us?

HELMUTH. Even then, Bruder Zoellner.

ZOELLNER. So be it.

HELMUTH. So be it.

The lights dim.

SCENE 9

The lights rise on WERNER *Kranz, who sits alone at a desk in the State Welfare Office, pondering a sheaf of* HELMUTH's *fliers. Finally, he lays them down and stares with a set expression, at the space in front of him. After a long pause, his hand resolutely reaches for a telephone.*

WERNER. *Zentral! Zentral! . . . Please give me the Secret State Police. . . .* That's right: The Gestapo. Investigative Division.

END ACT ONE

Act Two

SCENE 1

The following Sunday morning. Chapel of the Hamburg-St. Georg branch house. An organ prelude is heard. ZOELLNER *and two counselors sit on the stand. Elsewhere, lights delineate a section of the congregation where* JO-HANNES *and* KARL-HEINZ *are seated together. Suddenly* RUDI *rushes in and joins them.*

ZOELLNER. Dear brethren! We are grateful for your presence this morning—particularly in view of the urgent appeal which came to you last night that as many as possible be here this morning. Brother Sandmann, our first counselor, will first offer a word of prayer. Then we will transact an item of urgent and . . . regrettable business . . .

A murmur in the congregation. The boys do quick double takes at one another.

SANDMANN. Our Father in Heaven! We thy humble servants bow before Thee this morning to acknowledge Thy hand and Thy wisdom in all that transpires in our lives. Help us, we therefore pray, to be reconciled to what comes to us, to be thy submissive and obedient sons. Help us understand with our faith what might otherwise be a stumbling block to our hearts and our reason. And inasmuch as we are subject to political leaders, wherever we may find ourselves, we also pray that Thou wilt guide and inspire those who presently direct this nation.

KARL-HEINZ. What?

RUDI. What's he saying?

JOHANNES. Shh!

SANDMANN. *(Now visibly weeping.)* Direct them, if it be Thy will, to bring this war to a quick end and to usher in the blessings of peace to a weary and sorrowing world. We are grateful that they have permitted us still to worship Thee in Thy prescribed manner. We honor them for that and in turn ask Thee to prompt us all, as true and loyal citizens, to sustain them as our chosen leaders. In the name of Jesus Christ. Amen.

SANDMANN *sits down, and* ZOELLNER *returns to the pulpit.*

ZOELLNER. With great sorrow, we announce that Juergen Knopke, the son of Sister Luise Knopke, is reported fallen on the Eastern Front in defense of the Vaterland. . . . *(Gasps are heard in the congregation.)* Also, a quilting session will be held in the home of Relief Society president, Sister Wagner, this Wednesday evening. Any torn or ragged sheets, clothing, or toweling which can be donated for this purpose will be appreciated. The quilts are being made for our elderly and indigent members. . . . And now, in view of the nature of our next item of business, I must ask all investigators and all members of the Aaronic Priesthood, except for Brothers Schnibbe and Wobbe, to leave this meeting.

A few younger men rise and leave.

ZOELLNER. Now, brethren, it is my sad duty as your branch president to inform you that early this morning, at five o'clock, we, the branch presidency, conducted an elders' court in which one of our members was found in violation of his trust as a German citizen, actively engaged in the overthrow of the Nationalist Socialist regime and in undermining the national defense. We accordingly declare excommunicated from the Church of Jesus Christ of Latter-day Saints the seventeen-year-old Helmuth Guenther Huebener.

Gasp from the congregation.

JOHANNES. *(Abruptly standing and shouting.)* No!

JOHANNES *slowly sinks into his seat, then collapses against the bench in front of him as the other names are read.*

ZOELLNER. As two of Huebener's accomplices are still present, they will now be invited to leave with an escort from the State Police. . . .

Still more gasps. Four uniformed MEN *come forward from the rear of the congregation, laying hold of* KARL-HEINZ *and* RUDI, *lifting them from their seats and leading them out of the chapel.*

ZOELLNER. They will be conveyed to the Gestapo prison at Fulsbuettel, where the former Bruder Huebener is already incarcerated, awaiting interrogation, trial, and the fulfillment of justice.

The congregation, including two counselors, who in turn assist JOHANNES, *file out without a word, leaving only* ZOELLNER *at the pulpit. After the others have gone, a Gestapo* OFFICER *returns and comes to the pulpit.*

OFFICER. I would advise you to take care that there are no further incidents like this among your members, or the American Church, like the Jews and certain other devious minorities, will find itself and its members no longer among the living. . . . Is that understood?

ZOELLNER *nods his assent. The lights dim.*

SCENE 2

Several days later. An interrogation cell in the Gestapo prison at Fulsbuettel. Two Gestapo OFFICERS *sit before* RUDI, *with the beam from a bright lamp focused on his face.*

FIRST OFFICER. So you're even more stubborn than your friend Jonni Duewer. Well, you will talk before we are through with you—and the sooner the better. You still haven't learned what real pain is, but we can teach you. . . . Bring in the next one.

RUDI *is ushered out of the cell. As he disappears he is heard shouting.*

RUDI'S VOICE. I told them nothing, Karl-Heinz! Nothing!

ANOTHER VOICE. Shut up, you!

A slap is heard, then a moan. KARL-HEINZ *is quickly ushered in and seated before the lamp.*

FIRST OFFICER. *(To* KARL-HEINZ's *escort, in a rage.)* I thought you knew enough to wait until the interogee is out of sight. There must be no more communication between them!

SECOND OFFICER. Forgive me.

FIRST OFFICER. That is worth several demerits. And don't think I will forget!

SECOND OFFICER. Forgive me, Captain. It won't happen again.

FIRST OFFICER. And now for the snippy one—the one called Schnibbe. . . . Do you realize, Herr Schnibbe, that just last week you turned eighteen and became a fully accountable adult, that you are no longer a minor?

KARL-HEINZ. I know when I was born.

The FIRST OFFICER *nods to the* SECOND OFFICER, *who slaps* KARL-HEINZ.

FIRST OFFICER. Don't be smart! That's no way to begin a session like this. Besides, now that you are no longer a minor, like the others, you can be dealt with to the full extent of the law. And for a crime like the one you've committed, I suppose you know what the punishment will be?

KARL-HEINZ. What crime?

The FIRST OFFICER *nods, and the* SECOND OFFICER *slaps* KARL-HEINZ.

FIRST OFFICER. I told you not to be smart, punk! Now listen, I will square with you, because you need to cooperate with us, and I'm confident you will. So far Huebener has assumed the whole blame, but Huebener could not possibly have done this by himself. If you do not tell us what we are after, before Huebener or someone else does, your life won't be worth a pfennig—you will already be the late Karl-Heinz

Schnibbe, already in the past tense, poor Karl-Heinz, only eighteen years old, who probably never—tell me, puppy, have you ever known a woman?

KARL-HEINZ. No.

FIRST OFFICER. Or even a girl your own age?

KARL-HEINZ. Never.

FIRST OFFICER. I didn't think so. You see, I know a few things about you Mormons. It's part of my business to study oddities. . . . The late Karl-Heinz Schnibbe, who never really lived, who never even knew a girl. . . . who didn't even care if he lived or died. But surely I'm mistaken. You at least want to stay alive, don't you?

KARL-HEINZ. Of course I want to stay alive!

FIRST OFFICER. Even as a celibate Mormon?

KARL-HEINZ. Especially, as long as I'm unmarried, as a celibate Mormon.

FIRST OFFICER. Well then, speak! What do you say?

KARL-HEINZ. I say . . . I say . . . I'll take my chances with Huebener.

The FIRST OFFICER *slaps* KARL-HEINZ *himself, this time harder than ever.*

FIRST OFFICER. You filthy scum! You American lover!

SCENE 3

Several weeks later. HELMUTH *sits in a private cell in the same prison. He appears fatigued and visibly battered. A* GUARD *approaches, escorting* HELMUTH's *mother.*

GUARD. Suspect Huebener—Frau Emma Huebener. Ten minutes.

The GUARD *admits* EMMA, *then moves outside the cell, but within earshot.* HELMUTH *and* EMMA *embrace and weep.*

EMMA. My boy. My boy. At least you're still alive.

HELMUTH. Mother. How unhappy I've made you.

EMMA. What have they done to you?

HELMUTH. The beatings are over. They know I won't accuse the others.

EMMA. *(Desperately.)* My boy, don't take all the blame! We know that the others have put you up to this. Make them share your punishment.

HELMUTH. No. Only I am responsible. It was my idea. I persuaded the others.

EMMA. Are you sure?

HELMUTH. I'm sure. . . .

EMMA. Then I'll believe you, but Hugo never will. He blames the Church.

HELMUTH. The Church?

EMMA. Bruder Zoellner, our leaders.

HELMUTH. But how? They disapprove. They've opposed me all the way!

EMMA. He says it's because of what they taught you—they and the Church.

HELMUTH. Well, that's true, I suppose. At least I'd like to think so.

EMMA. And what about the other boys? They joined in too. Helmuth, don't be foolish. Let them share the responsibility. That way your punishment will at least be a little lighter. Remember, you're charged with—

HELMUTH. High treason. But, Mother, I'm still a minor. They can't execute me.

EMMA. Oh, Helmuth. Don't be so sure.

HELMUTH. According to the law we will only receive a reprimand and a very light sentence—all but Karl-Heinz. That's why it's important that . . . that *I* be fully responsible.

EMMA. But the law can be twisted, Helmuth.

HELMUTH. I know. But it's still better this way.

EMMA. Even if they only imprison you—it will be for many years . . . maybe for a lifetime.

HELMUTH. That wouldn't surprise me either. But you don't really think the war will last much longer, do you?

EMMA. No.

HELMUTH. Or that we will win?

EMMA. Shh! *(Looking around, then in a whisper.)* That's my one hope now, thanks especially to you and others like you. My son, you have made some difference.

HELMUTH. Well, we'd better not say any more about that. . . . How is Father? How are Grandmother and Grandfather? Why didn't they come, too?

EMMA. They would allow only one of us to see you. Your grandparents are still recovering—from the shock. It set them both back. And your father's even more confused about the Church than before. They love you so—each in their own way.

HELMUTH. Oh, Mutti, I'm sorry . . . so sorry, Mutti. . . . Do be patient with him. And Gerhard, what about Gerhard?

EMMA. He's well . . . and safe. . . .

HELMUTH. "Well?" "Safe?" What have they done to him?

EMMA. Oh, Helmuth, they traced your radio set to him.

HELMUTH. But he had nothing to do with—

EMMA. It didn't matter.

HELMUTH. What have they done to him?

EMMA. Expelled him from Officers' School. Reduced him to the lowest rank. . . .

HELMUTH. And sent him to the front lines. Where? To the east?

EMMA. Yes.

HELMUTH. I thought so. To fight the Russians.

EMMA. *(Wiping her eyes.)* I think he's relieved that he won't be an officer. . . .

HELMUTH. Any other "happy" news?

EMMA. Everything is about the same. . . . Oh, yes, Bruder Schwartz was sent to the concentration camp at Theresiendstadt.

HELMUTH. Old Solomon? Yes, it follows.

EMMA. And word has it he died there in the first week—from exposure. . . . But tell me—I may not be allowed another visit—when is your trial?

HELMUTH. Not before August. It's still months away. They'll try us, I've heard, in Berlin.

EMMA. So you're important to them. They want to make an example of you. Don't you understand that's why I'm so afraid for you?

HELMUTH. If they do, I'm ready. It can't help their cause.

EMMA. *(Breaking down.)* Oh, Helmuth, Helmuth!

HELMUTH. Please, Mutti. . . . Please. What's most important, I still feel good about myself, my . . . my eternal self.

EMMA. That's good . . . and you hold no grudge against Bruder Zoellner? (HELMUTH *does not answer.*) He had to do it, Helmuth. He had to hold that court and pronounce your excommunication.

HELMUTH. I guess he did.

EMMA. You can't believe that he wanted to.

HELMUTH. Why can't I?

EMMA. It was the one way he could protect us all. And the Church. After all, you'd used the branch house and its equipment. This way the Church wouldn't be implicated and could continue to function. He came to the house that same day. He could hardly talk, he wept so. . . . Oh, he still wishes you hadn't been so headstrong, that you had respected his authority and taken his advice. But he begged your forgiveness. I believe him, and for your sake, you must, too, Helmuth, although . . . although it's a lot to ask, I know. . . .

HELMUTH. The elders' court—I can forgive him that. But why did he have to denounce me? That was a breach of sacred trust. You see, I told him what we were doing, I admitted it to him, as a confession, on the condition that he wouldn't divulge it. And he agreed . . . he agreed to that.

EMMA. Oh, no!

HELMUTH. He is my priesthood leader. I thought I could trust him . . .

EMMA. Helmuth, are you sure *he* denounced you?

HELMUTH. They told me so.

EMMA. But can you believe *them*?

HELMUTH. No. Of course not. But who else could it have been? Bruder Zoellner is the only one who could have known. We were all arrested, including Jonni and Werner.

EMMA. I see. . . . Then how does that make you feel toward him—toward Bruder Zoellner and the others?

HELMUTH. Feel? A little confused, I have to admit.

EMMA. He is still your priesthood leader—

HELMUTH. Even if I no longer hold the priesthood?

EMMA. Still your branch president—

HELMUTH. *(Breaking into sobs)* Even if I am no longer a Latter-day Saint?

GUARD. Time is up!

EMMA. Oh, Helmuth! Don't forsake the Church!

HELMUTH. The Church has already forsaken me, Mother!

EMMA. Even then—even then . . . One thing will help bring me peace . . . to know your faith remained constant.

As the GUARD *opens the cell door,* EMMA *and* HELMUTH *embrace and kiss, then separate.*

EMMA. Goodbye, my son.

HELMUTH. Goodbye . . . Mutti.

The GUARD *leads* EMMA *off.* HELMUTH *stares after her, then sits on his cot. He picks up a well-thumbed triple combination as if to curse and fling it from him, then stops, opens it and begins to read aloud.*

HELMUTH. "If thou art called to pass through tribulation; if thou art in perils among false brethren . . . (*HELMUTH's pre-recorded voice takes over. Although we still hear his words, he appears to be reading silently.*) . . . if thou art accused with all manner of false accusations; if thine enemies fall upon thee; if they tear thee from the society of thy father and mother and brethren and sisters . . . and thou be dragged to prison, and thine enemies prowl around thee like wolves for the blood of the lamb; and if thou shouldst be cast into the pit, or into the hands of murderers, and the sentence of death passed upon thee; . . . if the very jaws of hell shall gape open the mouth wide after thee, know thou, my son, that all these things shall give thee experience, and shall be for thy good. The Son of Man hath descended below them all. Art thou greater than he?"

The GUARD *returns, admitting the interrogating* OFFICER *of Act Two, Scene 2.*

OFFICER. Well, Huebener, have you reconsidered? We are still willing to lighten your prosecution if you will attest that the others helped and encouraged you.

HELMUTH. *Encouraged?*

OFFICER. Ja, your leaders.

HELMUTH. Bruder Zoellner?

OFFICER. *(Laughing cynically.)* Ja, your "bruder," who denounced you. . . . Blame the Mormons for your traitorous ideas. Help us prove that they are an American front. Do that, and you won't suffer. You will become our star witness.

HELMUTH. Why do you want such a witness? So that you can deal with the Mormons as you have with the Jews?

OFFICER. *(Flaring up.)* You know nothing about that! . . . *(Regaining his composure.)* Just remember that you've been betrayed and who has betrayed you. Why do you still try to shield them, to sacrifice yourself so that they can continue to deceive others?

HELMUTH. If Bruder Zoellner really did betray me—

OFFICER. *(Hopefully.)* Ja?

HELMUTH. I still cannot.

OFFICER. *(Enraged.)* Denounce them! Denounce the Mormons! *(Slapping* HELMUTH *and screaming.)* How long do you think I can wait?

HELMUTH. No. No. No. I cannot. I'm still obliged to God.

OFFICER. *(Banging his fist.)* Do you know what this means?

HELMUTH. I understand . . .

OFFICER. *(Leaving the cell, then turning back.)* You stupid, stupid fool!

SCENE 4

August 11, 1942. Berlin. Courtroom of the Volksgericht, Germany's highest court. Three JUSTICES, *dressed in blood-red robes embroidered with symbols of the Third Reich, sit in closed session on the same stand which served earlier for the priesthood meetings. A* PROSECUTOR *and* DEFENSE COUNSELOR *stand beneath the justices, while* HELMUTH, *his hands and feet in chains,* KARL-HEINZ, RUDI, *and* JONNI *sit on a bench facing them, flanked by an armed guard.*

DEFENSE COUNSELOR. . . . In summation, therefore, I plead that the court make allowance for the defendants' youth and take account of the religious fanaticism which interfered with an otherwise normal inclination on the part of the three of them to be loyal, law-abiding sons of the Vaterland. The fourth is obviously unusually weak willed, highly impressionable, and to some extent the victim of the others' perverse influence. The defense rests.

CHIEF JUSTICE. Has the prosecution a final statement?

PROSECUTOR. Honorable judges. In the case here argued, we have taken great pains to stress the defendants' traitorous activity—their deliberately defiant monitoring of shortwave transmissions from the enemy and their reprehensible exploitation of said transmissions in an attempt to demoralize and incite doubt, disloyalty, and acts of rebellion among the populace—in fact, to agitate in the most treasonable manner for the overthrow both of the Fuehrer and the government, not to mention the deeply demoralizing effect of the defendants' propaganda as it sporadically reached the hands of discouraged soldiers at the front. This, too, has been established. . . . In other words, the defendants were not just playing innocent childlike games. The duplicating machine which served as their weapon was far more deadly in its effect than the most sophisticated machine gun trained directly and at pointblank range upon its victims. There is no difference—none whatsoever—between the actions of these defendants and those of the enemy. It is exactly as if they had worn the uniform of enemy soldiers and mercilessly assaulted us, therewith taking the lives of defenseless German citizens. They were quite literally in the employ of the Allies. Their subversive deeds have substantially disunited our people and consequently impeded the war effort, as such. . . . Now, as to the instigator of these crimes, who, by his own consistent admission, is chiefly responsible for the group's activity, the defendant Helmuth Huebener: We will no longer dispute contention. He has in fact proved it to our satisfaction, although he appears to have argued it so forcefully in an effort to spare one of his accomplices the full punishment that the law would have accorded to him as an adult—a dubious magnanimity for which Huebener himself must, I urge, be required to pay far more than he could have ever expected. . . . It is true that Huebener is technically a minor, but the court will recall that, as a part of the prosecution's case against him, intelligence tests were administered to the defendant Huebener, conclusively establishing that within this far-from-normal personality are monstrously combined a serious moral aberration, a totally deficient sense of social responsibility, together with the astounding intelligence, honored judges, of a thirty-year-old professor; for that is exactly what was required to author, so skillfully, yet so insidiously and heinously, the various tracts for whose existence he is solely responsible. The knowledge they imply of political history is deep, of human psychology—extremely subtle. May I be so bold to say that, had this Huebener seen fit instead to serve with these gifts on the side that throughout his life nurtured and befriended him and called him one of her sons, he would have found employment and recognition in the company and at the side of no less a patriot than Doktor Goebbels himself. . . . But my point is this, most honorable judges—that, because his talents and their employment have been so formidable, the defendant Huebener ought in all justice to be regarded as a man of those years which most approximate his actual mental age, for we are not to condemn the body but the mind of this despicable traitor. That, worthy judges, is why Huebener, not Schnibbe after all, but Huebener must be required to pay for his act of high treason as would any adult citizen in time of war. . . . The prosecution demands for the accomplices long and severe terms of prison at hard labor, but for Huebener . . . the full and ultimate punishment prescribed by the law itself—the death penalty! The prosecution rests.

CHIEF JUSTICE. Has the defense any final refutation?

DEFENSE COUNSELOR. The defense rests, your Honor.

CHIEF JUSTICE. The justices will now deliberate.

As if pre-rehearsed, the three JUSTICES *briefly whisper, then readily nod to one another in agreement.*

CHIEF JUSTICE. The defendants will now stand. *(They do so.)* The court is prepared to pronounce its decision and also, in view of its pressing schedule, the appropriate sentences. . . . There can be no doubt that, for reasons brought forth during this trial and subsequently proved to the court's unanimous satisfaction, the defendants are in varying degrees all guilty of high treason against the German nation. This court consequently finds said defendants guilty of the same and pronounces upon them the following penalties:

SECOND JUSTICE. According to Article 9 of the Law Code Governing Youthful Offenders Guilty of Crimes against the State—the defendants Wobbe, whose dissemination of subversive materials was especially extensive and the consequences of which were noticeably inflammatory: ten years' imprisonment; defendants Schnibbe and Duewer, for similar activity, the consequences of which proved adverse to a considerably lesser degree: five- and four-year imprisonments, respectively. We might add that defendant Duewer's desperate plea that his participation in this conspiracy was a ruse whose intent was to gather information with which to denounce fellow conspirators—that said plea has proved to be unsubstantiated and quite groundless. . . .

THIRD JUSTICE. In line with the persuasive reasoning of the prosecution and hence according to Article 73 of the Reich's Law Code Governing Adult Offenders Guilty of Crimes against the State—to the defendant Huebener, to one who, by virtue of his precocious and doubly dangerous masterminding of the whole affair, as the more severe punishment, a punishment befitting his criminality: the forfeiture of his life and the rights of citizenship during the remainder of his days. The defendant Huebener will therefore be deprived of his existence on October 27 of this year by agents of the State Execution Service at Berlin-Ploetzensee. Furthermore, as an example and a deterrent to others of a similar inclination, the aforesaid penalty shall be enacted by means of beheading with an axe. . . .

CHIEF JUSTICE. According to Article 60 of the Criminal Code, the five months' imprisonment served in advance of this trial and since the defendants' arraignment, will be reckoned against the sentences to which it is applicable. According to Article 465, the condemned or their kin will withstand all expenses pertaining to the case in question. . . . Have any of the condemned a final statement before they are returned to detention, there to fulfill the sentences which have been pronounced upon them? Wobbe?

RUDI. No.

CHIEF JUSTICE. Schnibbe?

KARL-HEINZ. Just wait, you butchers! Your turn will come!

CHIEF JUSTICE. *(As* GUARD *slaps* KARL-HEINZ.*)* Silence! You will still address the court with respect—if, that is, you do not wish to incur still more serious penalties. . . . Duewer?

JONNI. No, Your Honor.

CHIEF JUSTICE. That is better. . . . And, finally, the condemned Helmuth Huebener.

HELMUTH. . . . Thank you—

THIRD JUSTICE. Use the correct term of address!

HELMUTH. Thank you, Your Honors, for this privilege. May I raise just one matter which has received not the slightest consideration during this entire trial?

CHIEF JUSTICE. This trial has been most thoroughgoing. All relevant considerations have been deliberated. . . . But as you wish. . . .

HELMUTH. The most unjustly accused and condemned, the principal defendant, was never brought before this court. . . .

SECOND JUSTICE. And who is that? Is the defendant at last prepared to admit that there were other conspirators? Is the defendant finally admitting to his panic, his desperation, and ready to be sensible? Will he at last reveal who actually masterminded the whole affair? Who, besides yourself, is the "principal defendant," Herr Huebener?

HELMUTH. The truth.

THIRD JUSTICE. Please repeat yourself. The court must have misheard you.

HELMUTH. I said: "The truth." . . . The truth. . . . The simple truth. . . . Isn't it just a little paradoxical, Your Honors, that throughout the trial the possibility was never once even entertained—the possibility that our statements to the German people might in fact, despite their disfavor with the regime, represent the truth?

THIRD JUSTICE. What?

HELMUTH. And for that very reason be their own justification? I frequently asked the Defense Counsel for the opportunity I was never permitted: to argue, to demonstrate, or to present evidence that our statements about the present state of affairs, both here and abroad, are indeed truthful, absolutely truthful, and, as such, deserve vindication. . . .

The JUSTICES *briefly consult with one another in anxious whispers.*

CHIEF JUSTICE. In view of your demonstrated intelligence, Huebener, the court finds you incredibly naïve. In fact, I, for one, am curious to know what it is exactly that "makes you tick," as the saying goes. Can you instruct us?

HELMUTH. "How very strange that an obscure boy, of a little over fourteen years of age . . . should be thought a character of sufficient importance to attract the attention of great ones. . . . I was led to say in my heart: Why persecute me for telling the truth?. . . . I could not deny it, neither dared I do it; at least I knew that by so doing I would offend God and come under condemnation. . . . "

THIRD JUSTICE. What are you muttering?

HELMUTH. The words of a prophet, Your Honor.

THIRD JUSTICE. A prophet?

HELMUTH. Though you might not recognize him as such.

THIRD JUSTICE. Probably not. Prophets are not especially useful to the Third Reich. Besides, the court has no time to discuss prophets just now. There are too many others to condemn. *(*HELMUTH *smiles.)* To *try,* I mean. . . .

SECOND JUSTICE. Is that all then?

HELMUTH. I believe so, Your Honor.

SECOND JUSTICE. In that case, I have one more question before you leave our presence—again of a personal nature. Will you answer me? Honestly?

HELMUTH. I will try, Your Honor.

SECOND JUSTICE. It would be useful to the court to understand if you did what you did out of innermost conviction, or if in fact there wasn't just a touch of bravado, even exhibitionism to it as well. Did you not, perhaps, resort to this religious impulse after the fact, let us say, to make yourself look all the more noble?

HELMUTH. An honest question deserves an honest answer, Your Honor, and I must tell you that your question reflects the uncertainties in my own mind as I have sat in my cell and, with little else to do, pondered my motives. I cannot tell you how pure my motives have been. I only know that I could not do otherwise.

SECOND JUSTICE. If you are really that confused, why don't you recant your deeds?

CHIEF JUSTICE. It is still possible to lighten your sentence. And I personally assure you . . . *(eyeing the other* JUSTICES, *who nod back in agreement)* in fact, my colleagues and I guarantee that if you will at last cooperate, late as it is, it will make some difference—enough at least to spare your life. Think, therefore, think carefully before you answer me, Huebener. This is your last chance. We don't ask you to implicate anyone. If you only strike us as sufficiently contrite, as sufficiently convincing, I think I can assure you that—

HELMUTH. Spare yourself the words, your Honor. They can't change my convictions. . . . Of course I want to live. Of course I am tempted. But I cannot recant. I cannot recant what I have done.

THIRD JUSTICE. Are you sure?

HELMUTH. I am quite sure.

THIRD JUSTICE. Then we have nothing further to say either . . . except that you are a poor fool.

RUDI. Your Honor.

SECOND JUSTICE. You've had your turn.

RUDI. Please, Your Honors. It's not for me—it's for Helmuth.

SECOND JUSTICE. Well, what?

RUDI. Is an appeal possible?

CHIEF JUSTICE. This is a civilized court. An appeal is possible.

RUDI. Then we shall appeal!

CHIEF JUSTICE. As you wish.

KARL-HEINZ. Your Honors!

SECOND JUSTICE. Now what?

KARL-HEINZ. I have a question—just one question.

CHIEF JUSTICE. Well?

KARL-HEINZ. Your Honors . . . where is Rudolf Hess?

The CHIEF JUSTICE *signals to the* GUARD, *who again slaps* KARL-HEINZ, *this time more viciously.*

HELMUTH. *(Incensed.)* Your Honors!

CHIEF JUSTICE. Ja?

HELMUTH. I do have one last statement for the court.

SECOND JUSTICE. *(Hopefully.)* Ah, at last. And what is your statement?

HELMUTH. Just wait! Your turn will come!

The GUARD *offers to strike* HELMUTH, *but the* CHIEF JUSTICE *makes a restraining gesture. He stares at* HELMUTH, *and* HELMUTH *stares back as the lights slowly dim.*

SCENE 5

October 27, 1942. A cell at the Gestapo prison and execution site in Ploetzensee, Berlin. HELMUTH *sits on a bunk, writing on a note pad. As he does so, his voice is heard, representing his thoughts.*

HELMUTH'S VOICE. *(Pre-recorded.)* My dearest family, when you receive this letter I will be dead. But before my execution I have been granted one wish: to write to my loved ones. . . . I am very thankful to my Heavenly Father that this agonizing life is coming to an end this evening. I could not stand it any longer. My Father in Heaven knows that I have done nothing wrong. I am only sorry that in my last hour I have to break the Word of Wisdom. I have only two hours left. Then I must appear before my God. The appeal, initiated by yourselves and others courageous enough to take my part, did not succeed; but I did not expect that it would. . . . It is possible that I might have said or done things that could have mitigated my sentence without endangering the other defendants. But I felt much as did Luther at Worms: 'Here I stand. God help me, I can do no other. . . . ' And also like the prophet Joseph as, returning to Carthage, he declared: 'I am going as a Lamb to the slaughter, but I am calm as a summer's morn. I have a conscience void of offense toward God and toward all men. If they take my life, I shall die an innocent man, and my blood shall cry for vengeance, and it shall be said of me, "He was murdered in cold blood."' Truly, though, life is precious—just how precious one only fully understands in a moment like this—precious, and I and life about to part company, I would not change my course, had I to do it all over. My only regret is the sorrow and anguish I have caused all of you. Greet all the members for me. And tell Bruder Zoellner . . . tell Bruder Zoellner, even if he did denounce me, I forgive him. I plead for his forgiveness and that of any others whom I have caused anxiety or difficulty. Lastly, be assured of my love and my testimony of the gospel and the restored Church. . . . I know that God lives and that He will be the proper judge of this matter. . . . May our Heavenly Father bless us all to be worthy of His presence when we meet again. . . . Until our happy reunion in that better world, I remain, Your Helmuth.

As the lights fade a single note is sounded, as though played on a synthesizer, at first not unpleasant but becoming increasingly shrill and nearly deafening after the stage has darkened. The noise is accompanied by muffled, monotone VOICES *which become louder as the noise increases.*

FIRST VOICE. Over here.

SECOND VOICE. The head must hang over.

FIRST VOICE. So.

THIRD VOICE. Tighten that strap. Tighter.

FIRST VOICE. How sharp is the blade?

SECOND VOICE. It will do.

THIRD VOICE. Now stand back. Give him room.

FIRST VOICE. Is all ready?

SECOND VOICE. Why don't you scream like the others? Well, scream!

FIRST VOICE. Scream!!

THIRD VOICE. Scream!!

SECOND VOICE. Scream!!!

The noise and the VOICES *abruptly cease, punctuated by the heavy thud of a falling blade.*

SCENE 6

A month later. The Sudrows' living room, as in Act One, Scene 2. The Huebeners and Sudrows are seated as before. EMMA *is clearing dishes.*

EMMA. I am sorry we were so late for dinner, Mother.

ANNELIESE. We're happy when you and Hugo spend the evening with us—whatever the hour.

JOHANNES. Where is Bruder Zoellner this evening?

EMMA. I'm glad he didn't come sooner. We'd have never cleared the table in time.

JOHANNES. What will he try to say this evening?

ANNELIESE. He feels responsible.

EMMA. I know.

ANNELIESE. It's been a full month, and every evening he has to drop by—

JOHANNES. Last week in the middle of an air raid!

HUGO. He needn't bother. It can't change anything.

ANNELIESE. There's one thing you could still do, Hugo, that would make some difference. Not only for Bruder Zoellner's sake—

EMMA. That's right, Hugo, if you would only—

HUGO. Don't say it.

JOHANNES. All you'd have to do is to tell Arnold. He'd interview you and take care of the rest.

ANNELIESE. You'd only have to put on a white suit and step down into the water. . . .

HUGO. No! No! . . . Don't any of you understand? It isn't that simple.

A knock on the door.

EMMA. That must be him now.

EMMA *exits.*

HUGO. *(Changing the subject.)* Speaking of the air raids, isn't it time we had another?

ANNELIESE. Please, don't remind us!

EMMA *returns with* ZOELLNER.

ZOELLNER. Evening.

THE OTHERS. Good evening.

ANNELIESE. How are you this evening, Bruder Zoellner?

ZOELLNER. All right. Thank you. How are you all?

EMMA. Please, don't worry about us so.

ZOELLNER. I'm sorry.

JOHANNES. It's frosty these mornings, have you noticed? Should be a severe winter.

EMMA. Think of the troops in Russia.

ANNELIESE. And how will we manage at home—with so many already bombed out, and the fuel shortage.

HUGO. We'll manage.

EMMA. Let me help you with your coat.

ZOELLNER. If I just had some sort of sign. . . .

EMMA. Yes?

EMMA *helps* ZOELLNER *remove his coat.*

JOHANNES. What sort of sign?

ZOELLNER. I don't know. . . . Nothing supernatural. But some sort of assurance or manifestation, let us say, that what we have all been engaged in—what we have individually done—has a purpose.

JOHANNES. Like the mystery of the Atonement?

ZOELLNER. Why, yes, I suppose it's a little like that. . . .

EMMA. But remember Helmuth's letter. He forgave you.

ZOELLNER. It still didn't save his life. And he still didn't know that I didn't inform on him. He went to his death still suspecting me.

ANNELIESE. But Arnold—as soon as he was on the other side, he knew that wasn't so.

HUGO. Maybe that will have to be your cross, Arnold, just as wondering about himself after the excommunication was his. . . . *(ZOELLNER audibly sighs.)* A heavier cross by far than prison or what they finally did to his body.

ZOELLNER. I understand. Yes, that is right. But. . . .

HUGO. You could have done nothing to save him. The excommunication didn't deprive him of his body—just his peace of mind.

EMMA. Hugo, please.

HUGO. I'm sorry. Bitterness solves nothing. . . . And, as a matter of fact, I have gained something from all of this.

ZOELLNER. What is that?

HUGO. The way he took everything. The way he stood up under it all—that set me pondering, and I think now I understand the difference a little better between a reformer and a prophet. It took a prophet and a prophet's example to inspire Helmuth in what he did . . .

EMMA. *(Expectantly.)* Hugo . . . do you mean?

HUGO. No, my dear, it would be too ironic, I'm afraid, if an excommunicant brought about another man's conversion. I hope that doesn't offend you, Arnold.

ZOELLNER. What can I say? I wish it were otherwise. But I understand. Maybe someday, Hugo. . . .

HUGO. I don't know. Maybe someday.

ZOELLNER. You know, Helmuth also taught me something. I now realize that, although I was his priesthood leader, his bishop, Helmuth still had to act according to his . . . own light, that there are matters which a man must judge for himself and which the rest of us may not presume to understand. . . .

EMMA. *(Pressing his arm.)* There's one more bottle of cranberry juice. You remember, it was Helmuth's favorite. It's in the kitchen—I'll go get it . . . *(EMMA leaves, then quickly returns with a bottle of cranberry juice.)* Grandfather!

JOHANNES *assists her to pour it into glasses, then hands one to each of them.*

JOHANNES. We were saving it for another celebration, weren't we?

ANNELIESE. Yes, for the end of the war.

ANNELIESE. But I doubt some of us will ever live to see the end of the war.

EMMA. Odd, isn't it?

JOHANNES. What's that, my dear?

EMMA. Mother and I picked the berries and bottled the juice especially for Helmuth, because it was his favorite. But he never managed to drink any of it with us. . . .

A long pause. EMMA *stares distractedly into space. The others look at her empathetically.*

HUGO. *(With forced cheerfulness, breaking the melancholy mood.)* Isn't Helmuth—isn't his memory—worth toasting? Isn't that a special enough reason to celebrate? *(Toasting.)* To Helmuth. Also your peace of mind, friend Arnold. . . .

ALL BUT ZOELLNER. To Helmuth. . . .

They look encouragingly toward ZOELLNER.

ZOELLNER. *(Hesitant, then, as he raises his glass, breaking into a faint but distinct smile.)* To Helmuth. . . .

As they hold their glasses toward each other, the lights darken and the curtain closes.

CURTAIN

PROGRAM NOTE

To be handed to the audience as they exit.

Our account is now concluded. It is essentially a true account, even if certain principals have been given fictitious names. We cannot, of course, vouch for their exact words either, or even that the young Huebener had a penchant for cranberry juice. On the other hand, the wording of the various tracts attributed to him is for the most part a direct rendering of what he actually wrote. Certain liberties were, of course, taken to enhance our presentation's dramatic form. There is no evidence that the Nazis outright compelled Huebener's branch president to expel him from the Church either. Their actual influence in this respect has therefore been left ambiguous. Huebener's confession to his branch president—which serves as the philosophical crux of the play—is strictly conjectural and probably never occurred. The matter of Hugo Huebener's interest in the Church is also purely speculative; it seemed an appropriate circumstance, however—a case where "ought" has every right to contend with, if not outweigh, the "is." As for the story's aftermath, the facts are these—like life itself, both sad and reassuring: Helmuth Huebener's corpse was delivered to the Anatomical Institute of the University of Berlin. Its place of interment is unknown. His mother and grandparents perished just nine months later in July of the following year, during an air raid, and his stepfather had a heart attack shortly thereafter. Schnibbe and Wobbe served prison terms until April 1945, when they were enlisted in the Nazis' final, desperate stand against the Allied invasion. Wobbe was later captured and subsequently freed by the British. Schnibbe was sent by the Soviets to a concentration camp in Siberia, from which he was released after several years. Huebener was posthumously reinstated a member of the Church of Jesus Christ of Latter-day Saints upon review by the Church's General Authorities after the war, and today a plaque in Hamburg's Beberhaus, where Huebener served his apprenticeship with the State Welfare Agency, memorializes the young martyr. Also, in 1966, a street in a new section of the city, Hamburg-Lohnbruegge, and a Youth Home in the Huettenstrasse were named for him. Huebener has also served as inspiration to several foremost contemporary German authors—including Guenther Grass and the Nobel Prize-winner Heinrich Boell, who in their novels have made him a symbol of the modern German conscience, in his way a German Gandhi or Solzhenitsyn. Of all who participated in the anti-fascist resistance, Huebener was almost alone in refraining from violence or physical retaliation and not affiliating himself with some partisan cause. Few such men appear in any generation. Huebener was a true son of the twentieth century, of whom Latter-day Saints, Germans and the world at large can be justly proud. May we cherish his memory with gratitude . . . and reverence.

J. Golden

James Arrington

Based on the primary research and collection of James N. Kimball

About the Playwright

James Arrington could be considered the Hal Holbrook of Mormon drama. Like Holbrook, who is famous for his portrayal of Mark Twain, Arrington is chiefly known for his energetic one-man shows. This one-man-wonder form of drama is a comfortable fit for Arrington. It combines his tremendous talents, not only as a playwright, but also as a skilled, professionally trained performer. (Arrington received dramatic training from the prestigious American Conservatory Theater in San Francisco.) Arrington said that his focus on one-man shows came out of "necessity":

> I couldn't seem to get people to see me as the broad character actor I was. I was always what looked like a second-rate leading man. I wasn't physically distinctive for an obvious character actor, not skinny, not tall, not stout (I've taken care of that one now), no big Adam's apple or nose. I was also alertly looking for some way to make my way in the theatre, an opportunity that was unique to me. When I was about twenty-three, I went to see (kicking and screaming, actually) my first one-man show, *Will Rogers's USA* with James Whitmore, and I was again thunderstruck. I realized that here was an actor onstage alone (low overhead) who had the audience completely in his control (power) and HE determined the action, pace, rhythm, (art), AND didn't have to share his paycheck with anyone else (a living!) Wow. The combination was irresistible.[1]

Arrington didn't see too many drawbacks to the genre, except that "at a certain point the audience disappears or moves on. Life on the road can become grueling, and having the same haircut for thirty years has been annoying."[2] Yet Arrington struck a chord when his first shows came around, having strong audiences from the get-go: "Again, I think I was lucky to come along when I did. One-man shows were not around in Mormonism in those days, so I was an anomaly. I managed to hit the timing of it just right for my audience."[3]

---

1   Mahonri Stewart, "James Arrington," Interview, *Mormon Artist*, Issue 10 (June 2010): 51.
2   Ibid., 52.
3   Ibid.

But who to initially portray became an important decision for Arrington:

> It didn't take long for me to center on Mormon history, and of the characters in Mormon history perhaps none has been as carefully documented as Brigham Young. So there was plenty of material—in fact, way too much, I found out later. I also was very lucky in choosing a character that had some controversy surrounding him, plenty of documented speeches about all kinds of things, and an audience base that would be quite interested, possibly even enough to get over the idea of watching one guy for two hours.

Here's Brother Brigham was an immediate success. In 1976, Orson Scott Card had high praise for Arrington's inaugural depiction of the Lion of the Lord in his review of the premiere run of *Here's Brother Brigham*:

> He used little make-up, and yet his characterization was so detailed that more and more frequently throughout the play we found ourselves recognizing Brigham Young for a few chilling seconds. The man he showed us was warm—sometimes scorching—and we could understand both how he led thousands of people to a dry mountainland to build a God-oriented civilization, and how he antagonized most of the American public and even some Mormons.[4]

Card was especially impressed by Arrington's ability to do so much with so few resources to draw upon: "It was a small show, with a small set and a feeling of closeness. Arrington worked with a tiny budget, and his publicity was almost all from unpaid articles and word-of-mouth comment. But the house was nearly full every night."[5]

Of great help to Arrington was his father, Leonard Arrington, the famous LDS Church Historian, who had become a leader among his peers in Mormon history at a pivotal time in Mormon studies in the 1970s and 1980s. Arrington tapped into this powerful resource to help research *Here's Brother Brigham*:

> When I went down to his office to ask for help he simply selected about 12 (big, heavy, dusty, thick, small type, no pictures) books from his library and asked me to go ahead and read them. I was devastated. I'd never really been hot on books (except science fiction) and now I had to read history?! I kept them at arms length in my BYU apartment until I was compelled by guilt and time frame to start. I started with the thinnest one, with photos and larger type. But as I continued to read I started making connections and soon became quite conversant with Brigham, his life, mission, family, and the overview of his destiny and viewpoints. Then and only then, could I talk with my

---

4   Frederick Bliss and P. Q. Gump (pseud. of Orson Scott Card), "Reviews," *Sunstone* 1, no. 3 (1976): 90.
5   *Ibid.*

father intelligently about Brigham's world . . . Later on my mother once said to him, "Leonard, have you noticed how many new books and articles there are about Brigham Young?" (Including my father's seminal *American Moses*.) "Why yes," he replied offhandedly, "what do you think the effect of James's play was?" A greater compliment was never paid me.[6]

Yet it was not this initial success with his portrayal of Brigham Young that became Arrington's most recognizable creation. An entire family of nutty Mormons gathering for a family reunion (which require a lot of quick changes and a bit of cross dressing on Arrington's part) in his hilariously infamous *The Farley Family Reunion*, which premiered in 1980, have won Arrington not only a firm place in the tradition of Mormon drama, but also a nearly permanent place in the landscape of the Wasatch Front. The impetus for this clan of satirical Utahns came close on the heels of Arrington's first show:

> After the major success of *Here's Brother Brigham* I was still not seen as doing my greatest love: character acting. Although Brigham could certainly be seen as a character—and was—I just wasn't fulfilling my ambition to do broader characters. For years at parties I would arrive with my instrument (the actor's body is his instrument) on my back, so to speak, and would be asked to improvise characters and situations. Though I enjoyed those opportunities I always had this nagging feeling that there was something more substantial in it for me. Some of these improvisations began to recur . . . and I began to look for ways to use them in a more artistic effort. It wasn't till I read Don Marshall's wonderful little character book *The Rummage Sale* that I realized all these characters were in a family, and literally, I was the patriarch. Drawing from that, my improvisations, my real family, and my observations of Mormon culture over thirty years, I sat down and tapped out what was originally presented as a two-person show. Necessity again entered when I couldn't find enough work to hire an actress to work with me and I took it over, making it into the one-man show that is so recognizable today. I still think the earlier two-man show is a funnier script and concept, but a one-man show sure travels easier and pays the bills.[7]

The Farleys are certainly a tongue-in-cheek, broad satire of the idiosyncrasies of Mormons (specifically the culture born in Utah), but not everyone has had the innate sense of humor to appreciate the Farleys without getting offended:

> The Farleys have been received by countless audiences as just how I meant them to be: a warm satire. However, I have learned that some people

---

6   Stewart, "James Arrington," 53–54.
7   Ibid., 53.

just aren't born with a satire gene and those individuals have a very rough time with the Farleys, thinking they are entirely too simplistic (caricatured, cartoon-like) or that they are a mean-spirited judgment on Mormon society and should be avoided. I've had people in the audience stand up and demand their money back. What they don't realize is that the moment they leave, I have the last say . . . "Them's air cousins from (whatever miniscule town leaps to mind). They're never satisfied, but now we can all speak frankly." And we go on. *The Farley Family Reunion* isn't meant as a final judgment on my society, more of a mirror.[8]

Arrington senses that part of this defensiveness happens whenever one tries to mix criticism (no matter how good-natured or warmly funny it is) with one's culture, religious or otherwise. Not everyone can laugh at who they are:

I believe this is because our culture has been rather insular, and looking too closely appears to be judgmental, prejudiced, or, at worst, anti-Mormon. We're not fond of "disgruntled" members. Secondly, our missionary status and zeal as a church has not allowed us to really look hard at the difficulties and dramatic internal struggles of our people except in melodramatic terms. . . . As a missionary church we don't want to air our dirty laundry; we just don't want to show that our society is subject to less than perfection. Criticism and realism is best kept to oneself. Paraphrasing Cyrano de Bergerac, "I can say these things lightly enough about myself, but I allow no one else to do so" and then out comes the sword. The Farleys are in there somewhere. . . .[9]

But very many in Mormon culture have embraced the Farleys with open arms, being able to distinguish between Arrington's friendly satire from those who criticize the Church and its members in a mean-spirited attempt to tear down their progress. In her review of the *The Farley Family Reunion*, fellow ACT graduate Merilee Van Wagenen wrote that it took a playwright like Arrington, "who feels no need either to reinforce or ridicule Mormon society, to write a play—a comedy, strictly [about] our culture and completely free from self-consciousness."[10] After delighting in the zany characters presented to her, Van Wagenen continues:

In spite of this nonsense the characters are not revolting but endearing. Though unsophisticated and having achieved nothing by way of worldly success, (of the 47 Farleys attending college this year, most tried real hard for a while or got married), there is something healthy about characters who feel

---

8   Ibid.
9   Ibid., 54.
10 Merilee Van Wagenen, Review of *The Farley Family Reunion* by James Arrington, *Sunstone Magazine* 5, no. 6 (November–December 1980): 60.

no need to justify their place in the cosmos. Their idiosyncrasies are harmless. It is the extended family support system at its best. As we recognize some of our zany, pesky relatives and ward members in the play, we are almost persuaded to organize a family reunion of our own if we could be assured of as many laughs as we had at *The Farley Family Reunion*.[11]

Among the appreciative audience of Arrington's work have been high leaders in the LDS Church itself, including prophets and apostles:

> I performed [*Here's Brother Brigham*] for President Kimball in a post-conference dinner where I did a shortened version for all the brethren and their wives, a frightening and astounding experience. At the climax of that short show the lines say, "... Stand to your faith, straighten His paths, for the Lord's coming is nigh!" This phrase is at high intensity and volume, and when I say it I point my finger into the audience. This night I looked down my randomly pointing finger and there I was pointing straight at President Kimball whose widened eyes and intense concentration made him look completely convicted! I nearly fainted. I was grateful that he came up after the show and thanked me personally for the presentation.
>
> I performed with President Hinckley in the group on several different occasions, both before he was president and afterwards. He was always congenial and appreciative, though it's always a little nerve-wracking. I have also managed to perform in several circumstances where members of the leading brethren were in attendance. Once in St. George, one of the apostles was present and had to make a quick announcement at the pulpit before my talk. He sat with me and asked specifically that I not begin until he'd gotten back to his seat so he could "enjoy the whole thing." As complimented as I was, here was such an irony: Me the ersatz Brigham was speechifying while one of the Lord's actual prophets sat quietly watching. A strange juxtaposition for sure. He winked at me from the audience when he was settled and ready for me to begin. I actually think that over all the brethren are grateful for my Brigham Young. He can approach topics and say things quite powerfully that they would feel restrained from discussing. Odd, huh?[12]

The Farleys have been performed over 850 times (nearly all of them by Arrington), in three countries and a dozen states. Add upon that his many performances of the spin-offs *The Farley Family Christmas* and *Farley 2: The Next Gyration*, and the Farleys have become acquainted with thousands of audience members through its long history.[13]

---

11 *Ibid.*
12 Stewart, "James Arrington," 55.
13 "Bet You Didn't Know," *Deseret News*, June 9, 2003, *http://www.deseretnews.com/*

Brother Brigham isn't the only Church history legend to have been treated by Arrington's pen. *Tumuaki! Matthew Cowley of the Pacific*; *Wilford Woodruff: God's Fisherman* (written in collaboration with Tim Slover), and *J. Golden* have all been one-man shows centered around famous Mormon icons.

But whether it's these famous figures or the provincial Farleys, Arrington's experiences, and the gut responses of his audiences, have provided a wealth of experience and personal stories:

> The war stories of touring and producing shows all over the world include what you might expect from such kinds of strange instances, everything from arriving at a show dressed and prepared for the wrong character, being picketed (HBB in Orange County), being shut down by a thunder and lightning storm, and having my costume and makeup (beard) not arrive on the plane with me for a show that night. I think one of the most memorable experiences was performing the role of Matthew Cowley in the play *Tumuaki! Matthew Cowley of the Pacific* which I wrote and presented on the hundred-year anniversary of BYU-Hawaii. Many people who attended knew Brother Cowley personally, and at one point, a group of about 30 Maori men invited themselves up on stage to perform the Haka (their cultural war dance) with me. I've never had an experience quite like that . . . except in the second act when a high priestess from their culture came up and presented me with a priceless antique bird-feather cloak and tied it around my neck. I performed the rest of the show in that cloak. Amazing. I still have it.
>
> On occasion, I have been told fascinating stories by those who had specific and hidden information about some of the characters I've portrayed. For instance, everyone has a personal favorite J. Golden Kimball story, and I hear a new one or at least a take-off on an old one every time the show is done. I have been adopted into the Brigham Young family and continue to receive their family e-mails and *Wilford Woodruff: God's Fisherman* has played at Oxford, England.[14]

Extending beyond one-man shows, Arrington has also written a play about Joseph Smith (or more accurately how various people have viewed Joseph Smith) called *The Prophet* and was a collaborator with Marvin Payne and Steven Perry on the popular musical about the Mormon trek west *Trail of Dreams*. Recently he also teamed up with Mahonri Stewart to write *March of the Salt Soldiers: The Utah War*, to celebrate the sesquicentennial of the Utah War.

The almost strictly Mormon-centered themes of Arrington's work hasn't frightened off audiences. Rather the opposite, as he has been successfully performing his

---

article/988847/Bet-you-didn't-know-The-Farley-Family-Reunion.html?pg=all (accessed September 23, 2012).

14 Stewart, "James Arrington," 55.

shows for nearly three decades, with positive reviews abounding. But when asked about how his faith and his art intersect, Arrington hasn't been able to come up with an answer that he is completely satisfied with:

> [My faith and my art] are so intertwined that I can't have either of them without it leading to the other. I know that must sound a little strange, but I've always felt blessed and felt the hand of the Lord, if nothing else, giving me a slight push forward. I've always felt that my talent was given to me for a purpose, and purpose is what religion is all about; thus, they are deeply intertwined and hardly separable. Obviously, if I had to make a choice I would know to separate the two and I'm clear about the answer; theatre is the temple of man, but it's not a saving institution. I'm very clear about the difference.[15]

But, fortunately, theatre is not a matter of simply choosing between two masters. Arrington has proven that, with his faithful, albeit not always formal, portrayal of Mormonism, members of the LDS Church do not have to be afraid of seeing their culture and their history portrayed on the stage. They can sit back, engage, and enjoy a two-hour talk with Arrington about Mormonism's triumphs, tragedies, flaws, and glory. About Marvin Payne acting in the title role of Arrington's *J. Golden,* one reviewer wrote: "With the combined energy of James Arrington's pen and Marvin Payne's acting, the spell was woven. Where the pen left off and the acting began was a seamless boundary to detect. As the spell lulled my left brain critic to sleep, J. Golden sprang to life before my eyes. It was only a matter of sitting back and enjoying the experience from then on. . . . An evening watching J. Golden was an evening well spent, marvelously entertaining with a bit of thoughtfulness thrown in, just the right touch to avoid damaging the fun."[16]

And it is perhaps that "fun" for which Arrington's work is best known. Although often coupled with considerable wisdom and pathos, Arrington's sense of humor is evident whether it comes from the mouth of Heber Farley, Brigham Young, or J. Golden Kimball. Arrington has become one of Mormonism's top satirist and humorists, which is only one of the many reasons that, even after three decades of exposure to Arrington, audiences keep coming back.

---

15   Ibid., 57.
16   D. Michael Martindale, "J Golden," AML-List Review Archives, November 6, 2001, *http:// www.aml-online.org/Reviews/Review.aspx?id=3452* (accessed April 5, 2010).

About *J. Golden*

J. Golden premiered at the Nelke Theatre at BYU in the fall of 1982. It went on to play in various venues throughout the years including in Logan, Salt Lake City, St. George, and, notably, the Provo Tabernacle, where J. Golden Kimball actually preached. The first actor to play the role of J. Golden was Bruce Ackerman who shaved his head to achieve the likeness. The role was later taken on by Dalin Christiansen and then by Marvin Payne.

Act One

J. GOLDEN KIMBALL, *a tall, thin man, about seventy and balding, enters the stage which is sparsely furnished. A desk, a pulpit, a chair or two.*

J. GOLDEN. Good evening, brothers and sisters. I'm mighty happy to be here tonight. They just told me I'd better watch my "Ps" and "Qs." I don't know why everybody's so worried about me. I say what everybody else says.

Apostle Ballard gets up and says "Brethren and sisters, I haven't prepared a sermon today. What I'm going to say the Lord alone knows." And he'll preach 'em a fine sermon, too. I get up and say the same thing: "Brethren and sisters, God alone knows what I'm going to tell you." See? They all laugh. Because of that President Grant has asked me to write out my sermons these days and, of course, I have my discourse here in my pocket. He told me I had to write it. Didn't tell me I had to read it . . . so I won't.

Are there any reporters here tonight? I guess there is. I'm always afraid of these reporters. They always get things down just as I say it! See, I never know just how I will begin nor how I will end. I'm not highly cultured, and for me to be my natural self has proven somewhat dangerous.

I'm not going to announce any blood or thunder doctrine to you tonight. I've not been radical since I came very near to being operated on. Thought I was going to die. People said to me, "Why, Golden, you needn't be afraid, you'll get justice." "Well," I said, "that is exactly what I'm afraid of." I'm old enough to know a thing or two and I'm here to pass it on so some of you won't travel the same rocky ground I did. If you don't like what I have to say you can surely go to sleep like you do in Church; we'll wake you up when it's time to go home. (J. GOLDEN *gets on his glasses.*) Looking over you I do not discover that you are very distinguished in appearance. Why, you're no better looking than I am, and I look pretty bad. I'm only a remnant of what I ought to be. We would not take a very good picture, would we? Thank goodness the Lord doesn't judge on appearance or we'd all be damned!

One more thing before I get started. Everywhere I go among this people, they look at me with sympathy and pity and ask me how my health is. Only a few days ago, I walked down Main Street a couple of blocks and twelve people rushed up to inquire how I felt. I felt like kicking the last one. I want to say to you that when I'm walking around I'm alive and my head works, and that's just enough, thank the Lord!

I can tell my whole history in about five minutes flat, leaving out the bad parts of it. My whole name is Jonathon Golden Kimball. Most people call me Golden. I am one of the polygamous sons of Heber C. Kimball. Forty-three sons and not a bastard among 'em. Seventeen daughters and forty-six sons out of sixteen wives—quite an accomplishment. I don't know how many wives my father had. He never told me, mother said he never mentioned it to her either. You know I'm a native. Guess I look it, too, don't I? I was born in these valleys, on Capitol Hill six years after the pioneers arrived. I don't remember much about their hardships or famines . . . look like I passed through a famine, don't I?

Well, I'll tell you how I was brought up and then you can make up some excuse for my general make-up. Father died when I was fifteen; and for the next twelve years, I was as free as the birds that fly in the air! There was no restraint further than the counsel of my mother. I presume the following description of me when I was young is pretty true: "He shall have strong mental powers and be stupid in his own way." That's a part of my history I'm not making much noise about; I'm trying to forget some things I did. Nothing criminal, of course, but it was a well-known fact that you didn't fool with the Kimball boys. Why, I believe we were the terror of Salt Lake City.

Us boys used to meet up in the Eighteenth Ward block. We had a brother who was somewhat of a general, trained us boys—that is, when father was away. He'd get us behind the barn, put a chip on one of our shoulders and tell somebody to knock it off. Then we'd fight. When we asked why he did it, he said, "It makes you tough!"

My father had a wonderful garden with lots of fruits and vegetables in it. He told us we couldn't have any of the fruit. To prove it he fenced it in by an eight-foot wall. We got it anyhow. Boys do, y'know. This same brother, the General, would take one of the boys and dangle him over the wall on a rope, so he could load his shirt bosom and pockets with apples. Once Brother Tucker, the gardener, caught him holding the rope and took a willow to him, really lambasted him. Oh, I mean he really laid into him. After it was over, I went up to my brother who was feeling pretty bad. I said, "Cheer up. It will make you tough!" Already in trouble—at an early age, too.

So, I grew up in Salt Lake City, I've known this town all my life; it's not safe anymore. I would just as soon think of putting my daughters in a den of lions as send them to Salt Lake City. There is no longer safety for your children if you don't look after them—don't care who you are: apostle, prophets, evangelist or priest. There are no people in the world, where there is more laxity and freedom given to children than there is among the Latter-day Saints. I think we ought to feed them on a raw meat, cayenne pepper, and green cactus diet . . . that would stiffen their backbones!

I remember being in a far-off settlement not long ago for conference where they see few, if any, of the leading brethren. There was a great many young people there; and when I retired, I was kept awake all night by the boys and girls running the streets. Finally I got up towards morning, looked at my watch, and they were still roaming the streets at 4:30! I spoke to the stake president about it the next day and he said, yes, they had some problems all right, what with boys toting guns, etc. Well, I thought maybe it was time to get their attention.

(J. GOLDEN *approaches the pulpit.*) Go to hell! Go to hell! That's where you're goin' anyhow if you don't quit your damn foolishness! I heard last night you're all going around with six shooters in your hip pockets! Ya better watch out. The damn things will go off and blow your brains out! (J. GOLDEN *sits.*)

Oh, I gave up cussing entirely, you know. At least the way I used to. Well, I never intend to cuss. When I get up to speak, I'm not thinking about those words but they just come out. They're left over from my cowboy days—used to be my native language. And I can assure you that they are leftovers from a far larger vocabulary.

Can't drive mules if you can't swear, it's the only language they understand. I'll never know how Noah got two of those consarned, ornery critters on board the ark at the same time. Why, I've never know a mule to as much wiggle his ear unless he heard a few cuss words. When I stand up there, I never intend to use those words, but my mind works in a motion picture fashion, and things come up before me one after another in rapid succession, I'm not thinking about those words . . . then phhhft, there they are! Well, everybody's got some weakness. Mine's just more conspicuous.

Why, even President Grant swears . . . it's true. You say it isn't true? I heard him. It was summer. Crops were perishing for want of water. The people were starving. There were dead and dying cattle. I looked out at this terrible drought, and I said, "It's a damn shame, isn't it, Heber?" and Heber said, "Yes, it is."

When my father died, the families all divided up. We went up to Bear Lake and commenced to fight for life. God knows it was a hard fight, with poverty and terrible blizzards in the winter. Some years seemed we had nine months of winter and three months of late fall. Nothing grew. Still we survived, my brother Elias, and I, my sister Mary, and my dear mother Christeen Golden. The strange part of it was we never got discouraged. We hadn't enough sense to know when we'd failed. We had to hustle to earn a living, that's how I became a hustler—got in with some cowboys, and mule skinners, loggers. Went very quickly down the road to hell, I did. Seems like I've seen some of you on that road, too, eh?

One winter the call came for volunteers to go to the canyons to cut logs for the Logan Temple. I guess I was about twenty-five, and what are you going to do when you're twenty-five in Bear Lake country in the winter? So we went, we all went. Worked in snow to the waist, temperatures from 10 to 40 below. When we'd return to camp, our clothes were frozen stiff as a board from the waist down. Nobody got paid. Nobody even caught cold! Think of that! Do you read something into it? Good, you should.

One day C. O. Card, who ran the camp, gave me one of the worst jobs I ever had. He said, "Golden, I want you to take charge of the camp." That didn't seem so hard, but then he said my job was to get them to pray every morning and every evening and choose a different man every time *and*, we were to entirely stop swearing . . .

at all! Well, some of the prayers were downright funny, but I know the Lord heard every one of them.

But to cut out the swearing? Well, I thought about it and thought about it and decided if I could just get me and George to stop . . . Now George was the champion cusser of all time. He swore so perfectly and made such a science of it that I never thought he needed an ax to chop down those trees—just r'ar back and let out a jagged bunch of words and that tree would gladly fall down! Well, I made my way around the canyon to where he was chopping. We stood there in the snow four feet deep and way below zero. I said, "George, you've got to stop your swearing; those are orders. I know George, I know. . . . Now just hang on, George. We gotta do it, all of us; that's my orders. I've quit already, George, and, dammit, if I can do it, you can." And do you know that the whole camp fell in line when George did? It was astonishing!

Joe Morris was up there with us. He was the best man with oxen I ever saw. One time when we were hauling some of those temple logs to the sawmill, he turned the whip over to me. There were six yoke. I had never tackled half so many. "You can't learn any younger. Go ahead." So I took the whip and started in: "Heyah, heyah." Those oxen, dumb as they were knew a change had been made. "Heyah! Heyah!" Joe stood there and laughed. They lagged and some of them turned around to look at me. I fancied they were all laughing at my shrill voice. *(J. GOLDEN deepens his voice.)* "Heyah! Heyah! Come on, get up there, you!" I spoke quite respectable to those oxen for a time, but what good did it do? Then I started to cuss (it was after the manifesto on swearing, too, but I was mad and had to let loose). And, boy, did I cuss! Did I wax eloquent! Oh, I'm afraid I did. But did those oxen sit up and take notice? They sure did; you see, they were Church oxen, and when you talked that language to them they understood it.

You can see a training of that sort kicks hell out of you and makes a man as tough as a pine knot! But I wasn't meant to be a pine knot for long, at least in that condition, for an event occurred to me that has changed me from that day to this, and it impressed me with a feeling which never can be blotted out: it was that night in Bear Lake when I went into that log meetinghouse and heard a short, stout man with a thick German accent talk about education and the gospel. I shall never forget it. Never remembered exactly what he said, but something hit me that night and I knew there was more to life than I had. That man proved to be Karl G. Maeser.

Well, my brother, my mother, and I have made as great a sacrifice as I have ever seen to go down to Provo where we could attend Brigham Young Academy. Go to college.

From Brother Maeser, we not only learned academics, we learned what it is to be a Latter-day Saint. What it is to have character. "Whatever you are, don't be a scrub," he would say. Up to that point I didn't even know I was a scrub. It was news to me. "Always be yourself, but always be your better self." I've been trying to be the best I can and I'm still not good enough for some folks.

Well, I spent two years studying under Brother Maeser. Then one day, it was 1883, I had a petition for Salt Lake City to grade the street. I went to President Taylor's office to obtain a signature. Brother William Spence was in the office. He said, "Brother Kimball, President Taylor sent you a letter calling you on a mission, and he is disturbed because you have not answered." I said, "How could I answer it, when I never got it?" "Well, you better go and see him." "Right now? . . . Like this? If you say so . . . *(J. GOLDEN enters into the "office" area, looking awkward.)* P-P-Puh-President Taylor? Thank you, sir . . . Yes, I'm, yes . . . Oh, yes! *(Extends his hand to shake hands.)* Kimball, yes . . . Jonathan Golden. Yes, one of forty-six sons and not a b-b-bas—bad one among them. Oh yes, the first time I've been here since my father died . . . yes, fifteen years ago. Yes, a great man . . . I loved him, too. Well, Brother Spence mentioned you . . . Well, how could I answer a letter if I never got it? Are you sure that's what the Lord wants? . . . No, I guess if you didn't know, nobody else would . . . I'll give you my answer in one hour . . . *(He rushes out and then back.)* Uh, thank you for your kindness Brother, President Taylor, sir."

I'd been praying for it; I had been asking the Lord why I could not go. My friends went. Still I was not called. I went out on the street and the first man I met was Bishop Jenkins who had been in Bear Lake.

"Bishop . . . Bishop, I've been called on a mission. Well, don't act so surprised. Brother Jenkins, will you sign my note at the bank? You bet." So I put a hundred dollars in my pocket and went on a mission to the Southern States!

I had a terrible time! When I think of it now, I actually shudder. In the South, the elders were hounded, hunted, whipped, shot at, sometimes killed, and yet I can look you in the face and tell you it was the happiest time in all my life. That is what you get for being in the service of the Lord.

We got on that train, twenty-seven elders—farmers, cowboys, few educated—a pretty hard-looking crowd, me included; we were on our way to meet President B. H. Roberts, the President of the Tennessee Conference. The elders preached, and taught, and sang—advertised loudly their calling as preachers. I kept still for once in my life; silence is Golden. I hardly opened my mouth until I heard some men talking about us. They were asking each other their destinations. One said, "Oh, I'm going north—to ESCAPE THE MORMONS." Another said, " I am going south—to ESCAPE THE MORMONS." And the third said, "Well, I am going east—to ESCAPE THE MORMONS." Well, something welled up inside of me and I said, "Why don't you go to hell for I know there are no Mormons there!" That is how missionaries feel sometimes.

I saw another gentleman get on the train. I can visualize the man now. He knew we were a band of Mormon elders. The elders soon commenced an argument with the stranger; and before he got through, they were in grave doubt about their message of salvation. He gave them a training they never would forget. That man proved to be President B. H. Roberts.

Brother Roberts sent me and a son of an apostle into the Blue Mountains of Virginia. I had ten dollars in my pocket, I said, "Let's ride in a carriage, it'll be the last time we see one." I didn't know that I was a prophet, I wish I hadn't have been, but it came true. We walked, oh my, how we walked! I am a very poor walker. I'm not built for it. Some say it's quite comical to watch me but it's the only way I can work it. We traveled without purse or scrip and learned to trust in the Lord. Well, there was no one else to turn to.

Now, my friends, I've been among this people a considerable length of time. I've traveled among the people from Canada to Mexico, but I've never in all my labors felt the thrill and the flame of the Holy Spirit like I did when I was on my mission. You had to be a good missionary to survive in the South. Stalwart, strong, humble . . . a lot of persecution.

The Southern States, that's where I learned to pray with one eye open. I remember my companion praying. We had our eyes shut and our hands up like this. I thought he would never get through; when we said Amen, we looked back, and there were four men standing behind us with guns on their shoulders. That was the last time I prayed with two eyes shut! Those people would rather hear anything than the truth.

I suppose I should give you some idea of their "religion" for that is what they called it. It will commence with a hymn then comes the eloquent preaching. Some of the finest words you will ever hear and then comes the grand finish, which is always money. I remember one preacher who couldn't seem to get clear what the price of a soul was. He finally commenced at $3 and then fell to $2, then to $1.50. He knew who we were, asked me if I'd give him 50 cents. I told him yes, and I did. The price of their souls then came down to 25 cents, then to 10, and finally at five cents, Amen! Merchandising the souls of men! And to think that I went for 50 cents when I could've been saved for a nickel.

It reminds me of a story I heard. Three southerners were playing cards when meteors began to fall. Supposing the world was about to come to an end, they wanted to pray, but none of them knew how. One said, "Well, what would the preacher do?" He took off his hat and took up a collection.

They call it religion. But that is a misnomer, it is simply business as usual. When we showed up, it caused their business trouble and, oh, how they howled and cried.

They called us names and choked and chortled. Why, I remember once on passing a minister, he said, "Good morning, sons of the devil." I said, "Good morning, Father."

It is quite a thing to put your religion on the line and travel as a stranger in a strange land. You must learn the lesson of humility. I learned my lesson, in this Church, as every man will learn to do it.

There is nothing I dreaded worse than lying outside on the ground. Now, I walked hundreds and thousands of miles, and I never lay outdoors but twice—

though I want to confess to you I hustled; the Lord doesn't help people who do not hustle and move, after they pray and do their duty.

We were never at a loss to know what to do when we had the spirit of our calling. I prayed, and my companion prayed and we heard that voice—not very often, not as often as we should have done, but we heard it say, "This is the way, walk ye in it." I have heard the voice more than once. I heard that voice when I was a wild, reckless young man. I did not know what it was. I told my brother Elias, "I hear a voice; it tells me something a hundred miles away." And I knew all about it before my mother knew it, and Elias thought I was going crazy—so did I. But it was the right voice. I didn't know what it meant then, but I know what it means now.

When I reported to President Wilford Woodruff, that great prophet, he said, "Brother Kimball," he was so kind, "come over here and sit down by me here for just a minute." We only had a few minutes. He said, "Now, Brother Kimball, I have had visions, I have had revelations, I have seen angels, but the greatest of all is that still, small voice."

I have heard that voice. I am a witness, and I know that God lives! That's what I am telling these young boys going on missions. They were not called by their bishop or stake president—oh, they were recommended and their names properly endorsed, yet the Lord is their Shepherd.

One good mother told me her son had asked for more money for his mission or he'd be "licking the paste off the signboards." I said, "You don't find the Lord with money in your pocket. Let him lick!" Missionaries must learn to depend on the Lord and each other. My companions were all dear to me. I grew to love them as all missionaries should.

I had one companion, Elder Charles Welch, something of a poet. He influenced me to write some poetry while on my mission. It's the only time I tried it. I don't know if I could repeat it publicly. I don't suppose you'd want to hear it, would you? That's what I was afraid of:

> We are traveling to preach to the Christian world
> And oftimes there's many a slur at us hurled
> But still we intend to wander about
> Sometimes indoors and sometimes out.

Umm, something something . . .

> Some day we walk three miles and some days more
> And if we are forced we will travel a score
> As a rule we can stand a great deal of rest
> It is hard to determine which one like this best

There's more . . .

> But when we have finished our missions abroad
> We still wish to dwell with the people of God
> In the valleys of Utah 'tis the land of the free
> Of all the lands on earth 'tis choicest for me.

Well, I told you I was not highly cultured and I suppose I have just proven it to you.

Eighteen eighty-four was a hard year for the Church in the South. Brother Roberts called me to work in the mission office. I did not want to go, but I went anyway. It was a great experience. Whenever we start to get a toehold, the devil always kicks up a row. They tried to persecute and drive us out. I was the one at Shady Grove who got the first information that Elder Gibbs, Elder Berry, and the Condor boys had been killed by a mob at Cane Creek. It was terrible. I cannot describe my feelings. Why, I would have been there with them myself except that I missed my connection.

We hardly knew what to do. Brother Roberts and I were determined to bring out their bodies for a proper burial. We went out into a cornfield disguised as laborers. I said, "Brother Roberts, let *me* go! They know you in that section. You have preached there. They will kill you. Let me go." Well, he took one look at my long, greyhound figure and said, "No, Kimball, a disguise for you would be impossible. No, I am the president of the mission. The Lord will take care of me."

I never felt so helpless and alone as I did watching Brother Roberts leave that cornfield. I learned a great lesson that day. I watched a man of faith trust in God and do the right thing. I also realized that the devil won't just roll over and play possum, but some men will be required to give their lives that the gospel may be preached to all peoples. I have learned that gospel never has, nor ever will be preached without lives being lost. It may be the privilege of some of us to go and get killed for the sake of the kingdom.

It was a bad time for the elders, and it was a bad time for me, too. I'd never thought much about my health until I lost it. I got boils—called carbuncles, if you know what a carbuncle is. I don't know what kind of boils Job had, but if he had carbuncles I'm full of sympathy for him. Right on the heels of that I became thoroughly poisoned with malaria. I was yellow as parchment, and I was always pretty much on the run after that. Along the streets in Chattanooga, a stranger, a physician, said to me, "Young man, I don't know who you are, but if you don't do something for yourself, you will die." I said, "I will not, as I'm a 'Mormon.' You can't kill them."

About that time, Brother Morgan came down and relieved Brother Roberts. I was looking worse than ever. Brother Morgan looked me over carefully and said, "Brother Kimball, you better go straight home. It will only cost twenty-four dollars to send you home alive, but it will cost you three hundred to send you home dead." It was a matter of business in that office; we had no money. I said, "Brother Morgan, I don't want to go home. I believe I was called on this mission by revelation; at least they told me so in my blessing. Now, God has been good to me, and He has been faithful and true, and I want to test Him out; and if he can't take care of me, when I have been faithful and true as I have, and made the sacrifices I have, then He is not the God of my fathers." So I stayed, and God kept me alive . . . just barely, but I filled my mission.

While Brother Morgan was there, I asked him if he had any idea why it took them so long to call me on a mission. He said matter-of-factly he knew just why. It seems that he and Joseph F. Smith were looking over the list of names and came across my name. Brother Smith didn't know me and asked Brother Morgan, who only knew I had been a student. There happened to be a man who had lived in Bear Lake in the office and they asked him. He told them he was passing by one day when I was trying to lead a wild horse, and I was swearing at the horse. Brother Smith crossed my name off without further inquiry. It learnt me a lesson which is one of Solomon's sayings, "Seest thou a man that is hasty in his words, there is more hope of a fool than him."

When I was released, he said, "Brother Kimball, now you'd better go right straight home." I said, "Brother Morgan, I can't. You know the one great vision my mother had? It was that her son, her eldest son, should grow to manhood and go back to her people and let them see what Mormonism had done." So I went, and God kept me alive.

My mother's relatives told their old minister, who had preached there for thirty years, that unless he let Christeen Golden's son preach, they would leave his church. He was a clever old fellow. At any rate, while I was there, I secured the names of over one hundred and fifty of my mother's people. In the winter of 1884, my brother Elias and I accompanied her and we did the temple work for the Golden family, and I am still alive. I don't often look it, but I am.

Well, the time finally came when I received an honorable release from my labors. That's the only release I've ever gotten and I'm proud of it.

When I got back from the Southern States I went into the cattle business and I got married. I mean, I got married to Jennie Knowlton, and then went into debt.

I ask the husbands here if you have wives that look at everything just like you do? I would not give the snap of my finger for a woman that didn't fight for her rights. I am thankful that my wife happens to be one of that kind; and we don't always see things just alike. Why there isn't one man in a thousand who knows how to be good and kind to his wife. And there is one woman in 999 who knows when she is well treated.

When a man prepares to marry, he thinks he's getting an angel; and then after he does, he wishes he had. Oh, don't misunderstand me. I love women, sure I do, but I don't love 'em like my father did. I remember a bishop who felt badly because he didn't have anyone to preside over. I said, "If you can preside over your wife, that should be the greatest contribution you can make." And with his wife, my hat would be off to him.

Wives and debts go together somehow. If I could pass along any counsel to you brothers and sisters here tonight, it would be to stay out of debt. To be in debt is hell—it is the worst hell I have ever been in. Well, I ought to know, I spent enough time there . . . in debt, I mean. See, I am in sympathy with people. I know we have all been foolish. I am foolish. I don't think there is a bigger fool than an old fool. A man who has had experience ought to know better. Of all the investments I ever made in my life, all I got out of it was experience; the other fellow got my money.

Now, I can tell you how you keep out of debt; but I can't tell you how to get out after you get in. Had a man come to me the other day who wanted me to endorse his note. I'd sworn I'd never sign another note, not even for my wife. But he looked at me so pitifully, y'see, that I told him I'd sign it, although I was quite sure I couldn't pay it if he did not. I went to the bank and looked the man in the face. He said: "Mr. Kimball, haven't you got any collaterals?" I said, "Collaterals—I should say not! I haven't got a collateral of any kind." He said, "How do you expect me to take your endorsement?" I replied, "On my looks and general character. That is all I have got." And he turned me down; and I have been tickled to death ever since. Now that's the way to keep out of debt!

Just about the time things started to look good in the cattle business, they called me on another mission. There was no noise about it—"You are called on a mission for the Church." "Where to?" "Southern States." Figured I didn't do it right the first time, I guess.

I went this time as mission president. They said, "Brother Spry will take you down and turn the mission over to you."

In fact, when Elder Spry turned the mission over to me he handed me only thirty-five dollars. I said, "Is that all we've got?" "Yes." "How do you get your money?" "Why, we go to the Lord and ask him." "Well," I said, "I don't think he's very liberal."

The first mission conference was in West Virginia. I rode all day and all night on the train. I was ill. The train was six or seven hours late, so by the time I got there all the elders had left and I had to find my way to the conference as best I could. I had a long way to go, too. I didn't feel like I could do it, and I finally broke down. I went into the woods to pray. When I was a boy, my father did most of the praying. I can remember how he prayed, and I have been sorry many times that I can't pray like my father did; for he seemed to be close to God . . . there seemed to be a friendliness and when you heard him pray you would actually think the Lord was right there and if you opened your eyes you would see him. Well, adversity is a great teacher. I suppose when I prayed that time I was humble enough to talk to the Lord like my father used to. Oh, I told the Lord all about it. When I got through praying, I did not see anything; I failed to hear anything, but there was something came over me, a happiness, a joy that it isn't possible for mortal man to express; it started at the crown of my head and filled my whole body. I was actually so overjoyed and so happy that I whistled. The twenty miles that I walked to that conference was the happiest time I have ever had for I knew I was clothed upon with the Holy Spirit.

There is a hole in a doughnut, you know. My mother was a doughnut maker and when she showed me the doughnuts, I grieved over the hole. Some people say there is no hole in a doughnut. I always see the hole and forget about the doughnut.

Oh, but the South, the South! Sometimes I think the only way we'll ever redeem the South is to burn it up completely and baptize for the dead.

We stayed out of the cities, didn't go near them, we were always on the run, but I determined it was time to try—we had no money, so the only place we could secure was the courthouse. I told the Elders, "I will do the preaching, and if they kill me, you need not bother any further." The people were very prejudiced.

I had my Bible, and I am well acquainted with my Bible. I can't find anything in anybody else's Bible. I have owned this Bible for forty years and it is well marked and every subject traced in my own penmanship. I would not take money for this Bible. . . . Oh, well, we went to the courthouse. The building was crowded; among them were some of the city's leading men. But all those present were men; and we all knew what that meant. It is dangerous enough when women are present. At any rate, I made up my mind to preach the gospel as fervently and as humbly as ever a president of a mission preached.

(J. GOLDEN approaches his pulpit.) "Gentlemen, you have not come here to listen to the gospel of Jesus Christ. I know what you've come for. You have come to find out about the Mountain Meadows Massacre and polygamy, and God being my helper I will tell you the truth."

And I did. I talked to them for one hour. When the meeting was out, you could hear a pin drop. There was no comment, noise, or confusion. We went to our hotel. After a short time, a brass band played. I thought it meant trouble. I sent an elder to find out what it all meant. They told him: "We are serenading that big, long fellow." Imagine! A brass band for me! That is the only brass band I have ever had dispense music after one of my talks from that day to this. A brass band! Now the question I want to ask you, brothers and sisters, is: Was I moved upon the correct spirit? I told those elders, "Don't one of you dare repeat that sermon—it'll cost you your life," and I've never preached it since.

There's nothing like the mission field for the making of men. Every time a new group of missionaries come, there are a group of ignoramus elders like I was when I went. The Lord certainly watches over the Church, otherwise ignoramus missionaries would have destroyed it long ago. I liked to test out my missionaries, to see what they're made of, just like B. H. did with us, you remember.

Once I dressed myself up as a Catholic priest and went down to the railroad station to meet them. Well, they were expecting *someone*. Finally after the crowd dispersed, there was only me and them left, and I didn't pay them the least bit of attention. They got together and talked and waved their arms a bit. Finally a big, burly, rough-looking fellow was selected and sent over to me. "Pardon me, Mister Priest, would you be so kind, we're looking for the headquarters of the Mormon Church, could you kindly direct us as to where we should go?" "Hell! Go to hell, young man, if you are more of those damned Mormons come out here to pester us." Oh, I had him on the spit then . . . and I roasted him! "I'll tell you something, you overgrown mountain goat. The last thing we want around here is a group of good-for-nothing, low-down, wife-stealers." Oh, he was starting to steam up, but I didn't let him get a word in edgewise . . . "Your kind of sacrilege don't fit well with our people that with your pagan worship of Ole Joe Smith and that filthy rag of the Book of Marmon." They all looked whipped, and he was cooking just fine. So, I started quoting scripture to them and that did it! He knocked me down! Caught me right upside the face here with one and laid me flat. He weighed well over 200 pounds . . . and me, well, what could I do? It was my own fault. The other missionaries came rushing over and grabbed me up, dusted me off with many apologies. I wish you could have seen their faces when I told them who I was. I wish you could have seen *my* face before the doctor did.

Well, I confined Elder Adams—Alexander Adams was his name—to his room. I knew he thought I'd send him home. As I passed his door one night, I heard him praying; and he promised the Lord that if he could stay he would not only learn to read, but quote scripture as well as . . . J. Golden Kimball. So on the third day . . . there is a parallel there, somewhere, I went in. "Young man, I have determined that you are a defender of the truth, but you've got to learn how to control your damn temper. Now get out there and work!" He did and learned to read and quote scriptures and filled an honorable mission.

Now, brothers and sisters, I realize my reputation for wisdom has been greatly injured by repeating jokes and stories of the kind I just related to you. In the estimation of some people, because of my calling I should be as a solemn as an owl. It is considered a good thing to look wise, especially when not overburdened with information. Some people seldom, if ever, get a bright idea in their heads or a generous sentiment in their hearts. I say we need not pull long faces thinking it indicates faith and is more pleasing to the Lord. The Lord has said, "Cease from your light speeches, and excess laughter," but He surely is pleased with pleasant countenances and a happy people. I think it's best to get people good-natured and in a mood to take what you give them. You remember what my father used to say about giving the baby medicine: "Just tickle it under the chin and down goes the medicine." Besides, a laugh is worth a hundred groans in any market.

Some people are without souls, without love and bigness. They are halfway men. They never fight in the open. They are demagogues and place hunters. They are perched upon every anthill, croaking out their stump speeches for this or that man to hold office. They never give it a thought whether such a man will do good for the people or not. When the ants start to bite, they will call them Mormon ants—blame everything on the Church.

I remember a man very excited about these matters. He moved here from the East. He was a nonmember. I suppose he thought he'd sit back and reel in a million dollars from our members. When it didn't work out to suit him, he became very exercised and burst into my office one day with the cords on his neck stickin' out like this, y'know. He said, "Keep your hands off from the State, and you see to it that your General Authorities do the same."

I said, "Lookee here!" I don't think I had an overload of the Spirit myself. "Look here!" I wasn't very cool either. "My friend, you were not born here like I was. I love this country because my noble loved ones are buried over on that hill, sixty of them. When I was a child, I walked around the site of this great tabernacle with my father before it was built. My father's oxen and his mules and his wagons hauled rock for that temple. When I think about that building, every stone in it is a sermon to me. It tells of suffering; it tells of sacrifice; it preaches—every rock in it preaches a discourse. I can't tell you what that temple means to me, about our worship, our marriages, about the priesthood—but I want to tell you that I shall not be cowardly and stop my tongue. You must keep your hands off this *Church*, and you must respect the men that I honor or we will part ways. So don't blame all of your problems on the Mormons, for I will not stand for it."

There is an animal that, when it reaches out with its feelers and when it runs against anything, it pulls its feelers back and crawls into its shell and, I suppose, remains there and reflects until the scene changes. Most men when they run into an obstacle will plow around it. I have always gone right over it. It does a whole lot of good to see my team pull, to test the plow. I've broken many a plow and done considerable damage by not plowing around things.

I'm a good deal like my father. One day he was praying. I told you how he prayed. Suddenly he burst out in a laugh and he said: "Oh, Lord, forgive me. When I pray for some men, I just have to laugh."

With our most perfect organization, priesthood, and authority, we still have our troubles and skeletons in our closets. Men come to me occasionally, and shake me by the hand and say, "I am glad to shake hands with a good man." I never feel so cheap as when that happens. I have always been thankful that they did not know me so well as I know myself. . . . What is a good man anyways? I have had business dealings with good men, at least who claimed they were good, told me how good they were, and when they got through I didn't have anything left. What can God do for a man like that? You may baptize him every fifteen minutes; but if he does not repent, he will come up out of the water just as dishonest as ever. Baptizing him won't settle the trouble . . . not unless you keep him under.

I stand before you a transgressor, but I am trying to be saved, and that is all that God asks me to do. Any man who tries to do the right thing and continues to try is not a failure in the sight of God. I want you to be good to me, and help save me. If *I* can be saved, it is a great encouragement to every man, woman, and child in Israel. If you have weaknesses, try to overcome them. If you fail, try again; and if you then fail, keep trying, for God is merciful to His children. He is a good deal kinder to us than some who hold the priesthood are to each other. We are a good deal like Peter. I was that way. I would have cut more than one of their ears off, if there had been someone to stick them on again.

I feel aroused sometimes, and the palms of my hands just itch to take hold of the jaw-bone of an ass and beat these things into dull men's skulls. I would do it, too, if I had a jaw bone. So we, you and I, need some older men to put their hands on us younger boys and hold us down.

Sometimes it's hard to understand. Like the first time as mission president that I was bringing home an emigration of Saints and I had gone up to comfort my wife who was sick. Brother Roberts wired me to come down to Salt Lake immediately. They never asked me, they never consulted with me, they just sent for me, and that's how I was ordained as one of the First Council of the Seventy.

Oh, by the way, did you know that there are three great "tions" in this Church by which men are called to positions of authority? Revelation, inspiration . . . and relation. Oh, I never would have amounted to a damn thing in this Church, if my father hadn't been Heber C. Kimball. We're all related down there.

I am suddenly reminded of a little fellow who was sick. He went to the doctor who was an herbalist. The doctor gave him four herbs and told him to boil them in a quart of water and drink it all. The little fellow said, "I can't. I only hold a pint!" Well, I am wondering how much you people hold? Age changes one's capacity for holding, so I'll tell you all about my experiences as one of the Brethren after a few minutes.

I feel like saying, "Cheer up, the worst is yet to come."

Exit J. GOLDEN.

END ACT ONE

Act Two

J. GOLDEN enters, thumbs through a Bible and suddenly:

J. GOLDEN. Wanna hear a good J. Golden Kimball story? It seems that Uncle Golden—you know, they always call me "Uncle" Golden in these stories. I'd protest except that I am uncle to hundreds of children and I don't ever know who is telling the story. Well, it seems that Uncle Golden was taking some people from England on a tour of Salt Lake City. He pointed to one large building and said, "It took us several years to build this building." One of the tourists said, "Oh, we have one like that and we built it in six months." They passed an even larger building, and J. Golden said, "It took us a year to build that one." One of the tourists said, "I think we have one a great deal like that and our men built in four months." Then the group passed the magnificent Salt Lake Temple, and the tourist said, "Splendid, splendid, what is that building, Mr. Kimball?" J. Golden looked and said, "Hell if I know. Damned thing wasn't there yesterday!"

Now I didn't say that! I didn't ever do that. Sometimes I wished I had, but I didn't. It is an amusing story, but I didn't do it. Ha ha, no no.

Wanna hear another one? All right. One time in conference, when they started broadcasting conferences on the radio and speeches were to be timed appropriately, J. Golden got up to speak and President Grant told him to be careful not to go over time. Well, he stood up and said, "Hell, Heber, with this tin can in front of me and the Brethren looking over my shoulder, how the hell am I supposed to get the Spirit?!"

Now I didn't say that! I really didn't. I've never done that in conference. What I really said was, "You see that big clock over there? My eyes are not so good as they used to be, but with that great, big clock before me and this microphone in front of me, then tell a man to get the Holy Spirit!" Not as funny, is it?

Do you see? I am wrongly accused. Wrongly accused! People take it out on me. I suppose they put in my mouth what they'd like to say if they were there.

I'll tell you one more. Would you like to hear one more? All right, once, on a very windy day and in the dead of winter, the sidewalks and streets were all covered with snow but J. Golden liked to go over to ZCMI to have his egg salad sandwich for lunch. I do, too, it's delicious egg salad—besides it's a chance to get out of the office. Well, on this particular day, as he was about to cross the street, he noticed a large woman struggling with a lot of big packages coming opposite of him. As he crossed the street, she lost her direction and ran right into him. Because of the icy conditions of the street, they both went down. First J. Golden and the large woman on top of him. They slid steadily southward, him underneath and her on top until they hit the curb with a bump. "My goodness, Brother Kimball, I'm terribly sorry." He said,

"That's all right, Sister, but you'll have to get off here. This is as far as I go." Now that one is absolutely true! Yes, it is! And there's not a swear word in it!

I don't know. Seems all the stories these days are about either me or Mae West! And I don't think I deserve it. Why I don't swear nearly as much as people say I do. But it bothers the Brethren. They talk to me long and hard about quitting. President Grant talks the longest and the hardest. It's not easy for him. He's a banker, a financier. He doesn't know about cowboys.

Other people try to help me, too. I remember I was walking down the street during the Depression. People were out of work, shops closed down, and buildings vacant—it was terrible. A banker stepped out of his bank, his name was Orvil Adams, at Zion's Bank. He'd made a great fortune as a banker sitting in the bank all day saying "no" to people. Well, he stepped out of his bank, he said, "Come here, Golden, come here. I want to talk to you." I said, "What do you want, Orvil?" He said, "Well, you got to stop swearing, Golden. President Grant's not going to put up with it much longer; he won't let you speak at conference anymore if you don't stop swearing. Take my advice—give it up." I said, "Orvil, I don't think these are times when bankers should be giving advice to anybody." He didn't laugh much, but I've never known bankers that laughed much.

The Brethren try to help me all they can, and I appreciate that. They're good to me, but they don't understand me. They're teachers, bankers, businessmen. It's hard for them to appreciate my upbringing.

Take Rudger Clawson. Poor Rudger. He always gets assigned to travel with me. I feel so sorry for him sometimes. A friend of mine said, "They send you out together. It's an inspiration, Golden. Rudger puts them to sleep and you wake them up." Well, that's not a very nice thing to say about Rudger. But I know that my swearing bothers Rudger.

One time we were down on a conference in California, and I'd gotten carried away down there speaking, and I'd said a few cuss words. I could feel him wincing in the back of me there. Didn't make him comfortable at all. Well, we went from one conference to another, and after the third one, he got up early and was packing his suitcase. I said, "Where are ya going, Rudger?" "I'm going home, Golden. I can't stand it any longer. I can't stand you and your swearing. That's it. I'm taking the next train home to Salt Lake."

I felt awful. I like Rudger. We got along well outside of that. I couldn't think of anything to say, so I helped him pack. Well, I walked with him down to the train station; and as we sat there on the platform waiting for the train to come, I said, "Rudger, before you leave, I want to tell you one thing. You got to understand, Rudger. If I didn't put a few 'hells' and 'damns' in my talks, they wouldn't listen to me any more than they would listen to you." You know, he laughed a little bit. I'd never seen Rudger laugh before, but he laughed at that. He stayed and we finished the conference. But then I think he asked not to be assigned to me anymore, 'cause I didn't see him after that.

I do like to travel out for conferences to meet the Saints. Why, whenever I've attended a conference and returned home, I have felt that I amounted to something. But after I wandered around in Salt Lake, I've sort of lost that feeling sometimes and felt like a stranger among strangers.

I remember a long time ago when the Mutuals launched the *Era* magazine. I was on a trip with Francis M. Lyman to Panaca, Nevada. It was Sunday, a fast day, as I recall. Meetings had begun in the morning, and they kept them up all day long. I was pretty nearly dead at four o' clock when Brother Lyman called me and said, "Now, Brother Kimball, tell the people about the *Era*." So I did. "All you men that will subscribe to the *Era* magazine, if we let you go home right now, raise your right hand." There was not a single man who did not raise his hand and subscribe. I don't claim that was inspiration; it was good psychology. Really, they paid $2.00 to get out. I might've paid three myself . . .

I remember I went to Bighorn Stake. Oh, that's when I got in a lot of trouble with President Grant. I went up there and I was not impressed that those people were living the gospel and they asked me to speak to them. That was their mistake.

(J. GOLDEN *goes to the pulpit.*) "Brothers and sisters, it is good to be here with you today. I hope that what I say /may be taken and given in the correct spirit, for it is my whole desire to preach repentance to this generation. Now, they say the Lord sees the sparrow fall, and I guess He does. And they say He watches over everything you do, but you can't tell me the Lord is watching you all the time. Why, some of the things you're doing, if the Lord didn't turn His head, He would've sent the lot of you to hell long ago. Now, I have looked over your attendance records, and I have looked over your tithing records and it's not very impressive, brothers and sisters. And I can tell you that if you don't change your ways there won't be 10 percent of you that goes to the celestial kingdom!"

Oh, and I really gave it to them. Got carried away. Used some of the old cowboy vocabulary. . . . I offended every one of them, I guess. They called back to Salt Lake before I could get back.

The damn telephone gets me into so much trouble. It used to be that I could get back and deny what I'd said before the letters came in, but now they call. I can't beat the phone calls, so they're waiting for me when I get back.

President Grant was right there at the train station. He said, "Golden, I've got several phone calls from sisters up there who told me what you called 'em. It's a terrible thing, Golden, to call 'em names like that. I'm very disappointed." I said, "Now wait a minute, Heber. You've got to remember that's Wyoming. It's hard country up there, difficult country. It's a drab life, and they're used to rough talk. Why, they don't hardly feel welcome if you don't call them sons of b-b . . . " Well, he didn't seem to appreciate that explanation. Told me I had to go back up there and apologize to those people as soon as possible.

(J. GOLDEN *goes to the pulpit.*) "I have been sent here to apologize for a statement I made a few months ago. After looking things over again and with careful thought and much prayer, I will have to apologize for my rash remark. If you don't mend your ways, only *five* percent of you will make it to the celestial kingdom and not a damn bit more!"

Whenever the time comes that I cannot be frank and honest with the people, I will feel that my usefulness has come to an end.

And after that, President Grant grounded me: I had to travel with him. For eight months I didn't leave his side. Not more than two feet away from him. Bless his heart. The only thing that was hard for me was that he gave the same talk everywhere he went. I had it all memorized. You know, it's that talk about . . . "that which we persist in doing . . . not that the nature of the thing changes . . . " You've all heard that, I hope. If you haven't I'll give it to you. You know, he'd talk about having taken up two things—singing and baseball. How he couldn't play baseball or throw a ball or sing at all, and how he just kept after it, practiced and how eventually he became very good at it. And then he'd sing for them—he'd sing that song: "The Flag without a Stain." Oh, I don't know. I thought he could use some more practice myself. But he could sing some, better than me. He'd always say, "When I first started I couldn't tell one note from another." And after I'd heard him say that umpteen times I got up and said, "Brothers and sisters, I betcha if that note were a bank note, I'll bet Heber J. Grant could have told the difference." He never asked me to go with him after that.

It takes a lot of courage to say what you think. The trouble is we think things we ought not to say. I have often said things that I'm sorry I said, but I couldn't take it back! It keeps me pretty busy repenting, but if I could not repent I would be woefully discouraged . . . wouldn't you?

I don't mean to misuse President Grant. Lord knows, I sustain and uphold, with all my heart and soul, President Heber J. Grant as a prophet of God.

It's only two months ago that a young lawyer—I'm sure he considers himself one of those brilliant, young lawyers—undertook to criticize severely the President of the Church in my presence. I took out my pocket watch and said, "I am going to give you five minutes to name a better man." I haven't heard from him yet.

I pray God to bless President Grant. It isn't the man. We don't worship men. I don't. I have never believed you get on higher ground by worshipping a man. I sustain the Brethren, but I have learned that they are human. Just like you are, just like I am. But that does not take away from their power and authority in God's kingdom.

I have spent a few sleepless nights myself, regarding the doing and actions of men who were in positions of authority, but have concluded I am not responsible for anything I may regard as irregularities. Why, if the Lord cannot care for His

Church, what in the world can I do? I'm going to trust the Lord and His prophet, Heber J. Grant.

I've known these men. I've worked with them and seen their works. I knew President Joseph F. Smith very well. No man had a cleaner, a sweeter, a better record than Joseph F. Smith, and he was a prophet of God. Then there was President Lorenzo Snow. No man was ever kinder to Golden Kimball than Lorenzo Snow. He put his arm around me before he died, and said, "I need you, Golden. I need your help; God bless you." I felt like I was eight feet tall. I have felt big only once, and that was when I thought that God needed me. Then there was President Woodruff. I have personally stood by the side of that good man and he took time—it was not so precious to him that he could not sit by me and bear his testimony to me, you remember that. Before that was President Taylor, a most magnificent specimen of manhood, a man of God I always honored. Never was I in his presence that his bigness and majesty did not impress me. His personality was wonderful, and he looked and acted as a prophet. And I was born and raised in the days of Brother Brigham. I knew him from the time I was a small child, and I testify of his greatness. Brother Brigham was a builder, and he built well and firmly and he continued where the Prophet Joseph ended. One reason why he was so great was that he had great men beside him who were tried as gold seven times, who never faltered or fell by the wayside.

Think of it, my father among the rest, was driven from his home five times! And yet those men held up their hands, no matter how much their hearts were tried. I knew every one of them, and they were all prophets of God. Pray God we shall continue to have men of courage and faith to lead us.

I have learned that some of the greatest miracles and most marvelous events happened to the servants of God when they were in trouble. Peter imprisoned, and an angel of God coming to his rescue. In the days of the Book of Mormon, prisons were broken down and manifestations of God were made apparent. Why, some of the greatest revelations that God has ever given in this dispensation were given to Joseph Smith when he was in jail.

I saw it on my mission when the state of Tennessee passed a law that any man who preached polygamy was to be arrested and punished. A complaint was filed, and two of our elders were arrested. The jail was a little short of room, and I think the sheriff thought he'd embarrass them some so they were confined in two steel cages outside the jail. Neither one of these elders was anything special to look at, two green plowboys from Idaho, but the people gathered to have a peep at these two. They told me sometimes up to four hundred people gathered around. These two elders took advantage of it and commenced to sing and preach the gospel. Although I told you they were nothing special, something happened to them and people had never heard such preaching or beautiful singing in all their days. The elders almost regretted receiving their freedom. So I am inclined to advocate putting our elders in jail once in a while, when they are unable to get a hearing any other way.

These days I go down from my house, down Main Street, walk up in front of the Church Office Building, look up at my office, and say, "Go up, Golden, and do the Lord's work. It's all you know how to do. Go up there and get to work," and then I say, "Yes, but it's hell to have to work with some of those angels up there." I think some of us are sent to lead us and others are sent to try us. Some are spares and some are flats.

Heber Grant, bless his heart, he's tried to work with me. You see, it was Heber J. Grant's father, Jedediah M. Grant that introduced my mother to my father and brought her to Nauvoo. I think sometimes after Heber got to know me, he regretted that introduction.

Heber asked me to take young David McKay up to Brigham City for conference. Brother McKay, he's the superintendent of the Deseret Sunday School, a nice young man, probably go a long way in the Church. We had to leave very early in the morning. It was in the winter and it was cold—drove up in a sled with a team of horses. We got into Brigham City about 7:30. The meetings didn't start until 8:15, so I said, "Brother McKay, let's go over and have some breakfast." He said, "Fine. That's a good idea, Brother Kimball."

Now in Bear Lake Country, when it's cold in the morning like that you have to get yourself going. I don't know why the Lord saddled me with so many burdens, I really don't, but ya see, I was just dying, out of habit to have some coffee to get me going. Lord knows, I'm not a hypocrite, and that's why I'll tell you about my weaknesses. Maybe you can be smarter than I was. I hope so, but by the time President Grant and the Brethren got serious about the Word of Wisdom, it was too late for me. It's plagued me all my life. The time between cups of coffee has gotten longer and longer, and I'm overcoming it now, but I'm not entirely past it and on a cold morning like that—well, I guess you get my point.

So we went over to this restaurant on Main Street. The waitress walked up and said, "What do you gentlemen want?" and Brother McKay said, "We'll have some ham and eggs and two cups of hot chocolate." I could hardly control myself. She left the table. I excused myself and went to the men's room, but on the way I stuck my head into the kitchen and said, "Ma'am, would you mind putting some coffee into that one cup of hot chocolate, please?" She said, "Sure," which was awfully nice of her.

Washed my hands and came back and here she came with the ham and eggs and two cups of hot chocolate. She said, "Now, which one of you gentlemen wanted that coffee in his hot chocolate?" I said, "Aw, hell, put it in both of them!" Now young McKay is going around the Church telling that story all of the time. I wish he'd keep his mouth shut. It's disgusting.

You see, I'd just as soon go out with somebody who understands me. Take B. H. Roberts. He was senior to me in the First Council of the Seventy. Remember we'd met in the mission field. He'd ask for me to go with him. I liked B. H., and he liked me. Oh, I loved to listen to him talk. He was one of the great orators of the Church.

I must confess that when I first heard him preach I was awestruck, almost beaten into silence. It's been a fight all of my life to have to follow men who have great talents as public speakers, but I discovered that no man was ever created that could reach all the people. Why, even the Savior couldn't seem to make Himself understood sometimes.

The only trouble with B. H. was that he was such a fine speaker, he'd forget I was along. He'd talk and talk and talk. Got me pretty upset. One time we were down in West Texas, speaking. It was in the summer, and it was hot. Texas hot. He spoke for two hours and forty-two minutes! He talked about faith, repentance, the Holy Ghost, the Book of Mormon, the Pearl of Great Price, the Doctrine and Covenants, salvation, celestial life, universal theology—he covered everything. At length, he turns to me and says to me, "Golden, have I forgotten to tell these people anything?" I stood up and said, "Yes, B. H., you forgot to tell them that when you die off I'll be the senior member of the Council of the Seventy." That's the only thing he forgot to tell them, I swear, the only thing.

But I'd get even with him. See, I'd snore all night and he couldn't sleep. He'd talk all day, so I'd snore all night! Well, one night he woke me up in the middle of the night. He said, "Golden, wake up. Golden, I can't sleep. No, don't roll over, it doesn't do any good." I said, "What do you want me to do, B. H.?" He said, "Here, I brought you some adhesive tape. I want you to wear it." I said, "What do you mean?" He said, "I want you to put it over your mouth so I can get some sleep." Well, I leaned up on my elbow in my bed and said, "Well, B. H., I'll strike you a bargain. I'll wear it in the nighttime; you wear it in the daytime."

Well, he's gone now. Bless his heart. His wife said, "Golden, we'd like you to speak at the funeral, but we're afraid of what you might say." I understood. They wanted it to be a stately affair. So I dedicated the grave out in Centerville. We drove out there, got out of the car. I'd never seen a cemetery like that before in all my life. It was a mess, brothers and sisters. Picket fence was falling down, bottles and trash all over, the grass was growing long and out of control. Well, they lowered the casket in, and I looked around and said exactly what I was thinking: "This is a hell of a place to bury one of the Lord's anointed—shall we pray?" Well, they fixed it up after that. That's right. That nice cemetery in Centerville, they owe it to me.

Oh, I miss him. I miss B. H. I never felt inferior to him in his presence; he never made me feel that way. He had a greater intellect, greater intelligence. I have preached by his side many times, and after he got through preaching, I reached those he missed. He often said, "Our love is akin to that of David and Jonathan."

I am now what they call the Senior President of the First Council of Seventy. It is not altogether merit. It is the regular order of things because I have had the tenacity to outlive my fellow laborers. You want to know how to live a long life? Get an incurable disease! That is the only way. If you can get an incurable disease, like I did—malaria—you'll take care of yourself.

We are good deal like Coué. Have you ever read Coué's book? When I was sick, I read it from lid to lid. According to the story, many people have gotten over physical ailments—they call it mental—by repeating the words, "Every day and in every way, I am getting better and better." So, I went trotting around, saying: "Every day, in every way, I am getting better and better." Every morning when I got up, I was feeling worse and worse.

I have been administered to by some of the best men in this Church; no better men ever lived than the men who have administered to me, but I'm ashamed to say, I did not have the faith to be healed. I do have the faith and the gift to heal others. I don't think it. I don't imagine it. I have seen God heal the sick. I know it isn't me.

When I was mission president in Alabama, we asked the elders to assemble for conference. In those days, we had no place to meet but the woods. Well, they came straggling in, suffering, rather low-spirited, because they were all traveling without purse or scrip. One young elder there, I don't know what his trouble was, but one of his legs was as large as my body, and it looked like a great piece of raw meat—looked like it would burst. I took one look and I said, "Elder, I'm sorry, you'll have to stay here." He said, "Brother Kimball, I have been dreaming about this, and I have been thinking and talking about it. It would ruin my whole mission unless I can be at that meeting." "Well," I said, "if you feel that way, two of us elders will have to carry you up there. It's about a mile." When we got into the woods, I looked those elders over. I was not very well myself, but I said: "Brethren, what are you preaching?"

"We are preaching the gospel of Jesus Christ."

I said, "Are you telling these people that you have the power and authority, through faith, to heal the sick?"

They said: "Yes."

"Well, then, why don't you believe it?"

This young man spoke up and said, "I believe it!" The elders gathered around and he was anointed. I administered to him, and he was healed right in our presence. Every other elder that was sick was administered to, and they were all healed. When we went out of that priesthood meeting, there was a joy and a happiness that cannot be described. Those elders, many of them, had never seen one another until they had assembled in that conference. And yet before they left, they got down and cried. They cried.

I've been trying to be sick all of my life but I have rather fizzled out at it. I've had problems keeping myself running. I talked with President Grant, and I thought climate would help me. I was a little short on faith, so I tried climate for nine months, but I became very ill—very ill. My family was very anxious for me to live, for some reason. I hardly know what it is. I have been awfully neglectful of them. Pray not only for the leaders of the Church, brothers and sisters. Pray for their families. Leaders go out and tell you how to take care of your families, and they are away from theirs. My family wanted me to go through a physical examination. Had to have an X-ray of my lungs, and all that stuff. I was scared to death. Nothing in the world frightens me like an examination.

So I went to a young physician of some considerable renown. I could only think of that humorous incident in the Bible. I would quote it, but I never dare quote scripture, for after I get through quoting you wouldn't recognize it.

(J. GOLDEN *looks through his scriptures.*) I am a little like my father. Whenever he used to quote scripture, he would say, "Well, if that isn't in the Bible, it ought to be in it."

Oh, here it is: "Asa in the thirty and ninth year of his reign, as King, was diseased in his feet, until his disease was exceeding great: yet in his disease he sought not the Lord, but turned to the physician." See, he went to the doctor, too. Now listen: "And Asa died and slept with his fathers" (2 Chron. 16:12–13). Well, don't ya get it? Well, he went to the doctor and died, don't ya get it? Well, I thought it was funny.

Well, this doctor, he found one of my batteries is somewhat damaged—that is what they told me. He shot me so full of serum of iron and strychnia, at five dollars a shot! Five dollars!!! That pretty near broke my heart. This young man did not believe in God, man, or devil. I found that out. I told him I was a Mormon. He said, "You'll never get any better." I said, "Oh, yes, I will." "Oh, yes?" he said, "I'd like to know how." "Because I have a greater physician than you are." "And who is he?" I said, "The Lord Jesus Christ." He laughed and said, "There is nothing in it." He was drowned last year, and I am still alive. I may not be for long.

People move along at a pretty good clip these days. Everyone's in a hurry. They climb in their automobiles and it's, "Look out, Buster!" There is nothing else annoys me so much as for a man to run onto me with one of those great, powerful machines, and just before hitting me, honk his horn. *Beep, beep, beep, beep!* My legs go right out from under me. I can't even hit a trot. He is saying: "Get out of the way, we are coming!"

I got that the other night on First North Street here. I can see only one way at a time, and even then I am not quite clear at it, but I had to see four ways that night with these cars all parked up to the corner. So I started out and here came two machines around that corner, and they tried to beat each other through and caught me right in the center. The only thing that saved my life was my being thin! I am not trying to be funny. I am trying to be serious. Now, I don't want to get killed by one of those great, big machines. What I'm worried about is that they might not make a good job of it and leave me maimed for life.

That reminds me of another good J. Golden Kimball story I heard. Shall I tell it? One day Brother Kimball was standing on South Temple and Main. He was waiting for a chance to cross and had just started when a car whizzed by and struck the cuff of his pantleg. It startled him, and he shook his fist at the retreating car and said,

"You—you—damn you!! Hell of a lot of respect you have for the priesthood!" Now I didn't say that. I never said it. What I said was, "You son of perdition, have you no respect for the priesthood? Can't you tell the difference between a common gentile and one of the Lord's anointed?" I guess I told him.

Seems the Brethren have finally decided to only send me out on two kinds of assignments anymore. Those that are good for me and those that are bad for anyone else. I'm willing to do God's work, whatever the cost. I suppose they feel it costs me less. They sent me down to Thatcher, Arizona. Thatcher, that's where my brother Andrew's boy is from. Andrew, one of forty-six. He said, "Tell Spencer and Camilla hello for me." More than that, they asked me to stay the night. A nice young couple. Short, though. Very short.

Next day in conference, the stake president said, "We'd like to have you speak to all the Melchizedek Priesthood about the Word of Wisdom." I said, "You want *me* to talk to them about the Word of Wisdom?" He said, "Yes, didn't the Brethren tell you that's what we asked for?" See what I mean?

I told him I'd do my best.

(J. GOLDEN *goes to the pulpit.*) "Brethren, I'll ask you a couple of questions. How many of you have never had the puff of a cigarette in all your life? Would you please stand up?" Most of them stood up. I was amazed. Most of them stood up! "Very impressive. Well, now, of all those standing, how many of you have never had a swig of whisky in your whole life? If you have, sit down." One or two sat down, but that was all, the rest of them just stood there proudly, backs straight, looking at me. I didn't know what to say, I didn't . . . "Brethren, repent! You must cease being so pious and self righteous!"

They understood that. They really did. They thanked me afterwards. Stake president didn't say anything. He just walked away. Do you think I learned the lesson they meant me to?

Another time they sent me down to St. George. They said, "Go down, Golden, and speak to them. Buoy them up. Make them happy." I said, "You want me to make them happy? They're practically dead down there!" "We feel certain that you can do it." The rest of the Brethren go in the winter, but they always managed to send me down in the middle of August somehow.

It's 115° in the daytime, then would cool down to 98° at night and the next day go right back up again. I mean those people down there have paid a severe price. What with Indians, scorpions, snakes, heat . . . I don't know how they do it, and I told them so.

(J. GOLDEN *goes to the pulpit.*) "Brothers and sisters, it's hard for me to be here. I don't know how you do it, I really don't, brothers and sisters. I admire your tenacity. I take off my hat to those hard-handed, white-headed, broken-down men who have made it possible for us to exist in this mountain country. Why, if I had a house in

St. George and a house in hell, I'd rent out the one in St. George and live in hell . . . I really would."

They didn't seem to appreciate that. They called back to Salt Lake before I could get back! As a result, I had to go back down the next July and apologize.

I told them I was sorry I'd offended them, but I couldn't help the way I felt and I still felt the same way, and I preached them a fine sermon on faith, that God will bless all of those who have faith. I thought it was a powerful sermon . . .

I alone thought that because afterwards a woman came up to me—I was still on the stand—and she said, "I'm sick and tired of you Brethren coming down here and telling us about faith and what it takes to survive. I'm sick of it." She said, "You're the ones without any faith. We stay down here. You just come and go." I thought about that. I have thought about it considerably since that time and, you know, she was right, brothers and sisters.

I don't know. You expect a lot from us, I know. You expect us to be perfect according to how you think we ought to be perfect. None of us are—I'm not, you know that. No great light from Heaven causes us to lose all our faults simply because we work in the Lord's kingdom. At least, it never did for me. I have gained knowledge and information, just the same as you have gotten yours. But, I don't know—when we go out to conferences they ask me some of the strangest things. I can't understand some of the brothers and sisters. Why, sometimes I think the members of the Church are stone crazy!

I distinctly remember the time at a conference in Las Vegas, Nevada, we were singing a hymn . . .

(J. GOLDEN *begins to sing an LDS hymn.*) The fellow next to me leans over and says, "Brother Kimball, do you think that Jonah was really swallowed by a whale?" I said, "Well, I can't say for sure, but I'll tell ya, when I get to heaven, I'll ask him." He said, "What if he isn't there?" I said, "Well, then you'll have to ask him." (J. GOLDEN *goes back to singing.*)

A sister in Delta came up to me once, "Can I ask you a question?" "Sure. What is it, sister?" "Well, I've got two brothers. One is a very good, faithful man in the Church, done all that was asked of him, good family man, good father, husband. He was called home recently . . . he died. Left us and his family alone. My other brother's not worth anything. He drinks, smokes, beats his wife, chases other women. He's always out of work and still alive. Now how do you explain that, Brother Kimball?" I said, "It's the Lord's will, I guess." She said, "How can that be?" I said, "Well, it appears that the Lord doesn't want that jackass brother of yours any more than you do . . . " I wished she'd laughed as much as you did. She didn't think it was funny at all.

I don't know. Well, it's funny. The way you people look around and feel around, I'm wondering if you think I'm old. I am very glad to say that I am not as old as I feel. I guess I must be getting close to death because people are asking me strange things.

A sister down in Richfield approached me as I left the ward house. She said, "Brother Kimball, you're pretty close. You'll go on the other side soon, pretty soon. I wonder if you would mind giving my father a message," and she handed me an envelope. I said, "No, sister, no, I won't do it." She said, "Ya won't?" I said, "No, I'll be too busy to look all over hell for your father."

I want you to all give up your sinning, brothers and sisters. There is no joy in sin. . . . It may be lots of fun, at the time, but you can't enjoy the Spirit. You can't hear the voice, that still, small voice, when your words and actions shout so loud as to block it out. Now you need to get a little bit anxious, and go home and get a little healthful exercise. Don't sleep too much. Lie awake a little and think about this work. Hold your family prayers. They are important. I have always held a prayer with my family, although there are occasions that, by the time I got them all together, I'd lost the Spirit, somehow. Did you ever have that happen?

I want you to live within your means, too, brothers and sisters. Plan a budget. Don't live lavishly—save your money. Live within your means, dammit, even if you have to borrow to do so! Live within your means!

I think you ought to clean up this city, too. I drove around before I came here tonight. You need to fix your yards, paint your houses and your barns. . . . Some of you sisters could stand a little paint yourselves.

I realize that during the past thirty years I may have said some foolish things. I have, in my own way, given the people a good deal of chaff to get them to take a little wheat; but if some of you haven't got the sense to separate the wheat out of the chaff, then you can eat it! If a man in this Church ever does say a foolish thing, they will remember it to the very day of their death; and it is the only thing some of them do remember. I think they do mighty well to remember that.

I've been taught the truth of the gospel from my youth, just as I was taught that a peach grew on a peach tree. I can tell a peach when I see it on a peach tree; but I can't for the life of me tell how that peach grows on a peach tree, and neither can you. Now there are many things about this work that I don't comprehend, but because I cannot tell it all, it doesn't prove that it is not true. I have a conviction burning within me sometimes, like a living fire. There are a lot of things I do not know, but I have paid the price. I have eaten the bread of adversity. I have drunk the water of affliction, and I have found God. I have heard that still, small voice—and whenever I have followed it, I was right.

I love God, notwithstanding my weaknesses. I am not afraid to meet Him, for I know that He will understand me, and that is good deal more than some of you have been able to do.

I have a friend who says, "Uncle Golden seems to be very desirous of checking out and going on the other side to see if what he's been telling is true." Well, I'm not ready to check out just yet. I am thankful every minute . . . nearly every minute, that

I am alive and better informed about life and death—that there is an opportunity with all our weaknesses that we can repent. And if you take from me the joy, and the happiness, and the peace, and forgiveness, for heaven's sake, what have you got left? I wouldn't give you a nickel for the whole thing.

Now I want to notify my friends not to worry about me; that when I am dead—and it is an awful job to get there, I have found that out—when I die, I have made arrangements for a brass band. A brass band! I like the idea of lots of noise and confusion, people inquiring, "What is that?" "Why, Kimball's dead." Then it's, "Oh, oh, Kimball."

I may not have walked the strait and narrow, but I crossed it as often as I could. God bless you, brothers and sisters, good night.

THE END

Burdens of Earth

Susan Elizabeth Howe

About the Playwright

Poetry, more than drama, is Susan Howe's specialty. Her accomplishments as a poet are impressive, having published in *The New Yorker, Poetry, The Southern Review, Prairie Schooner,* and a number of other literary journals.[1] Her first volume of poetry, *Stone Spirits,* received high praise:

> The publication of *Stone Spirits* . . . is a welcome and refreshing landmark in western, LDS, and, well, human poetry. In some 39 poems divided into four sections, Howe uses western landscapes and motifs (stones, mountains, desert sands and flowers, elk horns, paintings) to probe, in telling imagery, as Professor Edward A. Geary writes in the foreword, "meditations on birth and death, on love and loss and suffering, on nature and art, nature and ethics, on the sense of menace and the necessity of risk-taking." Throughout this important collection of poems, "there is always," Geary concludes, "something western in the perspective: western light, western distance, western confidence. Each poem . . . represents in its own way a 'hike to the spiries,'" and each poem, I might add, probes the human condition from a profound Latter-day Saint perspective.[2]

Stone Spirits was awarded the Charles Redd Center Publication Prize, as well as the Association for Mormon Letters Poetry Prize, both in 1996. Her second book of poetry *To Lie with a Landscape* (in conjunction with Florida-based poet Terri Witek) is forthcoming. Howe has also served as editor for the *Tar River Poetry*, as poetry editor for two Mormon publications, *Exponent II* and *Dialogue: A Journal of Mormon Thought, The Denver Quarterly,* and *Thought*.[3] Howe was also named one of Mormon Literature and Creative Art's "75 Significant Mormon Poets."[4]

---

[1] Susan Elizabeth Howe, BYU School of Humanities Faculty Biography, *http://humanities.byu.edu/faculty/sh36* (accessed May 7, 2012).

[2] Richard H. Cracroft, "Book Nook: The LDS Literary Version of 'Das Ewig-Weibliche' Continues to Stir and Inspire," *BYU Magazine*, Spring 1998, *http://magazine.byu.edu/?act=view&a=356* (accessed March 14, 2001).

[3] Susan Elizabeth Howe, *Mormon Literature and Creative Arts*, *http://mormonlit.lib.byu.edu/lit_author.php?a_id=1601* (accessed April 27, 2012).

[4] Ibid.

Howe didn't originally intend to be a poet, though. Her first impulse was to focus on foreign languages:

> I wrote poetry in high school and my early college years, but just for myself—I had received no training, not even in high school English classes. In college, I majored in Spanish and minored in French, and then after graduating I immediately realized that I'd majored in the wrong subjects (though they have been useful in teaching me how language works as well as some of the relationships between English and other Romance languages). So I didn't begin to train in poetry until my master's and doctoral programs. Then I took several poetry writing classes even though I thought I would primarily be a fiction writer and a dramatist. One of the major forces in my development as a poet was a friend in my doctoral program, George Bilgere. He is a very fine poet, and for about a year we had a pact that we would write a new poem and exchange it every week. That constant writing helped me learn the discipline of poetry. What finally turned me to poetry as my primary art form was that I began publishing poems in literary journals before I even had any stories ready to send out. That was a clue to me that I was a better poet than fiction writer.[5]

Thus, over the past few decades, Howe has taken these experiences as a trained and skilled poet and applied them with equal skill to another medium: playwriting.

Her first play, *Burdens of Earth,* shows many of the qualities one would expect to find in a poet: introspection, fluidity of thought, and beautiful language. These qualities were especially effective in the subject matter of *Burdens of Earth*: Joseph Smith's imprisonment at Liberty Jail. Those tedious, cramped, and miasmic months in Liberty Jail are effectively raised to creative life by Howe.

One BYU student made the following insightful comment in his review of the play:

> One thing I noticed, which may have been intentional, was that the play doesn't seem to follow a storyline. Events, dialogue, and flashbacks occurred repeatedly as the Prophet came to a greater realization of the purpose of this crucible. The one thing the prisoners had was time. . . . I could see the symbolism Howe used in putting it in. The thoughts and ideas were provocative and poignant. Howe also chose to use a simple style, rather than one of pageantry, evoking images of the dreary reality of their dungeon prison.[6]

---

5 Doug Talley, "An Interview with Susan Elizabeth Howe," *Meridian Magazine*, 2003, http://ldsmag.net/poetry/030910interview.html (accessed April 13, 2012).

6 Ryan Reeder, "Burdens of Earth," March 8, 2001, http://geocities.com/ryan_reeder/papers/burdensofearth.html (accessed April 11, 2012).

But even more than evoking the mood and pathos of that season of discouragement in Mormon history, Howe accomplishes an even more complex task: making the Mormon Prophet imperfect while maintaining the prophetic mantle which faithful Latter-day Saints insist that he had. Noting that "the action of the play is largely psychological," reviewer Robert Paxton summed it up this way: "It tackles a difficult subject and a near-impossible character in a way that humanizes him. It makes Joseph accessible by bringing him into a smaller perspective, yet it manages to diminish neither the man nor the mantle. And that is no mean achievement."[7]

Although theatre critic Eric Snider thought that the play was in constant climax, thus creating "no climax at all," he also had a favorable impression of the play and the playwright's portrayal of the prophet:

> The play . . . is thoughtful and incisive. Joseph's dilemmas and demons are clearly defined without being oversimplified. The answers to his questions do come, but like the revelations they were, they come quietly and subtly . . .
>
> *Burdens of Earth* is commendable for presenting Joseph Smith in an unsentimentalized manner. It's the rare theatrical treatment of him that doesn't stoop to emotional manipulation or mushy sermonizing, making this a highly intelligent, theatrical and religious experience.[8]

Burdens of Earth obviously showcases Howe's faith with its focus on the Prophet Joseph Smith. However, when asked whether she believed in a "Mormon school" of writing, Howe responded:

> In my mind, the question you ask is a question of audience: Should there be a body of art created for a Mormon audience . . . or should Mormon artists consider the larger culture as the audience for their art? I think that our culture is mature enough to support art for both audiences, and that the artist's talent and interests will suggest the audience she should create for. Both can be subsumed under the category "Mormon art." But standards of craftsmanship should be high regardless of audience and regardless of medium. I am encouraged by the excellence that I see developing in Mormon art in so many different mediums—drama, film, the novel, visual art, and music as well as poetry. It seems to me that in many ways our culture is coming of age and that many very talented Mormons are using their gifts to bless our culture and the larger American culture as well. . . . The specific subject matter of my poems is not usually religious, but my perspective on my subject is often the result of

---

7   Robert Paxton, "HOWE—Burdens of Earth," AML-List Review Archive, May 28, 1997, *http://www.aml-online.org/Reviews/Review.aspx?id=3088* (accessed April 12, 2012).

8   Eric D. Snider: "Snide Remarks: Theater Review: Burdens of Earth," General Merriment, February 11, 2001, *http://www.ericdsnider.com/theater/burdens-of-earth/* (accessed April 13, 2012).

my faith. Flannery O'Connor said that her definition of Catholic art was the Catholic mind working on any subject. . . . That is a definition that I apply to Mormon poetry—a Mormon mind working on any subject.

Howe's poetic and thoughtful skill as a playwright has also served her well in her other plays, *A Dream for Katy: A Celebration of Mormon Women,* as well as the theatrical adaptation of a book of poetry she edited: *Discoveries: Two Centuries of Poems by Mormon Women.* It is this very mix of dream language and evocative emotion characteristic of all true poets that make her a valuable crossover into the Mormon theatre community.

About *Burdens of Earth*

Burdens of Earth was first presented in Brigham Young University's Pardoe Theatre on May 28, 1987, with the following cast:

CAST

Joseph Smith: Robert Nelson
Hyrum Smith / Phineas Hobart: Kyle Sumpter
Caleb Baldwin / Hansen Jacobs: Reed McColm
Alexander McRae / Oliver Cowdery: Alex Starr
Lyman Wight / Major Sam Burris: Daniel Hess

CREW

Director: Robert Nelson

PROGRAM NOTE

Drawn from Leonard J. Arrington, "Church Leader in Liberty Jail," *BYU Studies*, Autumn 1972, 20–22.

The Mormon people began locating in Missouri in 1831. Joseph Smith, the prophet and leader of the Church, received a revelation in July of that year designating Jackson County, Missouri, as the land "appointed and consecrated for the gathering of the Saints, . . . the land of promise . . . the place for the city of Zion." As Mormons began buying land there, however, they quickly encountered persecution from those who had already settled in the area.

The Mormons were mostly Easterners who disapproved of slavery. They often visited the Indians in the area, convinced of an obligation to bring them the gospel. Most of the old settlers, on the other hand, were from the South. They feared that the Mormons would incite their slaves to revolt and cause Indian uprisings. Furthermore, the Missourians viewed the Mormons as fanatics, mistrusting their ideas of gathering to build a religious society, a "Zion." Rather than lose financial and political control to the Mormon people, who usually acted as a group, the Missourians launched demands that the Saints relocate, demands backed up with mobs and vigilante action. In February 1833, the Saints were pushed out of Jackson County into neighboring Clay County, whose initially hospitable residents, within a year also urged the Mormons to move on. A county in northern Missouri, created especially for the Mormons, only delayed the inevitable clash. In 1838, Governor Lilburn W. Boggs, issued an "Order of Extermination": "The Mormons must be treated as enemies and must be exterminated or driven from the state, if necessary for the public good."

At that time, all of the Mormons' firearms were taken, their settlements were seized, and their leaders were captured, betrayed by one of their own men. General Samuel Lucas of the state militia held an overnight courtmartial, convicting Joseph Smith and other leaders of treason. General Lucas ordered General Alexander Doniphan to shoot them at dawn. Doniphan, upon receiving the order, wrote back to Lucas: "It is cold-blooded murder. I will not obey your order. My brigade will march for Liberty tomorrow morning at 8 o'clock; and if you execute these men, I will hold you responsible before an earthly tribunal, so help me God." His courageous response saved their lives.

Then the leaders were imprisoned, and the rest of the Mormons had to flee from the state. Joseph Smith, his brother Hyrum, Lyman Wight, Caleb Baldwin, and Alexander McRae were moved to Liberty Jail, where they remained until April 1839. During this time Joseph was deeply troubled by the Saints' loss of Zion, by the apostasy of Oliver Cowdery (who had been with Joseph since he began translating the Book of Mormon and had served as assistant president of the Church) and other early leaders, and by the suffering of the Saints. As he fought off despair and took the trials he was facing to the Lord, he received some of the most meaningful scripture in the Mormon Church today:

> And if thou shouldst be cast into the pit, or into the hands of murderers, and the sentence of death passed upon thee; if thou be cast into the deep; if the billowing surge conspire against thee; if fierce winds . . . combine to hedge up the way; and above all, if the very jaws of hell shall gape open the mouth wide after thee, know thou, my son, that all these things shall give thee experience and shall be for thy good. The Son of Man hath descended below them all; art thou greater than he? (D&C 122:7–8).

With few visitors and with drab and depressing surroundings, the principal escape for Joseph and his companions during their confinement was into their own minds and hearts.

CHARACTERS

JOSEPH SMITH

HYRUM SMITH / PHINEAS HOBART

CALEB BALDWIN / HANSON JACOBS

ALEXANDER MCRAE / OLIVER COWDERY

LYMAN WIGHT / MAJOR SAM BURRIS

As indicated, four actors play two roles, while Joseph Smith always remains Joseph Smith.

SET

TIME: March 1839. Winter has not broken. Night.

PLACE: Liberty, Missouri.

SET: Liberty Jail. Obviously a place of confinement with a feeling of confinement. The set may be similar to the LDS Church's restoration of the historical Liberty Jail in Liberty, Missouri. The jail has two levels—a dungeon and an upper floor. The levels may be juxtaposed rather than set directly on top of each other, but one must be above and the other below. The jail should occupy most of the stage—from the back to near the front. There is an area in front of the dungeon, however, where scenes that occur in Joseph's mind can be played on the lower level. On the upper level, the back wall and side walls of the jail are visible. The side walls are cut away diagonally with the high part toward the back of the stage, to show the strength and construction of the jail: hewn logs one foot thick on the inside, two feet of loose rocks in the middle, and one foot of mortared stone on the outside. The small windows (two feet wide by one foot high), set deep in side walls in the upper room, are grated with heavy iron bars. The same windows are in the lower room, but they are smaller, two feet by six inches. Or the set may be designed so that the barred windows are assumed to be downstage center, so that when a character looks out the window, he is looking directly at the audience. In the upper room, the furniture consists of one small, unpainted chair and one similar table. In the lower room are one hewn wooden bench against the middle of the wall, dirty straw ticks (several scattered about the floor and one leaning against the back wall behind the bench), and a few tattered blankets. A battered tin candleholder sits on the floor, and a lantern hangs on the back wall. Stretched between two of the walls, Lyman will put up a blanket partition (during Act One) behind which the prisoners, at times, go to sleep; this is their exit from the stage when they are not in the scene in progress. Upstage right, in the floor of the upper room, there is a hole and a ladder descending to the lower room. There is no curtain. The set is visible to the audience as they enter and find their seats.

Act One

Complete blackout. The light comes up from a lantern hanging on a nail in the center of the back wall of the dungeon. The light is dim at first and intensifies as it spreads outward, revealing each of the characters one by one. First, JOSEPH SMITH, *who is seated on a bench beneath the lantern, staring at nothing. He is thirty-three years old, about six feet tall, with light brown hair, blue eyes, a rather thin face, a high sloping forehead, and a protruding nose. When he stands, he walks with a slight limp. He is dressed in the fashionable black pants, vest, and ruffled shirt of the 1830s. The clothes are somewhat worn after five months of use in prison but are not excessively dirty; clean clothes are brought in to the prisoners every week. Lying in front of Joseph, about center stage, on a dirty straw tick is* HYRUM SMITH, *who resembles Joseph but is a little older, larger, and darker. Hyrum has propped himself on one elbow and begins singing a tune—"This Earth Was Once a Garden Place"—very slowly and sadly, leaving about five seconds of silence between each phrase. Sitting on the floor with his back against the left wall is* CALEB BALDWIN, *who is reading the Book of Mormon. He is older than the others, in his late forties, and dressed as a farmer. His foremost characteristics are his honesty and his loyalty to Joseph Smith. He is also talkative, even though he has lost his hearing in one ear. He sometimes turns his head or cups his hand around his good ear so he can hear. The other two characters,* ALEXANDER MCRAE *and* LYMAN WIGHT, *are lying on dirty straw ticks spread near the right wall. They are sharing one thin, worn blanket and trying to go to sleep for the night. Alexander is thirty-one. A tailor, he is well-dressed in the pants of a suit and a formal shirt of the period. He may speak with a Scottish accent. Lyman is fierce, intense, something of a fanatic, and often angry, especially now as he is trying to get to sleep. His clothing suggests his military leadership—a large belt, high boots, perhaps—but otherwise is much like the others. For as long as it takes Hyrum to sing one verse of the song, there is little action. It is very cold, and all the prisoners huddle under whatever protection they can find, taking up as little space as possible in an effort to keep warm. The sense of time—unrelieved, oppressive—weighs on Joseph, who is oblivious to the others. The light begins from the lantern, spreads down to include Joseph.*

HYRUM. *(Singing)* This earth was once a garden place . . . *(Light spreads to include* HYRUM.*)* . . . With all her glories common . . .

Light spreads to include others. CALEB *turns a page of his book.* ALEXANDER *turns over and pulls the blanket off* LYMAN. LYMAN *sits up, grabs the blanket back and pulls it off* ALEXANDER, *who reaches his arm out and retrieves his share as* LYMAN *lies down.*

HYRUM. *(Continuing his song)* . . . And men did live a holy race . . . And worship Jesus face to face . . . In Adam Ondi Ahman.

LYMAN. Some of us is trying to sleep, Hyrum.

CALEB. The Lord got Alma out. Right here. It says the power of God was upon Alma, and he got out.

LYMAN. Anyhow, we're never going back to Di Ahman.

ALEXANDER. Lyman, you sleeping or you talking to Hyrum?

LYMAN. Anyone who hogs the whole blanket every night's got no cause to scold.

HYRUM. It doesn't make it any better in here when you argue. Now I'm sorry I bothered you, and I'll be still.

LYMAN. If Alexander would just quiet down, we could get some rest.

CALEB. Look here, boys. I want to talk about this. Says right here that Alma and Amulek was in prison, and the Lord gave them power, and the prison fell down on their enemies and they got out.

The next three lines are spoken simultaneously.

HYRUM. Not now, Caleb.

ALEXANDER. It's too late for that.

LYMAN. Go to sleep, will you?

CALEB. *(Continuing)* Alma was the prophet. *(The others will not answer. They just turn over and act as though they're going to sleep.)* Joseph?

LYMAN. Leave him alone, Caleb.

CALEB. Brother Joseph?

JOSEPH. *(Aroused from his thoughts)* Oh. Yes, Caleb?

CALEB. You recall where Alma and Amulek was in prison and they'd suffered for a long time?

JOSEPH. Yes, Caleb. I do.

CALEB. And one day their enemies come to mock them—

JOSEPH. Yes.

CALEB. And Alma cried to the Lord, *(Reading)* "How long shall we suffer these great afflictions, O Lord? O Lord give us strength unto deliverance." And, Brother Joseph, the Lord heard them. The power of God came upon them and they burst their bands and they was loosed. The prison walls fell down.

JOSEPH. That's what happened all right.

CALEB. Because Alma was a prophet.

JOSEPH. Yes, a prophet.

CALEB. Brother Joseph, you're a prophet.

JOSEPH. Yes, I am.

CALEB. Then what are we still doin' in this jail?

JOSEPH. I—I suppose we're learning, Caleb. I'm learning. To have faith . . . and patience.

CALEB. There's no one has more faith than you.

JOSEPH. Now that they've finally gone up there, I think I'll go up and take a look at the night. Do you mind if I take the lantern, Caleb?

CALEB. Go ahead, I've finished my reading. Brother Joseph, don't you think if you pray for us, the Lord will deliver us, like he did Alma?

JOSEPH. Well, I will, Caleb. I have been.

> JOSEPH *takes the lantern, opens the trap door and climbs up the ladder into the upper room. The light goes with* JOSEPH. *He sets the lantern on the table, goes to the window.* HYRUM *follows* JOSEPH *up the ladder.*

HYRUM. Joseph?

JOSEPH. Yes?

HYRUM. Like a little company?

JOSEPH. No.

HYRUM. Well, then I won't stay long. Why do you come up here alone?

JOSEPH. So I can look out.

HYRUM. What do you look at?

JOSEPH. Different things. All that snow.

HYRUM. *(Peering through the bars)* Not much out there that interests me.

JOSEPH. Snow changes things. The ruts in the road are smoothed up and even, and the mud is gone, and the earth is cold and buried. And there are no tracks, no footprints, nothing else to see.

HYRUM. What is the matter?

JOSEPH. Nothing.

HYRUM. What are you thinking about?

JOSEPH. Well, if you really want to know, beetles.

HYRUM. Of course. Beetles.

JOSEPH. Do they die in the winter or do they hibernate like bears and groundhogs?

HYRUM. You know, sometimes you can be very strange.

JOSEPH. When we were boys, one day I found a beetle crawling up the rock pile behind our field. I had never seen such a beetle. So black, it was almost purple in the sun, over three inches long, and fat. Near the top of the rock pile there was a crevice too narrow for your hand, and it was crawling there, but I took a stick and blocked its path. It stopped for a moment, confused, and then turned aside, trying to get around the stick. But no matter how it turned, I kept blocking its path.

HYRUM. I don't like beetles.

JOSEPH. Finally it stopped trying to get around the stick. It bumped up against it, as if it were testing it with its head, and then it climbed up onto it to try and get over.

HYRUM. And I don't like to talk about them.

JOSEPH. So I picked up the stick. I kept the beetle crawling up and around that stick again and again. When it would reach the top, I'd turn the stick upside down. It crawled on and on and never really got anywhere. But when I finally tired and let it down, it wouldn't climb back onto the rocks. I finally had to hit the stick against a rock to jar it loose. The beetle fell, and I lost it. I hope I didn't kill it. *(Short pause.)* I wonder if they hibernate . . .

HYRUM. I don't want to talk about beetles—

JOSEPH. . . . or if the snow kills them.

HYRUM. —I want to talk about you.

JOSEPH. I am talking about me. Listen, can't you?

HYRUM. What is wrong?

JOSEPH. You know what's wrong. They've driven the Saints from this state. They tried to exterminate them, like insects. Those who didn't die from the cold or the journey have spent the winter camping in snow, surviving on nothing but air and a little parched corn. And I rot here, like a frozen potato, of no use to them or to anyone.

HYRUM. The Lord will take care of them.

JOSEPH. How can you think that now?

HYRUM. What are you saying?

JOSEPH. I don't know what to do, Hyrum. I don't know how to help them.

HYRUM. The Lord will let you know.

JOSEPH. Not this time. I try with all my soul to understand where we should go now, what we should do, and I think I have something, and then I pray, and it's as if my prayers echo off the walls. As if I'm only speaking to myself.

HYRUM. The Lord wouldn't abandon us here.

JOSEPH. What's wrong? Is it me? Have I failed in some way?

HYRUM. You have given everything. Your life. I don't see how you can do more than that.

JOSEPH. When I lost the manuscript of the Book of Mormon and the plates were taken from me, at least I understood my sin and could repent. But I don't know what sin is in me, what evil could have brought us here.

HYRUM. It is not you.

JOSEPH. Then why has the Lord left us in this jail? Why so much misery for the Saints? Misery and Missouri. For us, there hasn't been much difference between the two.

HYRUM. Can't you forget it for tonight? You need to rest. For one night, Joseph, think of yourself.

JOSEPH. It seems too much that I asked the Saints to come here.

HYRUM. You have been living in hell. Look at this jail.

JOSEPH. What about it?

HYRUM. Hold onto these bars.

JOSEPH. They're too cold.

HYRUM. Can you feel your toes?

JOSEPH. No. Can you? (HYRUM *shakes his head.*) Well, we're not walking anywhere.

HYRUM. Joseph, the cold has gotten inside you. Don't you hate it?

JOSEPH. It's not important.

HYRUM. Freezing is important. We can't just let ourselves freeze. You never stop being the prophet to be Joseph anymore. Joseph my brother would know when he was freezing.

JOSEPH. There's got to be something I don't understand. But I don't know what it is, and I don't know how to find out.

HYRUM *goes to the trap door and calls below.*

HYRUM. Caleb, come up here.

JOSEPH. What are you doing?

HYRUM. You're stewing over what's past, when there's nothing you can do about it. So I'm going to help you forget it. There's no better talker than Caleb, and he can talk this nonsense out of you. Caleb! Come up here, will you? Oh, he can't hear me.

HYRUM *goes to the ladder and begins to descend.*

JOSEPH. Hyrum, you're not listening to me.

HYRUM. I'm your brother. I don't have to.

HYRUM, *now in the lower level of the jail, goes to* CALEB *and shakes him.*

CALEB. Huh? Hyrum? What's the trouble?

HYRUM. Brother Joseph can't sleep, and I was wondering if you'd entertain him for a while.

CALEB. I ain't much at entertaining, but I guess we can sit and talk a spell.

HYRUM. That's what I had in mind. Caleb, I'm afraid Brother Joseph is a bit low tonight. Till he gets tired, now, keep his mind occupied, will you?

CALEB. Why, sure, Hyrum.

CALEB begins to climb the ladder to the upper level.

HYRUM. My bones are cold. I'm freezing. So I'm going to get under a blanket and see if I can get some sleep.

CALEB. Go right ahead. I'm happy to visit with Joseph.

But when CALEB gets up with JOSEPH, he finds he has nothing to say.

CALEB. *(To JOSEPH)* Well, now . . . *(Pause)* Cold tonight, ain't it?

JOSEPH. Guess so.

CALEB. Worse'n last night.

JOSEPH. Maybe.

CALEB. Seems like this winter won't never break.

JOSEPH. Caleb, you don't have to sit with me. You can go on back to bed.

CALEB. Oh, no, Joseph, I'm glad to. Hyrum says you're feeling poorly.

JOSEPH. I'm just thoughtful.

CALEB. Anything I can do for you?

JOSEPH. I was thinking about some of the Saints. You knew Hanson Jacobs, didn't you?

CALEB. This here coat I'm wearing was Hanson's own. Took it off his own back and threw it to me just as they was driving us away. You'd never think that an educated storekeeper like that would take up with an old farmer. But since we first met, we've been close as brothers.

JOSEPH. He was a farmer, too. Before he joined the Church.

CALEB. You're right. Yes, he was.

JOSEPH. I remember when he came to Kirtland. Just three years ago, wasn't it? Summer of '36.

CALEB. Never was a man prouder to meet you than Hanson Jacobs.

JOSEPH. And I sent him right on to Missouri.

The action of the play shifts to JOSEPH's mind. Each time that this happens in the play, the light changes, intensifies. CALEB becomes HANSON JACOBS. When he turns back around toward the prophet, his sleepy, unsure demeanor and his disheveled appearance are gone. He is stronger, more forceful. Has the bearing of a successful Eastern farmer.

CALEB/HANSON. Excuse me, sir. Are you Joseph Smith?

JOSEPH. What? Caleb?

HANSON. No, sir. I'm Hanson Jacobs. Please excuse me. I thought you were the prophet.

> HANSON *turns away, then pauses as if he doesn't know what to do now.* JOSEPH *seems to realize that he is remembering this. He turns to* HANSON, *calls after him.*

JOSEPH. No, you had me right. I am Joseph Smith. Are you new here?

HANSON. Just arrived in Kirtland today.

JOSEPH. Well, let me welcome you. Is there anything you need? Anything I can do for you?

HANSON. I guess I just wanted to meet the man who could get me to leave my farm and move into strange country.

JOSEPH. Then you must be one of the Saints.

HANSON. I'm no saint, sir. I joined this church, but I'm as stubborn as I ever was. You'll never make a saint out of me.

JOSEPH. If you've been baptized, we already have. This is the Church of the Latter-day Saints. And you're not the only stubborn one in it—most of us are. May be one of our best qualities.

HANSON. Whatever you say. Now that I've got into this outfit, I might as well go whole-hog. I didn't want to be a Mormonite, and now I am one. I don't particularly want to be a saint, either, but if you tell me I am, then I guess I am.

JOSEPH. Well, in time it'll all come natural. I didn't like it myself at first. Wanted a farm. Finding out that the Lord had other plans for me took some getting used to.

HANSON. You didn't want to be a prophet?

JOSEPH. Why would a fourteen-year-old boy want to be a prophet? I just wanted to belong to the Lord's church.

HANSON. Well, I'll be . . . And look at where you are now.

JOSEPH. Yup. I'm a Mormonite, too. You won't mind after a while. If you're stubborn enough, you may even come to like it—or at least not let it rile you. What brought you to the Church, anyway?

HANSON. My wife, Lucinda. She heard some of your missionaries preach one day on a street corner in our town. Of course my wife had to be the only one who would listen. She even spent some of the money we'd been saving for a new plowshare on a Book of Mormon. What I thought when my wife brought me a book and what I needed was a plow! And it wasn't even a good book like an almanac or cyclopedia. About some strange new religion. And then she expected me to read it! I was a staunch Presbyterian, and my father and grandfather before me. And there was my wife, carrying this Book of Mormon to Sunday services, flaunting it at me, telling me that it was of God. Our marriage had been good. We were happier than most. I watched us go from happiness to bitterness.

JOSEPH. You must love your wife very much.

HANSON. I do, but I try not to get carried away about it. I decided that we could try a compromise on the matter. I'd listen to what she wanted and then she'd do what I wanted.

JOSEPH. Did it work out that way?

HANSON. Not exactly. She appealed to my reason. If there's one thing I pride myself on, it's that I'm a reasonable man. She told me to read the book, and compare it to the Bible, and pray. So I figured, what could be wrong with that? I could study your Mormon book until I had it pinned down, and then I would show my wife what a farce it was.

JOSEPH. There are many with us who have tried that.

HANSON. I didn't come easy. I checked everything in the whole book against the Bible for any passage to disprove it. Found quite a few. But the more I read, the more I doubted my own efforts, and finally I had to admit to myself that your Book of Mormon was of God.

JOSEPH. Sir, I didn't write it. Couldn't have. I don't know that much. It was a gift from God that let me translate it. Your wife—Lucinda, is it?—must have been very pleased with you.

HANSON. You think I told her that she'd won out? No, sir. I didn't want my life to change. So I put the book away from me and tried to go on as if nothing had happened.

JOSEPH. And what did Lucinda do about that?

HANSON. Nothing. Absolutely nothing, and that's what finally got me. After she convinced me to read the damn book, she didn't say another word about it. When I wouldn't read it any more, she knew I knew it was from God. I kept waiting for her to jump on me, and she never mentioned it again. Sort of let me stew in my own juice, you might say. Six months, a year went by. Finally I couldn't stand the suspense. It made me madder than hell—oh, don't mind me, I'm still working on my swearing. One day last September during apple season, I thought about it all day in the orchard. By night I was spittin' mad, and I marched into the house for supper, pounded my fist on the table so's I broke one of our best plates, and said, "I've made a decision for this family. We're joining up with the Mormons, and I don't want to hear one word of back talk!" Lucinda was at the stove frying potatoes. She didn't say a thing. Just turned around slow and started crying. That's how I come to be here today.

JOSEPH. What took you so long to get here?

HANSON. Lucinda was with child. Both of us are getting on in years, you see, and we've lost five children at birth. So we didn't dare move until the baby was born and growing up healthy.

JOSEPH. And is your baby healthy?

HANSON. Like a moose. He's about as ornery as his father, to boot. This time, we were blessed. So now we're going to buy some land and raise him here with you folks. Guess if I can stand being a Mormonite, he can, too.

JOSEPH. If you want to settle for good then you don't want to stay here. You want to go to Missouri.

HANSON. When we've tromped the whole country to get to you? No, Brother Joseph. Long as the Church is here and you are here, I think this is where we'll want to stay.

JOSEPH. I am not the Church. I am only one person in it.

HANSON. But you are the prophet.

JOSEPH. Yes, I am. And I'm telling you to move on to Missouri. That is the center place of Zion.

HANSON. Why not here? What's wrong with Ohio?

JOSEPH. It is not the right place. There are blessings and promises awaiting us in Missouri. That is where we will gather, and where we will stay.

HANSON. Are you going to Missouri?

JOSEPH. Not now, but soon.

HANSON. I've just come four hundred miles with a wife and child to get to you, and you're telling me to keep traveling twice that far.

JOSEPH. That's right.

HANSON. And you are staying here.

JOSEPH. I am.

HANSON. That is too much to require.

JOSEPH. I know it is. And I'm sorry. But I have to ask it of you. Only this once.

HANSON. Well what if I won't go?

JOSEPH. You can do what you want. I just advise you to go to Missouri.

HANSON. Now don't go telling me I can do what I want, damn it. I can't do what I want any more. You're a prophet of God, and you have spoken. If I don't go, I'm sure to be sorry.

JOSEPH. Brother Hanson, try to understand me. I know what this will cost you and your family. But we need people in Missouri, and I am responsible to the Lord. You will be blessed if you go.

HANSON. I don't suppose you'd like to be the one to tell my wife.

JOSEPH. Uh... No. No, I wouldn't.

HANSON. Then damn it, I guess I will.

> HANSON *turns to leave and holds his position as* JOSEPH *calls him.*

JOSEPH. Hanson. (HANSON *turns around again.*) By joining the Church, what have you lost?

HANSON. I don't want to tell you that.

JOSEPH. Please, Hanson. I need to know.

HANSON. My heritage. My past. My father no longer owns me. He wouldn't accept my son into his house when he was born.

JOSEPH. Is it too much to lose?

HANSON. I don't know. It may be.

JOSEPH. Why did you give it up?

HANSON. Because it's true, isn't it? The Book of Mormon did come to you from God?

JOSEPH. Yes. It's true. Do you hate me for this?

HANSON. No. I don't hate you. But I guess I blame you.

JOSEPH. Why?

HANSON. For forcing me to choose. For giving me this knowledge that seems it will bring suffering no matter what I do with it. I blame you for that.

JOSEPH. In time, you may hate me.

HANSON. I know. I will either hate you or revere you.

> HANSON *turns away. Below,* LYMAN *begins snoring loudly. The lights in the upper level return to normal.* CALEB *resumes his identity and begins to descend the ladder.*

HYRUM. Alexander? You asleep?

ALEXANDER. With that roaring going on?

HYRUM. Wake him up, will you?

ALEXANDER. You wake him up, Hyrum.

HYRUM. Get Caleb. He'll do it.

ALEXANDER. You're closer to the ladder. You get him.

HYRUM. (*Getting up*) You're not one to put yourself out, are you, Alexander? (CALEB *has come down into the dungeon by this time.*) Caleb, you're the only one who can get Lyman to stop snoring. Will you shut him up?

CALEB. Of course, Hyrum. Nothing to it. Just turn him over on his side.

> CALEB *takes* LYMAN *by the arm and flips him over onto his side.* LYMAN *snorts and the snoring stops, but he ends up with his arm over* ALEXANDER. ALEXANDER, *awakened, has to extricate himself from* CALEB *and the*

blanket. Meanwhile HYRUM *has climbed to the upper level.*

HYRUM. Well. Takes care of that. You have a good visit with Caleb?

JOSEPH. Yes.

HYRUM. What did you talk about?

JOSEPH. Oh . . . uh . . . About how cold it is.

HYRUM. And then what?

JOSEPH. Well . . . just what we always talk about.

HYRUM. You didn't listen to him, did you?

JOSEPH. Hyrum, what do you think is the cost when someone has to give up his past for the gospel?

HYRUM. I don't know. We've all done it, haven't we?

JOSEPH. The gospel is our past, Hyrum, but for most, it's a choice—often a heartbreaking choice.

HYRUM. This is just what you shouldn't be doing, Joseph. You can't—

JOSEPH. Did you know that when Hanson Jacobs joined the Church, his father disowned him? He and his wife had to stay in their home for months, disgraced and abandoned by their family and friends. They were alone when their baby was born. And when they finally came to Ohio to be with the Saints, I asked him to bring his family here.

HYRUM. But he came. Willingly.

JOSEPH. Hanson would never say this, Hyrum, but in some way he must blame me for what he has lost. I think they need someone to blame, in that way. And if they need to lean on me, I will let them.

HYRUM. They should stand for themselves.

JOSEPH. No, Hyrum. We depend on each other. I lean, too.

HYRUM. You?

JOSEPH. I'm leaning on you right now. I depend on Mother and Father, on Emma. I couldn't go on without the strength of all the people who love me in spite of my being a prophet.

HYRUM. But we don't blame you for what's gone wrong. It's people like Oliver who blame you.

JOSEPH. Oliver. I still can't believe he could desert me and leave the Saints.

HYRUM. You were so much alike for so long.

JOSEPH. I loved him like I love you. And now we come as close to hating each other as two people can come. Hyrum, sometimes I think it's my fault that he's gone.

HYRUM. Joseph, that doesn't make any sense.

JOSEPH. I wonder if that's why the Lord won't help me.

> ALEXANDER *climbs into the upper level of the jail as* JOSEPH *finishes this remark.* HYRUM *and* JOSEPH *fall silent, as this isn't a conversation that they want* ALEXANDER *to hear.*

ALEXANDER. Well, now. (JOSEPH *and* HYRUM *look at him, but don't say anything in response.*) Lyman's snoring woke me up. I can't sleep. Do you think it's late enough to start digging now? While you're up here, I might as well get busy.

JOSEPH. Caleb was just up here, Alexander. We'd better wait long enough to be sure that he's asleep.

ALEXANDER. Then do you mind if I sit up here with you and talk a bit?

> JOSEPH *and* HYRUM *speak the next two lines simultaneously.*

JOSEPH. Alexander, I need some time to think.

HYRUM. No, Alexander, not at all.

> JOSEPH *and* HYRUM *stop and look at each other.*

HYRUM. No, Alexander, Brother Joseph here was just telling me that he'd like someone to talk to for a spell, and I can hardly keep my eyes open. So if you don't mind, you just have yourselves a visit and I'll go on down to bed.

ALEXANDER. Really, Joseph? I don't mean to be a bother to you.

JOSEPH. Then, Alexander—

HYRUM. There's nothing he'd like more. He's feeling a little low tonight. Some good conversation is just what he needs. And I'll wish you both good night.

> HYRUM *descends to the lower level.*

ALEXANDER. Brother Joseph, I can tell that you want to be alone, so I'll go on down.

JOSEPH. I've been thinking about Oliver. How did we lose him, Alexander?

ALEXANDER. If you ask me, he's a rascal and good riddance.

JOSEPH. Yes, well, I hope you're right.

ALEXANDER. Brother Joseph, I can't sleep. So later, when you've thought things over, will you call me? It might help you to talk a spell.

JOSEPH. Of course, Alexander.

ALEXANDER. You're sure it's too early to start digging? It would give me something to do.

JOSEPH. Just be sure that Caleb's asleep. You know what will happen if he finds out what we're doing.

> ALEXANDER *descends the ladder, to be scolded by* HYRUM.

HYRUM. Alexander, what are you doing? Get back up there and talk to him.

ALEXANDER. Brother Joseph says he wants to be left alone, and if he says he wants to be left alone, I'm going to leave him alone.

HYRUM. No, Alexander, not tonight. He's got a troubled spirit about him.

ALEXANDER. I didn't notice it. And if you're so concerned, why don't you go up there yourself?

HYRUM. All right, I will. (HYRUM *ascends to the upper level.*) Joseph, maybe you can get Alexander to leave you alone up here, but not me. I'm going to sit here, and we're going to talk about something pleasant whether you like it or not.

JOSEPH. Why have I lost Oliver? What did I do?

HYRUM. You didn't lose him. He betrayed you—all of us.

JOSEPH. He was sent to me. When I first learned the work God had for me to do, I dreamed about being the size of a bug so that I could disappear under a rock or a leaf. To represent Deity to the earth—me, a farm boy from a backwoods village nobody ever heard of. Emma and I were so alone. I prayed again and again for somebody—some other human being—who would share the responsibility with us. And then Oliver came.

> ALEXANDER *becomes* OLIVER *in* JOSEPH's *mind.* JOSEPH *hears* ALEXANDER *as* OLIVER *from below.*

ALEXANDER/OLIVER. Pardon me, ma'am. I'm looking for a Mr. Joseph Smith. Does he happen to be here?

HYRUM. Oh, no, Joseph. We're not going to talk about Oliver. We're going to talk about . . . about . . . wrestling.

JOSEPH. I didn't even have to search him out.

OLIVER. *(Below)* I've been boarding with his family. This is where they sent me to find him.

JOSEPH. The Lord sent him to find me.

HYRUM. How about it, Joseph? Do you think you can still throw me?

JOSEPH. Hyrum, I guess if you're not going to let me alone, I'd rather talk to Alexander.

HYRUM. Now that's what I like to hear. Remember, this is for your own good.

> HYRUM *once more descends the ladder, and then* JOSEPH *calls down to* ALEXANDER, *who has become* OLIVER *to him. The lighting changes again as* JOSEPH *remembers.*

OLIVER. It is most important that I find him.

JOSEPH. I'm up here. Won't you please come up?

> OLIVER, *formerly* ALEXANDER, *climbs through the hole to the upper level.*

He is wearing the same clothes, but with the addition of a hat. He has tied the scarf at his neck and carries a bundle of books. He looks tired, as if he has just completed a long journey.

OLIVER. I am Oliver Cowdery, sir, and you are—

JOSEPH. Joseph Smith.

OLIVER. I know. You look like your brothers. Mostly like Hyrum, I think.

JOSEPH. Hyrum?

OLIVER. A bit more handsome, I'd say, but very much like him. Well, Mr. Smith, I hardly know how to begin.

JOSEPH. Then let me begin for you. Oliver Cowdery, I knew you were coming.

OLIVER. You did?

JOSEPH. I prayed you here. There is much work to be done, and I need your help.

OLIVER. I prefer to think that coming was my own idea.

JOSEPH. Of course. If it is important to you.

OLIVER. Let me explain. I was a schoolteacher in Manchester, and I boarded with your family for a time.

JOSEPH. I hope they were good to you.

OLIVER. Very good, but very secretive, too. Several times I overheard talk of a golden book and a brother named Joseph, but when I asked, I was always diverted to another subject. Very effectively, too. "Yes, we do have a brother named Joseph, and wouldn't I please have some more potatoes and how was Sophronia doing with her arithmetic?"

JOSEPH. They have learned not to talk. People who have heard my story—sometimes they hate me and my family for it.

OLIVER. I hope I don't ever have to see that.

JOSEPH. If you befriend me, you will.

OLIVER. Perhaps you have too little faith in the goodness of others.

JOSEPH. I wish that were true.

OLIVER. Your family would tell me nothing for weeks. What I learned of you, I learned by eavesdropping—I know that is hardly honorable, but what else could I do? And gradually, they came to trust me a little. Finally, I confronted your father, and he told me the story—the angel, the golden plates. Something burned within me as I listened.

JOSEPH. Yes. That is why I went to the grove to pray.

OLIVER. I became consumed with a desire to help you. I want to write that book. I want to help translate it.

JOSEPH. Then you believe me? Believe this work is of God?

OLIVER. Of course it is. And some day you and I will be great in the sight of all people. It is the greatest work in the world.

JOSEPH. Yes, Mr. Cowdery, it is great. When the spirit of the Lord is with you and you learn something that has been hidden for centuries, you know that it is great.

OLIVER. That's what I am here for.

JOSEPH. You need to know this, too. Often it is drudgery, and sometimes it can be very much like hell.

OLIVER. I am not afraid of work.

JOSEPH. It's more than work. You may have to face lies, prejudice, the hatred of good people who cannot understand what you are doing. I'm afraid that someday you may even see yourself in jail.

OLIVER. You exaggerate to discourage me.

JOSEPH. Don't tell me I don't know what I have lived with for seven years. If you think this is going to be easy, you can't help.

OLIVER. All right. I understand. But I feel things differently than you. Maybe I will not suffer so much.

JOSEPH. Sir, you will suffer. You may even break under your pain. How can I make you see?

OLIVER. We disagree on this point. Can't we just disagree?

JOSEPH. No.

OLIVER. Why not?

JOSEPH. Because some day when I need you, you will blame me for not telling you and have your excuse to leave me.

OLIVER. Listen to me, sir. I have made my own decision to come—and not because you prayed me here. Knowing all that you have said, I choose to stay and help, if you want me to. And even if what you say about persecution is right, you can trust one thing. No matter what comes, Joseph Smith, I will be loyal to you.

JOSEPH. Oliver, Oliver. That's not true. You have betrayed and deserted me. Why? What happened to you?

OLIVER. Me? What about you? You're so blind you don't even know—

OLIVER, *too upset to continue, turns away.*

JOSEPH. Blind? What do you mean, Oliver?

JOSEPH *follows* OLIVER *and grabs him by the arm. The lights return to normal;* JOSEPH *has seized* ALEXANDER *rather than* OLIVER.

ALEXANDER. Brother Joseph, what are you doing? I'm Alexander, not Oliver.

JOSEPH. Sorry, Alexander. I don't know what I was thinking. Please forgive me.

ALEXANDER. Where are you? You haven't heard a word I've said in the last half hour.

JOSEPH. He said I was blind. Am I?

ALEXANDER. Who said you were blind?

JOSEPH. Oliver Cowdery.

ALEXANDER. Oliver Cowdery is a snake and a liar, and it doesn't matter what he says. You know that, Joseph.

> LYMAN's *snoring begins again.* HYRUM *and* ALEXANDER *groan;* CALEB *has gone to sleep with his good ear under his arm and isn't disturbed.*

ALEXANDER. Not again! I was just getting tired enough to sleep.

HYRUM. Caleb? Caleb? Well, at least now we know he's asleep. If that doesn't wake him up, nothing will. (HYRUM *gets up and goes to try to move* LYMAN.) Come on, you old horse, roll over.

LYMAN. *(Groggy)* Huh? Look out, boys, it's a mobber. You'll learn to come sneaking in here, you Missouri scum. (LYMAN *wrestles* HYRUM *down, then hits him in the jaw.* HYRUM *falls to the floor, and* LYMAN *throws the blanket he has been sleeping under over the fallen form.)* There, you low-down mobocracy mobber! How do you like it when we get a chance to defend ourselves? Huh? (ALEXANDER *hurries into the dungeon.* JOSEPH *grabs the lantern from the wall and also descends the ladder, bringing the light back into the dungeon. It reveals* LYMAN *kneeling over* HYRUM, *whom he has encased in the blanket.* CALEB *is sitting on his mat, trying to wake up.)* Brother Joseph, I got him. No telling what he might have done otherwise. Say, where's Hyrum?

JOSEPH. Under the blanket.

LYMAN. Huh? Hyrum? Now what were you doing, attacking me like that? You lost your mind?

HYRUM. You were snoring again. I was trying to turn you over.

LYMAN. *(Grouchy)* You got no call to disturb someone out of a sound sleep when it's night time and I need my rest so as to be ready for later, if you know what I mean. Now look at what I'm doing here.

> LYMAN *takes a blanket from the floor and throws it over a wire that is hung diagonally between two walls of the dungeon.*

HYRUM. None of us can sleep when you snore.

LYMAN. Well, I can't sleep with you talking and carrying on. There. When I go behind here to sleep, I better not be disturbed. And I'm just telling the rest of you that if you want to be left alone from the bothering of such as Hyrum, you better sleep back here too.

CALEB. Fine, Lyman. I'd like a little quiet myself. *(To the others)* If he snores again, I'll turn him over.

LYMAN. Alexander?

ALEXANDER *shrugs and follows the other two, who pick up straw ticks and go behind the blanket. This partition can serve as actors' exit from the stage when they are not in the scene in progress.*

HYRUM. Well, I'm not going to be sleepy for a while. I might as well go up where I won't disturb you.

JOSEPH. I'll come up with you.

They climb back to the upper level.

HYRUM. You sure you're not ready to get some sleep? We've got a long night's work ahead of us.

JOSEPH. Oliver said I was blind.

HYRUM. You haven't seen Oliver for months. Why do you let something bother you that happened so long ago?

JOSEPH. A prophet can't be blind. Maybe he's right. Maybe I'm not willing to admit . . . what I don't understand . . . what I fear. What I don't understand is what I fear. I let everything I am afraid of slip out of my head so I won't have to look at it. I have blinded myself to what I'm afraid to see.

HYRUM. What are you afraid to see?

JOSEPH. Something about Hanson Jacobs, about Oliver. And about all the scoundrels in Missouri. I'm afraid of them.

HYRUM. After what they've done to us, only a fool wouldn't be afraid of them.

JOSEPH. It's more than because of what they've done. Because the Lord has left them where they are. Because I hate them.

HYRUM. You have reason to hate them. Boggs and that extermination order. And General Lucas would have had us shot.

JOSEPH. They've destroyed our hope of Zion, and they still have power to harm us. Why?

LYMAN *climbs from the dungeon to the upper level.*

LYMAN. Well, I hope you know that now I can't sleep. That make you happy, Hyrum?

HYRUM. Well, Lyman, I can't sleep either, and I'm going to have some ugly bruises tomorrow. That make you happy?

LYMAN. Sorry about the bruises. I was having a dream that a mobber was bent over me, about to tie me up.

JOSEPH. We've had enough trouble with mobs to give us all nightmares, Lyman. Maybe dreams are how the fear comes out.

LYMAN. I'm not afraid of anybody, Joseph, and neither are you. Least of all the rascals in Missouri.

JOSEPH. I don't know, Lyman. Some of them are powerful and evil. Even the weak, petty ones became powerful in their hatred. I remember one I met in a tavern in Illinois as we were traveling here. We were almost to the Mississippi but we needed to rest for a while, so I'd ridden ahead to secure lodging for the night. Major something he called himself. He wanted the room I had taken.

> LYMAN *becomes* MAJOR BURRIS *to* JOSEPH. *The lights change, and in the background are the sounds of laughter and eating in the public room of the tavern, below.*

LYMAN/MAJOR BURRIS. Yes, Phineas. This will do.

JOSEPH. He was with one of the shiftiest rascals he could find to grovel around him, Phineas Hobart.

> HYRUM *assumes the character of* PHINEAS HOBART *and looks around as if he is inspecting the room. They don't see* JOSEPH.

PHINEAS. Yep. Room's fine. Better'n some.

JOSEPH. I was sitting in a corner, just about here, and I thought they were almost as worthless then as I do now.

MAJOR. And we won't have to associate with none of that riff-raff down below. Mormons coming in down there, Phineas.

PHINEAS. On their way to Missouri?

MAJOR. Unless we dissuade them.

PHINEAS. Vermin's the word for them. Lice. Fleas. They've infested the whole state.

JOSEPH. Good evening, gentlemen.

MAJOR. Oh. You startled me.

JOSEPH. Well, you startled me as well.

MAJOR. We sort of claimed this room as our own.

JOSEPH. Now so did I. My family and friends are just arriving. But no matter. We can make room for you, too.

MAJOR. Well, thank you. Where are you headed, sir?

JOSEPH. Missouri.

MAJOR. Why, we're from Missouri. Planning to settle there?

JOSEPH. I certainly am.

MAJOR. Well that's right smart of you. Missouri's a land with a future.

JOSEPH. I think so.

PHINEAS. Except that just now we got a bad case of vermin.

JOSEPH. You mentioned that already.

MAJOR. Mormons.

> JOSEPH *plays this situation out as if it were a joke.*

JOSEPH. Mormons. Interesting comparison.

MAJOR. It's an apt description, sir. If you'd lived around them, you'd know.

JOSEPH. Oh, I agree with you entirely. Insects, definitely.

PHINEAS. Vermin.

JOSEPH. Yes. Vermin.

MAJOR. Started out with one or two, creeping in silently, so we wouldn't notice. But Mormons have a habit of multiplying. Before we knew it, the land was crawling with them.

PHINEAS. They was trying to take us over, eat up everything they could get their hands on.

MAJOR. Buying up all the land. Said they were promised it by God.

PHINEAS. Interfering with the slaves.

MAJOR. Looking down their noses at us.

PHINEAS. We don't need no damn Yankee Mormons to tell us how to live, now, do we, sir?

MAJOR. They can't just tend to their own business like other folks.

JOSEPH. Vermin. Definitely vermin. What are you going to do about them?

MAJOR. What do you do with pests? Scare them off. Burn them out.

PHINEAS. Kill them if we have to.

MAJOR. Whatever it takes to get rid of them.

JOSEPH. Well, I have a suggestion for you. It'll help you get them out faster.

MAJOR. What is it, sir?

> JOSEPH *acts as if he is divulging confidential information.*

JOSEPH. Start at the top. It will leave them helpless.

MAJOR. We know. We've had our eyes on every move Partridge and his men have made for months.

JOSEPH. That's good, but I think you should go even higher.

MAJOR. You mean old Joe Smith? That deceiving epileptic scoundrel is scared of us. He knows how we'd take care of him. He won't stay in Missouri longer'n two days strung together.

JOSEPH. "Old Joe Smith" is someone to watch, but you better start higher than him.

MAJOR. There isn't anyone higher than him.

JOSEPH. Sure there is.

MAJOR. Smith's the prophet. No one on earth is more important to the Mormons than he is.

JOSEPH. What about someone who isn't on earth?

MAJOR. Now you're talking in riddles.

JOSEPH. I mean the Almighty. Start by dethroning God, and you won't have any trouble with the Mormons. If you don't start there, you may be taking on a little more than you can handle.

MAJOR. Are you some kind of a maniac?

JOSEPH. I have often been called one. My name is Smith.

MAJOR. Smith. Your given name?

JOSEPH. Joseph.

PHINEAS. Joseph Smith.

JOSEPH. The deceiving epileptic scoundrel himself; and despite your words, I am coming to Missouri to stay.

MAJOR. Well ... uh ... I meant what I said, Smith.

JOSEPH. Of course. And if you're really going to "take care of me," now is as good a time as any. Come on.

JOSEPH is ready to wrestle with either or both of them.

MAJOR. I won't have you bait me. I have friends, sir. And when we come after you, we'll set the terms.

JOSEPH. I'm sure you will, and I'm sure they won't be fair terms. Some people call that cowardice.

MAJOR. You can go ahead and talk big now. But don't get too sure of yourself, Smith. I figure you've got six months at the longest, before we get you. And that goes for your damn followers, too.

JOSEPH. I appreciate the warning. Believe me, sir, we won't let you push us out of our homes again. We'll stand behind the law—despite your Governor Boggs—and we'll be ready to defend ourselves. You see, Missouri is our home, our Zion. So let me warn you, whoever you are.

MAJOR. I am Samuel Burris, attorney, and major in the Missouri State Militia.

JOSEPH. I should have known that you were an attorney. And a major? I am duly impressed. Well, Mr. Major, let me say this to you. You are fighting the work of the Lord. In the end, you've got to lose. In the eyes of God, a major is less impressive than a stink bug.

MAJOR. I promise you, Joe Smith, some day we'll see you shot.

JOSEPH. Wait. It's my fault that you hate us, isn't it? Because I treated you like fools?

MAJOR. Who are you calling a fool?

Both PHINEAS *and the* MAJOR *look as though they are going to respond violently but then turn away.*

JOSEPH. What if I'd treated you with some decency and respect?

All three have moved into the same positions they were in when the following lines were spoken earlier.

JOSEPH. Good evening, gentlemen.

MAJOR. Oh, you startled me.

JOSEPH. I'm sorry. I didn't mean to.

MAJOR. We sort of claimed this room as our own.

JOSEPH. Now so did I. My family and friends are just arriving. But no matter. We can make room for you, too.

MAJOR. Well, thank you. Where are you headed, sir?

JOSEPH. Missouri.

MAJOR. Why, we're from Missouri. Planning to settle there?

JOSEPH. I certainly am.

MAJOR. Well, that's right smart of you. Missouri's a land with a future.

JOSEPH. I think so.

PHINEAS. Except that just now we got a bad case of vermin.

JOSEPH. I heard you mention that.

MAJOR. Mormons.

JOSEPH. What's wrong with Mormons?

MAJOR. If you'd lived around them, you'd know.

JOSEPH. Well I am one of them, and I don't know. You seem like reasonable men. Tell me why you dislike them, and perhaps I can get them to make it right with you.

MAJOR. Don't come to Missouri.

JOSEPH. What?

PHINEAS. The major said don't come to Missouri. What he means is that any Mormon stupid enough to try and move onto our land is going to find himself pushed off it before he knows what hit him.

JOSEPH. We don't want your land. We want to buy our own. Surely in Missouri there is room for more people.

MAJOR. Not for more Mormons.

JOSEPH. Why can't we live together in peace?

MAJOR. Because Mormons are not like other folk. They don't mix in. They live off by themselves, then come in swarms and take over.

PHINEAS. Act like they'll get dirty if they talk to you.

MAJOR. If you don't agree with what they want to do, they walk through you, sure they're right and the rest of the world can be damned.

PHINEAS. Missouri was ours first. Why should we let you holy Mormons, who stink all the way to heaven, decide for us how we'll live?

JOSEPH. We won't do that. We'll let you live as you choose.

MAJOR. Sir, you don't now and you never will. That Joseph Smith won't be happy till everyone's under his thumb—doing what he tells them to do.

JOSEPH. Not what I tell you to do—what the Lord tells you to do through me. But surely we won't force you. We'll leave you in peace and treat you as a good neighbor.

MAJOR. You'd treat me as a "good neighbor" just long enough to get the power to throw me out. I'll see myself in hell before I'll let you push me off my land.

PHINEAS. What do you mean, "what the Lord tells you to do"? You on speaking terms with God, too?

MAJOR. That's right, Phineas. I thought it was only Joe Smith claimed to talk to God. Or is that getting to be a general delusion among all Mormons?

JOSEPH. I am Joseph Smith. And we won't push you out. You have my word on it. We want to live in peace with you.

MAJOR. You are Joseph Smith?

JOSEPH. Yes, sir.

PHINEAS. Then you are the cause of a hell of a lot of trouble.

JOSEPH. Perhaps I am, but I want to stop that trouble, if you'll help me.

MAJOR. I was not aware, Phineas, of the size of the pest before us. Were you?

PHINEAS. No sireee.

MAJOR. Why, he's not a flea or a bedbug—this one's a genuine cockroach.

JOSEPH. Please, talk to me. We are a good people. We need a home.

MAJOR. You ever stepped on a cockroach big as him, Phineas? I've seen some six-inchers back home. When you put your foot on one, you can feel it wiggle.

JOSEPH. I'm asking you men to work with me. Help me.

MAJOR. When you push down a little, you can feel the shell crack, but the cockroach is still alive. You can tell because the legs keep running, trying to escape.

JOSEPH. There doesn't have to be violence.

MAJOR. That's when you wonder if cockroaches feel pain, because—they don't writhe, exactly, but they shudder.

JOSEPH. You won't listen to me at all. You can't even hear me.

MAJOR. I like to push my foot on down to the ground slow, so the insides don't get all over my boot, and so I can feel the life go out of them. There's something to that—knowing when you've made the thing dead.

JOSEPH. I was wrong. I couldn't change you.

MAJOR. Six months in Missouri, Smith, and that's how we'll kill you.

JOSEPH. Stop it! Please stop it!

As JOSEPH *cries out, the lights return to normal and* HYRUM *and* LYMAN *resume their identities.*

HYRUM. Joseph, what's wrong?

JOSEPH. Nothing. Why do you think something is wrong?

HYRUM. Well, you just let out a yell that about frightened my boots off.

JOSEPH. I did? I must have been thinking . . . dreaming or something.

HYRUM. What's wrong?

JOSEPH. Nothing. Nothing. But if you could leave me alone for a while, I'd be grateful.

LYMAN. Sure, Brother Joseph. Come on, Hyrum. You heard what Joseph said. *(*HYRUM *stays where he is.)* Hyrum, Joseph wants to be left alone.

HYRUM. In a minute, Lyman. You go on down. *(*LYMAN *descends.* HYRUM *speaks to* JOSEPH.*)* What's happening to you?

JOSEPH. Go to bed.

HYRUM. I'm not going to bed. Tell me.

JOSEPH. I've learned at least one thing I was blind to. I was better off being blind. There will always be persecution for us, Hyrum. For the Saints.

HYRUM. Why?

JOSEPH. We can never say we are happy with people as they are. We will always want them to repent and be baptized. To join the Church.

HYRUM. Yes, we will.

JOSEPH. They will always resent it.

HYRUM. Not all of them. Some will join us. Some who don't will understand.

JOSEPH. The few. But enough will hate us for what they see as our self-righteousness to join together in violence, wherever we go.

HYRUM. And what if that's true?

JOSEPH. I have been charged to give people the restored gospel, which should bring them peace, and I am giving them trials and suffering.

HYRUM. Not just suffering.

JOSEPH. Look at Hanson Jacobs—any of them—how they have been broken. The gospel should give them hope for eternal life. What they have received is misery for this one.

HYRUM. Joseph—

JOSEPH. Where are the Saints now, Hyrum? Not in Zion. In Illinois. And how long do you think it will be before the persecution starts? Two years? Why should it be any different there than it was here? Or in Ohio and New York? Where will we go next, Hyrum? Where on earth can we live without hatred?

HYRUM. I don't have all the answers—

JOSEPH. I know you don't.

HYRUM. —but that doesn't mean that there are none.

JOSEPH. I don't need false hope. I need to understand the truth. If neither you nor I can see peace for the Saints, if we have petitioned the Lord for months for help and we have been given no answers, if he won't even get us out of this jail, then it is time we looked at things as they are. We have no place to go. Nor do the Saints.

HYRUM. Let's give the Lord some time.

JOSEPH. I have given the Lord some time.

HYRUM. Apparently not enough.

JOSEPH. What is enough time? Until I am broken? Will that be enough time?

HYRUM. What are you going to do?

JOSEPH. Open my eyes to what else I have been refusing to see.

HYRUM. Stop this. It's changing you.

JOSEPH. I have to understand. Maybe I've failed, Hyrum. Maybe we'll never escape and everything will end for us here in this jail. I have to know if that's true.

HYRUM. You say the Lord isn't helping you. I don't think that's true. *(JOSEPH doesn't respond.)* Joseph, the Lord won't abandon you. *(More silence from JOSEPH.)* Why don't you answer me?

JOSEPH. What do you want me to say?

HYRUM. *(Not knowing what else to do.)* I'm going down now. We have to work soon. Get some sleep, will you?

JOSEPH. All right, Hyrum.

HYRUM. Joseph, please. Stop hurting yourself.

JOSEPH. Good night.

As HYRUM *descends the ladder, the light fades, the moonlight shining through the bars across* JOSEPH *fading last.*

END ACT ONE

Act Two

Scene: the same as Act One, but later. It is very dark, and at first nothing can be seen. There is the sound of scraping, a chisel on rock. The lights rise gradually, first revealing three forms in the jail—two in the dungeon and one in the upper level. As the lights come up, it can be seen that the two forms in the dungeon have moved the bench that was against the back wall and have removed from the wall a three-foot long section of the middle two logs. The men are working there, scraping out the hole they have made. The other form is on guard in the upper level, watching through the window for any movement outside the jail. As the lights become a bit brighter, it can be seen that the two forms in the dungeon are JOSEPH *and* ALEXANDER, *and the form keeping guard in the upper level is* HYRUM. LYMAN *and* CALEB *are offstage—sleeping behind the blanket partition.* JOSEPH *is in the hole doing the work. He passes a pail half-filled with small rocks to* ALEXANDER. *When the characters are in the dungeon, they move quietly and speak in low, intense tones, because they are trying not to awaken* CALEB.

ALEXANDER. Brother Joseph, you've been at this about an hour. Why don't you go up and take the watch and let Hyrum and me work on the hole.

JOSEPH. This is a well-built jail, Alexander.

ALEXANDER. I know, Joseph. How many auger handles did we break going through the logs?

JOSEPH. I've run into the stone wall on the outside. If we can just clear out some more of the loose rock we'll be ready to start on the wall.

ALEXANDER. Will the chisel hold out?

JOSEPH. It's so dull it just bounces off. Hardly loosens the rocks. It's not going to be easy to chip out the mortar around the big stones.

ALEXANDER. It'll take weeks.

JOSEPH. One thing we have is time. Well, I'll let you take over here, and I'll send Hyrum down.

JOSEPH gives ALEXANDER the pail and tools and climbs to the upper level. ALEXANDER takes JOSEPH's place in the hole and continues to work, but no more scraping is heard.

JOSEPH. Anything happening out there?

HYRUM. Joseph. Nothing that I can see. All seems to be still in Liberty, Missouri, tonight. How is our escape route coming?

JOSEPH. We have struck the outside wall. We're going to have to chip the mortar bit by bit until we can pry some of those stones out. I told Alexander that that was just the job for you.

HYRUM. Always thinking of others, aren't you, Joseph?

HYRUM starts toward the ladder.

JOSEPH. Hyrum. About what I said to you earlier tonight. I'm sorry.

HYRUM. I'm sorry you said it, too, Joseph. I don't want you to hurt yourself with such nonsense.

JOSEPH. You remember when we were boys, how I got that infection in my shoulder and then in my leg?

HYRUM. Of course.

JOSEPH. After my operation, you had to carry me around for so long. I must have been quite a burden to you.

HYRUM. I didn't mind.

JOSEPH. Do you think I would have died if they hadn't chipped out the bad bone?

HYRUM. We thought you might.

JOSEPH. I've always wondered, because it's left me with this limp, and I hate it.

HYRUM. Better the limp than losing your leg—or your life.

JOSEPH. Hyrum, that's what's happening to me now. I think there's a sickness in me. If I don't dig it out, I'm afraid it will kill me just the same way.

HYRUM. What do you mean?

JOSEPH. What if Oliver was right and I was wrong? What if he shouldn't have been excommunicated?

HYRUM. Stop doing this. I won't talk to you about it any longer. I'm going down to chip mortar. That will be more pleasant than listening to you torment yourself.

JOSEPH. All right, all right. I didn't mean to make you angry.

HYRUM. Stop brooding. Just look out the window. That's all you need to do tonight.

JOSEPH. Maybe you're right.

HYRUM descends and goes to the hole. JOSEPH waits till he is gone and then he kneels.

JOSEPH. Oh God, the Eternal Father . . . I don't know what I have done wrong. Why are the heavens closed over my head? Father, please, please. I am willing to accept any chastisement, any punishment, if Thou wilt help me learn what I've done wrong. O God, please bless me. I need to talk to those I didn't talk to, to see things I wasn't there to see. I will do whatever I have to do, know whatever I have to know, if Thou wilt let me lead this people. I ask thee . . . I beg Thee . . .

From below there is the clang of the file hitting a rock and a sharp cry of pain. ALEXANDER *has gashed his hand as he has been working on the mortar. He emerges from the hole holding his hand in pain. Joseph goes to the trap door and calls down to him.*

JOSEPH. Alexander, are you all right?

ALEXANDER. I hit some stubborn mortar and the chisel slipped. It will stop hurting in a minute.

HYRUM looks at the hand, which is bleeding, and wraps it in a handkerchief that he takes from his pocket.

HYRUM. That looks pretty bad, Alexander. You rest that hand and I'll take my turn in the hole.

JOSEPH looks straight ahead toward the audience. The light changes, and ALEXANDER *becomes* OLIVER COWDERY *again as he takes the handkerchief off his hand. Though* OLIVER *addresses* JOSEPH, *he is speaking to himself.*

OLIVER. So this is where eight years of my life have brought me. Eight years. You reign with your high council, and I am excommunicated. There isn't any room for disagreement in this church. Not if it's Joseph Smith you happen to disagree with. You aren't content to be what you were called to be, the mouthpiece for God in our time. You want to be a king. A petty king of a petty kingdom that hasn't got a chance of surviving.

JOSEPH. Is that what you think I want? Is that what you think of Zion? A petty kingdom?

OLIVER. You couldn't just give us the gospel of Jesus Christ. You had to start running our lives. Buy land in Jackson County, Missouri. No, don't sell it, even though they've run you off, even though you'll never live on it again and you're going broke paying the taxes. Jackson County, Missouri, is Zion, boys, and you've got to hang onto it. If they kill you, hang onto it.

JOSEPH. Don't you even understand Zion? We were right to excommunicate you.

OLIVER. By trying to build yourself a kingdom in the middle of a state, you got your people thrown out. I told you you were wrong, but you turned from me to your high council, because they only agree with you. You sure stopped listening to me.

JOSEPH. *(Furious.)* Oliver Cowdery, you're the one who stopped listening. How can you stand there and mock a vision of the Lord? Zion, Oliver. Our home. Our place of peace, where we can live bound by covenants of mutual friendship and love. We cannot be saved if we don't build Zion, to free us from every incumbrance beneath the celestial kingdom. I won't apologize for God's revelations, or for trying to bring them about. Do you think those vile Missourians will just give Zion to us? If we don't make ourselves independent from them and strong, they'll never leave us alone. You think I want to be a king? I want the salvation of our people, Oliver. I want them to have a home.

OLIVER ignores Joseph during this speech. Then OLIVER rises, turns around and addresses JOSEPH, although he can't see or hear JOSEPH. He is still talking to himself.

OLIVER. Oh, Joseph, I don't care about your mistakes. I love you. Why did you let them excommunicate me? Why?

JOSEPH. You were opposing me.

OLIVER. You abandoned me—

JOSEPH. You were wrong.

OLIVER. —and you let them hold that trial. When I got the letter telling me of the nine absurd charges, I wasn't even concerned. Who were they to try me? Did John the Baptist appear to any of them? Had they seen angels? I waited, because I knew, Joseph, that you would speak for me. And you didn't. I heard nothing for days, and then I realized that the decisions had already been made. Oh, I wrote them a letter, to make the official procedures smoother, but you excommunicated me, Joseph. You.

The light gradually returns to normal, as ALEXANDER goes to see how HYRUM is coming along with the digging.

JOSEPH. I excommunicated you? I wanted you to repent. Not to be excommunicated.... But you deserved it. You were condemning me publicly. Urging people to sue me. And you wouldn't come to me to ask my forgiveness. You were always so muleheaded. You acted as if you expected me . . . to come to you.

JOSEPH takes a quick look out the windows and then descends into the dungeon.

HYRUM. Where's Lyman? Why isn't he helping tonight? Anything wrong with him?

ALEXANDER. He's back there next to Caleb. I don't know how to wake Lyman without waking Caleb.

JOSEPH. Hyrum, could I have stopped Oliver's excommunication? Should I have gone to him?

This is so upsetting to HYRUM *that he rises up in the hole, bumping his head and starting a small avalanche of stones. He emerges from the hole coughing and sputtering.*

HYRUM. Joseph, see what your fretting made me do?

JOSEPH. I know that Oliver took up for a time with that Major Burris and Phineas Hobart. Oliver wouldn't stoop to company like that unless he had a reason. The reason must have been that he thought I had wronged him greatly.

HYRUM. Joseph, get in here and dig. If you won't stop this by yourself, I'm going to work it out of you. And I think Lyman could take a turn at digging, too. Alexander, let's go see if there's some way we can get him out here without disturbing Caleb.

ALEXANDER and HYRUM walk away from JOSEPH, who bends down into the hole and then suddenly stops. The light changes, and ALEXANDER and HYRUM become PHINEAS HOBART and OLIVER COWDERY.

PHINEAS. You Oliver Cowdery?

OLIVER. Yes, sir.

PHINEAS. *(Sneering)* Former assistant president of the Mormonites?

OLIVER. What of it?

PHINEAS. I hear they excommunicated you. You've gone about as low as you can go, Mr. Cowdery, bein' kicked out of an organization that respectable folk wouldn't have nothin' to do with in the first place.

OLIVER. If you have business with me, state it.

PHINEAS. Whoooeee! Ain't we actin' high and mighty? Now let's suppose I'm here for somebody else.

OLIVER. Who?

PHINEAS. Well, supposin' he was, say, an attorney in one of the neighborin' counties.

OLIVER. Anything else?

PHINEAS. A major in the state militia.

OLIVER. A Mormon-hater.

PHINEAS. With good reason.

OLIVER. Why are you here?

PHINEAS. Well, now, if I was sent by this gentleman, it was probably to offer you protection.

OLIVER. Protection? From what?

PHINEAS. From whatever—or whoever—might be trying to do you injury.

OLIVER. You, for example.

PHINEAS. I mean none other than Joe Smith hisself, and his brother Hyrum, and Sidney Rigdon, and every other Mormon bushwhacker they can get to go along with them.

OLIVER. I'm not afraid of them.

PHINEAS. Maybe you should be. Ain't you heard about that sermon Rigdon preached last Sunday?

OLIVER. From many of the good brethren. "If the salt hath lost its savor, it is good for nothing but to be trampled underfoot."

PHINEAS. Rigdon mentioned hangin'.

OLIVER. As long as Joseph Smith is leading them, I've got nothing to fear. That sermon was to frighten me into leaving. Having left the flock and being willing to talk about it, I'm a source of embarrassment to him.

PHINEAS. So you'd already made up your mind to quit the Mormonites before they—

OLIVER. No. Not at all. I would never leave of my own free will.

PHINEAS. Why not? You seem like a right smart man. How could Joe Smith delude you with talk about angels and gold Bibles?

OLIVER. Who are you?

PHINEAS. I'd just as soon keep names out of it, till I find what you mean to do.

OLIVER. Well, then, whoever you are, whoever may ask me that question, I will have to give the same answer. On the honor of my life, I was not deluded. Joseph Smith translated that "golden Bible" as you call it, by the power of God, and both he and I were visited and ordained by angels.

PHINEAS. You expect me to believe that?

OLIVER. It is my responsibility to say it, and I have. It is your responsibility to decide what you'll do with it.

PHINEAS. Then I think I'll let it alone. 'Cause if you're so all-fired sure about your angels, why did you get kicked out of your church?

OLIVER. I have nothing else to say to you.

PHINEAS. What about the protection? You know there's a pack of wolves hangin' around Joe Smith, just waitin' to do his bidding.

OLIVER. I would call most of them sheep.

PHINEAS. So's if he wanted something done, he wouldn't have to do it hisself. He'd only have to suggest it, nice and subtle, and his wolves'd take care of it.

OLIVER. You're right. There are a few wolves.

PHINEAS. A few. I can name you more'n a few.

OLIVER. What do you mean?

PHINEAS. Them that signed this letter says you got three days to get out of the county.

JOSEPH. But I had nothing to do with that.

PHINEAS *takes the letter from his pocket.*

OLIVER. You're bluffing.

PHINEAS. "Or face a more fatal calamity." Read it yourself, Mr. Cowdery.

OLIVER. These aren't signatures. The same hand that wrote the letter signed the names. Where did you get this?

PHINEAS. It's a copy of a letter. We have our ways of keepin' track.

OLIVER. I'm not that gullible.

PHINEAS. No, sir, you ain't so gullible as to believe there's some Mormons scares easy, that'll do anything to save their own skin—'specially if it don't involve no more than keepin' us informed as to what goes on in Far West.

OLIVER. No, I'm not.

PHINEAS. You don't have to believe me. The letter's comin' to you tonight. You see, Old Joe's name ain't on this thing, and if we made it up so you'd help us get him, we sure would've thought to sign his name. And, of course, you ain't so gullible as to imagine for a second that if Joe Smith doesn't sign it, he didn't have a thing to do with writin' it.

JOSEPH. Oliver, it wasn't me. Hyrum and Sidney wrote it.

PHINEAS. Joe Smith is either going to kill you or force you to run away.

OLIVER. What do you want from me?

PHINEAS. Help us get him.

OLIVER. How?

PHINEAS. In court.

OLIVER. In exchange for what?

PHINEAS. Protection from the Mormons, and from what's comin' to the Mormons in the future.

OLIVER. And you say this letter is coming tonight?

PHINEAS. Yup.

OLIVER. I hope you are wrong; but if it does come, then maybe we've got something to talk about.

PHINEAS. I can wait till then.

OLIVER. I'll meet you at the fence, where the poplars come down to the creek.

PHINEAS. What time?

OLIVER. After I get the letter. You're the one who knows so much about when that will be.

PHINEAS. I'll come about eleven tonight.

OLIVER. And bring your attorney along with you.

PHINEAS. I don't suppose you'd believe me if I told you he won't come.

OLIVER. If he wants Joseph Smith as much as I think he does, he'll come.

PHINEAS. You're a pretty smart man, Cowdery. Except about your Mormons.

The lights return to normal. HYRUM *and* ALEXANDER *still haven't attempted to wake* LYMAN *up and pause before the blanket.* JOSEPH *throws the tools down and climbs back to the upper level.*

ALEXANDER. Hyrum, are we going to wake him up, or are we going to pace back and forth here all night?

HYRUM. You saw what Lyman did the last time I tried to wake him up. And if we disturb Caleb and he sees what we're up to . . . I don't know what to do.

ALEXANDER. I'll try tickling his nose. That's how my children used to wake me up. May make him grouchy, but I think it will work.

HYRUM *holds aside the curtain, as* ALEXANDER *crouches beside Lyman to carry out his plan.*

LYMAN. Who's there? What?

ALEXANDER. Lyman, ssshhh. Caleb. Come out here.

LYMAN *growls like a bear, but quietly, and he does what* ALEXANDER *has asked him to do.*

LYMAN. Can't you leave a man to sleep in peace?

HYRUM. Aren't you going to help with the wall?

LYMAN. Hyrum, who did most of the work so far? Who bored through those logs with augers dull as you are? Now tell me, who was that?

HYRUM. We all worked on it.

LYMAN. But who got two inches to everybody else's half inch? Was it you, Hyrum?

HYRUM. No. It was you.

LYMAN. So I don't think I need you to tell me when to work. I'm coming in a half hour or so, and I'm going to work the rest of the night, and I'll get a damn sight more work done than any of you. But I'm also telling you that I need my sleep. So leave me alone! Do you understand, Hyrum? Alexander?

With this, LYMAN *flings the blanket aside, walks behind it, and lies down again.*

HYRUM. Well, he sure was grouchy. You were right about that.

ALEXANDER. Just watch, Hyrum. He'll be back.

> ALEXANDER *is right again. In about ten seconds,* LYMAN *reemerges from behind the blanket. He is still grouchy.*

LYMAN. And I suppose the two of you are just going to stand around here and let Brother Joseph do all of the work? Seems like somebody ought to offer him a hand. *(They all turn toward the hole to offer* JOSEPH *some help, only to find that* JOSEPH *isn't there.)* That's just fine now, isn't it? Brother Joseph up on the watch, and the two of you don't do a lick of work. Just think up ways to disturb people's sleep. Well, somebody better get something done here tonight, that's all I got to say.

> *With that,* LYMAN *goes to the hole, crawls into it, and begins working furiously.* HYRUM *and* ALEXANDER *are concerned about* JOSEPH.

ALEXANDER. Is he all right, Hyrum?

HYRUM. I'd better go talk to him.

> HYRUM *climbs into the upper level, and* ALEXANDER *goes to assist* LYMAN.

JOSEPH. Hyrum, you remember the letter we sent to Oliver, ordering him to get out of the county? We were wrong to do that.

HYRUM. *We* were wrong? You didn't write that letter. You didn't have anything to do with it.

JOSEPH. But why did you write it, Hyrum?

> HYRUM *is set to scold* JOSEPH, *but he is taken aback by this question.*

HYRUM. I don't know. It occurred to us after Sidney's sermon about the salt. It was time for Oliver to go.

JOSEPH. And do you know why Sidney gave that sermon? Because I wanted him to. Oh, I don't remember whether it was his idea or mine; but if I had objected, it never would have been spoken. I forced Oliver from the county, the same way the Missouri mobs forced us. I am no better than they are.

HYRUM. We were all part of it.

JOSEPH. All he wanted was to be heard.

HYRUM. You don't know that.

JOSEPH. And I failed him as a friend. I didn't go to him.

HYRUM. It wasn't that simple. Don't try to erase my responsibility, and Sidney's. We were all afraid he would break the Church down into a group of petty factions—

JOSEPH. There is the power of my call, the power of my influence, and the power of my will. I could have made things different for him. I chose not to.

HYRUM. You can't do everything. How do you know he would have bent to you? You are not admitting any influence but your own.

JOSEPH. That poor, floundering man. What did I put him through?

HYRUM. Don't take all the blame on yourself.

JOSEPH. What is mine, I must take.

HYRUM. All right, then. We did nothing. Oliver did nothing. You can just sit up here and be guilty. Yes, Joseph, the way I see it, everything is your fault.

> HYRUM *descends into the dungeon, and in his anger he becomes* PHINEAS HOBART. *As he does so, the lights change. There is silence, then the chirping of a cricket and the quiet sounds of a creek. Moonlight forms the shadow of the top of a poplar tree—from stage left to about center.* PHINEAS *looks around himself, then stumbles and recovers.* LYMAN *emerges from the hole to become* MAJOR BURRIS. OLIVER *is squatting down, hidden by the shadow.*

MAJOR. Watch it, will you? Mormons will hear us sure.

PHINEAS. Patch of moss.

MAJOR. I thought you said he would be here.

PHINEAS. He'll be along.

> OLIVER *stands up, snaps a twig in his hand.*

MAJOR. What was that?

PHINEAS. Nothing. Cricket maybe.

OLIVER. I've been waiting for you.

> PHINEAS *and the* MAJOR *are both startled.* PHINEAS *falls to the ground and the* MAJOR *tries to fade back into the darkness.*

PHINEAS. Don't shoot. Don't shoot. Mr. Cowdery? It's me, the one you talked to this afternoon.

OLIVER. I didn't mean to startle you.

MAJOR. Walk into the light.

OLIVER. Of course. And who are you?

MAJOR. I might be a friend. Someone who can help you out.

PHINEAS. You got the letter.

OLIVER. There were over eighty signatures. Joseph's wasn't one of them.

MAJOR. And you'll help us.

OLIVER. What do you want?

MAJOR. We want you to enter a lawsuit against Joseph Smith.

OLIVER. For what?

MAJOR. For threats against your life. I'll represent you. You might say I've made arrangements with a judge, and he'll see that justice is done.

OLIVER. Joseph has done nothing to me.

MAJOR. You just got that letter. What's the matter with you?

OLIVER. Joseph didn't write it. As far as I know, Joseph didn't know about it.

MAJOR. Of course Smith wrote it. Nothing happens to the Mormons that Joe Smith doesn't arrange.

OLIVER. You can't prove that he wrote it.

JOSEPH. It is not that I wrote it, but that I did nothing to keep it from being written.

MAJOR. Yes, we can. We have to prove it if we're taking it to court. We have to have a witness.

OLIVER. Who?

MAJOR. You said there's eighty names on that letter. All potential witnesses.

OLIVER. None of them will accuse Joseph.

MAJOR. Under oath, they'll have to. You choose any one of those men, Mr. Cowdery, and we'll put him in court and see what he has to say.

OLIVER. I won't harm Joseph Smith.

MAJOR. You've got to, damn you. He's trying to kill you.

OLIVER. He is not trying to kill me.

PHINEAS. You crazy, blind man. You've put out your own eyes.

MAJOR. Phineas, you're right. He has to be blind. He has to believe that Smith didn't betray him, didn't turn his back on him. Because if he did, then Oliver Cowdery would have to see that for a long time his life has been spent helping a cutthroat and that he has wasted his suffering.

OLIVER. He didn't write that letter. He didn't betray me.

MAJOR. Prove it. Stake something on it. You think he's not after your life? Then bring him to court.

OLIVER. Joseph would never try to harm me.

MAJOR. Prove it to yourself. You choose any of those eighty men for a witness. A witness in court, Cowdery. It's the only way you'll ever know.

OLIVER. No, I—

MAJOR. You want to be haunted by this for the rest of your life?

OLIVER. Hanson—Hanson Jacobs.

PHINEAS. Who?

OLIVER. Hanson Jacobs. He signed the letter. He'll tell the truth.

PHINEAS. Hanson Jacobs? Runs one of the dry goods stores in Far West, don't he? I seen him around.

MAJOR. Take this paper. My name's on it. You ride down and see me and we'll get the suit underway.

OLIVER. I won't file suit until I've seen Hanson Jacobs.

MAJOR. You don't need to see him. We'll just serve him with a subpoena, so he has to show up in court.

OLIVER. No. I want to hear his story before I make my decision about a trial.

MAJOR. If that's what you want—fine. Well, Mr. Cowdery, you're not such a fool after all. So you dare open your eyes and take a look at Joe Smith.

OLIVER. Get out of here. I'm tired of looking at you.

PHINEAS. Sure, Cowdery. You think we like to spend time with Mormon scum? We was already leaving.

They turn to walk away. The MAJOR *pauses and turns toward* OLIVER *again.*

MAJOR. You come soon.

PHINEAS *and the* MAJOR *go behind the curtain;* OLIVER *speaks to himself as if he is addressing Joseph.*

OLIVER. Oh, Joseph. You warned me of the wrong thing. I have always been afraid of persecution. But how could I know it would come from you?

JOSEPH. How am I to go on? How strong can I be without you?

OLIVER. What are you doing with the Church? Why wouldn't you listen to me?

JOSEPH. Why don't you understand Zion? Why did you speak against me?

During this exchange in JOSEPH's *mind,* HYRUM *climbs the ladder into the upper level. He breaks into* JOSEPH's *thoughts, and the lighting becomes normal again.*

HYRUM. Joseph, I'm sorry I got angry a while ago. But you just can't feel guilty for everything.

JOSEPH. I thought if we were united in an understanding of what is right, of what the Lord wants us to do, we could build a Zion like Enoch's. But we were never united.

HYRUM. We are united. What else can I do to show that I stand with you? What can any of us do?

JOSEPH. Hyrum. Stalwart, faithful Hyrum. You are always by my side and I know it, and I am deeply thankful to you. I was speaking of Oliver. I didn't understand him. I should have waited till he wasn't so angry. He didn't want to leave the Church. He didn't even want to harm me. I have hurt him so much.

HYRUM. But he has hurt you as well. He didn't understand you either. Joseph, he tried to force you to abandon the possibility of Zion. Can you forget that?

JOSEPH. I could have helped him to understand. But I didn't. I'm afraid I have scarred his life.

HYRUM. And what has he done to your life? Have you thought about that?

> LYMAN *has been working furiously on the hole in the dungeon and breaks the chisel.*

LYMAN. *(Crying out.)* Oh, damn! I broke the chisel. Split right in two. Damn that mortar, damn this jail, damn the whole state of Missouri. Oh, how can we get out of here?

> JOSEPH *and* HYRUM *hurry down to them.*

ALEXANDER. Wasn't much of a chisel anyway.

LYMAN. But I could use it. Oh, now what are we going to do?

JOSEPH. Use the auger bits. They'll still chip out mortar. It will be slow, but we'll keep working. We won't just sit here. We won't.

CALEB. *(Voice from behind the blanket.)* What's the matter, boys? Has something happened? Do you need any help?

HYRUM. It's nothing, Caleb. Lyman broke . . . uh . . . the handle on the pail. Don't worry about it. Go back to sleep.

> CALEB, *drowsy, comes from behind the blanket to see what is going on and realizes what the others have been doing.*

CALEB. It's the middle of the night. Why—there's a hole in the wall.

HYRUM. Oh . . . uh . . . Yes, there is.

ALEXANDER. Nothing to worry about.

CALEB. You're trying to break out.

LYMAN. No, Caleb. It was just there. One night the bench slipped and that tick fell down, and I saw that somebody had cut through the logs. We just took them out to see if the hole went all the way through.

ALEXANDER. We thought it might be the way the Lord's prepared for our escape.

CALEB. You're lying to me. You cut the logs out yourselves.

LYMAN. No, Caleb. I swear to you—

JOSEPH. Lyman, stop. Caleb, you've caught us.

CALEB. Why stop him, Joseph? Why not lie to old Caleb? You've been at it—how long? Must have been weeks of work on those logs. You're liars—all of you.

LYMAN. But we're not cowards, Caleb.

CALEB. Meaning I am one? *(*LYMAN *shrugs in agreement.)* What's the matter with you boys? They want an excuse to kill us. Any little excuse. And you give them a four-foot hole in the jail wall that will sit here till they find it. They'll kill us all.

HYRUM. Not if we finish it first and get away.

JOSEPH. We know it's a risk, Caleb. But it's the only way out. The only hope we've got.

CALEB. Joseph, we agreed that none of us would try anything that might put the others in danger. Well, what about me? Were you just going to leave me here alone? Give me up to them so you could get away? You ask for loyalty, Joseph Smith. You have no more loyalty than a tick.

HYRUM. Caleb, don't—

CALEB. Hyrum, shut up. You don't care for any of us but Joseph. You'd kill us all to save him.

JOSEPH. Of course, we wouldn't leave you, Caleb. We thought you might feel differently if the breach was already finished and the chance to get away was right there in front of you.

CALEB. I wouldn't feel differently. You're all young. Strong. But look at me. I can't keep up with you. I'm the one they'll catch.

JOSEPH. Caleb, I will stay with you. I promise.

CALEB. Joseph, I'm afraid. I don't want to hold you back, but I'm terrified.

JOSEPH. We won't go without you, Caleb. If you won't come, we'll give it up.

HYRUM. Missouri won't try us, won't free us, won't even let us be heard. We have to get ourselves out of here.

LYMAN. You want us to sit here till we rot, Caleb? Just to please you?

CALEB. I'm not holding you back any longer. There's a hole in the jail wall. Now we have to go, before they find it.

JOSEPH. Are you sure, Caleb?

CALEB. Sometimes everybody has to do what they can't do. This time I have to.

JOSEPH. I'll help you.

CALEB. Brother Joseph, there is something that would help me.

JOSEPH. What's that?

CALEB. I got to have faith that the Lord will get us out of here, since we have to go. And Brother Joseph, I trust that you're a prophet. If you will raise your arm to the square and tell us, in the name of the Lord, that we will be delivered, I know we'll be safe, because all along we have been. Will you do that for me?

JOSEPH. Caleb, I don't think—

HYRUM. What would be better would be for us to pray together. The Spirit will—

ALEXANDER. No, Hyrum. Caleb's right. I know I'd feel a lot better if Joseph would promise us in the name of the Lord. Like he did the night they courtmartialed us.

LYMAN. Because then it's a sure thing that the Lord will be with us. Then we just have to work till we get ourselves out. Will you do it, Joseph?

JOSEPH *begins to put his arm up, slowly, then stops. He looks at them and finally drops his arm.*

JOSEPH. No. We'd all better give it up.

JOSEPH goes to the hole and begins replacing the logs.

CALEB. Joseph, I'm willing to try. I just need you to help me with my faith.

ALEXANDER. What do you mean, Joseph? We're quitting?

JOSEPH. We would only fail again. We would fail.

ALEXANDER. We'll die if we just sit here.

CALEB. They'll find the hole.

JOSEPH. I tell you, we won't get out of here, and we will give each other more grief and pain. So go to bed. *(They have never heard anything like this from JOSEPH, and they are all shocked. They do not move, but just stand and look at him.)* I can't help you any more. Don't you understand that? I can't help you.

JOSEPH turns away and climbs the ladder into the upper level.

HYRUM. Please, go on back and try to get some sleep.

LYMAN. But, Hyrum—

HYRUM. Please.

They reluctantly agree and retire behind the blanket. HYRUM goes toward the ladder, stops, turns back into the dungeon, and kneels.

HYRUM. Father, please help him, because I don't know how to help him. He can't see beyond what has happened to us here. Blaming himself. Clinging to his own doubts, as if they explain something to him. He has borne this calling eighteen years. Alone eighteen years before Thee. Father, when—and how—are the burdens shared?

The light shifts to JOSEPH in the upper level.

JOSEPH. Well, Joseph, it's finally time to look at yourself. Who are you? A prophet of the Lord? No, that isn't Joseph Smith. That's a cloak under which I've been allowed to hide. But who am I? What have I done? . . . I just failed the men in this prison with me. And I have failed as a friend. Joseph Smith, who has been threatened and betrayed, who knows the value of a friend. But Oliver was waiting for my help before his trial, and I left him waiting. So. I'm not much of a leader anymore, nor a friend. What is there to me? The only good I can think of is that I've tried to surrender myself to God. And that is something—to forget Joseph and put on God, to reflect His truth and power to the earth. But I have remained Joseph through it all. Uneducated as a common field hand. No more knowledge of the world than I could get for myself. No skill at politics, certainly none at finance. Why did the Lord choose me? Who am I to stand for God? No one. I am bound by the very earth I walk on, limited by ignorance and fear and sorrow. Yet I was called! The Lord knew me, and He called me. Why did he choose me, and then let me fail? Why didn't He save the

Saints? When Oliver went to Hanson about that letter, why didn't God help them?

The light in the dungeon changes; ALEXANDER *and* CALEB *become* OLIVER *and* HANSON *to* JOSEPH. OLIVER, *in the shadows, watches* HANSON *work.* HANSON *folds up and lifts one of the straw ticks as if it is a heavy bolt of cloth and struggles with it to the bench, where he drops it as if he is loading it onto a wagon. Then he straightens his stiff back.*

HANSON. Damn. Must be getting old. Good thing to have a son. Few more years and he'll be working right here alongside of me. Yes, sir. Few more years.

OLIVER. Need some help?

HANSON. No, thanks. Not from you.

OLIVER. Too good to want help from an apostate?

HANSON. I'd accept help from an apostate. But not from a mobocrat.

OLIVER. Mobocrat?

HANSON. You heard me.

OLIVER. You're a fine one to call me a mobocrat. What'll you and the rest of the good brethren do if I'm still in Caldwell County day after tomorrow? Of the two of us, I'd say you were the mobocrat.

HANSON. Oliver, you are just trying to stir up trouble. Why do you want to take Brother Joseph to court?

OLIVER. How do you know about that?

HANSON. Look, I'm damn tired, and I got a damn long ride home tonight, so I don't care to play your games.

OLIVER. What are you talking about? I don't understand you.

HANSON. And I don't suppose you know anything about those scoundrels who visited me last night, either.

OLIVER. I have no dealings with scoundrels.

HANSON. Then what do you call them that sets fire to a man's barn? They cost me one of my cows and all next winter's hay.

OLIVER. Who did it? Why?

HANSON. You know that better than me. They were waiting for me after the fire burned itself down, and I went back to my house. Put a gun to the back of my head. Told me about your trial.

OLIVER. Hanson, I'm sorry. I had no idea they would do something like that.

HANSON. All right. So you didn't know about that raid. I believe you. But why do you hate the prophet?

OLIVER. You stubborn, closed-minded—(OLIVER *searches for the right word*)

Mormon. Look at me for a change. Joseph isn't the one who has been wronged. I've been cut off from the Church. I have to leave the county tomorrow unless I want violence done to me. That letter of Joseph's ought to warn you, too, Hanson. I have never seen a more blatant violation of law or a clearer indication of the dictatorship he is leading you to.

HANSON. Joseph?

OLIVER. It's time he learned he can't trample laws and other men's rights without hurting himself. That's why I'm taking him to court and why I chose you for the witness. I have to prove he is behind that letter, and I know you will tell the truth.

HANSON. Joseph didn't write that letter. He didn't even sign it. And I'll say that in court.

OLIVER. Joseph was responsible for the letter that threatened my life.

HANSON. Those who were responsible for it signed it. Did you just miss all those signatures at the end?

OLIVER. Joseph could get it done without putting his name to it. Seems that's how he prefers it when he's dealing with me. That's how he handled my excommunication.

HANSON. Joseph had nothing to do with it. Leave him alone.

OLIVER. You're lying to protect him.

HANSON. Oliver, you know who's lying, and why. They'd use anyone to get to Joseph. He had nothing to do with that letter. I'm ashamed I put my name to it. It was wrong. But Joseph didn't do it. The damn thing never would have been written, had it been up to him. I know you've been hurt, but, Oliver, why distort it? Why make it worse than it is?

OLIVER. Because I am excommunicated, Hanson. Can you imagine what that is? I have to understand why I was sacrificed.

HANSON. You've forgotten how to follow.

OLIVER. Follow? I should snivel along behind Joseph, when he is wrong? No church, especially not the true church of Jesus Christ, should control where you live, how you vote, what you do.

HANSON. The Lord can ask anything he wants of us.

OLIVER. It's not the Lord asking. It's Joseph Smith.

HANSON. He's a prophet.

OLIVER. He's a fallen prophet. I know you think I've lost the faith, but I've seen visions, too. And now Joseph has lost touch with God. He is leading you to violence and persecution. Needless, useless waste.

HANSON. You believe that, don't you?

OLIVER. Why else would I fight against someone with whom I've shared visions of the eternities?

HANSON. But Joseph still receives revelation.

OLIVER. No, it isn't from God. He's convinced himself. I never wanted to fight Joseph. But this Zion of his will bring catastrophe, and—I thought I had been betrayed.

HANSON. It's the Lord's Zion, and Brother Joseph hasn't betrayed you.

OLIVER. He didn't help me.

HANSON. What could he have done? To defend you, Joseph would have to deny his own teaching.

OLIVER. And you think I'm wrong, too.

HANSON. I trust the prophet.

OLIVER. Can't you see what this Zion idea will get you? The old Missourians are frightened, desperate. They've been watching this Joseph Smith, and they can see his power. More Saints coming in every day, all of you buying, voting, breathing together. They're afraid of losing their land. Do you think they'll just sit around watching it happen? No. They're going to do whatever they have to do to destroy Joseph now, before he destroys them.

HANSON. That's your opinion.

OLIVER. Because of what you've told me, I've decided not to file suit against Joseph.

HANSON. Good.

OLIVER. What do you think will happen to you when Burris finds out?

HANSON. What will happen to you?

OLIVER. I won't be here. I know I'll look like a coward when I leave Caldwell County, but I'll go. I don't want to see what happens to the rest of you.

HANSON. Well, if you leave, you won't have to.

OLIVER. Come with me, Hanson.

HANSON. I can take care of myself.

OLIVER. Will you risk your family?

HANSON. I can take care of them, too.

OLIVER. Not against those men.

HANSON. We will be fine.

OLIVER. Hanson, I'm trying to warn you.

HANSON. I know, but I can't run away. I didn't want to join this church. But I'll tell you something. I'm not ashamed of being a Mormon. In fact, I'm damn proud. And the longer I'm in the Church, the more I believe it's true. So I'm not going to run off because of trouble. I've given up too much for that.

OLIVER. I truly hope you will be spared.

HANSON. Oliver, I hope things change for you. I hope, some day, you can come back.

OLIVER. Thank you. But I'm afraid the Church may have to come to me. No one will believe this, but I have been fighting to save it. Fighting. And I've had to watch it all slip away because I won't bend from what I know. You won't reconsider and come with me?

HANSON. No.

OLIVER. Well, then, good-bye, Hanson. I'll be praying for you.

Light in dungeon returns to normal. HANSON *and* OLIVER *exit behind blanket partition.*

JOSEPH. If Zion was from the Lord, why weren't we protected as we tried to carry it out? The homes, the land—all taken. Gone. And the Saints. When they walked from this state, they left footprints of blood in the snow. I see it every time I look out that window—all the way to Illinois. A trail of smudged, fading sickness away from me and what I tried to get them to be. But the Lord gave me the knowledge of Zion in holy vision—the very spot that was the center place. I knew it when I first saw it. He commanded us to come here and to build a city of righteousness. It is as though he brought us here to fail. His revelation mocks me, mocks us all. *(*JOSEPH *kneels.)* Hear me, O God. I plead for thy people. They are a good people. They are not perfect, but they have sacrificed so much. Think of Hanson Jacobs, and what thy gospel cost him. Why wasn't his sacrifice acceptable? Father, what is required? Their faith is as important as their lives. Why have we violated that? Father, why have we betrayed them—both of us?

Near the end of JOSEPH's *prayer, before lights come up in the dungeon, there are sounds of furniture being thrown down and broken, glass shattering. Lights rise as* PHINEAS *and the* MAJOR *shove* HANSON *onto the floor. They are beating him and destroying his home.*

MAJOR. Now that was right stupid of you, staying out here alone to defend your farm. About as stupid as you not helping us when you had a chance. *(*MAJOR *kicks* HANSON *in the groin.)* Maybe you'll think twice before you cross us again.

PHINEAS. If you'd helped us take Joe Smith to trial, none of this would be happening to you.

MAJOR. Where's your two-bit prophet now, Jacobs? You were so bent on helping him—why isn't he helping you? *(*HANSON *doesn't answer.)* Captain Hobart, I don't like it when I'm ignored.

PHINEAS. *(Hitting* HANSON*)* You heard the major. Answer him. *(*HANSON *still doesn't answer.)* Major, maybe he don't know. We could tell him.

MAJOR. Now that's a fine idea, Captain. Because I want him to know.

PHINEAS. I guess you heard Far West is fallen, now, didn't you? *(No answer from* HANSON. PHINEAS *strikes him again.)* Answer me when I talk to you. Major, he don't learn.

MAJOR. Well, even if he can't talk, he can hear. Explain it to him.

PHINEAS. All right, Major. Jacobs, I was telling you about Far West. That's old Joe's Zion, ain't it? Two-bit frontier town, and he calls it Zion. Well, there ain't going to be no more Zion, and there ain't going to be no more Mormons in Far West. State militia is ruling Far West now. We've got your weapons and your leaders, too. Did you know that we've got Joe Smith?

HANSON. *(To himself.)* Not the prophet. Oh, no.

MAJOR. And the rest of you Mormons, too. I guess you heard of the order from Governor Boggs. Either you crawl out of this state, or we'll exterminate you. Like the insects you are. Phineas, tell him what's going to happen to his prophet tomorrow.

PHINEAS. General Lucas held a court martial, and Joe Smith and others was found guilty of treason. The general ordered Doniphan to shoot them tomorrow at dawn.

HANSON. Brother Joseph?

MAJOR. That will be the end of your prophet—and the end of you Mormons, too. (HANSON, *tied, lunges at the* MAJOR, *trying to batter him with his head. They both fall to the floor.)* Get him off me. (PHINEAS *easily pulls* HANSON *away.)* You damn fool Mormons. *(Hitting* HANSON.*)* Damn fools. We can do whatever we want to you now. Don't you understand that? Whatever we want.

PHINEAS. This one needs a lesson. I told him if he didn't help us, he'd lose more'n his barn.

MAJOR. You're right, Phineas. He was warned. Suppose, tonight, we take care of the rest of his stock and his house. Hear that, Mormon?

PHINEAS. And then his store.

HANSON. Not my store.

MAJOR. Well, he's finally found his voice.

HANSON. You stay away from my store.

PHINEAS. Now why do you suppose he's so all-fired concerned about his store? Think he might have his family hid in there? Sure hope nothin' happens to your family, Jacobs, 'cause you been such a fool.

HANSON. Please. I'll pay you.

PHINEAS. You ain't got nothin' to pay us with. You might not of known, but you ain't got nothin' at all. I guess I'll get on into Far West to see what I can find.

HANSON. I'm begging you. I'll do anything you say.

MAJOR. *(Kicking* HANSON, *knocking him down:)* Shut up, you. You had your chance for that. Captain, kill the stock before you go.

The MAJOR *and* PHINEAS *exit behind the blanket.* HANSON *lies prostrate on the ground.*

HANSON. Not my family. Dear God, no.

JOSEPH. Didst thou hear that, Father? He pled for Thy help. Did that mean nothing to Thee? I couldn't help him—I was chained in the mud in the middle of a field surrounded by five thousand men bent on killing me. But Thou—Thou art powerful. Thou art the great God, the ruler of earth and seas. Why didst Thou let them hurt his family? Why? I promised him blessings for coming to Missouri. Blessings? Blessings of devastation and promises that must have been lies. O God, for what hast Thou used me?

HANSON. *(Hysterical with grief.)* Joseph Smith. You hear me.

JOSEPH. Not me. Take it to God.

HANSON. Yes, you will hear me.

JOSEPH. It wasn't me—

HANSON. I gave up everything for what you taught me. You deceiver. You lied to me. You promised me a Zion, a home. You promised my family peace. Why didn't you kill us first? There would have been some mercy in that. Do you know what they did to my wife? You listen to this, you prophet. I want you to feel some of her shame. That Captain Hobart took ten men. Damn them all to hell. They pulled our son from her arms and threw him in the street. Then they tied her to a bench and they violated her. Ten of them, Joseph Smith. She banged her head on the edge of the bench again and again, trying to knock herself out, but she couldn't do it. She was conscious through it all. And my son—when they found him, he was clinging to a hitching post in the rain. He'd been there all night. They had to pry his fingers away. And now he's burning with a fever, and—he's going to die. You Joseph Smith, you prophet, why did you bring us to this? I wish I had never heard of you.

JOSEPH. Hanson, I—

HANSON. Leave me alone. Leave me and my family alone.

> HANSON *goes behind the blanket.* JOSEPH *is left alone.*

JOSEPH. Oh, God, why did I ever speak? What was it Thou hast taught me? This impossible truth I struggled years to learn? An abyss in which we can fail more completely, knowing the depth of our loss? We didn't have a chance of making it true. Why did I see the peace and joy of Zion if we can never build Zion? Why did I give Thy people truth to live by if they have to die? *(Defiant, almost sobbing.)* My God! Where art Thou? And where is the pavilion that covereth Thy hiding place? How long shall Thy hand be stayed, and Thine eye, yea, Thy pure eye, behold from the eternal heavens the wrongs of Thy people and of Thy servants and Thine ear be penetrated with their cries? Yea, O Lord, how long shall they suffer these wrongs and unlawful oppressions before Thine heart shall be softened towards them? O Lord God Almighty, maker of heaven, earth, and seas, and of all things that in them are, let Thine anger be kindled against our enemies; and in the fury of Thine heart, with thy sword avenge us of our wrongs. Or if Thou wilt not help us, at least, Father, leave us alone.

> JOSEPH *remains in place, head bowed, body bowed, throughout the next scene. The normal lighting comes up in the dungeon.* CALEB *and* ALEXANDER *have reopened the hole against the back wall.* CALEB *is sitting on the bench next to the hole, and* ALEXANDER *is standing behind him, watching.* CALEB *is holding the chisel and a small rock, tapping the chisel against the mortar in the large rocks of the outside wall.*

ALEXANDER. Caleb, I think you're right.

CALEB. You see, if we turn the broken chisel around and hammer on it with a rock, it'll work like a spike. Maybe not as good as a new chisel, but it's better than nothing.

ALEXANDER. Yes. It'll work! Lyman! Hyrum! Can you come here? We've got something to show you. We've found a way to use the broken chisel.

> HYRUM *and* LYMAN *emerge from behind the blanket.*

CALEB. Treat it like a spike, see? Plant it up against a piece of mortar, hold it steady, and hammer it with a rock.

LYMAN. Here, let me try it.

> LYMAN *holds the broken file too high and hits his own finger.*

CALEB. Oh, I guess you have to watch your fingers.

ALEXANDER. It'll work, at least till we can get another chisel brought in.

CALEB. Maybe if we tell Brother Joseph, it'll cheer him up. Especially if he knows that I thought of it.

HYRUM. That might be even better news for him. (HYRUM *goes to the ladder and calls up to* JOSEPH.) Joseph, come down and look at this. Caleb and Alexander have found a way to keep working on the escape. Joseph, what do you think about that? *(There is no answer from* JOSEPH.*)* Joseph?

> *Again there is no answer.*

CALEB. He won't answer. He thinks the escape is ruined because I wouldn't go along.

HYRUM. No, Caleb, that isn't it. Nothing's wrong. Why don't you all go back to bed. There's only an hour or two left of this abysmal night.

LYMAN. Hyrum, don't treat us like we're too dumb to know the nose at the end of your face. We been in this jail right alongside you. Right alongside Brother Joseph. Whatever's wrong, you should tell us.

HYRUM. Don't you know?

ALEXANDER. How could we know?

LYMAN. Hyrum, maybe I'm not as smart as you. But I know your brother is a prophet of God. Now if he's in trouble, I'm here to help him. We all want to help.

HYRUM. Joseph is afraid that he has failed.

ALEXANDER. He can't fail—he's the prophet. We couldn't go on without him.

HYRUM. We wouldn't want to, but we could. The Lord would choose another prophet in his place.

ALEXANDER. How can you say such a thing, when he's your own brother?

HYRUM. Because it's true.

ALEXANDER. Well, I want Joseph to keep telling us the will of the Lord.

HYRUM. So do I, Alexander. And I hope he can. But Joseph has carried such burdens for us all. He's been so discouraged.

LYMAN. I never thought—Hate to say it, but I never thought about how Joseph might feel. Did you?

ALEXANDER. I guess not. I never tried to. What can we do to help him?

CALEB. No, you're all wrong. Don't you see? It's me. I let you all down, and Joseph thinks I'll do it again. Maybe I should—

HYRUM. All I can think of is to pray. We can pray together.

> HYRUM *kneels down.* ALEXANDER *and* LYMAN *follow immediately.* CALEB *looks toward them, then toward the trap door.*

CALEB. Hyrum, I have to go up and talk to him. I'm the one got him so upset.

HYRUM. Caleb, believe me, it wasn't you.

CALEB. I have to go up there, Hyrum, or I won't be able to live with myself. *(*CALEB *ascends quickly into the upper level.)* Brother Joseph, I know you think you want to be alone, but I have to speak to you.

JOSEPH. Caleb, if I don't pray now, I may never pray again.

CALEB. Brother Joseph, I'm sorry for what I said when I thought you was all going to break out and leave me here. I'm just an old fool.

JOSEPH. Don't worry about it, Caleb. I understand.

CALEB. And I don't know why, but now I'm not scared. I think we can get out fine.

JOSEPH. *(Listless.)* I'm glad, Caleb.

CALEB. No, you're not. You're still angry with me. Because I said you didn't have any more loyalty than a tick.

JOSEPH. I had already forgotten that till you brought it up. I'm sure I'll forget it again, too. I just wish that other . . . other Saints who have suffered could recover as easily.

> *The light changes as the action again shifts to* JOSEPH's *mind.* CALEB *becomes* HANSON.

HANSON. Joseph? It's Hanson Jacobs. I'd like to see you.

JOSEPH. I don't think I can look you in the eyes. I'm sorry, Hanson, for what has happened to you.

HANSON. Joseph, we're depending on you. We need the guidance of our prophet more than ever now.

JOSEPH. How can you call me a prophet when your wife—

HANSON. We all got across the river safe, Joseph. Most of us. And we're ready to go on. We're waiting for you—and the Lord—to lead us.

JOSEPH. How can you trust me again?

HANSON. Joseph, that time, after my wife'd been—hurt. I'm sorry for what I said to you. It was the grief. A grief I think I gave you.

JOSEPH. There's no need for you to be sorry. It was the truth.

HANSON. Joseph, you're so lost in our pain that you can see only part of the truth. Now I'm asking you to look at it all.

JOSEPH. I see it all.

HANSON. I was the same way—after. Only your grief is worse than mine, because you feel it for all of us, don't you?

JOSEPH. I feel too little of what the Saints have suffered.

HANSON. It's time you let our suffering go.

JOSEPH. I can't let it go.

HANSON. Listen to me. The night Far West fell—when I became conscious, Burris and Hobart had set fire to my house. I just had time to crawl out before it fell. They'd shot my horses so I had to make my own way into town. I prayed to God all the time I was stumbling along that he'd protect my wife, my child; all night I prayed while I was trying to get to them. Well, I got there, and I found what Hobart and his men had done. I would have killed them if I'd had any weapon at all. The damn helplessness was the worst thing I've been through. So I sat in my store with my wife and my son, watching them suffer, and I settled down to hate. I hated Hobart, and that major, and I hated God. I hated you, too, and that's why I said those things I said. I wanted to punish someone; I wanted someone to feel the way I felt. So I sat there with my wife, hating, and waiting for my boy to die. Ten days. The rest began to leave, and I just sat there, watching my wife and my son.

JOSEPH. I know, Hanson. I know how you felt.

HANSON. No. Wait. He didn't die. My wife finally come around some and got from her bed. She asked me to give him a blessing. I said no. I figured we'd done enough turning to God. Next day, Lucinda got me to go out for a walk, but I didn't go more than half a mile. And when I got back, I found she'd had the elders come in to bless him.

Brother Joseph, do you know what I did? I interrupted the blessing, swore terrible things at them, and I threw them out. When they were gone, Lucinda began to look at me frightened, and she said, "You're one of them." I asked what she was talking about, but I knew. She was right. I sat all that day, alone with my boy, and I begun to see down into my heart. I realized I'd rather let my child die than turn back to God. When I saw that, I hated who I was. Then it come to me, like a waterfall over me, that I did it to myself.

JOSEPH. You had good cause—

HANSON. Oh, yes, I had cause for all the hate and grief in the world. But I settled into it as if I'd been waiting for it. Oh, Joseph, I even forgot the love of my wife. When she helped me see it, I made my choice. I won't be something dead, something finished. So I did what I had to do. Finally, just let my bitterness go. That's what I'm asking of you, Joseph. Just let it go.

JOSEPH. Your boy?

HANSON. I fell on my knees and asked the Lord to forgive me and to give him his life. Then my wife and I took him in our arms, and we blessed him. Right away the fever broke. He suffered some on the trek out of the state, but now he's fine.

JOSEPH. I felt that the Lord and I had destroyed you.

HANSON. No, Brother Joseph, you couldn't destroy me. I could only do that to myself. You see, that's what I've finally come to know—Lucinda and I made our own decisions. We believe the gospel you taught us is the truth, so we chose to try to follow you. So will you help us go on, Joseph?

JOSEPH. How can I ask you to suffer again?

HANSON. You don't ask us to suffer. You offer us the truth you have been given, the gospel of Jesus Christ. Sometimes the truth asks us to suffer. But all of us need our own trials to show us who we are. It isn't right that you should take them on yourself.

JOSEPH. Hanson. Thank you for this.

HANSON. Then you'll forgive me?

JOSEPH. Forgive you? There's nothing to forgive.

HANSON. Yes, there is. It took me a while. I had to come to understand.

JOSEPH. So did I. I have had a long, dark time. But I think I can go back to the Lord and hear him now.

> HANSON *turns to leave, hesitates, and turns back to* JOSEPH.

HANSON. Brother Joseph, I want to tell you something. I know you're a prophet of God. If I can ever help you in any way, please let me do it. It would be an honor to my life.

JOSEPH. You have helped me, Hanson. More than you'll ever know.

HANSON *turns to leave, crouches on the floor, and becomes* CALEB *again. He has been showing* JOSEPH *how to use the broken chisel as a spike. The lights have gradually been returning to normal.*

CALEB. So what do you think, Joseph?

JOSEPH. What do I think?

CALEB. Yes?

JOSEPH. About?

CALEB. About the escape. Using the broken chisel like a spike. What I've been telling you. If we keep working, we'll be through that wall in no time and on our way to Illinois.

JOSEPH. *(Finally hearing what* CALEB *is saying.)* Well, yes. It's worth a try. And it was your idea?

CALEB. I knew you'd like it. Joseph, we can get out of here. Yes sir, I think we can.

JOSEPH. Caleb, just give you enough time, and you always come around. Now we'd better set up shifts for tomorrow night. Why don't you go on down and tell the others to sleep some so that we can get going on that wall?

CALEB. Now you're sounding more like yourself.

JOSEPH. And Caleb, will you hand me the candle? There are some things I'd like to write down.

CALEB. Of course, Joseph. Happy to.

CALEB descends the ladder but doesn't say anything, though all are waiting for him to speak. He goes to the candle, picks it up, and turns back toward the ladder.

HYRUM. Caleb?

CALEB. Yes?

HYRUM. What happened?

CALEB. I'm not quite sure. I apologized. He said he forgave me. Then I explained about how we can use the broken chisel, but I don't think he heard a thing I said. Finally, just before I came down here, he said we should get some sleep so that tomorrow night we'll be ready to dig.

CALEB begins to climb the ladder.

HYRUM. He wants us to keep trying to escape?

CALEB. Well, of course.

HYRUM. Then he must be all right. What are you doing?

CALEB. He asked for the candle. Here you are, Brother Joseph.

He climbs the ladder, gives the candle to JOSEPH *and climbs down.* JOSEPH *takes the candle to the table, takes a quill, a bottle of ink, and some paper from a drawer, and begins to write a letter to the Church.*

HYRUM. Caleb, how is he?

CALEB. Brother Joseph? Just fine. Hyrum, you're too anxious about him. Joseph wasn't feeling like a failure. Nothing like that. You worry too much.

HYRUM. *(Understanding far more than the others about* JOSEPH's *struggle.)* Well, then, I'm relieved.

ALEXANDER. Why doesn't he come down?

CALEB. Said he had some things to write.

ALEXANDER. You mean we just have to sit here and wait for him?

HYRUM. No. It's time we got some sleep. Don't you agree, Lyman?

LYMAN. Only if Brother Joseph is all right.

CALEB. He's fine. Same as always.

LYMAN. In that case, I'd say we've had enough broken tools, complaining, noise, hogging of blankets, and carrying on for tonight, and I'm going back to get a few hours rest. And Alexander, don't forget what I said about the blanket. Now, good night!

ALEXANDER. Lyman, I think whoever gets to the blanket ought to have his say about the blanket. Doesn't that seem fair to you?

    ALEXANDER *races* LYMAN *for the blanket behind the partition.*

HYRUM. Caleb, thank you.

CALEB. Oh, I didn't do anything. You know what I think, Hyrum? I think Brother Joseph was just acting discouraged to scare some sense into me. Well, I guess if I have to be ready to dig tomorrow night, I better get a little sleep myself. Good night.

HYRUM. Now maybe it will be. Even in this jail.

    CALEB *goes behind the partition with the others;* HYRUM *settles on a tick against the ladder. The lights rise slightly on* JOSEPH, *who puts the quill down.*

JOSEPH. Oh, Father, I thank Thee for this knowledge. I thank Thee for that woman and that man. Their sorrow is not mine, and neither is their glory. What they have suffered was for Thy gospel, not for me, and what they have become for that is their own. Some day they will be holy, and I thank Thee for my part in their lives. *(Elated, with a sense of triumph:)* As well might man stretch forth his puny arm to stop the Missouri River in its course or turn it upstream as to hinder Thee from pouring down knowledge from heaven upon the heads of Thy Saints. Oh, Hanson, Lucinda, hold to your path. Continue as you have begun. Be full of charity towards all and let virtue always fill your thoughts. Then your confidence will wax strong in the presence of the Lord and the doctrines of the priesthood will distill upon your souls like the dews from heaven. The Holy Ghost will be your constant companion, and your scepters unchanging scepters of righteousness and truth. Your dominion will be an everlasting dominion and without compulsory means it will flow unto you forever and ever.

As JOSEPH *finishes speaking, the light on him begins to fade. The light on* HYRUM *is of the same diminishing intensity.*

HYRUM. *(Singing slowly, thoughtfully.)* . . . And men did live a holy race . . . *(Pause, with reverence.)* . . . And worship Jesus face to face . . . In Adam-Ondi-Ahman.

As HYRUM *sings, the spotlights fade to black.*

THE END

FINAL PROGRAM NOTE

The breach the prisoners made in the wall of the dungeon was discovered before they could escape. However one month later, in April 1839, the prisoners were ordered to Daviess County for trial. A grand jury brought in a bill against them for "murder, treason, burglary, arson, larceny, theft, and stealing." As they were being taken to another county, it became clear that some officials had connived to allow their escape. A guard even helped them saddle their horses. With the sheriff and other guards drunk and asleep, the five men escaped to Illinois, where they arrived on April 22. The guard who had helped them escape was beaten and tarred and feathered by a mob because he assisted them.

Matters of the Heart

Thom Duncan

About the Playwright

When Thom Duncan converted to the LDS Church at the age of fourteen, he also got involved in community theatre and Church roadshows. These two new elements in his life—his religion and his passion for theatre—began to slowly melt and mold together. He then started thinking about Mormon drama even before it became a true movement: "This was back in 1964 and there was a dearth of plays about Mormons. We had lots of stories to tell, but no one seemed to be telling them in any form, dramatic or fiction. I later learned that some work had previously been done but it had been spotty and academic. Few had attempted to write and produce a play that was about LDS for an actual LDS audience. I felt drawn to do that. Someone needed to dramatize our stories."[1]

Thus, Duncan got involved in Mormon drama during its genesis as a movement, becoming one of its early playwrights in the early 1970s. Contemporary with Orson Scott Card, Carol Lynn Pearson, Robert Elliott, and Martin Kelly, he was one of the pioneers of Mormon drama. Mentored by poet and BYU professor Max Golightly, Duncan's first play *A Sword, A Scepter, and a Scented Rose*, based on the Book of Mormon story about Ammon and the conversion of King Lamoni, premiered at BYU in 1971. It was followed the next year by one of the earliest musicals about Joseph Smith, called simply *Prophet*, with music by Jerry Jackman in its premiere version, and by Mark Steven Gelter in its 1999 revival at the Scera Theatre in Orem, Utah.

But, as with all movements, Mormon drama had its growing pains, and Duncan was no exception. Some pointed criticism was leveled at *Prophet*. Orson Scott Card said that the play "was heavy handed and relied too much on the questionable idea that Joseph Smith knew about his death throughout his life."[2] Mormon theatre critic Eric Snider not only took legitimate umbrage at the choice of Simond Ryder, a character who merits only a minor footnote in Church history,[3] as the show's ultimate vil-

---

1 Thom Duncan, email to Mahonri Stewart, February 21, 2008.
2 Orson Scott Card, "Mormon Shakespeares: A Study of Contemporary Mormon Theatre," *Sunstone Magazine* 1, no. 2 (Spring 1976): 61.
3 According to Mormon folklore, Ryder is famous for leaving the Church because Joseph Smith spelled his name wrong in a revelation. (His first name is misspelled to this day in D&C 52:37 as Simonds instead of the correct Symonds.) Mark Lyman Staker, "*Hearken, O Ye People*": *The Historical Setting of Joseph Smith's Ohio Revelations* (Salt Lake City: Greg Kofford Books, 2009), chap. 23, discusses this problem in detail, including providing several examples of Ryder's name spelled variously and without Ryder's complaint in

lain, but also said the show was "too long, too talky, too slow and it never really tells us anything."[4]

However, BYU playwriting professor Eric Samuelsen came to Duncan's rescue in response to Snider's review in a review of his own (which was as much a review of Snider's review as it was a review of the production), for he saw at the heart of the play its greatest strength: the relationship portrayed between Joseph Smith and his first wife Emma:[5] "The obstacle, for this Joseph, is his fear that his obedience will result in his death (not itself something he fears) which might in turn lead to his wife's apostasy (which is something genuinely to be feared). He will accept martyrdom if that's the will of God, but he'd be desperate at the thought that his wife's testimony will not survive his death. Folks, that's powerful, compelling conflict. It's true to the character of Joseph and Emma and it's one with tremendous, dramatic resonance."[6]

And thus Samuelsen picked up on Duncan's great talent as a writer: the portrayal of human relationships. Although Duncan started out with rather epic subject matter, derived from the Book of Mormon and the martyrdom of Joseph Smith, it was the personal stories that really mattered to Duncan. "I was never interested in telling THE story of Mormonism," Duncan wrote, "I found myself more interested in the people of Mormonism, or how the ideas and doctrines of Mormonism interfaced with real people."[7]

As Duncan's life moved on past the 1970s, he became engaged in a number of different attempts to found a Mormon-centered theatre company. His most recent attempt resulted in founding the Nauvoo Theatrical Society in 2005 with Scott Bronson and Paul Deurden.[8] Yet it was during one of his previous attempts to build such a com-

---

    contemporary local newspapers. I agree that Ryder was a poor choice, especially with such rich material presented by antagonists who are actually part of the Nauvoo era narrative, such as William and Jane Law, Thomas Ford, Thomas Sharp, Robert Foster (whom Duncan also uses) and the Higbee brothers.

4 Eric Snider, "Snide Remarks: Prophet," column on "Film Reviews-General Merriment," http://www.ericdsnider.com/theater/prophet/. The original review was posted on the AML-List on October 5, 1999 (accessed May 22, 2010).

5 Joseph and Emma were played powerfully in the 1999 production by Sam Payne and Johanne Frechette Perry. Their performances, and that of Marvin Payne as a guitar-toting angel, helped buoy a rather uneven, unsteady, but promising production.

6 Eric Samuelsen, "Thom Duncan's *Prophet*, and Eric Snider's Review of Same: A Review of a Review," The AML-List Review Archive, October 5, 1999, http://www.aml-online.org/Reviews/Review.aspx?id=3250 (accessed May 9, 2010).

7 Thom Duncan, email to Mahonri Stewart, February 21, 2008.

8 Duncan, email to Stewart, February 21, 2008, commented that the Nauvoo Theatrical Society "was the third iteration of my attempt to establish a full-time live theater dedicated solely to original Mormon plays. . . . There are many, many quality LDS dramas and comedies that have been written and are being written. Co-founders Scott Bronson, Paul Deurden, and I wanted to provide a venue for those plays. It was successful, in my opinion, in that, of the four shows we produced, each and every one was a quality production, given our limited budget. They were plays that needed to be seen by LDS

pany that *Matters of the Heart* premiered at Theater-in-the-Square on November 22, 1985. *Matters of the Heart* played to Duncan's biggest strengths as a playwright: character and relationships: "I worked with a man who told me that he (a liberal Mormon) and his father (a conservative Mormon) couldn't talk about religion without arguing. I was struck by this. Both members of a religion that promises them a life for all eternity as a family and they couldn't talk about it? I had previously become aware of an article in *Dialogue* by Richard Poll about two kinds of Mormons, 'Liahonas' and 'Iron Rodders,' which the author used as symbols to categorize the 'intellectual' Mormon and the 'true believer.' These metaphors rattled around in my head for a while."[9]

One of Mormon drama's most dedicated theatre critics, Nan McCulloch, picked up on this reference. In her review of the Nauvoo Theatrical Society's staged reading of *Matters of the Heart* in 2006, she wrote:

> Duncan uses Richard Poll's Iron Rod/Liahona dichotomy from his 1967 *Dialogue* essay to characterize the two men . . . *Matters of the Heart* is an insightful play with universal appeal. It intriguingly revisits Poll's ideology from the 1960s body of Mormon thought, but asks for a third option, accented by the need for honest self disclosure. . . . As useful as the dichotomy of rods and compasses is in the play, it is Alice, the long-suffering wife and mother, who seems to transcend the two poles and thus proves to be the most interesting voice in the play.[10]

And that is one of the remarkable features of *Matters of the Heart*, in which a missionary voluntarily comes home early and must meet the issue with his parents. Between the two poles of extreme obedience to a culture and the repudiation of that culture lies that "third option" which Alice represents. It is impressive that one can watch the play and be swayed by either Robert or Paul Baines,[11] and then rejoice in the balance that Alice gives to both of them.

The play also highlights Duncan's chief focus in his playwriting. Duncan has written that he has found himself "drawn to the 'forgotten' individuals in Mormonism."[12] His desire to "comfort the afflicted and afflict the comfortable" becomes all too apparent in this, his best work. Those on the outskirts of the community, those who strive and struggle, but strain to hold on, are those who most often find germination in his mind to be reborn on his stages and into his theaters.

---

audiences, and they were as well-done as we could possibly do them. NTS showed that there is a market, albeit a small but growing market for quality . . . LDS theatre."

9   Ibid.
10 Nan McCulloch, "Understandest Thou Me?" *Irreantum* 8, no. 2 (2006): 200–201.
11 For example, I felt much more akin to Robert, the stake president-father in the play, while, ironically, Duncan's own opinions align much more with the son, Paul. This ability to write both points of view fairly and sympathetically is a rare gift.
12 Duncan, email to Stewart, February 21, 2008.

About *Matters of the Heart*

Matters of the Heart premiered at Theater-in-the-Square, Provo, Utah on November 22, 1985 with the following cast and crew:

CAST

Alice Baines: Betty Jo Smith
Robert Baines: Robert Detweiler
Paul Baines: Tim Scherer

CREW

Director: Thomas F. Rogers

Matters of the Heart received a second production at Theater-in-the-Square II in 1986 with Richard Dutcher as Paul Baines. *Matters of the Heart* won the Utah Valley Theatre Guild Award as Best New Play of 1985.

CHARACTERS

Robert Baines, stake president, mid to late fifties
Alice Baines, Robert's wife, also mid to late fifties
Paul Baines, their son, twenty

SCENE

Part of the backyard and home of Robert and Alice Baines. Downstage left, at the edge of the neatly manicured lawn and trimming the downstage base of the house are various shrubs and flowers. Nearest the back steps leading up to the dining room, at stage right, and occupying a prominent spot in the row, is an azalea bush just starting to bloom. Downstage left of that area is a patio table. A walkway immediately in front of this flower garden begins at the back steps and curves around the edge of the house through a gate toward the front of the house and stage right.

The interior of the house: a living room and dining room, kitchen offstage, and hallway leading to offstage bedrooms. In the center of the dining room table sits an attractive bouquet of flowers in a crystal vase. On the upstage wall of the living room is a fireplace. A clock sits on the mantel above the fireplace, and a photograph of the five Baines sons. Stage left of the fireplace is the front door, and to the left of the door, where the stage left wall turns downstage left, is a coat closet. The left wall continues downstage left, eventually giving way to a hallway and other unseen rooms beyond. A couch and end table (on which sits a telephone), chair, and coffee table complete the living room décor. On the low coffee table in front of the couch rests an unfolded newspaper and some *Ensign* magazines. The house is furnished in bland, inoffensive contemporary furnishings, the kind that at first set one at ease but which very suddenly become boring because of their predictability. All the trappings expected in the home of a stake president are there: a floor-to-ceiling bookcase filled with Church books and classic literature, pictures of prophets and temples on the walls. On a small three-legged table in the upstage entryway is a set of Joseph Smith and Brigham Young bookends with leather-bound copies of the Standard Works stiffly upright between them.

Classical music fills the darkness.

Lights up.

Music continues under scene for a while and then fades out. Downstage right, ROBERT BAINES *hacks away at an azalea bush and surrounding plants. His thinning hair hangs in sweat-soaked strands across his forehead. He wears overalls, gardening gloves, beat-up shoes, a pair of glasses in his breast pocket, and a wristwatch. He works feverishly, his face is a mask of grim determination that borders on obsession.* ALICE BAINES *stands at the dining room table—two glasses of punch and a pitcher on a tray resting on the table before her—reading a letter. Her hair is neatly coiffed. She wears an apron over a conservative housedress and a silver chain around her neck connected to the pair of reading glasses she wears while reading the letter. After a few seconds, she puts the letter down on the table, lets her glasses hang free, and picks up the tray.* ALICE *exits the dining room, crosses out to where* ROBERT *is gardening. She sets the tray down on the nearby patio table, pours a drink in one of the glasses, and holds it out to* ROBERT.

ALICE. Strychnine. Sugarless.

Robert absent-mindedly takes the glass, raises it to his lips, stops short of taking a sip.

ROBERT. What did you say? *(Pause.* ALICE *laughs, joined by* ROBERT. ALICE *pours herself a glass.)* Was I doing it again?

ALICE. Totally oblivious.

ROBERT. *(Sips.)* Sorry.

ALICE. You know, if I ever wanted to do away with you, I'd do it while you were working on the garden.

ROBERT. What did you say? Strychnine?

ALICE. Sugarless.

ROBERT. The best kind. Artificially sweetened strychnine has been proven harmful to your health. Causes cancer.

ALICE. I thought you might like a little something to drink. You've been out here all morning.

ROBERT. I appreciate it.

ALICE. *(Re: the azalea bush)* How's it going?

ROBERT. I've got a call in to the guy at Three Pines Nursery. If he can't tell me what's wrong . . .

ALICE. You're out here every day, pruning it, watering it, digging the soil around it. If the other plants had feelings, they'd probably feel neglected.

ROBERT. A lot has to do with the time of year you plant, the amount of water. I may be giving it too much. I don't know. Could be a lot of things.

ALICE. Maybe you should have called the nursery earlier.

ROBERT. I planted every one of these shrubs and flowers. This is the first one to give me any trouble.

ALICE. I'm sure you know best.

ROBERT. I put this in the ground a year ago. It should be covered with flowers by now. About three feet high. *(Points.)* Nothing. (ROBERT *hacks away at another branch, adds it to the pile.* ALICE *reaches for them.*) No, I'll take care of them. *(Holds out glass.)* But I could use some more strychnine, though.

ALICE *pours him some as he empties the branches into a nearby plastic bag.*

ALICE. I've got his room ready. (ROBERT *stops with a handful of leaves, but only for a split second; now, as he continues to fill the bag, his movements are more direct, more forceful.*) Just the way he left it. A little more orderly, mind you . . . but everything's there: the posters, the stereo . . .

ROBERT *finishes tying the bag of leaves, his voice straining with exertion.*

ROBERT. Did you find that one album . . . his favorite?

ALICE. Prominently displayed on top of the tape deck.

ROBERT. *(Stands with some effort.)* How did you manage to get rid of all my things?

ALICE. Just don't open the hall closet without a hard hat.

ROBERT. Good. Everything needs to be exactly as he left it. It mustn't look like we wanted him to go so we could have his room for my den.

ALICE. I don't think he would—

ROBERT. Alice, he'll be going through a period of adjustment. Coming home early from a mission is traumatic enough. Everything needs to be as normal as possible. (ROBERT *sets the bag of leaves aside, goes up the steps, and enters the house, though not before Alice gives him a look that says: "Don't forget to clean your feet on the mat," which he does. Once inside, he crosses to the wall clock in the living room, compares the time with his watch. He speaks over his shoulder to* ALICE, *who has also entered the living room by now*) When did he say—?

ALICE. I called the airport. His plane arrived on time.

ROBERT. He's taking a taxi, wasn't that—?

ALICE. He seemed pretty rushed.

ROBERT *crosses stage left, looks off, we assume through a pair of open drapes and a window, out into the street.*

ROBERT. He hasn't talked to us in a year and when he calls from the airport, that's all he says? "Don't pick me up. I'll get a cab."

    ALICE *adjusts the flowers on the dining room table.*

ALICE. It was long distance. He wanted to save us money.

ROBERT. We could have afforded to talk to him for days—

ALICE. Well, maybe he had to make a fast connection.

ROBERT. Still, he could have said more than: "I'll get a cab." *(He looks at the clock again, then back out the "window.")* What's it take, forty minutes from the airport?

ALICE. I'm sure he'll be here any minute now.

    ROBERT *sits in the living room chair, starts riffling through a stack of papers and magazines on the coffee table.* ALICE *picks up the letter from the dining room table, crosses to the living room.*

ROBERT. *(To himself)* I still don't understand why he didn't want us to meet him. Alice, have you seen that letter—? *(*ALICE *thrusts the letter into his face.* ROBERT *takes it while fumbling his glasses on.)* President Andrews doesn't give us a clue as to why he's sending Paul home early . . . *(Reads:)* " . . . for reasons that Elder Baines would like to discuss with you himself." *(Pause.)* Thank Heavens he's still "Elder" Baines—

ALICE. Bob!

ROBERT. Sorry—

ALICE. You don't think for one minute that Paul would—?

ROBERT. *(Putting the letter in his breast pocket.)* No, of course not—

ALICE. Whatever his problem is, it's nothing that would endanger his membership in the Church. I know that.

ROBERT. Yes. Yes.

ALICE. Then . . . why . . . ?

ROBERT. I don't know. I'm just trying to figure this all out, that's all.

ALICE. Paul would never do anything like that.

ROBERT. *(Looks at his watch again)* Probably stuck in traffic. I heard on the news that there was an accident on the Twentieth South off ramp.

    ROBERT *sits on couch, opens the morning paper, scans the headlines.*

ALICE. Would it make a difference? *(*ROBERT *looks up at her.)* Would you love him just the same—if he came home excom—

    She can't finish the word. ROBERT *sits back in the chair, reads the paper.*

ROBERT. Of course I would.

ALICE. Because what he needs now, more than anything, is our understanding, our support . . . not our condemnation.

ROBERT. I know.

ALICE. Does he know that? That you would love him regardless of what he does?

ROBERT *doesn't answer.* ALICE *pulls the paper down from his face.*

ROBERT. You mean, did I tell him? Not in so many words. You don't sit your son down when he gets his call and say, "Paul, I'll love you even if you're the worst missionary in France." The father-son discussion prior to a son's mission is a time of encouragement.

ALICE. But he's not the worst missionary in France.

ROBERT *drops the paper to his lap, takes the letter from his breast pocket.*

ROBERT. That's what his mission president says. *(Scans the letter.)* "... one of the most effective missionaries in the field." He's not been excommunicated, and he's not sloughing on the job...

ALICE. Wait till he gets here. Let him tell us. What's more important is: How do we deal with it? How are you going to deal with it?

ROBERT. Me?

ALICE. Yes, you.

ROBERT. It's not bothering you?

ALICE. Yes, of course it is. I've seen the sidelong glances from the other women in Relief Society; I can almost hear their thoughts: "What did her son do, that he's being sent home early? What did she do wrong? If she, the wife of a stake president, can't do everything right, how can I ever hope to?"

ALICE, *who had been in perfect control up to this point, suddenly turns away, reaching for a hanky in her apron pocket.* ROBERT *is instantly on his feet, taking her by the shoulders.*

ROBERT. It's been rough for you, hasn't it?

ALICE. No, not at—

ROBERT. I don't mean just about Paul. I mean about everything. About being my wife—the notoriety...

ALICE. Bob, I'm sor—

ROBERT. Come on, now. Admit it. It's been rough, hasn't it? *(Pause.* ALICE *nods. He takes her face in his hands.)* Why haven't you told me before? Because you wanted to be strong, didn't you? You thought showing your true feelings would be a sign of weakness, didn't you? *(Pause.)* Believe me, I know the feeling. *(He stands, brings her with him, takes her into his arms.)* I think you were right the first time. What are we going to do about our son coming home early from his mission? *(He kisses her. Pulling away, he looks at the flowers on the dining room table.)* And those flowers look great right where they are.

ALICE. Then I'll move them, because you have terrible taste. *(She takes the flowers from the dining table, goes into the parlor where she puts the flowers on the mantelpiece. Robert follows her, stands looking at her work.)* Did they mind terribly that you're taking the rest of the day off?

ROBERT. No, they understand a father's anticipation toward seeing his son come home. *(Making a weak joke as he moves toward the front window)* Maybe not my particular anticipation—

>ALICE *has had to move some pictures of her other sons and their families from the mantelpiece to make room for the flowers. Now she picks up one, a photo of all five of her sons. She caresses the picture.*

ALICE. Robert?

ROBERT. Hmm?

ALICE. Are you going to let Paul give a homecoming talk? *(*ROBERT *seems hesitant.* ALICE *becomes more enthusiastic.)* It would be a wonderful experience for him!

ROBERT. Well . . . I . . . don't—

ALICE. Returned missionaries speak in Church all the time.

ROBERT. True, but—

ALICE. But not missionaries who come home early?

ROBERT. No. And it's not because they're second-class citizens or anything. The youth need to view the mission experience in a positive light. Granted, there are . . . some difficult aspects to missionary life, but they find that out soon enough.

ALICE. *(Firm)* Are you sure it's not because you . . . don't want people to know he's come home?

ROBERT. *(Pause)* Is that it, Alli? Am I ashamed of my own son? *(*ROBERT *sees her still holding the photo. He takes it from her, looks at it. Smiles.)* Do you remember the day we brought him home? You had him in the bassinet, and he rolled over onto his stomach, lifted his head, and looked around through those squinty eyes? *(*ALICE *laughs as* ROBERT *squints, moves his head like one of those plastic dogs in the back of some people's cars.)* It was in that split second, that frozen moment of time, that I saw the entire course of Paul's life stretching out before him. I knew then that, in the face of the unknown, Paul wouldn't shrink but would lift up his head and face life straight on—eyes squinty, maybe, but he would face it. And he was always like that—all through school. If a problem was too tough, he would bite his lip until he mastered it. . . . Do you remember how he spent days patiently trying to tie his shoe? Never getting frustrated, discouraged. None of the other boys were like that. That's what makes it so difficult to accept—this thing about Paul coming home early from his mission. I get the feeling he's . . . running away from something. And I can't understand that.

>*A knock on the door.* ALICE *rushes to the door, opens it.* PAUL *stands there,*

wearing his suit but without the missionary badge.

ALICE. Paul! You're home. *(She launches herself toward* PAUL, *who just drops his luggage to take her in his arms and swing her around. When she finally comes to a stop:)* Oh, Paul, I'm so glad you're back!

PAUL. Nobody can keep me away from your home cooking.

    ALICE *steps back, scrutinizes* PAUL.

ALICE. You've gained weight . . . you've lost a little hair . . .

PAUL. Mom, I've only been gone a year.

ROBERT. *(Awkward.)* Welcome home, son.

    There is an electric moment between the two men. ALICE *senses this, steps back to silently urge them on.*

PAUL. Thanks, Dad.

    ROBERT *makes the first move: puts out his hand, which* PAUL *takes.*

ROBERT. *(Feigns a wince.)* I see you've learned this missionary handshake well.

(Sincere.) Congratulations.

PAUL. For what?

ROBERT. Your last baptism. President Andrews told me in his letter that your convert is now branch president.

PAUL. Frère DuChamp was a wonderful man. I was very lucky.

ROBERT. Blessed.

PAUL. *(Pause)* Whatever.

    ALICE *sees the tension between the two men, tries to change the subject.*

ALICE. *(Taking* PAUL *by the arm, moving him into the parlor.)* What's his first name? "Friar?"

PAUL. The word's "frère." French for "brother."

ALICE. Well, Paul. Don't be so formal. Sit down. This is your house, too.

    She leads him to one end of the couch.

PAUL. *(Indicating the luggage sitting near the front door.)* But what about—?

ALICE. We'll take care of that, later. You just sit down. (ROBERT *starts to sit in the chair, but* ALICE *gets there first, forcing* ROBERT *to sit at the other end of the couch, closer to* PAUL. *Once* ROBERT *sits,* ALICE *immediately stands up.)* Oh, I'm so flustered, I forgot! I have some punch for us. Father, you keep our son occupied till I get back.

    Exiting, she gives ROBERT *a look that says, "Don't you sit in that chair!" After a slight pause:*

PAUL. Uh . . . how's the flower garden coming along?

ROBERT. Funny, you should ask. I was working at it just before you—but you probably knew that already. *(ROBERT stands, moves toward the dining room, where the sliding glass door will take them outside. PAUL follows. ALICE stands at the dining room table, mixing more drinks, setting out some brownies on a tray. ROBERT and PAUL pass by, on their way to the garden.)* I'm showing Paul the garden.

ALICE. Fine, dear.

ROBERT and PAUL go out the sliding glass door. A faint smile passes across ALICE's lips. ROBERT and PAUL stop before the brave azalea.

PAUL. That's new, isn't it?

ROBERT. Azalea. I planted it the day you entered the MTC. I work at it nearly every day. It was my way of reminding myself that, as it grew, you'd be growing in another kind of field.

PAUL. It seems pretty mature, now.

ROBERT notices that some stray branches still remain. He kneels to pick them up.

ROBERT. Your brothers will be here around five-thirty.

PAUL is suddenly animated.

PAUL. Rich, too?

ROBERT. He's taking the afternoon off and flying up. He probably won't be bringing Ruth.

PAUL. I wouldn't think so. Four kids—

ROBERT. Five, soon.

PAUL. She's pregnant again?

ROBERT. They called last night.

PAUL. Are they hoping for a girl this time?

ROBERT. Well, Ruth's practically given up hope after four boys. Of course, Richard wants five sons.

PAUL. *(Pause.)* Just like you.

ROBERT. Did we tell you he's been made a bishop?

PAUL. *(Quick.)* In a letter.

ROBERT. Yes, I suppose I did.

ALICE exits the dining room with three glasses, a refilled pitcher of punch, and some brownies.

ALICE. Here it is! Real Hawaiian punch. *(She crosses down to the patio table, sets down the tray. Neither of the men move.)* Well, get over here, you two.

They join her at the table.

PAUL. Hawaiian punch? The real thing?

ALICE. You're going to tell me they don't have this in France?

PAUL. No, I'm not. Because you already said it. But they also don't have Jell-O, decent ice cream, or white bread. There's a McDonald's on the Champs-Elysees, but in name only. Secret Sauce or no, those Frogs can't make a decent hamburger.

ALICE. "Frogs?"

PAUL. That's what we call the French people.

ROBERT. You call them "frogs?"

PAUL. Only among ourselves.

ROBERT. Do you call the Germans "krauts?"

PAUL. *(Indignant.)* No.

ROBERT. Do you call the Jews "hebes?"

PAUL. Of cour—

ROBERT. Do you call black people "n—?

PAUL. *(Cutting off his father.)* I get it, Dad. *(Pause, nearly abashed.)* I get it. (ALICE *and* ROBERT *share a look as* PAUL *takes a drink.*) Mom, this is great stuff.

ROBERT. Yes. Thank you, Mother. It's very delicious.

ALICE. So what are the fr—uh . . . the French people like?

PAUL. Just like you and me. Except they speak a different language.

ALICE. No, what I meant was: How do they react to the Church?

PAUL. France is a Catholic country. The most frequent response I ever heard at the door was, "*Je suis catholique et je reste catholique.*" "I'm a Catholic and I'll stay a Catholic."

ROBERT. Pretty rough, was it?

    PAUL *looks at* ROBERT.

PAUL. What do you mean, "rough?"

ROBERT. *(Fishing.)* It must have been discouraging. That's all I meant.

PAUL. *(Shrugs.)* Maybe a little.

ALICE. Did Dad tell you about Ruth?

PAUL. Yeah. Can you believe it? Another kid?

ALICE. I'll tell you, she's absolutely amazing. Still looks like she's nineteen.

ROBERT. I wouldn't say that.

ALICE. All right. Twenty-one, then.

PAUL. Well, what about you? You had five kids. Look at you.

ALICE. Me? I'm a mess.

PAUL. Dad, is she fishing for a compliment?

ROBERT. More like trolling, if you ask me.

PAUL. Mom, you're not a mess. You're the best-looking mother I've ever had.

All laugh politely.

ALICE. Go on, you two. You know what I mean. Ruth jogs every morning.

PAUL. So you do canning every morning.

ALICE. She does that, too! *(Again, laughter.)* Want some more punch?

PAUL *holds up his glass.* ROBERT *shakes his head.*

PAUL. Speaking of good-looking twenty-one-year-olds, how's Lisa?

ALICE. The reception was absolutely beautiful. And her husband is nice, too. You knew him, didn't you, Paul?

PAUL. I still can't believe he would do that to me—come off his mission and steal my girl. Some guys have no class.

ROBERT. It's nothing. You'll get over it.

PAUL. I am over it.

ROBERT. Good. She's not worth worrying about. You're a returned missionary. An RM at BYU has nothing to worry about as far as girls are concerned.

PAUL *seems very uneasy at this.*

PAUL. Yeah, I know. It's all image.

ROBERT. What is?

PAUL. It's all image. Going to BYU. Just like the mission field. White shirts, short hair. It sends out a message to people: "clean and wholesome." If you're an RM, you grow a mustache. That sends out a message to the girls. Clean, wholesome, spiritual. And ready.

There is no bitterness in this statement but ROBERT *doesn't know how to take it.*

ROBERT. Yes . . . well . . . unfortunately, appearances are everything in this telestial world we live in. In the afterlife—

PAUL. But why do we have to play the game? If we're trying to live a celestial law, why should we care about what the telestial world thinks?

ROBERT. You're right. Our sights should be set higher.

PAUL. So when are you going to start wearing colored shirts to Church?

Pause. PAUL *laughs, breaking the tension.* ROBERT *and* ALICE *join in, relieved that it was all a joke. Or was it?* ALICE *stands, moves toward the house.*

ALICE. Well, I'm going to make your favorite lunch, Paul.

PAUL. American food! I can't believe it. (PAUL *follows* ALICE *into the dining room.* ALICE *crosses into the off-stage kitchen, as* PAUL *blurs by her, crossing to the suitcases he left at front door.*) Oh, that reminds me, I've got something for you guys. (PAUL *rummages through one of his suitcases.* ALICE, *carrying a tray of luncheon meat and bread, a pitcher of milk and some glasses, enters from the kitchen, joining* ROBERT *as he enters from the backyard.* ROBERT's *and* ALICE's *eyes lock. Pause.*) These are for you guys. (PAUL *comes back into the dining room, holding two wrapped gifts.* PAUL, *with a little protest by* ALICE, *takes the lunch tray to the dining room table, and gives the presents to his parents.*) This isn't honest-to-gosh baloney, is it?

ALICE. It certainly is. *(Indicates gift.)* What did you go and do this for?

They are all now at the dining room table, standing or sitting.

PAUL. Just open them while I make a sandwich.

ROBERT. Thank you, son!

PAUL *dives into the fixings as his parents begin to unwrap the presents.*

PAUL. You know, the French don't even know what baloney is. I had to go to the American store in Paris whenever I was in Paris to get this.

ALICE *has opened her present by now: A glass figurine of one of the Relief Society monuments.* ALICE's *eyes well up in tears.*

ALICE. Oh, Paul, this is so lovely!

PAUL. One of the men in my last branch was a glass-blower by trade. I showed him a picture of the Relief Society's monument to women and he copied it.

ROBERT *has unwrapped a bound book, reads the title.*

ROBERT. "The Missionary Journal of Paul W. Baines." *(Thumbs through it.)* It's all typed and bound.

PAUL. The glass-blower's wife was a secretary who knew English. I had her type it for me.

ROBERT. *(Genuinely moved.)* Paul, this is wonderful! I'll treasure this always.

PAUL. You know, Mom, snails are good but they're nothing compared to a good old-fashioned baloney sandwich. *(Pause.)* So fill me in on the local scene. What's happened since I left?

ALICE. *(Setting the glass figurine on the coffee table.)* Let's see... Oh, Karl Thorne got his mission call to Japan.

PAUL. He finally straightened up enough to go, huh?

ROBERT. He said you inspired him to go.

PAUL. Me? Inspiring?

ROBERT. You were to Brother DuChamp.

ALICE. Have some milk.

ROBERT. Tell us about Brother DuChamp.

PAUL. What's there to tell?

ROBERT. Why didn't you write to us about him? He was baptized—

PAUL. A couple of months ago.

ROBERT. It was more than that.

PAUL. Guess I never got around to it. Anyway, it's all in the journal.

ALICE. Would you like another sandwich?

PAUL. No, thanks.

ALICE. Oh, that reminds me. Your trunk came last week!

> ROBERT *goes to the coat closet, pulls out* PAUL's *trunk. It is heavy.* PAUL *rushes over, eagerly starts unlatching it before* ROBERT *barely has it fully into the room.*

PAUL. I've got some other things in here. Things that were too heavy to bring in the suitcase.

ROBERT. Your mother had the delivery man put it in here.

> PAUL *opens the trunk, then sits on the couch and rummages around inside.*

ALICE. Your room is just like you left it.

PAUL. Same sheets and everything?

> ALICE *smiles. Finally,* PAUL *finds what he was looking for: A square red rock, which he hefts, showing it is heavy.*

ALICE. What's that?

PAUL. It's called a *pavé*. The French use it pave their streets. Makes skate-boarding real difficult. Maybe I'll use it as a paperweight. *(He pulls out some books.)* My French dictionary . . . and this book was given to me by one of the most beautiful Frenchwomen I've ever met. *(This comment piques the interest of* ROBERT *and* ALICE.*)* She was only seventeen. But she had the longest honey-blond hair that hung straight down her back. Incredibly mature for her age. And very spiritual. Not the weepy-eyed kind of spirituality a lot of girls have at her age—hers was real. The first time I met her was my very first day in the city. Le Havre. "The Harbor." On the northern coast of France, just across the English Channel from England. My companion picked me up at the train station; and as we walked in the *salle*—sorry—as we walked into the meeting room, a bunch of members were there, polishing the floor.

I was introduced around and Dominique—that was her name—said, "Come on, Elder Baines. Why don't you help?" She threw me a cloth and I did what everybody else was doing: threw the rag on the wooden floor and kind of moved it with my feet, like this. *(Does a version of the Twist.)* The thought went through my head: "Am I dancing with a girl? Isn't this against mission rules?" Anyway, when I left that town three months later, she was there at the train station. That's when she gave me this book on French grammar. As the train pulled away, I looked out the window . . . and she was waving at me. There were tears in her eyes. I told her in a letter that, if things didn't work out with Lisa and me, I would look her up. *(Back to reality.)* I guess I can do that now.

ALICE. She sounds like a lovely girl.

PAUL. She is. I have a picture of her here someplace.

ROBERT. You wrote to her?

PAUL. I know it was against mission rules. But I always got such an incredible spiritual uplift from that girl . . . I can't explain it.

ROBERT. I . . . see . . .

Reaching back into the trunk, PAUL *pulls out a hunk of metal shaped like a grenade.*

PAUL. Anybody know what this is?

ROBERT. Looks like a grenade.

PAUL *tosses it to his dad, who catches it handily.*

ALICE. Oh! No—

PAUL. Don't worry, Mom. It's dead. I found this on the beach at Normandy. I took it to an expert who told me it was used during World War II.

ROBERT. You'd think they'd have combed the beaches clean by now.

PAUL *pulls out a couple books, hefts them.*

PAUL. Hey, is my bookcase empty?

ALICE. I gave all your old science-fiction magazines to Ronnie. That is what you wanted me to do, isn't it?

ROBERT *looks at the books in* PAUL's *trunk.*

ROBERT. The *Journal of Discourses*. Where did you get those?

PAUL. There's a European Distribution center in Liège. I ordered them.

ROBERT. When did you have time to read them?

PAUL. Haven't read them all yet.

ROBERT. Didn't you have a prescribed reading list as missionaries?

PAUL. I read all those. The Book of Mormon six times. These were in between. You know me. Always the voracious reader.

ROBERT. You should have stayed with the scriptures. There's some questionable material—

PAUL. Questionable? Brigham Young. Heber C. Kimball. Orson Pratt. How can anything they say be considered questionable?

ROBERT. I don't know. I've never read them—

PAUL. Never read them! Dad, this is history! This is the Church in its infancy.

ROBERT. I've never read them simply because there is so much that the modern Church leaders have written that just to keep track—

PAUL. There's some great stuff in here! You know, if you were to preach some of these things today, half the Church would get up and walk out.

ROBERT. Precisely why we shouldn't read them. At least missionaries shouldn't read them. There's deep doctrine in there. I've heard of some missionaries who've lost their testimonies from reading the *Discourses*.

PAUL. Did you know there are over twenty different times, over as many years, that Brigham Young taught the Adam-God theory?

ROBERT. That's open to interpretation.

PAUL. There are accounts in journals relating to Orson Pratt, who didn't believe the doctrine, arguing with Brigham Young, who did.

ROBERT. Then if the books contain false doctrines, why did you read them?

PAUL. (*Shrugs.*) They were interesting.

ROBERT. I don't deny that there are many great truths in the *Journal of Discourses*. But the modern prophets have said that belief in Adam as our God is a false belief. Why Brigham Young taught it, or if he taught it as we understand the doctrine, I don't know. (*Pause.*) Anyway, this is not the time or place to get into this kind of discussion—if, indeed, there ever is a time or place. You're home safe and we're very glad. How was the flight over?

PAUL. Long. The food was good, but not as good as your home cooking. By the way, Mom, what's for dinner tonight?

ALICE. You haven't changed a bit, have you? Well, why don't you try and guess? What kind of meal would I make on such a special day?

PAUL. Hmm—let's see. Fried chicken?

ALICE. That's right.

PAUL. And for dessert, German chocolate cake!

ALICE. You guessed it.

PAUL. Do we have to wait for everyone to get here? (PAUL *remembers something. Starts rummaging in through one of the suitcases.)* I almost forgot. There's something else I want to show you in my suitcase, and Mom, you sidetracked me. *(He pulls out something wrapped in paper, holds it out before him as he now leads his mother and father to the dining room table. As* PAUL *puts the small package on the counter:)* Therefore, I cannot be held responsible for any damage to your olfactory nerves! *(He unwraps:)* Ta-TAH! French cheese. *(He acts the part of a French missionary.)* Bonjour, Madame. Et que voulez-vous aujourd-hui? Du fromage? Eh, bien, nous avons du camembert, du gruyére, et un peu de babybel. *(*ALICE *reacts to the smell of the camembert.)* Now do you see why I didn't want to send these along in the trunk? That took a month and a half to get here. Anyway, Mom, add this to the dinner menu tonight.

ALICE. None of this . . . is bad . . . is it?

PAUL. No. Just smells that way.

ALICE. If you say so . . .

    ALICE *exits into the kitchen with the cheese.* PAUL *goes back to the trunk.*

ROBERT. You're looking good, son.

PAUL. Thanks. So are you.

ROBERT. No, I mean it. So many young men come home from their missions all fat and out of shape.

PAUL. Well, I exercised every day. Didn't eat too many French pastries. *(Pause)* Coming home a year early helped a lot, too, I guess.

ROBERT. You seem to have picked up the lingo pretty well.

PAUL. Yeah. Wouldn't that surprise Mrs. Holt? She thought I'd never learn French. *(Pause.)* Dad, when you were on a mission, did they ever play pranks on new missionaries?

ROBERT. Oh, yes, I suppose—

PAUL. I bet they were never like the ones we pulled. This one happened to my first companion when he was a greenie. His first senior comp had this whole thing prearranged with one of the sisters in the local branch. Anyway, when the greenie arrives at the train station, this sister comes up, dressed like a hooker? Anyway, she makes a pass at the greenie, who, of course, refuses. Then she makes a pass at the senior comp. Well, he looks at the greenie, says, "I'll meet you back at the apartment," and walks off with the girl.

    ALICE *enters.*

ALICE. What in heaven's name are you talking about?

ROBERT. Oh, just some missionary hi-jinks, Mother.

ALICE. Paul, you didn't do anything like that, did you?

PAUL. *(Raising his arm to the square.)* Not on your life.

ALICE. I certainly hope not. Those kinds of things are not becoming a missionary . . . Is that cheese going to affect everything else in the refrigerator?

PAUL. Don't worry about it.

ALICE. If it does, I'll make you clean out the entire refrigerator, all by yourself.

PAUL. As long as I can have all the leftovers.

ALICE. It's a deal.

ROBERT. *(Gestures to* ALICE.*)* Mother—

> ALICE *suddenly remembers something and exits through the hallway stage left.*

PAUL. What's going on?

ROBERT. You just sit still, young man.

PAUL. Hey—

ROBERT. Hurry up, Mother. Paul's getting restless.

ALICE. *(Off.)* Coming!

> ALICE *enters with a gaily wrapped package held behind her back.*

ROBERT. Since we're all in a giving mood, we've got something for you.

PAUL. Me? What for?

ROBERT. What for? Because you're our son and we love you.

> ALICE *doesn't know what else to do, so, all a-flutter, gives* PAUL *the present.*

PAUL. You guys didn't need to do this. You gave me enough. You paid for my mission—

ROBERT. Open it and quit complaining.

> PAUL *opens the present, lifts out a sports shirt.*

PAUL. Wow! This is great!

ALICE. Your father picked it out.

ROBERT. Read the card.

PAUL. "Dear Son, Welcome back to the real world!" Thanks. My first Gentile shirt.

ALICE. I hope it fits. I wasn't sure if your size had changed.

> PAUL *sees something in the pocket.*

PAUL. What's this? (ROBERT *gestures to* ALICE. *They both watch in silence as* PAUL *takes out an envelope and opens it.* PAUL*'s expression changes to one of dismay as he reads it.)* I don't understand.

ROBERT. An all expense-paid scholarship to BYU! What do you think of that?

PAUL. I . . . I don't know what to think. How—?

ROBERT. I have friends on the board of trustees, you know.

PAUL. Thanks ... but ... (ROBERT *looks at* ALICE, *then back to* PAUL.) I'm not sure I want to go to BYU.

ROBERT. *(Pause.)* I see.

PAUL. I ... probably should have told you when you mentioned it before.

ALICE. May we ask why, Paul?

ROBERT. Brigham Young has always been our school. For three generations—

PAUL. I'm just not sure if that's where I want to go—

ROBERT. Where else is there?

PAUL. Lots of places. The U of U. There are some good schools in California—

ROBERT. *(Blasphemy!)* California? *(In control.)* But BYU is all you ever talked about before your mission.

PAUL. A lot has happened in a year. I've changed my mind about a lot of things.

ROBERT. That's obvious!

PAUL. Father!

ROBERT. Sorry. *(New tactic.)* But ... uh ... now that your mission is over, you'll be wanting to get married. What better place to find a wife than among the choice daughters of Zion? *(PAUL says nothing.)* You don't want to get married?

PAUL. Yes! But not right away. I ... I want to think about it first.

ROBERT. That's reasonable. Commendable. Marriage is important. You shouldn't rush into it. *(Pause.)* Just don't wait too long.

PAUL. I don't know how long it'll take. I want to be sure.

ROBERT. I mean ... there are certain ... urges in a young man ... that are very powerful ...

PAUL. You mean, "it's better to marry than to burn."

ROBERT. Your namesake couldn't have said it better.

PAUL. If and when I do marry, it won't be to legitimize my lust.

ROBERT. I wasn't saying—

PAUL. I know. I just want my brains and my heart to play a role in the marriage decision.

ROBERT. And they should. Most definitely they should. I couldn't agree more. So BYU is out of the picture?

PAUL. Not totally—

ROBERT. Do you know what kind of people they have down there in California?

PAUL. I certainly do. One of my companions was from L. A. The most spiritual elder I ever met—

ROBERT. I'm not talking about the California Saints, though some of them tend to be a bit liberal. But the other people—

PAUL. What about the "other" people?

ROBERT. They're . . . we'll, they just don't . . . uh . . . look at life the same way we do.

PAUL. Not many people do.

ROBERT. Their standards aren't as high as ours—

PAUL. And I might be corrupted, is that what you're—

ROBERT. No, of course not. You're stronger than that. I know that. But Satan's influence is powerful—

PAUL. Since when is BYU a bastion of virtue?

ROBERT. Granted, BYU has problems . . . like everywhere else. But they're not as widespread. It's a safer environment, that's all I'm saying.

PAUL. Have you ever thought that I might be a good influence to these "corrupted" Californians?

ROBERT. I wouldn't be surprised. You've always had great leadership skills. But it's not wise to play with fire. *(Pause.)* I just think you should reconsider BYU.

PAUL. I will. I told you, I haven't decided for sure yet. *(Pause.)* Until I do, maybe you should keep this. *(He hands* ROBERT *the scholarship.)* And thanks for the shirt. Sincerely. I really like it.

ALICE. You're welcome, son.

> *Awkward pause.* PAUL *stands.*

PAUL. I'm a little tired. Jet lag, I guess. I'd like to lie down for a while.

ALICE. Have a nice nap.

PAUL. Thanks, Mom, the sandwiches were great. Rat-hair baloney and all.

> PAUL *kisses her on the forehead. That isn't enough for her—she pulls him into a hug.*

ALICE. I want my Paul Hug.

> PAUL *exits through the hallway.*

ROBERT. I know they're supposed to change on their missions, but . . . I can't believe this. Did you notice how defensive he was?

ALICE. I wouldn't call it "defensive." "Careful," maybe.

ROBERT. But what has he got to be careful, or defensive, about? Before he left on his mission, we could talk about anything at any time. Now I can't get a straight answer out of him.

ALICE. I think he just needs some time to unwind.

ROBERT. Well, I hope that's all it is. Did you notice how he warms up to you and how he—tenses up—when he talks to me?

ALICE. No, I didn't.

ROBERT. I make him uncomfortable.

ALICE. Well, his father's never been a stake president before.

ROBERT. No, it's more than that.

ALICE. He might . . . be afraid to express his independence around you. Dear, you do give off a stern image.

ROBERT. I do? But that's only when I'm speaking. It's my style, I suppose. But, surely, Paul doesn't think I don't have any compassion.

ALICE. I'm sure he doesn't.

ROBERT. Something happened to him while he was out there, Mother, to change his mind about things. A young man doesn't go on a mission with the bright hope of the gospel in his eyes and one year later ask to be released—for no reason. Maybe it's that girl—what was her name . . . ?

ALICE. Dominique.

ROBERT. Maybe he's gone and fallen in love.

ALICE. Why didn't he bring her back home with him?

ROBERT. Maybe he will, Mother. Maybe he will.

ALICE. It sounded to me like he didn't know what to do in that department.

ROBERT. You're probably right. I'm just grasping at straws. *(Frustrated.)* Why doesn't he tell us, Mother?

ALICE. In his own due time, I'm sure he will.

ROBERT. He must know how all this is affecting us. *(Pause.)* Maybe that's what he's trying to do. Some strange transference of guilt.

ALICE. Bob, you're not thinking—?

ROBERT. I've seen some troubled missionaries do some strange things, Alice. For obvious reasons, we don't talk about it but we've had problems with some missionaries. This one missionary in the East Stake—

ALICE. Bob, I don't want to—

ROBERT. No, no. I'm not going to tell you his name. But some missionaries walked into class one morning in the MTC and found the chalked outline of a man's body on the floor, with a knife severing the heart. The missionary who drew that is in therapy now.

ALICE. How sad.

ROBERT. There's no denying that the extreme discipline of missionary work can take its toll on certain types of individuals. But Paul is not that type. He has four brothers who told him what the mission field was like. He went on that two-week mission when he was a priest. He got straight A's in Seminary. He was more prepared than any missionary I know. So why? *(Pause)* It's the influence of the world, that's what it is. Things were so much simpler when we were younger. We were more sheltered. The ways of the world were unknown to us. Everything was laid out before you in nice, neat little packages. If you were a boy, you went on a mission. There was no deciding to do. It was expected. If you were a girl, you grew up to be a mother. It never even occurred to young LDS women of our day to pursue a career. Everyone was in his rightful place.

ALICE. Concessions have had to be made.

ROBERT. I know. But how are we ever going to be a Zion people if we make concessions all the time?

ALICE. They stopped polygamy. Wasn't that a concession?

ROBERT. That was a commandment of God on which depended the future of the Church.

ALICE. So maybe these . . . modern concessions are for the same reason. After all, Bob, whether we like it or not, this is the world we're living in.

ROBERT. But we don't have to be of the world as much as we are.

ALICE. Isn't it true that many of these concessions were directed by the prophets?

ROBERT. Yes, but what caused the changes? That's the key factor. The weakness, the vanity of the people. God gives us what we ask for—either to our exaltation or our damnation.

ALICE. All I know is that if Paul is doing anything wrong—if he's making any kind of mistake—he'll eventually come to see that. He'll be all right.

ROBERT. I certainly hope so, Mother.

The glass figurine PAUL *gave* ALICE *sits on the coffee table.* ALICE *reaches down, picks it up.* ROBERT *sits in a chair, thumbing through the journal* PAUL *gave him, which is also on the coffee table.*

ALICE. This is so delicate. I'm almost afraid to touch it. Wasn't it sweet of Paul? These gifts?

ROBERT. *(Absent-mindedly.)* It certainly was.

ALICE. He's always been very thoughtful about things like this.

ROBERT. *(Ditto.)* Yes, he has.

ALICE. I'll never forget that time he brought home that handful of weeds and presented them to me as a bouquet of flowers.

ROBERT. You put them in a vase and we had to look at those dreadful things all through dinner.

ALICE. The other boys made fun of them, and you told them to be quiet.

ROBERT. Well, he was so proud of them. As if they were the most artistically designed bouquet in the whole world. I couldn't stand to see him disappointed. (ROBERT *looks at the journal in his hands.*) He must have done something on his mission to be proud of if he went to all this trouble of having his journal typed up.

ALICE. I think it shows a lot of respect for you as his father. He may be too embarrassed to tell you how he feels, but he's certainly capable of showing it. (ROBERT *hasn't been listening because he's been reading in the journal. Now, he sets it aside, though open, stands up and moves away, overcome with emotion.* ALICE *reaches for the book. She reads aloud.*) "Got my copy of the Stake Newsletter today. Read Dad's talk. It really blew me away. He said something in there that I have a lot of difficulty believing. He was talking about young men going on missions and said, 'To any of you prospective missionaries who might be considering whether you should go on a mission or not, I address these words: "My young brethren, you have no choice. The prophet has called you. You *must* go."'"

ROBERT. *(Pause.)* My son thinks I forced him to go on a mission.

ALICE. Well, you have to admit, those were strong words.

ROBERT. But they're true. The prophet said it's every young man's duty to go on a mission. That's pretty explicit language. When the prophet speaks, the thinking is done.

ALICE. Still there are ways to make that message a little more palatable.

ROBERT. All right, maybe I came on a little bit strong.

ALICE. Just "a bit"?

ROBERT. All right, "a lot." But I was straight and to the point. You have to admit that. I was straight and to the point.

ALICE. So's an ice pick.

ROBERT. What are you saying?

ALICE. I'm saying that this Church is filled with millions of individuals. With millions of different ways of looking at the gospel. And your son is one of those individuals.

ROBERT. But isn't the purpose of the gospel to turn those individuals into one heart and soul?

ALICE. Some are a little harder than others.

ROBERT. Why does Paul have to be one of them? The other boys were never like that. And Paul never was either. Until his mission.

ALICE. Do you remember, you told me once that Paul was your favorite?

ROBERT. Yes, yes.

ALICE. Could that have been because he was so different from the others? Don't we all tend to stand behind a file leader who's distinctive? Look at Joseph Smith. No more individualistic a man could be found in his time. He couldn't fit into a mold. Brigham Young was another one. If that's the reason you love Paul so much—because he is so different, then making him fit into a mold would lessen your love . . . wouldn't it?

ROBERT. I don't know. I don't know anything anymore. I thought I understood Paul but I don't. Maybe I never did. I do know one thing: He doesn't understand me if thinks I coerced him to go on a mission. I encouraged him. Maybe my language was a little—very harsh—but . . . I haven't been a stake president very long. I haven't learned the finesse of some of the other brethren. Maybe I was over-enthusiastic, but it's only because I so want Paul to do the right thing. I so want him to be happy.

ALICE. Even if what makes him happy differs from what you expect? Bob, all things considered, he is our son.

ROBERT. When I was called to my first position of leadership—elders' quorum president—President Jameson pulled a piece of string out of his pocket and laid it on the desk between us. "Brother Baines," he said, "I want you to push that piece of string across the desk to me and keep it perfectly straight." I tried and, of course, it just crumpled up under the pressure. "Now try and pull it from the front and keep it straight." That was much easier. "As you lead the brethren in your quorum," he told me, "don't stand behind them and push. Stand in front and gently, ever so gently, pull them toward you." *(Pause.)* I've tried to do that all my life. I've never forced anyone to obey the gospel. Where does Paul get the idea that I have? Mother, I'm trying to understand him. Believe me, I'm trying.

ALICE. I know you are, dear. And, remember, the most important thing you can do is let Paul tell you why he came home. *(Kisses him.)* I need to clean up the lunch things. (ALICE *looks at* ROBERT, *sees something in his face, an indication that he isn't listening to her, that he has decided something. She tries to stop him as he heads toward the telephone.*) Robert, don't—

ROBERT *punches in eleven numbers.*

ROBERT. Hello, this is President Baines. (PAUL *enters from the hallway, his hair a bit mussed from his brief nap, wearing house slippers and his "Gentile" shirt.*) Elder Paul Baines's father. Is President Andrews in? *(Pause.)* Well, then, could you leave him a message to call me? Thank you.

ROBERT *hangs up. Turning, he notices* PAUL *and* ALICE.

PAUL. You won't even allow me the dignity of telling you myself, will you? Well, I'm going to, anyway.

ALICE. Paul, you don't—

PAUL. Yes, I do, Mother! You wanted me to tell you about Frére DuChamp. All right, I will. But first, let me tell you about my last companion. Elder Wainwright was my first greenie—a farm boy from Salem, Utah. Spent his whole life on the farm. As innocent as they come. The very first door he ever knocked on, the lady slammed it in his face. He just stood there for a moment, overcome with shock. "What's the matter?" I said. I thought maybe he had narcolepsy or something. "I can't believe it," he said. "She didn't want to hear about the Church. How can anyone not want to know about the Church?" It wasn't just a question he tossed out to keep the conversation going between doors. He was actually flabbergasted! "You find that surprising?" I asked. He said: "I've never known anybody who wasn't a Mormon. I don't understand how anybody can live without the gospel." So let me tell you about Frére DuChamp. We found him about a month and a half later. It was nine-thirty at night and the rain had been coming down in solid sheets, it seemed at the time. We were soaked to the skin and probably should have been home in our warm beds, but there we were, thoughts of the pioneers running through our heads, along with strains of "Come, Come, Ye Saints." Onward, ever onward, in the grand tradition of Paul, Ammon, Parley P. Pratt, to spread the Word at all costs. There was one building left in this particular complex we'd been tracting. As we approached, I admit to having had second thoughts, thinking that maybe, since it was so late, we should go home. But then I remembered something they'd taught us at the MTC: "When you want to go home, just knock on one last door. The golden convert you seek may be waiting." So that's what I did. I knocked on just one more door. This little man answered the door. He was maybe in his thirties and his eyes seemed to brighten as he looked at us. Well, we did the usual spiel . . . and that was when he broke into tears . . . It turns out he'd been praying for God to send someone with the truth about religion to his door. He was indeed the golden contact we'd been seeking. He took all the lessons and was baptized the following Saturday. After his baptism, we were at his home for a little celebration. He went to the refrigerator and brought out some kind of cola drink. He put the bottle down as if it had suddenly caught fire and looked at my companion and me with the most woeful look on his face. "Is this against the Word of Wisdom? If it is, just tell me and I'll never drink it again. I'll do whatever you tell me." I just couldn't bear—. Finally, I called up President Andrews. This is why I came home. Because of a farm boy from Idaho to whom the very idea of a happy non-Mormon was incomprehensible and because of a little Frenchman who was willing to alter his complete lifestyle merely because I said so.

ROBERT. But Brother DuChamp was baptized months ago.

PAUL. It wasn't an easy decision to make, Dad. I had to think about it for a while.

ROBERT. Maybe you should have—

PAUL. I did. *(Pause.)* Like I said. It's all in the journal.

   PAUL *moves toward the front door.*

ROBERT. Where are you going?

PAUL. Wherever I want to.

> PAUL *exits out the front door. Pause.* ALICE *crosses to* ROBERT. ROBERT *takes her in his arms.* ROBERT *and* ALICE *break their embrace.* ROBERT *goes to the window, looks out.*

ROBERT. He's been going through a rebellious stage, that's all. He's been trained well. He'll cool off, then come back and apologize. After a few days, he'll probably ask to finish out his mission.

ALICE. "He's been trained well"? You make him sound like a circus animal.

ROBERT. I was just paraphrasing scripture: "Train up a child in the way he should go: and when he is old, he will not depart from it."

ALICE. Roger Grady did. He had good parents.

ROBERT. That's an isolated case—

ALICE. Lehi had two sons who never came back.

ROBERT. Yes . . .

ALICE. Elohim had a rebellious son.

ROBERT. Alice, are you siding with him and his radical ideas?

ALICE. What's so radical about a son wanting his father to love him?

ROBERT. My love for him is not the issue here. He obviously feels he's been coerced into going on his mission.

ALICE. Hasn't he?

ROBERT. You sound as though you're condoning his actions.

ALICE. *(Immediately regretting this sudden outburst.)* I'm not condoning anything. I just think I know how he feels.

ROBERT. What do you mean?

ALICE. Robert, it's . . . very difficult living in the shadow of a great man.

ROBERT. *(Slow, pained.)* You, too?

ALICE. Don't think I don't support you—

ROBERT. I can't very well ask to be released simply because my family finds it difficult to live with me.

ALICE. And I'm not asking you to.

ROBERT. I know. I know. This thing with Paul has me so upset, I don't know what I'm saying anymore . . .

ALICE. We'll figure out Paul together.

ROBERT. That's really the only way, isn't it? *(Pause.)* So what do you think? What's

Paul's problem?

ALICE. I think it's exactly what he says it is. He doesn't feel he can handle the responsibility.

ROBERT. When he said, "I'm going wherever I want to go?" When he left in a huff? And there's that passage in his journal. I think he's making some stand for independence.

ALICE. That, too.

ROBERT. Then I'm worried. Because the independent thinker has no place in the Church. "Let Thy will be done." Not ours. The whole plan of the Church is to subjugate our own egos to the Lord's. If Paul can't do that, then he's in for a difficult time for the rest of his life. I wish President Andrews would call back.

ALICE. You should have let Paul tell you at his convenience.

ROBERT. So you're saying I made my own son leave this house?

ALICE. Don't be so hard on yourself. I'm sure I'm part of the problem, too.

ROBERT. You—?

ALICE. And his brothers. We're all a family. We're all responsible to some degree for whatever's happening to Paul. He's zeroed in on you because you're the most visible.

ROBERT. Alice, I don't want to lose him. I love him.

ALICE. Then when he comes back, why don't you tell him?

ROBERT. He knows I love him.

ALICE. Does *he*?

ROBERT. It should be quite evident, I would think, after all these years. I've told him many times before. I've spent quality time with him. I've had personal priesthood interviews with him. We've played handball together. Exactly what I've done with all the other boys.

ALICE. But Paul isn't like the other boys. We've already established that. He needs to be treated differently. You need to let him be himself, right or wrong.

ROBERT. He's only twenty years old and obviously is not capable of making correct choices.

ALICE. Paul isn't some hardened criminal you're letting loose on society. He's a highly intelligent, spiritual young man who's going through some real emotional problems right now.

ROBERT. Why do I feel like it's you and him versus the mean ogre of a dad?

ALICE. I'm not taking sides. I can't take sides where matters of the heart are concerned. I love you both. I want you both to be happy, but each in your own way. And you're not a mean ogre. A little stubborn around the edges, maybe . . .

ROBERT. *(Pause.)* You know what I'd like, Alice? It's strange, because I haven't thought of this for many years—at least not since my mission. I wish that . . . somehow . . . I could just take everything that's in my heart and soul, everything I know and feel about this glorious Church and transfer it wholesale into Paul. If he could only see the great vision of this work as I do there'd be no problem, no conflict between us.

ALICE. And no growth.

ROBERT. *(Slight laugh.)* "Oh, that I were an angel," said Alma, who later realized he had sinned in his desire.

> ROBERT *stands looking out the window.* PAUL *enters from the side fence, crosses over, kneels to look at the azalea bush.* ROBERT *goes out, stands in silence behind his son. Pause. Without turning:*

PAUL. I . . . I just had to walk around for a little while.

ROBERT. That's all right.

> PAUL *stands.*

PAUL. What was it you said about planting an azalea bush? "I knew that as it matured in my garden, that you would be maturing in another field."

ROBERT. Paul, you don't—

PAUL. When I saw you on the telephone to President—

ROBERT. Son, I'm sorry about that. I should have waited and let you tell me.

PAUL. This whole thing—my coming home early—must have been a great shock to you.

> ROBERT *puts his arm around* PAUL *as they move toward the house.*

ROBERT. It did concern us somewhat.

PAUL. Dad, you always were one with the understatement when it came to expressing yourself. Admit it: My coming home early blew you away.

ROBERT. Well, I wouldn't say it in those words—

PAUL. Come on, now.

ROBERT. All right. It blew me away.

PAUL. Did you cry, Dad?

ROBERT. I . . . suppose . . .

PAUL. Did you?

ROBERT. I was disappointed, and . . . uh . . . yes, I did cry a bit.

> ALICE *comes over, hugs* PAUL.

ALICE. I know I did.

PAUL. Would it surprise you to know that I did, too? The night I decided to go home, I just lay in bed staring at the ceiling for the longest time. When it finally came to me that—whatever else I was—I just wasn't cut out to be a missionary . . . I cried. Because, more than anything, I wanted to be! I wanted to do such a good job, to please the Lord, you and Mom . . . myself. *(Pause.)* And after what seemed like maybe a half hour . . . this absolutely incredible feeling of peace swept over me. It started at the exact center of my chest and seemed to swirl outward—this fantastic feeling of . . . *warmth* that left my entire body tingling. And the more I thought about going home, the better it felt. When I thought that maybe I ought to reconsider, to stay, it started to fade. *(Pause.)* I didn't cry after that.

ROBERT. Are you telling me that God told you to come home early from your mission?

PAUL. I won't propose to speak for God. That's your job! *(Softer now.)* I'm just telling you that I felt good about my decision. I told you this because I think you'll come to feel good about it, too . . . in time.

ALICE *tries to avert what she senses is coming.*

ALICE. We're just glad you're home safe.

PAUL. Anyway, that's it. When I told President Andrews how I felt, when I was able to convince him that my wanting to leave wasn't just a case of homesickness, he agreed to send me home. I didn't want him to tell you because . . . because I knew how it might sound out of context.

ROBERT *is seething now, but still in control.*

ROBERT. So that's it? The reason you came home early? Explained "in context?"

ALICE. Robert—

ROBERT. Son, about this Brother DuChamp and your missionary companion. You know, you can't judge the truthfulness of the Church by the actions of a few.

PAUL. *(Exasperated.)* You still don't understand, do you? You think I'm judging the Church, that I've lost my testimony or something?

ROBERT. You said you came home because of them—

PAUL. That doesn't mean I lost my testimony of the Church. Or of missionary work, for that matter. If I lost anything, it was the testimony of myself. When I first got out—full of missionary zeal, determined to convert the world—I'd always been taught that the gospel was the only true path to happiness. But the longer I was over in France, the more French people I met who were content, absolutely content in their way of life—I even taught a man once who told me that the Holy Ghost had told him his church was true—

ROBERT. There are many sincere deluded people in the world.

PAUL. And then when Frère DuChamp told me what he did—that his eternal salvation rested in whatever I told him to do, I couldn't take it. Dad, I could hardly govern my own life, let alone the life of another person. To have someone follow me blindly when I could hardly see the way myself . . . I just wasn't ready for that.

ROBERT. Many recent converts exhibit such blind faith. The more mature they become, the more sure of themselves they become, the more they begin to think for themselves.

PAUL. Unless you're a young man going on a mission.

ROBERT. That's different. That's a direct call from the prophet.

PAUL. Is it? The prophet individually calls every missionary?

ROBERT. I don't claim to understand how inspiration works in every situation. But I've heard many young men bear testimony that, as far their personal growth was concerned, their mission came at just the right time, or they were sent to just the right place—

PAUL. I don't doubt that. I just know it didn't happen to me. I felt good about my decision to come home, that's all I can say.

ROBERT. Maybe you should have given your mission more of a chance—

PAUL. That's your solution to everything, isn't it? Whatever's wrong with the world, the gospel can fix.

ROBERT. No one's ever claimed the gospel was a magic curative. People have to use it correctly.

PAUL. And how do they do that, if not by using their free agency?

ROBERT. You're right—

PAUL. So do you see the dilemma? On the one hand, the Church tells people to follow the prophet: "He will not allow you to be led astray." On the other hand, we're told to use our free agency, to let the Spirit tell us what to do.

ROBERT. What do you think your free agency is, if not the freedom to follow the prophet?

PAUL. *(Another approach.)* Dad, why was the war in heaven fought?

ROBERT. You know the answer to that.

PAUL. It wasn't just because Lucifer wanted the glory of God, but because he wanted to FORCE PEOPLE TO BE GOOD! I think sometimes we get the impression that Lucifer's plan was to make us do horrible things against our will. But that wasn't it at all. He wanted to *make* us pay tithing. He wanted to *make* us go on missions, WHETHER WE WANTED TO OR NOT! *(Pause, softer.)* Can't you see that, even if it's for a good reason, no man should force another?

ROBERT. Neither I, nor anyone else, forced you to go on a mission!

PAUL. There are more subtle ways, more sure ways to force people. Peer pressure: "All my friends are going on missions. I guess I should go;" intimidation: "My young brethren, you have no choice!" Dad, I'm not saying that guys shouldn't go on missions. They should. If they want to.

ROBERT. You're beginning to sound like one of those Mormon intellectuals who—

PAUL. "The glory of God is intelligence."

ROBERT. A questioning mind is a faithless mind.

PAUL. "Let us reason together." Have you heard that passage before? With what do you reason if not your mind—your intellect?

ROBERT. Your intellect tempered with the Spirit. And when your reasoning disagrees with the revealed word of God, then your reasoning is faulty.

PAUL. Then what do you do if "the revealed word of God" differs with other "revealed words of God"?

ROBERT. Now you're talking nonsense.

PAUL. Am I? Brigham Young said, on many occasions, "You cannot get to the highest degree of heaven if you only have one wife." But today, if you marry another woman, you're exed. Two diametrically opposed statements. Which one's right?

ROBERT. They both are.

PAUL. Now you're talking nonsense.

ROBERT. Brigham Young's statement was true for his time.

PAUL. But isn't God an unchanging god, the "same yesterday, today, and forever"? Why two different doctrines a hundred years apart?

ROBERT. It's the same doctrine—the same principle—just the way of practicing it differs. Principles never change. Practices do.

PAUL. Maybe. But do the Saints know that? You should hear some of the incredible lengths people go to make it look like tithing, the Word of Wisdom, and Sunday School have always existed.

ROBERT. You can say what you like, but the Church is true and the prophet will never lead us astray. That's all that matters to me. That's my iron rod.

PAUL. Then if the prophet can do no wrong—

ROBERT. I didn't say that. No one is perfect. But God would not allow him to teach false doctrine.

PAUL. Then why does the Doctrine and Covenants provide for a court to try the prophet? If he could never lead us astray, there would be no need for a court. Look at the Book of Mormon—

ROBERT. Mother, are you noticing? First he blasphemes the prophet. Now it's the scriptures.

PAUL. If the Book of Mormon is without flaw, if there can be no mistake in it—

ROBERT. There have been typographical—

PAUL. Then why did Joseph Smith call it the "most correct book"? Why does it say on the title page, "If there be mistakes, they are the mistakes of men." If prophets can't make mistakes, then why the disclaimer?

ROBERT. So you're saying the prophet is just like any other men?

PAUL. No, I'm not! He's a very inspired human being, whose very opinion I highly praise. But I must reserve the right to decide for myself on his or anybody else's teaching. If I can't have that right, then free agency is a joke. Then the war in heaven never happened. *(Pause.)* Do you think I like what's happened to me? Sure, I felt good about coming home but I didn't feel good about what it would do to you—what you would think of me—(ALICE *tries to intervene.)* Mother, I know how he feels. And though I know that, in my particular case—as far as I'm concerned—I've done the right thing by coming home, it causes me no pleasure to know that I've been a disappointment to both of you.

ALICE. Paul—

PAUL. There's no use denying it, Mother! You know as well as I do that, in this society, a missionary who comes home early is just one step above a divorced woman in the hierarchy of "People with Whom It Is Not Wise to Associate." Do you think I look forward to that stereotype for the rest of my life?

ALICE. Paul, no true Latter-day Saint would feel that way—

PAUL. I'm not condemning the Church. It's just a few individuals. But many of those individuals are in leadership positions, and they're influencing others to the same close-minded kind of thinking.

ROBERT. All right, you've said your piece. Now let me give you my impressions of your experience. But first, I want you to know that this comes from the innermost depths of my love for you. And I hope you perceive it that way. *(Pause.)* You know perfectly well that there are many lying and deceiving spirits in the world today. And that, in the last days, they will deceive and lead astray even the very elect.

PAUL. Yes, but—

ROBERT. Please, Paul, let me continue. You said you felt good about your decision to come home. Isn't it just possible, isn't there just the slightest chance, that what you felt was a clever imitation?

PAUL. What is this? You think I'm possessed or something?

ALICE. Dear, what are you trying to say?

ROBERT. Isn't that possible?

PAUL. No.

ROBERT. Have you ever felt similar "good feelings?"

PAUL. No...

ROBERT. Then you have nothing to compare this to, do you?

PAUL. Well, no . . .

ROBERT. Then it could have been a . . . Satanic imitation, couldn't it have?

ALICE. *(Shocked)* Bob!

PAUL. I know what I felt!

ROBERT. But with nothing to compare it to, you have no way of knowing for sure that you received a manifestation from God or from some other source, do you?

PAUL. I never said it came from God in the first place. I just know that I felt good afterwards.

ROBERT. Son, the devil and his angels swing into high gear with missionaries and those in other positions of authority. They pull out all the stops and will do anything they can to discourage the servants of the Lord. *(Pause.)* I know. *(Pause.)* Because it happened to me. *(This drops like a lead balloon in the room.)* It was just after I got my call to the stake presidency. Do you remember the day it happened, Mother?

ALICE. I'll never forget it.

ROBERT. When we got back from the interview, we just sat around the house for the longest while, not saying anything. I suppose I must have looked miserable because your mother asked me, "Who died?" "Me," I said. "My old self has died. I'll never be the same again." Soon, thoughts started running through my head, thoughts like: "Who do you think you are, Robert Baines? You, a stake president? Ha!" I began to doubt, thinking of all the things I still had to do, of the change in my status in the eyes of my neighbors and friends. I, Robert M. Baines, would soon have the responsibility of speaking in the name of Jesus Christ to the entire stake, "as if from mine own mouth," the scripture says. I felt woefully inadequate. I went so far as to actually pick up the phone to tell them I couldn't do it. But I hung up, got down on my knees—*(Which he does now)*—right there in my office, and prayed until the horrible feeling was replaced by an overwhelming feeling of peace—true peace. Not transitory peace. Not false peace. But the kind of peace that can only come from Christ. *(Looks at* PAUL.*)* Kneel with me, Paul. *(*PAUL *stands.)* Alice, kneel with me and Paul and let's pray—let's each of us pray that the veil might be lifted from your eyes, that you might see the error of your way. Paul, kneel with me. Alice. *(*ALICE *kneels)* Come on, Paul.

PAUL. No.

ROBERT. Then Mother and I will pray. *(*ROBERT *takes* ALICE's *hand. She looks at* PAUL, *begging him with her eyes to join them; he doesn't. She then bows her head as* ROBERT *starts praying.)* Our Father in Heaven, we humbly kneel before Thee at this time . . .

PAUL. What are you trying to do?

ROBERT. *(Going on:)* . . . with a desire in our hearts that Thou shalt shed Thy Spirit upon this household—that our son, Paul, whom we both love more than life itself—may see the error of his ways, that he may repent of his weak faith . . .

PAUL. Please, stop . . .

ROBERT. . . . and recommit himself to the high and holy calling which is his, of proclaiming Thy word to the inhabitants of this mortal sphere . . .

PAUL. Dad, please . . .

ROBERT. Let him once again feel Thy love for him, that whatever evil influence hath overtaken him may be purged from his soul forever.

PAUL. I know what you're trying to do!

ROBERT. That he may return to full worthiness in thy Church and kingdom—

PAUL. WILL YOU SHUT UP, DAMMIT!

Silence. ALICE *breaks into tears, gets up and moves away.* ROBERT *stays on his knees.*

ROBERT. And forgive our son his sacrilege. In the name of Jesus Christ. Amen. (ROBERT *stands, moves to his son. Pause.*) What has made your heart so hard?

PAUL. It's not hard. How can it be . . . when it's broken in two?

PAUL, *barely able to hold back his anger, strides across the room and out the back door.* ALICE *casts a killer glance at* ROBERT, *who is not looking at her. The phone rings once, twice before it is answered by* ALICE.

ALICE. Hello?

She holds out the phone to ROBERT.

ROBERT. Hello. *(Pause.)* You think so? All right, I'll be right down. No, no. That's all right. I wasn't doing anything important.

ROBERT *hangs up the phone, goes to the front door to get his keys, turns to tell* ALICE *where he's going, thinks better of it, then turns to go out the front door. He sees* PAUL's *journal sitting on the coffee table, picks it up, then goes out the door.* PAUL *stands at the edge of the garden, looking away. Sound of garage door opening and car driving away.* ALICE *crosses down to* PAUL, *looks down, sees* ROBERT's *trowel on the ground, picks it up.* PAUL *enters.*

ALICE. He left his trowel out here. It'll get rusty.

PAUL. I heard him leave—

ALICE. The man at the nursery called, they spoke for a few minutes . . .

PAUL. *(Re: the azalea bush.)* Maybe it needs more water.

ALICE. He waters it every day.

PAUL. Maybe it gets too much.

ALICE. Did you know there's a history behind each of these plants?

PAUL. He likes to tell us, doesn't he?

ALICE *moves down the row.* PAUL *follows.*

ALICE. Whenever some milestone is reached in his life, he'll plant a shrub or a flower. This one is when David was born. This was when your father sold his first insurance policy. (ALICE *stops at the azalea bush*) And you know what this one is for?

PAUL. It's the only bush that's dying. Isn't that interesting?

ALICE. Your father is happiest when he's out here in the garden. He says it gives him time to think about things.

PAUL. I tried growing a little garden in one of the places I lived. I guess I didn't inherit his green thumb because nothing edible came up.

ALICE. I can't seem to make anything grow, either. I asked your father about that once. "Alice, it's more than just digging a hole and dropping in a seed. You've got to nurture these plants. And that means a lot of 'TLC.'" Tender Loving Care—that's the difference, I guess. *(Pause.)* You know your father's a frustrated gardener.

PAUL. Yeah...

ALICE. That's what he wanted to do when we first got married, did you know that? Open up his own nursery.

PAUL. Really? Then how did he ever get into insurance?

ALICE. That was because of me. I wouldn't let him become a gardener. It was our first... disagreement.

PAUL. What do you mean, you wouldn't let him?

ALICE. Security. I wanted the steady income—not that insurance was steadier, but it had more potential. I felt uneasy not knowing where our next meal was coming from. *(Pause.)* "Security." A word that's probably killed more dreams than anything else.

PAUL. How come I never knew about this?

ALICE *looks up, suddenly realizing what she has done.*

ALICE. Oh, no...!

PAUL. Something wrong?

ALICE. I... uh... your father...

PAUL. Don't tell me. I can guess. He never wanted you to tell us. (ALICE *nods.*) Why is that man so afraid of anybody seeing his weaknesses?

ALICE. He believes that being an example—

PAUL. It can drive you crazy, that's what being an example can do. Never doing anything because you're afraid someone looking over your shoulder will misconstrue your actions, and you'll be responsible for them going inactive or something.

ALICE. As he often tells me: "Avoid the appearance of evil."

PAUL. So Dad was afraid we'd figure he was weak because he gave in to his wife?

ALICE. He didn't "give in." He agreed with me.

PAUL. I bet he wouldn't call it that.

ALICE. Maybe so. Your father's a complex man, Paul. It's not easy to point at any one thing and say, "This is Robert Baines."

PAUL. *(Pause.)* So, how's it been? This "security" that Dad "agreed" to?

ALICE. As far as I'm concerned, wonderful. I've been able to feed and clothe five sons. He's given me a marvelous house. For me, it's all I asked for.

PAUL. But for him?

ALICE. For him? I don't know. Maybe he's gotten used to it.

PAUL. Maybe.

ALICE. At least I hope he has.

> A pause. She cries softly. PAUL *takes her in his arms.*

PAUL. Hey, Mom! What is it?

ALICE. Nothing.

PAUL. Teenage girls cry over nothing.

ALICE. Paul, you don't think—? It just suddenly occurred to me that maybe he never has gotten used to it.

PAUL. Has he ever told you that?

ALICE. No. And he never would. He'd keep it inside. He'd never let on.

PAUL. You know what I think? I think you're upset over what's happening between Dad and me.

ALICE. Should I not be? Two men whom I love are both trying to force their differing philosophies on the other.

PAUL. I wasn't—(ALICE *sends a look to him.)* Maybe I was. *(Pause.)* What do you think, Mom? I know how Dad feels about my coming home early. He made that clear enough. But what do you think?

ALICE. You're my son, whatever you do.

PAUL. You're saying you love me even though I did the wrong thing?

ALICE. *(Pause.)* Yes.

PAUL. *(Moving away.)* I thought for sure you'd understand.

ALICE. I do understand. I'm not sure you do, though.

PAUL. It did get pretty heavy there for a while, didn't it?

ALICE. Paul, he was in the middle of a prayer. You shouldn't have interrupted him in the middle of a prayer.

PAUL. He wasn't praying. He was intimidating. I won't be intimidated any more.

ALICE. Paul, your father only—

PAUL. "—wants what's good for me." But why is what he thinks is good for me different than what I think?

ALICE. You interrupted me. I was going to say that he only wants so desperately for you to make the right choices.

PAUL. As he sees what's right.

ALICE. Would that be so wrong? After all, he had many years of experience in the Church—

PAUL. Which only proves he's learned to toe the party line.

ALICE. Is there anything wrong with that?

PAUL. Yeah. If you're doing it because everybody else is.

ALICE. And you think that's what your father is doing?

PAUL. I'm not going to judge him.

ALICE. *(Pause.)* All right, let's pretend you're not judging him.

PAUL. Mom—

ALICE. Just tell me. Do you think your father is "toeing the party line," as you call it, just because everybody else is?

PAUL. No, of course not. I have no doubt he's absolutely sincere in the way he feels.

ALICE. But "wrong," is that what you're saying?

PAUL. I'm not going to answer that. Everyone's entitled to his own opinion.

ALICE. Even if it's a wrong opinion?

PAUL. Who's wrong? Who's right? That's what our whole argument was about in the first place.

ALICE. You must have some opinion. Even the most liberal-minded Mormon must have some opinion of what's right and wrong.

PAUL. I don't want to say he's wrong . . . I . . . can't say what I really think.

ALICE. Why can't you?

PAUL. Because . . . because it'll sound terribly conceited.

ALICE. Maybe I won't see it that way.

PAUL. Have you heard of that passage in the New Testament: "When I was a child, I spake as a child, I understood as a child, I thought as a child: but when I became a man—"

ALICE. "—I put away childish things." Something else by Paul.

PAUL. Well, when I used to have this absolute, unwavering faith, I . . . I was like a child.

ALICE. But now you've matured beyond that.

PAUL. Well, not matured, really. Not progressed, either. "Changed," I guess is the only word.

ALICE. There's another scripture you're forgetting about. "Whosoever shall not receive the kingdom of God as a little child, he shall not enter therein."

PAUL. I can't go back to the way I was. I can't just forget everything I've learned. I've tried.

ALICE. Maybe you should have told that to your father. Maybe if he saw how much agony this is causing you—

PAUL. He wouldn't listen. He only gives Tender Loving Care to his plants.

ALICE. At least his plants don't turn against him.

PAUL. Is that what you think, that I'm rebelling against Dad? I guess I didn't make myself clear.

ALICE. It was hard to find clarity in all that yelling.

PAUL. I tried to do it calmly, but when he wouldn't listen, I just . . . lost control, I guess.

ALICE. That's a good guess.

PAUL. It was my fault, wasn't it? The shouting match.

ALICE. Does it matter whose fault it was? What matters is how it made you feel.

PAUL. Well, it didn't turn out exactly the way I wanted it to. Not even close.

ALICE. How did you want it to turn out?

PAUL. I knew there'd be . . . communication . . . problems, but the reason I asked President Andrews not to say anything is because I wanted to confront those problems myself. I like to fight my own battles.

ALICE. And boy, can you fight!

PAUL. What I expected was: I'd come home, it'd be a little tense at first, but eventually everyone would relax a bit . . . and then I'd tell him.

ALICE. And he would understand, just like that?

PAUL. I guess it was kind of naive of me, wasn't it?

ALICE. You know, dear, those people who can totally change their lives instantly are very rare.

PAUL. I know that.

ALICE. For most of us, any change at all must come over a long period. With your father, that period is longer than with almost anyone.

PAUL. But he's changed—before? There must have been at least one time.

ALICE. There was. It was when I was pregnant with Andrew. Before that, whenever we went any place, your father would always drive the car. It was the unwritten law of the Baines household: "The Man Shall Drive." I had a license but he never let me use it when he was in the car. I asked him about it one time. I can't remember his exact words, but it was something to the effect that women, not being as mechanically inclined as men, weren't as good drivers.

PAUL. *(Almost mocking.)* That's unbelievable.

ALICE. Remember, your father was raised in Utah. Well, when it came time to deliver Andrew, your father was nowhere to be found. So I borrowed a neighbor's car and drove to the hospital myself. When your father learned that not only had I delivered a healthy baby boy, but that I had driven there safely, he turned to me and said—and these words I do remember exactly—"I always knew you could do it." I accepted that as an apology.

PAUL. And did he let you drive after that?

ALICE. Yes, but he'd always wear his seat belt. So, you see, if you want to change the way he thinks—

PAUL. I need to have a baby.

ALICE. You need to be patient and work at it, maybe for quite a long time.

PAUL. Mom, will he ever understand? Will it ever be—between him and me—like it used to be?

ALICE. No. But I think—with work—you'll come pretty close. I will tell you one thing, though. When your father finally comes around, don't expect him to come right out and say it. He may be straight and to the point in his preaching but he'll skirt the issue. He'll say something else. It'll be up to you to see it for what it is: an apology. *(Pause.)* Now it's your turn.

PAUL. What?

ALICE. We've been talking about your father and his weaknesses, as if he's the only one involved in this disagreement.

PAUL. Yeah, but at least he's gone and can't hear what we say.

ALICE. But you're the open-minded one. So let's get philosophical—

PAUL. You don't have to do that. I can take it.

ALICE. Then I'll let you have it. You, in your "open-mindedness" were as letter-of-the-law as he was. You can no more accept his way of looking at things than he can accept yours.

PAUL. I'm more honest with myself than he is.

ALICE. Are you? When you accepted your mission call, you made a commitment to serve for two years. You didn't follow through on that. Does that seem honest to you?

PAUL. I told you. I had no choice. I was ramrodded into the mission field.

ALICE. You always have a choice. You chose to give in to this "intimidation" as you called it. You would have been more honest with yourself—and us—if you had never gone in the first place.

PAUL. I know that! But I couldn't do that—then. I didn't know what I know now.

ALICE. You know what this whole thing sounds like to me? One gigantic case of rationalization.

PAUL. Mom—!

ALICE. What else can I think? You go out in the mission field, excited, vowing to convert the world, and then when it gets a little tough, you tuck your tail between your legs and come home.

PAUL. Do you really believe that?

ALICE. I don't want to, but I've seen precious little else to convince me otherwise.

PAUL. I would have expected this from Dad—

ALICE. You see, you're not the only one in the Church who has your philosophy. I've known quite a few. But there's danger in your way of looking at the gospel, just as there is in wearing blinders all the time. The danger is that, unless you try very hard, you end up questioning everything. And eventually, believing nothing. And a life without belief is a life without hope.

PAUL. Everything I told Dad—

ALICE. Everything you screamed at him.

PAUL. You don't believe any of it?

ALICE. Do you?

PAUL. Let's not get into that again. I was not being influenced by the devil.

ALICE. How do you know that?

PAUL. I already told you how. I had this . . . feeling.

ALICE. Feeling. You mean you didn't sit down and reason out why you shouldn't be on a mission?

PAUL. I told you, I thought about it—

ALICE. If this feeling didn't come from Satan, or wasn't a result of your own feelings of inadequacy, then where did it come from?

PAUL. *(Reluctant.)* I see what you're getting at.

ALICE. Then say it.

PAUL. God.

ALICE. And how do you know that, if not by faith? Don't you see that, sometimes, reasoning is not enough, that even the most "intellectual" Mormon needs to take a step into the darkness every now and then? So what am I telling you? You've said it yourself several times now: "No one is either black or white." There are elements of questioning in all of us.

PAUL. In you?

ALICE. Yes.

Pause. PAUL *looks at her. She starts to speak.*

PAUL. I know. Don't tell Dad.

Another pause.

ALICE. I never thought I would tell that to anyone.

PAUL. I know what you're feeling. Kind of a strange mixture of relief and agony— coalescing somewhere at the base of your heart. You feel like you want to burst with joy that you've finally come to terms with yourself but afraid that, if you do, nothing will come out but this oddly shaped, deformed mass that used to be called "perfect, child-like faith." (ALICE *looks at* PAUL. *Suddenly, she bursts into tears, folding into* PAUL's *arms*) Let it come, Mom. Let it come.

ALICE. Paul. Promise me one thing. Whatever else you tell your father when he gets home, don't—

PAUL. I won't.

ALICE. Because it would destroy him. He already thinks that you and I are teaming up against him. If he found out that I. . . . You know what he told me once? He said the reason he married me was . . . was because I was perfect. That's what he said. So, you mustn't.

PAUL. Don't worry.

ALICE. He just wouldn't know how to handle it. Not yet, anyway.

PAUL. Someday you'll have to do what I did. You'll have to tell him.

ALICE. I know.

PAUL. You know what I think?

ALICE. What?

PAUL. I think that every member of the Church questions things. But most are afraid to admit it, as if by ignoring it, it'll go away. Or maybe they think if they stand up in testimony meeting and say, "I know the gospel's true, but I'm not sure about the Church," they'll somehow be judged as weak in the faith. *(Pause)* What . . . sort of things do you question?

ALICE. So it's my turn, is it? Yes, I suppose I owe you an explanation.

PAUL. You do.

ALICE. You know how we're taught that—you won't think I'm an apostate, will you?

PAUL. Mom, you're talking to Mister Liberal-Minded.

ALICE. It's just that—well, I told this once to your father and he said I should stop thinking about it—that, since it wasn't essential to my salvation—I didn't need to be concerned.

PAUL. "It's not essential to my salvation." The Great Mormon Cop-Out.

ALICE. It has to do with . . . the Creation . . .

PAUL. Go on.

ALICE. Well, you know how we're taught that the world was created by Elohim, Jehovah, and Michael.

PAUL. Yes . . .

ALICE. Well, you see . . .

PAUL. Go ahead. There are no G.A.'s looking over your shoulder.

ALICE. I don't think that's all there is to it. There are—aspects—of the creation that carry a decidedly feminine slant. The flowers, for instance, rainbows . . . all the things of beauty. I'm not saying that a man couldn't have done all that . . . what I'm saying is . . . Don't you think it's possible that maybe . . . Heavenly Mother could have designed those things and given them to her husband to create? Is that such a heretical idea?

PAUL. *(Smiles)* I think it's a beautiful concept.

ALICE. Why are you smiling?

PAUL. I can't believe it. My mother, the Mormon feminist.

ALICE. I'm not!

PAUL. Just kidding.

ALICE. You got me off the subject, which was you.

PAUL. An old missionary trick I learned to keep contacts from rambling.

ALICE. I wasn't rambling.

PAUL. I know, I know.

ALICE. Well, Mr. Open-Minded. Am I right? About you and your father, I mean?

PAUL. Well . . .

ALICE. Come on, now.

PAUL. Yes, you're right.

ALICE. So what we have here are two grown men who aren't willing to just throw doctrine to the wind and let love tell their hearts what to do.

PAUL. I don't know if we ever can. Our basic philosophies seem so diametrically opposed. He's an Iron Rodder and I'm a Liahona.

ALICE. What does that mean?

PAUL. You remember Dad saying that the words of the prophets were his "iron rod?" That's the one basic difference between people like him and me. Some are like in Lehi's dream of the iron rod. As long as they hold on tight, they don't have to worry about anything. They can make it through every mist in a clear, straight line to that beautiful tree. There are others of us who are better symbolized by the Liahona. We don't have the whole picture—feel more comfortable without it, as a matter of fact. We prefer to sort of figure out where we're going one step at a time. I was an "Iron Rodder" before I went on my mission. I'm now a "Liahona." And you don't know how many sleepless nights I've spent praying that I could somehow undo what happened to me—that, in one fell swoop, I could be returned to those days when I had a simple faith. *(Pause.)* Is it a sin, Mom, to pray for ignorance?

ALICE. That's a very fascinating idea. But there's one thing you need to remember about those two objects. They were both made by the same God. He must have done that for some reason. Could not that reason have been that he wants both types of people in the Church? For whatever reason, I don't know. But maybe . . . maybe the Iron Rodder is there to keep the Liahona geared toward the basics. And the Liahona is there to push, pull, and to make noise so that the Iron Rodder will occasionally look up to get the whole picture. Maybe it's God's system of checks and balances—I don't know. What I do know is that you and he will have to figure out some way to get together and resolve this. Whether you give in to him, or he does, or you reach some kind of compromise, I don't care. It's just got to happen. *(Pause)* Or I won't make you any more baloney sandwiches. *(They hug each other. Sound of a car driving up.* ALICE *pulls away.* ROBERT *enters at the side of the house, struggling with a plant.* PAUL *moves to help him.)* What . . . ? Another azalea bush.

ROBERT. A healthy one. (ROBERT *and* PAUL *struggle with the plant, finally putting it on the ground near the old one.)* Thank you, Paul. Leonard told me what was wrong with the other plant. It was getting too much water. The azalea doesn't need a lot of water. In fact, it does better in dry ground. I knew that . . .

PAUL. So what's going to happen to the old one?

ROBERT. Leonard told me I should uproot it and plant this one in its place. Would you like to help me, Paul?

PAUL. Sure.

PAUL *grabs a nearby shovel and starts digging up the old plant.*

ROBERT. Oh, wait! Keep digging, Paul. There's something I've got to get in the house. (ROBERT *crosses to the Standard Works on the side table in the entryway.* PAUL *and* ALICE *look knowingly at each other.* ROBERT *come back out, hands the* Book of Mormon *to* ALICE, *who takes it, looks surprised.* ROBERT *turns to* PAUL.) Excellent job.

Let's get this other one ready to plant. (ROBERT *starts removing the cardboard pot holding the healthy bush.*) Alice, would you read that passage I have marked?

As ROBERT *and* PAUL *work the bush out of its container and into the hole* PAUL *dug:*

ALICE. "And it came to pass that the master of the vineyard went forth, and he saw that his—"

ROBERT. Azalea bush.

ALICE. "And he saw that his azalea bush began to decay, and he said: I will prune it, and dig about it, and nourish it, that perhaps it may shoot forth young and tender branches and it perish not. But behold, the main top thereof began to perish. The master of the vineyard said to his servant: It grieveth me that I should lose this tree."

ALICE *starts to choke.* PAUL *and* ROBERT *finally have the bush ready to put in the hole.* ROBERT *stands, takes over the reading chores as* PAUL *plants the bush.*

ROBERT. "But what could I have done more in my vineyard? I have nourished it, and I have digged about it, and I have pruned it. Who is it that has corrupted my vineyard? And the servant told his master: Is it not the loftiness, or the pride of thy vineyard? (PAUL *stops digging and listens as* ROBERT *continues reading.* ROBERT *is starting to choke up, too, as he reads.*) Have not the branches thereof overcome the roots which are good, growing faster than the strength of the roots? And the Lord of the vineyard said unto the servant: Let us go to and hew down the trees in the vineyard. What could I have done more for my vineyard? (PAUL *looks at* ROBERT, *who moves closer to* ALICE, *puts his arm around her.*) But behold, the servant said unto the Lord of the vineyard: Spare it a little longer. And the Lord said: Yea, I will spare it a little longer . . . (Pause. ROBERT *is really having trouble at this point, but he plugs away to the end.*) For it grieveth me that I should lose the trees of my vineyard."

ROBERT *closes the book, gives it to* ALICE, *then kneels down with* PAUL. *Together the two men tamp down the soil as Alice looks on, smiling.*

Slow fade to blackout.

THE END

Gadianton

Eric Samuelsen

About the Playwright

Eric Samuelsen is one of Mormonism's most prolific[1] and produced playwrights . . . as well as one of its best. Because he recently retired in 2012 as the professor of playwriting in Brigham Young University's Theatre and Media Arts program, the majority of his work has been produced on BYU stages. However, he has also had outside venues open up to his work, not only in other prominent theaters in Utah like Plan B Theatre Company and the Covey Center for the Arts, but he also in New York, California, Indiana, and Louisiana. He is considered a bit of a darling within the Mormon literary community, having won three Association for Mormon Letters Awards in Drama for his plays. However, even after the AML disqualified him from further awards because he had won them so often, the organization wasn't finished honoring him, and elected him as its president (2007–9).

With Samuelsen's father being an opera singer, he grew up in an environment that exposed him at a young age to the arts. In junior high, however, Samuelsen felt that his life took a horrific turn when he was bullied and two thugs carved a swastika in his arm with a switchblade. The bullying caused him great shame and distress, and it wasn't until high school when things turned around for him. In high school, Samuelsen said, two teachers "saved my life":

> One was an English teacher named Kenneth Mann who thought I had potential as a writer and put me in a creative writing workshop he taught. The other was the typing teacher—yes, high schools used to offer typing and filing as a class—who was an opera buff and knew of my father and got me involved in the school choir. So I got involved with choir, went from there to theater,

---

1 Samuelsen's produced plays include *Letter from a Prophet* (co-written by Charles Metten), *A Girl Who Blushes* (one act), *Playing the Game*, *Emma* (opera libretto, music by Murray Boren), *Sex and the New York Yankees* (one act), *Accommodations*, *The Seating of Senator Smoot*, *Gadianton*, *Without Romance*, *The Christmas Box* (adapted from the novel by Richard Paul Evans), *Three Women* (three one-act plays on Mormon women), *What Really Happened*, *The Way We're Wired*, *Magnificence* (translated/adapted from Middle English), *Peculiarities* (several one-acts, produced in several iterations), *A Love Affair with Electrons*, *Family*, *Miasma* (first done as a ten-minute play for Plan B SLAM Festival as "The Butcher, The Beggar, and the Bed-time Buddy"), "Blood Pudding" (a ten-minute play), "Behind the Blue Door" (a ten-minute play), "Burning Desire" (a ten-minute play), "Perfect Circle" (a ten-minute play), *Inversion*, *Intersection*, *Amerigo*, *The Plan*, and *Borderlands*.

wrote a column for the school newspaper, and became editor of the school creative writing magazine. Basically, I found my niche. So when I went to college, playwriting seemed like a natural next step.[2]

Samuelsen had a rough time in his freshman year of college. His frank analysis of himself at that time was that he was "full of myself and a pain in the rear. I was also in the process of flunking out. By my second semester of BYU, I had stopped going to classes completely, had lost my job, was broke, in debt, and productively spending my days feeling sorry for myself." It was also during this time that Samuelsen was exposed to one of Mormon drama's most lasting successes *Saturday's Warrior*, which caused a viscerally negative reaction in him: "It was my first experience with a most unpleasant and frightening emotion: a feeling of deep, overpowering alienation from my own culture." Although Samuelsen, ironically, would later become close friends with *Saturday's Warrior* playwright Doug Stewart and would soften his position on the play, yet he continued to hold passionate reservations about the play and the qualities it reflected in Mormon culture.[3]

In many ways, Samuelsen took an opposite course from ardent Mormon champions like Doug Stewart. Where Stewart became known for his passionate defense of Mormon culture, Samuelsen became known for his equally passionate criticism of Mormon culture. Always adhering to his college motto, "Affirm the faith, attack the culture," Samuelsen was intent on being intellectually and morally honest with his culture, even when his approach might offend others. Like the character Sam Sumpter in his play *Gadianton*, who loosely quotes the Book of Mormon prophet Nephi, Samuelsen cries, "Woe unto them who say: All is well in Zion, yea, Zion prospereth!" It would be more accurate to compare Samuelsen to a reformer like Martin Luther rather than an apologist like C. S. Lewis.

Then, after his somewhat disastrous first semester at BYU, Samuelsen went on an LDS mission to Norway. It was a providential call since the Norwegian dramatist Henrik Ibsen would become a major influence on Samuelsen. Samuelsen would become an expert on Ibsen, even writing his own translations of some of Ibsen's plays.

After his mission, Samuelsen returned to BYU to become one of the many Mormon dramatists to be influenced by the tutelage of playwriting professors Charles Whitman and Max Golightly. (Samuelsen also identifies an advanced writing seminar taught by Orson Scott Card as a major influence.)[4]

Whitman referred Samuelsen to BYU's Theatre Department Chair Charles Metten as a promising young writer. Metten was looking for someone to help him write a play about Joseph Smith's experience in Liberty Jail and asked Samuelsen to collaborate

---

2   Mahonri Stewart, "Eric Samuelsen," interview, *Mormon Artist*, Issue 14 (February/March 2011): 37–38.
3   Samuelsen, "*Saturday's Warrior*, Recalled on a Sunday Morning," *Irreantum Magazine* 8, no. 2 (2006).
4   Stewart, "Eric Samuelsen," 37–38.

with him. This play was *Letter from a Prophet*. Samuelsen comments: "The play was pretty bad, of course, but that didn't matter much. I learned so much from the experience. I learned how to build a scene, how to create a character through dialogue and action, how to connect moments to create suspense and interest. I've always been grateful to Dr. Whitman and Dr. Metten for a tremendous learning experience."[5]

Letter from a Prophet, Samuelsen's first produced work, set the pace for the large volume of work that he produced in years to come. He followed it with a play for Card called *Playing the Game*, which was produced at BYU, then accepted to the regional level of the Kennedy Center American College Theater Festival, followed by the libretto for an opera, *Emma*, about Joseph Smith's first wife, Emma Hale Smith.

After graduating from BYU, Samuelsen received a Ph.D. in theatre history and criticism from Indiana University. In Indiana Samuelsen also did some work as a radio announcer and radio sports show writer/host. Samuelsen comments: "I can well imagine an alternate universe where I went into radio professionally."[6]

In 1992 Samuelsen was hired as a professor at BYU, teaching theatre history and criticism, and soon after wrote the play *Accommodations*. This play was produced at BYU, won Samuelsen his first Association for Mormon Letters award, and relaunched his playwriting trajectory. In 1999, when Tim Slover went to teach at the University of Utah, Samuelsen took over as BYU's full-time playwriting professor.[7]

Some themes and trends resurface continually in Samuelsen's work: progressive politics, a compassionate stance toward human frailty, and the need for human connection. But a large majority of Samuelsen's work focuses on his Mormon heritage, with specifically Mormon characters and Mormon themes (although not exclusively so). When asked about Mormonism's influence on his work, Samuelsen replied:

> It was a sort of epiphany. When I got home from my mission in 1977, I had a summer job, and one Saturday, I was sitting at home, and the new *Ensign* had just arrived. It was the July 1977 *Ensign* dedicated to the arts, and it included President Kimball's talk "A Gospel Vision of the Arts." While I was on my mission, I'd thought a bit about what I was going to do with my life—that's fairly typcial, I suppose. And I'd thought that I'd like to be a writer. My father tried to discourage me—he was convinced that it was difficult to make a living and support a family as an artist. This despite the fact that he was supporting his family by working as an opera singer!
>
> Anyway, I'd been in theatre my whole life, I'd been around opera singers my whole life, and it just made sense, to try to write. And then I read that great talk by President Kimball. . . . What I loved about it was the implication that we could write about conflicts in our culture, about difficulties and struggles, about "apostasies and inner revolutions and counter-revolutions." I knew that

---

5   Ibid., 38.
6   Ibid.
7   Ibid.

day that I needed to write about my own culture. And that's what I've been drawn to. Of course, I write about other things as well, but I do seem to have found something of a niche.[8]

In nearly all of Samuelsen's plays, but most prominently in plays like *Gadianton* (in which he criticizes what he views as certain Mormons' willingness to adopt unethical business practices—targeting large-scale layoffs specifically), Samuelsen shows a strong sense of liberal ethics and overt political activism. He makes few, if any, attempts to hide his loyalty to "liberal" causes, which often goes against the grain in Utah's staunchly conservative political climate.

> I do feel something of a disconnect with Utah culture. . . . It scares me whenever anyone talks about any political proposal as "consistent with sound conservative principles." Who cares if something's a conservative idea or not? What matters is if it will work, if it will accomplish a good end or not. . . . At the same time, I do think that I have a certain distance from my own culture which enables me to write about it. I think my alienation from my culture goes hand in hand with my immersion in it. I don't think I'd be a very good playwright if I lived somewhere other than Utah. In fact, I did live in Indiana for years, and I'm a better playwright living here. I actually love Provo, in part because it's beautiful, in part because I have many good friends here, and in part because I'm too lazy to want to travel very far to do my home teaching.[9]

With *Gadianton*, Samuelsen's brave stances didn't go unchallenged. Previous to BYU's run of the play, the school's administration voiced some concern with the script, which led to meetings about rewrites. There were some heightened emotions, according to Samuelsen, but many of the rumors that cropped up about those meetings simply were not true:

> I was never threatened by anyone. The atmosphere in all meetings with members of the administration was sometimes tense, but also cordial, respectful, and forthright. The administration was understandably concerned that the play would be seen as a direct personal attack on specific, well-known members of the community. I shared those concerns, although I also wanted to defend my play. Jim Gordon did inform me, however, that if the play weren't rewritten, it could not be produced at BYU. In retrospect, I believe that this was a reasonable position for the university to take.[10]

---

8   Mahonri Stewart, "An Interview with Eric Samuelsen," A Motley Vision, *http://www.motleyvision.org/2006/an-interview-with-eric-samuelsen/* (posted March 2, 2006).
9   Ibid.
10 Eric Samuelsen, "Me, *Gadianton*, and BYU," *Sunstone*, Issue 119 (July 2001): 67.

The "personal attack" on a specific, well-known individual was thought to be directed at Alan Ashton, founder of WordPerfect and a former BYU professor. WordPerfect's massive layoffs in the 1990s made headlines and were thought by many to be the target of Samuelsen's fire. Ironically, Samuelsen never intended Ashton or WordPerfect to be his target. Rather, a company called NCR in the Midwest was the impetus for *Gadianton*:

> My brother Rob was employed by NCR at its corporate headquarters in Dayton, Ohio, and NCR had been purchased by AT&T, in what analysts now call one of the most foolish and destructive of all those mid-nineties mega-mergers. Rob and I talked on the phone a lot, and he told me about the atmosphere of paranoia and mistrust that now characterized his working environment. . . .
>
> I made every effort to distance the specifics of the play from those of the WordPerfect sale and layoffs. Fred Whitmore, the play's demonic protagonist, had no WordPerfect parallel, for example, though there were a couple of guys like him at NCR.
>
> As it turned out, I didn't do a very good job. I didn't know much about WordPerfect and didn't know, for example, that one of the WordPerfect chief executives was well known for playing tennis. I'd written a tennis-playing executive into the world of my fictional company, and that parallel, understandably, bothered people who knew the real man. I reiterate: I did not want to write a play attacking specific individuals in Utah Valley. I wanted to write a play about layoffs generally. If audiences spent all their time looking for specific parallels to specific contemporary events and individuals, the impact of the play would be, I thought, lessened.[11]

And "impact" is certainly something Samuelsen strives for in his plays. Despite the critique from some reviewers for the play's overt "message," for others it is exactly this sense of mission and purpose in Samuelsen's writing that give his plays their moral edge and passionate power. This transparency of purpose in Samuelsen's writing is, to some, an asset, rather than a liability.

Previous to its production at BYU, the Utah Shakespearean Festival honored the play with a warmly received staged reading as part of its New American Playwrights series. *Gadianton* also received the Association for Mormon Letters Best Drama prize for 1997.

In addition to the long line of Samuelsen's religious plays that have been produced by BYU, he has created some interesting alliances with other theaters in Utah. The Covey Center for the Arts and New Play Project continue BYU's trend of producing Samuelsen's Mormon/religious work. However, it's Samuelsen's growing relationship

---

11   *Ibid.*, 66.

with Plan B Theatre in Salt Lake City that has allowed Samuelsen to produce work that tries to reach beyond a Utah County audience.

> Discovering Plan B was a tremendous thing for me because I love the people there and I love the opportunity to write for a different audience than I had been writing for. I've enjoyed writing plays with a bit more political edge; it's really been liberating for me. I haven't abandoned LDS audiences, not at all. I have three new plays coming out . . . and two of them are overtly and directly LDS, so I've hardly left my roots behind. And this new audience I'm writing for is, after all, just 40 miles north in Salt Lake City. But Salt Lake is a pretty liberal town, and I feel like I'm among friends up there.[12]

It's important to note that Samuelsen can be seen as a passionate reformer rather than just a political preacher. Much like a Charles Dickens or an Upton Sinclair, Samuelsen often uses his plays as a voice toward reform in what he sees as excess or hypocrisy within his community, while always making sure to mark the distinction that he's attacking the immediate culture, not the principles of the religion which he strongly advocates. And it's not only his immediate Mormon surroundings to which Samuelsen applies his reformation language. For example, his play *Miasma* is an attack on America's meat industry, and his play *Amerigo* has four historical characters (Christopher Columbus, Amerigo Vespucci, Niccolo Machiavelli, and Sor Juana Ines de la Cruz) debating in Purgatory. The play is a satirical and biting treatment of American political and cultural identity. Such plays prove that Samuelsen is targeting bigger targets beyond his immediate community.

It is this societal reform that Samuelsen works for in his plays, not just depending on others to effect the changes he wishes to see. On one hand, as previously mentioned, he has expressed a feeling of "disconnect with Utah culture." Yet, on the other hand, he has a reverent focus on his religion that makes him one of the most thoroughly Mormon playwrights in LDS theatrical history—as well as one of its most skilled, distinct, and clear literary voices.

---

12 Stewart, "Eric Samuelsen," *Mormon Artist*, 39–41.

About *Gadianton*

Gadianton premiered on January 29 and ran through February 8, 1996, at Brigham Young University in the Margetts Theatre at the Harris Fine Arts Center. The cast and principal crew were as follows:

CAST

McKay: Jason Tatom
Karen: Katie Holsinger
Fred: Ben Hoppe
Cynthia: Megan Sanborn
Mahonri: Tim Slover
Brenda: Colleen Baum
Sam: Josh Brady
Helen: Amy Barrus
Chad: Ryan Rauzon
John: Danny Stiles
Con: Jeremy Hoop
Wilson: Rob Gardner
Erma: Rachel Davenport

CREW

Director: Bob Nelson
Dramaturg: Eric Samuelsen
Stage Manager: Felina Khong
Scenic Designers: R. Clifford, Angela Paskett
Costume Designer: Lara A. Beene
Lighting Designer: Roger Larsen
Sound Designer: Brian Davenport

CHARACTERS

MAIN CHARACTERS: (NOTE: The play requires SEVEN male and FOUR female actors. Each plays a major character, then doubles to take various minor characters. It should be noted that all the major characters, except for CYNTHIA, are Mormons.)

MCKAY TODD. An LDS bishop, early forties.
KAREN TODD. His wife.
FRED WHITMORE. An exec with ONTI, late thirties.
CYNTHIA WHITMORE. His wife.

MAHONRI WARD. Owner and CEO of ONTI, late fifties.
BRENDA BURDETT. Todd's assistant, late twenties.
SAM SUMPTER. Helen's assistant, early thirties.
HELEN BRYSON. ONTI's head of public relations, early thirties.
CHAD FIRMAGE. Fred Whitmore's administrative assistant, early twenties.
JOHN W. COGBURN. Former partner of Harry June's, late forties.
CON BRYSON. Helen's husband, employed at Empasse.

MINOR CHARACTERS:

HARRY JUNE. Owner of Empasse, ONTI's main competitor.
WILSON HACKETT. Southern Utah sheep farmer, ca. 1948.
ERMA MACKELPRANGER. St. George housewife, ca. 1953
GADIANTON, KISHKUMEN, SEEZORAM, SEANTUM and BETHESDA. Book of Mormon characters.
COOPER and SCOTT. Two execs, silent partners of MAHONRI WARD.
THE STAKE PRESIDENT. President of Fred's stake.
BIBI HALSTRUP. Karen Todd's sworn enemy.
Various other ONTI employees, security guards and reporters.

A note on notation: In this play, whenever an ellipsis (. . .) occurs, it is intended to represent a pause. A double dash (—) indicates an interrupted line. In other words, a double dash in the middle of a character's line indicates that the next speaking character is to begin speaking, the two characters speaking simultaneously. But an ellipsis in the middle of a line indicates a brief pause, a collecting of thoughts.

Act One

As lights come up, we see WILSON HACKETT *and* ERMA MACKELPRANGER.

WILSON HACKETT. . . . so like I said, I seen it maybe closer than most folks. That was our winter pasture anyhow, Frenchman Flats. Me, my daddy, and my brothers would drive our sheep out from Cedar. Prettiest piece a land God ever created, and 'bout the hardest to make a living off of. Daddy useta say, "only thing—it's good for is pretty."

ERMA MACKELPRANGER. And there she was, right in front of me. Susan Hayward. All that red hair. Got her autograph that very minute. 'My friend Erma. . . . ' Well, Erma Mackelpranger, actually, that's me, but she didn't rightly catch the last name, just kinda scribbled it off. My friend Erma Mcklprfflsk it says but that's okay. You can read her name real good. Right here—on this napkin.

WILSON HACKETT. Just filled the sky. And then, a few weeks later, in come the movie people.

ERMA MACKELPRANGER. We was pretty used to 'em.

WILSON HACKETT. Shop owners in town would jack up their prices ever time the movie crews come, but I couldn't get too excited. Livin' off the land, you don't develop much of a taste for movie-goin'. Except for the Duke, of course. Saw—ever one of *his*.

ERMA MACKELPRANGER. Said she was in town to make a movie—with John Wayne.

WILSON HACKETT. I wondered why they was filmin' so soon after the shot, all the dust just—startin' to settle.

ERMA MACKELPRANGER. Movie called *The Conquerer*, about Genghis Khan.

WILSON HACKETT. Saw the Duke once at Walgreen's, had this funny looking moustache all the way down his chin, a Fu Manchu kinda thing. John Wayne in a Chinese moustache? He just—plain looked ridiculous.

ERMA MACKELPRANGER. You'd see movie folk everwhere, the drugstore, the soda fountain. You'd hear 'em griping, onnaccounta liquor bein' hard to come by. But they found it somewheres,—and you'd see 'em drinking.

WILSON HACKETT. I gotta say, they worked hard. You'd see 'em every day, all covered with dust. Start every morning at 5:00—and knock off at nine, ten, eleven.

ERMA MACKELPRANGER. I saw Susan Hayward three times that summer. She rented a house in town, hired a babysitter for her two little ones. Just as—down to earth as anything.

WILSON HACKETT. All day riding horseback, stirring up that dust, rolling around in it. Right over by where they set it off—. I did wonder.

ERMA MACKELPRANGER. Then a few years later, Susan Hayward died. Brain cancer. Kinda funny how it turned out, since so many here in town was going the same way. People talked about it, the St. George curse hittin' her, too—after she stayed here.

WILSON HACKETT. Saw the movie as soon as it come to town. Them writers in Hollywood shoulda been more careful what—kinda stuff they wrote for the Duke.

ERMA MACKELPRANGER. John Wayne, Susan Hayward, the director, most of the crew. They all got St. George disease.

WOMAN. *(As she and* BISHOP MCKAY TODD *enter.)* Bishop?

WILSON HACKETT. Not a good enough movie to die for, that's for damn sure.

WOMAN. Bishop? Are you all right?

> WILSON *and* ERMA *exit.*

BISHOP TODD. I'm fine. I'm sorry, I have a spinal—condition, sometimes it gets . . .

WOMAN. Look, I can come back. This is just routine, temple recommend renewal.

BISHOP TODD. No, that's all right. Let me just stand, walk around. This won't take—but a minute.

WOMAN. It wouldn't be a problem for me to—.

BISHOP TODD. I'm fine.

> *Cross fade to* FRED WHITMORE.

FRED. I earned a BS in business from UC Santa Barbara—.

WOMAN. Honest? In all my dealings? *(With a chuckle.)* That's always a hard one for me.

FRED. Then my MBA in finance from Ohio State.

WOMAN. You know how it gets. April 15th rolls around—.

FRED. I was hired by Proctor and Gamble right out of graduate school and assigned to their corporate headquarters in Cincinatti.

WOMAN. *(Outraged.)* Denied! I've had a temple recommend for twenty-five years now, no one has ever denied—.

FRED. Since then, I've been with twelve different companies in the last eighteen years: Microsoft. Then, Citicorp in Omaha, the Dallas office of HP, TNR Enterprises in San Diego—.

WOMAN. Isn't that just how it goes? They make some nobody bishop—.

FRED. Now, ONTI. ONTI Enterprises.

WOMAN. . . . starts throwing his weight around. You listen to me, McKay Todd, if you think you're getting away with this, then you—.

FRED. I'm usually indispensable within a month, leave when the job starts to get too routine. Ride off into the sunset, leave the settlers to raise their crops alone.

BISHOP TODD. Next.

A MAN *enters, as the* WOMAN *exits.*

MAN. Bishop, what's all this about? They said you wanted to see me.

FRED. I've been called a hitman, a gunslinger, a hired hatchet. That's unfair.

BISHOP TODD. Is there anything in your relationship with your family that you need to tell me about?

FRED. If my recommendations occasionally include layoffs, that's hardly my fault. Every company has fat to trim.

BISHOP TODD. Well, for starters, your wife had a black eye in church a couple of weeks ago. Is there anything I should know about it?

FRED. But I'm also not a consultant.

MAN. The lying bitch. . . . What did she tell you?

BISHOP TODD. Nothing. She said she slipped in the shower . . .

MAN. Then that's exactly what happened.

FRED. Consultants consult. I work for the company, implement change from the inside. I take good companies . . . maybe a bit . . . screwed up . . . (*He falters momentarily.*) I establish systems, procedures, policies . . . (*A pause. He falters, looks briefly disoriented.* GADIANTON, *a man wearing biblical robes enters, looks quizzically at* FRED.) Sometimes . . . sometimes I sort of . . . don't know what . . . pain right between my ears. (*The man in the biblical robes exits.* FRED *shakes it off, back to business.*) Anyway, that's it. I see what others can't, cut where they'd rather not. And then I get restless.

MAN. (*Livid.*) A court! I just came here . . . (*Sputtering.*) You can't just . . . just take some suspicion—!

MAHONRI WARD *enters, holding a memo.*

WARD. (*Reading.*) "To Mahonri Ward, CEO ONTI."

FRED. My latest project. ONTI. ONTI Officemate, one of the great DOS spreadsheets. Ten years ago, just another start-up, today, a market share in the high teens. Part of that mid-eighties software boom. Rank amateurs, of course, as business people.

WARD. (*Reading.*) "I began with what I perceived—to be . . . "

FRED. . . . to be the company's—.

WARD. . . . basic operating policies—.

FRED. . . . and procedures, both written and unwritten.

BISHOP TODD *quickly takes off his suit coat and replaces it with an ink-stained smock.*

FRED. The company's unofficial management motto seems to be—.

WARD. Teach them correct principles, and let them govern themselves.

FRED. I've heard that phrase from at least four people in supervisory roles. While the phrase itself is new to me, it does have a nice Tom Peters ring to it. But this motto implies a strong commitment to training and education. I have seen little evidence of such a commitment.

> As BISHOP TODD *hustles across the stage, he is met by* HELEN BRYSON, *an attractive young woman in her late twenties, wearing a business suit. Flashback.*

HELEN. Hi, you must be Mr. Todd.

BISHOP TODD. McKay Todd, that's right.

HELEN. Helen Bryson, nice to meet you. I see you worked for the postal service?

BISHOP TODD. I used to. I had to—retire because of . . .

HELEN. Great, sounds perfect. Everyone in the company's been stuffing envelopes and licking stamps for weeks now.

BISHOP TODD. Everyone?

HELEN. Everyone from programmers to custodial staff. Well, theoretically. Mostly it's a job people have been trying to duck. Drives me nuts.

BISHOP TODD. So I'll report to you?

HELEN. Heavens, no. I'm head of media relations. Well, I guess I am. Mr. Ward just decided he needed a PR person one day, hired me. But I've done a little of everything. We're kinda improvising. We were handling a volume of 200 units a week, we come out with OfficeMate 3.0, Dataworld gives it a four-star review, and suddenly our sales are through the roof.

BISHOP TODD. Wow.

HELEN. You said it. Now we get to process all those orders.

BISHOP TODD. So I report to—.

HELEN. I have no idea. If you have a problem, ask Mr. Ward, Mahonri Ward, he's the main boss, his office is upstairs.

BISHOP TODD. What kind of volume are you expecting?

HELEN. Who knows? We did twenty-five hundred last week, and it's going to go way higher.

BISHOP TODD. Twenty-five . . . I'll need some help.

HELEN. Hire anyone you want, pay 'em whatever you think. Three-and-a-halfs are over there, five-and-a-quarters over there, manuals, I'm not sure, there's a box somewhere.

BISHOP TODD. Three-and-a-halfs—?

HELEN. Good luck. And listen, you get the mail going smoothly around here, and you'll be a hero.

BISHOP TODD takes off his smock, puts on his suit jacket. A WOMAN enters his office.

FRED. *(As WARD resumes reading.)* "While I certainly applaud the relaxed, informal corporate culture you've created—.

WARD. . . . that very informality can, at times, get in the way of productivity."

FRED. I have a few suggestions.

We see in spots a series of business people, all young, dressed with a kind of affluent informality.

FIRST WOMAN. No more baby showers?

MAN. Birthday parties?

ANOTHER WOMAN. Monday night picnics?

MAN. We're not sponsoring a little league team any more?

FIRST WOMAN. Or Girl Scouts?

WARD. Oh, sure we will. In the evenings, weekends. Just not on company time.

MAN. Give up rotisserie baseball?

FRED. Unless it has a direct bearing—.

WARD. . . . on the creation, manufacturing and sale of computer software, we must ask you to save it for your after-work hours.

FIRST WOMAN. After-work minutes, you mean.

They all laugh. Enter CHAD FIRMAGE, a young man in his twenties.

CHAD. Mr. Whitmore?

FRED. You must be my new assistant.

CHAD. Yes, sir. Chad Firmage.

FRED. Chad, my pleasure.

Enter an older woman, SISTER GUINNESS.

BISHOP TODD. Sister Guinness.

FRED. *(They shake hands.)* Sit down. Take it easy. Call me Fred. Drink?

CHAD. I'm not—.

FRED. Coke, Sprite?

CHAD. Uh, a Sprite'd be—.

FRED. Bill Gates always keeps a fridge full of cold Diet Coke. I figure'd I'd follow suit.

Ice?

BISHOP TODD. Sister Guinness. As you may have guessed, we have a calling in mind for you.

SISTER GUINNESS. *(Chuckling.)* I've never turned down a calling in my life; I don't expect to start now.

FRED. So you've been married what? Three months?

CHAD. Just three months ago yesterday.

SISTER GUINNESS. The nursery?

FRED. Been a good three months?

CHAD. Yes, sir.

FRED. Good. Because three months from now, you'll barely remember her name.

SISTER GUINNESS. Bishop Todd, I'm sixty-one years old!

FRED. If I were to say to you that this job requires an eighty-hour work week, what would you say?

SISTER GUINNESS. My child-rearing days are over!

She exits in a huff. The BISHOP *sighs, follows.*

FRED. Basically, we're talking fourteen-hour days, six days a week. Say seven a.m. to nine p.m.

CHAD. It sounds—like a pretty heavy . . .

FRED. Well, what I think, eighty hours, that's for wimps. Eighty hours strikes me as a minimum commitment.

CHAD. Minimum commitment—.

FRED. Six months with me, Chad, and you'll wish you never heard the name Fred Whitmore. You'll want to quit ten times a day. You'll fantasize killing me.

CHAD. I really don't think—.

FRED. I'll give you fifty jobs at once, and expect them all yesterday. Anything you do that's just slightly not the way I want it, and you'll wish you were never born. I'll expect you to sweat blood, I'll steal every idea you think of, and I never, ever say thanks. You still with me?

CHAD. Yes, sir.

FRED. Don't call me sir. You want out?

CHAD. No, si . . . No—.

FRED. Only fair to warn you, that three of my last four assistants had nervous breakdowns. One's still in the hospital. Took sleeping pills, some kinda brain damage.

CHAD. I was raised on a ranch. I've never been afraid of hard work.

FRED. Good. Because the other two recovered, and both made their first million before their thirtieth birthdays.

CHAD. You've got your man!

FRED. Good. Finish your coke. (CHAD *hurriedly swallows it. The man in biblical robes reenters, smiling enigmatically.*) So, cowboy, whaddya say? Let's head 'em up and move 'em out!

CHAD. Yes—.

FRED. I said, let's head 'em up and move 'em out!

CHAD. Okay.

FRED. I thought you were a cowboy! Head 'em up and moooooove em out!

CHAD. *(Without much enthusiasm.)* Eeehah!

FRED. HEAD 'EM UP AND MOOOOOOOVE 'EM OUT!

CHAD. EEEEHAH!

FRED. That just got you a raise.

The man in biblical robes exits. Lights up on WARD.

WARD. Look, we've had a lot of fun and we've had a lot of success. But we can't treat this like a hobby any more. We're in the big leagues now.

BISHOP TODD *takes off his suit coat, puts on the smock.*

FRED. Having made these few broader suggestions, I will proceed with a more in-depth examination of specific operations. (*He crosses to* BISHOP TODD, *with* CHAD.) Hi. Fred Whitmore.

BISHOP TODD. McKay Todd.

FRED. My assistant, Chad Firmage. So, you're head of the mail room operation?

BISHOP TODD. That's right.

FRED. Been here two years?

BISHOP TODD. Two years, eight—months . . .

FRED. Helen Bryson says you're a miracle worker.

BISHOP TODD. That's nice of her.

BISHOP TODD *twists his back and winces.*

FRED. Are you okay?

BISHOP TODD. I just have an intermittent spinal—problem . . . .

FRED. Gosh, that's a shame. I've had some back problems myself, know what you're going through. Okay, here's what I don't get. You have how many employees in this area? Sixty-five, seventy?

BISHOP TODD. Good heavens no. I supervise six workers.

FRED. Chad?

CHAD. *(Shuffling through records.)* Uh . . . company records say you've hired a total of . . . sixty-seven employees.

BISHOP TODD. But I don't supervise them.

FRED. Explain that to me.

BISHOP TODD. When I was hired, my job was to fill customers' orders, not just supervise the mail operation. I hired people to package, to copy data onto disks, to stuff envelopes; most of them were moved to manufacturing. And I hired in other areas of the company: customer support—.

FRED. *(Impatiently.)* Uh-huh. And now you're down to six?

BISHOP TODD. Just the mailroom, here.

FRED. Chad?

CHAD. These sixty-seven people. How did you go about hiring them?

BISHOP TODD. Well, I just—.

CHAD. Our records show no evidence of compliance with Equal Opportunity guidelines, no apps on file—.

BISHOP TODD. I wasn't told I had to. I just—.

FRED. Uh-huh?

BISHOP TODD. . . .looked for people who needed work. I'm a bishop, I see a lot of people who really need a break.

FRED. Chad, a bishop. That's a church thing?

CHAD. Head of a local congregation. Bishop, you hired your ward members?

BISHOP TODD. Am I in some kind of trouble?

FRED. Don't sweat it. We're just trying to get our act together upstairs.

BISHOP TODD. So I don't . . . report to you?

FRED. You don't know who you report to?

BISHOP TODD. So far, it hasn't really mattered.

FRED. For now, go ahead and report to me. Or to Chad. Now, let me see if I've got this straight. The mail goes out when?

BISHOP TODD. The truck's usually here between two and two-thirty.

FRED. So your big rush is in the mornings. And you sort and deliver incoming in the afternoons?

BISHOP TODD. Yes.

FRED. Chad?

CHAD. One possibility might be to stagger hours to use your employees more efficiently?

FRED. I am a great believer in delegation.

CHAD. Say if four of them came in at, six or seven, worked until two or three, the other two could work nine to five and handle the incoming in the afternoon?

BISHOP TODD. I suppose—.

CHAD. And you're salaried, right? Not hourly? So you could supervise the morning rush, stay 'til five, and it wouldn't cost the company any more money.

FRED. Just hypothetically.

BISHOP TODD. But I can't.

FRED. Oh?

BISHOP TODD. My wife has to go to work early to be home when the kids come home at three. So I have to get them off to school. I can't get here—.

FRED. If you had to, you could work all that out, couldn't you?

BISHOP TODD. Well, I—.

FRED. For an extra five grand a year?

BISHOP TODD. Five grand?

FRED. We'd still come out ahead. You ever finish an entire morning's rush before the incoming?

BISHOP TODD. Generally we . . . Is this an order?

FRED. What?

BISHOP TODD. Are you telling me I'm supposed to come in earlier? From now on? As my boss?

FRED. No, I don't do that. This is all just hypothetical.

BISHOP TODD. I see.

FRED. But you could, right? I can put that on my report?

BISHOP TODD. *(Pause.)* I suppose. If I had to.

FRED. Good.

CHAD. Good.

FRED. Good to talk to you, McKay is it? Or do I call you Bishop?

BISHOP TODD. McKay is fine.

FRED. You'll have to forgive me. I'm a new convert, still a little shaky on Mormon protocol. *(To the audience.)* In south Philly, all those Italians, I went to mass every

Sunday. In San Diego, I took up golf. Here, it's Mormon country, so I took the lessons and took the bath. I figure, to get along, go along. *(To* TODD.*)* Nice operation you have here.

BISHOP TODD. Thanks.

> *Wearily, peels off smock, puts on suit jacket.*

FRED. Chad? You got all that?

CHAD. Comes in earlier, reports to you, raise. Got it.

FRED. Okay, next we look at programming.

> *Enter* BRENDA BURDETT *to* BISHOP TODD's *office.*

BRENDA. Bishop Todd.

BISHOP TODD. Sister Burdett. Please sit down.

BRENDA. Bishop, it's . . . *(She breaks down briefly.)* I'm sorry. I didn't think I was going to do that.

BISHOP TODD. Is it Brian?

BRENDA. It's over, Bishop. It's all over.

FRED. *(To* CHAD.*)* Then user support afterwards. *(To audience.)* Something else, too, a project of my own. The very fact I'm here says something. Big secrecy, mysterious holes in Mr. Ward's schedule. Big secrets equal big money. And since I am here, maybe some of it can trickle down my way . . . .

> *He shrugs, exits.*

BRENDA. All that time, he lost all that weight, started working out, grew that little moustache, I thought it was for me. You know? Talking about spending more time with the kids, maybe quit smoking. I thought it was for me, for the family. All the time, it was someone else. Someone named M. M. McGinn. I lost my man to an initial.

BISHOP TODD. M.?

BRENDA. That's the name on the mailbox. Outside the mobile home where I caught him. M. Mary Jane? Margaret? Martha? Megan?

BISHOP TODD. Brenda, an initial doesn't seem that . . . conclusive to me.

BRENDA. Oh, it's plenty conclusive. Looked right in the window, caught 'em in the act. I could see part of her face, even. Black hair. Except he was still wearing his cowboy boots, you know? A guy with cowboy boots, is that supposed to be some kind of turn-on?

BISHOP TODD. When was this?

BRENDA. Last night.

BISHOP TODD. Oh, my.

BRENDA. Yeah, it was a great night, all right.

BISHOP TODD. You say you looked in. Did you talk to him? Is everything—?

BRENDA. I didn't exactly talk to him.

BISHOP TODD. I think you should, don't you?

BRENDA. It's not necessary, Bishop. He knows that I know and he knows that it's over. Next time we talk, it'll be in court.

BISHOP TODD. How do you—?

BRENDA. Went back to the house and got all his stuff. His clothes, his shoes, his guns, that two-point trophy buck he was so proud of, everything. Took two trips, but I loaded it all in the bed of his pickup, there in her driveway. Then . . . well, Bishop, I have a little confession to make.

BISHOP TODD. A confession?

BRENDA. I was about to leave, then I saw the hose goin' out from the trailer. She has this little pathetic patch of lawn out in front she was watering. So she was used to the sound of water runnin'. So I just stuck that hose in the back of the truck with all his things. Oh, he knows all right.

BISHOP TODD. Oh, my.

BRENDA. Bishop, I know I'm supposed to forgive him. I know I'm supposed to ask Heavenly Father for forgiveness for ruining all his stuff and all. And I will. When I'm good and ready.

BISHOP TODD. I understand. In the meantime—

BRENDA. Bishop, you know me. I'm not a whiner and I'm not a taker. But I got three kids, a brand-new mortgage, and I just lost 80% of my family income.

BISHOP TODD. The Church will help.

FRED and CHAD enter, with MAHONRI WARD.

FRED. So that's my report, Mr. Ward.

BISHOP TODD. We'll help with the mortgage, if you need us to. I'll call Sister Marchant to assess your food needs.

BRENDA. I'm gonna get a better job. That'll help.

BISHOP TODD. We have an opening in my department at ONTI, actually.

FRED. I tried to fudge together an organizational flow chart—

BRENDA. Well, that would be great. ONTI, they pay good. And I'll be able to get child support when the divorce comes through, not that I figure to collect it real often.

BISHOP TODD. Good. I know how traumatic this must be for you—

BRENDA. No, Bishop. I'm okay. *(Sudden emotion)* I would like to claw the bastard's eyeballs out. *(Takes a deep breath.)* But I'm gonna be okay.

WARD. A flow chart?

FRED. Who reports to who.

BISHOP TODD. And I promise, the Church will take action on this, too.

BRENDA. Well, that's up to you. Won't mean much to Brian either way. But there is one more thing.

BISHOP TODD. Yes?

BRENDA. Well, I mean, you had all those talks with us, and he wasn't working nights as much, and I started thinking things were getting better. I had some hope, you know, and it's dangerous, hope is.

BISHOP TODD. So?

BRENDA. Well, on top of everything . . . I think I'm pregnant.

Pause.

FRED. You can see the result—just a total mess.

BISHOP TODD. We'll see if we can help there too.

He and BRENDA *exit.*

WARD. We've never needed anything like a flow chart before.

CHAD. We've basically identified a three-tiered structure.

WARD. Look, I don't want to lose our flexibility, make things so rigid good ideas don't get listened to. That's the problem with these top-down structures.

FRED. I understand.

WARD. Our approach, if we have a problem, we send out for lunch and sit around a table 'til we've worked things out.

FRED. That kind of chaos can yield creative dividends.

WARD. That's what we've found.

FRED. Right, back when you had thirty-five employees. Right now you have over six thousand.

WARD. Well, okay. That's what you're supposed to do for us, help us get better organized.

FRED. Chad?

CHAD. We've roughed out a little tighter organization.

WARD. *(Looking at a chart.)* Very impressive.

FRED. We could implement the whole thing in a matter of months.

WARD. You said something about layoffs—.

FRED. Mr. Ward, layoffs is not a word we use. That's for outsiders, people who don't know a business cycle from a Schwinn. Rightsizing, that's the term for it.

WARD. Rightsizing.

FRED. And that's not a recommendation I'm necessarily making. I don't know your plans: expansion, acquisition, a merger. With your liquidity—.

WARD. I understand.

FRED. ... your market share ... you're an attractive target. Lean and mean, right? That's how you survive.

WARD. Yes.

FRED. All I'm saying, if rightsizing turns out to be necessary—.

WARD. I'm not going to lay anyone off.

FRED. I understand that.

WARD. I don't believe in it.

FRED. It can often lead to feelings of hostility and bitterness, absolutely.

WARD. We're not that desperate, not yet, not by a long shot.

FRED. Then I'll just file this part of my report?

WARD. Pitch it, delete the program. We're not laying people off, and that's final.

CHAD. So our restructuring proposal—?

WARD. I agree we need a tighter organization. Minus layoffs.

FRED. You're the boss. *(A buzzing sound.)* My phone.

CHAD. *(Takes cellular phone from pocket.)* I got it. Fred Whitmore's office.

WARD. Go ahead and take it.

CHAD. Yeah, he's here. Fred, I think it's your stake president.

FRED. *(Taking phone.)* My what? Fred Whitmore. Uh-huh. Yeah. Yeah?

WARD. Problems?

FRED. *(Shakes his head.)* Okay, I guess. Say about seven? Yeah. *(Hangs up.)* Weird.

WARD. Anything important?

FRED. I don't know. Chad?

CHAD. Yes?

FRED. What's a stake president?

> *He,* CHAD *and* WARD *exit.* SAM SUMPTER, *unkempt, with his head on his desk. Enter* HELEN.

SUMPTER. Hello, Helen.

HELEN. Oh, Sam. *(She sighs, and sits next to him.)* What is it this time? Let's see.

Trilateral Commission? Area 51? The Kennedy assassin—

SUMPTER. I can't do it. Can't can't can't can't, not any longer.

HELEN. Okay, it's work-related. What can't you do?

SUMPTER. The job, this place, this job—.

HELEN. Specifically, Sam.

SUMPTER. Specifically? *(Nods.)* All right. All right, all right, you asked for it. We work at a computer company, we make computer software, our product is used in offices across the country.

HELEN. So far I'm with you.

SUMPTER. Mostly women, right? Mostly secretaries, women, single parents, blue-collar wives. Typing at a PC. For hours. Every day. The same repeated movements, the same muscles worked, hour after hour. You see them, don't you? You see them? Elastic bandages on their wrists.

HELEN. Sam—.

SUMPTER. Carpal tunnel. Carpal tunnel syndrome, bandages on their wrists. Any office in the. . . . And they keep working, ruining their hands and their arms and and and their health and and and—.

HELEN. Sam, this is Helen.

SUMPTER. And I'm party to it. Me. To an an an an increase in the sum total of human misery. I'm party to it.

HELEN. Sam, you've got to stay away from those websites—.

SUMPTER. Carpal tunnel and and and and ozone depletion, sometimes I feel like I'm the only one—

HELEN. Frankly, Sam—.

SUMPTER. . . . who bothers to look, who bothers to read and think, and instead of just just just just nailing my ninety-five theses to the door—.

HELEN. *(Wearily.)* You nail anything to our door and I'll have you arrested.

SUMPTER. I chicken out. Bwaaack bwaack bwaack. I chicken. Right? Bwaaack bwaaaack. Every time. For a paycheck. A lousy few hundred shekels a week.

HELEN. Sam, the point is, if you want to continue getting that paycheck . . . you with me?

SUMPTER. I know I know I let you down I know—.

HELEN. Look, I won't fire you, Sam.

SUMPTER. You should.

HELEN. Probably I should. But I won't. Okay?

SUMPTER. Okay.

HELEN. Just . . . It's not enough to just . . . just overcome your moral scruples enough to walk in the door. You know?

SUMPTER. I know.

HELEN. There's a little matter of a press release I needed yesterday.

SUMPTER. Yes . . . yes, I'll get right . . . right on it.

HELEN. All right. *(Starts to go, then turns back.)* We have this conversation nearly every week, you know.

SUMPTER. I know I'm sorry, it's just that—.

HELEN. Sam, why not give it up? I mean, it's not like we make . . . missiles, or cigarettes or, I don't know, crack cocaine. . . . Are we really so awful?

SUMPTER. "All is well in Zion, yea—Zion prospereth."

HELEN. Give me a—.

SUMPTER. "ALL IS WELL—.

HELEN. I need that press release by this afternoon.

    BISHOP TODD, *wearing his work jacket. Enter* BRENDA.

BRENDA. Bishop? I got it!

BISHOP TODD. Brenda. I'm so delighted.

BRENDA. Bishop, I can't thank you enough for this.

BISHOP TODD. Did you ask about the insurance?

BRENDA. They say I'm covered. Twelve hundred dollar deductible, and I'll get that from Brian, the judge said.

BISHOP TODD. This is great news.

BRENDA. So, what do I do?

    Enter HARRY JUNE, *affable, friendly, ruthless, owner of* EMPASSE.

BISHOP TODD. Excuse me. *(Crosses to him.)* Can I help you?

JUNE. Actually, I'm waiting for someone. *(They shake hands.)* Harry June. Pleasure to meet you.

BISHOP TODD. *(A bit in awe.)* Mr. June. I mean, Brother . . . President . . . uh, McKay Todd. It's my pleasure.

JUNE. McKay Todd. Do I know you from somewhere?

BISHOP TODD. I don't . . . think—.

JUNE. You gave a talk at regional conference, didn't you? Last summer?

BISHOP TODD. *(Beaming.)* As a matter of fact . . . you remember my—.

JUNE. I always remember a good talk. Let's see, you talked about . . . .

BISHOP TODD. Hope.

JUNE. Hope, right. Well, it's good to see you again.

BISHOP TODD. Likewise.

> *Enter* WARD.

JUNE. Nice operation you have down here.

BISHOP TODD. Thanks.

WARD. Harry.

BISHOP TODD. Mr. Ward.

WARD. The elevator's down the hall. *(He and* JUNE *start to exit together. He turns back to* BISHOP TODD.*)* Your name is Todd, isn't it?

BISHOP TODD. McKay Todd. Yes, sir.

WARD. Well, just go on . . . with what you were doing.

BISHOP TODD. Yes, sir.

> *They exit.*

BRENDA. Wow. *The* Mahonri Ward?

BISHOP TODD. And *the* Harry June. Both of them.

BRENDA. Two of the richest guys in the Church.

BISHOP TODD. Probably a billion dollars, right here in our mail room.

BRENDA. Be great, wouldn't it?

BISHOP TODD. Yep.

BRENDA. How often do they come down here?

BISHOP TODD. Never. This is a first.

BRENDA. I'm impressed. My first day, too.

BISHOP TODD. Amazing.

BRENDA. So why are those two guys sneakin' around our mail room?

BISHOP TODD. I have no idea.

> *Pause.*

BRENDA. Well. None of my business. What do I do?

BISHOP TODD. You start working. Address labels are there, work orders over there.

BRENDA. Great. And, Bishop?

BISHOP TODD. Yes, Sister Burdett.

BRENDA. Thanks.

Lights down. Up on JUNE *and* WARD *in* WARD's *office. Two other execs,* SCOTT *and* COOPER, *are with them.*

JUNE. Seventeen a share.

SCOTT. *(Depressed.)* Seventeen.

JUNE. Right now, that's it. Fair market value.

WARD. *(Pause.)* Look Harry, we'll have to think about it.

JUNE. You do that. *(Checks his watch.)* Meantime, I have stake meetings. *(With genuine affection.)* It's great to see you again, Mahonri. You're a good man.

WARD. So are you.

JUNE. Mr. Scott, Mr. Cooper.

Nods affably, exits. A longish pause.

SCOTT. Seventeen.

COOPER. It's not like it's news to us.

SCOTT. It's what we warned you, Mahonri.

WARD. I know, Randy. *(Pacing.)* We're still profitable; that doesn't matter. We have no debt at all, doesn't matter. Market share, irrelevant.

COOPER. Wall Street doesn't like us.

SCOTT. That's what it comes down to.

WARD. Remember when we were at thirty?

COOPER. Not that long ago, either.

WARD. Okay, at seventeen, where does that leave us?

SCOTT. One-and-three quarters for you, close to three divided between Coop and me.

WARD. Not so bad, when you think of where we started.

COOPER. It's not enough.

WARD. Coop, Randy. I want out. I can't put it any simpler than that.

COOPER. It's what we've been talking about.

WARD. I'm not cut out for this. I've been doing some soul searching, wondering how suddenly, I came to run this . . . monster of a company. That was never my dream.

SCOTT. I know. We've talked—.

WARD. I'm a guy with an itch for making things simpler. That's all. I liked playing with software, I came up with a new application, then when we needed financing, I took us public. One thing led to another, and—.

SCOTT. And here we are.

WARD. Here we are.

COOPER. The fact is, Mahonri, I want this merger as badly as you do.

SCOTT. Both of us do.

WARD. I know.

COOPER. For you, this was a dream, a crusade even. For me, it was an investment.

SCOTT. Me too. And it's time to cash in.

COOPER. But not at seventeen dollars a share. Not for stock I bought at fifteen-and-a-quarter, some of it.

SCOTT. That one block, I bought at sixteen.

COOPER. That's ridiculous.

WARD. It's still a great deal of money.

COOPER. If it's worth nineteen, I want nineteen. If it's worth twenty-five, I want twenty-five.

SCOTT. It's been as high as thirty. Wish I'd sold then.

COOPER. Me, too. Figured I'd keep riding it up.

WARD. Realistically—.

COOPER. Realistically, there's no reason we can't get twenty-five.

SCOTT. We want what's ours.

COOPER. That's just how business works.

WARD. I know you've been talking to Con Bryson—.

SCOTT. The logistics are in place.

COOPER. We'll stock split two for one . . . .

SCOTT. . . . trade shares to make up the balance.

COOPER. We have a three-week window, and we pick the day, based on Nasdaq closing price.

SCOTT. Harry doesn't set the price. The market will.

WARD. But that puts the price out of our hands, doesn't it?

SCOTT. Mahonri, weren't you listening? Harry couldn't have made it clearer.

JUNE. *(Reappears in light.)* Windows hurt you.

WARD. We're recovering from Windows. Look at our books.

JUNE. Your stock's down to seventeen. *(A pause. Then, baiting the hook.)* Of course, if you could reduce costs substantially over the next few weeks—.

WARD. No.

JUNE. You're fat in engineering. And customer support, well—

WARD. User support is our trademark.

JUNE. Not cost effective.

WARD. Harry, people are afraid of computers. They like having a helpline—

JUNE. Officemate wholesales at forty dollars per unit. Each customer call costs you twelve—.

WARD. It's why we have customer loyalty—.

JUNE. I'm telling you what Wall Street's telling you. Unless you can reduce costs substantially over the next four months, the selling price is seventeen dollars a share.

Lights out on him.

WARD. Windows wasn't our fault.

SCOTT. It's Bill Gates, Mahonri.

WARD. When you have to buy the operating system from Microsoft *and* they're your main competitor—

COOPER. The Justice Department—.

SCOTT. They did investigate—.

WARD. But how they . . . I mean, no major . . . come on—.

SCOTT. No major violations of antitrust. It's Bill Gates. They'll never catch him.

COOPER. It's also irrelevant. We've all read Fred's memo on layoffs.

WARD. How did you get hold of that?

COOPER. Mahonri—.

WARD. I told him to throw that report away!

COOPER. Calm down.

SCOTT. It was my idea to hire him. Remember?

WARD. An efficiency consultant, you said.

COOPER. That's right. Reporting to the four of us, as majority stockholders.

WARD. Reporting to me, as CEO!

SCOTT. What, you think we're not going to check with him?

COOPER. You think we're not going to ask for his recommendations?

SCOTT. It's all laid out for us.

COOPER. Wall Street will fall right back in love.

WARD. Absolutely not.

COOPER. We can get twenty-five, minimum.

WARD. Or we can sell now at seventeen. And that's good enough for me.

Pause.

SCOTT. Not me.

COOPER. No way.

WARD. I am CEO of this company, gentlemen.

COOPER. Yes—.

WARD. I founded this company. I run this company!

COOPER. That's right. You do. And you're the biggest shareholder. With 38 percent of the stock. Mahonri, you're outvoted.

Lights down as they exit. Lights come up CHAD *and* FRED.

FRED. Well, seven o'clock. I've got an appointment.

CHAD. *(He starts to pick up.)* Right.

FRED. You going somewhere?

CHAD. *(A pause. Sits.)* No.

FRED. There's a programming report and Windows update. I'll need those first thing tomorrow.

CHAD. Okay.

FRED. Seven o'clock, Chad, is when *I* go home.

CHAD. Right. (FRED *exits.* CHAD *picks up phone with a sigh.)* Honey? Yeah. Gee, that sounds great. No. No, I'm still going to be another couple of hours. I dunno, maybe midnight. I know. I know. I know. *(Pause.)* Because I have to.

Lights up on CYNTHIA WHITMORE. *She is talking over a tape recorder, looking over some photographs.*

CYNTHIA. Search for America, chapter seven. Continuing. Grocery shopping. *(With breathless enthusiasm.)* A supermarket! Such a carefully constructed maze, herding us all, like mice, towards our water bottles and seed trays. Today, a bonus; older women smiling at you, handing out free samples of foods on special. Insert Photo Seven. *(Turns over a photograph.)* We're all collectors of persons, searchers for faces and hands and impressions. This is St. George, Utah, white America, variations are subtler, but patience, patience, more refined pleasures are often their own reward. Insert Photo Eight. A tattooed man, wearing a Harley-Davidson jacket and a stained tee-shirt glowered, daring us all to comment, as he laid just five things on the conveyer: cigarettes, chewing tobacco, beef jerky, beer, and a box of Lucky Charms. Insert Photo Nine. Two of the checkout ladies had bandaged wrists: carpal tunnel, they said. Photo Ten. And there was an Indian woman, tall and fat and proud, and when she would approach, everyone would make such an exaggerated show of nonchalance, checking their wristwatches. Insert Photos Eleven through Thirteen, sequence. The contempt on a checker's face as a man paid with food stamps. Photo

Fourteen. And I saw one very young-looking woman, with unwashed hair shining in the fluorescence. Photo Fifteen. She had two small children with her. Photo Sixteen, closeup. One of them was crying and you could see the streaks the tears made in the brown and gray of her cheeks. *(Enter* FRED. *She gestures for him to sit. He does, smiling.)* And each of the free sample stations was like a point of the True Cross, and the mother was feeding them cookies and punch and smoked sausage, the Body and Blood of Christ. Then she left, her children fed, without making a single purchase, and the baggers smiled at her kindly as she went out the door. Photo Seventeen, actually make that before that last sentence, then Eighteen now. And in the parking lot, a dispute over a parking space very nearly led to a fistfight! Nineteen and Twenty. Shouting, threats, obscenities; *(Turns off the tape recorder.)* Oh, it was marvelous, glorious! I'm going back again tomorrow. Hello, darling.

FRED. *(Kisses her absently.)* Hi, Cinny. Nice stuff. Kiss?

CYNTHIA. I thought we'd do Chinese tonight. Take-out?

We see WARD *enter, ring a doorbell.*

FRED. Fine.

JOHN WAYNE COGBURN *answers his door. Alcoholic, nasty.*

COGBURN. Yeah?

WARD. Brother Cogburn. My name is Mahonri Ward, and—

COGBURN. Get lost.

Slams the door closed. WARD *stares at it a moment, exits.*

CYNTHIA. Did you give Mahonri your report?

FRED. Wouldn't take it. Had to slip it through the back door to Coop. He'll know what to do with it. Something else, too.

CYNTHIA. Oh?

FRED. I had a meeting with a stake president.

The STAKE PRESIDENT *enters.* FRED *turns, acts out the scene while* CYNTHIA *watches.*

STAKE PRESIDENT. Brother Whitmore? You're probably wondering why I called you in this evening.

FRED. As a matter of fact—.

STAKE PRESIDENT. I'm here to extend you a calling.

FRED. *(Turns to* CYNTHIA.*)* You remember anything about callings?

CYNTHIA. They told us about it. It's a lay ministry, so everyone has a job to do, but it's like hierarchical; they call you, you don't get to choose.

FRED. You remember all that stuff better than me.

STAKE PRESIDENT. You are an elder, isn't that correct?

FRED. I honestly . . . I don't rememb—.

CYNTHIA. You are.

FRED. I thought I was a priest.

CYNTHIA. That was at first. Remember? It goes deacon, priest, elder, bishop, something like that?

FRED. I'm second to the top?

CYNTHIA. I think. The guys in the circle, hands on your head?

FRED. Oh, yeah.

STAKE PRESIDENT. You come very highly recommended for this present calling, and I'm very happy to extend to you . . .

FRED. *(Raising his hand, like a kid in school.)* Uh, President?

STAKE PRESIDENT. Yes, Brother Whitmore?

FRED. Who are you? And what's a calling?

CYNTHIA. You didn't.

FRED. Well, I didn't know.

CYNTHIA. You said, who are you? He's the stake president. That's like the head of a diocese, like a bishop in most churches.

FRED. I found that out.

STAKE PRESIDENT. Look, maybe we should take this a little more slowly.

CYNTHIA. Thank heavens.

STAKE PRESIDENT. A calling is . . . an opportunity. An opportunity for service.

FRED. *(Nodding.)* Gotcha.

STAKE PRESIDENT. Yes. An opportunity to serve your fellow man, while also serving the Lord.

FRED. Uh-huh.

STAKE PRESIDENT. Precisely. As, for example, I'm doing.

FRED. So you want me to take over your job?

STAKE PRESIDENT. I beg pardon?

FRED. This president stuff. You want me to take it on?

CYNTHIA. Fred!

STAKE PRESIDENT. No, no, I don't have the authority—.

FRED. Hey, organizational I can handle. That's what I do at work, supervise over six thousand people. Get people working together, that's my kinda gig. *(Stands to shake his hand.)* You got your man.

CYNTHIA. Oh, Fred. Don't you remember anything they told you?

FRED. Not much, frankly.

STAKE PRESIDENT. Brother Whitmore, you don't understand. Believe me, I would love to have you take over my job. But that's not . . . I have a different calling in mind.

FRED. I don't know. I mean, I'm like everyone. Good at some things. Not good at others.

STAKE PRESIDENT. Certainly.

FRED. What if you give me something I'm no good at? *(Turns to* CYNTHIA.*)* And so, of course, that's exactly what he did.

STAKE PRESIDENT. We want you to be stake drama specialist.

CYNTHIA. Drama? Did he say drama?

STAKE PRESIDENT. Specifically, we want you to direct the stake play.

The STAKE PRESIDENT *exits.*

CYNTHIA. You're kidding.

FRED. Wish I was. A play. Like that thing we saw that one time with all the cats?

CYNTHIA. I know what a play is, Fred. They have a theater?

FRED. In the stake building, he said. Anyway, every other year or so they do a dramatic thing, and this year, I'm in charge.

CYNTHIA. That's just insane.

FRED. Tell me about it.

CYNTHIA. You're a businessman, you don't know anything about drama.

FRED. Actually, I think it'll be okay. It's more organizational than anything. Every ward has a drama person called, and they get the people to be in it, I just have to coordinate it all.

CYNTHIA. Well, you can do that, I guess.

FRED. That's what I figured.

CYNTHIA. So what play are you doing? Do you get to choose?

FRED. Kinda. They gave me three scripts, I'm supposed to read them, let them know. They're all real Mormon.

CYNTHIA. Figures. *(Looking them over.) Man of Thunder: The Orrin Porter Rockwell Story.* Who's he?

FRED. Mountain man, pioneer guy. It's a musical. Whaddya think?

CYNTHIA. I can see it now. All these guys in furs leaping around singing. Next. *No Greater Crown.* That's got to be some Eastery . . . *(Opens script.)* Nope. Joseph Smith.

Check this one off.

FRED. Why?

CYNTHIA. Cast of characters. Forty-one men, three women. That leaves one.

FRED. *Gadianton!* With an exclamation point, no less.

CYNTHIA. I remember him, he was a bad guy in that book they had us read. *(A cassette tape falls out of the script.)* Looks like it's a musical too.

FRED. "An ancient American musical." What do you think?

CYNTHIA. Nice mix of men's and women's roles.

FRED. *(Clowning.)* We may have a winner—

CYNTHIA. Sounds dorky.

FRED. Who cares? They all sound dorky. You know, Cinny, this could be fun.

CYNTHIA. If you think so.

FRED. Hey, I've run everything else in my life. Why not a stake musical?

> *Opens the script. Lights down. Enter* WARD. *He knocks again on* COGBURN's *door.*

COGBURN. *(Drunk.)* Uh-huh.

FRED. All right, Act One Scene 1. The prophet Nephi surveys his people—.

WARD. Brother Cogburn. My name is Mahonri Ward. I've been assigned as your home teacher.

COGBURN. Tomorrow.

WARD. Very well. I think I can clear some time in the evening. Would seven be convenient?

COGBURN. Tomorrow.

WARD. Very well. I'll see you at seven.

COGBURN. Tomorrow.

> *He shuts the door. Exit* WARD. *Enter* HELEN *and* CON BRYSON. *He is listening to music.*

HELEN. Hi, honey.

CON. Shhh.

> *Enter* BISHOP TODD *and his wife* KAREN, *other side of the stage.*

BISHOP TODD. Hey.

KAREN. Shhh, I'm watching this.

HELEN. What is it?

CON. Vaughan Williams. "Fantasia on a theme by Thomas Tallis." Shh.

They listen together.

BISHOP TODD. Any messages?

KAREN. Your brother called.

BISHOP TODD. Dave?

KAREN. He said call him back. Now, quiet.

> BISHOP TODD *crosses to the kitchen, pours himself a glass of milk, goes back to the sofa, sits with* KAREN.

CON. Exquisite. I love those soaring violins.

HELEN. It's beautiful.

CON. So how was life in the salt mines?

HELEN. Not bad. Same old same old.

CON. More problems with your pet lunatic?

HELEN. Oh, Sam's always got an ax to grind. You know, some people play solitaire, surf the net. Sam complains about the world.

CON. Why don't you just can him?

HELEN. Well, when he wants to be, he's very, very good.

CON. Oh, listen, listen, this is my favorite part.

BISHOP TODD. What're you watching?

KAREN. They're making like jewelry cases out of wallpaper and these little boxes.

BISHOP TODD. For homemaking?

KAREN. It's something Bibi Halstrup doesn't know how to do. Maybe.

BISHOP TODD. This is about Sister Halstrup? Again?

KAREN. Just once, I want my ideas to be as good as her ideas.

BISHOP TODD. You don't have to compete with Bibi Halstrup.

KAREN. Shut up. I do, too. All right, you go under the lid, and glue it . . . there. This whole darn thing's gonna end up stuck to my fingers, I just know it.

HELEN. You know anything about . . . well, what's going on?

CON. Where?

HELEN. Harry June dropped by Mahonri's office today. Cooper and Scott were seen in the building, first time in eight months.

CON. No kidding.

HELEN. You know anything about any of this? (CON *makes a gesture "my lips are sealed."*) I figured you would. You can't tell me anything?

CON. I can't even tell you that I can't tell you. Please don't ask about this.

HELEN. The SEC does not have a bug in our living room.

CON. Did I say anything about the SEC?

HELEN. We're married, Con. We can't even exchange a little pillow talk?

CON. About our jobs? No.

HELEN. *(Defeated.)* All right.

CON. Listen to this. The pianissimo just crystal clear.

BISHOP TODD. It looks good.

KAREN. You're just saying that. She drives me crazy, McKay. Makes me feel like such a slug.

BISHOP TODD. Why?

KAREN. Hush. Okay, make a seam with the wallpaper, glue around the edges . . . got it.

HELEN. Rumor is that we've got a big layoff coming.

CON. No kidding?

HELEN. Cut it out, all right? I know you can't say anything.

CON. Given what's happened to your stock, is it such a big surprise? That's why Mahonri hired Fred Whitmore.

HELEN. I figured. He's working that assistant of his to death.

CON. That's one of his trademarks. He's the best, a real assassin.

HELEN. Mahonri says he's just a consultant. You know him?

CON. I know of him. We nearly hired him two years ago.

HELEN. So the rumors are true.

CON. What's to worry? You're head of your department. You're no target for the likes of him.

HELEN. Cold comfort, if friends are getting it right and left.

CON. Downsizing, riffing—.

HELEN. I heard another one today. Involuntary reduction of payroll.

CON. Yeah, whatever. It's normal business practice.

HELEN. I know, I know.

CON. People who don't know anything about market economics get all hot under the collar every time a company lays people off. Ignore them. It's just part of staying competitive. Just one more necessary evil—.

HELEN. Like lawyers—.

CON. Right. Or accountants—.

HELEN. OSHA.

CON. The SEC.

HELEN. The EEOC.

CON. The NLRB.

HELEN. The EPA.

CON. Ralph Nader.

HELEN. Sam Sumpter.

They share a laugh.

CON. Listen to this, will you? Exquisite.

KAREN. All right, I think I've got it now.

BISHOP TODD. Any mail?

KAREN. On the piano.

BISHOP TODD. Anything from the twins?

KAREN. Kimball wrote. Says the Swiss winters are getting to him, needs a new overcoat.

BISHOP TODD. What about Spence?

KAREN. You know the Guatemalan mail. Nothing for three weeks and then four all at once. *(Finishes the lid.)* Ta DA!

BISHOP TODD. It looks good. Better than anything Bibi Halstrup could ever dream of making.

KAREN. McKay, you're not taking this seriously.

BISHOP TODD. No, I guess I'm not.

KAREN. You don't have any idea what a woman like that does to your psyche. You know she irons her sheets?

BISHOP TODD. Karen, she's just another sister in the ward. I don't see anything special about her.

KAREN. PLUS she volunteers at the hospital, PLUS she takes night classes, PLUS she cans, not to mention genealogy, emergency preparedness, makes her own clothes—

BISHOP TODD. You make your own clothes.

KAREN. You don't have a clue, do you? You know what she is? She's the kind of person who never makes jello with ice cubes.

BISHOP TODD. What?

KAREN. You know. There's a fast way and a slow way to make jello, you don't use ice cubes the slow way and it tastes better but it takes like two days. Well, how'm I supposed to know I'm gonna wanna eat something two days from now that jello would be good with? So I always make jello at the last second, and that takes ice cubes and ends up watery. Well, not her. She's got her menus and her shopping lined up three weeks in advance. Knows exactly when she's gonna want jello, gets little shredded carrots in there, pineapple, marshmallows, I'm serving up this soupy glop and hoping the kids won't notice. Hush, I'm trying to get this all down.

BISHOP TODD. I'll call Dave.

KAREN. Quietly. *(Muttering.)* Okay, let the glue dry and . . . the flap comes up. They said thirty seconds, I held it at least forty-five, and the flap still—.

BISHOP TODD. Hi, Sally, it's McKay. Is Dave . . . Sally? Are you all right?

KAREN. . . . I don't believe it. Look at that, flapping like some kind of bird.

BISHOP TODD. Sally . . . please, can you . . . I know, I know, but I can't understan—.

KAREN. Maybe if I use a little more glue . . . .

BISHOP TODD. Sally . . . please. I don't know anything . . . that's why I called.

KAREN. Something wrong?

BISHOP TODD. I don't know, Sally seems pretty . . . Hi, Dave, what in the world is . . . No, she didn't . . . *(Long pause.)* Oh, no.

KAREN. What is it?

BISHOP TODD. Dave, I don't know . . . I see. The biopsy's when?

KAREN. Dave?

BISHOP TODD. *(Nodding.)* The point is, you don't know that. The doctors don't even . . . That's what they said, huh? Well, what about the blood tes . . . Oh. Uh-huh. Look, maybe Karen and I ought to . . . yeah, maybe next weekend. Meanwhile, keep your spirits up, okay? It may not be . . . I know . . . I know, but still. Okay? It may not be as bad . . . I know. I love you too. Give Sally a hug. Yeah, what a mess.

Hangs up.

KAREN. So what's going on?

BISHOP TODD. They found a lump on his testicle. They're having a biopsy tomorrow.

KAREN. Oh, no. How's Sally doing? Maybe I should call her?

BISHOP TODD. She's got company, friends from the ward. I think we should drive up there next weekend.

KAREN. Of course.

BISHOP TODD. That makes six.

KAREN. McKay—.

BISHOP TODD. Six in our family, if Dave goes too. Six.

KAREN. McKay Todd, I'm not going to listen to this.

BISHOP TODD. You think it's coincidence, Karen?

KAREN. Coincidence, accident—bad luck.

BISHOP TODD. *(Overlapping.)* It's this town. It's St. George. We were all living here when it happened, and now—.

KAREN. *(Furious.)* Now you just shut your mouth! *(He looks at her, startled.)* You shut up and listen to me! Your family has had some bad luck, some real health problems, and that's too bad and I'm sorry. But that's all it is! Bad luck! You're paranoid about this. You overreact. That's why you got fired at the post office, and I won't have it happen again!

BISHOP TODD. The postal service—.

KAREN. Shut up! It is not going to happen to you. It is not going to affect you, I will not listen to any more about it. *(Gently.)* I love you, McKay. I can't live without you. *(Frightened again.)* And all this, it's just a lot of nonsense, and I'm tired of it, tired of it! Do you hear me!

BISHOP TODD. I'm sorry.

KAREN. *(Pause.)* Next weekend is not good. We'll drive up to Boise in a couple of weeks.

BISHOP TODD. All right.

Slow blackout on them. Lights up on MAHONRI WARD, *visiting* COGBURN.

WARD. Brother Cogburn. I've been assigned as your home teacher.

COGBURN. Uh-huh.

WARD. My name is Mahonri Ward.

COGBURN. No kidding.

WARD. I thought perhaps for my first visit today, we could just get acquainted. Get to know each other a little.

COGBURN. Oh, I think that's a very good idea. Get acquainted.

WARD. Yes. Good.

COGBURN. Three hundred. At twenty-five a share. More like one seventy five at seventeen, but you'll get twenty-five, have no fear.

WARD. Excuse me?

COGBURN. Stock split, trade, merger, your take in the neighborhood of three. Right?

WARD. *(A long pause, utterly shocked.)* How did you know that?

COGBURN. I know a lot of things, Mahonri Ward. I think our visits are going to be very interesting.

Blackout. Lights up on BRENDA, *holding herself, her hand bloody.*

BRENDA. Oh, great. This is just great.

Enter WILSON HACKETT *and* ERMA MACKELPRANGER.

WILSON HACKETT. It was the shot they called Dirty Harry.

ERMA MACKELPRANGER. The biggest of the bunch, they said.

WILSON HACKETT. You could just see the size of it. Lit up the sky—.

ERMA MACKELPRANGER. Gray ash everwhere.

WILSON HACKETT. Army personnel come up to our camp. They had masks on their faces, gloves on their hands, and they told us, you boys better high-tail it outta here—. This here's a hot spot.

ERMA MACKELPRANGER. My sister Edna was picking peas when it happened. Was seventeen years old. Met Wayne Garrett couple years later; got married spring of '55. She got pregnant right away, but the baby never did develop, just formed a mass like a buncha grapes inside her.

WILSON HACKETT. Since it hit, what with everthing that happened . . . never could hold down a job. I do handyman work here and there, mend a fence or paint a stable. No family left anymore, so just try—to get by, day to day.

ERMA MACKELPRANGER. She died three years later of—cervical cancer.

WILSON HACKETT. Dirty Harry, they called it.

ERMA MACKELPRANGER. Biggest shot they ever tried.

WILSON HACKETT. Took the heart right out of me and mine, sure enough.

Blackout.

END ACT ONE

Act Two

As lights come up, we see WILSON HACKETT *and* ERMA MACKELPRANGER.

WILSON HACKETT. We come from the winter range out by Frenchman Flat, me, my brother, and my Dad, when we seen it, the whole sky lit up and then the mushroom cloud, and—the gray haze up the valley.

ERMA MACKELPRANGER. We tried to be careful, wash off our vegetables before we'd eat 'em. But the cow ate the grass, and we drank the milk from the cow—. No way to avoid it.

WILSON HACKETT. The ewes was miscarryin'. And the yearlin's started to die. And the wool, like you could practically pull it off with your hands.

ERMA MACKELPRANGER. My husband's brother bought him a geeger counter. He sat it down here on our flagstones, and it was really jumpin'.

WILSON HACKETT. And then the lambs was bein' born with two heads, some with their hearts outside of their bodies, skin like parchment so you could see right inside to their organs, and sometimes just a big bloody mess of legs and feet and heads and wool.

ERMA MACKELPRANGER. It ain't just cancer, you know. Degen'rative spinal problems.

WILSON HACKETT. Depression and craziness. Hyperthyroids.

ERMA MACKELPRANGER. Mental retarded: In our ward we went from zero to seven Down's syndromes in one Primary class. They all sat together in the front row; folks called 'em God's row of angels.

WILSON HACKETT. And some folks just plain felt like hell their whole entire lives.

BISHOP TODD. *(At work, in the smock, with* BRENDA, *who is seven months pregnant.)* So that's the situation.

WILSON HACKETT. Nothin' in particular. Just plain felt like hell.

BISHOP TODD. I come in at seven, work 'til three. Then you come in at nine, work 'til five.

WILSON and ERMA exit.

BRENDA. And I'm in charge?

BISHOP TODD. They're naming you assistant supervisor, and you'll be in charge from three 'til five.

BRENDA. The rest of the time, I'm like second in charge?

BISHOP TODD. That's right. *(BRENDA has no reaction.)* They're talking an extra two hundred a month for you.

BRENDA. That'd come in handy.

She winces in pain.

BISHOP TODD. Are you all right?

BRENDA. Just a little spotting, some cramps.

BISHOP TODD. Contractions?

BRENDA. It's still two months early.

BISHOP TODD. You need to see a doctor.

BRENDA. After work today.

BISHOP TODD. Okay.

He looks at her searchingly.

BRENDA. The baby's moving, everything's fine.

BISHOP TODD. Okay. Anyway, I told 'em you were the only person for the job.

BRENDA. 'Preciate it. I could sure use the money. Brian's already told me, the judge can take his truck away before he pays that deductible. After I soaked his stuff.

BISHOP TODD. I'm sorry, Brenda.

BRENDA. I'm better off out of it.

BISHOP TODD. The ward—.

BRENDA. If I need it, I'll ask. So, you come in at seven. What did your wife think?

Enter KAREN.

KAREN. So great. Suddenly it's my job to get the kids up and dressed and to school every morning.

BISHOP TODD. I told them it would be awkward.

KAREN. I have to be to work by seven-thirty myself.

BISHOP TODD. I know.

KAREN. The bus doesn't come 'til eight-forty- . . . three or whatever.

BISHOP TODD. I know.

KAREN. What if the kids miss it? Who drives home?

BISHOP TODD. Karen, I wasn't given any choice on this.

KAREN. And I just have to deal with it, is that it? Just "sorry, I have to be to work by seven from now on, I know it screws up your life but that's the way it goes."

BISHOP TODD. That's not fair.

KAREN. Neither is this.

BISHOP TODD. Look, the money's better—.

KAREN. Not much better, not like they promised you. How hard did you fight 'em on that?

BISHOP TODD. *(Pause.)* Not very.

KAREN. Just tail between your legs, whatever you say, boss.

BISHOP TODD. I suppose.

KAREN. And now this. And it's always me that makes the adjustments. This is not fair.

She exits.

BISHOP TODD. She took it pretty well.

BRENDA. *(Reading between the lines.)* Uh-huh. *(She starts to get to work.)* In the meantime, they do pay us pretty good.

BISHOP TODD. They sure do.

BRENDA. Long as it lasts.

As they exit, enter HELEN, WARD, FRED, CHAD.

HELEN. Nice girls don't get angry. I believe in it, being nice. It gets you out of things, and it gets you through things, and it also makes for pretty strong armor. . . . When I was nine, my father inherited his father's carpet outlet, which declined rapidly under his management, ending eventually in bankruptcy. He turned to drink and finally left the Church. His rages, his furious, impotent rages. I learned I could always deflect them with a smile and a giggle, and so that became my role. Niceness works. I don't think it's such a bad way to be, the peacemaker.

She crosses to where WARD, FRED, *and* CHAD *are seated.*

WARD. Helen.

HELEN. *(Wondering.)* Mahonri. *(Sitting.)* What's up?

WARD. You know Fred Whitmore, of course. And his assistant, Chad—.

CHAD. Chad Firmage.

HELEN. *(Still cordial.)* We've met.

WARD. Helen. Helen, when you build a company from scratch, when you begin with an idea, and pursue it, and obtain financing, and begin hiring others who share your vision . . . when you build a company, you don't always anticipate . . . you don't . . .

FRED. There are going to be some changes.

HELEN. *(Shocked, staring at* WARD.*)* Yes?

FRED. Major changes.

HELEN. Mahonri?

WARD. I'm sorry, Helen. I'm just very, very sorry this had to happen.

HELEN. Look, what is this? What's going on?

FRED. Chad?

CHAD. Over the past year, Fred and I have formed an in-house task force reporting directly to Mahonri, designed to look at ways to improve our cash position and profitability. After carefully evaluating every department in the company, we believe that we have a recommendation to make that will greatly enhance our company's position in this very competitive market.

HELEN. You're talking about layoffs.

FRED. *(A brief pause.)* That's right.

HELEN. How big?

CHAD. This will be quite a substantial rightsizing of the company.

HELEN. How many?

FRED. Chad?

CHAD. We're initially targeting approximately twelve hundred positions.

HELEN. Twelve hundred?

CHAD. In the initial restructuring. An additional eight hundred will go in the second wave, six months from now.

HELEN. Two thousand total. A third of the company.

FRED. That's right.

HELEN. That's . . . huge. *(Fighting for control. To* FRED.*)* And so you've told me about this . . . you've warned me of this, so I can begin preparing.

FRED. That's right.

HELEN. When?

FRED. Soon. And we make our preparations quietly. The timing's really crucial here.

HELEN. Press release, press conference? Both?

FRED. Looks like you're on top of things.

HELEN. Putting a happy gloss on unhappy news. My forte. *(Longish pause.)* Mahonri?

FRED. Yes?

HELEN. Can I ask a few questions?

FRED. Shoot.

HELEN. Mahonri. We're friends, aren't we? I've been here from the very beginning. Why are we doing this?

FRED. You see our stock price lately?

WARD. That's enough, Fred.

HELEN. So that's it. It's about the price of our stock?

WARD. That's right.

HELEN. Mahonri, we paid cash for these buildings. Every expansion came out of profits. Last year was the worst year of our last five, but we still had total profits—.

FRED. Chad?

CHAD. A figure down 64 percent from fiscal nineteen-—.

HELEN. *(For the first time, a bit of an edge to her voice.)* This is a profitable company with no debt . . . .

WARD. Because I took us public. We've been selling stock to keep us afloat. The Windows fiasco . . . This is necessary, Helen. If I want out, it's necessary. And I want out.

HELEN. I see.

FRED. Any more questions?

HELEN. We're still profitable, though. Right? We're in the world's most rapidly expanding market . . . *(Pleading.)* I still don't understand. Why is it necessary to fire two thousand people?

FRED. Not firing, Helen. Not canning. Rightsizing. Reshaping, for the future.

HELEN. I understand the distinction.

FRED. You don't seem all that supportive of this.

HELEN. I'm sorry. I'm . . . supportive.

FRED. We need team players on this.

HELEN. I understand.

FRED. Your job is safe.

HELEN. I appreciate that.

FRED. Don't fight it.

HELEN. No, I'm not. I'm not . . . but I do need to understand it. If I'm going to defend it. Publicly.

FRED. See, Chad, that's the sign of someone who is very, very good at her job. You see that?

CHAD. I do.

FRED. Immediate thought: How can I defend this, put my own feelings aside. Terrific.

Enter GADIANTON *and* KISHKUMEN, *two characters in biblical robes.*

CHAD. So. Shall I? *(A pause as* FRED *stares at them.)* Clarify the situation for her?

GADIANTON. So if we can gross 226 per unit at 100,000 per lot, we're looking at what, 14 percent above overhead?

CHAD. Fred?

KISHKUMEN. The boys at M&A think it's a real plum. Think they can finance it at eight, sell off those two divisions—.

GADIANTON. Okay, let's go for it. Fax these figures to Zeezrom at legal.

KISHKUMEN. All right. And I think that we should—.

FRED. Get out of here! Go!

GADIANTON *and* KISHKUMEN *exit. The others stare at him.*

WARD. Fred, are you all right?

FRED. Sorry. I'm sorry. *(Recovering.)* Tourette's. Sorry. I usually control it with medication, got in a hurry this morning.

HELEN. Maybe we should—.

FRED. Nah, I'm fine, just ignore me if I start cussin'. Right, Chad?

CHAD. *(Uncertainly.)* Right.

FRED. Helen, it's like this. Your entrepreneurs, your Bill Hewlitts and Stephen Jobs and Mahonri Wards, guys like that're kinda like your gunslingers in the old West. Guy rides in on his trusty palomino, forty-five in hand, and tames some desolate corner of the wilderness. Kills off the rattlesnakes, tears out the sagebrush, scares off the riffraff. Then in come the townspeople, and they set up a bank and a church and a blacksmith's shop and a general store, and they build homes. Comes a time the old gunslinger just doesn't fit in anymore. Then it's time to move on.

HELEN. So you already have a buyer, an offer on the table.

WARD. *(After a moment.)* Yes.

FRED. Again, not for public consumption, right? We can't tie the layoffs to the sale.

HELEN. I'm familiar with the relevant SEC regulations.

FRED. Exactly. See, fact is, being a gunslinger doesn't mean you necessarily can function great as mayor. You look at a town that's had a gunslinger in charge of it and the first thing you see is four blacksmiths, and three general stores, and five feedlots, and six churches, and you don't really need more'n one of any of 'em. That's why we call it rightsizing. Cutting down to just one of whatever it is you just can't live without.

HELEN. But those *extras*. They're not surplus, they're people. With mortgages and families and ties to the community.

FRED. Exactly, they're comfortable. Lost the fire in the belly. Lean and mean, Helen. That's how you survive.

HELEN. Of course. Lean and mean, of course.

FRED. Anything else?

HELEN. Let me just . . . If enough *is* coming in—.

FRED. Helen, that's irrelevant. We still have too many blacksmiths. Every horse in town's been shoed.

HELEN. Empasse is the buyer?

FRED. Can't tell you.

HELEN. Yes, in other words. After the layoffs?

FRED. After. You got a brand-new boss, don't want him to be the bad guy.

HELEN. Plus the purchase price is tied to price per share, and Wall Street will love a 30 percent layoff.

FRED. None of which you've heard from me.

HELEN. And how much are you getting, Mahonri?

WARD. *(Clears his throat.)* It's substantial.

HELEN. How much?

FRED. Helen, Mahonri stands to retire with a total package in excess of 300 million dollars.

HELEN. *(After a long pause.)* Not a bad golden parachute. Wow.

FRED. So how do we handle the PR problem?

HELEN. We leak it, say two weeks beforehand. Make it a rumor. Not that they don't already have an idea.

FRED. Excellent.

HELEN. Do what we can to soften the blow. Give them good references, maybe set up a job placement office in-house, give them a place they can see what's out there, serve them some cider and doughnuts—.

FRED. This is all terrific. Chad, you getting all this?

HELEN. Make the severance as generous as we possibly can.

WARD. Top priority. Fred, we're clear on that? I want the people we lay off to be treated with decency and generosity—.

FRED. Good severance is a must. And Chad, we instruct the guards to be extra cordial.

Pause.

HELEN. Guards?

CHAD. Well, we're firing a lot of programmers, Ms. Bryson. People who know how to use computers.

HELEN. Yes?

CHAD. Given much notice at all, they could do all sorts of damage. A virus, steal software, format hard drives. It's quite a risk.

HELEN. So you're escorting them out?

FRED. Armed guards. Plus a supervisor.

CHAD. It really is necessary.

HELEN. *(Pause.)* And I get to put a positive spin on that, too.

FRED. Sensational. You really are good at this, Helen.

HELEN. *(Empty.)* Thanks.

WARD. One more thing.

They all look at him, surprised.

HELEN. Yes, Mahonri?

WARD. Do this right, and you could be looking at a vice-presidency.

FRED. *(Not thrilled, but hiding it, enthusiastic.)* Now there's an idea.

HELEN. Marketing VP.

WARD. I know you've had your eye on it.

FRED. We'd have to clear it with Harry June, of course.

WARD. I'll talk to Harry personally.

HELEN. I'd get to do the trade shows.

FRED. I'm sure you'd be terrific.

WARD. I know you would.

FRED. Well, I think that's all for now. We should meet pretty much daily on this, Helen.

HELEN. Give me two days to clear off my desk.

FRED. Friday, then.

HELEN. And I left. Thinking: "You handled that okay." Niceness again to the rescue.

As she, CHAD *and* FRED *leave,* WARD *crosses to* COGBURN.

COGBURN. Three hundred million.

WARD. Brother Cogburn—.

COGBURN. Cut the crap, Mahonri. I know who you are and you know who I am. What do you want?

WARD. Brother Cogburn, I'm—.

COGBURN. I'm no brother of yours. Harry and John, all those years.

WARD. I'm not here to talk business.

COGBURN. Oh, I know. You got yourself assigned as my home teacher.

WARD. I was assigned—.

COGBURN. By the bishop? By chance, maybe? Drew my name out of a hat? Liar—.

WARD. You've refused home teachers in the past. It was thought that an old friend—.

COGBURN. I let you in.

WARD. A good start.

COGBURN. First of all. We were never friends. Business rivals, Empasse vs. ONTI. Then Harry June cut me loose and I became, what? Someone to feel sorry for?

WARD. I've never thought of you as a figure of pity.

COGBURN. No. I'm too damned rich. Come on. Why are you here?

WARD. Just your home teacher. That's all.

COGBURN. Afraid I'm going to hell.

WARD. I think you're living in hell, John. *(Pause.)* Look, can I speak candidly?

COGBURN. That'd be a change.

WARD. John, I want to be your friend, in the Church or out. And I look around and I see, well, a lot of mess. Whiskey bottles on the front lawn, unmowed—.

COGBURN. *(Mocking.)* Word of Wisdom problems.

WARD. Weeds in the garden, paint peeling. This was a very expensive home.

COGBURN. Two million dollars.

WARD. Really?

COGBURN. Bought it for two million dollars. Big screen TV that slides up into the ceiling. Jacuzzi. I love that tub. I've had lots of girls in that tub, Mahonri.

WARD. *(With distaste.)* I don't doubt it.

COGBURN. Ever since Catherine left me. I got eighty million dollars for my share of Empasse. Then I spent two million on the house, and two million on all the cars, and ten million on the divorce, and then I spent a bunch of it on broads and whiskey, and the rest I wasted, and know what I'm worth today?

WARD. I don't have any idea.

COGBURN. Eighty-four million. I spent and spent and spent and spent and it was still making more all the time. Like gerbils. Or guppies. Gerbils and guppies.

WARD. What about your children?

COGBURN. Gerbils and guppies!

WARD. John—.

COGBURN. Catherine stole 'em from me.

WARD. If the money makes you unhappy, why not give it up?

COGBURN. I could. You know. Heart or cancer or lungs or Jerry's kids or . . . culture stuff. Foundation for the Arts.

WARD. So why don't you?

COGBURN. Because you can't. You'll learn. You wouldn't have got it if you didn't want it. And then it's yours. And then it's you.

WARD. That doesn't happen with everyone.

COGBURN. Hah! Elbows back.

WARD. Excuse me?

COGBURN. I'm teachin' you how to be rich. Elbows back. Throws your chest out, your belly in. Mostly they want what's in your wallet, but pride, you have to try. Belly in. Big ring on the finger, ruby or emerald. Then flash the wallet in the bar and the next thing you know she's snuggled up real close.

WARD. John, what I'm saying is, I'd like to help you get your life back in order. (COGBURN *snorts with laughter.*) You're still a young man, talented, with a lifetime of service ahead of you. (COGBURN *snorts again.*) Let me help you.

COGBURN. *Squeeze* that camel through that eyehole.

WARD. John, let me just—.

COGBURN. *Squeeze* it through there.

WARD. —just clean the place up a little. You'd feel a lot better about yourself.

COGBURN. *Squeeze* that camel through.

WARD. John, let me help you. Please.

He begins to clean things up.

COGBURN. You pick up after me?

WARD. I don't mind.

Lights down on them. Enter HELEN.

HELEN. Everyone I see, I wonder. Him? Her? *(Enter* SUMPTER.*)* Him? *(He groans.)* Okay, Sam. What is it this time?

SUMPTER. I really can't anymore. I've hit the wall. I'm finished here.

HELEN. Sam, this is not a good day—.

SUMPTER. I know, I know, I'm sorry, I know—.

HELEN. Okay, thirty seconds, Sam.

SUMPTER. One word, then, Helen. One word. Cancer.

HELEN. You're saying our software causes cancer.

SUMPTER. Hear me out hear me out, picture it, cubicles and offices, hundreds, thousands of workers, women mostly, staring into the screens of their PCs. Computer screens emit electrical radiation, which has been proved, *proved, proved,* Helen, to increase incidence of breast cancer, bone cancer, lymphatic carcinoma, and . . . leukemia . . . and . . .

HELEN. Sam—.

SUMPTER. And blastoma, and—.

HELEN. Sam, no.

SUMPTER. Breast cancer. When was the last time you had your breasts examined? I'm asking as a friend.

HELEN. Sam, when was the last time you had your head examined?

SUMPTER. That's that's that's not—funny.

HELEN. Listen to yourself, Sam. You want to get rid of electricity?

SUMPTER. We're party to it, Helen! Breast cancer, malignant melanoma, our job is to . . . to to cover it up, put the best possible face on it, to to to . . . nothing's really wrong, people! Everything's fine! All is well in Zion, yea, Zion prospereth. And and and I can't, I just can't—.

HELEN. Aren't you overstating—.

SUMPTER. We are complicit, Helen! We are complicit.

HELEN. *(Troubled.)* You think so?

SUMPTER. Helen?

HELEN. We are, aren't we? Complicit.

SUMPTER. Glory be. I've finally gotten through to you, haven't I?

HELEN. No.

SUMPTER. I have. I can see it.

HELEN. Sam, tell me about your family.

SUMPTER. My family?

HELEN. That's right. Your wife's name is . . . Sharleen?

SUMPTER. Maureen.

HELEN. That's right. Maureen. Two kids?

SUMPTER. You've seen the picture, three kids, Helen, right here on the desk.

HELEN. Your oldest is a boy and then the two girls?

SUMPTER. Kyle just turned eleven.

HELEN. What would you do, Sam, if you didn't have this job?

SUMPTER. *(Suddenly frightened.)* What do you mean? What have you heard?

HELEN. Nothing. It's just that you've had these . . . scruples as long as I've known you. What would you do if you just couldn't take it, working here anymore?

SUMPTER. I'll never bother you with this nonsense again.

HELEN. Sam, that's not what I—.

SUMPTER. I know I'm a pain in the neck, but I do good work for you, you can't deny that. I don't spread dissension, you're the only one I complain to, but never again. Never again.

HELEN. Sam—.

SUMPTER. Never again.

HELEN. I didn't mean to—.

SUMPTER. Never again. What do you have for me?

HELEN. *(Sighs.)* I'm just trying to—.

SUMPTER. What do you have?

HELEN. *(After a pause.)* I've just been given a big project, something I've got to work on by myself. It means I've got to clear my desk for the next couple of weeks.

SUMPTER. Big changes?

HELEN. Yes, Sam.

SUMPTER. Bad changes?

HELEN. *(A long pause.)* I can't tell you any more.

SUMPTER. I've never complained to anyone but you.

HELEN. I know, Sam.

SUMPTER. I work hard, and I do good work. Good work, Helen.

HELEN. I know.

SUMPTER. Good work.

HELEN. I know.

They exit. Lights up on BISHOP TODD *as he talks with* KAREN, *as they sit at the kitchen table.*

KAREN. And another three-eighteen for the car payment, seven hundred to the missionary fund, twelve-seventy for the house . . .

BISHOP TODD. And we're short again.

KAREN. Even with your raise.

BISHOP TODD. Having the furnace go, that didn't help.

KAREN. Overcoat for Kimball, shoes for Joey and Lizzie—.

BISHOP TODD. Where can we cut back?

KAREN. Get the twins back from their missions.

BISHOP TODD. Eight more months. Meantime . . .

KAREN. Meantime, we got this.

BISHOP TODD. Another VISA?

KAREN. They're at five-point-nine. Discover's over 15 percent. We could transfer the balance over and cut our interest in half.

BISHOP TODD. We already have VISA.

KAREN. We have two VISAs. All under nine-point-nine except the Discover.

BISHOP TODD. We'd better do that, then.

KAREN. I'll fill it out. I'll need your signature in a sec.

Working on the form.

BISHOP TODD. Bibi Halstrup came by tonight.

KAREN. I'm not surprised.

BISHOP TODD. Complaining about Brenda Burdett.

KAREN. Uh-huh.

BISHOP TODD. Who, as it happens, was my very next appointment.

Enter BIBI HALSTRUP, *who is exactly as advertised.*

BIBI. Bishop Todd, really, I wouldn't be here if it weren't serious. As it was, I could barely fit it in between my aerobics class and my work at the genealogical library.

BRENDA. Bishop, I have to see you about something.

BISHOP TODD. *(To both.)* Go on.

BIBI. Bishop, I've always supported my Church leadership, even when I've been sure they've made a mistake, and then it's usually turned out to be me, wrong as usual.... *(Little laugh)* Silly me.

BISHOP TODD. You think I'm wrong about something, Sister Halstrup?

BIBI. Well, it's that Sister Burdett. The new Young Women's president?

BRENDA. Bishop, I went to the doctor. And they took that test, that amniocentesis. It's not good, Bishop. It's not good at all.

BIBI. I know she's been through a lot recently. What with the divorce and all, not her fault, I'm sure, I would never cast stones, some of us have an easier time keeping our husbands satisfied than others of us and no one's to blame. But really, Bishop—.

BRENDA. Bishop, the baby's not right. She's just not right. And I've got to know the Church's position on something because I've got a decision to make and I just don't know—

BIBI. Last week, she gave the Standards Night talk for the young women.

BISHOP TODD. I know. I was there, of course.

BIBI. And you approved of it!?!?!?

BISHOP TODD. There were times when it—.

BRENDA. All right, girls. Listen up. Time to talk about sex.

BIBI. Bishop, I have to say, I'm seriously considering withdrawing my daughters from the program.

BISHOP TODD. Standards Night is pretty much about the law of chastity. Isn't it?

BIBI. It is about the standards of the Church in regard to serious moral transgression!

BRENDA. Girls, you know the kind of guy I'm talking about. Gets that ol' tongue working when he kisses, keeps grabbin' at your tits. Real boobonic plague, you know what I'm sayin'? Well, you got two choices, girls, that moment in your life. One, you can go along with him. You know, it does feel good. Feels real good, get a guy rubbin' on your boobs like that. But see, the thing is, then *he's* in control. *He's* getting what *he* wants. And if *he's* in control, *you're* not. And the next thing you know, you're in the back seat of the car, feelin' all warm and soft. I ain't gonna kid you, girls, sex can feel just terrific.

KAREN. She gave this talk for *Standards Night*? In the *chapel*?

BISHOP TODD. Yeah, but you shoulda heard the rest of it.

BRENDA. . . . point is, after he's gone, you get to live with all the consequences, all by yourself. Consequences, that's just not a word in his vocabulary. And those consequences, they can get a little rough. Workin' all day at some no-account job, worried sick about your kids alone with who knows what kinda child care, comin' home and cleanin' the house by yourself. I been there. I am there. Hell of a lot of work for a little warmth in the belly. Second choice? You stay in control. And you say to him, "Buster, keep your hands to yourself." And you say it evertime he tries. Now I know what you're thinking. You're thinking, "If I say that, I'll lose him. I gotta let him feel me up, or I'll lose him for sure." Well, girls, if he cares for you even one little bit, you won't lose him. And if he don't, let me tell you something, and I want to hear you repeat it after me. HE. AIN'T. WORTH IT!

BISHOP TODD. *(To* BIBI. *Sighs.)* I'll have a talk with her.

BIBI. Well, I hope you do, because I do *not* allow that kind of smutty talk in my home, and I do *not* appreciate—.

BISHOP TODD. *(As he speaks, she cuts off.)* It's all right, Brenda. Just tell me the problem.

BRENDA. It's something called spina bifida.

BISHOP TODD. I've heard of it. A birth defect.

BRENDA. That's right. The baby's spinal cord is just like open, like there's no bone around it. There's a little sack at the base of the neck, they said, and it's full of spinal fluid, they said, and it could have part of the spinal cord. The baby might be paralyzed. It might be severely retarded. There's just no telling—

She breaks down.

BISHOP TODD. It's all right, Brenda. It's all right.

BRENDA. I'm sorry.

BISHOP TODD. It's okay.

BRENDA. It's just . . . the thought of it. All exposed up the back like that.

BISHOP TODD. Did the doctor—?

BRENDA. He said that some children have immediate surgery, and are fine, but that's not the usual thing.

BISHOP TODD. What can the Church do to help?

BRENDA. Well, in a case like this, where there's not much chance of a normal baby anyway, and when her problems could be severe ones . . .

Pause.

BISHOP TODD. Yes?

BRENDA. What's the Church's stand on abortion?

BISHOP TODD. *(Pause.)* That's not an option.

BRENDA. It is an option, even this late, the doctor said—.

BISHOP TODD. No.

BRENDA. What if I was to go ahead with it?

BISHOP TODD. It would be a terrible mistake.

BRENDA. What would you do?

BISHOP TODD. Just off the cuff . . . I would have to hold a court, and it's possible—.

BRENDA. Excommunication?

BISHOP TODD. We would take all extenuating circumstances—.

BRENDA. But it's possible.

BISHOP TODD. Yes. Abortion is actionable.

BRENDA. *(Pause.)* That bad, huh?

BISHOP TODD. That bad.

BRENDA. They're talking about layoffs at work, Bishop.

BISHOP TODD. I know.

BRENDA. I got least seniority in the mailroom.

BISHOP TODD. I know that, too.

BRENDA. I want this baby, Bishop. I can feel her inside me, she can't kick, but she . . . moves. I wanna hold her. In my arms.

BISHOP TODD. You will.

BRENDA. If I have to get another job, lose my benefits, this becomes a preexisting condition!

BISHOP TODD. I see.

BRENDA. We're talking reconstructive surgery, years of therapy. Not covered, if I lose my job.

BISHOP TODD. I don't know what to say.

BRENDA. So. You're my bishop, and you're my boss. You tell me what I should do.

BISHOP TODD. Wait.

BRENDA. For the axe to fall?

Pause.

BISHOP TODD. Let's pray it doesn't.

BRENDA *exits.*

KAREN. And you never did talk to her about Standards Night.

BISHOP TODD. No.

KAREN. You're gonna have to, you know.

BISHOP TODD. I know.

KAREN. Lizzie thought it was a great talk. But Bibi's probably right. You can't say "tits" in the chapel.

BISHOP TODD. I also know some of the girls in Young Women's. Bibi Halstrup's daughters included. Maybe some plain talk will make a difference.

KAREN. *(Crossing to him with the credit application.)* Maybe if you took the bus a couple times a week. Twenty bucks a week for gas doesn't help.

BISHOP TODD. Sure.

KAREN. And Boise will have to wait.

BISHOP TODD. Karen—.

KAREN. *(Sharply.)* I'm sorry. We can't afford it this month.

BISHOP TODD. He had the surgery last Friday. Double orchidectomy.

KAREN. So what are we supposed to do? Take out a second mortgage so you can go hold your brother's hand?

BISHOP TODD. Spend some time with him. Help out Sally.

KAREN. Not this month.

BISHOP TODD. Karen—.

KAREN. We can't afford it.

She exits. With a sigh he follows. Enter HELEN.

HELEN. Con?

CON. *(Sitting, listening to music, Samuel Barber's "Adagio for Strings.")* Shh. Listen.

HELEN. It's beautiful. Barber?

CON. Samuel Barber's "Adagio for Strings." I love this part, unison violins . . . .

HELEN. It really is beautiful.

CON. Lovely. Transporting.

HELEN. *(Persisting.)* Con?

CON. *(Sighs.)* Back to mundane reality. So. That press release, is that it?

HELEN. You don't have to feign interest, you know.

CON. My interest is quite genuine.

HELEN. But aesthetic pleasures first. Right?

CON. Always.

HELEN. Fine.

CON. My, my. Aren't we being snippish?

HELEN. *(After a moment.)* I'm sorry. Bad day, all right?

CON. Foot massage?

HELEN. That would be nice.

She takes off her shoes, he begins massaging her feet.

CON. So tell me all about it. I take it you haven't finished the press release?

HELEN. *(Aside, to the audience.)* Actually, the press releases were relatively easy. As it scrolls across the computer screen, you feel almost disembodied. Mouse, shade, copy, mouse, shade, delete. Lies appear and disappear, and soon the truth itself is lost in worries about phrasing, pace, flow. *(To CON.)* I've finished it, yes.

CON. So what's the problem?

HELEN. Con, do you ever get tired of all this?

CON. Of all what?

HELEN. This. Our jobs, our lives.

CON. The ONTI–Empasse tensions? Those will soon be solved.

HELEN. No, I know that. It's not the current emergency. It's just . . . everything.

CON. Can you specify?

HELEN. *(To audience.)* Grammar, spell-check, syntax: the computer functions become more crucial than the objective realities the text is intended to obscure. *(To CON.)* I'm beginning to hate my job.

CON. Too bad. I happen to love mine.

HELEN. I know you do.

CON. I love my work. I love the money. I love our home. I wish we weren't in St. George.

HELEN. *(To audience.)* And then you fax it, and that too seems unreal, a machine pulling paper through itself, and you think: that can't possibly be going anywhere.

CON. . . . two weeks in London every spring, two weeks in Paris every fall. New York and San Francisco for weekend jaunts. We get by.

HELEN. You don't wish that . . . .

Pause.

CON. What?

HELEN. You don't regret that we didn't have children?

CON. I haven't closed the door on that. When we're a little more settled—.

HELEN. I'm thirty-two years old.

CON. So maybe, within the next two or three years. . . . In the meantime, let's enjoy what we have together.

HELEN. I'm going to have to lie, Con. I'm going to have to stand there in front of all those reporters, and lie.

CON. Helen, you're head of public relations. It's your job to lie.

HELEN. I know.

CON. It's not like you're fooling anyone. Everyone's in on it.

HELEN. I know that, too.

CON. The reporters most of all. It's their job to be lied to.

HELEN. I know.

CON. It could even be illegal for you to tell the truth. As far as the SEC is concerned.

HELEN. Maybe so.

CON. So what's the big problem?

HELEN. I don't like it.

CON. *(Condescendingly.)* Innocent child.

HELEN. *(To the audience.)* And I stared at him for a moment. And the thought flickered through my head: Who are you? Who is it I married? *(Pause.)* Who am I?

CON. Come on. Let's go to bed.

HELEN. And we made love that night. To Barber's "Adagio for Strings."

They exit. Enter CYNTHIA, *who watches them with great interest.*

CYNTHIA. Something happened at the supermarket today, and it's got me a little worried. In front of me in line was a young man, he just had a few items, yet he waited behind a woman with a full cart, despite the fact that the next aisle was free. He got to her register, and the cashier looked up, and just stiffened, rang up his purchase without even looking at him. And he paid her, and then he leaned over, and whispered something to her, then picked up his purchase and left. Another of the cashiers saw him leave, and went up to her—"Ginger," her name-tag said—and she said, "Ginger? Are you all right?" And Ginger said, "He just told me he wants a divorce." I was entranced. The audacity! To go up to her while she was working and inform her of their upcoming divorce. Marvelous! She didn't cry. She told her friend she wanted to finish her shift; made a little joke about needing the money. And then she rang up my purchase, very controlled, just hanging on. And I wondered. The shock of it, the blow so soon. What would it take to break her down? Sympathy, I thought. A little female sympathy, and she'll lose it. And so, I stepped into the situation. As she was counting out my change, I leaned over, just as he had done, and I said, "I happened to overhear your situation. I just want you to know, I'm very sorry." And it worked! She burst into tears—I just barely got the shot—and raced out of the store, and another clerk had to finish the transaction! Should I have done that, I wonder? *(Enter* FRED.*)* I mean, am I invalidating the work by stepping into it?

FRED. Honey.

They kiss.

CYNTHIA. How was work?

FRED. Well, it's happening.

CYNTHIA. Marvelous. He went for the whole two thousand?

FRED. He had no choice. Twelve hundred at first, and then another eight. Look, I hope you don't mind....

CYNTHIA. What?

FRED. The stock's at seventeen. I emptied out our savings, see if I can figure out a way to buy a few thousand shares.

CYNTHIA. You handle the money, Fred. You think it's going up, fine.

FRED. There's gotta be a buy-out pending. See if I can launder it through Tony; I bet it doubles. Listen, I'm just going to grab a bite. Off to rehearsal.

CYNTHIA. Ah, yes, it's Thursday. Stake drama person.

FRED. You wanna come watch?

CYNTHIA. Do you mind?

FRED. You're more into that culture kinda stuff than me.

CYNTHIA. I will then. Just let me get my shoes. *(As he heads off.)* Fred?

FRED. Uh-huh?

CYNTHIA. When's it gonna happen?

FRED. What? The layoffs? Couple of weeks.

CYNTHIA. When it does . . . can I come to work with you?

FRED. Sure. Photo essay?

CYNTHIA. I think maybe so.

She exits. As she does, he sits, and enter SEANTUM, SEEZORAM, *and* BETHESDA, *three actors in badly fitting biblical robes.* SEANTUM *and* SEEZORAM *are wearing ridiculous-looking fake beards,* BETHESDA *is a woman.*

SEANTUM. So, Seezoram, my brother! I have found you alone, tonight, by the judgment seat of our people!

SEEZORAM. Guards! Guards!

SEANTUM. Call not for the guards, my brother! They are drunken with wine, prepared especially in its strength. I say unto you, tonight you shall die!

BETHESDA. Seantum, no!

SEANTUM. Bethesda! My wife!

BETHESDA. My husband, Seantum! Do not this wicked deed! Heed the words of the prophet Nephi, and forsake the evil counsel of Gadianton!

SEEZORAM. Listen to her, my brother!

SEANTUM AND BETHESDA. Shut up, Seezoram—.

BETHESDA. *(Sotto voce.)* Sorry, that's yours—.

SEANTUM. . . . you devil. Gadianton has told me of your nefarious plot! I know that you plotted to steal my precious birthright, and for that crime you must die like the villain you are!

BETHESDA. It is not true, Seantum! Gadianton has deceived you!

SEEZORAM. Please, my brother, please!

SEANTUM. False judge! Take that!

Stabs him. SEEZORAM *falls.*

SEEZORAM. I am wounded! Behold, I die! My life blood seeps out like spring rain through billowy clouds! But I testify, with my last breath, that I am a righteous judge! The prophet Nephi will sustain me! And I call on you, my brother Seantum, to repent this horrid deed!

SEANTUM. What have I done!

SEEZORAM. Repent!

BETHESDA. Seantum!

SEEZORAM. Repent!

He falls, dies horribly. Tableau.

FRED. Gadianton? Where's Gadianton?

BETHESDA. *(Under her breath.)* Whose line is it?

SEANTUM. I don't remember.

FRED. Gadianton!

Enter CHAD, *half in and half out of costume.*

CHAD. Sorry.

FRED. Keep on your toes, people. Chad, your evil laugh?

BETHESDA. *(Relieved.)* The evil laugh.

The other actors relax.

FRED. Let's do it. Seezoram?

SEEZORAM. Repent!

He dies horribly. Tableau. Enter CHAD, *as* GADIANTON. *He looks over the tableau, then laughs in a bloodcurdling fashion.*

FRED. And blackout. Good work people, it's really coming along. That's it for tonight. Hang up your costumes on the rack over there. We're back Saturday morning, eight o'clock. Lines were good tonight.

They all hang costumes on a costume rack, exit.

SEEZORAM. Fred, how was my death scene?

FRED. Good, fine. Listen, I was thinking, maybe we could get like fake blood stuff, put it in some kinda pouch in your mouth; you could bite down on it, bleed out the mouth for your death scene.

SEEZORAM. Cool!

FRED. What can I say? I'm a directing genius.

SEEZORAM. No doubt!

FRED. Could also be louder, Max.

SEEZORAM. I'll work on it.

He exits.

CYNTHIA. Fred, about the music?

FRED. Chad, don't take off yet.

CHAD. All right.

CYNTHIA. I wonder if the pianist can pick up the pace a little. Kishkumen's solo number? It's too slow.

CHAD. It's supposed to be kinda introspective.

FRED. Well, Kish can introspect a little faster.

CYNTHIA. I'm worried about her voice. Isn't Kishkumen a man?

FRED. With the beard no one'll notice. Anything else?

CYNTHIA. That comic number, the wicked Nephite rag?

CHAD. That's a fun song.

CYNTHIA. But it's a rag. Like ragtime? Scott Joplin?

FRED. It's gotta go faster, too.

CHAD. Look, she's just outside. You wanna talk to her?

CYNTHIA. That's a good idea.

CHAD. I'll go with you.

FRED. And don't miss your entrance next time.

CHAD. I'm sorry, Fred. I've been a little short of sleep.

FRED. Couple weeks, it'll all be over.

CHAD. Is that all for tonight?

FRED. Yeah, go home. Wake up your wife; maybe she'll let you boink her.

CHAD. *(Somberly, but hiding it.)* Yeah, maybe. See you tomorrow Fred.

> *He exits with* CYNTHIA. FRED *looks at his script, shouts to* CHAD.

FRED. And pick up the pace on that scene with Nephi! *(Grumbling to himself)* Damn thing lasts forever . . .

> *As he works, one of the costumes on the rack comes to life. It's* GADIANTON *from the earlier scenes.*

GADIANTON. Hello, Fred.

FRED. *(Not looking up.)* We're done tonight. Go home.

GADIANTON. Fred.

FRED. Look, I'm kinda busy . . . *(Looks up.)* Wait a . . . I've seen you before.

GADIANTON. Yes, you have seen me.

FRED. *(Shaking his head to clear it.)* Who are you?

GADIANTON. I'm Gadianton.

FRED. I'm leaving. *(He heads for the door. As he does,* GADIANTON *flies into the air, over his head, blocks his way.)* Look, I am not going nuts. That is not an option. I don't go nuts. That's not the kinda thing I do.

GADIANTON. You're not going nuts, Fred.

FRED. Then leave me alone.

GADIANTON. You're a Mormon now, Fred. You're required to accept certain myths as objective realities.

FRED. What are you doing here?

GADIANTON. Setting the record straight.

FRED. What record?

GADIANTON. The book, the play. They've got me all wrong. I'm misunderstood, just as you are.

FRED. I'm no Gadianton robber.

GADIANTON. Neither was I. I was a businessman. They called me a robber because the market was so tight.

FRED. A businessman.

GADIANTON. Buying low and selling high, marketing, finance.

FRED. What do you want?

GADIANTON. To be your friend. *(As CYNTHIA returns.)* Shhhhh—.

CYNTHIA. Fred, your pianist is not being terribly co-op . . . are you all right?

FRED. *(Recovering)* I don't know.

CYNTHIA. You look awful.

FRED. It's nothing.

CYNTHIA. Headache? *(He nods.)* It's probably just this play. Give anyone a headache.

FRED. You don't like the play?

CYNTHIA. Well, it is pretty awful. I mean, that book's supposed to be scripture, and they turn it into this cheesy melodrama. Gadianton, robber and fiend.

Mimes twitching a villainous moustache, she gives her own blood-curdling laugh.

GADIANTON. Listen to her, Fred. A businessman. "Thus they did have free intercourse one with another, to buy and to sell, and to get gain—. "

FRED. *(Interrupting him.)* To get gain.

CYNTHIA. What?

FRED. Laissez-faire economics. Zero-sum-game kinda market.

CYNTHIA. Fred, why don't you lie down or something?

FRED. Zero sum game. Pot's too small; for me to gain, you have to lose; for me to lose . . . Lean and mean.

CYNTHIA. Fred? Cut it out, okay?

FRED. *(Shakes his head, comes to.)* Sorry, Cinny. Sorry.

CYNTHIA. I'm worried about you.

FRED. Just woolgathering, thinking about the play. So you don't think I should do it?

CYNTHIA. Oh, no, do the play. It's just silly fun; who cares? I mean, it's not like the real Gadianton's going to come back and sue you for defamation of character, right?

FRED. *(Laughs with her.)* Right.

Suddenly overcome with pain.

CYNTHIA. Fred? Are you all right?

FRED. Killer headache.

CYNTHIA. Fred, I think I'd better drive. Can you wait here?

FRED. I think so.

CYNTHIA. Let me get the car.

FRED. You go do that.

> *He sits. She exits.*

GADIANTON. Fred—

FRED. Leave me alone!

GADIANTON. But, Fred, I'm your greatest admirer.

FRED. What do you want from me?

GADIANTON. Watch.

> *Lights up on* HELEN, *standing in the middle of a press conference, surrounded by reporters.*

REPORTER TWO. Helen, is there any truth to the rumor that these layoffs are related to or part of plans to sell the company, possibly to Empasse or some other major software supplier?

HELEN. *(Lying smoothly.)* I am aware of no plans to sell ONTI.

REPORTER THREE. So you deny that Mahonri Ward is trying to sell the company?

HELEN. As far as I know, Mahonri Ward will still be running things twenty years from now.

REPORTER ONE. Do you know of any further layoffs after these twelve hundred?

HELEN. I have heard rumors of a so-called "second wave." As far as I know, there is no truth to them whatsoever.

REPORTER TWO. Ms. Bryson. ONTI is a profitable company, in a rapidly expanding market. Why this massive layoff?

HELEN. Mr. Jones, for a town to function properly, it needs certain craftsmen—say, a blacksmith, and a tailor, and a butcher, and a baker. But let's suppose . . .

GADIANTON. Beautiful.

HELEN. *(Finishing.)* . . . that's why we don't really call it "a layoff." We prefer the term—

HELEN AND FRED. *(Simultaneously.)* "rightsizing."

GADIANTON. Rightsizing. Lovely word.

HELEN. *(She stares at* FRED. *In a whisper.)* Rightsizing. . . . Rightsizing. . . .

> Pause.

FRED. *(Simultaneously. Quietly.)* Good girl.

GADIANTON. Fred. A little advice. When you take over the company. That's your new Kishkumen. Your right-hand man. *(He flies out.)* I'm very proud of you.

> FRED *stares after him. Enter* ERMA MACKELPRANGER *and* WILSON HACKETT.

ERMA MACKELPRANGER. So finally some newspaper folks come snoopin', and they wrote up our problems, the AEC got scared and had hearings—up to Salt Lake.

WILSON HACKETT. Army said that sometimes they'd cancel tests 'cause the wind was blowing "the wrong direction." 'Nother words, west, towards L. A. or Vegas. What I wanna know is, if the tests wasn't dangerous, how could there be a "right" or "wrong" direction—for the wind?

ERMA MACKELPRANGER. Poisoned the air we breathed, the grass our children played on, the milk we drank, the water we washed up in—.

WILSON HACKETT. I went to them hearings for one day. All these men in suits, talkin' so reasonable.

ERMA MACKELPRANGER. I just wanted to stand up and scream, "Shut up! Shut up, you dumb people! Don't you know they're killing us!" But I didn't.

WILSON HACKETT. The fact is, we was patriotic people! God-fearing, flag-salutin', army-volunteerin' people. And they treat us like—makes me sick!

ERMA MACKELPRANGER. *(A warning.)* Wilson . . . .

WILSON HACKETT. *(Conspiratorial.)* Eisenhower knew. We all voted for him, and he knew the whole time.

ERMA MACKELPRANGER. He never—.

WILSON HACKETT. He said: "We can afford to sacrifice a few thousand people out there in the—interest of national security."

ERMA MACKELPRANGER. Don't talk dirty about the president—. Them's just rumors.

WILSON HACKETT. He was a damned politician!

ERMA MACKELPRANGER. He was a Republican!

Enter BISHOP TODD.

BISHOP TODD. We call ourselves downwinders; the word's a badge of honor. But it's just stories people tell. My father, my mother, my brothers Wilford and Lorenzo. . . . Could just be bad luck. It's just that . . . .When you grow up with mushroom clouds and red sunsets routine facts of life, and you see your entire family, one by one . . . then, for the rest of your life, every headache, every stubbed toe, every twinge in the back, every bruise . . .

Enter KAREN. *Lights up on* HELEN *and* CON *on other half of the stage.*

KAREN. McKay! It's seven-fifteen!

BISHOP TODD. And you wonder if that's the first sign. Of what's going to kill you.

CON. My. We're certainly dawdling this morning.

Music swells. The "Dies Irae" from the Mozart Requiem.

BISHOP TODD AND HELEN. *(Simultaneously.)* I know. I'm sorry.

KAREN. You're supposed to be at work!

BISHOP TODD. It's today, Karen.

KAREN. The layoffs?

He nods.

HELEN. Just couldn't face it.

CON. *(Incredulously.)* Couldn't face it?

KAREN. Now you listen to me, McKay. We need that job. You know what our finances are like.

BISHOP TODD. Karen, I'm not in—any danger.

HELEN. I think I'm—safe enough.

KAREN. You will be if you—don't get in.

CON. I'm not sure anyone's—completely safe.

BISHOP TODD. It's Brenda I'm worried about. And some of the others. Sister Maxie, Brother Hales, Sister Frederickson—.

HELEN. I'm mostly worried about Sam.

KAREN. So what?

CON. Sam's a joke!

BISHOP TODD. I'm their supervisor, Karen. It'll be my job to escort them off—the premises.

HELEN. Me, and two armed guards.

CON. Helen, you know why that's necessary.

KAREN. Then get in and do it.

BISHOP TODD. Karen—.

HELEN. Con, will you please turn off that music—.

KAREN. We need the money, McKay. This is no time for scruples.

CON. Sorry. I thought you might appreciate—

HELEN. This morning, it's more than I can handle.

CON. I thought the "Dies Irae" might be appropriate—.

HELEN. Well, it's not.

CON. You're in business, Helen. Lean and mean.

HELEN. I know.

Reluctantly, she and BISHOP TODD *pull themselves up, exit. Lights up on* FRED *and* CHAD, *sitting.*

FRED. ... optimist sees the glass and says, "It's half full." Pessimist says, "It's half empty." Corporate exec says, "You know, you're really got more water in that glass than you need."

He and CHAD *laugh.*

CHAD. Okay okay, I've got one. How many software engineers does it take to change a light bulb?

FRED. I know this one.

TOGETHER. Two fewer than it took last week!

FRED. Knock knock.

CHAD. Who's there?

FRED. Not you anymore.

He laughs.

CHAD. Hey, no fair, you stole that one from an old Dilbert.

FRED. Yeah? I wondered where I'd heard it.

CHAD. *(After a pause.)* Seems kinda strange, doesn't it?

FRED. What?

CHAD. Rush rush rush the last few weeks. Then today, the biggest day in the history of the company, and we don't really have much.

FRED. I was just thinking about the good old days.

CHAD. Oh, yeah?

FRED. Watching you. Late nights, early mornings. Takes me back.

CHAD. Where did you get your start? If you don't mind my asking.

FRED. Not at all. P & G.

CHAD. Proctor and Gamble, huh? In the Midwest?

FRED. Yeah. Spent three years in Cincinnati, at corporate, rooting for the Reds and Bengals. The devil's company.

CHAD. What?

FRED. The trademark?

CHAD. Trademark? Oh, you mean that genie thing?

FRED. That's right. Fundamentalist wackos decided that the P & G trademark, the genie guy with the lantern, was a sign of devil worship. It even made Donahue. We all thought it was pretty funny, the devil's company, like the boss was Satan's CEO? Very inside joke, you understand. If anyone found out, every Bible-thumping housewife in America woulda turned in her Tide.

CHAD. So, you were there three years? Where'd you go then?

FRED. Redmond.

CHAD. Microsoft! No kidding!

FRED. Yeah, that was me. Twenty-seven years old and rubbing shoulders with Bill Gates. Best two years of my life.

CHAD. Bill Gates? You met him? You worked with him?

FRED. I worked with him every day. Personally.

CHAD. What's he like? I mean really?

FRED. *(Admiringly.)* Smarter, tougher, meaner, quicker. You practically lived in your suit, and he got there earlier and left later than everyone. The best of the best of the best.

CHAD. Why'd you leave?

FRED. I was stupid. See, I wasn't technical, wasn't one of Bill's Smart Guys. He likes engineers. I was a bean counter. I got another offer and, like a dummy, took it.

CHAD. You've done well for yourself.

FRED. When you've had filet mignon, it's hard to get used to meatloaf.

CHAD. Fred . . . ?

FRED. Yeah?

CHAD. Could I . . . you know . . . hack it?

FRED. You?

CHAD. He likes young guys. I'm a hard worker, I've shown you that.

FRED. So?

CHAD. Well, when I finish here. Couple years down the road, maybe. Could I work for Microsoft?

FRED. Why is a manhole cover round?

CHAD. What?

FRED. Why is a manhole cover round? Answer me.

CHAD. Well . . . I don't really know. They just started doing it that way, I guess, and—.

FRED. I just invented a terrific new hot dog. Project how many can I expect to sell at baseball games next season, major and minor league.

CHAD. Hot dogs? I'm not sure. I mean, some people don't even like—.

FRED. Invent a new currency. If most purchases are under a hundred, what are your four lowest bill denominations?

CHAD. Bill denominations? What are you—.

FRED. *(Starts to leave.)* I'll need that marketing report on my desk by five o'clock tonight.

CHAD. Wait. Just a second. You didn't even answer—my question.

FRED. Answer is no. You couldn't work for Microsoft.

CHAD. Why?

FRED. Because you're not smart enough.

He exits. CHAD *stares after him, dumbfounded. Lights down. Enter* BISHOP TODD, BRENDA.

BRENDA. *(Tense.)* It's started.

BISHOP TODD. What's happening?

BRENDA. Saw a woman out in the parking lot. Crying so hard she couldn't get her key in the lock of her car. Guard had to help her.

BISHOP TODD. Did you recognize her?

BRENDA. Real short dark-haired lady, worked in Payroll?

BISHOP TODD. I know who you mean. Can't place a name.

BRENDA. Me, neither. So what do we do?

BISHOP TODD. Treat it like a normal workday.

BRENDA. Yeah, that's real likely. You sleep a wink last night?

BISHOP TODD. Mail still needs to go out.

BRENDA. I know. But normal, it ain't. Let's get going, people.

Lights down on them. HELEN *with* SAM.

HELEN. Come on, Sam, my press conference is in twenty minutes.

SAM. Just waiting for it to print.

HELEN. You sent the fax Friday. They all coming?

SAM. *The Spectrum,* the *Sun, Las Vegas Review,* even the *L. A. Times.* Two live remotes, but I couldn't see which stations.

HELEN. I look okay?

SAM. You look super. Helen—?

HELEN. What?

SAM. You heard anything—?

HELEN. No, Sam, I haven't. Not one way or another.

She exits.

BRENDA. *(Looking through papers.)* They say mostly supervisors, or assistant supervisors.

BISHOP TODD. Who said that?

BRENDA. Guy I met in the lunchroom. Said mostly assistants.

BISHOP TODD. You or me, in other words.

BRENDA. That's what he said.

BISHOP TODD. We're pretty understaffed down here. I was even about to request another afternoon person. Maybe we'll be okay.

BRENDA. Maybe.

Enter HELEN, *press conference.*

HELEN. That's right, a supervisor, and two security guards.

BISHOP TODD. How's the baby?

BRENDA. Six more weeks. Had another ultrasound. She hardly moves at all, but the picture . . . it helps to see her.

BISHOP TODD. Have you . . . made any decision?

BRENDA. Let's just survive today, okay, Bishop?

HELEN. I know this seems harsh, but the fact is, it is necessary.

BISHOP TODD. All right.

HELEN. They'll have the opportunity tomorrow or Friday to pick up personal belongings.

Enter CYNTHIA.

CYNTHIA. Fred told me they would start at nine, but I was disappointed, I must say, because when I pulled into the parking lot, I was almost hit by a car pulling out, the driver crying. . . . And I still had my lens cap on! When something is to start at nine, then that's when it should start.

BRENDA. Brother Warner was the first to go.

CYNTHIA, BRENDA *and* HELEN *overlap these quick speeches.* CYNTHIA *snapping.*

CYNTHIA. Man leaving . . . half walking half running, body so rigid he—nearly tripped down the step.

BRENDA. Sister Lakey—.

HELEN. All computer access codes—.

BRENDA. Brother Rockwood—. Brother Smith.

HELEN. . . . will be changed.

BRENDA. Brother Parmley—.

CYNTHIA. A cubicle in Personnel, empty. On the desk, a five-by-seven family photograph. A man—a woman, chubby little kids.

BRENDA. Mr. Daletski, the HR guy who helped me with insurance stuff. Mrs. Ramirez, who—always had flowers on her desk.

HELEN. Yes, we do have concerns about sabotage.

BRENDA. Brother Bentley. Sister Enos—. Brother Rahm.

CYNTHIA. And a man typing blindly, staring straight ahead. Empty cubicles—to either side.

BRENDA. Brother Walters—just married a few months.

HELEN. Yes, plus a supervisor—if possible.

BRENDA. Sister Breinholt. Brother Chandler—. Sister Ludlow.

HELEN. Seniority is a factor—absolutely.

CYNTHIA. Two men embracing, tall blond, little oriental.

BISHOP TODD. And I found myself thinking about Mahonri Ward. Wondering if I could talk to him.

WARD. Hello, Fred.

Enter FRED. GADIANTON, *enters, watches.*

FRED. Mahonri. Big day, huh?

WARD. At least it'll soon be over.

FRED. Yep.

WARD. Just a few more hours.

Pause.

FRED. I think it was a good idea for you to come in today. I know you didn't want to—.

WARD. No.

FRED. But I like the message it sends.

WARD. Yes.

Pause.

FRED. You coming in.

WARD. Yes.

Pause.

FRED. Well, I'll keep on top of things.

WARD. This is just useless.

FRED. Excuse me?

WARD. I don't run this company any more. Why did I even bother?

FRED. Support, solidarity.

WARD. People I started with, people I hired. Coming in and begging. Begging for this assistant or that secretary. That's what today's going to be.

FRED. I'll keep 'em out, Mahonri, they can come to me.

WARD. I don't think so. I've always had an open door. I'm not changing that today. If it makes them feel better to have someone to yell at, I'm here.

FRED. Whatever you want.

Pause.

WARD. Get out.

FRED. Right. (*He exits.*) Man.

GADIANTON. Don't worry, Fred.

FRED. What's with him?

GADIANTON. It's nothing. If anyone gets in to see him, he'll just undercut you. I'll take charge here.

FRED. Thanks.

He exits. Lights back up on HELEN *and* CYNTHIA.

BRENDA. Look, maybe this isn't the time, but . . .

BISHOP TODD. What is it?

BRENDA. See, Alice wants off at three-thirty to be with her kindergartener, wants to switch to mornings. Now Brett thinks that . . . Bishop, are you listening?

BISHOP TODD. I'm sorry. It's about Alice. Whatever you suggest, I'm sure it'll be fine.

BRENDA. It's not that easy, Bishop.

BISHOP TODD. Brenda. I'm sorry. Keep on top of things here for a sec. I have to go talk to someone.

BRENDA. Whatever you say.

Lights down. BISHOP TODD *exits.*

HELEN. Every effort will be made to treat people with respect and courtesy.

CYNTHIA. Programming. Two young men in their early twenties watch, as an older man's escorted out. His hair slicked—back, shoes polished.

BRENDA. Sister Hansen. Sister Yamaguchi—. Brother Mendez.

CYNTHIA. On every wall, posters: motivational sayings, "Proper planning prevents poor performance," the P's—all highlighted.

HELEN. Yes, we recognize that it is a volatile—situation.

CYNTHIA. The boss leaves. The door shuts, young guys give each other high fives.

GADIANTON. I'm sorry, but Mr. Ward isn't seeing anyone today.

BISHOP TODD. Is he in?

GADIANTON. I can't answer that. He's not seeing anyone—.

BISHOP TODD. Look, I'm from the mailroom. We have a major disaster happening, and I was told I reported directly to him.

GADIANTON. What kind of disaster?

BISHOP TODD. I'm supposed to tell Mr. Ward directly.

GADIANTON. Well, tell it to Mr. Whitmore.

BISHOP TODD. My job is to tell Mr. Ward.

GADIANTON. Well, my job is to screen Mr. Ward's appointments. And today he just can't fit you in.

BISHOP TODD. Five minutes, that's all, I'll take five minutes and—

GADIANTON. *(Simultaneously)* I've told you, he's not seeing anyone. You might as well—

WARD, *up by the door.*

WARD. It's okay. Send him in.

HELEN. Usually, we subcontract our security through—Diamond Security.

BRENDA. Mr. Kovaks. Mr. Greenfield. Dorothy and Carrie Ann—, from the cafeteria.

CYNTHIA. Customer Support. Chair after empty chair, phone lights flashing.

BRENDA. Mr. Bjarnson—. Sister Bridges.

CYNTHIA. And over it all, the voices. Courteous—. Tense. Frightened. Helpful.

BRENDA. Brother Marchant—. Brother Guinness.

HELEN. Today, we thought it might be better not to use people the employees already know.

BISHOP TODD. And so I told him the entire story, the ruined clothes in the bed of the truck, the Standards Night talk, spina bifida. And he sat there, his face in shadow. And whenever I paused, he'd just say quietly:

WARD. Go on.

BISHOP TODD. Mr. Ward, we're short-handed down there anyway. If you lay anyone off, we're just not going to be able to get the mail out on time, not the way we have been. Anyway, I know she's an assistant supervisor, and I know they're the people you're targeting. But I'm begging you. Don't . . . .

Pause.

WARD. *(After a long pause.)* Bishop Todd. What a remarkable story. You care about your . . . you care and that's good. I just have this feeling that all across the company today, that kind of pain . . . *(Long pause.)* I hate this.

BISHOP TODD. You can't stop it?

WARD. I even voted against it. . . . There's a limit to what a CEO can do, especially. . . . Well, I can do some things still. *(Writing at his desk.)* Take this note to Fred Whitmore. One less layoff in the mail room . . . I'll try to call him as well. *(Finishes the note.)* I can't do this for everyone. But this strikes me as an exceptional case.

BISHOP TODD. Thank you, Mr. Ward. *(He starts to exit.)* I take this to Mr. Whitmore?

WARD. He's running the layoff.

BISHOP TODD. I thought this was your company.

WARD. Not any longer.

As BISHOP TODD *leaves.*

HELEN. The guards have been instructed to act only if necessary to prevent bodily injury or the—destruction of company property.

CYNTHIA. And then someone tried to take my camera away from me.

BRENDA. Sister Douglas. Brother Alvarez—. Brother Taylor.

CYNTHIA. Tried to take it out of my hands and smash it against a wall.

HELEN. Any further questions?

CYNTHIA. A guard stopped him, the flash went off, and I think, accidently, he may have gotten a shot of his own face in closeup. I hope so. I've never seen such rage.

CHAD. I'm sorry. Mr. Whitmore isn't in right now.

BISHOP TODD. When do you expect him?

CHAD. I'm never sure. He's usually in and out.

BISHOP TODD. It's rather important.

CHAD. You're welcome to wait. I'd call him, but he didn't even take his phone.

BISHOP TODD. I'll wait.

Phone rings.

CHAD. *(On the phone.)* Excuse me. Honey, this is not a good . . . we've talked about this. . . . Honey, there's absolutely nothing I can. . . . We've had this conversation before.

HELEN. Any questions?

Spotlight on her, alone and vulnerable.

CYNTHIA. I'm not sure I've ever done better work. The looks, their faces.

HELEN. 'Cause if you don't have any, I sure do.

She crosses back to SAM.

SAM. How did it go?

HELEN. Pretty awful.

The "Dies Irae" starts again.

SAM. Good.

HELEN. Good?

SAM. It should be awful. You should feel awful. I do. We're doing an awful thing. And we're defending it. We should feel bad.

HELEN. Well, I do.

SAM. Good.

A pause.

HELEN. Sam . . . .

SAM. *(Warily.)* Yes?

HELEN. Sam, look. I don't know how to say this—.

SAM. Helen?

HELEN. I want you to know that this is no reflection on your work. You can expect, and you deserve, an outstanding letter of recommendation.

SAM. You knew all day, didn't you—?

HELEN. Sam, I'm terribly, terribly—.

SAM. Shut up.

HELEN. I'm afraid, I'm going to have to . . . *(Nearly loses control.)* . . . to ask you to remove your hands from your computer now.

SAM. *(Hands up.)* Fine.

HELEN. Thank you—. Now, I'm going to have to ask you to accompany me . . .

SAM. *(Speaking simultaneously.)* You are doing something despicable. I hope you know that—.

HELEN. *(Stops him.)* Sam.

SAM. Go on.

HELEN. Accompany me out of the building to your car.

SAM. Let's go.

HELEN. Sam . . . Look, you're supposed to come back tomorrow for personal effects, but if you want to . . . I don't know. The picture of your family—.

SAM. Keep it. *(Hands it to her.)* Put it on your desk.

He exits.

HELEN. So, Ms. Vice-President.

BRENDA. Brother Flandro. Brother Houghton. Sister Pomeroy.

HELEN. What do you do now?

BRENDA. Fred Whitmore better watch out. I know where he parks.

Lights down on her. WARD *suddenly gets up. He crosses to* COGBURN, *but* WARD's *no longer depressed, quite energized, in fact.*

WARD. Well, John, all finished. The yard is trimmed, the clippings are gone, garden's weeded. Come out and see.

COGBURN. *(Still a bit stunned, amazed.)* I saw.

WARD. But you haven't seen the paint job. Come on out.

COGBURN. In a second.

WARD. Whatever you say. The point is, John, we're getting you cleaned up. Okay?

COGBURN. For all the good it's gonna do.

WARD. I don't expect it to solve all your problems. I'm just trying to encourage you to—

COGBURN. To what?

WARD. To make a start, John. To get your life back in order.

COGBURN. Why?

WARD. I told you, John. I've been assigned as your home teacher. And I care about you.

COGBURN *stares at him in amazement. He looks as though he may cry. Suddenly, as he stares at* WARD, *he begins to chuckle. The chuckle expands into a laugh, a braying, harsh, ugly, laugh.*

WARD. John, what's the matter? *(The laugh turns into a coughing fit.* COGBURN *doubles over, but still laughing predominates.)* Can I help you? *(He reaches over to pat* COGBURN *on the back.)* John?

COGBURN. Don't touch me.

WARD. *(Friendly but puzzled.)* Do you mind sharing the joke?

COGBURN. The joke? The joke is you!

WARD. I don't understand—.

COGBURN. I figured it out. I did! The yard and the paint job, it's all outside the house, isn't it?

WARD. I told you, I'm trying to—.

COGBURN. This isn't about home teaching! Not about me! It's about the house!

WARD. It's about you.

COGBURN. It's about property values!

WARD. *(Pause.)* You can't really believe—.

COGBURN. This house is the disgrace of the neighborhood, and you don't want it to drag down property values.

Laughing again.

WARD. John, that's ridiculous.

COGBURN. I don't believe you—.

WARD. I'm your—home teacher.

COGBURN. How does it feel?

WARD. What?

COGBURN. Every good deed, every charity you give to . . . you'll hear the whispers. "What are his motives?" Mistrust and suspicion. That's you.

WARD. I don't believe that.

COGBURN. Every friend you make, you'll wonder, could just be about the money. Every conversation, that's underneath. "Maybe he'll give me money." You're not a home teacher. You're not even Mahonri Ward anymore. You're three hundred million dollars, and that's all you are for the rest of your life.

WARD. What are you doing? Why are you saying this?

COGBURN. I'm teaching you how to be rich.

WARD, stunned, backs away from COGBURN, sits across from where BISHOP TODD sits, sleeping in his chair.

BISHOP TODD. *(Light shift indicates a dream sequence. The "Dies Irae" begins.)* Mahonri Ward. Welcome. I'm your bishop. And this disciplinary council is now in session.

WARD. But I haven't done anything to warrant a court. *(As he lists his good deeds, BISHOP TODD begins the charge against him. They speak simultaneously.)* I pay my tithing, and I attend my meetings regularly, and I abstain from tobacco, alcohol, coffee, tea, white sugar, and soups hotter than my body temperature, and I obey the law of chastity and am honest in my dealings with my fellow man including all traffic ordinances, and serve faithfully in my calling as home teacher as my brother John Cogburn will surely attest.

BISHOP TODD. *(Simultaneously.)* You willfully and with full knowledge and intent did commit an act of economic violence against your brothers and sisters in the gospel, depriving them of their ability to earn an honest livelihood by the sweat of their brow and thus trampling on the poor but honest at heart in order that the stockholders of this company might get gain. *(Continuing after WARD finishes.)* And the stockholders did flourish, and their flourishing came at the cost of their brothers and sisters!

Shadowy figures in the background begin to appear.

HARRY JUNE. Stock's rising. It's up twelve dollars a share.

BISHOP TODD. Members of the court, how find you?

As they speak, his head droops.

GADIANTON. Not guilty.

HELEN. It's normal business practice. Not guilty.

CYNTHIA. Not guilty.

FRED. Not guilty.

COOPER AND SCOTT. Not guilty.

> *The entire company begins echoing, whispering "Not guilty." The bishop slowly retreats to his chair, head on his desk.*

WARD. *(As the whispering fades.)* I'm not guilty. I'm not. I'm not.

COGBURN. *(Simultaneously.)* No one will ever believe in your innocence. Not for the rest of your life.

> *He and* WARD *exit. Lights to normal.* BISHOP TODD *is asleep.*

CHAD. *(On the phone.)* . . . whatever you think you have to do.

FRED. *(Enters, sees the* BISHOP *sleeping.)* Chad, what's going on? Who is this?

CHAD. Guy named Todd. Works down in the mailroom.

FRED. We can him?

CHAD. He's not on the list. *(Crosses to* BISHOP TODD.*)* Mr. Todd? Wake up.

BISHOP TODD. *(Wakes.)* What? *(Notices* FRED.*)* Mr. Whitmore. I'm so sorry.

FRED. Whaddya need?

BISHOP TODD. *(Still trying to clear his head.)* This won't take more than a moment of your time.

FRED. No, it won't.

BISHOP TODD. I'm sorry. McKay Todd, from the mailroom, you said I could report to you if I—

FRED. I remember.

BISHOP TODD. I have an assistant. Her name is Brenda, Brenda Burdett. Can I ask . . . is she on the . . . is she supposed to be—

FRED. Chad?

CHAD. *(Checks the computer.)* Brenda Burdett. Yep. One of the last ones, this afternoon.

BISHOP TODD. I have a note from Mr. Ward for you. *(Hands it over.)* To lay her off would be a terrible mistake. I'm her bishop, you see. Believe me when I say that you would be destroying her life.

FRED. *(Reads the note carefully. A pause. He crumples the note and throws it away.)* The thing is, McKay, we don't make mistakes. Did this whole thing, twelve hundred lay-offs, and we didn't make a single mistake. Can you think of one, Chad?

CHAD. No, not a one.

FRED. She's, what? Chad?

CHAD. Assistant supervisor in the mailroom.

FRED. Right. See, that can't possibly be a mistake.

BISHOP TODD. But a human mistake, not a tactical or ... functional ... but—.

FRED. Oh, a *human* mistake. That's what you're saying we made.

BISHOP TODD. I didn't mean—.

FRED. See, that could happen. We could make a *human* mistake. That could happen, couldn't it, Chad?

CHAD. Sure. We're only human.

FRED. Right. We make all kinda *human* mistakes. Like what fr'instance?

CHAD. Well—.

FRED. I know. Like we put the assistant when we shoulda put the supervisor, that kinda thing. That what you're talking about?

BISHOP TODD. I ... don't—.

FRED. Like we shouldn't lay her off. Like we should lay you off instead. Is that the kinda mistake we made? *(A pause.)* Is it?

KAREN. And another three-eighteen for the car payment, eleven-seventy for the house.

BRENDA. I want this baby, Bishop.

KAREN. We need the money, McKay. This is no time for scruples.

FRED. Is it?

BRENDA. I can feel her inside me, kicking and pushing ... and I ... I wanna hold her. In my arms.

KAREN. Seven hundred a month for the twins—.

FRED. IS IT?

BISHOP TODD. Yes.

KAREN. McKay?

FRED. Excuse me?

BISHOP TODD. Yes. I'm saying that that's the kind of human mistake you made.

FRED. You're kidding.

KAREN. You did what?

FRED. I didn't even mean it serious. Maybe I said it wrong, got you confused.

BISHOP TODD. I understood.

FRED. She gets your job. You get the boot.

BISHOP TODD. I know.

KAREN. *(Livid.)* WHY?

BISHOP TODD. Because I'm bishop of this ward, Karen. How could I work for a company that just laid off thirty of my ward members? Who I hired? How could I look at them each Sunday?

KAREN. *(A pause. Terrified.)* But what are we going to do?

BISHOP TODD. I don't know.

FRED. All right. That's what you want. Chad, escort him to his car. You can come back tomorrow for your personal stuff. *(CHAD leads BISHOP TODD out. GADIANTON sits on FRED's desk.)* Wild.

GADIANTON. I've seen his type before. He just woulda been a troublemaker.

FRED. Still. Weird stuff. *(Enter CHAD.)* Everything go okay?

CHAD. He just went out to his car.

FRED. He say anything to you?

CHAD. He talked to me.

FRED. What about?

CHAD. My marriage.

FRED. Bummer. *(Enter CYNTHIA.)* Hi, honey.

CHAD. Mrs. Whitmore.

CYNTHIA. Are you ready to go home?

FRED. Just about, couple more things. You have a good day?

CYNTHIA. Marvelous.

FRED. Okay, Chad, you make that change on the Burdett thing?

CHAD. Got it.

FRED. And the second wave list? The next eight hundred?

CHAD. It's in the computer.

FRED. Good. Chad, just one more thing.

CHAD. *(Turns to him.)* Yep.

FRED. Take your hands off the computer. Let me escort you to your car. *(The security guards appear over his shoulder.)*

CHAD. That's awfully nice of you, Fred, but don't—*(Pause. He gets it.)* No.

FRED. Move away from the computer.

CHAD. Fred. Come on.

FRED. I want you to move away *now*.

CHAD. *(Complying.)* I've done everything you asked me to. Everything. I've worked—

FRED. Sure. You've done fine.

CHAD. I've worked—.

FRED. The job's done, Chad. We're *(with a break between the words)* rightsizing. You don't fit.

CHAD. Fred, my wife . . . the eighty-hour weeks, the days—.

FRED. Like I said, I've got no complaints about your work. You'll get a good letter from me. This is not personal.

CHAD. She's left me, Fred. Because of this job. She told me today, she's leaving.

FRED. Then you learned something about her, too. Didn't you?

A pause. CYNTHIA *takes* CHAD's *picture.* CHAD *leaves, almost running.*

GADIANTON. Very nice.

CYNTHIA. Last shot on the roll.

FRED. I'll take you home. We gotta big day tomorrow.

END ACT TWO

Epilogue

Enter ERMA MACKELPRANGER *and* WILSON HACKETT, *followed by the other characters as they speak.*

ERMA MACKELPRANGER. The government finally did admit they done—something wrong.

WILSON HACKETT. 'Bout time, you ask me.

GADIANTON. Nobody dies and nobody is injured.

BISHOP TODD. A few weeks later I got a job as a—high school custodian.

GADIANTON. While some lose their jobs, they're soon—employed elsewhere.

BISHOP TODD. The twins were able—to finish their missions.

KAREN. Bibi Halstrup's oldest daughter just—got pregnant. Unmarried.

GADIANTON. There's nothing wrong—with it.

BRENDA. The baby survived the birth—and surgery.

GADIANTON. It's a common practice,—perfectly ethical.

BRENDA. She'll be partly paralyzed—for life.

GADIANTON. Momentarily painful, but not—at all damaging.

BRENDA. My other kids do real—good with her.

HELEN. I still work for—ONTI.

GADIANTON. The company is stronger—for it.

HELEN. ONTI slash Empasse, as we're calling it—since the merger.

GADIANTON. More efficient,—a better investment.

FRED. I cleared a quarter mill on the—merger and sale.

HELEN. Con and I are separated.

FRED. I'm running the ONTI half.

GADIANTON. A company that isn't profitable hurts—its stockholders.

FRED. Harry June and I—get along great.

CYNTHIA. And I'm enjoying Idaho more—than ever.

CHAD. After my divorce, I went back to school, and earned—an MBA.

GADIANTON. No one likes it—.

CHAD. I was hired by P & G and moved—to Cincinnati.

GADIANTON. But everyone learns something, and most are—better off.

SAM. I attempted suicide. For the insurance. Failed. Twice.

WARD. I founded a trust fund, to support the arts—and local charities.

GADIANTON. It is, after all, just money—. Just a job.

WARD. And I remain a devoted—home teacher.

BISHOP TODD. Dave's cancer is in remission. And I'm still bishop.

GADIANTON. There's nothing wrong.

BISHOP TODD. For a while, half the ward was receiving Church assistance. But one by one, people—got jobs.

FRED. We're lean and mean now, boy. Every piece in place. Ready to take on Microsoft.

GADIANTON. There's nothing wrong.

FRED. Even the play was a big success. The Church, the company, Harry.

GADIANTON. There's nothing wrong.

ERMA MACKELPRANGER. Government promised all the downwinders—a financial settlement.

FRED. I gotta say, I feel right at home—in this valley.

GADIANTON. There's nothing wrong.

WILSON HACKETT. Ain't nobody got it yet, and I doubt we ever will.

GADIANTON. There's nothing wrong.

FINAL BLACKOUT

ACKNOWLEDGMENTS

I owe a lot of people big time for the help they gave me while I was writing *Gadianton*. I went into this project knowing next to nothing about the computer industry or the world of big business. As I tried to educate myself, the following books were particularly helpful: W. E. ("Pete") Peterson's *Almost Perfect: How a Bunch of Regular Guys Built WordPerfect Corporation*, Daniel Ichbiah's *The Making of Microsoft*, and James Wallace's *Hard Drive: Bill Gates and the Making of the Microsoft Empire*. David M. Gordon's *Fat and Mean: The Corporate Squeeze of Working Americans and the Myth of Managerial "Downsizing"* was a delightful polemic and greatly influenced my thinking.

Since this play is largely philosophical in nature, I chose to read a number of books on business ethics, and found Jacqueline Dunckel's *Good Ethics, Good Business*, Dorothy Maddox's *Ethics in Business: A Guide for Managers*, and O. C. Ferrell's *In Pursuit of Ethics* valuable. I was indebted to the Maddox book in particular for what it did *not* say on the ethics of rightsizing.

I also found Carole Gallagher's *American Ground Zero: The Secret Nuclear War* to be most thought-provoking and disturbing, so much so that it is largely responsible for the play's greatest flaw, its tendency to zip off into narrative tangents. And, of course, I read and re-read the book of Helaman in the Book of Mormon, especially chapters 1–11.

On a more personal level, I am grateful to my brother, Rob Samuelsen, a man who proves that businessmen can be both ethical and moral. Lisa Hawkins provided me a valuable clue to the character of Harry June. Jim D'Arc offered friendly criticism and encouragement at a time when the play seemed just too weird. My colleagues Bob Nelson and Tim Slover offered invaluable comments, and Tim was likewise willing to lend us his home for our first reading. Tim was also a superb Mahonri in our first production. Good friends like Blaine Sundrud, Darise Error, and Carrie Morgan took the time to read and critique scenes while they were being written. I am enormously grateful to Jerry Crawford, George Judy, Doug Cook, and the New Playwrights series of the Utah Shakespearean Festival, and to Doug Stewart and Robert Paxton of the Tuacahn Mormon Arts Festival, both of which venues were invaluable in the development of this script. Bob Nelson directed our first production, at BYU, and did his usual brilliant job.

I loved our cast, and must thank them all: Jason Tatom, Ben Hoppe, Ryan Rauzon, Jeremy Hoop, Tim Slover, Josh Brady, Rob Gardner, Danny Stiles, Amy Barrus, Katie Holsinger, Rachel Davenport, Megan Sanborn and Colleen Baum; I love all you guys. Above all, I must thank my wife, Annette, for her usual boundless patience at a time when my attention was always drawn at least two places.

Hancock County

Tim Slover

About the Playwright

Perhaps short only of Neil LaBute, Tim Slover is the Mormon playwright who has seen the most success outside the confines of Utah. Slover has had his work produced Off-Broadway; in Canada; by the Lamb's Players Theatre in San Diego (the third largest repertory company in the USA); at the Fulton Opera House; and on numerous other stages across the country.

Although Slover had written and produced a number of plays in his early career, including *The Dreambuilder* and *March Tale*, it wasn't until his most famous work *Joyful Noise* (about the dramatic backstory of George Frederic Handel's composition of *Messiah*), that his work began reaching more national stages.

> When friend and filmmaker David West suggested that we might do a movie about G. F. Handel and the writing of his *Messiah*, what came into my mind immediately were the half-remembered legends about the composer: Didn't he write the oratorio in some miraculously short period of time? Didn't he refuse to eat while writing? Didn't the music more or less come to him directly by God, carried on a silver salver by musically inclined angels, who were already humming the "Hallelujah Chorus"?[1]

West went onto other projects, but the history of Handel kept rattling around in Slover's head. Slover had previously found great delight in writing historical stories and he found that he had an appetite for more:

> I had recently written another historical play and found that I liked the process of reading biographies and source documents and critical editions, and then finding the story in the manuscripts. Actually, what I liked best was finding a place in the history that said something like, "Here in the life of Alexander the Great, a shroud is drawn over his activities. Historians have no idea what he was up to in August." Aha! I'll set my play in August! The gap in the narrative is the place where imagination can dwell.
> I set about reading to confirm all the legends about Handel. I didn't really

---

[1] Tim Slover, "Mormon Director Takes a Small Bite Out of the Big Apple," *Meridian Magazine*, http://www.meridianmagazine.com/arts/000114joyfulnoise.html (accessed May 15, 2012).

find them. True, he had written *Messiah* in about three weeks. But then, he had written just about all his oratorios in three weeks. His hectic entrepreneurial schedule only allowed him a certain amount of time to compose, and he had learned to make the most of it. The music didn't come down from a cloud; it came as a logical—but nevertheless inspired—next step after earlier oratorios. And goodness gracious, look at this: the man was on the brink of quitting when he began *Messiah*, he'd had so many recent failures. I began to think there was a good play in this history.[2]

Joyful Noise had ecstatic audience responses in its first production (and a second encore production the next year) at BYU. Yet it wasn't until the well-respected, Christian-based Lamb's Players Theatre in San Diego took an interest in the script that the play started making some ripples on the national scene: "An amazing thing happened. People from beyond the Pinecone Curtain began to like the play. It was invited to a playwriting workshop sponsored by Lamb's Players Theatre in San Diego, thanks to a generous friend and playwright who recommended the play, sight unseen. At Lamb's, I met some of the most extraordinary, compassionate, committed, flat-out talented artists I have ever known."[3]

The Lamb's Players production of *Joyful Noise* was very successful.[4] One reviewer, comparing it to Peter Shaffer's *Amadeus*, said that there was "much to enjoy in the play" and was "an interesting and often funny story that is as much about the politics of art as its creation."[5]

The successful run in San Diego eventually led to its Off-Broadway run in the Lamb's Theatre in New York (ironically, despite the similar names, it was not the same theater organization as that in San Diego) and the work was subsequently published by the prominent Samuel French, Inc. Although the *New York Times* took issue with its "aggressive comedy,"[6] the run has generally been seen as a success and continues to receive subsequent productions across the country.

Slover was slightly stunned by the chain of events that led his play to be produced in one of the theatre capitals of the world:

> I'm a forty-three-year old Mormon, and a play of mine is going to New York City. It's something I've hoped for for so long that, now that it's happened, I can't quite take it in. I hoped for it when I was in my twenties. I had

---

2   Ibid.
3   Ibid.
4   It conducted a revival of the play for its 2009–10 season.
5   Elyse Sommer, "A *Curtain Up* Review: *Joyful Noise*," *Curtain Up*, February 14, 2000, http://www.curtainup.com/joyfulnoise.html (accessed May 17, 2012).
6   Anthony Tommasini, "Handel's Holy Work, Born of Scandal," *New York Times*, February 29, 2000, http://theater.nytimes.com/2000/02/29/theater/theater-review-handel-s-holy-work-born-of-scandal.html (accessed May 11, 2011).

a few role models back then, twenty-somethings whose plays went to New York: Sam Shepard, Christopher Durang, Tom Stoppard, the wunderkinds. I hoped for it in my thirties. More role models: Harold Pinter, Sam Shepard (again), Peter Shaffer.

By their forties, most people give up on the foolish things they wanted when they were in their twenties. . . . By their forties, most people have learned the value and the sweet joy of just living a good life that doesn't harm anybody and may help someone every once in a while. I'm not being cute here: I fervently believe that living a mostly harmless life is about the highest achievement a white middle-aged, middle-class man can aspire to. Look at all the folks who haven't done that.[7]

Hot off this attention from *Joyful Noise*, Slover was then drawn to a story that emerged more from his Mormon roots. Slover claims that the original idea for *Hancock County* came from Don Oscarson, a generous patron of the Mormon arts: "The genesis and funding for the project came from Don Oscarson who had a passion for *The Carthage Conspiracy*, written by Dallin H. Oaks and Marvin Hill. However, to transform a history into a drama that captured the heart of the characters, Tim Slover had to ask probing questions, because 'the answers would give me the play.'"[8]

Latching onto this suggestion, Slover began to do the research and work on the play: "My research for the play led me to the conclusion that it was a story about a place, a not unusual place in the America of either the nineteenth or twenty-first centuries, where diverse cultures with potentially competing interests must try to coexist, if not harmonize, as each pursues its vision of American life. In Hancock County in the 1840s, the experiment failed. But the fear and intolerance which marked that failure might be instructive."[9]

The play was performed in BYU's Pardoe Theatre in early 2002; and once again, praise poured out for Slover's work: "*Hancock County* is a very fine play; an intelligent, thrilling, tightly drawn courtroom drama/tragedy that unfolds into a meditation on America, violence, and forgiveness. It bears comparison to Robert Bolt's *A Man for All Seasons*. . . . Slover gets a rollicking, frontier, Mark Twain-like quality to the story that draws you in like good historical fiction. The clash of visions between competing groups is a subject that will never go out of style."[10]

Eric Snider's review painted the production in equally glowing terms: "It is a clear, rich drama that is satisfying even when it doesn't go the way that we want [it] to. . . .

---

7   Slover, "Mormon Director Takes a Small Bite Out of the Big Apple."
8   "Hancock County: A New Play about the Trial of the Murderers of Joseph Smith," *Meridian Magazine*, April 27, 2001, http://www.ldsmag.com/arts/020215hancock.html (accessed May 18, 2012).
9   Ibid.
10 R. W. Rasband, "Hancock County," AML Review Archive, February 15, 2002, http://mormonletters.org/Reviews/Review.aspx?id=3484 (accessed May 18, 2012).

Whether LDS Church History is your thing or not, *Hancock County* is an engrossing depiction of it."[11]

Slover has had many successes, not only from audience satisfaction with his productions, but also as marked by an impressive list of awards and honors. His awards include an Emmy (for his screenplay *A More Perfect Union*), The George Washington Freedom Medal, the Grand Prize in the Writers Digest 65th Annual Writers' Competition, a Sunstone Moonstone Award, The Christopher Brian Wolk Award for Excellence in Playwriting, second place in the American Screenwriters Association International Playwriting Competition, a Hopwood Award in Drama, a Von Hess Foundation Grant, and four Association for Mormon Letters Awards in Drama.

Yet it is the content of his plays that draws the most attention. The fact that his plays often emerge from famous historical figures (a short list includes William Shakespeare, Benjamin Franklin, Alexander Hamilton, George Frederic Handel, Butch Cassidy, and Brigham Young) tends to give his work some epic weight. He also adds a much-appreciated dash of humor to his scripts. However, in the end, it is the sense of redemption, running like a bright red thread throughout all of his work, that gives his plays the majority of their power. This recurring theme was so clear to Chris Clark, who directed *Joyful Noise* for the Nauvoo Theatrical Society, that he purposely set the play in tan, white, and beige tones, then had bright red items (such as a red handkerchief or a pair of ruby earrings) given to characters when they experienced a moment of redemption. The blood of Christ imagery was a powerful reminder of what Slover's plays are really about.

Slover's main characters are often flawed, even what Mormons would consider sinful, and, as a result, have often become social outcasts. Josiah Lamborn, the hard-drinking, swearing prosecutor guilty of taking bribes in *Hancock County*, articulates this recurring archetype effectively in his closing monologue, referencing Joseph Smith's King Follett discourse. The fact that Joseph Smith thought that a sinful, dirty man like himself had the potential to become a *god*—it was stunning to him. But it is exactly that philosophy that makes all of Slover's work so distinctly Mormon, whether the play in question has LDS characters. The sense of grace, of atonement, and of eternal progression shows that Slover has taken to heart his religious heritage. Sinners as his characters are—as we all are—yet he knows that there is a brilliant hope for a purer and brighter state of being. These themes and the skill in which they are wrought are what make his work an essential part of Mormon drama.

---

11 Eric Snider, "Hancock CountyHas Good Timing for Audience Appeal," *Provo Daily Herald*, February 19, 2002, http://www.heraldextra.com/entertainment/hancock-county-has-good-timing-for-audience-appeal/article_f6d28ddf-f770-5abd-8583-2ca49536ee0b.html (accessed May 18, 2012).

About *Hancock County*

Hancock County premiered February 13 and ran through March 2, 2002, at Brigham Young University's Pardoe Theatre in the Harris Fine Arts Center. It was commissioned by the BYU Department of Theatre and Media Arts with support from the R. Don and Shirley Oscarson Discovery Grant. The cast and principal crew were as follows:

CAST

Josiah Lamborn: Marvin Payne
Eliza Graham: Stephanie Foster Breinholt
Thomas Sharp: Robert Gibbs
Orville Browning: R. Jeremy Selim
Brigham Young: Scott Bronson
Ann Fleming: Anna McKeown
Richard Young: Bob Nelson

CREW

Director: Tim Threlfall
Stage Manager: Michelle Rupp Gibbs
Scenic Designer/Lighting Designer: Rory Scanlon
Costume Designer: Emily Hoem
Sound Designer: Loraleigh Bowyer
Hair and Makeup Designer: Teresa Marie Easton
Assistant Stage Managers: Jeanette Pratt
Angela Wolfe

*"If you will not accuse me, I will not accuse you.
If you will throw a cloak of charity over my sins, I will over yours."*
—Joseph Smith

*For Gene England,
who all his days lifted up an ensign of peace*

CHARACTERS

ANN FLEMING, 32, proprietress of Warsaw House

ELIZA GRAHAM, 33, Ann's niece, cook at Warsaw House

ORVILLE BROWNING, 39, attorney

RICHARD YOUNG, 47, judge

JOSIAH LAMBORN, 36, attorney

BRIGHAM YOUNG, 44, leader of the Mormon Church; same actor also plays

WILLIAM DANIELS, 19, witness

THOMAS SHARP, 31, defendant, editor of the *Warsaw Signal*; same actor also plays

FRANK WORRELL, 24, witness

All also play neutral actors and occasionally take other roles for a few moments.

Act One

SCENE 1

Neutral playing space. As the audience enters the theater, they hear the murmur and rush of the Mississippi River. At curtain seven ACTORS *in modern dress enter the playing space.* THIRD *and* SEVENTH ACTORS *are women. Two actors carry large standing easels with pads of paper attached. They position them so that one or the other is clearly visible to all parts of the audience. With markers they draw three sides of Hancock County.*

FIRST ACTOR (YOUNG). Hancock County. A square of prairie on the edge of Illinois.

SECOND ACTOR (BROWNING). (*The actors draw in the river to form the fourth side.*) Its western corner cut off by the wide, meandering Mississippi River.

THIRD ACTOR (ELIZA). It is 1844. Hancock County has the largest population in the state.

FOURTH ACTOR (SHARP). 22,559 inhabitants. Half are members of a new religion, the Mormons. That half grows larger every month.

FIFTH ACTOR (LAMBORN). "My general invitation is, let all who will, come. Come and partake of the poverty of Nauvoo." Joseph Smith, the Mormon prophet.

SIXTH ACTOR (BRIGHAM). Many established citizens fear the Mormons' growing power.

SEVENTH ACTOR (ANN). Resent their buying up of land.

FIRST ACTOR (YOUNG). And hate their religious views.

SECOND ACTOR (BROWNING). "This deluded, fanatical, and ignorant sect is about to be poured upon us by thousands, and thus like the locusts of Egypt wither away every vestige of godliness." Reverend B. F. Morris.

THIRD ACTOR (ELIZA). The tension between the Mormons and the old settlers is hemmed into a hectic triangle, with three cities at the points.

FOURTH ACTOR (SHARP). (*They draw a star and write the name on the paper.*) Carthage, the county seat. Population 300.

FIFTH ACTOR (LAMBORN). Except during circuit court weeks in May and October, when the town swells up like a tick feeding on a steer.

SIXTH ACTOR (BRIGHAM). (*The actors draw a circle and write the name.*) Warsaw.

Population 500. Home to Thomas Sharp and his populist newspaper, the *Warsaw Signal*.

SEVENTH ACTOR (ANN). (*They draw a circle and write the name.*) And Nauvoo, population 11,000, the biggest city in Illinois. Ten times bigger than Warsaw and Carthage put together.

FIRST ACTOR (YOUNG). Nauvoo is the Mormons' Zion. Their kingdom of God on earth—

SECOND ACTOR (BROWNING). —built after what was left of them ran for their lives from their first kingdom of God across the river in Missouri.

THIRD ACTOR (ELIZA). Their leader is Joseph Smith: prophet, mayor, general of the Nauvoo Legion, and chief judge all rolled into one.

FOURTH ACTOR (SHARP). His followers revere him.

SIXTH ACTOR (BRIGHAM). "The honest-in-heart ran together and gathered around him and loved him as they did their own lives." Brigham Young.

FIFTH ACTOR (LAMBORN). His detractors are equally passionate.

SEVENTH ACTOR (ANN). June 5, 1844. A new, anti-Mormon newspaper in Nauvoo prints its first edition.

THIRD ACTOR (ELIZA). "We pledge our unmitigated disobedience to Joseph Smith, the self-constituted monarch, and to his gross moral imperfections." *The Nauvoo Expositor*.

SECOND ACTOR (BROWNING). The next day, the Nauvoo City Council orders the press destroyed.

SEVENTH ACTOR (ANN). A detachment from the Nauvoo Legion smashes the press and scatters the type.

FIRST ACTOR (YOUNG). In Warsaw, editor Thomas Sharp is quick to react.

FOURTH ACTOR (SHARP). "We hasten to inform you of the outrage perpetrated by the ruthless, lawless band of Mormon mobocrats upon our rights and interests, at the dictum of that unprincipled wretch, Joe Smith." *The Warsaw Signal*.

SIXTH ACTOR (BRIGHAM). Within days, Joseph and his brother, Hyrum, are in jail at Carthage, awaiting a hearing.

FIRST ACTOR (YOUNG). And that is where they are murdered.

THIRD *and* SEVENTH ACTORS *tear the sheets of paper off and exit with them. Underneath are simple outlines of standing men, one on each sheet, both alike.*

FIFTH ACTOR (LAMBORN). June 27, 1844. Hot and humid. A sky full of clouds gives way to glaring sun.

SECOND ACTOR (BROWNING). Seven men from the Carthage militia guard the jail.

SIXTH ACTOR (BRIGHAM). Inside with Joseph and Hyrum are two friends, Church leaders Willard Richards and John Taylor.

Commotion, getting louder.

FOURTH ACTOR (SHARP). 5:00 p.m. Between one and two hundred discharged soldiers from the Warsaw militia smear their faces with gunpowder and make for the jail.

FIRST ACTOR (YOUNG). "A party of men are coming to take Joe Smith and hang him in the square! Come on, you cowards, damn you, come on! Those boys guarding the jail will all be killed!" Tom Marsh, officer in the Carthage militia.

FIFTH ACTOR (LAMBORN). In the event, not one guard receives even a scratch—

SIXTH ACTOR (BRIGHAM). —despite the hundreds of rounds fired.

FIRST ACTOR (YOUNG). Now some in the crowd below begin firing up into the second-story window.

Gunfire.

FOURTH ACTOR (SHARP). Others rush up the steps inside the jail to the room where the four men are held.

SECOND ACTOR (BROWNING). Now Joseph and his brother prepare to fire pistols smuggled in to them earlier.

FIRST ACTOR (YOUNG). All brace themselves against the door.

Gunfire, wood shattering.

SIXTH ACTOR (BRIGHAM). Now the men with the blackened faces fire on the door, shattering a panel four feet three inches from the floor.

SIXTH ACTOR (BRIGHAM). The prisoners jump back. Hyrum Smith fires his revolver, hitting no one.

FIFTH ACTOR (LAMBORN). A shot through the door hits Hyrum in the face, on the right side of his nose.

Gunshot. An ACTOR makes a red mark on the face of the outline of a man.

SECOND ACTOR (BROWNING). A second shot through the jail window hits Hyrum in the back.

Gunshot. The ACTOR marks the shot in red.

FIRST ACTOR (YOUNG). Hyrum falls to the floor, face up.

FIFTH ACTOR (LAMBORN). "I am a dead man," he says.

FOURTH ACTOR (SHARP). He never moves again.

SECOND ACTOR (BROWNING). He is forty-four years old.

FIRST ACTOR (YOUNG). And now his brother bends over him.

SIXTH ACTOR (BRIGHAM). "Oh, my poor, dear brother Hyrum," he says.

SECOND ACTOR (BROWNING). Now Joseph flings open the door and fires all six shots at his enemies on the other side. He throws the gun down and slams the door.

FIFTH ACTOR (LAMBORN). Now, with his cane, John Taylor tries to beat down the barrels of the guns sticking through the hole.

Gunfire. Smoke begins to seep into the playing space.

FOURTH ACTOR (SHARP). A barrage of bullets blows him back from the door, and he is grievously wounded, but survives.

FIFTH ACTOR (LAMBORN). Now Joseph runs to the window, hoping to jump. Crossfire hits him from the hole in the door and through the window from the yard below.

FIRST ACTOR (YOUNG). One ball in the right collar bone.

Gunshot. Red mark on the Joseph outline.

SECOND ACTOR (BROWNING). One ball in the chest.

Gunshot. Red mark.

SIXTH ACTOR (BRIGHAM). Two in the back.

Gunshots. Red marks.

FOURTH ACTOR (SHARP). And now he falls through the window to the ground below.

FIFTH ACTOR (LAMBORN). "Oh Lord, my God," he says.

SECOND ACTOR (BROWNING). "He raised himself up against the well curb. He drew up one leg and stretched out the other and died." Thomas Dixon, eyewitness.

SIXTH ACTOR (BRIGHAM). He is thirty-eight years old.

FOURTH ACTOR (SHARP). "Carthage Jail, 8:05 o'clock p.m. Joseph and Hyrum are dead. (FIFTH *and* SIXTH ACTORS *tear the outlines of Joseph and Hyrum from the easels.*) Taylor wounded. I am well. The citizens here are afraid of the Mormons attacking them. I promise them no!" Willard Richards.

FIFTH and SIXTH ACTORS carry the outlines through and around the playing space. It is a stylized funeral procession.

FIRST ACTOR (YOUNG). The Mormons do not attack.

SECOND ACTOR (BROWNING). Instead, they grieve, in their thousands.

FOURTH ACTOR (SHARP). "The very streets of Nauvoo seemed to mourn." Vilate Kimball.

FIRST ACTOR (YOUNG). The news hit "like a thunderbolt, crushing the people to earth." Emily Dow Partridge.

FIFTH and SIXTH ACTORS exit with the outlines.

FOURTH ACTOR (SHARP). Afraid their enemies would try to desecrate the bodies of the Smiths—

SECOND ACTOR (BROWNING). —they hold a public funeral for coffins filled with sand and rocks, and then secretly bury the brothers in unmarked graves.

FOURTH ACTOR (SHARP). Governor Thomas Ford, to the Illinois House of Representatives:

FIRST ACTOR (YOUNG). (*Taking a speech from a pocket and reading it*): "The state will find and prosecute the perpetrators of this bloody deed. They will be brought before a court of justice in Hancock County. We will vindicate the violated honor of the state of Illinois."

The men leave, revealing two women, in period dress, and a wooden table with an accounts book, an open strong box, a bucket, and a scrub brush on it.

SCENE 2

Saturday, May 17, 1845. Warsaw House, Warsaw/Hamilton House, Carthage/Temple Site & Mansion House, Nauvoo. Early morning. ELIZA GRAHAM, *thirty-three, thin, and used to hard work, will take up her task of scrubbing the table in a moment. But right now she is examining the bruises on the arms of another woman,* ANN FLEMING, *32. Just under the surface,* ANN *is always a little bit scared. At the moment, she stands with her blouse unbuttoned so that she and* ELIZA *can examine her arms. She fights back tears.*

ANN. I told you. It didn't leave hardly a mark on either arm. It ain't bad, at all.

ELIZA. I can see bruises starting.

ANN. Where? (*She examines the back of her upper arm.*) Oh. Well, that won't show, will it?

ELIZA. Is that all you're worried about, Ann?

ANN. (*She shrugs her blouse back on.*) My head aches a bit. He shook me pretty good, I guess. You didn't see it, did you?

ELIZA. No, I was out back, checking on the stove.

ANN. Nor hear nothing?

ELIZA. I heard his voice raised is all.

ANN. Poor man. He's so worried.

ELIZA. Don't see why he takes his worry out on you, though.

ANN. Now listen, Eliza. Mr. Fleming didn't take nothing out on me. It ain't like he planned it. He just exploded. You know how black powder explodes.

ELIZA. You're my kin, Ann. I can't help worrying for you.

ANN. Well, don't go blaming my husband. Please.

ELIZA. What set him off this time?

ANN. Don't say "this time." There ain't so many times.

ELIZA. There aren't so few either.

ANN. It's his money worries getting worse, is all. We ain't bringing enough money into the tavern with just the drinkers, Mr. Fleming says. (ELIZA *begins scrubbing the table.*) If we're going to make Warsaw House go, we got to get more boarders. Like they do over to Hamilton House in Carthage. (*She breaks down a little.*) And I've tried.

ELIZA *comforts her, putting her arms around her.*

ELIZA. I know you have.

Ann resists because receiving comfort feels like disloyalty to her husband.

ANN. No. Now, I'm all right. I'm getting back to work. (*She returns to her business, which is going over the accounts. She picks up a bundle of cash.*) Oh, I meant to tell you. The Larimores are short. They're a whole dollar short almost.

ELIZA *stops scrubbing, considers.*

ELIZA. The Larimores? I don't think so. Is that January?

ANN. (*Looks at paper wrapped around bundle.*) That's what you wrote down on the paper.

ELIZA. Then they're not short. January they left for five days upriver to visit Abraham's father's cousin, remember?

ANN. 'Course I don't remember. That's why I got you. So they ain't short?

ELIZA. No. (ANN *puts the bundle into the box, takes out another—Mr. Fox's—while* ELIZA *watches.*) And neither is Mr. Fox. Least not yet. It's June 16 he's supposed to pay us in stove wood.

ANN. Do you remember everything?

ELIZA. Listen, Ann, I'll do this reckoning. You hate it.

ANN. You don't mind?

ELIZA. I don't mind a bit. I'll do it later.

ANN. All right. Thank you. I do feel a bit . . . peculiar.

ELIZA *finishes her scrubbing.*

ELIZA. (*Sighs.*) That's the last of them. We're ready for breakfast. I think I'll go to bed an hour. I was up late with supper. Do you mind?

ANN. 'Course not. Adeline can manage. Or Ashbel can come in if we get a lot. (ELIZA *turns to go.*) Or wait, Eliza. Wait just a minute. There's something else. (ELIZA *turns, wearily.*) Won't you sit down? (ELIZA *sits;* ANN *paces nervously.*) We need to talk just a little bit.

> *They disappear for the moment.* ORVILLE BROWNING, *thirty-nine, sits at a table, contemplating his cup of coffee. Ambient noise of a busy tavern/inn: Hamilton House, Carthage.* BROWNING's *puritanical religiosity is complemented by his careful grooming and vests of extravagant design. For a moment he sips contentedly, reflecting on his past successes and anticipating his future triumphs. Then* RICHARD YOUNG, *forty-seven, enters the room, carrying traveling bags and dusty from a long trip.* YOUNG *is handsome, unfailingly cordial.* BROWNING, *who has been watching for him, sees him before he sees* BROWNING.

BROWNING. Judge! Judge Young! (YOUNG *looks around.* BROWNING *is at his elbow, hand outstretched.*) It's Orville Browning, Judge. Welcome to Carthage.

YOUNG. (*Not quite placing him.*) Mr. Browning.

BROWNING. I'm counsel for the defense, Judge. I'm representing the men accused of murdering the Smiths.

YOUNG. Oh, yes. Of course. Forgive me, Mr. Browning. The journey has wearied me.

BROWNING. (*Indicating the table.*) Will you join me?

YOUNG. I'm just on the way up to my room.

BROWNING. You've come from Quincy?

YOUNG. And from Springfield yesterday. So I believe a spell of rest will do me good.

BROWNING. I took the liberty of ordering you a breakfast, Judge.

YOUNG. Breakfast?

BROWNING. They say it's the best in Carthage. It should be out in under three minutes.

YOUNG. (*Deciding to sit down.*) Well, all right. Thank you, Mr. Browning.

BROWNING. Not at all.

YOUNG. You seem to have anticipated my arrival.

BROWNING. I made the journey two days ago. Sabbath travel is abhorrent to me.

YOUNG. Ah yes, I believe I recall that now.

BROWNING. "Six days may work be done; but in the seventh is the sabbath of rest, holy to the Lord."

YOUNG. I respect your devotion, sir.

BROWNING. "Whosoever doeth any work in the sabbath day, he shall surely be put to death."

YOUNG. Yes. Not in Illinois, of course.

BROWNING. (*Smiles.*) No. Has Murray arrived yet?

YOUNG. Who? Oh. Hadn't you heard? He's retired from the case.

BROWNING. Has he? I can't say I blame him.

YOUNG. The governor has asked Josiah Lamborn to step in.

BROWNING. (*Surprised and dismayed, but struggling not to show it.*) Josiah Lamborn? Really?

YOUNG. Bit of a tall order for him, with so little time to prepare.

BROWNING. (*Still trying to take it in.*) That changes things.

YOUNG. Oh? Why is that?

BROWNING. Murray McConell's a man of integrity. But Josiah Lamborn . . .

YOUNG. You have a low opinion of him?

BROWNING. Well, the profaneness. Lately, the drinking.

YOUNG. Yes, that's a pity, isn't it?

BROWNING. And he took bribes.

YOUNG. Once or twice. Allegedly.

BROWNING. When he was attorney general of Illinois! He brought shame to an honorable profession. I believe he should have been disbarred.

YOUNG. (*Mildly.*) Well, he did some fine work for the state, I thought.

BROWNING *pulls back. He was getting too heated, and that would defeat his main purpose.*

BROWNING. You're right, of course. You're a compassionate man, Judge. It's an honor to have you sitting on this case.

YOUNG. (*Sighs.*) I never thought I'd be out circuit-riding again. But Governor Ford wants a genuine Supreme Court judge, so here I am.

BROWNING. He hopes the trial will discredit you, of course.

YOUNG. Who does? The governor? Why would he hope that?

BROWNING. Because you're opposing him in the next election. Aren't you?

YOUNG. I've heard that rumor.

BROWNING. I fervently hope it's more than a rumor.

YOUNG. You say this as a Whig?

BROWNING. We feel—myself and an influential segment of our party—we feel Illinois needs someone above politics now. She needs a statesman.

YOUNG. (*Savoring the word a little.*) A statesman.

BROWNING. We think it's you, sir.

YOUNG. Do you?

BROWNING. Yes, sir, we do. We all feel it would be an honor to support a man of your caliber.

YOUNG. (*Pleased.*) Well, that's very gratifying. That's really very gratifying, Mr. Browning.

BROWNING. So we mustn't let this trial besmirch your reputation in any way.

YOUNG. (*Thoughtfully.*) No. No, we mustn't. That's a good point.

BROWNING. You can count on me, sir.

YOUNG. Thank you.

BROWNING. Speaking of the trial, there's just a small issue . . .

YOUNG. Yes?

BROWNING. Yes. It's about jury selection.

YOUNG. Really? Well, what's troubling you, Mr. Browning?

> BROWNING *and* YOUNG *both leave as* BRIGHAM YOUNG, *forty-four, beardless, burly, in shirtsleeves, comes on quietly to work on a window frame.* BRIGHAM *conveys an impatient competence, as though he were often just a little behind in a crucial timetable known only to him. At the moment, it would be easier to believe him to be a good glazier than the leader of a church.* JOSIAH LAMBORN, *thirty-six, comes on. He is tall, thin, soberly and carelessly dressed.* BRIGHAM *looks up to see* JOSIAH *take a well-practiced swig from a hip flask and then replace it in a coat pocket. Now* JOSIAH *sees* BRIGHAM.

LAMBORN. I wonder if you could help me out here. I'm looking for Brigham Young.

BRIGHAM. Why don't you try the Mansion House? He's generally down there.

LAMBORN. Well damn it, they told me down there he was up here.

BRIGHAM. They did, did they?

LAMBORN. Said he was up here working on this thing. (*Looks up at temple.*) What is this, the next state capitol?

BRIGHAM. It's a temple.

LAMBORN. A temple? Well, I'll be damned. Do you know where Young is?

BRIGHAM. I might. You are, sir?

LAMBORN. Josiah Lamborn.

BRIGHAM. You're the attorney general.

LAMBORN. Former attorney general.

BRIGHAM. You're prosecuting in the murder trial.

LAMBORN. *Trials,* with an s. There's two of them. Joseph Smith now, save his brother for later.

BRIGHAM. Really? What advantage is there in that?

LAMBORN. Oh, keeps it simple for the jury. Look, mister, you go on working on your temple. I'll find Young. He must be around here somewhere.

BRIGHAM. (*Sticks out his hand*) You've found him, Mr. Lamborn. (LAMBORN *takes his hand.*) You must forgive me. There are so many writs out against me these days, I have to be careful about people I don't know. I've told them that at the Mansion House. They don't seem to listen.

LAMBORN. It's an honor to meet you, sir. Now I'm not real sure about your position here. I know to you folks Joseph Smith—

BRIGHAM. Joseph was the Prophet, Mr. Lamborn. I'm just president of the council. And the Twelve.

LAMBORN. Well, that sounds important. The twelve what?

BRIGHAM. Apostles.

LAMBORN. Apostles? Like in the Bible?

BRIGHAM. Yes.

LAMBORN. (*Surprised and amused.*) Are you sure?

BRIGHAM. (*Just a hint of severity.*) What were you expecting?

LAMBORN. Well, someone . . . more sort of . . . (*Changes his mind.*) Listen, you can't go by me, I ain't a religious man.

BRIGHAM. Just now, of course, I'm a glazier. What Joseph began, we will finish. Even if, like Israel of old, we must do it with a trowel in one hand and a sword in the other.

LAMBORN. I guess what I'm driving at, is what should I call you?

BRIGHAM. What do you think of the windows?

LAMBORN. The windows?

BRIGHAM. The way they catch the sun.

LAMBORN. That's your part, the windows?

BRIGHAM. That's right.

LAMBORN. Well, there's certainly a lot of them.

This was not the answer he was hoping for.

BRIGHAM. I think you better call me Mr. Young. And now you'll have to excuse me. This window needs to be in that wall before the council meeting at noon.

LAMBORN. Can I give you a hand? I've got awful important things to talk to you about before the trial. And I only got a couple of days.

BRIGHAM. That depends, Mr. Lamborn. Let me see your hands. (LAMBORN *holds his hands out uncertainly.*) No, I don't think you can. You go on back down to the Mansion House and take some refreshment. I'll be with you presently.

LAMBORN *starts to go, turns back.*

LAMBORN. This case can be won, Mr. Young. I can win it.

They exit as ANN *and* ELIZA *return. Now it is* ELIZA *who is pacing, agitated.* ANN *tries to soothe her.*

ANN. Now, please, Eliza, please, you got to understand. Mr. Fleming—

ELIZA. That's why Mr. Fleming turned into black powder.

ANN. What?

ELIZA. That's why he shook you.

ANN. Now—

ELIZA. He wanted to kick me out and you said no.

ANN. He ain't kicking you out. It ain't permanent. It's only for court week coming up. We can make some money, Mr. Fleming says. Then you'll come back.

ELIZA. Do you promise, Ann? Do you swear it?

ANN. Of course. Two weeks and you'll be right back in your rooms, all right? (ELIZA *doesn't respond.* ANN *becomes more importunate, taking a silly line.*) All right, Lizey, dear, who's everything nice and not a scrap of bad in her?

ELIZA. (*Smiling, relenting.*) Oh, all right.

ANN. Good! Now, will you still do the reckoning later on?

ELIZA. (*Looking down at the box in her hand, which she had forgotten.*) Of course I will.

ANN. You got a head for it. (*She puts an affectionate arm around* ELIZA, *strokes her head.*) Everything stays right in there.

The bell rings outside. The two women look at one another for a moment before TOM SHARP, *thirty-one, wanders in. He is editor of the* Warsaw Signal *newspaper.* SHARP *is an intelligent and clever man, perpetually convinced of the soundness of his own beliefs.*

SHARP. Good morning.

ANN. Why, Mr. Sharp, good morning. Look, Eliza, it's Mr. Sharp. We haven't seen you in here for a month of Sundays.

SHARP. I'm just on the way to my newspaper.

ANN. Well, we'll get you some breakfast.

SHARP. Just coffee, I think. Did you see the sky last night, Ann?

ANN. We was in all night with guests.

SHARP. Just about half a moon shining down on the river. The willows hanging over the slip. Beautiful.

ANN. I'll get you your coffee, Mr. Sharp.

SHARP. Oh, Eliza can get it, can't she?

ELIZA. Sure. I'll just make some.

    ELIZA *exits. As soon as she is gone:*

ANN. (*Confidentially.*) Mr. Sharp, do you know of any persons of upstanding character who might like to board here at Warsaw House? At least for court week. Looks like we got a vacancy or two.

SHARP. Oh. Then you must know about the indictments.

ANN. About the what?

SHARP. Folks accused of the Smith murders. Two of your boarders are indicted.

ANN. (*Not taking it in.*) Two of my boarders . . .

SHARP. Are being put on trial for the murder of old Joe Smith.

ANN. No! That can't be.

SHARP. Oh, don't worry. Nobody's taking it seriously.

ANN. Who's on trial?

SHARP. Well, Senator Davis for one. Listen, while she's getting the coffee. I'm just wondering. I heard a rumor. Is Eliza Graham a Mormon?

ANN. What?

SHARP. I'm just wondering.

ANN. Why? I don't understand.

SHARP. Just answer my—

ELIZA. (*Returning with the coffee.*) Looks like Mr. Fleming made some before he left for Boston.

    ELIZA *pours* SHARP's *coffee.*

SHARP. Thank you, Eliza.

ANN. Who else, Mr. Sharp? Who else besides Senator Davis?

ELIZA. What about Senator Davis?

ANN. Eliza, he's on trial for murder, Mr. Sharp says.

ELIZA. No.

ANN. Yes!

SHARP. My oath.

ANN. Now who else from here, Mr. Sharp? (*Realizing and blurting it out.*) Of course! Mr. Aldrich!

SHARP. Yes. (*Surprised into being almost menacing.*) That's right. How do you come to know that?

Immediately ANN *knows she has said the wrong thing.*

ANN. Well. It was in the newspaper, wasn't it?

SHARP. Not that I know of. I haven't printed a word of this yet.

ANN. Well then, some other paper, I guess.

SHARP. Which paper?

ANN *is flustered, tries to gather her wits.*

ELIZA. No, I think Mr. Fleming heard it, didn't he, Ann?

ANN. That's right. Of course. It was Mr. Fleming told us.

SHARP. He did? That's peculiar.

ELIZA. Isn't it though?

SHARP. Well, it's humorous, really. Accusing men like that of murder. Men who practically built the county. As I say, nobody's taking it seriously.

ANN. No.

SHARP. I mean the governor's got to indict somebody. Might as well be his enemies.

ANN. I'm sure you're right. Mr. Fleming reads your editorials.

ELIZA. Though we keep ourselves to ourselves mostly.

SHARP. I'll tell you, though. Whoever did put bullets in Smith, we ought to pin medals on them. They were patriots. That's what I'm on my way to print in the paper this morning. They put an end to the career of a tyrant.

ANN. A tyrant.

SHARP. Joe Smith, the tin-horn Jesus. He'd just about taken us all over. Well, you know that. Him and his mob of immigrant foreigners.

ELIZA. There's no law against being a religious man, so far as I know.

SHARP. Well, no, no law against being religious. Long as you're building up the kingdom of God, instead of one for yourself. (*Getting agitated*) Long as you don't make yourself mayor, judge, jury, and general of the biggest army in the state. That's what Smith did. I don't understand how you can defend him.

ELIZA. I'm certainly not defending him.

SHARP. Did you know he was running for president? How'd you like to have Joe Smith in charge of the United States of America, telling you what God says you got to do?

ANN. Are you sure we can't get you breakfast, Mr. Sharp? There won't be no charge.

SHARP. And what about freedom of the press? That's about the most sacred thing in the Constitution.

ELIZA. I'm sure you're right.

SHARP. Old Joe ran roughshod right over it. He just smashed up the *Expositor* when it dared to print the truth about him. When a tyrant takes away the precious freedoms of the people—well, what did George Washington do? What did Thomas Jefferson do? I tell you, whoever put bullets in him ought to get medals.

ANN. I never heard it put quite so plain, before. Did you, Eliza?

ELIZA. No.

SHARP. All right then. Listen, I apologize. It just makes my blood boil. A tyrant gets turned into a martyr and the folks who stopped him go on trial. That's not right. That's not American.

ANN. You're right.

SHARP. And I'll tell you another thing, ladies. Whoever testifies against these patriots . . .

ANN. What?

SHARP. Well, let's just leave it at this: there's been killing already, hasn't there? (*Fishing for a coin and putting it on the table.*) Thanks for the coffee. (*He turns to go, then back casually.*) Oh. I should mention. I'm one of the defendants.

ANN. Mr. Sharp!

SHARP. Oh, I'm not surprised. Everybody attacks the press. Now, neither of you heard any talk in here about those killings, did you?

ANN. No.

SHARP. I mean, last year when it happened? Or later on? You know how people talk in a tavern sometimes.

ANN. Goodness, no.

SHARP. Eliza?

ELIZA. I generally don't pay attention to what people say in here.

SHARP. Good girl. Well, it looks to be another fine day. I'm going to go out and breathe the free air. Keep safe. Remember, this new man Brigham Young's still got the Mormon army.

He leaves. The two women stand in silence for a moment. ANN *is extremely frightened.* ELIZA *is icy calm and suddenly very weary.*

ANN. Eliza.

ELIZA. What.

ANN. Eliza, why did he say all them things?

ELIZA. Because he's threatening us, of course. He knows what we heard that night, and he's warning us not to testify.

ANN. But we wouldn't. Months and months, we haven't told a soul.

ELIZA. Until you bring up Mr. Aldrich.

ANN. It just slipped out.

ELIZA. We got to be real careful now, 'til court week's done.

ANN. If we talked, we'd lose everything. Don't he know that? Mr. Fleming'd take a fit.

ELIZA. Mr. Fleming will make sure you don't come before the court. Listen to me. You'll never have to testify. It's going to be all right.

ANN. (*Suddenly remembering.*) Eliza! Mr. Sharp asked was you a Mormon.

ELIZA. He did?

ANN. Yes.

ELIZA. (*Instantly, she knows what this means.*) I have to leave. Tonight. I guess I'll go on back to Nauvoo.

ANN. Why?

Fear makes ELIZA *suddenly irritated.*

ELIZA. Oh, Ann, can't you remember anything? I testified. To the grand jury last year.

ANN. But you didn't tell them nothing, did you?

ELIZA. No! Of course not! But I'm—whatever that is—I'm on record. The folks from the court will come looking for me to testify again. I thought they wouldn't, but Mr. Sharp must think they will. And I'm not a good liar.

ANN. Eliza, you can't tell nobody. Not one soul. Even in Nauvoo. You can't!

ELIZA. There's nobody I'm talking to in Nauvoo. Now you never told Mr. Fleming what you heard that night—

ANN. You know I didn't. Of course not.

ELIZA. So we're all right there.

ANN. (*She starts to cry.*) Oh, lordy, why'd Mr. Sharp talk about killing?

ELIZA. Listen. We'll make it through this all right. You'll be safe here. And nobody'll come after me in Nauvoo. Just *don't talk* about it.

They disappear as BRIGHAM *and* LAMBORN *appear mid-conversation at the Mansion House.* LAMBORN *has got a lot of papers spread out, not neatly, on a table. He takes a pull from his hip flask, leaves it on the table.*

LAMBORN. All right. Let me boil the case down to its essentials.

BRIGHAM. Are you a drunkard, Mr. Lamborn?

LAMBORN. This? This clarifies the mind, is all. Half the time I fill it with sarsaparilla. Now—

BRIGHAM. Were you in this habit as attorney general?

LAMBORN. Look, Mr. Young, in my experience, the practice of law requires the occasional stiff one.

BRIGHAM. It does not inspire confidence.

    LAMBORN *taps the flask.*

LAMBORN. There. I just became a teetotaler. Now. No one knows who actually shot your man, Smith.

BRIGHAM. Which is why this trial has always been a lost cause.

LAMBORN. No, it ain't. Because you don't have to pull a trigger to be guilty of murder. Look. I'm Tom Sharp. I'm the editor of the *Warsaw Signal*. I hate you Mormons. So I tag along with the militia. And when the governor sends word to discharge it, I give the men a fire-breathing speech—telling them to go on out to the jail and end the tyranny and lawlessness of old Joe Smith while they got the chance.

BRIGHAM. Mr. Lamborn!

LAMBORN. If Sharp did that—if he incited to murder—if any of the defendants did—then they're just as guilty as if they fired the shots. That's the law.

BRIGHAM. (*Considering.*) Conspiracy...

LAMBORN. Yes, sir, Mr. Young. Conspiracy to commit murder. And now here's where you come in. You help me get witnesses from your people. Folks who heard a defendant conspire—or boasted about the murders afterwards.

BRIGHAM. I see.

LAMBORN. (*Looking through papers.*) How about John Taylor? He was in the jail.

BRIGHAM. He gave his affidavit.

LAMBORN. It would be a whole lot better if he showed up to tell his story to the jury.

BRIGHAM. He has still not completely recovered from his wounds.

LAMBORN. Even better. Can he limp?

BRIGHAM. Elder Taylor will not return to Carthage. His life is in danger there.

LAMBORN. But if you talk to him—

BRIGHAM. Why don't you get your witnesses from the militia? A hundred men heard Sharp and the rest of them.

LAMBORN. Oh, I will. I'll compel their testimonies and get what I can. But they're hostile, and they'll lie. Now. (*Picking up another sheet of paper.*) How about Mr. Daniel Jones? His affidavit's promising.

BRIGHAM. I'm thinking of sending him on a preaching mission.

LAMBORN. Sending him on a—! (*Finds more papers.*) All right. How about Stephen Markham? He was there or thereabouts.

BRIGHAM. I'm thinking of sending him on a mission, too.

LAMBORN. Mr. Young. Can you explain to me why you're being so damn unhelpful? I got to face Orville Browning in that courtroom. You don't know what that means.

BRIGHAM. What do you get out of all this, Mr. Lamborn?

LAMBORN. I get to see murderers convicted.

BRIGHAM. I may look like a Vermont yokel to you, Mr. Lamborn. Some day laborer who got put in charge of a church for a joke. That doesn't mean I am.

LAMBORN *takes a moment to decide.*

LAMBORN. All right. Here's what I get. I get back into the charmed circle. Nobody wanted this case, Mr. Young. Two prosecutors quit. Do you want to know why? Because being on the Mormon side is a losing proposition. That means when I win, I ain't the disgraced attorney general anymore. I'm the best damn attorney in Illinois. That honest enough for you?

BRIGHAM. Yep. Now here's what I want. To finish the Prophet's temple and keep my people safe. Consider their danger if they testify.

LAMBORN. The state will provide them protection.

BRIGHAM. Like it did for Joseph and Hyrum.

LAMBORN. Mr. Young—

BRIGHAM. Do you know what a night-rider is?

LAMBORN. No.

BRIGHAM. We do. Because they ride to our houses at night and set fire to them. Thirty homes since the murders.

LAMBORN. Well, that's terrible, of course. Still—

BRIGHAM. If you stir things up, I think it'll get worse.

LAMBORN. I can compel Mormon witnesses, you know.

BRIGHAM. You can. And I can continue to send them on missions.

LAMBORN. Mr. Young, don't you want your prophet avenged?

BRIGHAM. I want to put a saddle on a horse this second and get my hands around the neck of anyone who even thought of harming him.

LAMBORN. Well, don't you think God wants that, too?

BRIGHAM. The will of the Lord and what I want aren't the same thing.

LAMBORN. Well, what if he tells you to get me some witnesses?

BRIGHAM. Then, Mr. Lamborn, I'll pass the news on to you.

LAMBORN. Good. I hope he tells you soon.

LAMBORN *picks up his flask and leaves.* BRIGHAM *is alone.*

BRIGHAM. So do I.

BRIGHAM *leaves as* ELIZA *and* ANN *come on. They are at Warsaw House.* ELIZA *has a traveling bag. She is ready to go to Nauvoo.*

ANN. Oh, Eliza. Now that you're really leaving . . .

ELIZA. Will you talk to Mr. Fleming? Make sure he knows I'm coming back?

ANN. You know I will. (*Thinking of it for the first time.*) Eliza, where you going to stay in Nauvoo?

ELIZA. There's a place I can go back to, I think.

ANN. Maybe you'll like it better there now.

ELIZA. I liked it well enough before, mostly.

ANN. I'll come visit you, maybe.

ELIZA. Good. I'd like that. Now, don't say anything, remember. We're the silent sisters, right?

ANN. That's us.

SCENE 3

Sunday, May 18, 1845. Mansion House/Browning's room at Hamilton House, Carthage/Warsaw House/Grove, Nauvoo/Mansion House/Browning's room. ELIZA *turns and is in the Mansion House, Nauvoo, talking to* BRIGHAM YOUNG. *He is on his way to his office, carrying papers.*

BRIGHAM. Sister Eliza . . . Graham, isn't it?

ELIZA. Yes.

BRIGHAM. Welcome back to the Mansion House.

ELIZA. Thank you.

BRIGHAM. We still use the wing in the back for the hotel.

ELIZA. I remember.

BRIGHAM. Of course. Well. Will you be content with your old duties?

ELIZA. Thank you. I'll only be troubling you a couple of weeks.

BRIGHAM. They tell me you make the best breakfasts in the county.

ELIZA. Oh, anybody can cook.

BRIGHAM. No, Sister Eliza. I can assure you from personal experience: not everybody can cook. Now, good breakfasts improve relations with our neighbors. We sorely need that.

ELIZA. I'll do my best while I'm here.

Brigham gazes around the room for a moment. He is unable to resist bringing up the subject.

BRIGHAM. They tell me it was in this room. This is where everybody came to see the bodies.

ELIZA. Yes.

BRIGHAM. I wasn't here. I was back east. Apparently . . . they plugged up Joseph's wounds with cotton. They soaked it in camphor so the . . . smell . . .

Emotion he doesn't want to show keeps him from going on.

ELIZA. I heard that.

BRIGHAM. You didn't come?

ELIZA. No.

BRIGHAM. Oh.

ELIZA. I'm not much in the Church these days.

BRIGHAM. I see.

ELIZA. Am I still welcome?

BRIGHAM. Tell me. What do you think of the temple so far?

ELIZA. Oh, it's beautiful! Truly.

BRIGHAM. What do you think of the windows?

ELIZA. They're beautiful.

BRIGHAM. (*Smiles.*) You stay here as long as you like.

BRIGHAM leaves for his office while ELIZA puts on an apron and leaves for the kitchen. BROWNING comes on in his room at Hamilton House. He puts on his coat, takes his hat, cane, and Bible and starts to leave the room. SHARP knocks.

BROWNING. Yes.

SHARP. I wondered if I might have a moment. (BROWNING *opens the door.*) May I come in?

BROWNING. It is the Sabbath. I am on my way to church.

SHARP. I'm here on behalf of the other defendants.

BROWNING. Nevertheless.

SHARP. Mr. Browning, the trial begins tomorrow. We need to know your defense. Our defense.

BROWNING. This day hath the Almighty hallowed. I will not profane it. If your wish is that He sustain us in this trial, I enjoin you to search for Him in prayer all this day.

He gets a considerable distance before SHARP *blurts out:*

SHARP. You defended Joe Smith once. People say you were his friend. How do we know you'll do a good job for us?

BROWNING *turns to face* SHARP.

BROWNING. Whom God places in my way to defend, I defend. He sustains me, Mr. Sharp, and insures the victory. Particularly when my opponent is also His.

SHARP. You mean Joe Smith?

BROWNING. I mean Josiah Lamborn.

SHARP. Look. We're innocent. All of us.

BROWNING. I must ask you never again to speak to me on that subject. That is a matter entirely between you and the Almighty. It does not concern me at all.

He walks off, leaving SHARP *in some confusion. After a moment, he leaves in the other direction as* LAMBORN *comes into Warsaw House. He is in mid-conversation with a very suspicious* ANN.

LAMBORN. (*Frowning at his piece of paper.*) Mrs. Fleming, is it?

ANN. That's right.

LAMBORN. Is your husband in?

ANN. No, he ain't, but there's big strong fellas just a call away if I need them.

LAMBORN. Oh, you won't need them. I'm a lawyer, ma'am.

ANN. That ain't entirely reassuring.

LAMBORN. I'm here on court business. I'd like to ask Mr. Fleming—

ANN. He ain't got nothing to say about court business.

LAMBORN. Well—

ANN. Neither do I. Want some coffee?

LAMBORN. Well, what about (*looks at paper*) Miss Eliza Graham?

ANN. She ain't here.

LAMBORN. Do you mind telling me where she went?

ANN. Yes, I would. She's just—gone.

LAMBORN. Well, that's kind of peculiar, ain't it? To be just gone?

ANN. No, it ain't. It ain't the least peculiar to go visiting folks when you want to.

LAMBORN. (*He scribbles his name and address on a piece of paper.*) I'm staying over at Hamilton House in Carthage. Would you mind letting me know the next time she stops in from Nauvoo?

ANN. Sure.

LAMBORN. (*Looks up at* ANN.) Nauvoo, huh? (*Takes the paper back.*) Thanks, Mrs. Fleming. I'll have that coffee some other time.

He leaves. ANN *looks stricken.* BRIGHAM *comes on to address a large body of (unseen) Mormons in the grove. Ambient outdoor sounds.*

BRIGHAM. Brothers and sisters, I feel like shouting hallelujah that ever I knew Joseph Smith. He was our beloved Prophet. He communed with angels and with the great Jehovah himself. And he brought before our eyes the things of God. (ELIZA *comes on to listen to* BRIGHAM.) Now, tomorrow begins the court trial of the lawless men who killed him.

LAMBORN *comes on, holding some disorganized papers. He sees* ELIZA *and approaches her. He consults a paper.*

LAMBORN. Miss Eliza Graham?

She turns to look at him apprehensively.

BRIGHAM. Some of you have been called to be jurors. A few have volunteered to give testimony. May the Lord bless you and protect you.

LAMBORN. Do you mind if we have a talk? Down at the Mansion House?

BRIGHAM. For all the rest, we will attend to our own business and go nowhere within miles of Carthage. We will keep the peace, and we charge all others to do the same.

BRIGHAM *leaves. Ambient sounds out.* ELIZA *and* LAMBORN *are now mid-conversation in the Mansion House.*

ELIZA. It's a lost cause. Everybody says so.

LAMBORN. It ain't a lost cause! Listen, there's going to be plenty of Mormons on the jury. There has to be. It's the law. You people make up half the county.

ELIZA. What do you mean, "you people"?

LAMBORN. Oh, you're going to tell me you're not a Mormon? You just happened to move to Nauvoo this week?

ELIZA. What if I told you I'm not?

LAMBORN. Well, are you or ain't you?

ELIZA. I got nothing to say. I already told everything to the grand jury last year.

LAMBORN *shuffles his papers, finds the sheets he wants.*

LAMBORN. Yeah, but the thing is, I've read your testimony, and it's a couple jiggers short of a full drink.

ELIZA. What?

LAMBORN. It's incomplete, Miss Graham. That's why it caught my eye. Oh, I ain't saying you told lies. But the questions weren't very good, were they?

ELIZA. What do you mean?

LAMBORN. (*Consulting the transcript sheet.*) "Did you hear gunshots at any time?" "Do you harbor personal feelings against any defendant?" Pretty easy questions to answer without saying much.

ELIZA. I . . . I told the truth.

LAMBORN. Miss Eliza Graham. Up until yesterday, you spent pretty much every day working and living in the one place everybody in Warsaw came to talk. Now suddenly, at the start of court week, you pack up all your things and move out here. And you're telling me you don't have a story to tell?

ELIZA. I can't remember any more than I told the grand jury.

LAMBORN. You can't remember.

ELIZA. No.

LAMBORN. Are you scared, Miss Graham?

ELIZA. Why don't you compel my testimony, if you don't believe me? I heard you been doing that with militia fellas around the county. Why don't you get Sam Fleming to haul me over to Carthage?

LAMBORN. Would you tell the truth if I did? Or would you forget the same things you forgot to tell the grand jury?

ELIZA. I got nothing to say.

She walks quickly away from LAMBORN, *who gazes after her.* BROWNING *comes on in his room in Carthage. He is in shirtsleeves, taking his tie off, preparing for bed. A knock.*

BROWNING. Who is it?

SHARP. (*Off.*) It's Thomas Sharp, Mr. Browning.

BROWNING *opens the "door."*

BROWNING. It is exceedingly late, Mr. Sharp.

SHARP. Right. It's past midnight. It's no longer Sunday. May I come in?

BROWNING. This is iniquitous.

SHARP. Yes, I apologize. We're a little anxious, as I'm sure you can appreciate.

BROWNING. Come in, then.

SHARP. Thank you.

BROWNING *lets him in. They sit.*

SHARP. Mr. Browning, there's something I want to say.

SHARP *hesitates for a moment, not sure how to begin.*

BROWNING. Yes?

SHARP. Just . . . hear me out. Will you?

BROWNING. Of course, Mr. Sharp. You're my client.

SHARP *gets up, goes to look out a window.*

SHARP. If you get up at dawn, and you look out—that way (*indicates the direction*) you can watch the sun bring the prairie alive, foot by foot. And then, when it hits the river, it turns it into silver.

BROWNING. Why are you telling me this?

SHARP. Because it's how we feel. This is our place. It's our home. It was our Zion, until the Mormons came and overran it.

BROWNING. (*He stands.*) Thank you, Mr. Sharp. I appreciate your feelings. (*He begins to usher* SHARP *out the door.*) Now, if there is nothing further, a good night's sleep is the best arrow an attorney has in his quiver.

SHARP. Wait. Wait! What about our defense?

BROWNING. What about it, Mr. Sharp?

SHARP. Well, here's what we've been thinking. We figure we can get twenty-five, maybe thirty, witnesses testifying to our character, our stature in the community. We're all prominent men.

BROWNING. I have no intention of calling character witnesses. I will advance no positive case. There is none to be made.

SHARP. But—

BROWNING. It is well known that the Warsaw militia killed Joseph Smith.

SHARP. Well, yes, but—

BROWNING. Four of you defendants are officers in that militia.

SHARP. Now, wait. Hold on. Just because—

BROWNING. And your newspaper bellowed for Smith's death and justified the murder afterwards.

SHARP. You believe we're guilty!

BROWNING. (*Irritated.*) Mr. Sharp, I will not ask you again: Do not bring up that irrelevant subject! Now, if it would ease your mind to learn my intentions, I will explain. But briefly. I need my sleep.

SHARP. All right.

BROWNING. First, Mr. Lamborn will present his witnesses—

SHARP. He won't find any witnesses.

BROWNING. You made sure of that, did you? (*With distaste:*) Are you sure you've threatened everybody?

SHARP. Listen. We've got a right to look after ourselves. That's in the United States Constitution.

BROWNING. Lamborn always finds witnesses, believe me. It will then be my task to bring to light their defects, their secret sins. Everyone has them. I guarantee he'll find no witness I can't impeach.

SHARP. And that's it?

BROWNING. You claim Smith's death wasn't a murder, isn't that right?

SHARP. It wasn't. It was an execution, a just execution for his crimes. He was a tyrant, a violent, bloody Napoleon. He—

BROWNING. Yes, yes. Well, we need another execution.

SHARP. Damn it, Browning, what are you talking about?

BROWNING. His body is gone. His character remains. We must execute his character. I will demonstrate that Smith was so odious, so dangerous that the public was only safe with him dead.

SHARP. Now you're making sense. Here's where I can help. I'll—

BROWNING. You can assist by sitting quietly in the courtroom and looking as innocent as possible. And getting me a copy of the *Expositor* newspaper.

SHARP. That's all you need?

BROWNING. That and a new jury. Don't worry. I've been working on that, too.

SCENE 4

Monday, May 19, and Wednesday, May 21, 1845. Judge's chambers, Carthage court/Brigham's office, Mansion House/Hamilton House/Courtroom/Temple Site. SHARP *disappears and* YOUNG *and* LAMBORN *join* BROWNING. YOUNG *begins to speak immediately, while entering.* BROWNING *straightens his tie, rolls down his sleeves, and picks up a large book.* YOUNG *and* LAMBORN *read documents which we understand have just given them by* BROWNING. *Throughout,* BROWNING *tries to acknowledge* LAMBORN *as little as possible, directing all his energies toward* YOUNG.

YOUNG. This is certainly an unusual request to make of the court, Mr. Browning.

LAMBORN. Unusual, hell, it's a damn freak of nature!

BROWNING. Judge, will you please direct counsel for the prosecution not to blaspheme?

LAMBORN. I'll tell you what's blasphemous, Richard. (*He reads his copy.*) "Hancock County commissioners are very much prejudiced. They chose the panel of jurors in such an unfair manner as to imperil the defendants' rights and lives." Now that's a downright obscenity.

BROWNING. Does prosecution deny that two-thirds of the county commissioners are Mormon?

LAMBORN. What I deny, Orville, is that the jury panel is unfair and oppressive just because it's got some Mormons on it.

BROWNING. Judge, this is a formal affidavit requesting that you quash this prejudiced panel.

LAMBORN. Look who signed it, Richard.

YOUNG. Signed by the defendants. That is unusual.

LAMBORN. Orville, you can't quash a jury panel because the defendants don't like who's on it!

YOUNG. What's your precedent, Mr. Browning?

BROWNING *opens his volume and shows the relevant passage.*

BROWNING. *Blackstone*, Volume 4. You'll note that if there is a "tolerable ground of suspicion" that those selecting jurors are prejudiced, the court may select a new panel.

YOUNG. And you're saying the county commissioners are prejudiced because they're Mormons.

BROWNING. Well, surely.

LAMBORN. Why?

BROWNING. Is it likely that they would stop at anything to see the blood of their prophet avenged?

LAMBORN. Well then, why didn't they pick all Mormons for the panel? Why less than half?

BROWNING. (*Turning to* LAMBORN *at last.*) Why surely, Mr. Lamborn, you of all people understand the importance of creating the illusion of honesty.

LAMBORN. Richard, there's a procedure to follow here. If Orville wants to impeach the county commissioners, you've got to hold a hearing, and he's got to produce evidence of prejudice.

YOUNG. We don't have time for that. The whole case has got to be decided this week. I'm due in Springfield.

LAMBORN. Orville, name me one single case in the whole history of U.S. jurisprudence where a panel of legally selected jurors has been set aside because the defendants asked the judge pretty please.

BROWNING. Stop calling me by my Christian name. We are not intimates. Admittedly,

Judge, there is no precedent—

LAMBORN. Right.

BROWNING. —but there has never been a case like this.

LAMBORN. It's a murder case. There's been plenty of those.

BROWNING. No. This is a test of whether or not a court will uphold what it means to be American. How do you think it feels? To put your life's blood into farms and towns. And then to watch while a horde of strangers—many of them foreigners—moves in to threaten all you've built.

LAMBORN. Don't you like foreigners, Orville?

BROWNING. You go to the polls, but the horde always outvotes you because its—its Napoleon—is telling it how to vote.

LAMBORN. What's your evidence for that? *The Warsaw Signal*?

BROWNING. So it creates county commissioners and a jury to convict innocent men. Judge, I put it to you. Will anything happen to the horde this time? Or will tyranny continue to reign? It's in your hands. What would a statesman do?

LAMBORN. Richard, if you quash this panel, it'll be a signal that you don't intend to conduct a fair trial. My friendly witnesses'll run for cover. And I ain't got that many.

YOUNG. Are you accusing me of impropriety? You?

LAMBORN. (*Suddenly realizing.*) Wait a minute. You two already talked about this, didn't you?

YOUNG. Enough. I've heard enough.

LAMBORN. You cooked this up earlier.

YOUNG. I'm going to accept the defendants' affidavit. The panel of jurors is hereby quashed. I will direct Sheriff Deming to select a new panel—

BROWNING. Well, actually, Judge, remember: Sheriff Deming is named in the affidavit. He, too, is prejudiced.

YOUNG. Ah. Well then, the next selector is—

BROWNING. —the coroner, who, unfortunately, is a justice of the peace in Nauvoo, and so—

LAMBORN. Here's an idea. Why don't you just ask the defendants who they want on the jury?

> LAMBORN *turns and is immediately in conversation with* BRIGHAM *in Nauvoo.*

BRIGHAM. First the judge allows indicted murderers to roam the county freely. And now he dismisses the entire panel of jurors!

LAMBORN. It ain't good, I know.

BRIGHAM. There's not one Mormon on that jury now. This is justice in Hancock County!

LAMBORN. I can still win the case, if I get the witnesses.

BRIGHAM *takes a letter from his pocket and unfolds it.*

BRIGHAM. Mr. Lamborn, you must be the last man in Illinois not to know what this trial is really about. Listen. (*Reads*) "The people of Hancock County cannot rise above the prejudices excited by your religion. I confess I do not foresee the time when you will be permitted to enjoy quiet. Signed, the Honorable Thomas Ford, Governor of Illinois."

LAMBORN *grabs the letter, surprised.*

LAMBORN. When did he send this?

BRIGHAM. Three weeks ago. So you see, the governor's not looking for a conviction. He's looking for an eviction. Ours.

LAMBORN. How could Tom Ford . . . ?

BRIGHAM. The trial is just to clear his name before the next election. And we will no longer have anything to do with it.

LAMBORN. Is that God speaking to you? Is that the will of the Lord?

BRIGHAM. It is the will of Brigham Young!

BRIGHAM *leaves as* ELIZA *comes on. Immediately* LAMBORN *is in mid-conversation with her.*

LAMBORN. Miss Graham, witnesses are deserting this case like paint peeling off in July. I know you got a story to tell.

ELIZA. If I do, I'm not telling it to a room full of guns and not a Mormon on the jury. I'm sorry. Good-bye, Mr. Lamborn.

LAMBORN. Yeah, good-bye. Only I don't understand you people, I really don't. I thought this "Brother Joseph" meant something to you.

ELIZA. (*Heatedly*) You listen to me. Tom Sharp said he'd make trouble for me and my aunt. He talked about killing. Am I supposed to risk that for—for a man who . . .

LAMBORN. Who what? A man who what?

ELIZA. Nothing. I never wished him any harm. But now he's dead, I don't have to go risking myself and my kin for Joseph Smith.

LAMBORN. You got something against him?

ELIZA. Of course not.

LAMBORN. Don't you people more or less worship the man?

ELIZA. No. They . . . revere him.

LAMBORN. Well, then?

ELIZA. Well, that doesn't mean everything he did or said was perfectly right!

LAMBORN. Oh. See, I thought the idea was, Smith got his news straight from God. Otherwise why keep him on the payroll?

ELIZA. Don't say such things.

LAMBORN. All the time getting revelations for you. So why don't you do something for him and testify?

ELIZA. Revelations! Well, they can't all have been revelations, can they?

> ELIZA *turns and is in* BRIGHAM's *office at Mansion House.*
> LAMBORN *exits.*

ELIZA. He keeps at me to testify.

BRIGHAM. I'll tell him to stop.

ELIZA. He said none of us cares about the Prophet.

BRIGHAM. It's a lawyer's trick, Sister Eliza, to apply pressure.

ELIZA. I don't know what to do.

BRIGHAM. And you figure I've got some counsel for you.

ELIZA. That's what I . . . hoped.

BRIGHAM. Only, you aren't much in the Church these days. Right?

ELIZA. No. You're right. I should go.

BRIGHAM. Well, to be honest, on the subject of this trial, the heavens seem to be brass.

ELIZA. Oh.

BRIGHAM. And I'll tell you why. I've got so much anger piled up around my spirit right now, the Lord can't clear away the brush. At this moment, I would rather have a six-shooter than all the lawyers in Illinois. Sorry.

ELIZA. Well, I'll—I guess I'll head on back downstairs. (*But she can't. Suddenly blurting out.*) How can . . . how can a revelation . . . How can something that comes from God hurt people? How can that happen? If it hurts someone, it can't come from God, can it?

BRIGHAM. Seems unlikely.

ELIZA. Right.

BRIGHAM. (*Quietly.*) But there are what you might call precedents. The book of Job. Abraham and Isaac. Paul with rocks flung at his head in Lystra. Christ in Gethsemane. Joseph and Hyrum in Carthage Jail.

ELIZA. Oh.

BRIGHAM. I don't know, Sister Eliza. I'm afraid it may just be that hurt and the will of the Lord do sometimes travel the same road. But if they do, in the end, I know that road leads straight to His arms.

ELIZA *disappears as* ANN *comes on and talks as though through a door.*

ANN. I'm sorry I upset you, dear, but you was insistent to know, so I told you. Dear. Mr. Fleming. Please don't take on and be upset. I hate it when you shut yourself up like this. Won't you come out?

Drum roll. BRIGHAM *turns and is at the temple site. Ambient early morning noises.*

BRIGHAM. Brother Pitt, members of the Nauvoo Legion band, thank you for that stirring march. And now we all thank the Lord that the final capstone has been laid to the temple.

ANN. All right then, you just stay in there for a spell. But honest, I think everything'll turn out right. We just have to make sure we don't . . . we don't tell no one about that night. Because you know Eliza won't. She's too scared. I've almost forgot it, myself, we been so busy.

BRIGHAM. It is a fine edifice, an edifice of beauty and grandeur. I believe the windows are particularly fine.

ANN. So we just won't talk about it. Eliza says that's the right thing. Or would you rather . . . would you rather we do something else?

BRIGHAM. I now pray the Almighty to defend us in this place and sustain us until it is finished inside and out and we have all got our endowments.

ANN. Mr. Fleming? Dear? You know I'll do what you think is right. Long as I don't have to go to court. I don't think I could do that. . . . I can't do that.

BRIGHAM. And now, Brother Pitt, a final hymn.

The actors playing BROWNING, LAMBORN, *and* SHARP, *now neutral again, come on as* ANN *and* BRIGHAM *disappear.*

FIFTH ACTOR (LAMBORN). The circuit court comes to Hancock County twice each year, in May and October.

SECOND ACTOR (BROWNING). It stays a week, clears up whatever business is put before it, and then moves on to another patch of Illinois prairie.

FOURTH ACTOR (SHARP). It is May 24, an especially clement spring Saturday. Two hundred Hancock County citizens crowd into the second-story courtroom in Carthage.

SECOND ACTOR (BROWNING). Roughly the same number as the mob that killed the Smiths.

Growing crowd noise.

FIFTH ACTOR (LAMBORN). "Almost everybody attending court comes armed to the teeth—as if this were a militia muster instead of a trial." *The St. Louis Missouri Republican.*

YOUNG *takes his place at the bench. He takes a gavel from a small black valise.*

SECOND ACTOR (BROWNING). "The decision of Judge Young to quash the jury is considered a great victory for the defendants." *The Burlington Hawkeye.*

The ACTORS *playing* BRIGHAM, ELIZA, *and* ANN, *now neutral again, come on with the red-marked body outline of Joseph Smith. They hang it high above the stage. It will preside, like a ghost, over the trial. Then they exit. Meanwhile:*

FOURTH ACTOR (SHARP). "The impression appears to be that the Mormons will not attempt a very rigorous prosecution." *The Sangamo Journal.*

LAMBORN, SHARP, *and* BROWNING *take their places in the chairs,* SHARP *beside* BROWNING. YOUNG *bangs his gavel.*

YOUNG. (*Reading.*) The state of Illinois charges that the defendants, not having the fear of God before their eyes, unlawfully, willfully, and of their own malice aforethought did cause to be killed and murdered Joseph Smith, Junior. Levi Williams, Mark Aldrich, William N. Grover, Jacob C. Davis, Thomas C. Sharp. (*He looks up.*) How do you plead?

Blackout.

END ACT ONE

Act Two

SCENE 1

Saturday, May 24, 1845. Courtroom[12]/Mansion House. Lights up to reveal YOUNG *at the judge's bench,* BROWNING *in his chair, with* SHARP *beside him, and* LAMBORN *up and ready to go. Ambient noise of a loud and noisy armed crowd. During the trial scenes, the actors will address the audience as though they are the jury—or, at other times, the spectators.*

YOUNG. (*He bangs his gavel, addresses the audience.*) Order! Order! There will be order

---

[12] Alternative version of this opening appears at end of play

in my courtroom. This is not Missouri! (*He bangs again.*) I caution you spectators that I will remove the rowdy from my court. There are another two hundred outside ready to take your place, so you will not be missed.

LAMBORN. Hell's bells, a man can't hear himself think.

BROWNING *leaps to his feet.*

BROWNING. Your Honor, surely the dignity of this court will be better served if counsel for the state does not besmirch it with his odious oaths.

YOUNG. Yes. Save your tavern expressions for the tavern, Mr. Lamborn. They have no place in my court.

LAMBORN. Oh, I guess we're not going in for freedom of speech here, members of the jury.

YOUNG. Consider yourself warned, Mr. Lamborn.

LAMBORN. Your Honor. I'm supposed to go first in this tea party, but my witnesses for today haven't shown their faces.

SHARP. I guess the citizens of Hancock County just don't have anything to say to you, Mr. Lamborn.

Crowd noise of agreement. YOUNG *bangs his gavel.*

YOUNG. Quiet! (*He points his gavel at a couple of people in the audience.*) You. And you. Court Deputy Fleming will accompany you both out of my court. After which, he will fetch the men on Mr. Lamborn's witness list.

LAMBORN. Your Honor, where are the other four defendants in this case?

BROWNING. Released on recognizance bonds, as you know. They are not required to attend all sessions.

LAMBORN. Oh. I suppose Tom Sharp here is just covering the trial for his newspaper. These men are charged with murder! And yet, members of the jury, they're not spending a night in jail. You suppose the Smith brothers wish they'd been so lucky?

YOUNG. Mr. Lamborn, Mr. Browning, you are both out of order. And Mr. Browning.

BROWNING. (*Standing.*) Your Honor.

YOUNG. Please counsel your client that the court will look with little favor on any further outbursts from him. Proceed with your opening statement, Mr. Lamborn.

LAMBORN *turns to a section of the audience.*

LAMBORN. Yes, Your Honor. All right. The state's case is conspiracy. What does that mean? This fellow, Tom Sharp, yelled for Joseph Smith's blood in his newspaper. (*Pulls out a copy of the* Signal.) Listen to this.

BROWNING. Objection, Your Honor.

LAMBORN. You can't object to my opening statement, Orville. It ain't polite.

BROWNING. Your Honor, Mr. Lamborn is about to read a newspaper article to the jury. That's hearsay evidence. It's not admissible.

LAMBORN. It ain't hearsay evidence. (*Indicating* SHARP.) Your client wrote it. He called for the (*finding the word*) "extermination" of the Smiths. That's a direct quote.

BROWNING. You allege that he wrote it. It isn't a signed editorial.

LAMBORN. It's his newspaper! Mr. Sharp, did you write this editorial?

> BROWNING *lays a hand on* SHARP's *arm to make sure he doesn't reply.* LAMBORN *turns to the jury.*

YOUNG. Mr. Sharp is not in the witness stand, Mr. Lamborn. I will allow this objection.

LAMBORN. Well, hell.

YOUNG. I have cautioned you about swearing. Do you want me to find you in contempt?

LAMBORN. No, sir. I don't fancy my chances for a safe night at Carthage jail.

YOUNG. Have you concluded your opening statement, Mr. Lamborn?

LAMBORN. Just about, Your Honor. (*Back to the jury.*) Now look, none of you is a Mormon, thanks to Mr. Browning. And neither am I. So we don't care two spits in the wind about the man who got murdered in the jail down the street, do we? He wasn't our prophet. And he wasn't popular around here apparently. But now, let's just suppose for a moment that you got to be unpopular with some folks in Hancock County. Think you'd still like to be protected by the law? Or would you prefer the rule of Tom Sharp, the exterminator? That's all I got to say for now.

> *He sits.*

YOUNG. Mr. Browning.

> BROWNING *stands.*

BROWNING. Thank you, Your Honor. Gentlemen of the jury, two men were killed in Carthage jail last June. No one disputes that tragic fact. However, some might say that the death of Joseph Smith was not a murder, at all but an extra-legal execution for black and serious crimes. Some might say that his tyranny, his unlawful control of the courts and elections—

> LAMBORN *leaps up.*

LAMBORN. Your Honor!

YOUNG. Yes, Mr. Lamborn. (LAMBORN *looks around, bewildered.*) Are you objecting?

LAMBORN. I'm bewildered, Your Honor. I thought we were trying murderers here, but Orville seems to be libeling their victim.

YOUNG. I'm going to overrule your bewilderment. Continue, Mr. Browning.

BROWNING. Now who are the men wrongfully accused of this execution? A state senator. A clergyman. Officers in the militia. A newspaper editor. Respected citizens. Lovers of liberty. Who was Smith? That he was in jail for treason against the state, you know.

LAMBORN. A trumped-up charge!

BROWNING. That Smith destroyed that sacred engine of the people's freedom, the newspaper press, you also know.

LAMBORN. He abated a public nuisance!

YOUNG. Mr. Lamborn!

BROWNING. But what you do not yet know are the revelations printed about him in that newspaper. They are why he destroyed it. (*Takes out* Expositor *to read to the jury.*) Here. Let me read to you the true character of Joseph Smith.

LAMBORN. Objection!

BROWNING. Why? Are you afraid to let the jury hear about the depraved depths to which this man had sunk?

LAMBORN. Now this really is hearsay evidence, Your Honor. A pack of lies printed by his enemies. If I can't read my newspaper, Orville, you sure as hell can't read yours!

YOUNG. Mr. Lamborn is correct. The objection is sustained. And we'll recess until the prosecution's witnesses arrive.

> YOUNG *bangs his gavel. All disappear as a table is banged down in the middle of the courtroom.* ELIZA *is scrubbing it as* ANN *enters, looking very worried and frightened. She is carrying a bag of* ELIZA's *belongings.*

ANN. Here you are. Thank goodness.

> ELIZA *stretches her back. She's been working a while and is pleased and surprised to see her aunt.*

ELIZA. Ann!

ANN. I thought I'd never find you. I been walking through these streets. People told me you were up here at the . . . the . . .

ELIZA. The Mansion House, they call it. (*Taking her hands.*) How are you?

ANN. I had no idea Nauvoo was this big. All these streets—straight line this way, straight line that way. (*Lowering her voice and looking around.*) And I couldn't be sure if people could tell I ain't a Mormon.

ELIZA. No one's going to hurt you here.

ANN. That's not what they say in Warsaw.

ELIZA. They've been good to me. They gave me something to do and a place to stay. (*Hugging* ANN.) Oh, but I miss family, though! It's a treat to see you.

ANN. The accounts is all in a heap already.

ELIZA. Oh, well, don't worry. You know I'll set it all back straight again. Ann, you want to see the kitchen here!

ANN. No, I can't stay long. Mr. Fleming'll take on.

ELIZA. He doesn't know you're here?

ANN. Lordy, no! I ain't such a fool as that! I brought your things. (*She hands her the bag.*) Books you left, your sewing frame.

ELIZA. You shouldn't have gone to the bother. I'll be back in a week.

ANN. Well . . .

ELIZA. Ann? I'll be back in a week. Won't I?

ANN. (*Breaking down.*) Oh, Eliza. I'm sorry.

ELIZA. But I was coming back. Few days after court week, same as we planned. Soon as everything calmed down. (ANN *doesn't say anything, and* ELIZA *gets suspicious.*) You didn't tell Mr. Fleming about that night?

ANN. I couldn't help it. You know how he gets. I'm sorry. I'm sorry. I got to go now. Don't be mad at me.

> ELIZA *embraces* ANN *fiercely.*

ELIZA. I'm not mad at you, Annie.

ANN. I may not . . . I may not get to see you again.

ELIZA. Why? Ann? Why?

ANN. Good-bye.

> *She runs out. Table out. Now in the courtroom a chair is placed facing away from the audience. No one sits in it, but* BROWNING *and* SHARP *now neutral actors again, stand together in front of the judge's bench.* LAMBORN *stands in front of them, examining "witnesses" in the empty chair. The actors answer his questions with an easy confidence.*

LAMBORN. John Peyton. (*Consulting his ever-present papers.*) According to your grand jury testimony, you were in the Warsaw militia. That right?

FIRST ACTOR (YOUNG). Sure.

LAMBORN. Sure. Nothing wrong with that. Now you heard Tom Sharp hootin' and hollerin', trying to get folks stirred up to go attack that jail after the Governor discharged them.

FIRST ACTOR (YOUNG). I might have.

LAMBORN. That's what you told the grand jury last October.

FIRST ACTOR (YOUNG). Well, sure, then.

LAMBORN. What did Sharp say?

FIRST ACTOR (YOUNG). Don't know what you mean.

LAMBORN. Did he say anything about killing Joseph Smith?

FIRST ACTOR (YOUNG). No.

LAMBORN. Well, did anybody say anything? You said somebody was getting that crowd of soldiers going.

FIRST ACTOR (YOUNG). Well, sure.

LAMBORN. Well, who said what, Mr. Peyton?

FIRST ACTOR (YOUNG). I couldn't tell. I don't know what their intentions was.

LAMBORN. (*Consulting paper.*) Jonas Hobert. You told the grand jury you heard firing and come running to the jail from your home. That correct?

SECOND ACTOR (BROWNING). Yes, sir.

LAMBORN. You know all the defendants by sight, except Grover?

SECOND ACTOR (BROWNING). I do.

LAMBORN. You see any of them at the jail?

SECOND ACTOR (BROWNING). No, sir.

LAMBORN. There was over a hundred people milling around with guns. You see anybody you knew there?

SECOND ACTOR (BROWNING). No, sir. Not one person.

LAMBORN. Mr. George Walker, you were in the militia, too.

FOURTH ACTOR (SHARP). I didn't see nothing, and I didn't hear nothing. And I don't know anybody.

SECOND ACTOR (BROWNING). "No, I never heard these men talk about the murders before or after—or any time." Canfield Hamilton.

FIRST ACTOR (YOUNG). "I didn't want to hear anything. And I wouldn't have heard anything if anybody wanted to tell me." Captain John Wilson.

LAMBORN. Your Honor, I'm calling Frank Worrell to the stand.

> YOUNG *and* BROWNING *resume their roles, going back to their places.* SHARP *now plays* FRANK WORRELL *(24). He sits in the witness chair.*

YOUNG. Do you swear to tell this court the entire truth, fearing Almighty God?

WORRELL. I do.

LAMBORN. Well, Mr. Worrell, you going to lie to me like all those other fellas?

WORRELL. (*To* YOUNG.) Do I have to answer that?

YOUNG. Mr. Lamborn is making a rhetorical point, Mr. Worrell.

LAMBORN. Let me give you some questions you do have to answer. You're a soldier in the Carthage Greys sometimes, aren't you?

WORRELL. I'm proud to be a lieutenant in the Greys.

LAMBORN. And what was your job on the day the Smiths were murdered?

WORRELL. I was in charge of the seven-man detail guarding the jail.

LAMBORN. You was guarding the jail the Smiths was in?

WORRELL. Yes.

LAMBORN. Just let me get this straight, Mr. Worrell. There you are with six other fellas. You're standing with, what, muskets? In front of the door to the jail?

WORRELL. Of course.

LAMBORN. What were you doing that for?

WORRELL. It's what we was ordered to do.

LAMBORN. Who gave that order?

WORRELL. The governor.

LAMBORN. Oh, he thought, just maybe, the Smiths might be in some danger?

WORRELL. I guess.

LAMBORN. All right. So here comes a hundred or more of the Warsaw militia ready to attack the jail you're guarding. (*As though thinking of it for the first time:*) Oh. What's your other job, Mr. Worrell?

WORRELL. What?

LAMBORN. All you militia men volunteer your time. You don't get paid for it. That's what makes it patriotic.

WORRELL. Yes, sir.

LAMBORN. So what do you do to make money?

WORRELL. I own a store.

LAMBORN. It's a good one, too, gentlemen of the jury. I bought me this collar there, and I got no complaints. You all ought to stop on in to Mr. Worrell's store.

WORRELL. (*Pleased.*) Well, thank you.

LAMBORN. (*To the jury.*) Actually, I think a lot of you do. I saw a lot of traffic in that store. In fact, Mr. Worrell, how many folks visit your store?

WORRELL. Oh, about all the county stops in from time to time.

LAMBORN. So I suppose you know about everyone in the county.

WORRELL. Well, I know a fair few. I'd say about a third by sight and name.

LAMBORN. Heavens. That's a lot. So there they are, bearing down on you.

WORRELL. Who?

LAMBORN. Fellas who do their buying in your store. Dressed up as the Warsaw militia. How many did you recognize?

WORRELL. Oh. (*Thinks.*) I didn't recognize any of them.

LAMBORN. Not one?

BROWNING. The witness has answered Mr. Lamborn's question.

LAMBORN. Well, I just find that incredible, Mr. Worrell. Here you supply sundries to the whole county, and you didn't recognize one soul in that group of a hundred or so. Is that what you're saying?

WORRELL. Their faces was blackened. And there was a lot of smoke once they commenced firing their pieces.

LAMBORN. You're sure. Not one? Think, man!

BROWNING. He's badgering the witness, Your Honor.

LAMBORN. Well, hell, he's my witness!

YOUNG. Take another line of questioning, Mr. Lamborn.

LAMBORN. Mr. Worrell, what did you do when that big horde of unrecognizable fellas came storming down on you?

WORRELL. We did our duty.

LAMBORN. You mean you fired your muskets?

WORRELL. We did.

LAMBORN. Anybody get shot?

WORRELL. No.

LAMBORN. How close was this mob of liquored-up soldiers when you fired at it?

WORRELL. About eight feet away.

LAMBORN. You and your guard detail fired on them, point blank, and not one soldier took a bullet?

WORRELL. That's right.

LAMBORN. Lieutenant Frank Worrell, did you load your guns with blank cartridges, so that when you fired there would be no danger to the mob attacking the jail?

BROWNING *leaps to his feet.*

BROWNING. Your Honor, the witness does not have to answer that incriminating question!

LAMBORN. And did that mob know by prior arrangement that you'd be firing blanks?

BROWNING. Mr. Worrell is not on trial!

LAMBORN. Your Honor, I'm trying to establish conspiracy. If Frank here and his men fired blanks, it must have been because somebody told them to. And those somebodies are the defendants.

BROWNING. You don't know that.

LAMBORN. We'll all start to know it when Lieutenant Worrell answers my questions.

BROWNING. Your Honor, in the interest of fairness, in the interest of *statesmanship*—

LAMBORN. What's statesmanship got to do with it?

BROWNING. —I must ask you not to let this persecution go any further.

LAMBORN. Your Honor, will you please direct the witness to answer my question? Did he load and fire blank cartridges? Your Honor? Judge Young? Richard!?

> YOUNG *is deeply worried and not a little frightened. Everyone leaves except* LAMBORN *who slumps into the witness chair, now a chair in the dining room of Mansion House late at night. He loosens his tie, takes out his flask, and gulps.* ELIZA *enters. She watches him for a moment.*

ELIZA. Mr. Lamborn?

> LAMBORN, *surprised, puts his flask away, wipes his mouth, and tries to look presentable.*

LAMBORN. Ah, my silent witness.

ELIZA. What are you doing here?

LAMBORN. Well, seeing as how tomorrow's a day off, I figured I'd spend the night in Nauvoo. (*He gets wearily to his feet.*) I am not drunk, Miss Graham. Drunk is not something I ever seem to get. Good night.

> *He starts to leave,* ELIZA *watching him.*

ELIZA. How . . . how is the trial going? We don't get much news here.

LAMBORN. Oh, the trial? Let's see. I got witnesses who don't have the smallest inclination to tell the truth—Orville doesn't even cross-examine them. And I got a judge who won't compel testimony from an eyewitness to the shooting because he's already started his campaign for governor. Trial's going about like I expected. 'Course you can't blame poor Richard. He's scared to death. (*Fishes for a scrap of paper, hands it to* ELIZA.) Here. Look at this. (*She takes it, reads.*) You can see why it seems prudent to spend the night here.

ELIZA. You can't go back.

LAMBORN. Oh, they ain't really going to lynch me.

ELIZA. You don't know that. You don't know what people can do.

LAMBORN. Well, of course I ain't a woman of the world like you, but I got a pretty fair idea.

ELIZA. (*Noticing a small cut on his hand for the first time.*) What happened to your hand?

LAMBORN. (*Holds up his hand, frowns at it.*) Fear of strangers.

ELIZA. Hold on. I've got something. (*She produces a bandage roll and a bottle of something to clean the wound. She tears off a square of bandage and soaks it.*) There are terrible people in Carthage.

LAMBORN. I agree. 'Course this happened in Nauvoo. (ELIZA *applies the soaked bandage to clean the wound.*) Oww. (*She wraps the wound expertly while* LAMBORN *talks.*) Some boys didn't like the look of me, I guess. Happily, Mr. Young was on the other side of the street. So you see, Miss Graham, it's dangerous everywhere, depending on who you are.

ELIZA. (*Finishing up.*) What would I have to say?

LAMBORN. I beg your pardon?

ELIZA. Would I have to face all those people?

LAMBORN. There ain't no way around it. I wish there was.

ELIZA. You say none of us cares about the Prophet.

LAMBORN. That's what it seems like.

ELIZA. To me, Joseph Smith was Moses and John the Baptist and the Archangel Gabriel practically.

LAMBORN. If you say so.

ELIZA. And then, a couple of years ago, they were just opening this part of the Mansion House. Emma—that's the Prophet's wife—she'd been clear to St. Louis to buy furniture and linens and silverware. I remember it like it was yesterday. There was a new red carpet. And the Prophet and Sister Emma decided to make a party of it. They used to do like that all the time: everything was a celebration. So I was flying around, helping get everything ready, singing a hymn I was so happy.

ELIZA. Around noon I came up into the passageway from the private part of the house.

She stops, remembering, suddenly sober.

LAMBORN. Yes?

ELIZA. And there was Sister Emma, just standing there. Her eyes were red, and her face was terrible with grief. I was going to walk on and leave her private, but she spied me. "Oh Sister Eliza," she said. She looked so stricken, I took her hands. She just clung to me then and sobbed and sobbed. And then she . . . she told me. And my heart just broke up into pieces.

LAMBORN. Now wait. Wait. I'm just not following this.

ELIZA. Have you ever heard of spiritual wifery, Mr. Lamborn?

LAMBORN. No, I can't say—

ELIZA. Joseph Smith took another wife. People don't know this. Lots of Mormons don't know it. But it's true. And it broke Sister Emma's heart.

LAMBORN. Well.

ELIZA. She said it came from God. And Brother Brigham says sometimes God asks painful, unhappy things. And I guess he's right, if you read your Bible. "He's still the Prophet," Sister Emma kept saying. She believed it, too. She stayed loyal 'til the day he died. But my belief in him just flew away like sparks from a fire.

LAMBORN. Son of a gun.

ELIZA. In my heart, I quit the Church that day.

LAMBORN. Well, if you think Smith got it wrong over this thing—which he might not have, stranger things have happened in heaven and earth—but if he did—you're supposed to forgive him, ain't you?

ELIZA. Why should I?

LAMBORN. Well, don't the Bible say something about not judging? Ain't you believers supposed to forgive and forget?

ELIZA. That's what everybody says when they're the ones who did wrong. Forgive and forget. Well, I can't forget anything. I remember everything—from what color my first dress was to what date the whiskey's coming down from Boston.

LAMBORN. You do?

ELIZA. Yes! Every damn detail of my life!

LAMBORN. Listen to me. Orville Browning once told me—this was after he defended him in '41—he said after an hour's conversation, he thought Joseph Smith was the greatest man in America. 'Course he wouldn't say that now.

ELIZA. You're just trying to get me to testify.

LAMBORN. Of course I am. (*Impulsively, almost unconsciously, he takes her hand.*) But it don't make this any less true: People ain't all one thing. Not one of us. Governor Ford's head is full of moonbeams half the time, but it don't make me want to quit being a citizen of Illinois.

ELIZA. It's not the same thing.

LAMBORN. You think your Prophet made some mistakes. You think maybe he did a couple of good things, too?

ELIZA. He poured the light of heaven down on our heads.

LAMBORN. Well, which is he then? His mistakes or his miracles? Let me tell you something. When I was attorney general, I took two bribes, Miss Graham. It was pure, unadulterated damn foolishness and wrong as it could be. But, believe it or not, those two bribes don't sum up my entire life.

He looks down, notices he has been holding ELIZA's *hand and, self-conscious now, releases it.*

ELIZA. I didn't tell the truth—least, not all I knew—to the grand jury.

LAMBORN. No, I didn't figure you did.

ELIZA. What do you think of me now?

LAMBORN. *(Holds up his bandaged hand.)* I think you bandage a hand about as good as anyone I ever met.

ELIZA. What would I have to say in there?

LAMBORN. Eliza, you'd have to say the truth.

SCENE 2

Sunday, May 25, 1845. Grove/Church, Carthage. LAMBORN *disappears as* ELIZA *turns and is standing next to* BRIGHAM. *At the same time,* ANN *enters with* BROWNING. *The four* ACTORS *take out hymnals and sing a verse of* "Come, Thou Long-Expected Jesus."

ELIZA, BRIGHAM, ANN, BROWNING. "Come, thou long-expected Jesus,

Born to set thy people free.

From our fears and sins release us;

Let us find our strength in thee."

They split, ANN *and* BROWNING *going to one side of the stage while* BRIGHAM *and* ELIZA *go to the other.* BRIGHAM *and* BROWNING *come forward to preach while the women disappear.* BRIGHAM *is giving a sermon in the grove in Nauvoo.* BROWNING *is speaking from the pulpit in Carthage.*

BROWNING. I am delighted to speak this Sabbath day in your lovely Carthage church.

BRIGHAM. We're leaving the county, brothers and sisters. We're leaving the state of Illinois and the whole country.

BROWNING. And I am likewise delighted to be passing time in your beautiful county on the banks of the rolling Mississippi.

BRIGHAM. The valley of the Great Salt Lake. Fremont says it is a country which rivals in richness the alpine regions of Switzerland.

BROWNING. Surely it is as a fertile Canaan, overflowing with milk and honey.

BRIGHAM. That's where the Lord will lead us, to a land where there is none to set fire to our houses and granaries.

BROWNING. Most of you know that God hath granted me the privilege of defending five of your county's most sober and honorable citizens.

BRIGHAM. When the autumn comes, plant no winter wheat. We will be gone before its harvest. Let that be a sign to our enemies. They may come and buy our farms and every building.

BROWNING. Here to Hancock County, they have come to build their homes and their lives, and here, found innocent of wrongdoing by a jury of their peers, they will stay.

BRIGHAM. Prepare yourselves, for we are going. Going like the great camp of Israel out of Egypt forever.

BROWNING. Let us now turn to our Sabbath text in Exodus: "Keep thee far from a false matter; and the innocent and righteous slay thou not."

SCENE 3

Monday, May 26, 1845. Courtroom/Lamborn's room at Hamilton House, Carthage/Street, Carthage. BRIGHAM *sits in the witness chair, head down. When he raises it, he will be the witness* WILLIAM DANIELS, *nineteen.* YOUNG *takes his place at the bench.* LAMBORN *and* BROWNING *also take their places.* LAMBORN *turns to* WILLIAM, *asking him the final question of his examination.*

LAMBORN. All right, Mr. Daniels, to sum up, will you tell the jury just one more time what you heard Tom Sharp here tell the Warsaw militia?

DANIELS. Yes, sir. Mr. Sharp said they might never again get the Prophet into their power and they ought to hasten to Carthage to execute him.

LAMBORN. And what did the militia do?

DANIELS. Some went home. Most of them cheered and started for the jail.

LAMBORN. Sure sounds like conspiracy to me, gentlemen of the jury. Thank you, Mr. Daniels; you're all through.

 BROWNING *gets up.*

BROWNING. A moment, Mr. Lamborn.

LAMBORN. Well, Mr. Daniels, you must have impressed learned counsel for the defense. He's actually deigning to cross-examine you.

 LAMBORN *takes his seat.*

BROWNING. Mr. Daniels. Do you go by William?

DANIELS. Yes, sir.

BROWNING. How old are you, William?

DANIELS. I'm nineteen.

BROWNING. Nineteen. And you're a Mormon.

DANIELS. Yes, sir.

BROWNING. Are you a good one?

DANIELS. I think so.

BROWNING. Are you a truthful one? Is telling the truth part of the peculiar Mormon religion?

DANIELS. Sure.

BROWNING. Good. (*Goes to chair, gets a small pamphlet.*) I have here a small book entitled "A Correct Account of the Murder of Generals Joseph and Hyrum Smith." It says its author is "William W. Daniels, an Eyewitness."

LAMBORN. Objection. Mr. Daniels has already given his testimony about his book.

BROWNING. Your Honor, I am trying to establish this witness's credibility. If he exaggerated events in his book, he may have exaggerated his testimony.

YOUNG. I'll allow it.

BROWNING. Did you write this book, William?

DANIELS. Well. Mostly.

BROWNING. Just explain to the jury what that means.

DANIELS. I had some help composing it.

BROWNING. Oh. Well that doesn't seem very honest, does it? The cover proclaims that you and you, alone, are the author.

DANIELS. Well, Lyman Littlefield wrote it down, but it was my story.

BROWNING. I see. Is it a true story?

DANIELS. Yes, it is. Just like it says on the cover.

BROWNING. (*Flipping through the book.*) All right then. Your book states that a man ran toward Smith while he was lying on the ground.

DANIELS. That's right. Right after he died.

BROWNING. Then suddenly there was a "marvelous light."

DANIELS. It was like a flash.

BROWNING. Your book says it was a "streak."

DANIELS. Well, a streak, then.

BROWNING. Tell me, right now, from your own memory, William, what did that man have in his hand? And remember that you are under oath to Almighty God to tell the truth.

DANIELS. He had . . . he had a flute in his hand.

BROWNING. A flute? But your book says he had a bowie knife and that he was going to cut Smith's head off for the reward in Missouri.

DANIELS. Well—

BROWNING. What stopped him from cutting off Smith's head with that flute? It was the marvelous flash of light, wasn't it?

DANIELS. No. Yes!

BROWNING. Your book says it made him stop like a frozen statue. Now, before God, did that really happen?

DANIELS. They put that in the book? I didn't say that!

BROWNING. Do you sell this book for money and also exhibit a painting of the scene to gullible Mormons?

DANIELS. Well, what if I do? A man's got to make his way in the world!

BROWNING. No more questions, Your Honor.

DANIELS. I only charge 50 cents!

Uproar from the spectators. YOUNG *bangs his gavel.*

YOUNG. You may retire from the court, Mr. Daniels. The deputy of the court will see you to your wagon.

DANIELS *gets up to go.*

DANIELS. I'm sorry, Mr. Lamborn.

LAMBORN. You did your best, William. You get on home to Nauvoo now, quick as you can.

DANIELS *leaves.*

YOUNG. Do you have another witness, Mr. Lamborn?

LAMBORN. I'm waiting for one. I was hoping she'd show up this morning.

BROWNING. I am not aware of this witness, Your Honor.

LAMBORN. Doesn't seem to matter, Orville, since she ain't here.

BROWNING. Your Honor, if Mr. Lamborn has concluded his case, defense is prepared to go forward right now.

YOUNG. Mr. Lamborn?

LAMBORN. (*Looking through his papers.*) No. Hold on. Hold on. Let me see here. I call Mr. Benjamin Brackenbury!

All but LAMBORN *and* YOUNG *exit.* LAMBORN *sits despondently on a chair. He is in his room at Hamilton House. He pulls his flask from a coat pocket, takes a drink.* YOUNG *approaches him.*

YOUNG. Josiah?

LAMBORN. There's probably another chair somewhere.

YOUNG. *(Pulling up a chair.)* How are you feeling?

LAMBORN. Little run down. Why?

YOUNG. Too bad about your man, Brackenbury. I'm sorry.

LAMBORN. Drunk on the day of the murder. Trust Orville to worm that out of him.

YOUNG. He's a skillful advocate.

LAMBORN. Say what you want about him, he is that. Oh my. I would dearly like to beat that sanctimonious Sunday School teacher.

YOUNG. You won't. You know that. The jury's against you.

    LAMBORN *raises his flask.*

LAMBORN. Here's to our fine jury. Sterling characters all. You know something, Richard? I loved being attorney general.

YOUNG. You did a lot of good.

LAMBORN. Along with the bad. And that's what people remember.

YOUNG. That's not so.

LAMBORN. No? Richard, when you're governor, you going to appoint me to the bench?

YOUNG. Josiah . . .

LAMBORN. That's what I thought. (LAMBORN *raises his flask again.*) Here's to the charmed circle.

YOUNG. Look, you've had death threats on this case, haven't you?

LAMBORN. So have you. So what? What do you want me to do, Richard, quit?

YOUNG. Yes.

LAMBORN. Oh.

YOUNG. You can't win this case.

LAMBORN. I have never, *never* retired from a case!

YOUNG. This one is different. Your life may be in danger. I'm concerned about you.

LAMBORN. That goes straight to my heart.

    LAMBORN *takes a swig from the flask.*

YOUNG. *(Grabs the flask.)* And when are you going to give up this rot-gut, man? It's killing you. (LAMBORN *grabs it back.*) What are you being paid?

LAMBORN. A hundred dollars.

YOUNG. A hundred dollars? For the entire proceeding?

LAMBORN. That's right.

YOUNG. Well I'd say you've done your hundred dollars worth, counselor. What does Governor Ford expect you to do—get us both killed?

> YOUNG *walks out.* BROWNING *walks across the street, on his way to his room, his hands full of papers.* SHARP *pursues him, very agitated. They pass right by* LAMBORN, *though they are in a different place.*

SHARP. Why can't I testify? I have a lot to say.

> LAMBORN *leaves.*

BROWNING. Defendants in murder trials do not take the stand. That's state law.

SHARP. But I want to talk about the sacred freedom of the press! I want to talk about the land!

> BROWNING *wheels on* SHARP.

BROWNING. Mr. Sharp, it may interest you to know that my research for this trial has included you. Your love for this land is actuated by your fervent wish to speculate, a wish thwarted by Mormon land purchases.

SHARP. That's a damn lie!

BROWNING. And all this caterwauling about freedom of the press. Your *Warsaw Signal* was an abject failure until you hit on the scheme to increase its circulation by screaming like Beelzebub at the Mormons. One wonders, Mr. Sharp, when you've finally driven them out, and you no longer have an easy target to boost sales, how long you'll be interested in the sacred freedom of the press!

SHARP. How dare you, sir!

BROWNING. Now heed me. This trial is proceeding exactly as planned. Lamborn produced not one witness who credibly linked you or any of the defendants to the murders.

SHARP. Executions! Not murders! Exterminations by men who love this country and its freedoms!

BROWNING. Now it's our turn. I have secured a dozen men who will pour scorn on Lamborn's witnesses. That was the plan, Mr. Sharp, remember? The case is won. You will go free.

> *He stalks off.* SHARP *is dumbfounded for a moment, but only for a moment.*

SHARP. Browning! Wait!

> *He takes off after him.*

SCENE 4

Tuesday, May 27. Courtroom and Anteroom /Brigham's Office, Mansion House/Warsaw House/Mansion House. Courtroom noises. YOUNG, LAMBORN, *and* BROWNING *take their places.* LAMBORN *approaches the bench to speak confidentially to* YOUNG, *while* BROWNING *arranges his papers at his chair.*

LAMBORN. Look, can we adjourn 'til this afternoon? Maybe I can get to Nauvoo and find my witness.

YOUNG. Your witness was to appear yesterday. Let's get this done, Josiah.

LAMBORN. But Richard—

YOUNG *bangs his gavel. Noise subsides.*

YOUNG. If that concludes Mr. Lamborn's case for the state . . . ?

LAMBORN. (*Defeated.*) All right. I'm done.

YOUNG. Mr. Browning, please proceed.

BROWNING. Thank you, Your Honor. Gentlemen of the jury, the prosecution's case rests entirely—

SHARP *sees* ELIZA *standing at the back of the spectator gallery of the courtroom. He stands up, in shock.*

YOUNG. Mr. Sharp! What is it?

SHARP *is speechless.* LAMBORN *sees who it is, and leaps to his feet.*

LAMBORN. Eliza!

Murmuring in the crowd. YOUNG *bangs his gavel.* SHARP *starts whispering fiercely to* BROWNING.

YOUNG. Order! (*Noise subsides.*) Mr. Lamborn, who is this woman?

LAMBORN. My witness. Your Honor, I need a short recess. The state asks for— a minute.

YOUNG. Mr. Browning?

He looks up from where SHARP *is frantically whispering to him.*

BROWNING. Fine.

He goes back to SHARP'*s whispering.* YOUNG *bangs his gavel.*

YOUNG. One minute recess.

Although they stay onstage, everyone except LAMBORN *and* ELIZA *is out of the scene. These two do not move, but it is understood that they are in the anteroom of the court.*

LAMBORN. I ain't sure, but I think I'm surprised to see you.

ELIZA. Well, you shouldn't be. Seems to me I heard a fella say once, in mighty bad English, "People ain't all one thing."

LAMBORN. Listen. Browning'll cut up rough. He'll call you a liar.

ELIZA. You look terrible. What have you been eating?

LAMBORN. Whiskey, mostly. Come on.

>YOUNG *bangs his gavel and the courtroom comes back to life.* BROWNING *and a panicked* SHARP *are still whispering away.*

YOUNG. Witness for the state will take the stand.

>BROWNING *is immediately on his feet.*

BROWNING. Your Honor, you cannot allow this witness. The state has concluded its case.

YOUNG. Defense will present its case after this witness has testified.

BROWNING. Judge, I must warn you: this irregular decision will be seen as unfair.

YOUNG. Is that so, Mr. Browning? By whom?

BROWNING. People of importance. People who make political judgments about who is and who is not a statesman.

>YOUNG *hesitates.*

LAMBORN. Oh, no. Yeah, go ahead and be a statesman again, Governor.

YOUNG. No. I will not compromise Illinois jurisprudence to please you, Mr. Browning. Or your people.

BROWNING. (*Smiling smoothly.*) So be it.

LAMBORN. Well now, ain't that a kick in the pants.

YOUNG. (*Bangs gavel thunderously.*) Sit down, both of you. This witness will take the stand. (ELIZA *comes to the witness chair and sits down.*) Do you swear to tell this court the entire truth, fearing Almighty God?

ELIZA. Yes.

YOUNG. Proceed, Mr. Lamborn.

LAMBORN. I got to tell you, members of the jury, this witness never sat still long enough for me to depose her. So I guess we'll all hear her story together. (*To* ELIZA.) Miss Graham. Will you tell this court what you know?

ELIZA. I work . . . I used to work . . . for my relatives at Warsaw House. I used to get meals there, clean, take care of the boarders' rooms some. Last summer, late at night, on June the 27th, Ann Fleming and I were working late. And a lot of men came in. . . .

She falters, momentarily frightened.

YOUNG. Do you need a minute, Miss Graham?

ELIZA. (*Shakes her head, recovering.*) No. These men, they stayed for hours. They wanted meals.

LAMBORN. Who were they?

ELIZA. They were . . . most of them were in the Warsaw militia.

LAMBORN. Were any of them the defendants, Miss Graham?

ELIZA. (*Nods slowly.*) Mr. Sharp was there.

SHARP *leaps to his feet.*

SHARP. That's a damned lie!

YOUNG. Order!

ELIZA. (*In a rush.*) No, it's not, Mr. Sharp. I've been scared to say it, but you were there. Ann asked you how you got on at Carthage. And you said . . . You said, we have finished the leading men of the Mormon Church.

SHARP. I never said that!

ELIZA. You did say it!

YOUNG. Mr. Browning, restrain your client.

BROWNING. (*Pulling him down.*) Sit down!

ELIZA. You said, we killed old Joe. And they all said it. There were about sixty men. And Mr. Davis was there, and Mr. Grover. They were all boasting and laughing. We killed old Joe, we killed old Joe. And they did. (*Breaking down.*) I know they did. They killed the Prophet.

Silence, except for the sound of ELIZA's *emotion.* BROWNING *has his head in his hands.* LAMBORN *stands somberly. After a moment,* YOUNG *speaks.*

YOUNG. We'll adjourn until 2:00 for Mr. Browning's questioning of this witness.

All disappear, leaving only BROWNING *and* LAMBORN. *They are in a room off the courtroom.*

BROWNING. You rehearsed her, I assume.

LAMBORN. You assume what you want, Orville.

BROWNING. She seems like a nice woman. It's a shame. I'll have to be a little insistent when I question her.

LAMBORN. What's that supposed to mean?

BROWNING. I've got her grand jury testimony.

LAMBORN. So have I.

BROWNING. Then you know she lied. And you know my cross-examination will end whatever welcome she may have left in this county. Or . . .

LAMBORN. Or what?

BROWNING. My clients are prepared to settle this case.

LAMBORN. You been reading dime novels again? You can't settle a murder case with the state of Illinois.

BROWNING. No. I mean we are prepared to settle with you personally.

LAMBORN. With me personally.

BROWNING. For a substantial amount.

LAMBORN. Why, Orville Browning, are you attempting to bribe me into retiring from the case?

BROWNING. Certainly not. I'm making, on behalf of my clients, a legitimate settlement offer.

LAMBORN. Bribery is what you tried to get me disbarred for.

BROWNING. This is not bribery. This is ensuring that justice is done. Those men are innocent . . . Josiah.

LAMBORN. (*Mock surprise.*) "Josiah." Are we intimates now, Orville?

BROWNING. (*He takes out an envelope filled with money.*) My clients are prepared to offer five hundred dollars.

LAMBORN. (*Suddenly sober.*) Five hundred dollars?

BROWNING. (*He puts the envelope in* LAMBORN'*s hands.*) An amount which no doubt purchases a large quantity of liquor.

LAMBORN. It sure does. Eliza Graham's testimony must have really rattled you.

BROWNING. Well?

LAMBORN. What do I have to do?

BROWNING. Admit your lack of evidence in your closing argument.

LAMBORN. And you?

BROWNING. I spare your weeping witness.

    LAMBORN *opens the envelope and looks in.*

LAMBORN. There's a lot of money in here.

BROWNING. (*This encourages him.*) I won't call any defense witnesses. We'll go right to closing and finish this today.

    LAMBORN *starts laughing.*

LAMBORN. Oh, Orville, I believe God must be a mite disappointed in you today.

BROWNING. (*He snatches back the envelope.*) His sacred name is a blasphemy in your mouth! It is His will I follow.

LAMBORN. What, he whispered in your ear: Go bribe counsel for the prosecution; I'll look the other way?

BROWNING. It is His will that I win.

The two men are eye to eye and toe to toe now. A physical fight might ensue, but YOUNG *bangs his gavel, and all are back in the courtroom.*

YOUNG. You may proceed, Mr. Browning.

BROWNING. Miss Graham. May I call you Eliza?

ELIZA. No. I don't think so.

BROWNING. (*To the jury.*) Take note of this witness's hostility, members of the jury. Well, Miss Graham, you seem to recollect a lot of detail about a night that happened a year ago. You even remember direct quotations: who said what to whom. Why is that?

ELIZA. The night stands out in my memory.

BROWNING. You have a remarkable memory. Which means, I suppose, that you could just as easily recall other statements made at roughly the same time.

ELIZA. I guess so.

BROWNING. Good. Miss Graham, I assume you heard Joe Smith preach.

ELIZA. (*Immediately nervous.*) Lots of folks did. Whether they were Mormons or not.

LAMBORN. Objection. What's this got to do with the price of cattle? I'd like to know.

BROWNING. Your Honor, I'm simply testing this witness's memory.

LAMBORN. Oh.

YOUNG. I'll allow it—if it's a reasonable test. The witness's memory is relevant. Unless the state has an objection?

LAMBORN. No, you carry on, Orville.

BROWNING. Thank you, Your Honor. Now (*goes to briefcase and pulls out a document*), I happen to have one of Mr. Smith's strange sermons, the last he gave before his decease a year ago. It was about the recently deceased Mr. King Follett. Were you present for that sermon?

ELIZA. Most all Mr. Follett's friends went.

BROWNING. I suppose you recall it, then. It was memorable, apparently.

ELIZA. I think so.

BROWNING. Can you recall what Smith said on that occasion about the Almighty? Here, counselor. (*Hands the document to* LAMBORN.) You'll tell us if Miss Graham's recollections are correct.

ELIZA. About God?

BROWNING. Yes, about God in the beginning, as he put it. I assume someone with a good memory would recall it.

ELIZA. I remember he said, "I will go back to the beginning before the world was, to show what kind of being God is."

LAMBORN. I'll be damned. That's word for word.

BROWNING *snatches the document and scans it.*

ELIZA. "Open your ears and hear, all ye ends of the earth—"

BROWNING. Thank you, Miss Graham—

LAMBORN *snatches the document back. He keeps it.*

ELIZA. "—for I am going to prove it to you by the Bible—"

BROWNING. That will do, Miss Graham. I'm sure we're all impressed by your parlor trick.

LAMBORN. You want her to remember anything else for you, Orville?

This isn't going well for BROWNING. *He's getting a little frayed and desperate. He picks up some papers—*ELIZA's *grand jury testimony.*

BROWNING. Miss Graham, are you a Mormon?

LAMBORN. Objection. There's no way that's relevant to what this witness saw and heard. Unless counsel is claiming Mormons have different eyes and ears than the rest of mankind.

SHARP. They do. They perceive what their leaders tell them to perceive.

YOUNG. Mr. Sharp.

BROWNING. I have some character questions, Your Honor, based on Miss Graham's grand jury testimony last year.

YOUNG. I'm going to let the witness answer the question. And I don't want to hear a peep from anyone.

BROWNING. (*To* ELIZA.) Well, Miss Graham?

ELIZA. Yes. I'm a Mormon.

BROWNING. Did you keep that a secret from people in Warsaw?

ELIZA. My kin knew.

BROWNING. What about everyone else? The customers who came into the tavern, for instance. Did you lie to them?

ELIZA. I wasn't feeling so much like a Mormon.

BROWNING. I repeat, did you lie to the citizens of Warsaw?

ELIZA. I . . . was afraid. There's some bad feelings about Mormons there.

BROWNING. So. Sometimes you lie when you're afraid. (*Looks at a paper.*) Such as when you testified to the grand jury last fall that you didn't know anything about the killings. (ELIZA *is silent.*) Your Honor?

YOUNG. Answer counsel's question, Miss Graham.

LAMBORN *is on his feet.*

LAMBORN. You look at that grand jury transcript, members of the jury—

YOUNG. You'll have your chance to re-direct, Mr. Lamborn. Go on, Miss Graham.

ELIZA. I didn't tell them anything I didn't have to.

BROWNING. (*To the jury.*) You see? This witness lies when it suits her.

ELIZA. But I'm telling the truth now. I swear it. And there's nothing I'm getting out of it, except maybe my only kin in trouble and me the object of Mr. Sharp's next hateful editorial.

SHARP. Oh, you can count on it.

BROWNING. An oath, Miss Graham, is a terrible thing. It puts your soul in the palm of God's hand.

ELIZA. I know that.

BROWNING. And when you break it, God's hand closes over you. Yet you, an oath-breaker, come in here expecting this honest jury to believe you. Why should they? Why are you suddenly telling the truth now?

ELIZA. Because someone has to! They died. Those men. Somebody has to care about that, no matter what.

BROWNING *is taken aback. His next speech is completely sincere.*

BROWNING. Miss Graham, I respect your depth of feeling. It may surprise you to learn that I knew your prophet.

ELIZA. (*Glancing at* LAMBORN.) I know that. So then, you understand.

BROWNING. I do. Indeed, I do. I expect you're a widow now, Miss Graham.

ELIZA. (*Puzzled*) No. Why would you . . . ? I've never been married.

BROWNING. Oh. Does that mean Joseph Smith just made you his spiritual wife?

ELIZA. (*Appalled.*) What?

LAMBORN *is on his feet again.*

LAMBORN. Objection! Objection!

BROWNING. Isn't it true that spiritual wifery is the gross immorality the *Expositor* press exposed?

ELIZA. I don't know.

BROWNING. Isn't that why Smith had it destroyed?

ELIZA. I—

BROWNING. Has Brigham Young made you his plural wife?

LAMBORN. Objection! This is just pure offensive!

YOUNG. Yes, it is. Does it have a point, Mr. Browning?

BROWNING. Your Honor, I'm demonstrating collusion between this witness and Mormon leaders.

YOUNG. Then do so properly. The jury is directed to disregard this line of questioning.

BROWNING. I have just one more question, Your Honor. (*A sudden outburst of verbal violence:*) Miss Graham, did Brigham Young send you to lie to this court?

ELIZA. Nobody sent me! And I'll tell you something, Mr. Browning. There may be things in Nauvoo you find peculiar. But one thing's for certain: there are two women there still grieving so hard they don't know if they want to take their next breath, because their husbands were gunned down. And children who won't ever get over it. And God knows I heard what I heard at Fleming's Tavern!

> *Everyone stays in place except* LAMBORN *who leaves the court briefly to join* BRIGHAM *in his office at Mansion House.* BRIGHAM *stands, looking out a window.*

BRIGHAM. I used to like looking out the east window, toward the temple. Now I always find myself here, looking west, across the river. Do you ever think about making a fresh start, Mr. Lamborn?

LAMBORN. Just about every day.

BRIGHAM. (*Turning to* LAMBORN.) Then you know what it feels like to be a Mormon. That's about all we've had is fresh starts. Will you tell me about the trial?

LAMBORN. Well, Orville Browning's paraded his character assassins up there one by one.

BRIGHAM. So. It's not going well.

LAMBORN. I'm pleased to report to you, sir, that's it's going exceedingly well. Orville hasn't scratched Eliza Graham's testimony. And he's about run out of ammunition.

BRIGHAM. And then you adjourn?

LAMBORN. Then we recess before closing arguments.

BRIGHAM. Will you come and see me again during the recess? I would come your way, but—

LAMBORN. I know. All them writs out against you. Can't say I blame you.

> BRIGHAM *disappears as* BROWNING *turns and is in Warsaw House, talking to* ANN.

BROWNING. Mrs. Fleming? I'm Orville Browning, attorney-at-law.

ANN. No! I got nothing to say to you attorney-at-laws!

BROWNING. I think in this case you do, ma'am. Your husband sent me.

This surprises and worries ANN.

ANN. Oh.

LAMBORN *turns and is talking to* ELIZA *at the Mansion House.*

LAMBORN. What you did in that courtroom yesterday. That was . . . glorious.

ELIZA. Josiah, when this is over, will you let me cook you a decent meal?

LAMBORN. Hell's bells, Eliza, why are you always trying to shove food at me?

ELIZA. Well, if that's how you feel—

LAMBORN. I accept. Thank you very much.

SCENE 5

Wednesday and Thursday, May 28-29. Courtroom/Brigham's Office, Mansion House. YOUNG *bangs his gavel* LAMBORN *and* SHARP *take their places in the court as* ELIZA *exits and* BROWNING *escorts* ANN *to the witness chair. There is a bruise visible on her face.*

YOUNG. Mrs. Fleming, do you swear to tell this court the entire truth, fearing Almighty God?

ANN. (*Quietly.*) All right.

YOUNG. (*Concerned.*) Are you in distress, Mrs. Fleming?

ANN. No, sir. No.

YOUNG. We'll only detain you a short time.

ANN. (*To the jury.*) Mr. Fleming was away, in St. Louis. He wasn't near our place that night.

BROWNING. Yes, yes, Mrs. Fleming. That's fine.

ANN. It's important everybody knows Mr. Fleming was away.

BROWNING. Thank you. Yes. Now, the night you speak of. Was that June 27 of last year?

ANN. Yes.

BROWNING. Will you please tell us all what happened that night?

ANN. Nothing happened. Nothing bad happened.

BROWNING. Eliza Graham, told us quite a story about a lot of men showing up that night at Warsaw House.

ANN. I never saw them.

BROWNING. She said Thomas Sharp was among them.

ANN. No. No. That definitely did not happen. Mr. Sharp wasn't there that night any time.

BROWNING. Well, then, I suppose he couldn't very well have said anything about the killings in Carthage.

ANN. I told you. He wasn't there.

BROWNING. Mrs. Fleming, I understand Miss Graham is your relative, but in the interests of justice to these accused men, I must ask you: Why would she lie about all these things?

ANN. I don't know. Eliza's a good woman.

BROWNING. Well, she lied to some folks about being a Mormon, didn't she? (*No reply.*) Mrs. Fleming?

ANN. Yes.

BROWNING. So, in your opinion, is Eliza Graham a liar?

ANN. I . . . I guess so.

BROWNING. Thank you, Mrs. Fleming.

He takes his seat.

YOUNG. Mr. Lamborn?

LAMBORN *stands, shakes his head sadly.*

LAMBORN. Oh, Mrs. Fleming. I wanted you to be a witness on my side. Why didn't you show up?

ANN. Mr. Fleming advised against it.

LAMBORN. Your husband?

ANN. Yes.

LAMBORN. The same Sam Fleming who is deputy of the court this week and is standing right over there?

She looks the direction he is pointing and then away.

ANN. Yes.

LAMBORN. But you're here now. How come? No, don't tell me. Mr. Fleming advised it. After he heard Eliza Graham's testimony.

ANN. I come to tell the truth.

LAMBORN. Well, that's a very good idea. And something of a novelty here this week. (*Gently.*) Mrs. Fleming, how'd you get those bruises on your face?

BROWNING *is up.*

BROWNING. Objection, Your Honor!

LAMBORN. On what possible grounds?

BROWNING. That information is hardly relevant to Mrs. Fleming's testimony!

LAMBORN. Oh, it's very relevant, members of the jury. Because a good cuff can make you say just about whatever someone wants you to, can't it? Who hit you, Mrs. Fleming?

ANN. Nobody. Nobody.

YOUNG. I'm going to excuse this witness right now. (*To* ANN.) You go on home, ma'am. And Mr. Fleming, I'd like to see you in the clerk's office.

All disappear except LAMBORN, *who joins* BRIGHAM *in his office.* LAMBORN *is jubilant.*

LAMBORN. They didn't believe her. Nobody in the jury did.

BRIGHAM. And they did believe Sister Eliza?

LAMBORN. I'd say the jury considers Eliza Graham's testimony holy writ.

BRIGHAM. So there's actually a chance . . . ?

LAMBORN. There's a very good chance, Mr. Young. Hell, *I* may run for governor now.

BRIGHAM. You've done a remarkable thing, Mr. Lamborn.

LAMBORN. I certainly have. I'm going to win this case.

BRIGHAM. Yes. That's the problem.

LAMBORN. What are you talking about?

BRIGHAM. I've come to believe . . . that it would be better if you didn't win it.

LAMBORN. No. I'm not hearing this. What are you saying? That you want to see your prophet's murderers just walk away?

BRIGHAM. You know that's the last thing I want.

LAMBORN. Well then? Oh now, wait a minute. Are you telling me Brigham Young has finally heard the word of God? Damn it, of course I'm supposed to win! I told you what this case means to me.

BRIGHAM. Mr. Lamborn—

LAMBORN. And what about Eliza?

BRIGHAM. Mr. Lamborn—

LAMBORN. It's too late anyway. All that's left is closing arguments. Judas Priest, everybody's after me to lose this case! At least Orville offered me money!

BRIGHAM. I can only tell you what I believe and why I believe it. What you do after that is entirely up to you. Will you hear me out?

Immediately, BROWNING *is addressing the jury.* LAMBORN *sits quietly in his chair, head down.* YOUNG *comes on, sits on another chair behind. A third chair is empty. It is* BROWNING's, *who is in the middle of addressing the jury.*

BROWNING. In summation, members of the jury, I confess myself surprised, but gratified, that the light of truth has burst upon Mr. Lamborn here at the end of the trial. He has repudiated all his perjured witnesses. You are now free to return these good and innocent men to their rightful place as leaders in your community. I know you will do your duty before Almighty God. The defense rests.

He and YOUNG *leave.* LAMBORN *stands and someone takes his chair away. He is in the Mansion House in Nauvoo, waiting for* ELIZA. *She enters, dressed to go out, carrying covered dishes. She sees him, then, without speaking, starts to leave.*

LAMBORN. Eliza! Hold on.

ELIZA. I have to get these meals up to the temple.

LAMBORN. Just give me a minute. I want to explain it to you.

ELIZA. It doesn't matter. I knew it was a lost cause. I told you that at the beginning.

LAMBORN. You told the truth—hell, I know that.

ELIZA. I guess that's why you figured you had to lump me in with all those liars.

LAMBORN. (*He takes her hand.*) Will you listen to me, Eliza?

She removes her hand from his.

ELIZA. How much money did you get for it?

She leaves. LAMBORN *is stunned.*

SCENE 6

Friday, May 30. Courtroom/Warsaw House/Mansion House/Neutral playing space. YOUNG *and* BROWNING *reappear in their places. It is the courtroom.*

YOUNG. The jury will now withdraw to consider its verdict.

LAMBORN. Wait.

YOUNG. Yes, Mr. Lamborn? You have already given your closing argument.

LAMBORN. The prosecution gets one last say before the jury retires, don't it? Ain't that the procedure?

YOUNG. Do you have something to say?

LAMBORN. Yes. I do.

> YOUNG *and* BROWNING *leave, but* LAMBORN *stays on. He takes Joseph Smith's sermon from a pocket and silently reads it.* ANN *comes on with a covered dish. She is talking through the "door" to her husband.*

ANN. Things is good again now, right, Mr. Fleming? I know you won't do nothing like that again. It's all in the past, I know that. So there ain't no need to bring it up again, and I ain't going to. I got some river fish here for you, cooked like you like. We'll get plenty of boarders now is the good news, won't we? Well, you just come on out when you're ready. (*She turns to go, hesitates, turns back.*) Mr. Fleming. You know . . . you know I love you.

> BRIGHAM *and* ELIZA *come on. They are at the Mansion House in* BRIGHAM YOUNG's *office, in mid-conversation.* ANN *leaves.*

ELIZA. He told the jury my testimony might be unreliable. In his closing argument.

BRIGHAM. Forgive him, Sister Eliza.

ELIZA. He made me out a liar. And those men are guilty. I know they are.

BRIGHAM. What do you think will happen if the jury comes to that conclusion?

ELIZA. What do you mean?

BRIGHAM. You were in that courtroom. What was it like?

ELIZA. Like being in the midst of a mob.

BRIGHAM. We know that look: our enemies howling for our blood. And that's not all. There must be a hundred right here in Nauvoo just waiting for an excuse to take vengeance.

ELIZA. Not vengeance. Justice.

BRIGHAM. Well, justice is a long road. It goes right through the grave and beyond. And I'm not the toll-keeper on that road. Are you? Now, I'm not Joseph. I'm just plain Brigham. But maybe the Lord can speak to Brigham, too, if he talks slow enough. I believe these murderers have to go unpunished.

ELIZA. Why?

BRIGHAM. So our people can get out of here alive. And without the blood of our enemies on their hands. So none of us has to look back on what we did here with shame.

ELIZA. Did you tell Josiah to renounce my testimony?

BRIGHAM. No. I just told him what I told you. What he did was entirely his decision.

ELIZA. Those men are murderers. I can't just forget that.

BRIGHAM. Sister Eliza, maybe some things we have to let go of so we can go on.

ELIZA. But how can we bear it?

BRIGHAM. We can't. I loved Joseph. And Hyrum. I loved them. I believe Mr. Lamborn has honored their memories. Come west with us, Sister Eliza. Will you?

YOUNG *comes on. The* ACTORS, *except* LAMBORN, *are now sometimes neutral, sometimes in character.*

YOUNG. Mr. Browning. Are your clients prepared to abide the judgment of this court?

SEVENTH ACTOR (ANN). After the trial, Judge Richard M. Young sought the Democratic nomination for governor. He lost.

BROWNING. They are, Your Honor.

SIXTH ACTOR (BRIGHAM). Orville Browning had a spectacular career, becoming a founder of the Republican Party and Secretary of the Interior under President Andrew Johnson.

SHARP. We're ready and confident, Your Honor.

THIRD ACTOR (ELIZA). Thomas Sharp was elected mayor of Warsaw three times in succession and then to a four-year term as judge of Hancock County.

YOUNG. (*He opens a piece of paper, reads.*) The jury finds the defendants not guilty as charged in the indictment.

BROWNING. The Almighty hath delivered me the victory.

SEVENTH ACTOR (ANN). September 10, 1845. Hancock County night riders burn down a Mormon village.

FOURTH ACTOR (SHARP). By the end of October, a hundred Mormon homes have been put to the torch.

FIRST ACTOR (YOUNG). November 19. Two thousand five hundred wagons are ready to leave Nauvoo.

LAMBORN *turns to face* ELIZA.

ELIZA. You did a good thing.

LAMBORN. I know it, and I'm sorry. Won't happen again. What are you going to do now?

ELIZA. Well, I can't stay here anymore.

LAMBORN. No, I wouldn't recommend it.

ELIZA. I've lost my kin.

LAMBORN. I'm sorry.

ELIZA. What about you?

LAMBORN. Me?

ELIZA. What are you going to do? You could . . . come west with us.

LAMBORN. I ain't a Mormon.

ELIZA. No, and I don't recommend you join up. You wouldn't like it a bit.

LAMBORN. I got to admit, it don't look like much fun.

ELIZA. But you could still come. Say you'll come.

LAMBORN. I have to go east. I got another case over in Mason County I got to go lose.

ELIZA. Oh.

LAMBORN. Eliza, do you really want me to go with you?

ELIZA. (*Putting a hand on his cheek.*) Yes. I do.

LAMBORN. (*Putting his hand over hers.*) Well, hell. That's the most beautiful thing anybody ever said to me.

ELIZA. (*Maybe he'll come!*) Really?

LAMBORN. Truly.

ELIZA. (*But then she knows he won't.*) But.

LAMBORN. But. It's like I . . . I come up over a rise, and look down into some green valley, and I see lots of folks walking around down there, taking their ease in each other's company, and I think, "That's where I want to be." But then I look down at my feet. I see my path just don't go that way.

ELIZA. Josiah, it's just a matter of believing you can make a new start.

LAMBORN. What I'm trying to say is, that ain't for everybody.

ELIZA. No, I don't guess it is. (*She kisses him briefly. It is a poignant moment, both knowing, reluctantly, that they will not share a life together. Then:*) All right then. You know where I'll be. About a million miles west of anyplace any decent person's ever heard of.

LAMBORN. I'm sorry, Eliza.

ELIZA. Don't be sorry for me.

LAMBORN. I ain't sorry for you.

> ELIZA *leaves* LAMBORN, *who returns to his manuscript.*

SEVENTH ACTOR (ANN). February 4, 1846. The first wagons roll across the frozen Mississippi.

BRIGHAM. Well, come on, you Saints. It's time for the Camp of Israel to depart.

SECOND ACTOR (BROWNING). By acclamation, Brigham Young was made second prophet of the Mormon Church at Winter Quarters, Nebraska.

BRIGHAM. Let all who journey with us organize into companies.

> LAMBORN *steps forward to make his final prosecutor's statement.*

LAMBORN. Members of the jury. You're about to retire into that room back there and find these men, these murderers, innocent.

FIRST ACTOR (YOUNG). Josiah Lamborn's career was not so illustrious.

LAMBORN. No, it's all right. I know you are. I helped you do it. It wasn't hard, since to you, murder just ain't murder if you happen to dislike the victim.

BRIGHAM. Let each company provide themselves with teams and wagons, provisions and clothing. For we are going.

LAMBORN. Well, I want to tell you, you're doing the right thing. Oh, not because of Joseph Smith's morals or his militia—hell, you all got one of those. No. It's his ideas. (*Holds up the manuscript.*) I've been reading them. And they're so dangerous and pernicious that you folks had no choice but to kill him.

BRIGHAM. Unlike Israel of old, we must leave the bones of our Joseph in Egypt.

LAMBORN. Just listen to what he wrote.

FIRST ACTOR (YOUNG). Two years after the trial, in Green County, Illinois, Josiah Lamborn died of delirium tremens.

LAMBORN. *(Reads:)* "Hold out to the end, and we shall be resurrected and become like Gods." As far as I can make out, this man believed that human beings can turn into gods. How's that for blasphemy, members of the jury? But just try to grasp it for a moment if you can. All our meanness and our fear, and our little hatreds, and our weakness, all turned into glory. (*He begins to laugh, a low chuckle.*) Now imagine someone actually believing that. (*The chuckle rumbles on for a few moments threatening to turn into tears. He stops laughing, looks up once more into the audience. Three gunshots.*) Oh Lord, my God.

BRIGHAM. Farewell, Illinois.

ELIZA. Good-bye, Hancock County.

Lights down to black, except on the outline of Joseph Smith. Then, blackout.

THE END

Act Two (alternate beginning)

SCENE 1

Saturday, May 24, 1845, Courtroom/Mansion House. Lights up to reveal YOUNG *at the judge's bench.* SECOND ACTOR (BROWNING), FOURTH ACTOR (SHARP) *and* FIFTH ACTOR (LAMBORN) *stand in place. The noise of a loud and noisy armed crowd, which has played through the end of the intermission, fades to nothing.*

FOURTH ACTOR (SHARP). Court week, 1845.

FIFTH ACTOR (LAMBORN). The noise and tumult of those attending the trial is often so deafening—

Noisy crowd abruptly punches in for a three-count, then cuts out suddenly. We are establishing the crowd and will not hear it again, though all will occasionally respond as if it were there.

SECOND ACTOR (BROWNING). —that Judge Young must frequently call for—

YOUNG *bangs his gavel and the other* ACTORS *resume their roles. When* YOUNG *speaks he will address the audience as though they were the courtroom spectators or jury, establishing the precedent that all will follow.*

YOUNG. Order! Order! There will be order in my courtroom. This is not Missouri! (*He bangs again.*) I caution you spectators that I will remove the rowdy from my court. There are another two hundred outside ready to take your place, so you will not be missed.

Stones

J. Scott Bronson

About the Author

Although he certainly was an actor and dramatist even at a young age, J. Scott Bronson wasn't necessarily on the path to become a playwright when he was majoring in theatre at Brigham Young University. He was participating in the Mormon theatre scene, having acted in productions of Thomas Rogers's *Journey to Gologotha* (previously titled *God's Fools*) and Robert Lauer's *Digger*, but hadn't yet made the leap as a playwright. When he took a creative writing class from the late Susan Ream that all changed:

> For the final project I wrote a one-act play [called *Heartlight*]. I showed it to one of my theatre professors, Charles Whitman. He read it, handed it back to me, and said, "Great. Write another act." This wasn't part of any class, but I wrote another act and gave it to him. "Great," he said. "You got a third one?" So I wrote another act and turned that in to him. The next semester he and Max Golightly and Bob Nelson started a new program in the department. It was then called PDA (Playwright/Director/Actor workshop) but now it's WDA (Writer/[Dramaturg]/Actor workshop). That play was chosen for the very first workshop. Over the course of the next few years, I was in the workshop as a writer three times and as a director once.[1]

Bronson's debut did not go without some controversy. Bronson admits, "The structure was a bit odd, and there wasn't really a plot."[2] So the fact that it got put on during BYU's main season, November 8–24, 1984, in BYU's Margetts Theatre, caused some jealousy and frustration from members of the workshop and other students within the department:

> It got a review that completely vilified it. The reviewer was scandalized by a "thoroughly disgusting line in the third act" (I assumed she was referring to this line: "He doesn't know his butt from a hole in the ground.") and the fact that she thought I had used the Lord's name in vain. When his father dies, the character of Gene says, "Oh, dear God." I happened to be in the theater office when the Department Chair, Harold Oaks, stopped Dr. Whitman to ask about

---

1 Ben Crowder. "Scott Bronson," Interview, *Mormon Artist*, Issue 2 (November 2008), *http://mormonartist.net/issue-2/scott-bronson/* (accessed May 18, 2012).
2 Scott Bronson, email to Mahonri Stewart, January 30, 2009.

this taking of the Lord's name in vain. Dr. Whitman said, "Harold, it is not a vanity. It is a wonderful, prayerful supplication to God. I'm not taking it out." Dr. Oaks said, "Okay." That was nice. *Heartlight* was chosen to represent the school at the big Festvention thing and there were some students who didn't like that. It was an interesting time.[3]

Bronson went on to produce several more plays after *Heartlight*, including *Arthur's Place*[4] and *City of Peace*[5] (with music by Arlen Card), plus a number of short works, including "Confessions," which won the first Sunstone One-Act Playwriting Contest. Yet with these opportunities and successes under his belt, Bronson's best and most influential play was yet to come.

After writing *Heartlight,* Bronson was talking with his friend Barta Heiner, an experienced actor in her own right and a well-respected member of BYU's theatre faculty. Bronson asked Heiner what he should write next. She said, "I've always wanted to direct a play about Abraham and Isaac." The play began shaping itself in Bronson's mind, and immediately he knew the title would be *Altars:* "I don't know why I knew those things; I just did. . . . I knew what it was to be a son, but I had no idea what it was to be a father. Then in 1992, when I'd been a father for five years and had two children, I just started writing it. I thought it was going to be a full-length play, but I couldn't get it there—I came out to about fifty pages, maybe. I tried to team it up with a couple of other plays but there was just never anything right about that, so it sat around for a long time."[6]

But *Altars* was only half of what would become *Stones*. Bronson concluded that there ought to be a companion piece for *Altars*, since full-length evenings of theatre were easier to sell, and he thought that, like *Altars,* the subject matter ought to come from the Bible. It would be seven years after Bronson finished *Altars* that he would finally zero in on the elusive second half of his groundbreaking work.

Bronson had been considering writing a play about Jesus Christ, one that would touch upon both His humanity and His godhood, someone "approachable and understandable, instead of some faraway incomprehensible thing in the sky." A moment of what some might call inspiration occurred after he dropped off his car for repairs and was walking home. The vital elements of the play starting fleshing themselves out in his mind. And, as with *Altars*, he already had a title formed immediately in his mind: *Tombs.*

> It blossomed immediately in my head and I thought, "That will be a great play to write someday, but there's no way I'm ready now." Then there was this almost physical thing; I didn't hear the words, but I definitely felt the phrase somewhere in my heart or head, "Write it now." So I started working on it right away. I had a small role acting in *Wait until Dark* at Provo Theatre

---

3   Ibid.
4   Performed September 25–October 11, 1986, in BYU's Margetts Theatre.
5   Performed October 5–December 9, 1990, in BYU's Margetts Theatre.
6   Crowder, "Scott Bronson."

Company and had an hour and a half in between scenes, so most nights I sat there and worked on the play. It took—I don't know—two to four months to write it.[7]

Stones premiered at the Little Brown Theatre in Springville, Utah, November 23–December 6, 2001. It then had subsequent performances at the Nauvoo Theatrical Society's Center Street Theatre in Orem (March 20–April 26, 2003) and Provo's Covey Center for the Arts (April 4–26, 2008).

If Bronson's first forays into playwriting didn't immediately catch the admiration of his peers, *Stones* certainly did not have that problem. Universally applauded in nearly all of the reviews written about the play, the critical acclaim was unifying in its praise. Eric Snider, writing for the *Provo Daily Herald*, wrote, "The emotional intensity is palpable, and *Stones* is a cathartic, enriching experience."[8] Nan McCulloch wrote on AML-List that, "Scott Bronson, missionary man, has reached a pinnacle of perfection that few of us will equal. Would that we all could leave this earth with a legacy so profound."[9] Sharon Haddock at the *Deseret Morning News* called the play "powerful" and "riveting."[10]

After a brief attempt to start the Nauvoo Theatrical Society[11] with Thom Duncan, Bronson is now the artistic director for the Little Theater in the Covey Center for the Arts in Provo, Utah, where Mormon dramas continue to pepper their theatrical seasons.[12] His work there has resulted in some high-quality productions, making miracles

---

7   Bronson, email to Stewart, January 30, 2009. Bronson wrote about this experience: "I hesitate to claim that there was divine inspiration—even if I felt from time to time that there was—because I don't want to make people feel like they have to like it. If they don't, they don't. I don't for a minute believe that that means they are not in tune with the Spirit. I will say this: when the thought came into my head—while walking home from Doug's Auto Repair on State Street in Orem—that a play consisting of a dialogue between Jesus and his mother would be a good thing to write someday, a spirit of uncertain identification kicked me in the pants and said, 'Write it now.'"

8   Eric Snider, "*Stones* a Cathartic, Enriching Experience," *Provo Daily Herald*, November 29, 2001. http://www.heraldextra.com/entertainment/stones-a-cathartic-enriching-experience/article_cd5e59df-c3b2-515b-be73-115aab5f531d.html (accessed September 24, 2012).

9   Nan McCulloch, "*Stones* (drama)," reviewed on March 31, 2003, AML-List Review Archive, http://www.aml-online.org/Reviews/Review.aspx?id=3615 (accessed May 21, 2012).

10 Sharon Haddock, "'*Stones* Offers Solid Storytelling and Acting," *Deseret Morning News*, April 7, 2008, http://www.deseretnews.com/article/695267572/Stones-offers-solid-storytelling-and-acting.html?pg=all (accessed April 15, 2008).

11 For more about the Nauvoo Theatrical Society, see "Mustard Seed: An Introduction to Mormon Drama" and Thom Duncan: "About the Playwright," both in this volume.

12 They include Bronson's *Dial Tones*, a revival of Bronson's *Stones*, Steven Kapp Perry and Marvin Payne's *Wedlocked*, a set of short plays called *An Anthology of Love*, Jeffrey Hatcher's adaptation of *Turn of the Screw*, Tim Slover's *Joyful Noise*, and Steven Kapp Perry's *Polly: A One-Woman Musical*.

out of the meager materials allowed by the small theater in the upstairs section of the Arts Center.

Part of *Stones*'s appeal, and that of Bronson's other work, is the emotional connection it makes with its audience. This is not to say that Bronson relies on emotionalism. In no way does his work ever come across as anti-intellectual or overly sentimental. Quite the opposite, his work is full of depth and wisdom. Yet in every production of *Stones*, many audience members have been moved to tears, showing that Bronson's work is rooted as much in the heart as in the head, that there is something truly visceral in his plays. Bronson has put it this way, "Some people write to make us think. Some people write to make us feel. I'd like to think that I write to move us to thought."[13]

But there seems to be something even more than that. Bronson's plays are rooted in a special spirit, perhaps even the Holy Spirit. And it is this spiritual edge in Bronson's work that he seems most invested in:

> A theater can be a holy place. A play can be a sacrament. It can be a testament, even an expiation. The stage is the altar where the offering is laid and burnt in the fire of breath, brio, the vigor of human lives whose words, thoughts and deeds rise like prayers with the sustaining vote of laughter, tears and applause from the audience.
>
> Am I a propagandist if I claim that the intent of all my artistic labors is to build the kingdom of God? Some will say that the two concepts—propaganda and art—cannot coexist on the same plane. I think that's hogwash. If the purpose of propaganda is to spread ideas or information in the service of a cause, how does art not fit into that definition? Any artist that is honest with him or herself will admit that an artist's core intent is to get everyone else in the world to think just like them. That's as much propaganda as a political ad. If an artist has no purpose for creating and disseminating their work then it's onanistic and can demand no involvement from any community.[14]

In this way, Bronson is truly a self-professed "missionary man." He is not distancing himself from spirituality or religious messages. His intent is not to make great art. His intent is to serve the Lord. The fact that in serving the Lord he creates great art is merely an afterthought.

---

13 Bronson, email to Stewart.
14 Scott Bronson, "How Did I Wind Up on the Mormon Stage?" *Irreantum Magazine* 8, no. 2 (2006), 7.

About *Stones*

Stones premiered at the Little Brown Theatre in Springville, Utah, November 23 through December 6, 2001, with the following cast:

CAST

Son: Elwon Bakly
Father: J. Scott Bronson
Mother: Kathryn Laycock Little

CREW

Director: J. Scott Bronson

Stones was next produced at The Nauvoo Theatrical Society's Center Street Theatre in Orem, Utah, March 20–April 26, 2003, and again, April 2–26, 2008, at the Covey Center for the Arts, in Provo, Utah. The play was produced for the third time at the Covey Center for the Arts on April 23–24, 2010. Then it moved to the Kit Carson Amphitheater in San Diego, California, April 28–May 1, 2010. The original director and cast have been used for each production since its premiere.

Altars

*For Barta
because she asked for it.*

CHARACTERS

The FATHER, old, but looking younger.
The SON, around thirty.
The MOTHER, old, and still beautiful.

SETTING

The place is the top of a mountain.
The time is past.

SET

I think the play will best be served on an arena or thrust stage. Intimacy, I believe, is vital. Several blocks of irregular geometric shapes should be placed in apparent randomness to represent stones. Everything is black except for the gleaming silver of the knife's blade, and the hands and heads of the actors.

COSTUMES

These should definitely not be flowing robes and sandals, the type of thing you would normally associate with a biblical period. I suggest something nondescript—timeless, if you will—like long sleeves and no collar for the shirts, no pockets or zippers or buttons on the pants. Then sashes or cords about the waist.

> *Lights up. Pause. The* SON *enters carrying a bundle of sticks upon his back. He drops the bundle and sits on one of the stones to catch his breath. Soon the* FATHER *enters wearing the knife in a leather sheath and carrying the vessel which contains the fire. He sits opposite the* SON *to catch his breath as well. Pause.*

FATHER. I won't be able to make a climb like that too many more times.

SON. As many times as you need to.

FATHER. I pray it is never again.

> *Pause.*

SON. How is the fire?

FATHER. Burning still.

SON. Fortunately there is no wind here for it to contend with.

FATHER. Yes. Fortunate.

Pause.

SON. Shall we begin?

FATHER. No. Not yet. Rest.

Pause.

SON. Father?

FATHER. Yes?

SON. What will the sacrifice be? You haven't told me yet.

FATHER. I said—

SON. You said that the Lord would provide.

FATHER. Yes.

SON. There's nothing here—

FATHER. We are here.

SON. —to sacrifice.

FATHER. Not yet.

SON. When?

FATHER. Patience. The Lord will provide.

Pause.

SON. Father, are you that tired?

FATHER. What?

SON. You look . . . defeated.

FATHER. It was a long walk for this old body.

SON. And for this young body.

FATHER. It's a healthier body.

SON. It serves me.

FATHER. Good. May it serve you for . . . for—.

SON. What is it?

FATHER. I am tired. More than I thought.

SON. Rest then. I will build the altar.

FATHER. Wait. It will wait. Sit with me.

SON. I'd prefer to finish this. I'm hungry.

FATHER. You're supposed to rejoice in fasting.

SON. Well, normally I do.

FATHER. I know. So rejoice with me for a while.

SON. Yes, Father.

FATHER. Don't be so sullen.

SON. Yes, Father.

FATHER. That's my cheerful boy. *(Pause.)* Besides, you never liked building altars.

SON. It's hard work.

FATHER. But that's not why you don't like it.

SON. No, I suppose it's not.

FATHER. Does it still embarrass you?

SON. Well . . . yes, but—.

Pause.

FATHER. But?

SON. It's not pride.

FATHER. How do you mean?

SON. I mean . . . It doesn't matter to me that everyone knows I was afraid of the blood.

FATHER. I think every child is afraid the first time he spills the blood of a lamb.

SON. I don't know why it embarrasses me, but, sometimes, after all these years, I still . . . I pity that little lamb.

FATHER. Oh, that shouldn't embarrass you. You should pity the lamb.

SON. Yes, I suppose I should.

Pause. Light change. The SON *is now in darkness while the* FATHER *is isolated in a small area of light.*

SON. *(Off. As a young boy.)* I'm ready, Father.

FATHER. What?

SON. *(Entering the light.)* I'm ready.

FATHER. Oh, are you?

SON. Yes.

FATHER. Bring the wood over here. *(The* SON *drags the bundle center.)* That's good right there. Have you brought the lamb?

SON. Yes, Father. Here.

The SON *drags a [pantomimed] lamb into the light and the* FATHER *inspects it.*

FATHER. This is the runt, isn't it? *(Pause.)* Well?

SON. Yes, but—

FATHER. What did I tell you? *(Pause.)* What?

SON. That I should bring . . . the choicest lamb.

FATHER. Correct.

SON. But, he's my favorite, Father.

   Pause.

FATHER. He's my favorite, too.

SON. Then—

FATHER. Bring him. *(The* SON *leaves the light. The* FATHER *sighs.)* Why did I choose to be a father? *(The* SON *returns. Pause.)* Good. Let me hold him. *(The* SON *holds his lamb, unmoving.)* Son. *(Pause.)* I won't hurt him. *(Finally the* SON *gives up his lamb.)* Now place some wood on the altar. *(The* SON *pushes a stone into the light and places a few sticks upon it, then stands back and stares at the altar. The* FATHER *offers the lamb to the* SON.) Here.

   The SON *holds the lamb for a while. The* FATHER *offers the knife to the* SON *who turns from it and places the lamb upon the altar. Pause.*

SON. He is silent.

FATHER. Yes.

SON. He does not fight.

FATHER. He trusts you. Hold him like this. *(The* FATHER *helps the* SON *get a good grip on the lamb. The* SON *holds it down for some time then holds his hand out for the knife. The* FATHER *places the knife in his hand.)* Cut here.

   Pause. The SON *cuts then immediately drops the knife and cries out staring at his hand in horror.*

SON. Oh, Father! Look! *(He looks down at the lamb and cries out again. He backs away from the altar.)* It's so hot. Oh, father, it burns me! Take it off! Please take it off. I hurt him! I hurt him! Why did I hurt him? *(The* FATHER *is holding the* SON *now.)* Why? Why? Why? It's his blood—he's bleeding—I made him bleed—I made him bleed. Take it off—wash it off!

FATHER. *(Holding the* SON, *overlapping.)* Stop now. Hush. Hush. No. No more. No more. That's it. Quiet now. Yes. Now. Now—look at this. Look. See this? This hand too has spilled blood. Has been bathed in blood. But it washes off. It does wash off. Do you understand? Yes? Now go. Wash your hand.

SON. Yes, Father.

The SON *leaves.*

FATHER. Oh, why did I want to be a father?

Light change. Pause.

SON. I slept that night with my hand buried in the sand.

FATHER. I remember.

SON. Now that I think about it, though, it's not the lamb I pity at all. It's myself. And that's wrong.

FATHER. I think you pity the lamb as well. That's not so wrong.

Pause.

SON. Well, enough about my childish past. Let's build an altar.

FATHER. You build, I'll watch.

SON. Of course.

FATHER. Of course.

Pause.

SON. Are you really just going to watch?

FATHER. I'll supervise from over here.

SON. All right.

FATHER. That stone will start a good foundation.

SON. Thank you. I thought so, too.

FATHER. That stone over there looks like it will fit well right here.

SON. Thank you.

The SON *picks up the indicated stone and brings it to the foundation stone.*

FATHER. You are still young and strong.

SON. You're not so frail yourself.

Pause.

FATHER. I am so pleased with you. I always have been. You know that.

SON. Yes.

FATHER. It was the greatest day of my life when you were born.

SON. It was the greatest day of my life too. Though I imagine, if I ever have a son of my own, my outlook might change.

FATHER. If?

SON. Nothing is certain.

Pause.

FATHER. No, you're right, nothing is certain. Your mother certainly believed she'd never have a son, and yet, here you are.

SON. Here I am.

FATHER. Until you were born, I don't think your mother really believed that she was actually going to have a son. She'd waited so many years, and was long past her birthing age. You truly were a miracle. An answer to so many desperate prayers. *(Pause.)* She loves you more than she loves anything else in this life.

SON. More than you?

FATHER. Maybe.

SON. I love her.

FATHER. I know you do. And that's more important than any feelings you have for me.

SON. I love you, too, Father.

FATHER. I know. But your mother . . . is more important.

SON. Yes, sir.

Pause.

FATHER. I'll help you. *(The FATHER struggles to lift a stone. The SON hurries to help him. Together they fit it to the altar.)* Thank you.

SON. You're welcome.

FATHER. I need to rest.

SON. Are you all right?

FATHER. *(As he sits.)* No.

SON. What is it?

FATHER. Your mother—

SON. What?

FATHER. She will—, she won't . . .

SON. What, Father? Please—.

FATHER. God has required . . . of me . . . of you . . . a most difficult thing.

SON. Is Mother all right?

FATHER. Yes. For now.

SON. Is something going to happen—?

FATHER. Not—. Not to your mother.

SON. To whom then?

Pause.

FATHER. The sacrifice . . . today— *(Pause.)* The lamb for the altar . . . is . . . *(Pause.)* It is you, my son.

Pause.

SON. I thought— *(Pause.)* Why?

FATHER. I—*(Pause.)* If the Lord should require even all that we have . . . then we must give it. *(Pause.)* You are all that I have.

Pause.

SON. And the Lord has required it.

FATHER. Yes.

SON. Then we m—. *(Pause.)* We must . . . do . . . what the Lord requires.

FATHER. Yes.

SON. Yes. *(Pause.)* Oh—!

FATHER. Son—

SON. You did not tell Mother.

FATHER. No. Oh, no. She would not have let you leave.

SON. I wish I hadn't.

FATHER. It is God's will.

SON. But why? Why does He will this?

FATHER. I don't know.

SON. It seems . . . capricious. I'm sorry.

FATHER. I understand.

SON. Do you? How? How is it you're able to understand how I feel? *(Pause.)* Will Mother understand when you return with nothing more than ashes and my blood on your hands and on your garments?

FATHER. Your mother—. Your mother's heart will break. As mine has broken a thousand times already. A thousand times since we left your mother, I have watched myself draw this knife across your throat. A thousand times I have seen your blood pour out upon the stone and the sand and felt it, hot and sticky, upon this hand. A thousand times I have died when I killed you. A thousand times I have wished that I were already dead so that your soul might have passed through this day in the light of life rather than the shadow of death. *(Pause.)* But God has willed otherwise.

Pause.

SON. Your devotion is greater than mine, I fear.

FATHER. Not likely. Already I have held in my heart thoughts even your brother would deem unworthy.

SON. They must be evil thoughts indeed.

FATHER. Thoughts that should have rent the veil between me and the Adversary and cast me into his midst.

SON. How can this be, Father? How can I believe that this is necessary? *(Pause.)* Do you believe it? Or is this just a test?

FATHER. I believe it, and it is a test. That must be won. By performing the deed.

SON. Will you force me if I refuse?

FATHER. No.

SON. I must go like the lamb, silent and trusting.

FATHER. Yes.

SON. Except that I know what the knife will do.

FATHER. Yes.

Pause.

SON. I am not ready.

FATHER. Nor am I.

Pause.

SON. I will finish building the altar.

Light change. All is dark except for a pool of light around the altar. The FATHER and the SON are both out of the light. The FATHER's voice is heard in the darkness.

FATHER. Hurry, son.

SON. What?

FATHER. I said, hurry.

SON. I'm busy, Father.

FATHER. Busy?

SON. Yes.

FATHER. *(Stepping into the light.)* Too busy to help your father?

SON. Yes.

FATHER. Come out here, son. *(Pause.)* Now.

SON. *(Stepping into the light.)* Yes, Father?

FATHER. I need your help.

SON. Is there no one else?

FATHER. It is time to build the altar. I want you to help me.

SON. I thought—

FATHER. Your brother is hunting.

SON. Why?

FATHER. He thought we needed more meat.

SON. We have plenty.

FATHER. I know.

> *Pause.*

SON. He wanted out of building the altar.

FATHER. More than likely. He doesn't like building altars any more than you do.

SON. You let him go?

FATHER. I did.

SON. Why?

FATHER. Because I knew that you were still here. *(Pause.)* I hoped that you would help me.

SON. You expect a lot of me.

FATHER. Yes, I do.

SON. Why?

FATHER. Fathers always expect a lot of their sons.

SON. But you expect more of me than you do of him.

FATHER. Yes.

SON. Why?

FATHER. I want you to be better than your brother.

SON. Why?

FATHER. You are my son.

SON. My brother is not your son?

FATHER. He is not your mother's son.

SON. Doesn't that already make me better than him?

FATHER. It makes you my birthright son. You have to earn "better."

SON. How?

FATHER. By helping me build an altar.

> *Pause.*

SON. I don't like building altars.

FATHER. I know that.

SON. I just want you to know that.

FATHER. Thank you.

Pause.

SON. If we stayed in one place and stopped moving around, we wouldn't have to do this so often.

FATHER. You're right. But this is difficult land. We must go to where we can survive. And so, from time to time, we must move. And we must build an altar wherever we go.

SON. I suppose if I have to—

FATHER. No. You don't have to.

SON. I don't?

FATHER. Not at all. *(Pause.)* But I will be happy to receive your assistance if you are willing to give it.

Pause.

SON. I think I should be willing.

FATHER. Are you willing?

SON. If I must—

FATHER. No.

SON. What?

Pause.

FATHER. God has made a promise to me that through me a nation would be born. That means that through you a nation will be born. As a patriarch, you must learn to serve. I know you are still young, perhaps too young to grasp this, but you must learn to serve willingly, giving freely, begrudging nothing of those you serve. *(Pause.)* Would you like to help me?

Pause.

SON. Yes.

FATHER. Thank you.

Light change as the SON *moves to pick up a stone and begin building. He works in silence while the* FATHER *watches. Occasionally they share a look. Mostly, however, they watch each other while the other is not looking. Finally:*

SON. Has God told you if you will have another son?

Pause.

FATHER. No.

SON. No, you're not, or no, He hasn't?

FATHER. He has said nothing about it.

SON. Then we're proceeding blindly?

FATHER. What do you mean?

SON. How will you father a nation without a son? Or will it be through my brother after all?

FATHER. I don't know. I had thought—I had hoped—I've always believed that it would be through you.

SON. Isn't that what he promised?

FATHER. I've always assumed that. Perhaps I was wrong.

SON. But you've kept your part of the covenant. You removed the foreskin of every male of your household, including yourself, and me when I was eight days old. You have fulfilled your part. How will he fulfill his?

FATHER. He satisfied one impossible demand by giving me you. He can satisfy another.

SON. Mother was already long past birthing age when I was born and it's been more than thirty years since then. How can her body accommodate?

FATHER. You know the answer to that.

SON. Yes. The Lord will provide. *(Pause.)* Oh, Father, please don't make me do this.

FATHER. I won't. But it must be done.

Pause.

SON. I know. *(Pause.)* I have known from the moment you announced that we were taking a journey how this journey would end.

FATHER. How could you have known? I gave nothing away. Even your mother did not suspect, and she knows me better than I know myself. If she had known, we never would have gotten away. How did you know?

SON. I begged the issue. I boasted. *(Pause.)* I was swollen with pride, and the Lord took me at my word.

FATHER. What are you talking about?

SON. My brother was speaking highly of himself—

FATHER. Your brother often speaks highly of himself.

SON. Well, occasionally it gets to be too much for me.

FATHER. Me, too.

SON. Then you can understand what a temptation it is to challenge his pride.

FATHER. Yes. I can understand. *(Pause.)* What was he puffed up about this time?

SON. His circumcision.

Pause.

FATHER. Is it better than yours?

SON. If you ask him, yes.

FATHER. How is that?

SON. I was but eight days old, a mere infant when my foreskin was removed. I don't remember the pain.

FATHER. Ah. And I assume he told you that he bore the pain as a man, not like a bawling child?

SON. Of course.

FATHER. Of course. The truth is that he wasn't quite that aged; and although he was a sturdy boy, on this occasion he wasn't exactly the man he pretended to be. I would not say that is necessarily shameful, however, for circumcision is indeed a painful process to endure, and I believe I may have shed a tear or two myself over the matter. *(Pause. The* FATHER *smiles.)* As I remember it, he held his water all day, trying to avoid the pain he thought releasing it would bring. We did not tell him that it was not painful. And as it turned out, he could not hold it all night. Many of the servants laughed. *(Pause.)* I laughed.

They laugh. A little. Pause.

SON. I wish I had known that before I boasted of my own capacity to bear pain. *(Pause.)* I said to him that if God should require it, I would willingly lay down my life, as a sacrifice, upon a burning altar. *(Pause.)* God must have been listening.

FATHER. Or your brother told him.

SON. He doesn't often speak to the Lord as far as I know. Though he may have in this case. *(Pause. Falling to his knees:)* Father, help me.

The FATHER *goes to the* SON. *The* SON *embraces the* FATHER *about the knees. The* FATHER *holds the* SON's *head in his hands.*

FATHER. I know, child. I'm sorry. *(Pause.)* I love you. You will—. *(Pause.)* The Lord will—. *(Pause.)* I—. *(Pause.)* I can't—. *(Pause.)* I can't . . . I can't believe the Lord wants me to do this. I mean—.

SON. Why, Father?

FATHER. Why? Why would a true god require that a man kill his own son? That is only in the purview of invented gods of stone and clay.

SON. But the true God has required it, hasn't He?

FATHER. Yes. But I don't know why. It makes no sense. It's wrong.

SON. Can the true God command us to do something that is wrong?

FATHER. I—. I suspect I don't know the answer to that any more. But it is the question that has haunted me—tortured me—for three days. Since the moment we left your mother standing there, in front of her tent, smiling . . . confident of your return.

(Pause.) Your mother believes she will see you again.

SON. She will.

FATHER. In this life! *(Pause.)* If I cannot take you back to her, as you are now, alive—full of warm blood and . . . passions—how can I return to her at all? How?

    Pause.

SON. But how can we disobey God?

FATHER. Like that! In an instant. We can pick up the wood, we can pick up the fire, and we can walk back down the side of this mountain, and I can take you to your mother's tent and . . . and . . .

SON. God won't allow that.

FATHER. Oh yes, He will. He will allow us to do anything we choose to do. He allowed one man to kill his brother in cold blood simply because of jealousy. Because, you see, the flesh and the blood of man is not as important as the spirit of man—

SON. Which is why we must do this.

FATHER. True. You're . . . true.

    Pause.

SON. Father, I don't want to die. *(Pause.)* But I will.

FATHER. Oh, dying's easy. You don't need strength to die. You need strength to live. You need even more strength to kill . . . your own son.

    Pause.

SON. If the Lord has required it, then will he not strengthen you for it?

FATHER. Yes. Of course. If I ask Him.

SON. Then do it.

FATHER. I don't want to.

SON. Father—

FATHER. Listen, Son. Many of God's commandments are easy to obey. Return a tenth of all your wealth to God. Erase your sins in the waters of baptism. Remove the foreskin of every male of your household. *(Pause.)* Some commandments are more difficult to obey. Cut your son's throat and burn his flesh upon the altar of God. That is not an easy thing to do no matter how obedient I want to be. I want to keep my son. My true son. *(Pause.)* The day that I was born was a great day for my father. Friends came to the house, and they celebrated long into the night. When they left, it was still dark outside; and they looked up and saw an omen in the sky—an omen that told them that I was to become a great man and that I would one day supplant the king. These men feared the king. So they imparted their supposed knowledge to him. The king then offered my father silver and jewels for my life. But my father, though he, too, feared the king, though he followed after the king's idolatry, set about to secure my safety by delivering to the king my half-brother just recently born to my father's concubine. The grateful king took that child by the feet, swung with all his might, and smashed its head against the stone of the floor before his throne. My father passively watched this . . . his son's . . . murder. *(Pause.)* Of course, I never knew of this until I was an adult when the mother of that child, the concubine, told me about it on a day when she had been particularly provoked by my mere existence. I don't know what was special about that day, only that she meant to hurt me. To make me feel guilty about something that I really had nothing to do with. Well, I was hurt. I felt guilty. But my guilt became anger. Not for her, or the king even, but for my father. I hated him. I hated his gods. I blamed them—I blamed his belief in them—for all the bloodletting, for there was more than the loss of that child—so much more—that I'd pretended not to see. So much blood. *(Pause.)* In my righteous fury, I mocked my father's gods. I brought them an offering. I took a lamb into their presence, into the courtyard where they all stood, stiff, upright, silent, blind, unconcerned like so many dead trees. I wandered among them, tempting them with the blood of the lamb, offering them the innocent flesh. Nothing. None of them partook. *(Pause.)* I took an axe into the courtyard and smashed and hacked to bits all of the gods that would not answer me. That would not accept my offering. I killed them. And there was no blood. How can a real god not bleed when you kill it? *(Pause.)* I left one god standing. I told my father that his great stone god had destroyed the others because they desired the sacrifice over him. Somehow my father knew that I was lying. He knew that his stone god was incapable of such a deed. *(Pause.)* So he turned me over to the priests, the, the, the necromancers, the astrologers, the . . . turned me over to them to become a sacrifice—an offering—to those bloodless gods. *(Pause.)* Can I describe to you what it feels like to lie with your back upon that cold lifeless stone? Can I make you smell the fear as it rises within you and strangles your thoughts and reason as you feel the knife grip your flesh here—*(He grabs the* SON *by the throat.)* Knowing that you are a dead man? *(Pause. He releases his grip. Pause.)* The angel of the Lord stayed the knife . . . then guided me to this desert. Here—this is where I am to establish a foundation for a progeny that will fill the earth. *(Pause.)* How can I do that without you? *(Pause.)* Knowing what it's like to lie on one of these . . . I— *(Pause.)* I couldn't face you.

> Pause. The SON *rubs his injured throat. At one point he tries to say something, but nothing comes. He tries to make eye contact with the* FATHER *but is ignored. Finally the* SON *decides to finish building the altar. He works alone. Eventually the* FATHER *joins in the work. They place the last stone together. Pause.*

SON. I don't want to die, and you don't want to kill me. And yet, neither of us wants to rebel against the will of God.

FATHER. Would I rather become the father of nations or remain the father of one?

SON. Are they mutually exclusive?

FATHER. They must be.

SON. Why? How do you know that?

FATHER. How else can it be?

SON. You have another son—

FATHER. I don't want it to be through him—

SON. Maybe God does!

FATHER. I don't believe that! Do you?

SON. I don't know. How would I know? *(Pause.)* What I want to believe is that somehow we can go through with this . . . and I won't have to die.

FATHER. We cannot proceed with the assumption that the angel of the Lord will intercede for you as he did for me. *(Pause.)* We must proceed. And we must proceed with the assumption that you will die.

SON. I don't understand what—why we're being tested this way—what's going on here. Why this is—. It doesn't make sense to me. What kind of test is this?

Sudden light change as he speaks the last line. The MOTHER *is now standing where the* FATHER *stood.*

MOTHER. I don't know.

SON. Mother, how am I supposed to deal with this? How am I supposed to react?

MOTHER. I don't think your father really considered your feelings.

SON. Exactly!

MOTHER. Or mine.

SON. Why?

MOTHER. Should he have?

SON. Of course.

MOTHER. Why?

SON. Mother, why—, why don't y— *(A vocal sigh.)* You exasperate me.

MOTHER. I'm sorry.

SON. No, you're not. You're proud of yourself. You enjoy doing this to me.

MOTHER. I haven't done anything to you.

SON. You've taken Father's side.

MOTHER. You don't even know what your father's side is.

SON. I know he's brought that murderer back into our midst.

MOTHER. Your brother is not a murderer.

SON. He was about to kill me with an arrow. You caught him. You told me that.

MOTHER. That was long ago. You were a child. He was young.

SON. Old enough to want to kill out of jealousy. It was serious enough that you asked Father to exile him and his mother. To send them out into the desert.

MOTHER. Yes?

SON. Father exiled them. He banished them.

MOTHER. Yes.

SON. And now he's brought them back. Prepared a feast, a celebration. Surely Father can't expect me to greet them with open loving arms.

MOTHER. He is your brother.

SON. Half-brother. Who tried to kill me.

MOTHER. Perhaps he's changed.

SON. Oh, Mother.

MOTHER. It's possible.

SON. Yes, but it's not very probable.

MOTHER. Oh, so you're able to look on the heart of a man now.

SON. Mother, he tried to kill me!

MOTHER. And we banished him! He has been wandering about on those dry sands for many years. He has a family now, and they live like nomads, moving their tents from place to place, wandering to and fro, living by their cunning. A very hard life.

SON. The same life we live.

MOTHER. Yes, and the kind of life that could change a man. Your brother has returned. Your father loves him and has welcomed him into this home as he would any stranger, as you would any stranger, and expects the rest of his household to do likewise.

SON. He expects a lot of me.

MOTHER. Fathers are like that.

SON. Mother, I have spent so much of my life hating him!

MOTHER. Then it is time for you to change.

SON. How? I hate him! How can I eat with him? How can I bear to look at him? How can Father expect me to sleep in the same house with him? It requires too much of me. I can't do it.

MOTHER. *(With his face in her hands.)* Hush. Hush. Calm yourself. Look at me. Please look at me. *(Pause.)* There now. That's it. *(Pause.)* Better now?

SON. Mother—

MOTHER. Son. You must submit.

SON. I ca—

MOTHER. You can . . . do it. *(Pause. Stroking his hair and face.)* You are strong enough. *(Pause.)* You can do anything you want to do. *(Pause.)* You can do anything that you know is right.

Pause. The FATHER *enters.*

FATHER. Are you two going to join the feast?

MOTHER. Shortly. *(Pause.)* My son was just about to thank the Lord for the safe return of his brother.

FATHER. I see.

Pause.

MOTHER. I will look in on preparations for the feast. Soon we can all rejoice together.

She exits. Pause. Light change. Pause.

FATHER. Well?

SON. I am ready.

FATHER. I am— *(Pause.)* I have . . . *(Pause.)* Forgive me for the way I have spoken here today. I do not doubt God or his wisdom. I simply— *(Pause.)* I am ashamed of my own inability to understand . . . my lack of . . . I'm sorry.

The SON *takes his father by the hand and leads him to the altar. They kneel. Pause.*

SON. Great God, our Father . . . through the blood I am to shed this day, sanctify this deed—.

Pause.

FATHER. And give us strength to obey Thy will in all things. Enable us to perform—.

Pause.

SON. Amen.

They stand. They embrace and kiss each other on the neck.

FATHER. Amen.

They look at each other and smile. They rest their foreheads together.

SON. Father? When the sacrifice is complete—when the fire has died—take what shall remain of me . . . the ashes . . . and give them to my mother and say to her . . . "this is the sweet smelling savor of your son." *(Pause.)* I wish I could have said good-bye to her.

Pause.

FATHER. Perhaps she will understand that it is a glorious honor to be deemed by the Lord a worthy sacrifice. Then perhaps she will forgive me.

Pause.

SON. *(Offering his sash to the* FATHER.*)* Father, bind me ... tightly, so that I cannot move. So that I do not ruin the sacrifice.

Pause. The FATHER *begins to tie up the* SON *using both their sashes. As he works, the light around the altar begins to intensify and shrink, leaving most of the stage in darkness while the light around the altar should be almost difficult to look at by the time we reach blackout. The* FATHER *places wood around the* SON's *body. The* FATHER *places his hands upon the* SON's *body—almost a blessing. He reaches over to close the* SON's *eyes but the* SON *refuses this gesture. The* FATHER *draws the knife and holds it flat on the* SON's *chest. The* FATHER *will not look at the* SON *as he brings the knife, very hesitantly, to the* SON's *throat.*

SON. Father ... please?

Slowly the FATHER *turns to look at the* SON. *He removes the knife from the* SON's *throat and with his free hand strokes the* SON's *face.*

FATHER. My son—

Maintaining eye contact the FATHER *kneels on the* SON's *chest ... then raises the knife into the air very swiftly—the* SON *gasps as:*

BLACKOUT

Tombs

For my mother
The first miracle of my life

CHARACTERS

The MOTHER, middle-aged.

The SON, around thirty.

The FATHER, just past middle age.

SETTING

The place is a tomb.

The time is past.

SET

Same blocks from *Altars*; different configuration. A low bench and the lower portion of the entrance to the tomb.

COSTUMES

The same as for *Altars* but without the sashes.

> *Lights up. The* MOTHER *is sweeping the floor. After a time she moves to the bench and dusts it with a small white cloth. Then she sits on the bench. She runs her hand along the edge of it. She stretches out on her side—almost in a fetal position. Then she rolls to her back and stares at the ceiling. She places the cloth over her face. Pause. The* SON *appears in the entrance. Pause.*

SON. Mother.

MOTHER. *(Sitting up suddenly.)* What?

SON. I frightened you. I'm sorry.

MOTHER. No. No. Stay. Please stay. *(Pause. The* SON *sits next to his mother and takes her hand. Pause.)* I was—. I just—. It's so cold. Hard.

SON. Mother, his body will feel none of it. And his spirit . . . right now his spirit feels nothing but joy.

Pause.

MOTHER. Truly? *(The* SON *nods. Then she nods.)* He was a good man, wasn't he? He deserves that kind of joy.

SON. Yes. He was—is—a good man. A very good man. Father put me into his care . . . trusted him to rear the Son of Man.

MOTHER. The Son of Man. *(Pause.)* What about the Son of Woman?

SON. One and the same. *(Pause.)* It's not like you to be bitter.

MOTHER. I'm not bitter. Not really. I just don't want you to forget that you also have a mother.

SON. The best mother any son could have. How could I possibly forget you?

MOTHER. You may be the son of God, but like all men—people—you can become preoccupied to the point of excluding other concerns. Or perhaps you inherited that from me.

SON. What could so infect me that it would push my mother from my mind and my heart?

MOTHER. Oh, I know I'll always be in your heart. Even if you weren't a god, I think your heart could hold all the world. But not your mind. Your mind holds only one thing at any given time.

SON. That's true of everyone. I hope you have noticed, however, that your influence on me has taken deep root. I have learned a great deal from you.

MOTHER. Really. I know it must be true, but at this moment I feel as empty as an ancient desert well. As if I have always been.

SON. Mother—

MOTHER. Your deep-rooted learning was not watered from my well.

SON. It was. It is.

Pause.

MOTHER. Bitterness and self-pity. All in one day. Aren't you pleased you were here to witness it? *(Pause.)* He's been gone for such a short time. I remember every hour I spent with him. But now, none of it seems real. As if the memories are someone else's, and I never really knew him at all.

SON. It's a terrible, hollow feeling to lose someone so dear.

MOTHER. It is. You feel the same way?

SON. I understand your feelings.

MOTHER. But you don't share them.

SON. Not quite.

The MOTHER *takes a deep breath.*

MOTHER. I'm ready.

SON. No. No sermons.

MOTHER. Actually, I could use a sermon right now.

SON. Time enough for sermons later.

MOTHER. But that's not what I meant. You have something to tell me. What is it?

SON. I miss him too, Mother. And, like you, my memories of him already feel like shadows.

MOTHER. That wasn't it. *(She looks him deeply in the eyes.)* You're hiding something. When did you begin this practice?

SON. When I was certain that I was about to hurt someone I love quite dearly.

MOTHER. And perhaps you feel that I am too fragile at this moment to hear whatever news it is that you have for me.

SON. Perhaps. I was counting on it.

MOTHER. Fine. You'll tell me when you're ready. But don't for a minute think that we will get out of this tomb before you have confessed all.

SON. Whatever you say.

MOTHER. That's right. Your mother has spoken. *(Suddenly, she breaks into tears. The* SON *holds her until she stops.)* I'm sorry.

SON. For what?

MOTHER. Oh, admit it, son . . . you want to teach right now. You can't help yourself. You are a teacher. Isn't that why Father sent you? *(Pause.)* Aren't you going to tell me that my grief is pointless? That it profits me nothing in the long run? That I should have a broader, more eternal view of my husband's death?

SON. Never be ashamed of expressing your grief. There's no sin in feeling sorrow. Especially for a lost love.

MOTHER. But he's not lost, is he? I've heard you speak on this very subject before. He'll be mine again one day . . . I'll be his . . . forever. And if I could express my faith in that as well as I express my grief, I wouldn't feel the grief at all. My soul would be comforted by a divine peace. Isn't that what you want to tell me?

SON. No, Mother. I meant what I said . . . no sermons just yet.

MOTHER. Don't hold back, son. What is it?

SON. The sermons will come. Soon. Soon, too, will come the time when your faith, if it is sufficient, will allow you to throw your griefs upon another who will bear them for you. I wish that time were now. But, it cannot be. I am not yet ready.

MOTHER. What are you saying?

SON. I—

MOTHER. Actually... what are you not saying?

SON. I'd rather not say just yet. I'm not ready for that either.

MOTHER. Don't do that. No. Perhaps I am too fragile right now. Too fragile to know that something... portentous is about to happen... to you perhaps... and not be allowed to know what it is. I will not permit you to drop ominous statements like that and let them lie. It fills me with more dread than I can bear. Especially now. Oh, this is worse than when we lost you at the temple.

SON. I wasn't lost.

MOTHER. Your father and I didn't know where you were.

SON. As I told you then, I was about my Father's business.

MOTHER. Yes, without indulging in the courtesy of informing your stepfather and your wet-nurse.

He shoots her a look. Pause.

SON. I apologized for that.

Light change. The FATHER *appears.*

FATHER. Apologies, no matter how sincere, can't heal some wounds.

MOTHER. He's already explained himself.

FATHER. Yes, yes... he's about his Father's business. I'm sure that it's terribly important that this brilliant twelve-year-old prophet who has been put into our care be about the business of disabusing these doddering old fools of their unworthy traditions.

SON. They're not fools.

FATHER. Then they're foolish.

SON. Why?

FATHER. Because they won't listen to you.

SON. What?

FATHER. They think you're a curiosity. Do you suppose even one of them will change because of the things you've been teaching and expounding for the last three days? If they actually believed any of the things you've told them, they would be plotting your death right now. *(Pause.)* They think you're quaint.

Pause.

SON. I thought you were going to lecture me.

FATHER. I'm getting there. But first I want you to know that I know just how truly brilliant you are. I know that what you taught them is true, and comes from God. I know who you are, what you are, and why you are here. I know what your mission is... will be. And for a long time it intimidated me. Frightened me. But now, I know who I am. I know what I am. And why I'm here. It's a blessing and an honor for God to have put you into our care. But he did so because he trusts us. He chose us because He knows we can teach you something. As brilliant as you are, you have much to learn. And you are teachable. I know that you talk with Father every day, and I'm sure that He communicates with you . . . somehow. Whether through visions, dreams, or angelic manifestations, I know he is teaching you. My sense is that those teachings have more to do with . . . the eternities. The verities of heaven. If I'm wrong, don't tell me. I rather like believing that I'm right.

SON. You are.

FATHER. Really. Well, then. That makes what I'm going to say now even more pertinent. This is the lecture you were waiting for.

SON. I'm listening.

FATHER. Some things can be learned only through experience. I'm sure you understand that . . . in theory. What, perhaps though, has escaped your understanding is that, despite these angelic tutorials, you still need the experience of living and growing with a family. With a family is where you will best learn the practical application of such concepts as respect and courtesy—two things that you failed to exhibit when you left us to be about your Father's business. Your mother has been sick with fear for three days. That's not just an expression. She has been sick. So much so she can hardly stand now without aid.

SON. Mother, you have no need to fear. I am in Father's hands.

FATHER. Don't tempt God, young man. You may have angels attending you but that doesn't allow you the privilege to blithely stroll along the brink of a cliff. Your enemies may throw you off and if God wants to save you, you will be saved. If you throw yourself over the cliff, God will let you fall. We are the subjects of the test. God is not. Do you understand?

SON. Yes, sir.

Pause.

FATHER. We love you so very much. One day you may understand just how much. I hope you will.

SON. I will.

FATHER. Good. Because then you will understand why we were so frightened for you. And why that fear has turned to anger. And why that anger will be set aside. We are so grateful to have you back with us. So grateful that you are safe. *(Pause.)* Please forgive my sharp words.

SON. No. You are right. It is I who must apologize. I must try to . . . learn to . . . *(Pause)* to include . . . more people in the decisions I make.

FATHER. Yes. Good. Thank you.

The SON *kisses his mother on the cheek and exits. Pause.*

MOTHER. Why did you say they would be plotting his death?

FATHER. What?

MOTHER. Don't play this game with me. Please just answer my question.

FATHER. I just wanted to scare the boy a little.

MOTHER. Do you really think I'm going to believe that? *(Pause.)* Why do you think those men would be plotting his death? *(Pause.)* What did he say to them? What was he telling them?

FATHER. The truth.

MOTHER. About himself?

FATHER. Very nearly. He was speaking in hypotheticals. He was leading them to the truth.

MOTHER. What is he thinking?

FATHER. He's thinking that he will change the world.

MOTHER. By getting himself killed?

FATHER. I believe that's the plan.

Light change. The FATHER *disappears.*

MOTHER. I have never been so frightened. Not before or since . . . until now. What's going to happen?

SON. Mother, you have no need to fear. I am in Father's hands.

MOTHER. You've said that before . . . and I believe it. But, for some reason, it doesn't comfort me.

SON. Comfort will come. In its own time.

MOTHER. Everything in its season. Is that it?

SON. Yes.

MOTHER. Is your season upon us?

SON. Yes.

MOTHER. What does that mean?

SON. It means I will be leaving soon.

MOTHER. To do what?

SON. Teach. As you said, I'm a teacher.

MOTHER. Where will you go?

SON. Everywhere Father leads me.

MOTHER. Will I ever see you again?

SON. Oh, yes. You will see me.

MOTHER. When will you leave?

SON. Soon.

> *Pause.*

MOTHER. Please don't.

SON. Mother—

MOTHER. I don't want you to go—

SON. This is what I was born to do.

> *Pause.*

MOTHER. I know.

SON. Do you?

MOTHER. Yes.

SON. You know the purpose of my existence?

MOTHER. Of course.

SON. How do you know?

MOTHER. You're not the only one to receive visitors.

SON. I know that, but . . . I thought—. I was told . . .

MOTHER. What?

SON. That I was the only one who knew about . . .

MOTHER. That you're the Mediator? That you will be despised and persecuted of men? That you will bear the burden of the world and men will want to kill you? Yes, I know about that. I've heard you and others read the scriptures. I know what they mean. I know who you are. And what you are. At least I think I do. Maybe there's more to it. *(Pause.)* I love you. You can't know how much I love you. You can't know how badly I need you right now. You can't leave. *(Pause.)* You say nothing.

SON. I don't want to hurt you, Mother.

MOTHER. Oh, you could never hurt me. There was a great deal of pain when you were born . . . but never has there been an ounce of hurt. *(Pause.)* It's ironic, but I imagine some day people will celebrate your birth. There will be songs written about the beauty of that holy night. About the angels who sang. About the kings from the east, and the shepherds and the inn. But no one will sing about the blood and the pain and the sweat and the pain and the tears and that incredible pain. But it was all a part of it. They'll sing about the manger and the gently lowing cattle, but they won't sing about the hearty scent of animal dung. About the grunting and the groaning. They will see your birth as a miracle, and they will assume that it was silent and easy. They won't ever imagine that you came into this world just like every other babe that is born, through the bloody, watery womb of a screeching, straining mortal woman of flesh and bone. The miracle of your birth is who your father is, not your mother.

SON. No, Mother. No man could have done what you did. Not even the Eternal Man who is my Father. If he could have, he would have. *(Pause.)* Only a woman. And he chose you. Do you know what it means that in all Father's creations He chose you to bear the Son of God? That He trusted you to raise me to be a god? *(Pause.)* You are the greatest miracle of my life. Believe that.

MOTHER. I'll try. *(Pause.)* I wish your brothers and sisters felt the same way.

SON. *(Laughing.)* Some day they will. Give them time.

MOTHER. Oh yes, on my deathbed, they'll all be gathered around uttering whispered prayers assuring God and me that they honor me as the greatest miracle of their lives.

SON. Yes, I believe they will. And they'll mean it. Just as I do, with all my heart, mind, and soul.

MOTHER. Thank you. *(Pause. She kisses him. Touches his face, his hair.)* You are a miracle, too.

SON. Yes, well, a child born of a virgin is a rather miraculous thing.

MOTHER. That's not what I mean. To me you were the most . . . I don't know. It's impossible to describe. Just to touch your perfect, smooth skin. To look into your eyes and try to imagine what you were thinking. To watch you crawl around picking up everything in your path and putting it in your mouth. Everything about you was, still is, a miracle to me.

SON. Even if I were not the Son of God you would feel that way. A mother's first child . . . well, if you can't describe it, how can I?

MOTHER. Perhaps you're right. Perhaps the miracle is in discovering how to be a mother.

SON. Then every mother everywhere could know that miracle if they would follow your example.

MOTHER. I don't deserve that.

SON. Of course you—

She stops him with a gesture.

MOTHER. Please don't. I appreciate and cherish your honor for me. It is a wonderful gift, especially coming from you. But, any more than that is . . . too much. I'm afraid I wouldn't believe even you if you were to bestow upon me more praise than I deserve. I could never live up to it. I may allow you to call me a miracle or even an angel . . . maybe. But never . . . never the perfect mother.

SON. But to me—

MOTHER. Don't! *(Pause.)* Listen, if you're going to begin teaching people, there's something you need to understand about people. We don't love better by reaching for perfection. We approach perfection by loving better. Does that make sense?

SON. Perfect sense.

MOTHER. Was that meant to be funny?

SON. Possibly.

MOTHER. Now that I think about it, I suppose it is possible that to you I might have seemed like a perfect mother because I did love you so very much. But it was easy to love you. So easy.

SON. More than the others?

MOTHER. It must seem that way. But not really. It's just that . . . my heart went out to you so much. I was always so afraid for you.

SON. Why?

MOTHER. Because . . . because . . . you're so submissive. To a parent, that's . . . a dream come true, a completely obedient child. Who couldn't be grateful for that? But you tended to let people take advantage of you. I hated that. You always seemed to be in so much pain. And I can't bear to see you in pain.

SON. And yet, every pain that I brought to you over the years—every cut, scrape, bruise, and hurt feeling that I had was soothed, treated, kissed, and healed by your love.

Light change. The SON *gasps in pain and holds his hand out to his mother.*

MOTHER. What's this? What have you done now? You're bleeding. *(Using her white cloth, she begins to wipe at the wound on his hand.)* How did you do this?

SON. Working with Father in his shop.

MOTHER. Well, I assumed that much. But how? What made this hole?

SON. A nail.

MOTHER. How did you manage to impale yourself with a nail?

SON. Daydreaming, if you ask Father.

MOTHER. *(As she wraps his hand, turning the cloth into a bandage.)* Mm-hm. It's not very deep. You'll be all right.

SON. Thank you.

MOTHER. You're welcome. And what were you daydreaming about?

SON. I wasn't.

MOTHER. No?

SON. No. Not really.

MOTHER. I see. So then, what distracted you?

SON. A vision.

Pause.

MOTHER. Of what?

SON. A wooden cross. Nails. And a man wearing a crown of thorns.

MOTHER. What man?

SON. I couldn't see his face.

Pause.

MOTHER. Thorns?

SON. Yes. It appeared to be quite painful. There was a great deal of blood.

MOTHER. There was no more to the vision?

SON. No.

MOTHER. What do you think it means?

SON. I don't know.

Pause.

MOTHER. That poor man. *(Pause.)* How did you do it?

SON. I had dropped a nail . . . I bent to pick it up . . . and . . . the vision came. When it was gone, I felt pain in my palm. My hand was gripped in a tight fist over the nail.

Pause.

MOTHER. And your father accused you of daydreaming.

SON. Yes.

MOTHER. Did you tell him it was a vision?

SON. No.

MOTHER. Why?

SON. I . . . don't know.

MOTHER. Are you afraid of him?

SON. No. *(Pause.)* No.

MOTHER. What are you afraid of? *(Pause.)* Your father is a wise man. He could help you to understand these visions. He knows that you commune with angels. He doesn't chide you for that. Why do you think that he would chide you for having visions?

SON. It's not that. I'm certain that he can help me understand them. I think that . . . I think that I don't want to understand them . . . yet.

Pause.

MOTHER. Ah. I see. *(Pause.)* When you're ready . . . go to him, tell him of your visions.

SON. I will.

MOTHER. In the meantime, always bring them to me, and we'll wonder about them together.

Pause.

SON. Yes.

Light change.

MOTHER. Who else was there to help you bear the pain?

SON. Not many. Not many that I trusted.

MOTHER. Your father—

SON. Yes . . . but not until I was ready to know the full weight of the pain that they brought. You understood what my visions were before I did.

MOTHER. Yes. And no. I knew they were given to you to prepare you—to strengthen you. For what, I didn't know. I still don't.

Pause.

SON. You let me work through all that by myself. You helped me carry the weight of the confusion of not knowing. And when I was ready, Father helped me carry the weight of certainty.

MOTHER. Yes.

SON. How did you do it?

MOTHER. I don't know.

Pause.

SON. Well, it's not over.

MOTHER. I know. It's just about to begin. Isn't it?

SON. Yes.

MOTHER. Without your father to help you.

SON. My true Father will be with me.

MOTHER. Of course. I simply meant . . .

SON. I know what you meant. I'm sorry. I shouldn't be so quick to correct.

MOTHER. But you are correct.

SON. Yes, I'm correct, but so what? That doesn't mean I need to be insensitive to the memory of the man who raised me as if he were my true father. I owe him more respect than that. Besides, you are correct as well. His wisdom and calming influence would be great comforts to me now as I prepare for my mission. I am sorry he is gone.

Pause.

MOTHER. Thank you.

Pause.

SON. I was sent to bring you home.

MOTHER. Were you?

SON. Yes.

MOTHER. Why?

SON. We all know that this tomb will never be just right. It will never be clean enough or comfortable enough for the remains of such a good man. You will never be ready to lay him down.

MOTHER. That's true, I suppose.

SON. But he is gone.

MOTHER. Though happy, you said.

SON. Yes. (MOTHER *closes her eyes. Long pause.*) Mother—

MOTHER. What will you teach?

SON. What?

MOTHER. What will your message be as you go about teaching? That you are the Son of God?

SON. That we must all love one another.

MOTHER. Then you won't tell them who you are?

SON. Oh yes. I will. It is by that authority that I will teach them.

MOTHER. You'll put yourself in so much danger telling people that.

SON. Be that as it may, I will tell them.

MOTHER. Why?

SON. Because my message must come from a position of supreme authority.

MOTHER. "Love one another" is such a radical idea that it can only be taught by the Son of God?

SON. The depths to which I will ask them to go in order to practice true God-like love for their fellow beings is indeed a radical concept. Very frightening in fact for those of insufficient faith.

Pause.

MOTHER. Is it . . . possible for mere mortals to love that deeply?

SON. You do.

MOTHER. How? What have I done to demonstrate the kind of love you're talking about?

SON. Simply by placing the interests of others before your own.

MOTHER. What mother couldn't do that for her children or her husband or even—

SON. Yes, yes, very true. Even the heathen can love its own. But I will require that they love their enemies as well. They must embrace all people within the limits of their love. Everyone.

Pause.

MOTHER. That's impossible.

SON. That's what many will believe. But they are wrong. You do it every day.

MOTHER. I don't—

SON. Every day, Mother. Please forgive the reproving tone I am using, but you need to understand just how worthy you are. I don't know, perhaps you won't admit to your own goodness because you fear becoming too prideful. I wouldn't worry about that if I were you, for surely we must know—must be able to acknowledge—when we are doing, or have done, something right and good in the world. We must know that we are, or are not, following Father's commandments. We all know the difference between what is right and what is wrong, and we know which path we tread. We know. *(Pause.)* We know.

MOTHER. Not always.

SON. Mother, you taught your children, every day, that all men, all women—all people—are worthy of our love. As you mediated all those petty little differences between us children you made us understand that we should always think of the Other before ourselves.

MOTHER. I don't recall—

SON. By asking us these questions: How do you know that's what she meant? Do you think his intention was to hurt you? What do you suppose he feels about that? Is she truly as angry as you say? And you expected answers. And none of us could ever give them to you . . . because we were only thinking of ourselves.

MOTHER. Yes, but I was only talking about your siblings, not . . . the whole world.

SON. But your actions belie that claim. I watched you. When you had a difference with someone you always kept your feelings in check until you were fairly certain that you knew their true position. This extended even to those who oppress our people, our so-called enemies. *(Pause.)* This is what I will preach.

MOTHER. That we should love . . . include our enemies?

SON. Yes.

MOTHER. They will kill you for that.

SON. Yes, they will.

MOTHER *reacts with a small outcry which she immediately tries to contain.*

MOTHER. Don't do it. Don't go to them. Don't give them your life if all they're going to do is throw it away.

SON. Some of them won't. Some will listen. Some will hear me.

MOTHER. Enough to make it worth your effort?

SON. Oh, yes. If it saves only one . . . it will be worth the effort.

MOTHER. You didn't learn that from me. My love isn't great enough to allow me to open my arms to all the world and yet be content to embrace one soul.

SON. That will never be asked of you.

MOTHER. Only you. And I have no doubt that you can do it.

SON. But I won't have to. I already know many souls that will accept my sacrifice.

She looks at him sharply.

MOTHER. Sacrifice?

SON. Yes.

MOTHER. You're just going to give yourself to them?

SON. Yes.

MOTHER. Why? Shouldn't they have to earn your death?

SON. No. That is a gift. It's my life they will have to earn.

She stares at him for a long time.

MOTHER. And you have lived a remarkable life. But nothing you have done so far seems, to me at least, to have been anything that would be of such value that all of humankind should want to purchase it. Pardon me if I speak blasphemy.

SON. No. You are correct. But what I will do will be so valuable to them that the cost of purchasing it will be their own lives. *(Stunned, she opens her mouth to speak, but he cuts her off.)* What I mean is, that in order for humankind to make . . . what I will do effective in their lives, they will have to give their lives—live their lives for me . . . for my cause.

MOTHER. What could cost that— *(Pause.)* What will you do?

Pause.

SON. I— *(Pause.)* I . . . will—

MOTHER. You're shaking. What's wrong?

Light change. The SON *falls into a kneeling position in pale moonlight.*

SON. Father . . . I am ashamed to confess . . . that I am frightened. So very frightened. I have seen this moment in vision numerous times, and I have been preparing. Angels . . . have administered to me . . . guided me . . . I should be ready. And yet—. *(Pause.)* Father . . . I know you can do all things . . . that if it were possible you could remove this bitter cup . . . that I might not drink it. If it is possible . . . Father, please spare me the horror . . . the agony of this deed. *(Pause.)* Forgive me. I know that it is not possible. If it were an easy load to bear . . . any man could bear it. I am not any man. I am Your Son. *(Pause.)* Send me help, Father. Please strengthen me for the task. Otherwise, I fear I will lose heart and follow my own will, which is to shrink from Your will. Please, Father, help me. *(Pause. A bright, white light appears near the* SON. *The* SON *gains strength from this communion. Slowly, he is calmed. The white light fades. Pause.)* Father . . . Your will . . . not mine be done.

> *Immediately the* SON *is stricken with pain—however, this pain is not yet beyond any he has already suffered in his life. It is not yet beyond the pain that any other person has likely suffered. The* SON *bears most of this pain in silence. But, as the pain increases, vocalizations occur from time to time—deep groanings or hissings—but nothing very demonstrative. As his Atonement proceeds, the light around the* SON *begins to widen as it turns red. And as the* SON'S *pain increases the red deepens. If possible, it might be a nice effect to have the red light engulf the audience as well as the entire stage. At the ultimate moment, when the light is at its deepest, broadest red—when the Son can bear no more pain without dying—he opens his mouth to scream, but . . . Light change. And all that emerges is a whisper:*

SON. Mother.

She is there in an instant, holding her son, rocking him.

MOTHER. Hush. Hush, son. It's over now. The vision is gone. *(She strokes his head and continues to rock him as he calms down. Pause.)* You're all right. Everything's all right now.

Slowly, he regains his composure. He looks into his mother's eyes and smiles.

SON. Thank you. Thank you, Mother.

Looking into his eyes, she can still see the terror.

MOTHER. What did you see? *(Still breathing heavily, he cannot answer.)* What?

Pause.

SON. I saw . . . the end.

MOTHER. The end of what?

SON. Not the end . . . the beginning. Of me. My beginning, really.

Pause. His mother can hardly contain her emotions.

MOTHER. What happens?

Pause.

SON. We should go.

MOTHER. What happens! *(Pause.)* What happens!

SON. I will bear the weight . . . the pain . . . the sorrow, the guilt of all the sins, of all the people, of all the times, of all the worlds . . . at one moment.

MOTHER. No.

SON. Yes.

MOTHER. No man can do that.

SON. But the Son of Man will.

MOTHER. Don't. Please don't. It will kill you—.

SON. No—.

MOTHER. I can't bury my husband and my son on the same day—.

SON. It won't kill me. And it's not going to happen today.

MOTHER. Yes it is. *(Pause.)* If you tell me today . . . it happens today. And every day until I die.

Pause.

SON. It's going to happen. It must.

MOTHER. Why must it?

SON. Otherwise there is no salvation.

MOTHER. None?

SON. None at all.

Pause.

MOTHER. I see. *(Pause.)* And it won't kill you?

SON. Not quite.

Pause.

MOTHER. How is it then that you . . . ? How will you die? Who will kill you?

SON. Mother—

MOTHER. Tell me!

Pause.

SON. I will die on a cross. Soldiers will take my clothing and drive nails through my palms . . . and through my wrists and my feet. They will place a braid of thorns upon my head and they will call me King. (MOTHER *quietly sobs.*) After six hours, I will give up the ghost. They will pierce my side, and the fluids of a broken heart will flow out. And they will take me to a tomb much like this one.

MOTHER. All this for our salvation?

SON. Yes.

Pause.

MOTHER. Is there no other way?

SON. There is no other way. *(Pause.)* And I want you to be there.

MOTHER. NO!

SON. Please—.

MOTHER. No! No. No. I can't watch that happen. I can't even think about it.

She collapses, nearly fainting.

SON. Mother! *(He holds her, keeps her from falling all the way to the floor.)* Mother.

MOTHER. Oh, son. *(Pause.)* How can you ask that of me?

SON. I need you, Mother. I'll need you there. *(As his own tears begin to flow:)* In the last hour . . . the great God, my Father, will leave me. I must have you there. I must see your face . . . your sweet face. I must.

Pause.

MOTHER. Then I will be there.

SON. *(Embracing her tightly:)* Thank you. Thank you.

Pause.

MOTHER. Are you sure that you can do these things? How can it be possible?

SON. Yes . . . I can do it all. I will do it all. My body will endure the pain because God is my father. My heart will endure because you are my mother.

Weeping, she covers his face with kisses. As well as his palms, his wrists.

MOTHER. God bless you, my son. God bless you. For all the people, of all the times, of all the worlds, I thank you. Thank you. *(Pause.)* Thank you.

BLACKOUT

Farewell to Eden

Mahonri Mackay Stewart

About the Author

Mahonri Stewart was taking an introduction to theatre class at Utah Valley State College (later Utah Valley University), and the instructor, Mormon playwright and actor James Arrington, assigned the class to write a ten-minute scene. Stewart had already been working on the rough beginnings of a full-length period piece,[1] so he decided to write a scene from that pre-existing concept. The scene was read in front of class and Arrington liked what he saw. As he later told a reporter: "I slapped my hand down on the table, and said, 'Ladies and gentlemen, we have a playwright [in our midst]!' . . . I took Mahonri aside after class and said, 'This is a scene from a three-act play, isn't it?' And it was. There was such excellence of effort. His characters were believable and likable and interesting."

To Arrington, the next step was obvious. Stewart should write the play and bring it to him for a critique, "because if it's good, we'll produce it here at UVSC."[2]

Nearly a dozen drafts later, the result of this turning point in Stewart's life was the premiere of his first full-length play, *Farewell to Eden*, on November 13, 2003, in UVSC's Black Box Theater. Naturally, Arrington, who had become a mentor to Stewart, directed the production.

Of that first run, BYU playwriting professor Eric Samuelsen wrote: "I had high expectations, which the play more than lived up to. Mahonri Stewart: remember that name . . . There's genuine wit and bite in the dialogue, and the characters are sharply drawn. . . . It's a tremendous debut."

---

1   "I was sitting in the Provo Temple during an endowment session. I had just returned from my mission to Australia and was pondering the big "WHAT NEXT?" At that juncture you're feeling kind of vulnerable. On a mission your life had been prescripted and focused and deeply meaningful for a couple of years, but afterwards you are thrown back into a whole gamut of choices and possibilities and terrifying realities that need to be taken care of. *I* was thrown into that gamut, that whirlpool of possibilities . . . not all of them reassuring. That's when the voice came into my mind. It was clear and precise, very calm: "Write a British play." That small shard of personal revelation was specific enough, but also open enough, to give me both direction and freedom. I knew I could write a play. I went home comforted and motivated." Mahonri Stewart, "Farewell to Eden: 10 Years Later," *And My Soul Hungered*, http://mahonristewart.blogspot.com/2013/04/farewell-to-eden-reflections-10-years.html (accessed May 6, 2013).

2   Elizabeth Bennett, "The Play's His Thing," *Provo Daily Herald*, October 2004, Life and Style, B1–B2.

The play went on to have an extended, sold-out run. Subsequently, it was accepted as one of five full-length productions to compete in the regional level of the Kennedy Center American College Theater Festival, held that year in San Bernardino, California. During the festival, KC/ACTF playwriting chair and New York University playwriting professor Gary Garrison said that *Farewell to Eden* was one of the "most intelligently written plays I have read in a decade."[3] Stewart was then invited to attend the KC/ACTF's National Festival in Washington, D. C., where he went on to receive a "National Selection Team Fellowship Award" and second place for the KC/ACTF's "National Playwriting Award."

Farewell to Eden had a revival produced by Stewart's organization, Zion Theatre Company, at the Provo Theatre, January 15–25, 2010. The *Deseret News* said of the revival: "*Farewell to Eden* is brilliant. It's complicated, not very predictable and has a lot of depth and characterization."[4] Nan McCulloch wrote in her review for the Association for Mormon Letters:

> *Farewell to Eden* is intelligent and extremely well-written. . . . *Farewell to Eden* will have widespread appeal for mainstream audiences and for Mormons, though it is most certainly not a Mormon play. It is a morality play without being didactic. There were no last minute conversions or declarations of love, no happy endings tied up with pretty bows and no forever afters into the sunset. Thoroughly Mormon Mahonri has written a fine crossover piece.[5]

After *Farewell to Eden*, UVU went on to produce Stewart's *Legends of Sleepy Hollow*,[6] loosely based on Washington Irving's short story. (Incidentally, the cast included Anne Ogden, who would become Stewart's wife.) That script would later win the Hale Centre Theatre's "Ruth and Nathan Hale Comedy Playwriting Award" (with *Farewell to Eden* taking second place; thus, Stewart won both top prizes that same year).

Since then Stewart has had a good many more of his plays receive full productions: *Friends of God*,[7] about the events leading up to the martyrdom of Mormon prophet

---

3   This conversation occurred between Gary Garrison, James Arrington, and Mahonri Stewart at the festival.

4   Sharon Haddock, "*Farewell to Eden* Absorbing, but Bleak," *Deseret News*, January 18, 2010, http://www.deseretnews.com/article/705359376/Farewell-to-Eden-absorbing-but-bleak.html (accessed September 24, 2012).

5   Nan McCulloch "Farewell to Eden," AML-Discussion Board, http://forums.mormonletters.org/yah_poststt838_STEWART-Farewell-to-Eden.aspx; and AML Review Archives, http://aml-online.org/Reviews/Review.aspx?id=4660 (accessed May 27, 2012).

6   Performed by UVU in the Black Box Theater on October 14–23, 2004. Another production was put up by Zion Theatre Company at the Castle Outdoor Amphitheater in Provo, Utah, October 7–15, 2011.

7   Performed by Art City Playhouse in Springville, Utah, January 15–30, 2006.

Joseph Smith; *Rings of the Tree*,[8] a theological fantasy which has manifested itself into two versions, a more traditional version and a multimedia version; *Swallow the Sun*,[9] about the early life of C. S. Lewis; *Prometheus Unbound*,[10] an allegory for Christianity using Greek myths and archetypes; *March of the Salt Soldiers: The Utah War*,[11] which he co-wrote with James Arrington; *Uneaten Cantaloupe*,[12] an "anti-absurdist" farce; *The Opposing Wheel*[13] (a modern Arthurian fantasy); *A Roof Overhead* (a drama about a Mormon family who take in an atheistic tenant which creates cultural tensions between the two groups)[14]; as well as three sets of short plays, *Immortal Hearts and Other Plays*,[15] *Jinn and Other Myths*,[16] and *The Death of Eurydice and Other Short Plays*.[17]

One of Stewart's more well-known plays is *The Fading Flower*, which tells the story of Joseph Smith's family many years after his martyrdom. Although the play deals with all of Joseph's children, including Joseph Smith III and Julia Murdock Smith, the crux of the play's action centers around the relationship between the little known but fascinating figure of the Smiths' youngest son, David Hyrum Smith, and his mother, Emma.

Although a negative review in the *Deseret News* said the play needed some "trimming and tightening,"[18] Nan McCulloch's review for the Association for Mormon Letters gave the play high praise:

---

8   The traditional theater version was performed in UVU's Black Box Theater on September 6–8, 2007. The multimedia version was performed by Zion Theatre Company at the Off Broadway Theatre in Salt Lake City, February 3–4, 2012, and at the Grove Theatre in Pleasant Grove, Utah, on February 7–13, 2012.
9   Performed by the New Play Project at Provo Theatre Company, May 16–24, 2008.
10 Performed by the BYU Experimental Theatre Company in the Nelke Theatre, July 31–August 9, 2008.
11 Premiered at UVU in the Center Stage and Ragan Theaters on September 10, 2008. It also had performances at the Salt Lake Public Library and the Caine Lyric Theatre in Logan, Utah.
12 Performed by the New Play Project at Provo Theatre Company, November 7–15, 2008.
13 Performed by Zion Theatre Company at the Castle Theatre in Provo, Utah, on September 2–10.
14 Performed by Zion Theatre Company at the Little Brown Theatre in Springville, Utah, April 16–28, 2012. It received a second production through Binary Theatre Company in Tempe, Arizona, October 12–21, 2012.
15 Performed by Zion Theatre Company at the Provo Theatre in Provo, Utah, on July 16–19, 2011.
16 Performed by Zion Theatre Company at the Off Broadway Theatre in Salt Lake City on November 18–19, 2011.
17 Performed by Zion Theatre Company at the Off Broadway Theatre in Salt Lake City on August 10–18, 2012.
18 Sharon Haddock, "*The Fading Flower* Tells Little Known Story," *Deseret News*, Wednesday, June 3, 2009.

Stewart is ever the writer of brilliant dialogue. This piece is so powerful and beautifully written it demands competent actors to match the material. These talented and sensitive actors are up for the task and are superb as they bring to life some of the most important players in our early church history. . . . I am appreciative of Stewart's courage in writing this bold, candid, historically authentic work honoring Emma Hale Smith. The play is an important historical achievement.[19]

When interviewed by *Mormon Artist* about the inspiration for *The Fading Flower* Stewart gave the following reply:

I was on the last leg of my mission when I had a dream where I saw a black-and-white photograph of Joseph and Emma Smith's family. Joseph was a kind of ghost standing to the side, and Emma and the children were all very somber-looking, except for Julia, who was in bright color (which is significant because she becomes a kind of truth teller in the play). I woke up with this very intense, beautiful feeling and had all of these thoughts tumbling into my head. I had to grab a pencil, and then I was writing down all these things that really surprised me—things about Emma, things about Joseph F. Smith visiting her while he was on his mission, a whole slew of things I had no clue about but (when I did my research later) ended up being true.[20]

That initial dream and the following research after his mission became the basis for *The Fading Flower*. Stewart's play *Swallow the Sun* is another of his plays that has received attention. The play centered on the conversion to Christianity of the young C. S. Lewis, author of the *Chronicles of Narnia* and other seminal Christian fiction/apologetics. The play generated a lot of interest, due to C. S. Lewis's popularity among Mormons. The *Deseret News* called it an "intriguing and compelling production. . . . The play has a fascination about it that holds the audience's attention. . . . The story line is wonderful."[21]

Although New Play Project's first production of the play was positively received, the Utah Theatre Bloggers wrote a scathing review of Zion Theatre Company's 2012 remount of the show calling it a "step down" from C. S. Lewis and took strong issue with both the script and the cast.[22] However, Front Row Reviewers Utah had a polar opposite

---

19   Nan McCulloch, "The New Play Project: *Fading Flower* (drama)," May 30, 2009, Association for Mormon Letters, *http://www.aml-online.org/Reviews/Review.aspx?id=4565* (May 30, 2012).
20   David Habben, "Mahonri Stewart," interviewed for *Mormon Artist*, Issue 5 (May 2009): 33.
21   Roger L. Hardy, "*Swallow the Sun* Compelling Conversion Story," *Deseret News*, May 20, 2008, *http://www.deseretnews.com/article/700227342/Swallow-the-Sun-compelling-conversion-story.html?pg=al* (accessed August 7, 2012).
22   Julia Shumway, "*Swallow the Sun* Is a Significant Step Down from the Source Material,"

reaction of the show (even down to the Ken Foody's portrayal of C. S. Lewis), giving an extremely positive review of the show. Front Row Reviewers said that "you will laugh, you will think, and you will enjoy it."[23] Meanwhile Scott Hales at *The Low-Tech World* wrote, "As a play *Swallow the Sun* is well-written, funny, and thought provoking. . . . *Swallow the Sun* is a captivating journey from doubt to belief."[24] Jerry Earl Johnston, a religion writer at the *Deseret News*, also reviewed the play very positively. Johnston appreciated that Stewart didn't avoid the controversies in the life of C. S. Lewis: "To his credit, playwright Stewart doesn't gloss over such things, but allows them to find their own level. He lets the audience decide what to think, while lobbying for us to dwell on Lewis's incredible insights into Christianity and the souls who choose to embrace it. I liked the play very much."[25]

Having long loved the work of C. S. Lewis, Stewart had some very meaningful experiences in writing the play, tapping into parts of himself that lay even beyond his love for Lewis's books:

> After my son Hyrum Irving was born, and I was with my wife at the hospital for a couple of days, she finally sent me home. . . . I got home from the hospital. I was filled with very poignant, spiritual feelings as I finished it and, unconsciously, placed my son's initials into C. S. Lewis's final line: "I am HIS."
>
> The play is also very connected to my dad, George Stewart . . . so in my mind it's connected to him and to my son in very strong ways. In many ways, it's a play about fathers and sons, including C. S. Lewis's (and, consequently, my) relationship with his (my) Heavenly Father.[26]

The Fading Flower and *Swallow the Sun* were both published in 2012 by Zarahemla Books, to positive reviews.[27]

Utah Theatre Bloggers, August 29, 2012 (accessed September 10, 2012).

23   Jennifer Mustoe and Caden Mustoe, "Mahonri Stewart's *Swallow the Sun* Will Inspire You—and Make You Laugh," August 25, 2012, http://www.frontrowreviewersutah.com/?p=168 (accessed September 10, 2012).

24   Scott Hales, "Faith in Darkness: A Review of Zion Theatre Company's 2012 Production of Mahonri Stewart's *Swallow the Sun*," *The Low Tech World*, September 5, 2012, http://www.low-techworld.org/2012/09/faint-in-darkness-review-of-zion.html (accessed September 10, 2012).

25   Jerry Earl Johnston, "Play Captures C. S. Lewis—Warts and All," *Deseret News*, September 16, 2012 (accessed September 24, 2012).

26   Habben, "Mahonri Stewart," 33–34.

27   See Laura Craner, "Bizarre and Beautiful Stories: a review of Mahonri Stewart's new book of plays," *A Motley Vision*, June 20, 2012, http://www.motleyvision.org/2012/review-of-mahonris-book-of-plays; Scott Hales, "Truth and Madness: A Review of Mahonri Stewart's *The Fading Flower* and *Swallow the Sun*," *The Low Tech World*, July 6, 2012, http://www.low-techworld.org/2012/07/truth-and-madness-review-of-mahonri.html; and David Allred, "*The Fading Flower* and *Swallow the Sun*," Association for Mormon Letters Discussion Board,

Besides his obvious debt to James Arrington's mentorship, Stewart also credits a great deal of his inspiration to Mormon playwrights whose plays he would watch at BYU in the late 1990s and 2000s—playwrights like Arrington, Elizabeth Hansen, Tim Slover, but most especially Eric Samuelsen:

> I was a freshman in high school. My familiarity with Mormon theatre up to that point was pretty much limited to participating in BYU's summer theatre camp for youth (EFY[28] for drama geeks) and watching the VHS versions of *Saturday's Warrior* and *My Turn on Earth* (which, like many Mormons of my generation, my family had grown up with). C. S. Lewis had recently ignited my imagination towards religious literature through a book of his poetry which I had stumbled upon at the library—thus I was exploring religious themes through my own poetry and early playwriting. Yet it was a general Christian religiousness, with very little strong-flavored Mormonism.[29]

In high school Stewart frequently attended the plays presented by BYU's Theatre Department, and thus it was a seemingly natural occurrence that his parents should take him to attend Eric Samuelsen's *The Seating of Senator Smoot*, playing in BYU's Margetts Theatre. Little did Stewart know that the production would change the direction he would take in his life: "Samuelsen's *The Seating of Senator Smoot* was certainly not the *Saturday's Warrior* I had grown up with. Here was something more challenging, more bold—and it created a change on my inner, spiritual geography." Then the following year he would see Samuelsen's next play *Gadianton*: "Even more than *Senator Smoot*, this play struck very deep chords within me. I didn't then, nor do I now consider myself, a liberal (I rather buck at political labels, actually. I think they're too confining). Yet this play was able to present to me the plight of the "laborer in Zion" . . . in such an intelligent, persuasive and spiritually personal way, [that the] natural barriers and prejudices I had built up in myself melted against the sheer humanity and vision of Samuelsen's work."[30]

Stewart's heightened use of language has often been cited in reviews of his work, both positively and negatively. He often purposely uses a heightened and poetic style of speech. This approach has not been without its detractors, a fact he is cognizant of:

> One of my greatest strengths is also my greatest weakness: my love for the English language. In my period pieces, it usually works in my favor, but it also

---

June 25, 2012, http://forums.mormonletters.org/yaf_postst1284_Stewart-The-Fading-Flower-and-Swallow-the-Sun-reviewed-by-David-Allred.aspx (accessed September 13, 2012).

28 EFY (Especially for Youth) is a religiously oriented, summer youth camp held for teenagers by Brigham Young University.

29 Mahonri Stewart, "Mormon Theater: The Fabulous Invalid," *A Motley Vision*, posted April 29, 2006; http://www.motleyvision.org/2006/mormon-theater-the-fabulous-invalid (accessed September 14, 2012).

30 Ibid.

comes back to bite me sometimes. I'm wordy. Certain friends have affectionately termed some segments in my plays as "Mahonrilogues." I'm starting to become more aware of that, though.[31]

However, with his critics, Stewart has also had supporters of his style and work. McCulloch, in writing about Stewart's *Swallow the Sun*, said: "Stewart is a master writer of rich dialogue, clever and scintillating in the style of Oscar Wilde and George Bernard Shaw. This is a very good play, befitting a fascinating, worthy protagonist in the historical character of C. S. Lewis, whose thoughtful writings on Christian themes include *The Screwtape Letters* and *The Chronicles of Narnia*."[32]

In addressing Stewart's "wordiness," Scott Hales wrote of *Swallow the Sun*, "Critics of Stewart's often cite wordiness as one of his flaws, but the eruption of language that occurs in this play hardly seems out of place for character like [C. S. Lewis] and his friends, all of whom are artists and thinkers that love the sound of their own voice."[33]

In her review of Stewart's play *Rings of the Tree*, McCulloch once again praised Stewart's style: "*Rings of the Tree* has broad appeal. . . . The thought-provoking plot twists and turns make the play interesting and keep the audience fully engaged. This is a play you can't leave at the theater, you take it home with you. Stewart has a gift for writing dialogue. His conversations are well thought out and go a long way to developing the characters."[34]

McCulloch has also noted various themes that crop up again and again in Stewart's work. In addition to his recurring Mormon elements, she has noted another strong pattern, "I have come to expect Stewart's heroines to be feminists. That seems to be a hallmark in most of his plays."[35]

Stewart has also mentioned that mythology plays into much of his work, especially in *Rings of the Tree*, *Swallow the Sun*, *Prometheus Unbound*, "Jinn," "The Death of Eurydice," *Manifest*, and *The Opposing Wheel*: "I'm in love with the ideas that C. S. Lewis and J. R. R. Tolkien discussed about Christianity being the 'true myth.' I believe that the Holy Ghost has revealed truths in many cultures and many mythologies, a kind of pre-existent memory that comes tumbling out in the form of stories. It connects in my mind to the psychologist Carl Jung's idea of a collective consciousness, and to Joseph Campbell's recurring mythical archetypes he discusses in *A Hero of a Thousand Faces*."[36]

---

31 Habben, "Mahonri Stewart," 32–33.
32 Nan McCulloch, "Understandest Thou Me?" *Irreantum* 8, no. 2 (2006): 203.
33 Hales, "Faith in Darkness: A Review of Zion Theatre Company's 2012 Production of Mahonri Stewart's *Swallow the Sun*."
34 Nan McCulloch, "*Rings of the Tree* (drama)," AML-List, September 2007. http://www.aml-online.org/Reviews/Review.aspx?id=4172 (accessed November 3, 2010).
35 Nan McCulloch, "*Farewell to Eden*," Association for Mormon Letters Discussion Board, January 20, 2010, http://forums.mormonletters.org/yaf_postst838_STEWART-Farewell-to-Eden.aspx (accessed September 24, 2012).
36 Mahonri Stewart, "Manifestation: Personal Revelation and Art," *Proving Contraries*,

These elements, combined with Stewart's desire to recapture a lost sensibility rather than to march to a contemporary drummer, has given his work a distinct aesthetic, which has exposed him to the skeptical criticism of some and the praise of others.

One thing Stewart has made clear is that, even when his plays will not always be Mormon-centric, his beliefs will always be visible in the subtext:

> I really can't separate my beliefs from my work, even when it's disguised. It's too much infused into who I am. Some people have called me out on that. They seem almost embarrassed for me at times, and a little patronizing. One of the times that happened was when *Farewell to Eden* went to the KC/ACTF regional festival . . . We had hugely positive responses from the non-Mormon audiences and judges . . . Ironically, however, when I approached a professor from BYU about it, he was extremely critical. The Mormon elements were too much for him. That jarred me and I've thought about it a lot since then.

After graduating from UVU, Stewart and his family moved to Arizona to accept a job as a theatre and creative writing teacher for a charter school in Mesa. While teaching in Arizona, Stewart applied to Arizona State University's MFA program for a degree in dramatic writing, was accepted, and is currently working toward that degree. He also founded Zion Theatre Company in 2010, which is continuing to produce his work, as well as the work of others, in Utah.

Two controversial productions of Stewart's *A Roof Overhead* were produced, one in April 2012 by Zion Theatre Company at the Little Brown Theatre in Springville, Utah, and the other in October 2012 by Arizona State University's Binary Theatre Company, with a largely non-Mormon cast. The play polarized critics and audiences, earning both praise and criticism. Some saw the play as too aggressive against secularists, while, oppositely, some saw it as too positive toward the secular characters and aggressive toward its Mormon characters.[37] Contradicting that position, some saw it as too pro-Mormon, even calling it "Mormon apologetics."[38] Yet there were many who were moved by the performance, with reports of emotional outpourings at the play's cathartic ending being common, responding to its themes of love and tolerance, despite the play's heightened conflicts between ideologies.

In the Association for Mormon Letters blog *Dawning of a Brighter Day*, James Goldberg called the play a "flagrant foul," taking strong issue with the play's commentary on New Atheism; hyperbolically calling the show a "blood libel" against atheists (which is a bit of a paradox, considering the play promotes tolerance for opposing beliefs); and

---

http://provingcontraries.blogspot.com/2009/12/manifestations-personal-revelation-and.html (accessed May 30, 2012).

37 One audience member asked a member of the cast, "Why does he hate Mormons so much?"
38 Russell Warne, "A Roof Overhead Needs Remodeling," Utah Theatre Bloggers, April 23, 2012, http://www.utahtheatrebloggers.com/10840/a_roof_overhead_needs_room_for_improvement (accessed September 8, 2012).

calling it a "moral obligation" to oppose the play.[39] On the other side of the debate, Margaret Blair Young's review of *A Roof Overhead*, also for *Dawning of a Brighter Day*, was very positive (especially appreciating Stewart's feminist themes touching on diversity and the Divine Feminine): "Stewart's characters are all strong, all opinionated, and all delightfully quirky in ways that help the audience suspend disbelief. An audience member could come to the play over several performances and glean new insights to his various themes of diversity, family bonds and the dimensions of maternal influence."

Despite the strong criticism some had against the play, the Association for Mormon Letters honored *A Roof Overhead* with the Award for Drama in 2012. In the citation of the award, the judge said:

> *A Roof Overhead* . . . exemplifies what I like most about Mormon theatre: real Mormons, in real situations, who do their best to overcome their weaknesses, who don't always succeed in the time-frame of the play, yet leave the audience with hope that a resolution will be forthcoming . . .
>
> You couldn't find a more diverse (and interesting) set of characters. . . .
>
> As to be expected with a Mahonri Stewart play, the title *A Roof Overhead* is thematically telling. What happens under the roof of this home full of loving but flawed people is what draws us into their lives . . . even when the characters steer us into uncomfortable areas that still challenge many members of the Church today (like, for instance, Blacks and the Priesthood), we are presented with multiple sides of those issues in a fair and balanced manner. . . . The father Maxwell Fielding is fond of saying throughout the play, "It's about being fair." *A Roof Overhead* is nothing if not fair.
>
> Stewart's skill at dialogue and characterization, mingled with just the right amount of humor, drama, and pathos, anchors us to the play . . .
>
> What this play says to Mormons is, "We are not alone in the world. We need to learn to get along with others of different, or sometimes, no faith."[40]

Stewart has now been brought full circle in his experience as a playwright, as a tenth anniversary production of *Farewell to Eden* was produced by Zion Theatre Company at the Echo Theatre in Provo, Utah, on April 15-27, 2013. As far as can be currently deduced, the revival was universally praised by all the critics who wrote about the production.

Blair Howell at the *Deseret News* called it a "finely crafted play" and a "uniquely rewarding character study that is so splendidly played as to make it highly recommended."[41]

---

39 James Goldberg, "In Defense of Grumpiness: A Review of 'Brothers,' 'Quietly,' and A Roof Overhead," August 9, 2012, *http://blog.mormonletters.org/?p=4912* (accessed September 19, 2012).

40 Margaret Blair Young, "Report on AML Conference 2013 and List of Awards," *Dawning of a Brighter Day*, March 31, 2013, *http://blog.mormonletters.org/?p=6111*, accessed April 8, 2013.

41 "Theatre Review: 'Farewell to Eden' is Richly Rewarding Character Study," April 21, 2013,

Kara Henry at *Front Row Reviewers* said, "The script is one that makes me, a former English major, wish I was back in school so I could trot off to write a paper about its symbolism or perhaps deconstruct it from a feminist point of view. . . . Witty banter, symbolism, broad range of characters, historical figures popping in and out, romantic stories that avoid clichés, and did I mention witty banter and fully fleshed out characters? Please sign me up."[42]

Even Russell Warne at the Utah Theatre Bloggers, who had previously been very critical of Stewart's work, was highly complimentary of the script and production. Warne called *Farewell to Eden* a "highly literary script" that is "full of plot twists and authentic character development. . . . This production probably has the most pleasantly understated acting that audiences can find in Northern Utah right now. This tenth anniversary production of the play would be a thought provoking experience for anyone who catches *Farewell to Eden*."[43]

Mormon writer and former Association for Mormon Letters president Marilyn Brown was enthusiastic about *Farewell to Eden* and considered it an indicator of the kind of work that is coming of age in Mormon drama:

> [*Farewell to Eden*] is successful because 1) in the timeless style of Shakespeare, it relentlessly develops one major character (supported well by others, of course) until we fully see both her radiance and flaws, 2) it follows a timeline of integrated scenes that furnish variety and action leading to an appropriate climax and denouement, and 3) the "Mormonism" is almost incidental, yet organic to the story, not solicitous . . . or suspect. . . . I admit I'm getting more and more impatient to see great Mormon literature before I die! Thanks to Mahonri, we're coming closer. *Eden* is a work of art that aspiring Mormon writers should STUDY!! For now—if anybody is rising to the top—one of our best is Mahonri Stewart. I loved his *A Roof Overhead* and now this *Farewell to Eden*. So a big hooray for quality! It's coming![44]

Section C 13.

42 "*Farewell to Eden* is Gloriously Entertaining," http://frontrowreviewersutah.com/?p=1171 (accessed May 6, 2013).

43 "Say Hello to *Farewell to Eden*," http://utahtheatrebloggers.com/15248/say-hello-to-farewell-to-eden (accessed May 6, 2013).

44 Andrew Hall, "This Week in Mormon Literature, April 29, 2013," *Dawning of a Brighter Day*, http://blog.mormonletters.org/?p=6302 (accessed May 6, 2013).

About *Farewell to Eden*

Farewell to Eden premiered at Utah Valley State College in the Black Box Theater, November 13–22, 2003. It also played at California State University in San Bernardino in February 2004 for the Kennedy Center American College Theater Festival. The original cast and crew were:

CAST

Georgiana Highett: Margie Johnson
Stephen Lockhart: Aaron Wilden
Thomas Highett: Brandon Michael West
Catherine Highett: Amber James
Darrel Fredericks: Samuel Snow Schofield
Mary: Angela Youmans
Harold Lowe: Kenneth F. Brown
Esther Whitefield: Tatum Langton
Hannah Whitefield: Fallon R. Hanson
Brigham Young: Sam Davis
John Taylor: Russ Bennett

CREW

Director: James Arrington
Stage Manager: Sarah Dawn Barley
Scenic Designer: Randy Seely
Costume Designer: Mary Haddock
Lighting Designer: Devan Byrne

Farewell to Eden was produced by Zion Theatre Company at the Provo Theatre, January 15–25, 2010, with the following cast and crew:

CAST

Georgiana Highett: Jamie Denison
Stephen Lockhart: William McAllister
Thomas Highett: Derrick Legler
Catherine Highett: Rebecca Minson
Darrel Fredericks: Amos Omer
Mary: Kaye Woodworth
Esther Whitefield: Hailey Nebeker

Hannah Whitefield: Tanika Little
Brigham Young: Thom Neil
John Taylor: Jeff Bond
Harold Lowe: G. Randall King

CREW

Director: Kathryn Little
Stage Manager: Andrew Cannon
Costume and Scenic Designer: Anna-Marie Johnson

The ten-year anniversary production of *Farewell to Eden* was produced by Zion Theatre Company at the Echo Theatre, April 15–27, 2013, with the following cast and crew:

CAST

Georgiana Highett: Sarah Stewart[45]
Stephen Lockhart: Joseph Vernon Reidhead
Thomas Highett: Kevin O'Keefe
Catherine Highett: Cabrielle Andersen
Darrel Fredericks: Wes 'Milosh' Tolman
Mary: Debra L. Woods
Esther Whitefield: Mckenzie Steele Foster
Hannah Whitefield: Heather McGregor
Harold Lowe/Brigham Young: Matthew Davis
John Taylor: Patrick Newman

CREW

Director: Ronnie Stringfellow
Stage Manager: Matthew Fife
Scenic Designer: Ronn Andersen
Costume Designer: Brooke Wilkins
Lighting Designer: Jeffrey and Julianna Blake
Music Composition: Nathaniel Drew
Poster Design: Liz Pulido

---

45 Incidentally, Mahonri Stewart's sister.

*Dedicated to
James Arrington,
who has done so much to encourage
and improve this play. He has become
a trusted mentor and made this
playwright believe his craft is worthwhile.*

TIME: 1840

PLACE: Edenbridge, England

Act One

SCENE 1

The Highett Household, a wealthy home, well furnished, and with two portraits. The portraits are of Alexander and Susan Highett, both of whom are now deceased. Enter GEORGIANA HIGHETT, CATHERINE HIGHETT, THOMAS HIGHETT, *and* HAROLD LOWE. GEORGIANA *is in her mid- to late twenties, perhaps even in her thirties. It is obvious that she is high born, but she is not obviously beautiful. Her dress is severe and shows no sign of lace or embroidery.* THOMAS *is in his late twenties and* CATHERINE *is anywhere from eighteen to twenty.* CATHERINE *has a distinct beauty to her.* HAROLD *is nearly sixty, a dignified gentleman of the upper classes. All three of the Highett siblings wear black armbands signifying mourning.*

HAROLD. A very sad business, Miss Georgiana.

GEORGIANA. We do appreciate your kindness in visiting us so often. I don't think Father ever had a truer friend than you, Mr. Lowe. After Mother's death, Father found great comfort in you.

HAROLD. Ah, Susan—he wept like a child over that woman. The only tears I ever saw him shed.

GEORGIANA. And now you give the same kindness to his children. What you have done for our family will not be forgotten.

HAROLD. Don't forget that I find great comfort in all of you, Miss Georgiana. Your father's death will not be the end of the Highett line.

THOMAS. Yes, the torch must go on and all that. We keep Father's works alive.

HAROLD. I assume that you have taken over the estate and your father's business, Thomas? You have a good sense for it.

THOMAS. I make an effort.

CATHERINE. Thomas has surprised us all, really.

HAROLD. And how do you fare, Catherine?

CATHERINE. It has been hard. But I'm slowly easing myself back into society.

GEORGIANA. Not even Catherine has been able to stomach such things at a time like this. It was the first instance I had ever seen her miss a dance. That was more earth-shattering than if Parliament had suddenly been invaded by the French.

CATHERINE. And, of course, you're back to your sharp tongue.

THOMAS. It was nice for a while during our mourning process, Mr. Lowe, that these two were finally learning to be civil to each other.

HAROLD. Well, at least you have all survived with your humor intact.

CATHERINE. Ah, the wit of intelligent company heals all wounds. Isn't that right, Georgiana?

GEORGIANA. I wouldn't know, Catherine. You haven't said an intelligent thing for years.

HAROLD. It looks like things are back to status quo then. All is well.

GEORGIANA. Not all is well yet, Mr. Lowe. We've still much to pass through until our mourning is done.

HAROLD. He was so proud of what you were becoming, Georgiana. He used to tell me all sorts of stories. Always bragging and bullying about his daughter. I hear that you've made quite the name for yourself. The president of Edenbridge's debating society. On the council for the Philosophical Association. A political advocate. You occupy prominent positions. Especially for a woman.

GEORGIANA. Yes, *for a woman*. You might as well put me in a zoo of rare species. Along with the unicorns and the phoenixes. Right now I'm a spectacle, a curiosity. Nothing more.

HAROLD. I have something here for you, Georgiana.

HAROLD *takes out a rectangular box and hands it to* GEORGIANA.

GEORGIANA. For me?

CATHERINE. What is it?

HAROLD. Open it, dear.

GEORGIANA *opens the box to find an ornately carved dagger.*

GEORGIANA. Whatever could you have—oh! It's—it's magnificent.

HAROLD. Your father gave it to me.

GEORGIANA. Truly?

HAROLD. He said, "Keep it sharp, Harold. Keep it sharp. Cut off all those that oppose you with a keen, dangerous wit. Dissect their logic, dig out their arguments, slice through all of their defenses." I think it's appropriate to pass it onto you now, Georgiana. You are truly your father's daughter.

CATHERINE. And what does that make me?

GEORGIANA. Your father's *other* daughter.

HAROLD. I've brought you and Thomas your favorites—

HAROLD *brandishes a candy box.*

CATHERINE. Sweets! Oh, Mr. Lowe, you always remember the sweets!

THOMAS *nabs the sweets before* CATHERINE *can get to them.*

THOMAS. *(With an impish smile.) My* sweets!

CATHERINE. Thomas!

Exit CATHERINE *and* THOMAS.

HAROLD. Especially with your father's passing, I thought it important to give this gift to you now—I have had it in mind to pass it on to you for many years now.

GEORGIANA. Thank you. I will stay true to the gift.

HAROLD. You will do great things. There will be those who try to stop you. Just remember that you are a stronger force and a keener mind.

GEORGIANA. A Highett.

HAROLD. A Highett. But I ought to leave now, if I am to make it back to London in time.

GEORGIANA. Thomas! Catherine! I can't thank you enough, Mr. Lowe. You've been very thoughtful.

Enter THOMAS *and* CATHERINE.

GEORGIANA. You're welcome, my dear.

THOMAS. Good-bye, Mr. Lowe.

CATHERINE. Good-bye.

HAROLD. Farewell to you all, for now.

Exit HAROLD.

CATHERINE. So why do *you* get the dagger?

GEORGIANA. Obviously, Mr. Lowe thinks the symbolism applies to me. You're not sharp enough to cut bread.

CATHERINE. It's a *family* heirloom.

THOMAS. Oh, stop it, you two. May I see it, Georgiana?

>   THOMAS *takes the dagger and inspects it curiously.*

THOMAS. My, it's a rather frightening-looking thing, isn't it?

GEORGIANA. It's noble.

>   THOMAS *lunges forward with the dagger.*

THOMAS. Tally ho!

GEORGIANA. Oh, do be careful with it, you silly boy!

CATHERINE. Men and their toys. You are such a sparrow, Thomas.

>   THOMAS *brandishes the dagger about, swiping it in the air and playing at a mock battle.*

THOMAS. Nice. This is nice. *(Considering the dagger.)* Just think of it—Thomas the Conqueror! Does the dagger match my shoes?

GEORGIANA. I think it's time to give it back, young Master Thomas—

THOMAS. You seem to forget that *I'm* the oldest here.

GEORGIANA. The oldest, perhaps, but who's the wisest?

THOMAS. You know, I've always thought I could be a military man. Just think of me in a war outfit. With brass buttons. Lots of brass buttons. And the other shiny things they put on you.

GEORGIANA. Medals?

THOMAS. And the dangly yellow things on the shoulders—and, and a sword. A sharp sword to match the dagger. And a plume of feathers on my hat. All along here, like this! Like the Romans used to wear on their helmets.

GEORGIANA. If you want a complete Roman outfit, we can probably get you a leather skirt.

THOMAS. Shiny boots! And white gloves! Ah, and Miss Jane Fields would be a perfect woman to stand by such a noble-looking man.

CATHERINE. You can't be serious.

THOMAS. Well, I must say that the gloves would be a necessity.

CATHERINE. Not the gloves. Jane Fields.

THOMAS. Why not? Miss Fields is a lovely woman.

CATHERINE. That hyena? She is as loud as a parrot. Does it not bother you that just three years ago she was a factory girl? It's vulgar.

THOMAS. It is not. She is a sweet girl. She calls me *Teddy*. And money is a definite attraction—you can't deny that. Her father worked hard in that factory and he worked smart.

CATHERINE. Smart? That donkey?

THOMAS. Are you so obsessed with the animal kingdom?

CATHERINE. Such class jumping ought to be guarded against!

THOMAS. Whatever you may think of Mr. Fields's personal manners, he is a mechanical and economic genius. He made himself indispensable there.

GEORGIANA. Thomas, are you being serious? This isn't one of your larks?

THOMAS. What about me is not serious? Am I painted up like some jester with bells and cap? What about me does not appear *serious?!*

Pause. GEORGIANA *and* CATHERINE *look at* THOMAS, *at each other and then look away.*

THOMAS. Well, Father would have approved. You know that he would have, Georgiana.

GEORGIANA *gazes at* THOMAS *momentarily, sincerely considering his statement. She looks back at her father's portrait, something stirring deep within her. But then, almost coldly:*

GEORGIANA. Papa still understood propriety.

THOMAS, *genuinely surprised by this response, goes to* GEORGIANA *and takes her by the hands.*

THOMAS. Please, Georgie, I would like your approval.

GEORGIANA. You are supposed to be the head of this family now.

THOMAS. But as we have seen, what is supposed to be, *(presenting* GEORGIANA *with the dagger)* and what is, are two different things.

GEORGIANA. I don't like Jane Fields, Thomas.

This visibly hurts THOMAS *for the slightest of moments, but then he checks himself and once again puts on the fop.*

THOMAS. Well, la dee da, you're always so serious, Georgie! Let's finish our card game—

CATHERINE. Yes, I was winning—

They begin to sit at the card table. Enter MARY.

MARY. Miss Georgiana, there is a gentleman here for you. Should I bring him in?

GEORGIANA. Did he leave his name?

MARY. Darrel Fredericks, mum.

CATHERINE. The publisher? What could he possibly want with *you*, Georgiana?

GEORGIANA. Well, do you think a publisher would wish to see you? To publish your autobiography perhaps? My, that would be fascinating reading. Chapter One, "Our Noble Heroine Gets Up and Does Her Hair." Chapter Two, "Our Estimable Heroine Goes to a Dinner Party." Chapter Three, "Our Majestic Heroine Goes into Town to Buy a Hat."

THOMAS. Didn't you see them at the assembly the other night, Catherine?

CATHERINE. No. Was Mr. Fredericks there?

GEORGIANA. You must have been too caught up with Mr. Johnson to notice. And Mr. James—and Mr. Baker—and Mr. Evanson—

THOMAS. He was paying the most rapt attention to Georgiana. Now where in the game were—

CATHERINE. To *Georgiana*? But he's so very handsome—very respected—

GEORGIANA. You are delightfully vain, aren't you, Catherine?

CATHERINE. Please, don't get me wrong, dear Georgiana—

GEORGIANA. No, I think I understand you quite clearly. I told Mr. Fredericks the other night that he was welcome to come to our home any time he pleased. We run in many of the same circles—thus, he and I are very well acquainted. Please, see him in, Mary.

MARY. Like a cricket on a skillet, mum.

Exit MARY.

GEORGIANA. Let's see if we can crack into the motivations of a man who would woo a she-troll.

THOMAS. Nonsense, Georgiana. *(Back to the cards.)* Ah, I can't remember where we were—

CATHERINE. I was winning.

GEORGIANA. Let's have Mr. Fredericks take a hand and we'll start over.

CATHERINE. But I was winning!

Enter MARY *with* DARREL FREDERICKS.

MARY. Mr. Darrel Fredericks.

Exit MARY.

DARREL. Miss Highett!

GEORGIANA. Why, Darrel, it is wonderful to see you again! I was wondering when you would take up my invitation. Sit down and play cards with us. Come, we've placed the table by the windows to take advantage of the warmth of the sun.

CATHERINE. Yes, it was so chilly this morning!

DARREL. *(Looking out the windows.)* Oh, what a beautiful view you have! And those gardens! What it would be to possess such gardens!

GEORGIANA. Come, Darrel, play!

They all sit to play.

DARREL. A pleasure. Certainly.

GEORGIANA. You will, of course, call me Georgiana, won't you? We've known each other long enough. I absolutely detest those wretched formalities.

DARREL. Of course.

GEORGIANA. I was just talking about you, Darrel. He is quite the accomplished man, you see, Catherine.

DARREL. All I can claim is my humble printing company.

GEORGIANA. Note how modest he is.

DARREL. We don't publish only books, but newspapers, journals, periodicals, and notices as well. But you are the one who most certainly impressed me, Georgiana. You're a woman of nobility. You're a woman of gentle feeling.

GEORGIANA. And my beauty?

DARREL. Why, that of a Greek goddess.

GEORGIANA. A Greek goddess! Note that, Catherine, a "Greek goddess." Artemis, the chaste huntress? Athene, the goddess of wisdom?

DARREL. Aphrodite, the goddess of beauty.

GEORGIANA. You are a detestable liar.

DARREL. Pardon me?

GEORGIANA. *(Laughs.)* I am hardly one of those simple women you are accustomed to luring in. You are as transparent as water.

DARREL. I don't understand what you mean.

GEORGIANA. Do you deny that you go from wealthy woman to wealthy woman, as if they were no more than sculptures in a museum, crafted for your own enjoyment?

CATHERINE. Georgiana, your manners are enough to repel an elephant.

THOMAS. Catherine!

GEORGIANA. Again with the animals—my, oh, my! Well, Catherine, let's see if I can come up with a few animals of my own.

CATHERINE. Look how she's treated this good gentleman here—

GEORGIANA. Suddenly Mr. Fredericks has become as fragile as a humming bird.

DARREL. *(To* CATHERINE.*)* Actually, I actually did not come to see your sister, Catherine. I came to see you.

GEORGIANA. As deceptive as a chameleon.

DARREL. I was hoping that through Georgiana I would meet the fair Catherine whom

I have heard so much about.

GEORGIANA. And as cunning as a fox.

DARREL. Since I was well acquainted with Georgiana, I was hoping that, through our friendship, she would introduce me to you.

CATHERINE. You came to see me?

GEORGIANA. You must be the most simple woman alive, Catherine.

CATHERINE. I did not know you were the jealous type.

GEORGIANA. Yes, as jealous as if you were dancing with a giant scorpion.

DARREL. Please, Georgiana, enough with the animals!

GEORGIANA. A shrieking owl.

CATHERINE. Someone ought to take those blades out of your mouth.

GEORGIANA. And someone ought to take that champagne out of your brain.

THOMAS. Now come, let us all be reasonable.

CATHERINE. You resent the fact that, when I am happily married, you will be an old spinster forever.

GEORGIANA. If you are going to marry the likes of Darrel Fredericks, I doubt you will ever be happy!

DARREL. Marry?

CATHERINE. I am sure Darrel would make a fine husband.

DARREL. *Husband?!*

GEORGIANA. I shall not marry because I will not have any man who is not worth having.

CATHERINE. Really, Georgiana, how could you be so rude to poor Mr. Fredericks?

DARREL. Poor? Ha! Really, ladies—

GEORGIANA. Most men seem to build up this flittering bird of a woman—a docile, brainless thing of insignificance—like *this* girl *(motioning to* CATHERINE*)*. If men desire such a tender beast, I do not find many men worth having.

THOMAS. On behalf of my gender, I'm flattered.

GEORGIANA. But do not fret, Darrel. You must understand that I am not so mean-spirited as I seem. I just like a nice battle. For me, it's a sign of affection. By the way—*(putting down her cards)* I win.

DARREL. *(Standing.)* You know, I am not very good at these games of chance. Perhaps I should leave you to enjoy yourselves.

CATHERINE. Oh please, do not feel compelled to leave on account of my sister, Darrel.

GEORGIANA. *(With a smile.)* Yes, I enjoy a good farce.

CATHERINE. Come, I want to show you the new furnishings in the ballroom—then you must see the gardens up close!

DARREL. I do not think Georgiana would like me to—

CATHERINE. But *I* would like you to.

DARREL. Well—all right then.

THOMAS. Let's all go together!

All look at THOMAS, *stupefied.*

THOMAS. As a group, you know, what.

GEORGIANA. *(Dryly.)* I am delighted. Thrilled. Ecstatic.

Exit CATHERINE *and* DARREL. THOMAS *grabs* GEORGIANA *before she can leave.*

THOMAS. Behave yourself.

GEORGIANA. I always behave myself.

THOMAS. No, you don't.

GEORGIANA. I can't help it that she doesn't know when she is being insulted.

THOMAS. Oh, she knows *when* she is being insulted. She just does not know *how* she is being insulted.

GEORGIANA. *(Laughs.)* What would I do without you, Thomas?

THOMAS. With Catherine as your sole company? Die of boredom, I suppose.

THOMAS *and* GEORGIANA *laugh and exit. After some moments, enter* MARY *with* STEPHEN LOCKHART. STEPHEN *is a handsome gentleman of the upper classes.*

MARY. My, we're in the mire with visitors today, aren't we? As stuffed as a duck on Christmas, I dare say. Sounds like they're in the ballroom.

MARY *heads toward the ballroom.*

STEPHEN. You don't recognize me, do you, Mary?

MARY. Should I? What did you say your name was again, sir?

STEPHEN. Stephen Lockhart.

MARY. Lockhart—oh my! Little Stevie Lockhart from Edenbridge School!

STEPHEN. Yes, the little school brat! Ha, ha! I was wondering when you would catch on.

MARY. Why, you have grown taller, sir—and filled out nicely! Imagine! Those were dramatic times in this household, sir.

STEPHEN. Yes, I remember. You should have heard the kind of things being bandied about when Georgiana and Catherine were allowed to enroll. The only girls ever allowed, you remember!

MARY. It made quite the fuss.

STEPHEN. Mister Highett and the schoolmaster called it their "great experiment"—their women's revolution didn't last long, however. He died soon after Catherine graduated and those two are still the only females to have graduated from Edenbridge School.

MARY. Don't tell them I told you this, but they used to come home crying.

STEPHEN. Georgiana as well?

MARY. Aye. The poor dears.

STEPHEN. Strange, I can't imagine Georgie crying. She always showed such a strong face. She took it bravely.

MARY. Oh, she has plenty of pluck, sir. She may rub some the wrong way, but whatever else can be said about her, she has plenty of pluck.

STEPHEN. Oh, this is strange being back. Edenbridge—this lovely piece of paradise! I loved it here. Graduating from Eden's school was like being cast out of paradise.

MARY. Childhood memories run deep, don't they, sir?

STEPHEN. Yes, they do. I am glad to see that you are just as free with the guests as you always were, Mary.

MARY. The Highetts have never been very strict with me about that sort o' thing. Oh, I can be proper when there's need, but you're practically family! You'll take a bit of cheek from an old woman. When you know the family as well as I do, then you can drop some of the formalities in the right company. I changed their nappies. They can't put on airs with me.

STEPHEN. Ah, *you* hold the family secrets! Surely there couldn't be any truly damaging information against them?

MARY. Every family has its unpleasant histories, sir. There's a thorn under every rose.

Enter GEORGIANA *and* DARREL. *They are too caught up in their argument to notice* STEPHEN *or* MARY *at first.*

GEORGIANA. Why do you persist in pursuing *my* company?

DARREL. Because Catherine and Thomas cannot keep up with my long legs, so I wish to amuse my time with you. How did you say it before? Oh, yes—"I enjoy a good farce."

GEORGIANA. The venom of your mouth would certainly cause the death of anyone, if your lips were not so small and petite.

DARREL. Oh, if you knew what else I have done with these lips, you would be jealous.

GEORGIANA. Hardly. The dim-witted damsels you court are simply moving, breathing pieces of porcelain with cotton in their heads.

Enter THOMAS *and* CATHERINE.

THOMAS. My, you two sprint when you argue, don't you?

CATHERINE. Why, who is this, Mary?

MARY. Prepare yourself, mum. This is Mr. Stephen Lockhart, mum!

GEORGIANA. *(Startled, noticing* STEPHEN *and* MARY *for the first time.)* Lockhart? Stephen—can it be?

STEPHEN. It certainly is, Georgie!

The three HIGHETTS *circle* STEPHEN *for a moment, much like birds of prey, but with the opposite intent. All of them speak simultaneously.*

GEORGIANA. *(Goes to* STEPHEN.*)* Stephen! Thomas, Catherine, it is Stephen!

THOMAS. Is that really you, old boy? Why I thought—

CATHERINE. It can't be—is it really—?

GEORGIANA. Why, I had never dreamed that I may see you again after graduation—I was devastated at the thought—

THOMAS. —you would have been far from here—well, how is that old cricket arm? Do you remember when—?

CATHERINE. I would hope you would forgive me for that time—

GEORGIANA. —but here you are! My confidante, my ally, my childhood friend! Could that possibly be you?

STEPHEN. *(Laughs.)* One at a time, one at a time! I did not die, you know.

The Highetts make a circle around STEPHEN, *chanting something quite enthusiastically in Latin, which is understood to be a relic from their childhood with* STEPHEN, *for* STEPHEN *joins in the chant. They laugh heartily.*

THOMAS. Why, it is good to see you, chap! You are a regular prodigal!

CATHERINE. My, oh, my, it *is* Stephen. I did not even recognize you. You're—you are quite different now.

STEPHEN. Well, I am taller.

CATHERINE. You did much more than grow taller.

STEPHEN. And you were that little girl who always made fun of her older sister's awkward friend.

CATHERINE. I would hope that you would consider that I had grown out of that peevish phase.

GEORGIANA. I wouldn't.

CATHERINE. I am much more adult than when you last saw me, am I not?

DARREL. *(Clearing his throat.)* Mm-hm!

CATHERINE. This is—uh—Darrel. Darrel—uh, yes, Mr. Darrel Fredericks.

STEPHEN. Mr. Stephen Lockhart. It is a pleasure to meet you, sir.

DARREL. I am sure it is.

GEORGIANA. You are a burst of sunshine in a dark time, Stephen.

STEPHEN. Yes, I read about your father's death. That is part of the reason that I thought I would come. My sincere condolences.

CATHERINE. Yes, Georgiana, he is sunshine! You are an absolute beacon, Stephen. I just hope that I have become as beautiful as you are handsome.

GEORGIANA. I believe that is the most blatant thing I have ever heard you say, Catherine—and that is saying a bit. Why, you have embarrassed Stephen. Hasn't she, Stephen?

STEPHEN. Well—

CATHERINE. Oh stop being a prude, Georgiana. It was a perfectly appropriate thing to say. Wasn't it, Stephen?

STEPHEN. I suppose I could say—

GEORGIANA. Do not feel compelled to answer that, Stephen. Well, Catherine, Darrel has come to see you and Stephen has come to see me—

CATHERINE. But—

GEORGIANA. So perhaps you and Thomas can show Darrel around the gardens, while I catch up with my dear friend.

CATHERINE. Oh, but—

DARREL. Yes, my dear, for once I agree with your sister.

> DARREL *takes* CATHERINE *by the arm and the two exit along with* THOMAS. *Exit* MARY.

GEORGIANA. Well, Stephen, you have changed, my friend!

STEPHEN. Have I?

GEORGIANA. Why, where is the ungainly, fumbling friend of mine? Where are his tousled hair and freckles? Where is my awkward, little, rich boy? All I see before me is a confident, polished gentleman.

STEPHEN. And you, Georgie! I am hearing all sorts of rumors!

GEORGIANA. It's rot—do not believe a word of it.

STEPHEN. But I *do* believe it. I knew you would turn into something impressive.

GEORGIANA. I am hardly something impressive.

STEPHEN. You were *always* something impressive. I am sure your father was very pleased.

STEPHEN. What a blow that must have been to you, Georgie.

GEORGIANA. The ache is beginning to recede. It was unexpected, but those last few days with him—he tried to instill strength in us. He wanted us to keep rising higher. Rising Highett. So the best way to comfort me at this time is not to dwell upon it. Especially with you here. Give me a way to serve you. Is there anything I can help *you* with?

STEPHEN. Can I be honest?

GEORGIANA. Hello, Honest.

STEPHEN. I will be frank then.

GEORGIANA. Hello, Frank.

STEPHEN. Oh, our childhood games! I had almost forgotten.

GEORGIANA. I hadn't.

STEPHEN. Oh, it is a joy to be with you again, Georgie—but I must admit, I had planned this trip even before I heard about your father. There is actually something I need assistance with. I heard that you could help me.

GEORGIANA. In what way?

STEPHEN. Do you remember my ambitions to be a writer?

GEORGIANA. Yes, I thought they were foolish notions at the time.

STEPHEN. I have finished something decent, Georgiana. Much more than decent actually. I dare say it is rather good! A period piece. A drama!

GEORGIANA. What is it about?

STEPHEN. Honor! Terror! Oppression! Revenge!

GEORGIANA. Amusing. You must let me read it.

STEPHEN. Oh, Georgie, how do I ask you this? I hear that you have become very influential. You are not far from London here and they say you go into the city to your home there quite a bit—people say that you *know* people and that people *know* you. People like publishers.

GEORGIANA. I see. *(Pause, disappointed, but then recovering:)* I am sure that I can find someone to take a look at it.

STEPHEN. Truly?

GEORGIANA. Publishers, publishers. I know quite a few, but which would be most suitable— There is Darrel—

STEPHEN. Is he a publisher?

GEORGIANA. Yes. Well, he says so. On second thought, I would not suggest *him*—why, of course! Our family knows a fine editor named Harold Lowe who was dear friend of my father's. Oh, if you had only been here earlier, he came by.

STEPHEN. Truly?!

GEORGIANA. *(Looking at Stephen squarely, having a sudden thought.)* Stephen—I wonder—

STEPHEN. You wonder what?

GEORGIANA. Hm. I think I know how I want to do this—why shouldn't we make a fine time of this?

STEPHEN. What do you mean?

GEORGIANA. Do you dance better than you used to?

STEPHEN. I always danced well!

GEORGIANA. Hm?

STEPHEN. Well—for someone my age I danced remarkably.

GEORGIANA. Hm?

STEPHEN. Ah, blast it all, Georgie! Yes, I dance better than I used to.

GEORGIANA. Good, because Harold's family loves assemblies, parties, balls, and the like. If I were to host one here and begged his presence—why, I am sure he would come.

STEPHEN. Oh, Georgiana, that is a wonderful idea! I knew I could count on your sharp mind. You always did impress me.

GEORGIANA. I did?

STEPHEN. There was no person in that school—boy or girl—more intelligent than you. There was no one so witty as you.

GEORGIANA. And you favored that?

STEPHEN. Why else would have I spent so much time with you?

GEORGIANA. I thought that we outcasts just naturally came together.

STEPHEN. But we are outcasts no longer.

GEORGIANA. You surprise me, Stephen.

STEPHEN. Why so?

GEORGIANA. I see you so differently now. You—you have changed.

STEPHEN. How so?

GEORGIANA. You seem to have more—never mind.

STEPHEN. Ah, always the sphinx, aren't you? Very well, keep your secrets. I will discover them someday.

GEORGIANA. I assure you, it will be quite the remarkable man to learn the secrets I hold.

STEPHEN. And you do not think that I am up to the challenge?

GEORGIANA. Perhaps you are.

STEPHEN. Well, this Oedipus will have to solve your riddles another day then, for I am afraid I must leave you early.

GEORGIANA. So soon?

STEPHEN. There is some business I have to attend to in the area, but I shall be back before the end of the day with manuscript in hand. Then we can *really* talk as we used to. I will find Mary to see me out.

GEORGIANA. Don't bother, she is right behind the door. Aren't you, Mary?

Enter MARY.

MARY. I was just polishing the silver, mum.

GEORGIANA. Mary loves a good bit of gossip. She has an ear that is shaped well for keyholes.

MARY. Innocent as a lamb in the butter, mum.

STEPHEN. I don't think I understand your analogy, Mary.

MARY. Oh, sir, there is a kind of wisdom that comes with age that nobody else seems to quite understand.

STEPHEN. I—I see. *(Back to* GEORGIANA.*)* Well, thank you again.

GEORGIANA. The pleasure is mine. I look forward to seeing you tonight.

STEPHEN. Good-bye then, dear friend.

MARY and STEPHEN *exit.* GEORGIANA *looks after them wistfully. She twirls and drops herself on a couch, with what almost sounds like a surprisingly girlish giggle.*

SCENE 2

Enter DARREL *and* CATHERINE *in riding outfits.*

CATHERINE. —and then she said that I had not the sense to discern a jackal from a labrador. And she said that the labrador had more intelligence than I did! She said it much better than that, though—am I not so cruelly mistreated, Darrel?

DARREL. A regular martyr, my dear.

CATHERINE. Oh, she and Thomas are as thick as thieves! They have always been like that! And then there I am left out in the cold. I so wanted to be like them growing up.

To be considered witty and intelligent—but I couldn't keep up, you see. You know what else she *dared* say? Why, she blatantly—

DARREL. Shh. Enough talking.

CATHERINE. Oh, but—

DARREL. Really. You're done.

CATHERINE. But—

DARREL. You are exceptionally taking today, Catherine.

CATHERINE. Truly?

Enter MARY. *She gives* DARREL *a piercing stare.*

MARY. Mum, Jeffrey has finished stripping down the horses. Is there anything else you wish him to do with them?

CATHERINE. Uh, no, no. That is quite all right, Mary. Put them in the stables.

MARY. If you need me, mum, I will be as accessible as a cat looking for a rat.

CATHERINE. That won't be needed, Mary.

Exit MARY *with another withering look at* DARREL.

CATHERINE. So you think I am "taking," even in this outfit?

DARREL. Yes. When I saw you on that horse, you looked so elegant and noble. A truly romantic figure.

CATHERINE. Do you truly think so?

DARREL. You know I do. I adore you. You are a dear, beautiful woman.

CATHERINE. *(With a discreet smile.)* So you say.

DARREL. I can do much more than say it.

DARREL *goes in to kiss* CATHERINE. CATHERINE, *caught off guard, pulls away.*

CATHERINE. What are you doing?

DARREL. I was trying to kiss you.

CATHERINE. I am not cheap, Mr. Fredericks.

DARREL. Oh, it is "Mr. Fredericks" now?

CATHERINE. Yes, and it will continue to be so until you remember that you are with a lady. I am a woman of high society.

DARREL. *(Laughs.)* You are made of the same mettle I am, Catherine. Your marionettes and shadow shows do not fool me. You put on the proper face, which is good. We can't have anyone suspecting us, can we?

DARREL *once again draws in, but* CATHERINE *draws back.*

CATHERINE. I am in earnest, Mr. Fredericks.

DARREL. Do not pretend with *me*. I have seen your concealed looks and unblushing thoughts. I attract you and it's certainly not because of my virtue. Nor yours.

Enter MARY *in a rush, with a cart with various items for tea.*

MARY. Shall I serve tea, mum?

CATHERINE. Thank you, Mary!

MARY. Would Mr. Fredericks like to continue to be a burden and join you?

DARREL. *(Giving* MARY *an annoyed glance.)* I do not think that is necessary.

MARY. As you wish, sir. Anything to please you, sir.

Exit MARY.

DARREL. That maid of yours is quite the snoop, isn't she?

CATHERINE. Mary? She is harmless.

DARREL. I'm not so sure. Well, I suppose I will see you in a couple of days when I call by again.

CATHERINE. Darrel—I am all torn up. I am not sure if I want you to go.

DARREL. Catherine, I consider myself a progressive man. You are the dearest of women to me. You have something which I find very exciting—alluring, you see. You are like an exotic spice mixed with the sweetness of cinnamon. Fragrant, almost—narcotic. Like opium. I shall love you to the day I die.

DARREL *goes to exit.*

CATHERINE. Wait. Mr. Fredericks, I—Darrel—

CATHERINE *walks over to* DARREL, *lifts her head and closes her eyes, offering herself for an innocent kiss.* DARREL *smiles and lunges into a much more passionate kiss than* CATHERINE *had expected. She resists at first, but then melts into it, giving up her resistance. Enter* MARY.

MARY. My, my, mum! I am sorry to interrupt and all, but—

CATHERINE. *(Jolting away from the kiss.)* Mary!

DARREL. Oh, I swear.

MARY. Oh, but it is most important, sir.

DARREL. I am sure it is.

CATHERINE. What is it, Mary?

MARY. I—er—

CATHERINE. *What is it?*

MARY. I can't tell you in the presence of Mr. Fredericks! It's a very delicate family matter!

DARREL. Very well. Good-bye, dear Catherine.

CATHERINE. Good-bye, Darrel.

Exit DARREL.

CATHERINE. Nothing is wrong, is it, Mary?

MARY. Miss Catherine, your fox has a pleasant appearance to him, such a red-haired furry fellow. But you don't trust a fox with chickens. You don't let him near your best birds, mum.

CATHERINE. You and your farmyard analogies! Honestly, who would put foxes with chickens! I am not stupid, Mary.

As CATHERINE *turns to exit, she runs into a pillar. Flustered,* CATHERINE *exits.* MARY *smiles and then exits as well.*

SCENE 3

GEORGIANA *reading a book. She is intent upon its contents, engrossed.* THOMAS *enters, sneaking up on* GEORGIANA *from behind. He pounces on her and begins to poke her, giggling mischievously.* GEORGIANA *laughs as he tickles her.*

GEORGIANA. What—oh, stop it, Thomas! *(Laughs, but then slaps away his hands.)* I said stop it!

THOMAS. Has some gypsy had you under a trance?

GEORGIANA. What do you mean?

THOMAS. I have been calling you for twenty minutes!

GEORGIANA. You have?

THOMAS. Are you ill?

GEORGIANA. No. No, I am quite fine.

THOMAS. What is that you have your nose in?

GEORGIANA. Nothing.

THOMAS. Oh, now you do have me intrigued—

GEORGIANA. Really, Thomas, it is nothing of consequence.

THOMAS *swipes the book from* GEORGIANA.

GEORGIANA. Thomas, give that back!

THOMAS. Why, it can't be—

GEORGIANA. At once. Give it back!

THOMAS. What a farce! What a delight!

GEORGIANA. Thomas!

THOMAS. A romance! Has the end of the world finally come? Is *this* what kept you up so late last night, Georgiana?

GEORGIANA. It is fine literature.

THOMAS. Jane Austen? Never heard of her. But I am sure she is very skillful in telling a maudlin story of swooning maidens. *(Acting.)* Oh, Reginald! Save me! I am all alone in this big, gothic castle!

GEORGIANA. Do not be childish.

THOMAS. I hardly recognize you, Georgiana. The severe spinster has become sentimental.

GEORGIANA *grabs back the book.*

GEORGIANA. Do not make a fool of yourself, Thomas. I have read nearly every other book in the house. My options are becoming rather narrow.

THOMAS. Narrow, indeed!

GEORGIANA. Put it aside, there is another matter I want to address.

THOMAS. That formal, eh? Out with it.

GEORGIANA. I wish to host a ball here and—

THOMAS. Wait—did you say a ball?

GEORGIANA. Yes, a ball.

THOMAS. Truly, you have been transformed! Catherine, come in here!

GEORGIANA. Oh, Thomas, you traitor, please, do not—

THOMAS. Why? Are you embarrassed?

GEORGIANA. I am no such thing!

THOMAS. Oh, of course not—I do not think that you have been embarrassed your whole life. Completely unruffled. Catherine, come here!

GEORGIANA. Thomas, please, don't make this into something bigger than it is!

THOMAS. Catherine!

Enter CATHERINE.

CATHERINE. What are you off about?

THOMAS. Georgiana wants to host a ball.

CATHERINE. *(Peering at* GEORGIANA *suspiciously.)* Thomas, our sister has been replaced with an evil twin.

GEORGIANA. I have always enjoyed going to balls and assemblies with you, Catherine.

CATHERINE. Yes, to play cards or talk your serious talks. But when have you ever been known to *dance* at a dance, Georgiana?

GEORGIANA. I know how to dance.

CATHERINE. It is one thing to know *how* to dance, yet it is a completely different thing to be *known* to dance. Of course, that may be no fault of your own. One has to be asked first.

THOMAS. That is enough, Catherine. Tell me, do you dispute the idea of a ball?

CATHERINE. Of course not.

THOMAS. Good. I think it is high time! We will prepare the invitations, hire the musicians, prepare some elegant food, and have a fine time.

CATHERINE. I have been just aching for something like this. Father's death has been such a foggy darkness!

They all look to Alexander Highett's portrait.

THOMAS. Yes. We must pay no disrespect to Father.

GEORGIANA. No, I agree with Catherine for once. Our mourning is over.

GEORGIANA *takes off her black armband.*

CATHERINE. It is high time!

CATHERINE, *too, tears off her armband. The two sisters look at* THOMAS.

THOMAS. Father would not want us to grieve forever!

THOMAS *tears off his armband as well.*

THOMAS. We shall make this the grandest ball that this area has ever seen then! We will need to get you a new dress, Georgiana.

GEORGIANA. I have plenty of dresses.

THOMAS. Yes, they all make you look like a mortician's wife. They are not suitable. That new dress you showed me yesterday, Catherine, where did you get it?

CATHERINE. Well, it is a bit embarrassing, but it was a dingy little shop run by two young women. But the dress was so well made that I decided to buy it anyway.

THOMAS. It is the most beautiful dress I have seen you wear. We will invite the dressmakers here to measure you, Georgiana. They will do splendidly.

GEORGIANA. Thomas—

THOMAS. No arguments, Georgiana. The matter is decided and you have no say in it. Mary!

Enter MARY.

MARY. Yes, sir.

THOMAS. I thought you might be listening in, Mary.

MARY. I was just polishing the silver, sir.

THOMAS. Taking that comfortable spot of yours by the door while doing so, I am sure. Catherine will write down some directions for you to a dress shop.

MARY. Yes, the one on Dover Lane.

THOMAS. Tell the two dressmakers that if they can come by with some of their designs that I will make it worth their while. Give them instructions how to get here.

MARY. I will be there and back again faster than a hound after a fox, sir.

Exit MARY.

GEORGIANA. Then I shall pay for it. I will not babied. Anyway, I do have some sense. I was planning on purchasing a new dress—I just did not want to make a big scene out of it.

CATHERINE. Why this will be a treat to see you play the part of the stylish creature.

GEORGIANA. Now do not think that this will be a regular thing with me.

CATHERINE. A treat nonetheless. Oh, all the planning—invitations, musicians, food, silverware, and china! And the guest list—the guest list—oh, the guest list!

Exit CATHERINE *in a near panic.*

THOMAS. *(Pause.)* So is it Stephen?

GEORGIANA. Pardon me?

THOMAS. Stephen. I am not blind, Georgiana. The ball, the romance novel—you are behaving peculiarly, and there is only one thing that I know that causes that kind of peculiarity.

GEORGIANA. Don't be absurd!

THOMAS. It is not absurd.

GEORGIANA. It is an embarrassing accusation.

THOMAS. It is not a crime to be in love.

GEORGIANA. I'm not!

THOMAS. Look at your behavior.

GEORGIANA. Don't you remember? I am the one who is to never marry.

THOMAS. Oh, dear Georgiana, you are more vulnerable than I thought.

GEORGIANA. Do not mistake this, Thomas, I—

THOMAS. I saw that he came again the other day—and the next—and the next—

GEORGIANA. What is your point?

THOMAS. What was it that he brought with him?

GEORGIANA. His manuscript. He wanted to show me some parts of it.

THOMAS. I see.

GEORGIANA. Truly, Thomas, it is not what you think.

THOMAS. Could it be that someone has truly penetrated your armored heart?

GEORGIANA. How can you—

THOMAS. Look at me.

GEORGIANA. What?

THOMAS. Look at me.

GEORGIANA. You are treating me like a child.

THOMAS. Look at me. *(She does so.)* Ha! Just what I suspected! You are gone.

GEORGIANA. Gone? Gone where?

THOMAS. Oh, Georgiana, be frank with your brother for once—*(takes her by the chin and looks again.)* Gone!

GEORGIANA. Thomas!

THOMAS. Gone, gone, gone, gone!

GEORGIANA. Oh, stop being being foolish. How can I say this in a way that you will understand?

THOMAS. It is not surgery, my dear.

GEORGIANA. Thomas—

THOMAS. Anyone can be wounded by Cupid's arrow—even you!

GEORGIANA. Thomas, please!

THOMAS. Yes?

THOMAS *begins investigating* GEORGIANA's *person in mildly intrusive ways.*

GEORGIANA. Thomas—what—what are you doing now?

THOMAS. Looking for the arrow, of course.

GEORGIANA *pushes* THOMAS *away.*

GEORGIANA. Thomas, please, be serious! This is painful!

THOMAS. All right.

He takes her by the hands with a mock serious expression.

GEORGIANA. Truly serious!

THOMAS. *(This time sincerely supportive.)* Go on.

GEORGIANA. I must ask you something—something—

THOMAS. Something personal?

GEORGIANA. Yes. Something personal.

THOMAS. Go on.

GEORGIANA. How can I—make myself—more—

THOMAS. Say it.

GEORGIANA. —more attractive to a man?

THOMAS. I never thought I'd hear you say that!

GEORGIANA. I'm in earnest. Please, Thomas!

THOMAS. I don't know. How should I know?

GEORGIANA. You are a man, aren't you? Tell me what to do.

THOMAS. *(Pause.)* I am really enjoying this moment very much, you know.

GEORGIANA. Thomas! I—I know it sounds like foolishness—I have always ridiculed it as foolishness! But I have never—never wanted to look—well, attractive for a man. I thought I had more dignity than that, but it is—

THOMAS. It is a good move. If you want him as a man, treat him like a man by behaving like a *woman*.

GEORGIANA. Pardon?

THOMAS. Ornament your hair. Burn your old wardrobe.

GEORGIANA. Burn? Remember who you are talking to, Thomas.

THOMAS. Dear Georgiana! There's something hidden up in you. Something none of us have seen. It is there. Let it out. You just have to help it, that's all.

GEORGIANA. Do you really think so?

THOMAS. Absolutely.

GEORGIANA. But I never expected, if I were to feel such, that I would be—

THOMAS. Yes?

GEORGIANA. Well—

THOMAS. Hm?

GEORGIANA. Frightened.

THOMAS. Ah, yes.

GEORGIANA. Where does fear play into matters of the heart?

THOMAS. Welcome to your first taste of humility. Celebrate it, my dear.

GEORGIANA. It is ironic. I always thought you the fool of the family, Thomas. Yet you have turned to be the wisest of us all.

THOMAS. Now do be careful with that. It is our little secret. The disguise of the fool is a convenient device and I am not likely to part with it.

SCENE 4

GEORGIANA *with the two dressmakers,* ESTHER *and* HANNAH WHITEFIELD. *The two dressmakers are both pretty,* ESTHER *more distinctively than* HANNAH, *but they both have the appearances of the laboring class. They have brought several dolls and a carrying case.*

ESTHER. What is it that you don't like about that dress, Miss? If it is the color—

GEORGIANA. It is not the color. There is too much lace.

ESTHER. What if we were to take off the lace up 'ere—would that suit you, Miss?

GEORGIANA. No, it just will not do. I will not be made up like one of these dolls, you understand. I do have some dignity.

ESTHER. That I can see, Miss. Of course, Miss. Hannah, bring over the one in green. Now this one is bit plainer, but—

GEORGIANA. Yes, it is plainer. Too plain. Something else.

ESTHER. Yes, of course. Hannah, the one with the train—

GEORGIANA. Oh no, that one is an abomination!

ESTHER. The one next to it then.

> HANNAH *brings over one of the models and* GEORGIANA *circles it, inspecting it closely. The dressmakers note her thoughtfulness hopefully.*

GEORGIANA. Certainly not.

ESTHER. Yes, of course. 'Ere are two more. Bring them both over, Hannah.

> HANNAH *brings over the two remaining dolls.* GEORGIANA, *again, inspects them, deliberating between the two.*

GEORGIANA. That one is unbearable, but that one—I like that one.

HANNAH. Exc'llent choice, Miss.

GEORGIANA. But the colors are terrible. Can you change the red and green to purple and green?

ESTHER. Yes, Miss.

GEORGIANA. I should hope so.

ESTHER. Now, if we can measure you, Miss 'Ighett. Hannah, will you please get out the measuring equipment?

> *Enter* MARY.

MARY. Mr. Lockhart is here to see you, Miss Georgiana.

STEPHEN *enters, barging in.*

STEPHEN. Hello! Sorry to barge in, but I'm barging in!

STEPHEN *laughs. Exit* MARY.

GEORGIANA. Stephen! Oh! I wasn't expecting you for another hour.

STEPHEN. Yes, I didn't intend to be so early. Mary tried to stop me, but that only intrigued me more. I thought I may finally be able to solve one of the cultish riddles of womanhood, if it was that clandestine! *(Noting the dolls)* Why, I'll be stumped. Are you buying gifts for children?

GEORGIANA. Well, not exactly. I—perhaps it is best to say—how can I—

Enter CATHERINE.

CATHERINE. Stephen! I thought I heard your voice and here you are!

GEORGIANA. It is for Catherine! Yes, these are dressmakers who have come to show me the designs for a birthday present I am having made for her! *(To* CATHERINE.*)* Sorry to spoil the surprise for you, my dear.

CATHERINE. A birthday present for me?

GEORGIANA. Why, of course, dear sister. Come over here, and we will have these two take your measurements.

CATHERINE. Why, I think I have harshly misjudged you, Georgiana. You are a dear sister, indeed. For you to remember my birthday! And for you to think of such a thoughtful way to express your affections and apologies and adoration and—

GEORGIANA. *(Out of* STEPHEN's *hearing.)* Be quiet, Catherine. Don't you know that your birthday is not for another six months?

CATHERINE. Oh. Well, yes, I did think you were preparing for it a tad bit early.

GEORGIANA. The dress is not for you. I do not want Stephen to know it is mine until the ball.

CATHERINE. But I was so looking forward to a new dress—

GEORGIANA. Go!

CATHERINE, ESTHER, *and* HANNAH *step into a side room, from which they can still be heard and vice versa.*

GEORGIANA. *(Back to* STEPHEN.*)* Now, before we get to your manuscript *(bringing him to the dolls)* tell me what you think of these.

STEPHEN. Very pretty dolls. Let's see—

GEORGIANA. No, no, the dresses.

STEPHEN. Ah, yes.

GEORGIANA. Which one is your favorite?

CATHERINE. *(From the other room.)* I like the blue and yellow one.

GEORGIANA. Of course, the most gaudy. This doesn't concern you, Catherine.

GEORGIANA. So which would be your choice?

    STEPHEN *circles the dolls, inspecting them.*

STEPHEN. This one! With the lace.

GEORGIANA. That one?

STEPHEN. Yes. It is modest, but has an innate grace in its design. It is a beautiful piece of craftsmanship.

ESTHER AND HANNAH. *(From the other room.)* Thank you, sir!

GEORGIANA. *(Darts an annoyed look, then back to* STEPHEN.*)* We really need thicker walls in this part of the house. Now, there are others. What do you think of this one?

STEPHEN. It is rather, umm, severe.

GEORGIANA. Severe?

STEPHEN. Yes. Where is its elegance and softness? Where is its beauty?

GEORGIANA. It has strength.

STEPHEN. Strong? This is for Catherine, is it not? She is a pretty girl, who should have a pretty dress.

GEORGIANA. I do not think that even Catherine should be so debased.

STEPHEN. Georgiana, there are certain things men and women do simply to please each other. There is no pride in it—it is a humble submission to each other's feelings.

    CATHERINE, ESTHER, *and* HANNAH *have finished and have now re-entered.*

CATHERINE. I adore being measured. It always means something is coming.

    Enter MARY *with* DARREL.

MARY. Mr. Fredericks, mum.

DARREL. Ah, Good evening, beautiful Miss Catherine. Good evening, frightful Miss Georgiana. *(Picking up one of the dolls, amused.)* Revisiting your childhood?

GEORGIANA. Why, do you want to play dolls with me?

DARREL. And are these two young girls your playmates? Rather rough additions to your social circle, if you ask me.

GEORGIANA. My relationship is purely professional with these two. They are making m—er, Catherine a dress for a ball we are having.

DARREL. Yes, I am sure that Catherine has told you that I will be attending.

GEORGIANA. That is quite all right. I will not notice you. We will seat you behind the orchestra.

DARREL. 'Tis true, you are no respecter of persons. You will shuffle me off, as you have your meager playmates.

Enter THOMAS, *ecstatically, almost as if he were in an insane daze, making wild movements and gestures, his voice rising and falling in a frenzied pitch.*

THOMAS. Repent, repent, repent! Ye wicked sinners, ye vile men and women of Babylon, know ye not that the day shall come when the earth shall shake to and fro like a drunken man? This very house shall topple upon us! Repent, repent, repent!

DARREL. What on earth?!

GEORGIANA. What sort of bizarre thing have you got yourself involved in now?

THOMAS. Today I got religion! *(Laughs.)* It was most entertaining. I'll show you! Mary?

Enter MARY.

MARY. Yes, sir?

THOMAS. Can you bring in the gentlemen at the door, please?

MARY. Yes, sir.

Exit MARY.

GEORGIANA. You didn't—

THOMAS. I brought the religion home with me.

CATHERINE. *Whom* did you bring with you?

Enter MARY *with* BRIGHAM YOUNG *and* JOHN TAYLOR.

THOMAS. My dear friends and family, we have apostles in our midst! Welcome Misters Brigham Young and John Taylor! They are preachers from America! They followed me home—can I keep them?

There is a shocked pause.

GEORGIANA. This must be a joke.

THOMAS. Well, I admit, *I* think it is rather a novel treat, but I think you will find *them* very serious. Latter-day Saints is what they call themselves. I just stumbled upon them, really, and opened them like Pandora's box!

JOHN. Not so much like Pandora's box, sir. We have something much better to give the world. We have the truth.

STEPHEN. The truth! *(Laughs.)* He has the truth! And I am sure he will sell it to us at a discount.

THOMAS. I was just walking absent-mindedly through Liverpool and I heard this man's *(motioning to* BRIGHAM*)* strong accent. I stopped to discover that a whole group had gathered to hear him preach about Jesus, oh, and angels and scripture and fa-la-la! Afterwards, if you can imagine, they told me to repent and be baptized right where I stood! Without any water in sight! We had a pleasant talk anyway, and

I even bought a book off them.

GEORGIANA. That still does not explain why you brought them here.

THOMAS. I told them that, if they were brave enough, they could have a whole house of infidels to preach to. And here you all are! Introductions: these are my two lovely sisters Miss Georgiana and Miss Catherine Highett, and this is Mr. Stephen Lockhart, and then Mr. Darrel Fredericks.

JOHN. It is a pleasure.

BRIGHAM. Nice to meet you, folks.

THOMAS. I think that you will get more than you bargained for, gentlemen, especially between my sister Georgiana and our friend Darrel. They are quite accomplished debaters—they are able to practice quite often on each other.

DARREL. Actually, I am already well acquainted with Mr. Young and Mr. Taylor.

THOMAS. Why, Darrel, have *you* had a visit from an angel?

DARREL. A self-proclaimed agnostic like myself? Hardly. Yet I would dare say I am friends with these two gentlemen.

JOHN. Yes, we have—met with Mr. Fredericks.

CATHERINE. You do not speak much like an American, Mr. Taylor.

JOHN. Unlike Brother Brigham, I was born in England. And who are these two young ladies?

CATHERINE. Do not fret yourself, Mr. Taylor. They are just a couple of dressmakers.

JOHN. Dressmakers have names, do they not? *(To* ESTHER *and* HANNAH.*)* I am John Taylor.

ESTHER. Yes, gov'nor. I'm Esther Whitefield. This is my sister Hannah.

JOHN. Miss Esther, Miss Hannah, it is our honor.

BRIGHAM. *(To* MARY.*)* And who are you, ma'am?

MARY. Just one of the servants, sir.

BRIGHAM. Why, what a coincidence, I'm a servant myself. I serve God.

MARY. Well then, sir, you might say that I serve Mammon.

BRIGHAM. It is not too late to switch sides, you know.

MARY. Mary, sir. I'm Mary.

CATHERINE. Excuse me, gentlemen, but is it some strange American custom to mingle with the hired help while neglecting your hosts?

GEORGIANA. It does not surprise me that religion does so well over there in your rough country, Mr. Young. Why, the ignorant are always looking for another barrel to keep their superstitions afloat. Intelligence, science and noble philosophy are expected in *England*.

JOHN. Philosophy? Fried froth.

GEORGIANA. Pardon me?

JOHN. In Paris they have a sort of exceedingly light cake. It is so light that you could blow it away. You could eat all day of it, and never be satisfied. Somebody asked me what the name of it was. I said, I do not know the proper name, but in the absence of one, I can give it one—I call it fried froth, or the philosophies of men.

GEORGIANA. Oh, and you are so substantial?

BRIGHAM. Ma'am, we carry God's truth restored—

THOMAS. Yes, yes, to make it short, an angel visited a young man and led him to an ancient record. He translated it by the power of God, etcetera, etcetera, etcetera. So thank you very much, gentlemen! *(Begins to usher them out.)* Now if you could—

HANNAH. Did he say angel?

GEORGIANA. Who do you think we are, gentlemen? Fairy tales are for children, not us.

JOHN. Do you not believe in God, miss?

GEORGIANA. I believe in myself. Whether there is a god does not much concern me.

BRIGHAM. There are greater truths than you understand, ma'am. Greater powers, greater beings.

STEPHEN. Where is your proof, sir? It's still just a story to me. You are talking to a writer, a man who knows how to craft believable stories.

BRIGHAM. So you like stories? I've got a story. There was once a farmer who bought a plot of land in a far-off country, away from civilization. A man came along to him selling seeds, saying, "These seeds will sustain your life." The farmer asked him, "How can I trust you? How can I trust the seed will do what you tell me it will do?"

GEORGIANA. And how did he answer, rabbi?

BRIGHAM. The man with the seeds said, "You don't have to trust me. Here, eat the fruit that is produced by that seed." The farmer asked, "How do I know it's not poisoned?" The man said, "Trust me." The farmer said, "I trust proof." Soon enough, having put no seeds in the ground and no food in his mouth, but weeds and acorns, the farmer starved and died.

THOMAS. Ha! A regular parable, right in our own house. That was lovely. *(Again, trying to usher them out.)* Thank you very, very much, gentlemen!

GEORGIANA. Well, you never answered whether the seeds were poisoned or not.

BRIGHAM. I thought that was obvious.

GEORGIANA. No, sir, not so obvious at all. Gentlemen, the converts you will make will be nothing more than the ignorant, poor classes of England, so you will do us a favor, if you can export them out of here into your own country.

DARREL. Now wait a minute, Georgiana.

GEORGIANA. You of all people can't possibly be defending these Bible wailers, Mr. Fredericks!

DARREL. Please, Georgiana, I have something to say. Unlike the rest of you, I have spent some time with these men and their associates, but more importantly, time among the class of people they convert—the class of people you have so degraded.

GEORGIANA. Am I incorrect in my estimations of their ignorance?

DARREL. Whatever your prejudices about the laborers are, Georgiana, these people are supporting us. They are the ones making our bread, they are the ones building our homes, they are the ones building our trains and carriages. Men and women like Mary here and the dressmakers are the ones who literally make the clothes on our backs. If they will go to America and build the Latter-day Saints into a great nation, we would molder and rot. Can you make a dress? Can you forge a horseshoe or cook a feast? Without these "lower" classes, Georgiana, what are you good for?

Stunned by the direct insult, everyone looks to GEORGIANA *to see how she'll respond.* GEORGIANA *coolly regards* DARREL *and then looks away from him, as if he hardly mattered at all. She then addresses the two missionaries.*

GEORGIANA. *(Pause.)* Then I would like to thank Thomas's guests for coming, but we shall not detain them any longer.

DARREL. *(Refusing to be ignored.)* What, no rebuttal?

GEORGIANA. With all the due respect Papa paid to the "captains of industry," Mr. Fredericks, I hardly expect a middle-class man such as yourself to understand.

DARREL. Your dear "Papa" certainly liked to dabble in business himself . . .

GEORGIANA. But, you see, Darrel, my Father played with business because it was his hobby . . .

THOMAS. Georgiana, don't . . .

GEORGIANA. . . . you do so because you have work to survive. That is the difference between you and me, Mr. Fredericks. That is the gulf that shall always divide us, for better or worse. Mary, please see these good gentlemen back to the carriage and instruct the driver that they are to go anywhere they please . . . as long as it is away from here.

THOMAS. Oh, dear!

CATHERINE. What is it, Thomas?

THOMAS. *Carmen!*

CATHERINE. Who?

THOMAS. The opera!

GEORGIANA. Oh, heavens!

CATHERINE. Oh, yes! How could have we forgotten! Good afternoon all!

GEORGIANA. Oh, Stephen! I had forgotten to ask you. We have an extra seat in the box. I was hoping you would want to come with us.

STEPHEN. Well, I am hardly dressed for the opera.

THOMAS. You can borrow something of mine, Stephen. *(With a sly wink)* Or Catherine has this lovely, scarlet cloak which would look stunning on you! But we must hurry! We will have to push the horses all day, if the carriage is to get to London in time! *(To everyone else.)* I am sorry, everyone. Mary will see you all out.

Exit GEORGIANA, STEPHEN, THOMAS, *and* CATHERINE.

MARY. Whoosh, swish! You get used the commotion around here. I will go get all of your things.

Exit MARY.

ESTHER. *(To* DARREL.*)* Gov'nor, thank you for defending us.

DARREL. *(Genuinely.)* You're welcome, ladies. Now, Mr. Young and Mr. Taylor, I should like to speak to you about our prior business.

BRIGHAM. We have already given our answer, Mr. Fredericks.

DARREL. Yes, but I don't think you realized the full implications of what I was offering you. That little paper of yours—oh, what was it called? The Apocalyptic Moon?

JOHN. *The Millennial Star.*

DARREL. Yes, that's it. Now let us be frank. You haven't the talent nor the know-how to run a successful newspaper. My paper can help you.

JOHN. We have already gone through this—

DARREL. I have been thinking about opening a religious section to my newspaper—you know, a place for the exploration of faith.

BRIGHAM. We do not need help, sir.

DARREL. You have already excited a great deal of antipathy against you among the local clergies. But, if you put my major newspaper behind you, it will give you credibility. Then it won't matter who is against you, for your popularity would be enormous!

BRIGHAM. Mr. Fredericks, if I now had in my possession sufficient money, I could buy the favor of the publishers of newspapers and control their presses, though I expect popularity would send us to hell.

DARREL. Yet unpopularity certainly won't fill your pews. Let us be practical, Mr. Young.

BRIGHAM. I am the most practical man upon this planet, sir. Your *Daily Hornet* is the sinking ship, not ours.

DARREL. Whatever do you mean?

JOHN. We have investigated, and you are not in the most promising situation, Mr. Fredericks. People do not seem to like the negative and accusatory views in your paper. We will place ourselves in God's hands, thank you.

DARREL. You hustling bullies! I will not be dealt with in this manner! You have made a dangerous enemy today, gentlemen.

JOHN. Mr. Fredericks—

DARREL. You soon shall find a poisonous editorial about your church in *The Daily Hornet*.

HANNAH. You are just wrenched up a bit, sir. These are honest men. *(Touching his arm.)* Please—

DARREL. Don't touch me! How dare you take such liberties!

ESTHER. She 'as meant you no 'arm!

DARREL. Just leave me alone. . . . just leave me alone!

    DARREL *goes to exit and* MARY *enters handing him his cane, cloak, and hat.*

MARY. Hope you have a pleasant day, sir.

DARREL. Behind there the whole time!

MARY. Just polishing the silver.

    Exit DARREL, *furious.*

JOHN. Pay no mind to him, ladies.

ESTHER. Oh, 'ow do we know that you ain't no better than them with your fine, 'igh ways? You could betray us, too. You turned like a dog on Mr. Fredericks. Why not us?

BRIGHAM. Ladies, Mr. Fredericks only defended us for flattery to help his paper. The Bible warns us to be as wise as serpents and as harmless as doves. Good evening, ladies. *(Goes to leave, but then turns back.)* Where are you both headed?

HANNAH. Dover Lane, sir.

BRIGHAM. There's some rough streets between here and there. May we chaperone you?

JOHN. *(Taking his cane from* MARY.*)* Yes, if anyone gives us any trouble, I have this cane which I call the "rascal beater."

HANNAH. We would appreciate the assistance and the company, wouldn't we, Esther? And there's some questions I want to ask you.

    Exit BRIGHAM, JOHN, ESTHER, *and* HANNAH.

SCENE 5

DARREL *and* CATHERINE *are in a passionate kiss.* CATHERINE *tries to extricate herself.*

CATHERINE. Darrel—

DARREL *continues.*

CATHERINE. Darrel, give me a chance to breathe!

DARREL. Come now, this is nothing new to you.

CATHERINE. But right here in the open—where anyone can see—

DARREL. Ah, gentle Catherine—has Georgiana been telling you how much of a villain I am?

CATHERINE. How can I trust you, Darrel?

DARREL. How can you trust anybody? There is a point when you simply have faith.

CATHERINE. Oh, you have taken up religion, have you?

DARREL. Oh, I preach a different kind of sermon than they do. *(He takes* CATHERINE *in his arms.)*

CATHERINE. *(With a smile.)* You're wicked.

DARREL. And so are you, but you look good in it.

CATHERINE. You charmer.

DARREL. Once I started to investigate your family, then I understood what a rare treasure you all were.

CATHERINE. I thought you first were drawn to me as an individual?

DARREL. So I was. Yet I always make sure I know where I am standing, darling.

CATHERINE. And what did you find?

DARREL. More than you can imagine.

CATHERINE. I don't understand.

DARREL. All in good time, my dear.

DARREL *and* CATHERINE *once again kiss, but then they hear voices approaching. They both stop and listen to them coming closer.*

CATHERINE. Oh, I am sure to get another scolding for being with you alone again.

DARREL. Shh.

DARREL *abruptly takes* CATHERINE *by the hand and they hide behind a couch in a far corner. Enter* GEORGIANA, STEPHEN, MARY, ESTHER, *and*

HANNAH.

GEORGIANA. I had forgotten all about the fitting that you had with—Catherine today. I hardly know where she could be. Stephen can you stay here, while we look for Catherine?

STEPHEN. Oh, I can help you look, I'm sure.

GEORGIANA. No! No. Catherine may come in here and I will need someone to stay while I look through the estate outside. *(To the dressmakers.)* Which one of you has the measuring tools?

HANNAH. *(Holding up her bag.)* I do.

GEORGIANA. Then you come with me in case we find Catherine—so we can *measure* her immediately.

HANNAH. I understand, miss.

GEORGIANA. Come then.

Exit GEORGIANA *and* HANNAH.

STEPHEN. That was strange.

MARY. Oh—Mr. Lockhart, I really am quite busy. Miss Whitefield, come with me, please, and I'll situate you in a different—

STEPHEN. Oh, you can leave her in here, Mary.

MARY. Are you sure that's wise, sir?

STEPHEN. What, are you afraid something's going to happen?

MARY. *(Nearly under her breath.)* Foxes and chickens—

STEPHEN. Pardon me?

MARY. Barnyard thoughts, sir. I'll be about my business.

Exit MARY.

ESTHER. So 'ave you told 'er?

STEPHEN. About what?

ESTHER. Our little scrap in the street.

STEPHEN. I happened upon your little street meeting with Mr. Young and Mr. Taylor quite by chance. Our little debate was hardly of enough consequence to bring up to anyone.

ESTHER. Ah—I'm nothin' of *cons'quence*, am I, sir? None of us are.

STEPHEN. I didn't say that.

ESTHER. But you meant it.

STEPHEN. We just inhabit different worlds.

ESTHER. No, Mr. Lock'art, we in'abit the same world. The same cont'nent, the same country, the same city even. And at this very moment, to both of our discomfortures, we're even in'abit the same room.

STEPHEN. Miss Whitefield, please—

ESTHER. Sir, you're a writer, aren't you?

STEPHEN. Why, do you think you have read my books?

ESTHER. I—I can't read.

STEPHEN. *(Laughs.)* Yes, that would make it quite difficult!

ESTHER. Please, sir, don't make fun o' me.

STEPHEN. I am sorry. I believe you were trying to drive a point, weren't you?

ESTHER. What do you write about?

STEPHEN. Why?

ESTHER. Nothin'.

STEPHEN. You can speak your mind.

ESTHER. Because—because writers get into peoples 'eads, sir. That can be a good or bad thing.

STEPHEN. You are afraid that I will corrupt everyone, are you?

ESTHER. Sir, the other day you said that we were only talkin' to Mister Taylor and Mister Young because we were poor. Why?

STEPHEN. People of a—well, people in your station are much more likely to try to reach for religion, while people in my station much more readily recognize the manipulation those preachers put upon others. We are in a higher class for a reason.

ESTHER. Why? 'Cause you were born there?

STEPHEN. No, because we stay there. Certain conditions of living create a certain kind of individual. In your realms of society there are thieves, there are murderers, there are drunks and, if I may be indelicate, there are ladies of the night. The morals of your people bring down society.

ESTHER. Sir—per'aps you 'aven't been 'mong my kind o' people much—but recently, I 'ave 'ad a chance to be 'mong yours. And you know what I find?

STEPHEN. Let me guess, you think we're all "snobs." Posh, eh?

ESTHER. No, sir, that is not what I was goin' to say. I wasn't goin' to say that at all. I was goin' to say that I found some very lovely people. I found that being among a diff'rent people helps you understand them. You should judge a person, sir, by the choices they have put before them, not the choices that they don't.

STEPHEN. Why, Miss Whitefield, have you ever thought of going into forensics?

ESTHER. I'm not that kind o' girl, sir!

STEPHEN. Oh no, you do not understand what I mean. You've got a sharper mind than I gave you credit for. You know, I enjoy talking to you.

ESTHER. Why, sir, is that a compliment?

STEPHEN. You earned it. You have impressed me, Miss—

ESTHER. Whitefield. Esther Whitefield.

STEPHEN. Miss Whitefield. Why—this may sound strange, but can I see you again?

ESTHER. Me, sir?

STEPHEN. *(Taking* ESTHER *by the hands.)* Why, yes. I have enjoyed our talk—I would enjoy another.

ESTHER. Truly? Why—I don't know, sir. That would be nice, I guess. Very nice.

> *The two stand in silence for several moments, and as they gaze at each other, there is an electric moment when it appears that they might kiss.* MARY *enters in a rush.*

MARY. Oh my.

STEPHEN. Mary!

MARY. Excuse me, sir!

STEPHEN. Weren't you supposed to be busy doing something?

MARY. I was polishing the silver—

STEPHEN. —behind the door, I know. Blast it all, Mary! Why don't you—?

MARY. Miss Georgiana is coming, so you two better look less—*comfortable* with each other.

> STEPHEN *and* ESTHER *realize that they're still holding hands. They drop their hands, create some distance from each other and try to look "less comfortable." Enter* GEORGIANA *and* HANNAH.

GEORGIANA. I am sorry, Miss Whitefield, but your sister and I were not able to find Catherine. You will just have to come another day.

ESTHER. As you wish, Miss Highett.

GEORGIANA. Good day.

> ESTHER *takes* HANNAH *by the hand, and the two scurry out.* MARY *exits behind them.*

GEORGIANA. Now, Stephen, finally we can discuss your story. Let us start where we left off, shall we?

STEPHEN. *(Emerging from a private reverie, as he looked after* ESTHER *when she left.)* Hm? What is that?

GEORGIANA. We were deep into your story. Your manuscript.

STEPHEN. Oh, yes. That.

GEORGIANA. Now, Stephen, it shows wonderful promise! You have proven yourself rather profound, you know. I especially love your depiction of the lower classes and their surroundings. The filth, the grubbiness, the immorality—why, it's perfectly accurate.

STEPHEN. Now, Georgiana, it still is a *rough* draft. I am not sure whether I am keeping—

GEORGIANA. Oh, writers dream of such a rough draft! You are well on your way! Mr. Lowe will be so impressed.

STEPHEN. Really, Georgiana, I am not sure if it deserves that kind of praise.

GEORGIANA. Here, are my new notes. I have written here that on page 310—

STEPHEN. You know, Georgie, I am not quite in the mood for this today.

GEORGIANA. What do you mean? We have had such good sessions—

STEPHEN. I know, Georgiana, but my mind is elsewhere. Maybe another day.

GEORGIANA. Are you all right?

STEPHEN. Oh, I think so.

GEORGIANA. You do know that you can trust me? If there is anything that I can help with, I am your friend and confidante.

STEPHEN. Yes, I know. But there is a certain matter I need to think over—

GEORGIANA. Think over?

STEPHEN. A matter of the heart—

GEORGIANA. *(Caught off guard.)* Truly?

STEPHEN. I have grown—very—well, how would I say it at this stage? I have grown very fond of someone. But I cannot discuss it now. Excuse me, dear friend.

Exit STEPHEN. GEORGIANA *looks after him, bewildered.*

GEORGIANA. *(With a hopeful smile)* Could it be?

She sits on the couch that CATHERINE *and* DARREL *have been hiding behind.* CATHERINE *squeals from behind it.* GEORGIANA *jolts up, shrieking in return, twirling around to look at the couch in confusion.*

DARREL. *(To* CATHERINE.*)* You are the model of subtlety and stealth, my dear.

DARREL *and* CATHERINE *rise from behind the couch, revealing themselves.*

GEORGIANA. What are you two doing back there?

DARREL. Trying not to sneeze.

DARREL *wipes the dust from his clothes.*

GEORGIANA. You spies! You were eavesdropping!

DARREL. Which you ought to be glad of, dear Georgiana.

CATHERINE. Darrel—

GEORGIANA. What do you mean?

DARREL. There is quite a bit going on under your own roof that you are not aware of.

CATHERINE. Darrel, don't—

GEORGIANA. What are you concealing, Catherine? Well—out with it!

CATHERINE. It is nothing you need worry about, Georgiana.

DARREL. Believe it or not, your sister is trying to protect your heart.

GEORGIANA. My heart?

DARREL. Yes, I know, popular opinion states that you haven't got one.

CATHERINE. Darrel! You promised!

GEORGIANA. Will you stop this taunting? What kind of libelous rumors are going about that would involve my heart?

DARREL. You know, Georgiana, I am the only friend you have right now. I am the only one willing to tell you the truth.

GEORGIANA. Good! If you have something to say, then say it. I will have none of your manipulations.

DARREL. Did you not wonder why your dear Mr. Lockhart dismissed you so easily just now?

GEORGIANA. He did not—

DARREL. Yes, he did.

GEORGIANA. I am sure that he has his reasons.

DARREL. Yes, he certainly has his reasons. It has a lot to do with that little dressmaker of yours. The very pretty one.

CATHERINE. Darrel!

DARREL. There are certain attractions that blind men even to poverty.

GEORGIANA. What?

CATHERINE. Stephen is an honorable man.

DARREL. Whatever his honor dictates in the matter, the fact still remains that Catherine and I overheard his declaration of affection.

CATHERINE. *Interest.*

DARREL. *Affection.* Why, he was absolutely singing the praises of that absolutely stunning little pauper. Ask Catherine, she will tell you the same thing.

GEORGIANA. Catherine?

CATHERINE. I—I—Darrel!

GEORGIANA. Catherine, just tell me it is not true.

CATHERINE. I wish I could.

GEORGIANA. It can't be true. I know better of Stephen.

CATHERINE. I am sorry, Georgiana. I truly—

GEORGIANA. It is a lie. What are you plotting?

DARREL. No plot. Just concern.

GEORGIANA. Ha!

DARREL. Georgiana, I know this may be hard to believe, but I am watching out for you in this matter. I view it as a personal point of honor to shield you from harm.

GEORGIANA. What does it matter to me? Stephen is his own man and I never entertained an idea of—of—

CATHERINE. Georgie—

GEORGIANA. Oh, I see what you are thinking—you were thinking that I dared to dream—how could you think that I could scarcely hope to dream that Stephen and I—to dream that—

CATHERINE. Georgiana, let us talk about this later.

GEORGIANA. Excuse me.

> GEORGIANA *exits, repressing the emotions that are running through her.* CATHERINE *turns on* DARREL.

CATHERINE. You cruel man!

DARREL. Would have you preferred for me to keep her in ignorance?

CATHERINE. You have never cared a shilling for my sister!

DARREL. Are you so sure of that?

> *This catches* CATHERINE *off guard.*

CATHERINE. Who are you?

DARREL. Who are *you*?

> *Unable to answer this question,* CATHERINE *exits the room, desperately confused.* DARREL, *somber, walks over to a window and looks out at the Highetts' garden, as if he desires to take solace from them. Lights fade to black.*

SCENE 6

GEORGIANA *is beneath the portrait of her father, holding the dagger which Mr. Lowe had given her. She is staring up at the portrait, talking to her father.*

GEORGIANA. "Keep it sharp. Keep it sharp—Cut off all those that oppose you . . . slice through all of their defenses . . . "

    MARY *enters.*

MARY. Esther Whitefield is here, Miss Georgiana.

GEORGIANA. Let her in.

MARY. Are you upset, mum?

GEORGIANA. That is none of your business, Mary.

MARY. Yes, mum.

    MARY *exits.* ESTHER *enters.* GEORGIANA *places the dagger back in its case.*

GEORGIANA. You are late.

ESTHER. I am sorry, miss.

GEORGIANA. Where is your sister?

ESTHER. She is very ill, miss.

GEORGIANA. Well, I will have to do with you then.

ESTHER. We did not expect this kind of emergency.

GEORGIANA. No excuses. Where is my dress?

ESTHER. There's been some delays, miss. Sorry, miss.

GEORGIANA. Delays!

ESTHER. The sickness, miss.

GEORGIANA. If you expect me to pay you more for your time, then you are mistaken. I will not be cheated.

ESTHER. We do not expect more.

GEORGIANA. You simply failed to meet your deadline.

    MARY *enters with* BRIGHAM.

MARY. Why look at that, mum—we have another visitor!

BRIGHAM. Really I didn't need to—

MARY. Go on, sir.

GEORGIANA. Ha. What foul fate has brought you to us, Mr. Young? I had hoped not to see you in my home again. Nothing has been the same since the curse of your last visit.

BRIGHAM. I was just going to deliver this invitation—I ran into Thomas and he told me to drop it off here. I came to invite you and your family to a meeting we're having, ma'am.

GEORGIANA. You are an ignorant fool, if you think that I would attend any of your spiritual circuses.

MARY. Now try to be kinder, mum.

ESTHER. Brigham Young deserves anybody's respect.

GEORGIANA. Are you contradicting me, dressmaker?

ESTHER. Forgive me, miss, I didn't mean—

BRIGHAM. You don't have to do this, Sister Esther.

GEORGIANA. *Sister* Esther? Have you joined with these religionists, Miss Whitefield?

ESTHER. My sister has, but I have not—

GEORGIANA. Well, at least you have some sense.

ESTHER. But— *(Slight pause. A decisive moment.)* I believe they are good people and you were absolutely cruel to them the last time they were here. They have done nothing but good for my sister since she joined them.

GEORGIANA. You are a fool.

ESTHER. I'm not alone in my foolery, you heartless witch.

GEORGIANA. You siren! I will have no more of you, dressmaker! Have your sister bring me my completed dress immediately!

ESTHER. As soon as we—

GEORGIANA. You better have it here within the week, or I will cut your pay into half.

ESTHER. We need that money, miss—

GEORGIANA. Then you better be quick about it.

BRIGHAM. Miss Highett, she has done nothing—

GEORGIANA. Nothing? Perhaps you should know the character of those who follow you, Mr. Young. This young seductress tried to reach past her station to my friend Mr. Stephen Lockhart. Right in this very room! Do you deny it?

ESTHER. It wasn't like that—you must believe me, Mr. Young. It wasn't like that—

BRIGHAM. I believe you.

ESTHER. How did she even know we talked?

MARY. Oh, don't look at *me*.

GEORGIANA. Even with all your charms and pretty gazes, you were quite simple to think that Stephen would last on your hooks. Your face and figure may have been cut into a fine gown, but you are still coarse! And rough! And no amount of lace or finery could ever change what you were born into!

BRIGHAM. Sister Whitefield, perhaps it's time we should both leave.

GEORGIANA. Do not come back, Mr. Young. You are not welcome here. Neither of you will ever be tolerated here.

BRIGHAM. Miss Highett—

GEORGIANA. My life has been nothing but a storm and a fury since you have come into my life, Mr. Young. If there is a God, perhaps he is trying to tell me something about you and your religion.

BRIGHAM. But what is it that he is trying to say? God extends His hand to you, ma'am, but if you reject it, you reject the only force which will save you from the coming storms.

GEORGIANA. See them out, Mary.

MARY. *(To BRIGHAM and ESTHER.)* I'm sorry about all of this.

BRIGHAM. God's work is not through in this house.

GEORGIANA. God is not welcome in this house!

Before BRIGHAM and ESTHER can leave, DARREL enters.

BRIGHAM. Good day, Mr. Fredericks.

DARREL. A better one with you leaving, I assure you, Mr. Young.

Exit BRIGHAM and ESTHER.

GEORGIANA. I get rid of one nuisance only to receive another. Do you want to see Catherine, Darrel?

DARREL. I am here to see Thomas.

GEORGIANA. I hope you are not here for what I think you are.

DARREL. I am not.

GEORGIANA. Good. The last thing I need is you as a brother in-law. Mary?

Enter MARY.

MARY. Yes, mum?

GEORGIANA. Fetch Thomas for Mr. Fredericks.

MARY. So the fox wants a go at the rooster as well then, eh?

DARREL. Just get him, will you?

Exit MARY.

GEORGIANA. So why the sudden interest in male camaraderie?

DARREL. It is none of your business.

GEORGIANA. I suppose it is not. But I do not trust you, Darrel. I never have.

DARREL. I learned never to trust anybody years ago, Georgiana. Especially women.

GEORGIANA. Perhaps there is some wisdom in that—especially *this* woman. Don't trust me, Darrel. Don't trust me at all.

Enter THOMAS.

THOMAS. Hello, Darrel.

GEORGIANA. Good-bye, Darrel.

Exit GEORGIANA.

THOMAS. How are you, Darrel?

DARREL. As always, Thomas. As always.

THOMAS. I am surprised that you asked to see *me*. Do you plan on asking me for my sister's hand in marriage?

DARREL. Not yet.

THOMAS. *(Laughs.)* I never know quite what to make of you, Darrel.

DARREL. As it should be.

THOMAS. Cloaked in mystery, our cunning thinker.

DARREL. I know your secrets, Thomas.

THOMAS. Pardon me?

DARREL. I won't small talk. I won't play with you. I came here with a purpose. Don't play the fool with me.

THOMAS. I thought it was well understood that it was no act.

DARREL. Yes, the foppish Thomas Highett. Fool, clown, and high-brow fellow. Who would guess that he is an embezzler?

THOMAS *stops cold. His face falls, as he stares stunned at* DARREL. *His manner immediately changes.*

THOMAS. What the devil!

DARREL. I am a businessman, Thomas. I looked into your assets long ago.

THOMAS. You what?

DARREL. I always know where I am standing. I found out that your fortune was much more than your shipping business in Liverpool or your family inheritance ought to suggest, as considerable as the returns from those are.

THOMAS. What are you doing looking at—?!

DARREL. I also found out why you have shown so much attention to Jane Fields. Her father has been helping you embezzle money, I presume, in return for your help in establishing him as a respectable figure.

THOMAS. That's a serious charge, sir!

DARREL. Yes, it is. And it is a true charge. You marrying his daughter will lend them some of that credibility which they have lacked and in return he has been slowly sucking money from his company and into your bank coffers. Am I accurate thus far? *(Pause.)* Your silence is illuminating.

THOMAS. Look here, what is it that you want?

DARREL. In return for your continual support of my publishing company, I will turn a blind eye to the corruption I have seen and will not report it to the authorities.

THOMAS. So all of your involvement with my sister has been a ploy to get at me?

DARREL. I want to be tied to you by blood, Thomas. I will need your unerring support no matter which of your sisters I marry.

THOMAS. Did you say "which?"

DARREL. Somehow your sister Catherine has developed a conscience. It was the last thing I expected. In any case, Georgiana was the one I was going to try for in the first place—but you saw how that went.

THOMAS. Why would a man like you prefer—?

DARREL. Oh, the world doesn't understand the value of a woman like Georgiana—and I'm not only talking about her excellent mind. These stupid men gallop like studs after pretty ponies like Catherine. But I tell you from experience, it's the plain women who make the most attentive lovers . . .

THOMAS. Here now! You are talking about my sisters!

DARREL. They are always somebody's sisters, Thomas. Or daughters, or mothers, or . . . wives. (DARREL *is sincerely disturbed by his own talk for a moment. But as quickly as it came, it is gone, shrugging off the brief battle with emotion that just came across him.*) I can have my fun with pretty women, surely, but a wife *(giving the word "wife" a bitter emphasis)* needs to be something else. Georgiana is a rare species.

THOMAS. And you think that I'll just submit to you?

At this DARREL *zeroes in on* THOMAS *and, with the swiftness of a viper, pushes* THOMAS *against a wall and grabs his throat.*

DARREL. I know what your game is, and I am prepared for it. I have partners in this. You must understand that there is more than one wolf on your trail. Tricky little rogue though you are, do you think your wits can handle my whole pack of professionals?

THOMAS *struggles against* DARREL's *strong grip, but* DARREL *only knocks him back harder.*

DARREL. Let me hear you say that you understand.

THOMAS. I understand.

> DARREL *loosens his grip and lets* THOMAS *go.* THOMAS *falls to the floor, struggling for air, massaging his neck. He looks up resentfully at* DARREL.

DARREL. Good. I'll be back in the morning to discuss the details. In the meantime, we have a clear understanding. *(Pause.)* Do we not?

THOMAS. Yes, we do.

DARREL. Good.

> *Exit* DARREL. THOMAS *stares him and then turns over a chair violently.*

THOMAS. Blast!

> *Blackout.*

END ACT ONE

Act Two

SCENE 1

> *A room in the Highett household.* GEORGIANA *is in her new dress, as* HANNAH *works on the last touches and ties up the back of the dress.*

GEORGIANA. *(Tersely.)* Are you almost through yet, dressmaker?

HANNAH. Almost, miss. Almost.

GEORGIANA. I ought to dock some of your pay for finishing it late. *(Uncomfortable silence.)* What would you think of that?

HANNAH. It is late, miss, I admit.

GEORGIANA. Yes, you could not accuse me of not being fair.

HANNAH. No, miss.

GEORGIANA. I am sure that you will be glad to leave this house anyway. I suppose you curse the day that you came in here.

HANNAH. It's been a blessing.

GEORGIANA. Pardon me?

HANNAH. Nothing but good has happened to me since I came here, miss.

GEORGIANA. Good?

HANNAH. Yes, miss.

GEORGIANA. That is ridiculous. I have heard of optimism, but I still do not see how you could say such. Especially since I have threatened to cut your pay.

HANNAH. We met Misters Young and Taylor here, miss.

GEORGIANA. Do not mention those names here, dressmaker.

HANNAH. I beg your pardon. *(Looking over the finished dress.)* It is done, miss.

GEORGIANA. Well, let us see it then.

> HANNAH *brings* GEORGIANA *to the mirror.* GEORGIANA *is dumbfounded.*

GEORGIANA. Oh my.

HANNAH. Is there anything wrong with it?

GEORGIANA. I can't believe how beautiful—it is.

HANNAH. If I may say so, miss, it suits you.

GEORGIANA. Does it? It is so different than anything I have ever worn. I look so—light. Why, you have transformed me! You could make even a rhinoceros look beautiful.

HANNAH. We changed the dress to fit your natural beauties, Miss Highett.

GEORGIANA. Natural beauties?

HANNAH. Yes, miss.

GEORGIANA. Such as what?

HANNAH. Well, if miss would allow me—

GEORGIANA. Yes, yes, show me!

> GEORGIANA *sits herself into a chair in front of the mirror.* HANNAH *is hesitant.*

GEORGIANA. Well, get to it. I give you permission.

HANNAH. Yes, miss.

> HANNAH *steps behind* GEORGIANA *and lets down* GEORGIANA's *hair.*

GEORGIANA. Be careful now.

HANNAH. Yes, miss. Now look at your eyes, miss—their shape, their color—aren't they beautiful? And see this? Miss's hair? It is very rich and very beautiful. When we picked a shade of color, we made sure it would point out its highlights.

GEORGIANA. Yes, I see that.

HANNAH. If Miss is agreeable and would pardon me making the suggestion, Miss might want to do a little more with such beautiful hair. Having it tied into that tight bun all the time may not be exactly the effect that Miss would desire on a day such as the ball. With your permission, miss, may I?

GEORGIANA. Yes.

HANNAH. (HANNAH *begins working on* GEORGIANA's *hair.*) Perhaps you could bring it up like this. Or like this. With a hot iron, you could have ringlets on the sides of your face here and here. There is so much that could be done with it, if Miss desires it and it is agreeable with her.

GEORGIANA. Do you truly think it is beautiful?

HANNAH. I think *you're* quite beautiful, miss. If you don't mind me saying so, that is.

GEORGIANA. Poppycock. My face, what can you do for that?

HANNAH. Pardon me saying so, miss, but there's nothing wrong with your face. It's only that—

GEORGIANA. Out with it. I want to hear it.

HANNAH. Pardon me for saying—it's not your face. It's your expression.

GEORGIANA. My expression! What do you mean?

HANNAH. When a woman has something to—live for, a purpose, meaning—then all of the tightness disappears and she becomes more pleasant to look at. Miss is very perceptive to see that, for Miss has been using it, and she has been becoming beautiful, yes?

GEORGIANA. Well, you cannot decorate the soul, Miss Whitefield.

HANNAH. If you don't mind me speaking my mind—

GEORGIANA. Proceed.

HANNAH. Respectfully, I disagree. A soul can be refined. Mine has.

GEORGIANA. Yes, you have changed religions, correct? So you have been refined in what way?

HANNAH. I daresn't say, miss.

GEORGIANA. Come now, out with it.

HANNAH. This is close to me, intimate—this is sacred to me. I will only discuss it, if it can remain sacred.

GEORGIANA. All right then, sacred. What do you have to tell me?

HANNAH. May I speak frankly, miss?

GEORGIANA. Of course.

HANNAH. Miss and I are the same.

GEORGIANA. That's preposterous. *(Pause.)* What do you mean?

HANNAH. In my temperament, I can seem condescending to others.

GEORGIANA. Condescending? Yes, I can see that—

HANNAH. I get so afraid. As if someday everything will suddenly break. For years I have thought if I were righteous enough, kind enough, strong enough, I could prevent that day from happening.

GEORGIANA. What day?

HANNAH. The day when it suddenly all unravels.

GEORGIANA. Unravels.

HANNAH. Torn to shreds.

GEORGIANA. Shreds. How do you prevent that?

HANNAH. *(Pause.)* I'm not sure.

Enter THOMAS. THOMAS *sees* GEORGIANA *and is stunned by the change.*

THOMAS. Georgiana?

GEORGIANA. What is it, Thomas?

THOMAS. Why, you are—

GEORGIANA. Yes?

THOMAS. You are absolutely—you are absolutely beautiful!

GEORGIANA. Thomas, really—

THOMAS *feigns staggering back and falls over a couch or chair.*

THOMAS. I'm blinded by your beauty! I'm blinded! Honestly, I can't see! Like Saul of Tarsus!

GEORGIANA. *(Annoyed.)* Thomas—

THOMAS *goes to his knees and starts bowing and groveling to* GEORGIANA.

THOMAS. Oh, please, have mercy on me, Goddess of Beauty!

GEORGIANA. I am not in the mood for your games, Thomas.

THOMAS. *(Getting up suddenly.)* Actually, I am being rather serious, dear. You really do look splendid in that dress. But, Stephen is here.

GEORGIANA. What? What is Stephen doing here?

THOMAS. I invited him to go hunting with me. I am sorry, I, uh—forgot that your dressmaker was going to be over.

GEORGIANA. Oh, Thomas, what a stupid thing to do! Let me talk to him before you go off—but, oh, hurry, Thomas, go get Charlotte and Angelina to help me out of this thing.

Exit THOMAS.

HANNAH. Perhaps I should take my leave—

GEORGIANA. You can get your pay from Mary, Miss Whitefield. I will give you the full price. Plus tell Mary that I am giving you a 10 percent bonus for such quality work.

HANNAH. Oh, thank you so very much! We truly needed—

GEORGIANA. He simply can't see this dress yet.

HANNAH. I don't know how to—

GEORGIANA. Oh, don't be a fool. Go. Go!

HANNAH. Yes, miss.

Exit HANNAH. GEORGIANA *goes to the door, calling out.*

GEORGIANA. Angelina. Angelina!

SCENE 2

We're back in the drawing room. STEPHEN *waits. Enter* HANNAH.

STEPHEN. Oh. Miss Whitefield. I did not know that you were here.

HANNAH. Well, yes. I'm just on my way out, sir.

HANNAH *goes to leave,* STEPHEN *calls out to her and stops her.*

STEPHEN. Miss Whitefield!

HANNAH. Yes, Mr. Lockhart?

STEPHEN. How is Esther?

HANNAH. My sister is well, thank you.

STEPHEN. Do you—do you suppose she would mind if I—if I paid her a visit this afternoon?

HANNAH. Mr. Lockhart—

STEPHEN. She did tell you about the talk that I had with her, didn't she?

HANNAH. Yes.

STEPHEN. Then you understand that I expressed—interest to her?

HANNAH. Yes.

STEPHEN. Good. Is today a bad day to visit then?

HANNAH. I think any day is a bad day to visit.

STEPHEN. What do you mean? What are you telling me?

HANNAH. She—she was flattered.

STEPHEN. Flattered?

HANNAH. She told me that if you and I were able to talk today when I came by—she told me to give you her apologies and she hopes that you will have no ill feelings towards her because of her refusal.

STEPHEN. You are in earnest?

HANNAH. Regretfully so.

STEPHEN. But why?

HANNAH. She—she was flattered. But we—she has decided to—Mr. Lockhart, you are in no position to honorably make a future with my sister.

STEPHEN. Are you the one who pressed this decision upon her?

HANNAH. Esther makes—her own decisions, she—

STEPHEN. What a farce! I suppose this has much more to do with your ignorant superstitions than anything! Well, let your sister know that your religious tyranny has destroyed any chance we may have had at happiness together.

HANNAH. Esther makes her own decisions, she—she happens to desire somebody who would share what is most precious with her. What is most true.

STEPHEN. You know nothing of truth!

This startles HANNAH. *After a shocked pause, she curtsies.*

HANNAH. Good day to you, sir.

HANNAH *turns to leave, but then stops. She gathers her courage and turns back to* STEPHEN.

HANNAH. I may not have your education, but I have experienced things in this religion that would knock you off your high place, sir! Supernatural things, spectacular things—sacred things.

STEPHEN. And what if another preacher came along just as schooled in the art of deception? What then!

HANNAH. Who is the true deceiver here, sir? Mr. Young and Mr. Taylor—or you? Or have you just deceived yourself?

STEPHEN. You do not know what you are talking about . . .

HANNAH. Don't I?

STEPHEN. It is not pragmatic. All it does is make you discontent . . .

HANNAH. I did not need this religion to be made *discontent*! And I am a lucky one. I don't have to go into those factories and risk my hand and life to a spinning jenny. I don't have to prance as a strumpet in desperation. I have not been thrust that low, but I have seen it and smelled it and heard it!

STEPHEN. Well, that's the way God planned it, isn't it?

HANNAH. No, it's the way that man has made it.

STEPHEN. Things are the way they are.

HANNAH. And you benefit.

STEPHEN. *I* benefit?!

HANNAH. Don't you, sir? While my people work and slave, your people live off our sweat, you build upon our foundations, you oppress us for our labor! While you grow richer and fatter, with more and more leisure time, we work our bones raw and dwindle away into specters of poverty.

STEPHEN. Why, how dare you accuse me of . . .

HANNAH. Am I not correct, sir?

STEPHEN. I—you are not—you and Esther must be able to— *(Pause)* oh dear.

HANNAH. Sir?

STEPHEN. You are right—you're absolutely right.

HANNAH. I—I didn't mean to be contrary.

STEPHEN. Oh, yes, you did. Thank heaven for that.

HANNAH. Sir—

STEPHEN. Why have hidden yourself, Miss Whitefield?

HANNAH. I beg your pardon?

STEPHEN. I find you to be quite remarkable. Yet only now have I thought so. You have been so silent before—now I find your voice to be quite thrilling.

HANNAH. I'd better go, Mr. Lockhart.

STEPHEN. Wait. Can I see you again?

HANNAH. Mr. Lockhart—

STEPHEN. I have seen something in you—

HANNAH. What you've seen in me is what you saw in my sister—women who know who they are and what they believe.

STEPHEN. Please—

HANNAH. Sir, you went from Miss Highett, to my sister and now you speak sweetly to me—what next? You didn't want them. You don't want me.

STEPHEN. How could you possibly know what I want?

HANNAH. You want a crutch to hold you up.

   HANNAH *picks up her bag and is about to leave.*

STEPHEN. You've wounded me—

HANNAH. Frankly, you deserved it.

STEPHEN. Such strength—such confidence. Where do you get it?

HANNAH. Good-bye, Mr. Lockhart.

STEPHEN. The book—Is it that apostle's book? *(HANNAH is leaving.)* Please! Wait! Thomas said that they gave him a book—is that the book?

HANNAH. Yes.

STEPHEN. I like books.

HANNAH. Yes?

STEPHEN. May I borrow *your* book?

HANNAH. My book?

STEPHEN. Yes, yes—the one you read from. You have one in your bag there, don't you?

HANNAH. How did you know?

STEPHEN. I have great powers of deduction.

HANNAH. *(Taking out her Book of Mormon.)* Sir, this book is precious to me.

STEPHEN. I will return it to you. I promise.

> HANNAH *considers it a moment and then hands* STEPHEN *her Book of Mormon.*

STEPHEN. Thank you, Miss Whitefield.

HANNAH. Don't be too quick to cast it aside as foolishness, Mr. Lockhart. Make you sure you understand a thing before you try to condemn it.

SCENE 3

> GEORGIANA *and* MARY. GEORGIANA *is appareled in her new dress and her hair is styled and decorated. She is self-conscious about her appearance, as if she were exposed in a very vulnerable way. Music is playing from the ballroom, as the ball is in full sway.*

GEORGIANA. Is it hot in here? I feel it is very hot. I am sure it is even worse in there with all the people.

MARY. Come now, Miss Georgiana, you must go in there. Your guests are all waiting and you look—

GEORGIANA. *(She goes, but then stops.)* I can't. I just can't. I don't see why I got this thing together. I forgot how uncomfortable it gets with all of the heat, the odor, the perspiration—

MARY. Mr. Lockhart has been asking after you.

GEORGIANA. Of course he has. He needs me to introduce him to Mr. Lowe—who, by the way, has not arrived!

MARY. Miss Georgiana—

GEORGIANA. How would *you* like it, Mary, if a man only hung about you because you knew some influential people.

MARY. Now you know that's not the case.

GEORGIANA. Do I, Mary? Do I?

MARY. Well, if that's the case, then tonight he has something else coming to him. You look splendid, mum.

GEORGIANA. You're my maid, Mary. You're paid to say that.

MARY. Now, mum, that's like making a cat bark. You know that I have only ever said what I want to.

GEORGIANA. *(Seeing* STEPHEN *approaching.)* Oh, no!

GEORGIANA *turns her back toward* STEPHEN *as he enters.*

STEPHEN. Mary, where's Georgiana? I have been looking for her all evening.

MARY *points at* GEORGIANA.

GEORGIANA. I am sorry I have left you waiting, Stephen. I—

GEORGIANA *turns around.*

STEPHEN. Georgiana—

GEORGIANA. What? What is it?

STEPHEN. Why, you are—Georgiana! You're lovely.

GEORGIANA. I . . .

STEPHEN. Splendid, smashing—beautiful.

GEORGIANA. I am not either—It's just a new dress.

STEPHEN. It is not the dress. I am humbled to be in your presence.

STEPHEN *bows.*

GEORGIANA. Stephen, stop it, this is embarrassing.

STEPHEN. Mary, are you embarrassed?

MARY. No, sir.

STEPHEN. Then you must be the only one who feels so, Georgiana. If you had looked into the mirror, perhaps you would have felt differently.

GEORGIANA. I—I don't know how to explain myself.

The music changes.

STEPHEN. Recognize the music, Georgiana?

GEORGIANA. Why, of course! Graduation! This was the song in which you asked me to dance. I'm surprised you remember that.

STEPHEN. Dance with me!

GEORGIANA. Oh, Stephen I just can't go in—

STEPHEN. All right. Then let us dance here.

GEORGIANA. Pardon me?

STEPHEN. We can hear the music. Let us have one song when we're not bumping into everybody in those dreadful lines. I want you to myself for a moment.

GEORGIANA simply nods, a kind of sweet embarrassment coming over her. They start to dance.

STEPHEN. Remember, my uncomfortable suit coat? I felt so embarrassed.

GEORGIANA. You were adorable. I am the one who ought to have felt embarrassed.

STEPHEN. I remember that you wore a beautiful dress.

GEORGIANA. Yes, it was Catherine's. A bit tight.

STEPHEN. I didn't notice. I just thought—oh, never mind.

GEORGIANA. You thought what?

STEPHEN. I remember thinking that you were my favorite girl in the world. *(Pause)* Perhaps I shouldn't have told you that just now.

GEORGIANA. I think you should have told me it *then*.

The music stops. They stare at each other for a moment. They kiss and then separate, still staring at each other. DARREL *and* CATHERINE *enter.*

DARREL. Have we interrupted a private moment?

STEPHEN. Good evening, Darrel.

DARREL. Er—good evening, Stephen. Georgiana, is that really you?

GEORGIANA. Good evening, Darrel. You look absolutely splendid tonight, Catherine.

CATHERINE. I—so do you, Georgiana. You look—like a queen.

DARREL. The dance is in the other room, you know.

STEPHEN. Oh, I see that they want our spot, Georgiana. Should we give it to them?

GEORGIANA. Why not? And you truly do look stunning tonight, Catherine. You are certainly at top form.

STEPHEN *and* GEORGIANA *exit.* MARY *exits satisfied.*

CATHERINE. Did you hear that? Georgiana was—well, she was—kind to me.

DARREL. What did you think of the woman Thomas is escorting around out there?

CATHERINE. Jane Fields? Well . . .

DARREL. She is a detestable woman. She has no sense of propriety at all.

CATHERINE. If she can make Thomas happy, then she is quite suitable to me.

DARREL. What? You used to detest her, I thought.

CATHERINE. Well, now I don't. I think I am starting to look at people a little differently now.

DARREL. Oh dear, you have become a wretched moralist haven't you?

> DARREL *suddenly gives a start when* HAROLD LOWE *is seen in the doorway.*

CATHERINE. What is wrong, Darrel?

DARREL. What is Harold Lowe doing here?

> DARREL *attempts to retreat from the room before* CATHERINE *stops him.*

CATHERINE. Do you know each other?

DARREL. I must leave.

CATHERINE. Darrel, wait—

DARREL. I am sorry, Catherine, but I will have to quit the ball early.

CATHERINE. Why? We have planned this for weeks.

DARREL. A personal matter, my dear.

> HAROLD *tips his hat with a smile as* DARREL *tries to pass him.* HAROLD *prevents him for a moment.*

HAROLD. It has been some time, sir.

DARREL. Get out of my way, old man.

HAROLD. What are you up to these days? The usual?

DARREL. Get out of my way.

HAROLD. Yes, yes, always your "way." That is the important thing. No matter who gets crushed in the meantime.

DARREL. I don't need your lectures.

HAROLD. Yes, yes, avoid the lectures. Avoid the morality. Avoid those voices from the past. Avoid the voice of conscience.

DARREL. Get out of my way!

> DARREL *pushes his way past* HAROLD *and exits.* HAROLD *comes over to* CATHERINE.

HAROLD. I had hoped that I had been misinformed when I heard that you were involved with that scoundrel, Catherine.

CATHERINE. How do you know him?

HAROLD. He wanted to become a partner with me. I investigated his past and found some very malignant pieces of information.

CATHERINE. Oh dear—oh, no, no, no—

HAROLD. I am afraid so. Catherine—

CATHERINE. I am not sure that I want to hear this.

HAROLD. Catherine, dear, Mr. Fredericks is already married. He left behind a wife in London—a wife who is expecting their first child. Even when he was still with her, he was unfaithful. At the time he was so steeped in debt because of his gambling that he simply fled London and came here under a different identity. Now it appears that he is attempting to hook himself into your family's fortune.

CATHERINE. *(Crying.)* I have been a fool.

HAROLD. I am afraid to cause you pain, my dear, but I do it to prevent a deeper hurt. Be rid of him and do not get caught in his snares.

CATHERINE. Excuse me. This is a bit overwhelming.

CATHERINE goes to exit, but HAROLD stops her.

HAROLD. Catherine, how extensive was your relationship with that man?

CATHERINE. How dare you—how dare you accuse me of that!

HAROLD. *(Pause.)* I have not accused you of anything.

Exit CATHERINE, retreating. HAROLD looks after her with a mixture of concern and suspicion. Enter GEORGIANA and STEPHEN.

GEORGIANA. I thought I saw you come in, Harold!

HAROLD. Georgiana, my girl!

GEORGIANA. Harold, I have been waiting all evening for you! I have some very important things I want to bring up to you. But first, this is my friend Stephen Lockhart. He has been wanting to meet you.

STEPHEN. Sir.

HAROLD. A pleasure.

GEORGIANA. I think that you will both benefit from the meeting.

HAROLD. If he has your approval, Georgiana, I am sure we will. So I imagine you have a manuscript you want to show me, Mr. Lockhart?

STEPHEN. Am I that transparent?

HAROLD. Sir, I can spot a writer from a mile away.

SCENE 4

Enter THOMAS *and* MARY.

THOMAS. Mary, I don't understand your line of questioning.

MARY. All I am trying to say, Mr. Thomas, is that I think it odd that you spend so much time with Mr. Fredericks nowadays.

THOMAS. I have no personal friendship with the man. We are doing a bit of business together, that's all.

MARY. Business?

THOMAS. Yes, business.

MARY. Is that what you call it?

THOMAS. Call what? Why wouldn't it be called business?

MARY. The walls have ears, sir.

THOMAS. —and flies and windows and pictures. What are you saying, Mary?

MARY. I overheard your conversation with Mr. Fredericks.

THOMAS. Mary—you were behind the door!

MARY. Polishing the silver, sir. I polish it nearly every day. And I know a great deal more than you think—things about this family. I know it all more intimately than you do. Sir, that Darrel Fredericks is not a nice man. Not a nice man at all. He's invaded this house in more than one way, and I won't stand by as he tries to destroy it.

THOMAS. Mary, you don't understand. I am too caught up with it now.

MARY. Say that you were at a picnic, sir. And this hornet comes upon your food.

THOMAS. Hornet?

MARY. Yes, a pest, an insect, a hornet with spindly legs, black eyes, and a fearsome sting. Say this hornet tries to infest your food. Do you swat him away?

THOMAS. No, because he will sting my hand.

MARY. So what do you do then, sir?

THOMAS. I deputize him, give him a regiment and send him off to India.

MARY. Seriously, sir, what do you do?

THOMAS. I don't know.

MARY. But say you have a stick, sir. A big stick. So when this hornet falls upon your food, what do you do then? Do you smash the hornet and the food together?

THOMAS. Yes, to save the rest of the food.

MARY. Then, sir, my suggestion about Darrel Fredericks, is to find a stick. A big one.

A book flies into the room. GEORGIANA *is heard off stage.*

GEORGIANA. *(Off stage.)* Romantic rubbish! You make a woman dissatisfied! I don't know why I read such things.

THOMAS. Oh, do you think she's in one of her moods? Perhaps I should go in and—

MARY. Don't touch the kettle while it's hot, sir.

THOMAS. Is a retreat in order then?

MARY. Aye.

Exit THOMAS *and* MARY. *Enter* CATHERINE. *She picks up the book.*

CATHERINE. Georgiana?

Enter GEORGIANA.

GEORGIANA. What is it, Catherine?

CATHERINE. I am worried about you.

GEORGIANA. No need to worry.

CATHERINE. Something is wrong.

GEORGIANA. Nothing is wrong.

CATHERINE. Something has been wrong since the ball.

GEORGIANA. Do I need to repeat myself? Nothing is wrong.

CATHERINE. You have been watching the windows for a week now. You are waiting for him to come.

GEORGIANA. For whom to come?

CATHERINE. I may not have your kind of mind, but I'm not stupid.

GEORGIANA. What do you care about it?

CATHERINE. I care about you.

GEORGIANA. Since when?

CATHERINE. Georgie—

GEORGIANA. You are serious, aren't you?

CATHERINE. How did the ball go? He showed interest, didn't he? *(Silence)* Didn't he?

GEORGIANA. Yes.

CATHERINE. He expressed that interest?

GEORGIANA. You could say that.

CATHERINE. But since then he hasn't come.

GEORGIANA. He hasn't come. Catherine, is it possible that a man could regard—could have affection for a woman like me?

CATHERINE. Oh, Georgiana—

Enter MARY.

MARY. *(Gleefully.)* Mr. Lockhart is here to see you, mum.

GEORGIANA. Stephen?

MARY. I thought that might cheer up your spirits. I'll bring him right in.

Exit MARY.

GEORGIANA. Oh, Catherine, he's come!

GEORGIANA *embraces* CATHERINE. *They both laugh. They separate, somewhat embarrassed.*

GEORGIANA. We haven't done that for some time, have we?

CATHERINE. Good luck, Georgie.

Exit CATHERINE. *Enter* STEPHEN.

STEPHEN. Good evening, Miss Highett.

GEORGIANA. It's so good to see you, Stephen.

STEPHEN. As it is to see you.

GEORGIANA. I wondered what took so long for you to come by since the ball. What could have possibly detained you for so—*(Seeing his hesitation.)* Something's wrong, isn't it?

STEPHEN. I—I don't know what to say.

GEORGIANA. Stephen, what is wrong? You look so rigid.

STEPHEN. Please, sit down. I have something to tell you—

GEORGIANA. Why are you so formal? What is it? Trust me.

STEPHEN. Well—I—

GEORGIANA. Stephen?

STEPHEN. I'm trying—I—oh, dear—

GEORGIANA. You can tell me.

STEPHEN. I'm leaving.

GEORGIANA. Leaving?

STEPHEN. To America.

GEORGIANA. America? America! Whatever for? When will you be back?

STEPHEN. I have come to thank you for your friendship, Georgiana. It has meant a great deal to me all these years and—

GEORGIANA. What is this about?

STEPHEN. It is a personal decision.

GEORGIANA. A personal decision you cannot share with me? *(Pause.)* Stephen, I thought—well, after the ball we were so close—

STEPHEN. I hope that you did not misinterpret—

GEORGIANA. You kissed me.

STEPHEN. I know—I know. I meant it—I meant it then.

GEORGIANA. *Then?*

STEPHEN. It was a mistake. I am sorry.

GEORGIANA. It was not a mistake—

STEPHEN. Yes, it was. I acted rashly. I am deeply sorry.

GEORGIANA. That is not the sort of thing a woman wants to hear about her first kiss.

STEPHEN. I feel—I have been tortured with guilt about the whole thing.

GEORGIANA. Oh, spare me of any prepared speeches you have to ease my—

STEPHEN. I have joined the Latter-day Saints. There. I said it.

GEORGIANA. Oh. *(She sits.)* Oh dear. It is about the dressmaker then.

STEPHEN. No, it is not that.

GEORGIANA. She is a pretty girl.

STEPHEN. I am sincere in my conversion.

GEORGIANA. It *is* the dressmaker!

STEPHEN. Do not jump to such a dramatic conclusion—

GEORGIANA. Dramatic? No, a man like you falling for such a girl is absolutely trivial. It is beneath you!

STEPHEN. Georgiana, this has nothing to do with the dressmakers. And, my poor darling, it has nothing to do with you.

GEORGIANA. Who has it to do with then?

STEPHEN. It has everything to do with me. Me! I—I have been searching, inquiring, but I didn't know it. Not really. Yet now—

GEORGIANA. You are a dyed-in-the-wool heathen like I am. Are you foolish enough to abandon all of your security for the sake of a dressmaker?

STEPHEN. I have already said—

GEORGIANA. Will you abandon the vigor of our friendship for such gutter children?

STEPHEN. Do not make them a part of this. They are women of goodness. Women of gentleness.

GEORGIANA. Women of weakness. Stop creating goddesses out of the delicate, porcelain-faced nymphs of the ignorant!

STEPHEN. Georgiana, how can you be so vain? Can't you see that it is the ugliest part of you?

GEORGIANA. Vain? Vain am I? With a face like mine? I am not one of these crystallized corpses of beauty!

STEPHEN. Please—

GEORGIANA. What feminine qualities, what prancing movements, what horrid lace and velvet do I possess to make me vain?

STEPHEN. It is the conceit of your mind, your own self-regard.

GEORGIANA. You are defensive because I have intellect and depth, while these religionists have nothing, but a polished husk! Emotionalism!

STEPHEN. Georgie . . .

GEORGIANA. What, do I threaten you? Do you feel as if I will debunk your manhood?

STEPHEN. Georgiana—

GEORGIANA. Is the mind of an intelligent, sophisticated woman too much for you? Is this dressmaker so much more to your liking because she will bend to you?

STEPHEN. Georgiana! This is not a contest between you and Esther!

GEORGIANA. Tell me why else you would take this fantastic journey?

STEPHEN. It is true belief. *My* belief. It sat well with me—there was truth in it.

GEORGIANA. Truth?! There is no truth, only ranting and raving and flinging the name of God about as if it actually meant something!

STEPHEN. And that is the difference between us. It does mean something to *me*, Georgiana. I am a believer now—I think, deep down, I always was. But deep down you never have been.

GEORGIANA. Belief—belief in what? Will you abandon the pinnacle of the world for that wild-eyed beast of a nation?

STEPHEN. I was brought up a gentleman, but I have cultivated the soul of a beggar. This is *my* decision. I will not be a laborer for this world. Better to be the servant of God than to be the slave of social pharisees.

GEORGIANA. Pharisees! Do not be deceived!

STEPHEN. *(Temper rising.)* I am not deceived! Georgiana, I do not need England's social structure to buoy me up. And I do not need your approval or that of any man, woman, or devil!

GEORGIANA. Stop it! *(Pause. They both attempt to regain their composure and repress their emotions.)* Then you are a convert?

STEPHEN. Yes.

GEORGIANA. One of the religious faithful?

STEPHEN. Yes.

GEORGIANA. Oh.

STEPHEN. Georgiana—

GEORGIANA. Your writing? What is to happen with that?

STEPHEN. It is nothing to me. Now my once vain ambition can give up my prominent future and not despair about it.

GEORGIANA. So nothing is the same for you anymore. Your writing means nothing, your country means nothing, your society means nothing?

STEPHEN. Not what they once did.

GEORGIANA. And am I nothing as well?

STEPHEN. Oh, Georgiana—

GEORGIANA. I deserve an answer.

STEPHEN. I care for you—deeply. But I cannot stay.

GEORGIANA. Do you love me, Stephen?

STEPHEN. Love—I hardly know what love is.

GEORGIANA. I have changed—I have put on a new dress, a new face—

STEPHEN. I love you, Georgiana. I always have, I think—but not in that sense. It is like with the dressmakers. I admired them. I mistook that for love. They lifted me to a point, and you lifted me even higher, but it is even greater hands that bore the piercing of nails that have truly brought me bravery.

GEORGIANA. So are you here to cut me loose or ask me to go with you?

STEPHEN. What kind of question is *that*?

GEORGIANA. I—I will not sacrifice my life on your altar! I will not be controlled by the dictates of a man I have never seen nor a god I have never heard.

STEPHEN. I understand. In fact your feelings have simplified the matter for me greatly.

GEORGIANA. Stephen, I would give up everything for you. You are substance. I can hold you in my hands. If you could just abandon this quest of Quixote.

STEPHEN. Our ships are sailing in different directions—we grow more distant every moment.

GEORGIANA. It doesn't have to be this way.

STEPHEN. I came here to say good-bye, Georgiana.

GEORGIANA. Stephen, don't go. I need you.

STEPHEN. And I once thought that I needed you.

GEORGIANA. Then stay.

STEPHEN. No. I can't.

GEORGIANA. Stephen—

STEPHEN. I believe in this, Georgiana. You and I—we are too different—

GEORGIANA. We are the same!

STEPHEN. No. We are not the same. There is a part of me that you have never known, for it is foreign to you—it was foreign to me. Yet I have discovered a piece of it and now I am in search for the rest. There is something that I long for which you have never sought, never understood, never acknowledged.

GEORGIANA. If it is love, I can love—I do—

STEPHEN. That is not it either.

GEORGIANA. Did you hear what I just said?

STEPHEN. Good-bye, Georgiana.

    STEPHEN *exits.* GEORGIANA *can't hold the emotion any longer and exits.*

SCENE 5

The dressmakers' shop and home. HANNAH *and* ESTHER *are packing a trunk. We see that they are very poor and can maintain only a minimally professional atmosphere without much to decorate or refine the place with. However, the work that sits on the dress frames is magnificent. Quality dresses, some made for women of a more modest income, while some are made for women of a higher station. Although we see this distinction in the dresses, it is obvious that both kinds have been made with craftsmanship, an eye for detail, and a lot of love.*

HANNAH. And I still can't convince you to come with me?

ESTHER. I—I admire the people of your faith, Hannah. But I don't feel it like you do.

HANNAH. I know. But America. It could be a new start for us.

ESTHER. Edenbridge is my home. It's always been my home. It's been yours, too.

HANNAH. I—I never belonged here. Except with you.

ESTHER. Are you sure about this, Hannah? I know you believe in this, but . . . America is so far.

HANNAH. I want to be with my people.

> *There is a knock.* HANNAH *and* ESTHER *look at each other, confused.*

HANNAH. Who could that be at this hour?

ESTHER. I'll get it.

> ESTHER *goes to the door. In the door frame stands a regal woman in a hooded cloak.*

ESTHER. Can we . . . can we help you, mum?

> *The woman takes back her hood to reveal* GEORGIANA. GEORGIANA's *expression is hard, icy, a calm exterior just barely concealing the wild fury underneath, which is only betrayed by the heat in her eyes. Without so much as waiting for an invitation to come inside, she makes her way in, almost pushing* ESTHER *out of the way to do so. She carries a valise with her.*

ESTHER. Miss Highett? Why, this is a surprise. It's looking pretty murky outside. Would you like some tea to warm you up?

GEORGIANA. Don't put on your false kindnesses with me, you hypocrite.

ESTHER. This is about Stephen, isn't it?

GEORGIANA. You ought to call him Mr. Lockhart.

> *Intimidated into silence,* ESTHER *watches* GEORGIANA *as she makes her way around the shop inspecting it with condescension and arrogance.* GEORGIANA *walks among the dresses, looking at them as if they were actual people, but people of a lower order. She seems a cruel queen amid their lifeless forms. She stops at one particularly beautiful dress and stares it down.*

GEORGIANA. Headless. Armless. How appropriate.

ESTHER. Miss?

GEORGIANA. *(With a touch of tendernesss.)* I almost pity them.

> *She starts gently touching the dress, her fingers smoothly gliding down its fabric, feeling its quality and care, and she almost understands it for a moment. She looks it over, and we see her rare vulnerability come through once again.*

GEORGIANA. They have fashioned us into a thing of beauty, it is true. But with no eyes to see with, no arms to act. Blind and crippled. Is this what these men have created us to be?

> GEORGIANA's *soft eyes harden once more.* ESTHER *becomes more and more nervous at this bizarre behavior. We see* HANNAH *approach, unseen by* GEORGIANA. *She looks as startled as* ESTHER. *In the meantime,* GEORGIANA *is almost in her own world of thought, as if the dressmakers didn't even exist. It's just her and the dress.*

GEORGIANA. Or is it we who wanted it, who willed it? We . . . I—I so much wanted to be admired . . . beautiful. Did I allow this?

ESTHER. Miss Highett, I have ended whatever chances I could have had at Mr. Lockhart's heart. You can still . . .

GEORGIANA. I do not want to hear it! I do not want to hear your pities or your sympathies or your condolences!

ESTHER. You don't understand . . .

> GEORGIANA *reaches into her valise and pulls out the dress which the dressmakers had created for her.* ESTHER *gasps, not at the revelation of the dress, but at the other object Georgiana pulls out: her father's dagger.*

GEORGIANA. Yes, you know every stitch in this dress—this horrid shroud!

ESTHER. We have meant you no harm!

> *Having knocked, but being unheard,* STEPHEN *enters unnoticed by* GEORGIANA.

GEORGIANA. You and your sister so earnestly said that I was beautiful—you said that this fitted me! Well, have this for your troubles and cares!

> *With very purposeful and skilled strokes,* GEORGIANA *stabs into the dress and starts shredding it with the very sharp and effective dagger. The dressmakers watch horrified at this display of rage and deliberate destruction. In an almost graceful fit of fury,* GEORGIANA *completely destroys the dress.*

GEORGIANA. I do not want your beauty! I do not want your dependence! I will not debase myself with your embarrassing costume any longer!

> ESTHER *goes down her knees, touching the remains of the dress with some remorse. She then looks up, angry.*

ESTHER. For all your eloquence and fury, miss, you've become nothing but a jilted spinster.

> GEORGIANA *harshly slaps* ESTHER. ESTHER *shrieks, and* HANNAH *lunges forward grabbing* GEORGIANA *by the shoulder.* GEORGIANA *in surprise and fear, twirls, lifting the dagger which slices through* HANNAH's *dress and into her upper arm.* HANNAH *screams and clutches her arm, as* GEORGIANA *steps back in shock.* ESTHER *rushes to grab some disinfectant and clean bandages and immediately begins to attempt to stop the bleeding.* STEPHEN *lunges forward to the dressmaker's aid.*

STEPHEN. Georgiana!

GEORGIANA. Stephen?

STEPHEN. Georgiana, have you lost your mind?!

GEORGIANA. Stephen, please, it's not what it looks like . . .

STEPHEN. Then why do you have a dagger in your hand?! If you want to vent your jealousy, come at me! If you want to strike some one, strike me!

> STEPHEN *approaches* GEORGIANA, *and in an instinct that surprises even her, she lifts the dagger against* STEPHEN. STEPHEN *stops, shocked to have his friend turn a dagger on him.* GEORGIANA, *wide-eyed and afraid, looks at* STEPHEN *defensively, but then back down at the dagger. In a moment of comprehension, she lowers the dagger and stares back up at* STEPHEN. *She then turns and flees out the door.* STEPHEN *turns back and once again helps* ESTHER *with* HANNAH's *wound, as* HANNAH *winces and cries in pain.*

SCENE 6

The Highett Mansion, the drawing room. A terrible thunderstorm is heard outside. CATHERINE *enters with* DARREL *trailing behind her.*

CATHERINE. Get away from me!

DARREL. Catherine, darling—

CATHERINE. I am no longer your darling!

DARREL. What has gotten into you?

CATHERINE. I know, Darrel! I know all of it!

DARREL. What do you know?

CATHERINE. I know that you are a scoundrel and that I will no longer be a part of anything that you have touched.

> *Exit* CATHERINE. *Enter* THOMAS.

THOMAS. My, things are just unraveling for you, aren't they?

DARREL. Thomas, my friend—

THOMAS. I am not your friend.

DARREL. You are my partner. *(Wrapping his arm across* THOMAS's *shoulder.)* Now you understand that lovers, they have their little spats every once in a while. Women can be so emotional. Go to her, calm her down, and tell her that I just want to talk things through. I love your sister. She must know that.

THOMAS. Love? Love! You love no one.

DARREL. Thomas, why antagonize me? We are partners. We are in business together.

THOMAS. We are no longer in business together!

DARREL. *(Quietly threatening.)* Oh, yes we are. Many business partners dislike one another, but they each have something the other wants. You have my future, and I have your past. Now, be a good partner, and go in there and do what you must to get Catherine back into my arms.

Enter GEORGIANA. She is disheveled, rain-soaked, and very fierce looking. The dagger, which she still has been carrying, is placed aside as GEORGIANA takes off her wet gloves, cloak, etc.

DARREL. I have been waiting for you.

GEORGIANA. You—get out! Get out! Get out!

DARREL. Catherine and I—we are having a bit of trouble at the moment. Thomas, go bring her in here.

THOMAS. What are you up to?

DARREL. I said do it.

THOMAS hesitates, then exits.

GEORGIANA. You slithering creature, what are you plotting?

DARREL. You always assume the worst.

GEORGIANA. Only when you are around. You have the smell of filth wherever you go.

DARREL. Ah, that scent was already *here*. I just uncovered it.

Enter THOMAS with CATHERINE, who is reluctant to return.

DARREL. The whole picturesque family! Now listen, all of you. I am sick of this little dance, so I am cutting off the music and will be straightforward with you. I am here to propose a marriage. A marriage of convenience.

GEORGIANA. Darrel, will your arrogance ever cease?

DARREL. All you have to do now is decide whether it's Georgiana or Catherine who marries me. I don't care who anymore, as long as I am tied to this family.

CATHERINE goes to DARREL and slaps him.

CATHERINE. You already have a wife. You have a child! I will never—

DARREL. You tart!

DARREL slaps CATHERINE, but much more fiercely. CATHERINE crumbles to the floor. THOMAS grabs his father's dagger and raises it against DARREL.

THOMAS. Don't *ever* touch her again!

DARREL. *(Cautiously.)* Do you not see where you are? I have much to offer all of you.

GEORGIANA. You are not in a position to offer us anything.

DARREL. Georgiana, please, tell your brother to lower the dagger.

GEORGIANA. If he didn't grab it, I would have.

DARREL. You are an intelligent woman. You must see your family for what it really is.

Look at how Thomas threatens me. And your sister, she provoked me. You think that I am the villain? Your family is the greatest enemy you have.

GEORGIANA. They are no such thing!

DARREL. You truly think so? Do you think that Catherine and I have had a pure, platonic relationship? Her reputation would be ruined, if the world discovered her secret life with me.

GEORGIANA. Catherine?

CATHERINE. Georgie—no, no, no, no—

DARREL. And Thomas! Now this will be a shock to you!

GEORGIANA. Thomas is as pure as snow!

THOMAS. Georgiana—

GEORGIANA. Thomas...

DARREL. Naive! You are so naive! The great intellect, Georgiana Highett! The sentinel of wisdom is ignorant of what goes on in her own house! Your sweet brother, your dear brother, why, he is a criminal. He is guilty of embezzlement, bribes, graft. Your whole fortune is now caught up in illegal affairs.

GEORGIANA. Thomas?

THOMAS. It's true. I am sorry—so desperately sorry—

GEORGIANA. What have you done with Father's fortune?

THOMAS. You don't understand, Georgiana. It was Father who got me started into the whole wretched business!

GEORGIANA. What?

DARREL. The embezzling has been going on for years, hasn't it, Thomas? Long before he ever knew about it. Your father built you up on that kind of money.

GEORGIANA. No.

DARREL. He overspent your inherited fortune, so he had to find another way. That's why he went into business, that is why he started to—he apparently started only with those people who he felt had betrayed him—but then he kept getting more involved.

GEORGIANA. That is not true—

THOMAS. Georgiana—when Father first told me about it, I was shocked. But then I just got deeper and deeper into it as Father got more and more persuasive. My wits hadn't a chance. But since his death, I have been trying to pay it off, to get it all worked out honestly again. I've been making deals, agreements. I have still had to—*borrow* small amounts, but you must believe me that I am trying to work it all out!

DARREL. I have enough evidence to throw your brother into prison. So, if you care for your reputation, if you care for your brother, if you care for your family's name and fortune—

GEORGIANA. Out! I will have none of it. I will *not* be blackmailed by you, nor will I let you blackmail my family. If I have to, I will grind you down with my own hands!

> DARREL *charges toward* THOMAS, *wrenches the dagger from him, and points it at all of them threateningly.*

DARREL. Now, all of you listen. I am a reasonable man. I don't want any of this to get messy. But I know your secrets. Forget any advances I made towards Georgiana or Catherine or anybody. For all I care, I wouldn't give a single pound for such sirens anymore. I want in the profits of your business, Thomas, or I'll reveal everything.

> GEORGIANA *begins to laugh.*

DARREL. Why are you laughing, you ugly gorgon?

GEORGIANA. You toad. You utterly worthless creature.

DARREL. Shut your mouth or I'll cut it off!

GEORGIANA. Could you be more predictable? Our classic villain!

DARREL. Don't you dare tempt me too far.

GEORGIANA. Oh, you are such a brave man.

> GEORGIANA *laughs again.*

DARREL. I am deadly serious, Georgiana.

GEORGIANA. No, you are afraid. Afraid and desperate. Harold Lowe told me what you are.

DARREL. I will reveal everything!

GEORGIANA. Do it then. Reveal everything. But I will tell you this: Whether you do or not, it matters not to us, for we shall see you fall with us, Mr. Fredericks.

DARREL. Fall? Why, don't you see, I am at my high point.

GEORGIANA. Until tomorrow.

DARREL. What do you mean by that?

GEORGIANA. I received a letter yesterday. Why, yes, from Mr. Harold Lowe. He told me that he was well acquainted with your dealings. He knows all about your failing business and your desperation to find capital to save yourself with. He had a list of your transactions and past history—why, I believe nearly every one of the seven deadly sins were included—and tomorrow in his paper which is read by multitudes in London, he is going to publish an article, an exposé of sorts. He is going to publish it about you, Darrel.

DARREL. You're lying.

GEORGIANA. No, by the terror I see come upon you, I see that you believe me quite readily. Oh, Darrel Fredericks, our great oppressor! Where is your triumph now?

DARREL. I will kill you all!

> GEORGIANA *goes directly to* DARREL *and places herself right at the dagger's point.*

GEORGIANA. Then thrust the dagger, Darrel! But be ready for the curse that will come upon you afterward.

DARREL. You do not frighten me with your curses.

GEORGIANA. You are nothing. A lie. Not even real.

> DARREL *maintains his gaze with* GEORGIANA *as long as he can, until he trembles, and looks away for a moment. Then he looks up again with an empty, frightened gaze. He is near tears and we see something pitiable in* DARREL.

DARREL. Georgiana . . .

GEORGIANA. Oh, such softness now? Are you really going to pretend you love me now? For I am about sick to death of man's fickle love!

> DARREL's *demeanor has completely changed. He does not seem threatening, nor even afraid any more, just overcome by an emptiness and loss. Despite* GEORGIANA's *statements otherwise, we see a bright glimpse of sad humanity within him, lost and wayward as it is.*

DARREL. Georgiana . . . dear Georgiana . . . aren't you as tired as I am?

> GEORGIANA *is startled at* DARREL's *meek pronouncement.* DARREL, *more out of exhaustion than fear, drops the dagger and exits. There is a long pause.*

THOMAS. Bravo, Georgiana.

CATHERINE. Why, you were magnificent! We are saved.

GEORGIANA. No. We certainly are not "saved."

THOMAS. You bruised that serpent's head! You smashed him! He won't dare threaten us again!

GEORGIANA. No.

CATHERINE. You have sent him into the dark where he belongs.

GEORGIANA. No, no, you don't understand. He was not the real enemy, he was not—

THOMAS. There's nothing to—

GEORGIANA. There was no letter! There will be no article!

CATHERINE. What?

GEORGIANA. I made it all up to frighten him away.

THOMAS. Why, it was a bold, convincing choice—

GEORGIANA. No.

THOMAS. You have given us our future back. You have given us—

GEORGIANA. No! Stop it! I do not want any more of your reassurances of smooth roads and conquering opposition! Look at me. Look at yourselves. We have been revealed!

CATHERINE. No one need know—

GEORGIANA. None of us is wholesome or worthy. Stephen was right to cut himself off from us!

THOMAS. Georgiana, calm down—

GEORGIANA. I have been calm my whole life, Thomas! I have been full of an arrogant smugness as our lives have been threatened and our principles have been prostituted.

THOMAS. We have won. *You* have won, Georgiana.

GEORGIANA. Won what? My dignity, my confidence? What have you won, Catherine? Your virtue? What have you won, Thomas? Your personal honor, your integrity? We are no better than Darrel Fredericks! We have our own sins to answer for!

> CATHERINE *goes and embraces* GEORGIANA. GEORGIANA *struggles, trying to tear away from her, which makes* CATHERINE *cling to her even tighter. They both collapse to their knees and* GEORGIANA *sobs and shakes with intense emotion.*

GEORGIANA. I have nothing left but this wretched face and proud heart!

> *They continue in this position and intense emotion as* THOMAS *sinks into a chair, now knowing full well what he has led his family into. His eyes are empty, nearly emotionless, as he listens to the cries of his sisters.*

SCENE 7

The mansion has been stripped down, the expensive furnishings and ornamentations gone. All that remains is the portrait of Alexander Highett. Enter MARY, *trying to carry in a large trunk which is obviously too large for her, huffing and puffing as she goes.*

MARY. Blimey!

> MARY *throws down the trunk and sits down on it, exhausted. Enter* STEPHEN.

STEPHEN. Mary?

MARY. Why, Mr. Lockhart! Who let you in?

STEPHEN. Well—I actually let myself in. Nobody answered and so I thought all the servants were—gone.

MARY. So they are, sir. I am the last relic to leave. I have gathered me things.

STEPHEN. *(Looking amazed at the luggage.)* So I can see. Mary, that luggage is nearly as big as you are!

MARY. Call me sentimental, sir. I'm a bit of a collector of past memorabilia.

STEPHEN. *(Looking about at the bare house.)* My, they have had to sell nearly everything, haven't they?

MARY. All auctioned off, sir. When Master Thomas turned himself in, the courts were lenient with him, especially since the majority of the damage had been done by his father. But all debts had to be paid—with considerable interest. But haven't you heard, sir? The house has been sold, too.

STEPHEN. The house! My poor friends.

MARY. Poor indeed. They'll have barely enough to scrape by for a while, especially compared with what they're used to. Their father's fortune, their father's business—all gone.

STEPHEN. They must be devastated.

MARY. No, sir. Not at all.

STEPHEN. What do you mean?

MARY. I've never seen them stronger, sir—happier.

STEPHEN. Happier?

MARY. Aye. They weep and mourn, of course, sir, but I've seen something grow in them. Sometimes it's better to get something new than to fix something old, if you catch my drift.

STEPHEN. But—has no one stood forth to help them?

MARY. They've tried, sir. Mr. Lowe, why he was nearly red in the face when they told him that they didn't want his help—

STEPHEN. They—they did that?

MARY. Aye.

STEPHEN. Georgiana—is she here?

MARY. I don't manage things here like I used to. Are you here to—?

STEPHEN. I don't know why I am here. I felt—compelled.

MARY. I see.

STEPHEN. Mary—I know that perhaps I may not be as to close to you as the Highetts are, but—

MARY. There's always room for another duckling under *my* wings—*(holding out her arms)* albeit short wings, sir. Quack.

STEPHEN. Mary—you know the Highetts better than they know themselves—I need your counsel. What would you say—how do you suppose—ah, blast. I do not even know what I am trying to say.

MARY. Do you love Miss Georgiana?

STEPHEN. There. You have hit the question.

MARY. *(Pause.)* Well?

STEPHEN. I—well—who's to—ah, you must understand, Mary, I don't rightly know.

MARY. Her heart's not some baby rattle for you to play with, sir.

STEPHEN. Yes. I see that.

MARY. Very good then, sir.

STEPHEN. So what do you suggest I—?

MARY. I don't suggest anything. I think it's about time you all started making your own decisions. Don't you? *(Pause.)* Sir? *(Pause.)* Sir?

STEPHEN. That is not very helpful, Mary.

MARY. Not to disagree, sir, but yes it is. You both need the elements. But I best be going. Miss Georgiana's been mighty fine to me. She's found me a new position and is even having me driven over there in a fancy coach. Imagine *me* in a fancy coach!

STEPHEN. That is wonderful, Mary.

MARY. But I've got to get me things down there—the coach won't wait forever—and this *beast* is heavy!

STEPHEN. Yes, it looks quite heavy.

MARY. If only I could find someone to help me.

STEPHEN. Well, we could call one of the butlers—

MARY. There are no more servants, sir.

STEPHEN. Well, then we could call the gardeners, perhaps.

MARY. No more servants—

STEPHEN. But then the—

MARY. There is no one, sir. And I'm not a servant here anymore either!

    Pause. STEPHEN *winks at* MARY.

MARY. *(Throws her arms up in the air.)* Oooh! No kindness for an old woman!

STEPHEN. Oh, yes. Right—that leaves just me then, doesn't it?

MARY. As far as I can see, sir.

STEPHEN. Yes. Well. Let me take it for you then, I suppose.

MARY. *(Feigning resistance.)* But, sir—

STEPHEN. *(Suddenly feeling quite gentlemanly.)* No arguments. Let someone serve *you* for once. You just wait here and rest a bit.

MARY. Why, thank you sir, I—

STEPHEN. I'll be back in a moment.

> *Exit* STEPHEN *with the luggage.* MARY *chuckles, but then stands in silence for a moment, feeling suddenly small in the big, empty house. Feeling awkward and is if she suddenly wants to be occupied, she takes off her shawl and begins dusting with it. She stops, places her hands on the fireplace mantle and, overwhelmed with tender emotions, she weeps. Enter* GEORGIANA, *her harsh and severe appearance is gone. Her hair is down and she is attired in a simple but graceful white dress. This makes her even more beautiful than her ball gown did.*

GEORGIANA. I thought I heard voices. Mary, who were you talking to— *(Noting her tears.)* Mary?

MARY. Pardon me, mum.

GEORGIANA. Oh, Mary— (GEORGIANA *goes to* MARY *and embraces her.*) I understand.

MARY. No, no, you don't! Miss Georgiana, you'll have to go through many more years and much more experience, and the raising of children, before you understand a heart like mine! But I don't mean to chide—don't mind the tears of a sentimental old hen, mum.

GEORGIANA. Mary, I wish—

> *Enter* STEPHEN.

STEPHEN. The coach is ready for you, Mary—ah.

> STEPHEN *and* GEORGIANA *are both very surprised. Long, tense pause.*

STEPHEN. Georgiana.

MARY. My, my, I believe that's me cue! *(Embracing* GEORGIANA.*)* I love you, dearie. Good-bye. *(With an impish smile.)* Imagine—*me* in a fancy coach!

> *Exit* MARY, *as if she had suddenly been made into a duchess.*

GEORGIANA. So.

STEPHEN. So.

GEORGIANA. *(Simultaneously)* Stephen, I—

STEPHEN. *(Simultaneously)* Georgiana, if only—

> *They both stop.*

GEORGIANA. You must understand that—

STEPHEN. I hope that—

They both stop.

GEORGIANA. It's not at all what it—

STEPHEN. Ever since we—

They both stop. Then they smile sheepishly.

STEPHEN. You—you look absolutely splendid, Georgie. You know, I don't think I've seen your hair down like that since we were children.

GEORGIANA. So you are not angry with me anymore?

STEPHEN. Would it matter, if I were?

GEORGIANA. I think it might.

STEPHEN. Then no, I am not angry. You were under a lot of strain. Are you angry with me?

GEORGIANA. No.

STEPHEN. Then where does that leave us? At the beginning?

GEORGIANA. No. We can never go back to the beginning.

STEPHEN. Why not? Georgiana, think back to when we were children. It was so much more simple then, was it not? The love we felt for each other back then was so simple.

GEORGIANA. Love?

STEPHEN. *(Taking her by the hands.)* Can't we go back to it?

GEORGIANA. *(Pausing, then taking her hands gently away.)* No. We must go beyond it. Stephen, what of the dressmakers?

STEPHEN. What of them?

GEORGIANA. Is the one—is Hannah all right?

STEPHEN. The wound looked worse than it was. After we stopped the bleeding, she was fine.

GEORGIANA. Good. Very good. Are—have you promised yourself to—?

STEPHEN. No. I no longer have any romantic intentions toward—*either* of them. They have been true friends—nothing more.

GEORGIANA. *(Afraid, but hopeful)* But—then are—are you still going to America?

STEPHEN. Yes. I leave to Liverpool tomorrow and then off on a ship.

GEORGIANA. To follow your God?

STEPHEN. Yes.

GEORGIANA. God is stripping me of *all* my comforts.

STEPHEN. Georgiana—if God is truly the God of those that mourn, of those acquainted with grief, if He is truly the God of the downtrodden and the outcast—then you are closer to Him than you have ever been in your life. You are now in His domain and His sphere.

GEORGIANA. Edenbridge did not have room for either of us, did it, Stephen?

STEPHEN. Perhaps we outgrew it.

GEORGIANA. Just as we outgrew each other.

STEPHEN. Georgie, do you really think—

GEORGIANA. No, listen to me for a minute. You say you loved our life when we were children. Well, life is more complicated than it was and we can't change that. I sometimes think that somewhere along the line that you may have saved my soul, but—

STEPHEN. I think you saved mine—

GEORGIANA. I said *listen*. The day may come when we will see each other again in happier circumstances, but as for today, we are traveling to different countries and if we are to truly discover our purposes we must learn to let go of our—securities.

STEPHEN. Can't we travel to the same country? You with me, or me with you?

GEORGIANA. Not different countries, but different paths—

STEPHEN. We'll merge them into the same path.

GEORGIANA. Different *realms,* Stephen. You came to me before with such commitment and determination—don't lose that. You saw clearly then, see clearly now.

STEPHEN. But, Georgie—

GEORGIANA. Let me go, Stephen. Follow your vision.

STEPHEN. I—of—of course. You're right.

GEORGIANA. Good. Good, you understand.

STEPHEN. Then—then this is genuinely good-bye?

GEORGIANA. For now.

STEPHEN. Do you think we will ever—

GEORGIANA. I don't know. Time will tell.

STEPHEN. Then this truly may be our last moment?

GEORGIANA. Perhaps.

STEPHEN. Then let me just say this—it was not a mistake.

GEORGIANA. The kiss?

STEPHEN. Not just the kiss—everything. Farewell, dear friend.

> STEPHEN *takes her by both hands and presses each of them, one after another, against his lips.* GEORGIANA *fights against the emotion this token causes.* STEPHEN *stares into her eyes one last time and then exits. Pause.*

GEORGIANA. You can come in now, Mary. *(No response. She goes to the door and looks behind it.)* Mary? *(MARY is not there. This absence is poignant to GEORGIANA.)* The world has changed. *(Looking towards the portrait.)* One last thing—

> GEORGIANA *goes to the portrait and lifts it. Scrutinizing it, she places it back above the mantle.*

GEORGIANA. We were going to take you with us, Father—but now I suppose we must not.

> GEORGIANA *takes the dagger from a bag she had put aside and places it upon the mantle beneath her father's portrait.*

GEORGIANA. You will remain here, in the house you fashioned for us. You are the cherubim to watch over what you have created, and this will be your flaming sword.

> GEORGIANA *turns to leave, but then turns and gazes at the house. She looks back at her father's portrait and the dagger. She lets out a short, gentle laugh, but then it catches in her throat, as she struggles with the threat that the laugh may become tears.*

GEORGIANA. No. No more crying. We are in another domain, another sphere.

> GEORGIANA *exits. As the lights fade, a light on the portrait and the dagger remains until those, too, fade to black out.*

CURTAIN

Martyrs' Crossing

Melissa Leilani Larson

About the Playwright

Melissa Leilani Larson hadn't been involved in theatre when she was an undergraduate at Brigham Young University, instead majoring in English with an emphasis in creative writing. Before graduating in 1998, she fatefully took a playwriting course from Elizabeth Hansen. As a result of the class, and subsequent advanced classes from Eric Samuelsen, she was surprised to find that she had become a playwright.

Her first play was a period piece titled *Lady in Waiting*, about Anne Bolyn, the executed second wife of King Henry VIII. Since *Lady in Waiting*'s premiere, it has been produced by three universities[1] and was the winner of the Arlene R. & William P. Lewis Playwriting Contest for Women in 2001.

One of Mormonism's finest and most devoted drama critics, Nan McCulloch, saw Larson's next play *Wake Me When It's Over*, which premiered in the Nelke Theatre, July 17–22, 2002, and was thoroughly impressed by her talent:

> My husband and I drove to California the day after seeing the play and we spent lots of time talking about it. The play is about a young man who has chronic fatigue syndrome. I know several people who have this disease, so I have a frame of reference. Although Ben and Grace love each other, the reality of their complex, somewhat hopeless situation calls for more than love to exact a solution. . . . Even when their strained situation is most obvious, the love that they feel for each other comes through. They are darling together. Ben has joined a chat room to talk to other people who share his disease. He establishes a friendship with a girl and they frequently talk. One day Grace, unknown to Ben, joins him and azure_skies for a conversation . . . It seemed obvious where this triangle was heading. I was so relieved that I was wrong. The outcome of the play is not predictable . . . Melissa shows wisdom beyond her years.[2]

Wake Me When It's Over went on to win the 2002 Vera Hinckley Mayhew Award and an honorable mention in the 2002 Association for Mormon Letters Best Drama

---

1 This play premiered at Brigham Young University in the Nelke Theatre, August 1–11, 2001; Brigham Young University–Hawaii (June 2002) and California State-Los Angeles (May 2003).

2 Nan McCulloch, "*Wake Me When It's Over* (drama)," *Association for Mormon Letters Review Archive*, June 23, 2002, http://mormonletters.org/Reviews/Review.aspx?id=3535 (accessed July 10, 2002).

Category. Her film screenplay of *Standing Still Standing* also won first place in the 2006 LDS Film Festival.

After *Wake Me When It's Over,* Larson adapted John Gay's *The Beggar's Opera* for the BYU main stage. It enjoyed a successful run and several sold-out houses in March 2004.

After graduating from BYU, Larson went on to receive her MFA in playwriting from the University of Iowa. In Iowa she had a number of plays produced, making it a very productive time in her career. She contributed the vignette "A Place Apart," about an early liaison of Louis XIV, to David Schweizer's new collaborative collage *Versailles,* which premiered on the Iowa main stage in March 2007. Other work at Iowa included the Gallery Series productions *Hope Falls* and *A Flickering,* as well as *The Church of St. Pinky at Katy, Texas,* which appeared in the 2007 Iowa New Play Festival.

Larson's most significant piece performed in Iowa, however, was her work on Joan of Arc, *Martyrs' Crossing.* The play was produced at the 2005 Iowa New Play Festival, winning the IRAM Best New Play award (under the title *An Experiment in Sainthood*).

The play did not initially originate in Iowa, however. A workshop version of the play had been performed in Utah at the short-lived Provo Fringe Festival, April 15–17, 2004, at the Provo Arts Center—its first amateur performance.

After seeing Larson's *Martyrs' Crossing* at the Provo Fringe Festival, BYU playwriting professor Eric Samuelsen warmly praised his former student: "With this play, one of the finest young playwrights in Mormondom took a great leap forward, writing and directing with confidence and skill." He goes on to explain how Larson had given audiences a "Mormon Joan," noting the prominent presence of the two Saints Catherine and Margaret, the spirits whom the real Joan cited as her heavenly guides:

> How is this Mormon? Not, as you might expect, by emphasizing the reality of Joan's voices, the reality of revelation itself. Instead, Larson focuses on agency, on the difficulty of figuring out who God is and what He wants, and the way He lets us sort of muddle through. And the play suggests that this uncertainty, this confusion extends to the Spirit world.
>
> Margaret and Catherine are specifically portrayed as heavenly messengers, post-mortal spirits, who have been given the responsibility of looking after Joan, but without specific instructions as to what that means. They exceed their authority at times, they give Joan contradictory information, they quarrel between themselves as to tactics and consequences. In other words, Margaret and Catherine have a Church calling. They know God has called them to be messengers, and they have sort of vague, general ideas as to what they're supposed to do. The specifics are up to them, and they get a lot wrong along the way. . . . Death and agency and revelation; that's the world Melissa has explored with this play. I loved it.[3]

---

3   "*Martyrs' Crossing* (drama)," *Association for Mormon Letters Review Archive,* April 19, 2004, http://mormonletters.org/Reviews/Review.aspx?id=3705 (accessed September 22, 2012).

After the initial workshop in Provo, Utah and then *Martyrs' Crossing*'s success in Iowa, BYU once again produced Larson's work, performing the play (this time titled *Angels Unaware*) in the Margetts Theatre, March 8–25, 2006 (it has since gone back to its original title). Writing for the *Deseret News*, Genelle Pugmire called BYU's production of the play, "a stunning story,"[4] and then later named it in the *Deseret News*' "Theater in Review" as the best play of the year in Utah Valley.[5] In 2006, the play won a KC/ACTF Meritorious Achievement, Excellence in Playwriting Award. The BYU production was featured in Andy Lorimer's Rocky Mountain Emmy-winning documentary *A Cathartic Space* and was also part of the WorkShop Theater Company's Sundays at Six reading series in New York in June 2008.

In a review for the Association for Mormon Letters, Mahonri Stewart wrote of BYU's production of *Angels Unaware*: "The play is powerful, it is moving, it is beautiful. The spirituality that is infused in the very bones and sinews of the play make it radiate.... [T]ears poured down my face. Not because of emotional manipulation or melodrama, but because at that moment, the Spirit rushed through me and I felt as if I was about to burst with light.... [I]n a show that is focused on the spiritual and the religious, the play edifies."[6]

Larson's most recent work includes an adaptation of Jane Austen's *Persuasion*, which premiered in November 2009 at Concordia University. *Persuasion* then had subsequent productions on March 16–April 1, 2011 on BYU's Pardoe main stage, which McCulloch referred to as a "pure delight,"[7] as well as a production by Zion Theatre Company September 7–22 at the Off Broadway Theatre in Salt Lake City to sold-out audiences and overwhelmingly positive reviews.[8] Larson continues to show her passion for Jane Austen, as she plans on adapting all of Austen's work.

Larson's other recent achievements are a revival of *Wake Me When It's Over* (revised and retitled *Standing Still Standing*, presented at the Provo Theatre's Bluelight Stage, July 10–27, 2009) and *Flickering*, which the Bluelight Stage company presented January 29, 2010. Another production of *Martyrs' Crossing* was presented by Rising Star

---

4   Genelle Pugmire, "*Angels Unaware*: Story of French Heroine Is a Story of Inspiring Impact," *Deseret News*, March 16, 2006.
5   Sharon Haddock, Rodger Hardy, and Genelle Pugmire; "Year-End Theater Wrap Up," *Deseret Morning News*, December 26, 2006, http://www.deseretnews.com/article/650218078/Year-end-theater-wrap-up.html?ph=all (accessed September 25, 2011).
6   Mahonri Stewart, "*Angels Unaware*: A Story of Joan of Arc (Drama)," *Association for Mormon Letters Review Archive*, March 12, 2006, http://mormonletters.org/Reviews/Review.aspx?id=3902 (accessed September 14, 2012).
7   Nan McCulloch, "*Persuasion* (drama)," *Association for Mormon Letters Review Archive*, December 14, 2008, http://www.aml-online.org/Reviews/Review.aspx?id=4479 (accessed September 15, 2012).
8   See Kara Henry, "Zion Theatre Company's *Persuasion* Would Make Jane Austen Proud," Front Row Reviewers Utah, September 8, 2012, http://frontrowreviewersutah.com/?p=279 (accessed September 25, 2012); Amber Peck, "*Persuasion* feels like Austen to Me," Utah Theatre Bloggers, September 12, 2012, http://utahtheatrebloggers.com/1288/persuasion-feels-like-Austen-to-me (accessed September 25, 2012);

Production in Kelso, Washington, in March 2011. Beyond those successes, however, Larson in 2009 offered a powerful play, a true trailblazer: *Little Happy Secrets*.

A myriad of plays have addressed the issue of same-gender attraction and Mormonism, notably non-Mormon Tony Kushner's Pulitzer Prize-winning *Angels in America* (1993) and Mormon Carol Lynn Pearson's *Facing East* (2006). However, many of these dramas have taken the secular side of the debate. In *Little Happy Secrets*,[9] Larson takes a stance deeply rooted in a commitment to her faith. She has created a religiously orthodox Mormon character named Claire and made her the focus. Never detouring into homophobia or prejudice, Larson always portrays all of her characters in a compassionate light, a realistic light. Yet Larson shows a young Mormon woman who struggles with her homosexuality (and never gets over it), who yet remains with the Church. It's a delicate balance that strives to be compassionate to both those who struggle with same-sex attraction, as well as to straight—and often uncomprehending—members of the Church of Jesus Christ of Latter-day Saints and its policies.

McCulloch once again praises Larson's superb writing ability and insight: "I still recognized the sensitive, gracefully intelligent style I have come to appreciate from Melissa. For me, this play is unique. I have seen plays about gay men struggling with their same-sex attraction, then leaving the church. This is the first Mormon play I have seen about a young woman struggling, but choosing to stay. It is past time to broach this subject and Larson has done it well."[10]

Gideon Burton, a BYU professor of English and a very active commentator/advocate of Mormon literature, theatre, and cinema, praised *Little Happy Secrets* after seeing the New Play Project's production. In his review, he commended its skill in avoiding easy sensationalism:

> No one should mistake the play, reducing it to a political or religious complaint. No such rhetoric ever surfaces, because this is a play more about faith and Christ-like love than anything else. This is a play that pushes some of the darkness into the light, gently and authentically, and in so doing shows a love and respect for those who struggle—both those that struggle with homosexuality, and those that struggle with those strugglers. It united people who thought they might be divided. It depicted realistic yearnings and deep feelings—both for God and for those creatures with whom we interact and who, male or female, give us a reason to make life worth it. *Little Happy Secrets* should not be a best-kept secret. It is a brave and reverent Mormon play representing a great success for its creative personnel, for New Play Project, and for Mormon theatre generally."[11]

---

9   *Little Happy Secrets* premiered at the Provo Theatre, March 19–21, 23, 2009, through the New Play Project. Southern Utah University's Stage Two produced the play in January 2011 and the play was part of Salt Lake Acting Company's Fearless Fringe Festival in August 2011. A radio play version is available on Larson's website: *http://melissaleilanilarson.com/*.
10 Nan McCulloch, email to Melissa Leilani Larson, copy in my possession courtesy of Larson.
11 Gideon Burton, "A Brave and Reverent Mormon Play: *Little Happy Secrets*," Gideon

In 2009, Larson won one of the highest honors in Mormon literature, the Association for Mormon Letters Award in Best Drama, for *Little Happy Secrets*. Based on her success with one of the best Mormon plays to come out in a decade; her impressive, cumulative work; her deft ability to write convincingly in both period and modern styles; her major accomplishments at a young age; and her mature, philosophical outlook, Larson is one of the best of the next generation of Mormon playwrights. She is representative of the power that the next wave of Mormon dramatists have, not only to achieve what their predecessors have, but far surpass it. If Larson is indicative of her current peers, then Eric Samuelsen was very correct in exclaiming, "Man, but Mormon drama's in good hands right now."[12]

Burton's Blog, March 21, 2009, *http://gideonburton.typepad.com/gideon_burtons_blog/2009/03/little-happy-secrets-review.html* (accessed April 11, 2009).

12 Eric Samuelsen, LARSON: *"Martyrs' Crossing* (drama)," AML-Review Archive, *http://www.aml-online.org/Reviews/Review.aspx?id=3705* (accessed September 25, 2012).

About *Martyrs' Crossing*

Martyrs' Crossing was first produced as a workshop entitled *Martyrs' Crossing: An Experiment in Sainthood* as part of the premiere season of the Provo Fringe Festival. The production ran April 15–17, 2004, at the Provo Arts Center, with the following company:

CAST

Catherine: Bryn Fairclough
Margaret: Joni H. Clausen
Joan: Ashley Ogzewalla
Michael: Clay Bunker
Charles: Tim Lewis
Cauchon: Matthew Carlin
Ensemble: Joshua Karoly
Christopher M. Lowry

CREW

Director: Melissa Leilani Larson
Production Design: Jennifer Brass Jenkins
Lighting Design: Shane Withers
Sound Design: Emily Severson
Hair & Make-up Design: Sarah Lock
Assistant Costume Design: Bethani Jensen
Stage Manager: Annike VerHoef
Assistant Stage Manager: Katrina Paxman
Deck Crew: Ellinor Bergqvist
Lightboard Operator: Emily G. Ray

Then titled *An Experiment in Sainthood*, the play was subsequently produced as part of the annual Iowa New Play Festival, with Alan MacVey as acting director of theatre and Art Borreca as head of the Iowa Playwrights Workshop. The production took place May 6, 2005, in the David Thayer Theatre at The University of Iowa, with the following company:

CAST

Catherine: Christy Sullivan
Margaret: Abby McMillin
Joan: Leslie Koppenhaver
Michael: Tae Geun Kim
Charles: Jeff Worden
Cauchon: Jack Bisbee
Ensemble: Rebecca Miller, Diana Selwyn,
Elizabeth Steele, Nicole Vespa

CREW

Director: Scott Pardue
Choreographer: Cassandra Bednall
Dramaturg: Jessica Dart
Scenic Design: Cassandra Reardon
Lighting Design: Annie Croner
Costume Design: Emma Tremmel
Sound Design/Composer: Chris G. Haug
Stage Manager: Brett M. Van Fleet
Assistant Stage Manager: Marc Black
Deck Crew: Brian Finley, Jacy Fitzpatrick, Ryan Karloff

The play was then produced as *Angels Unaware: A Story of Joan of Arc* on the mainstage season at Brigham Young University, with Rodger D. Sorenson serving as artistic director and as the Mary Lou Fulton Chair of Theatre & Media Arts. It ran from March 8 through 25, 2006, in the Margetts Arena Theatre with the following company:

CAST

Catherine: Amanda Schütz
Margaret: Jennie Pardoe
Joan: Hollie Beard
Michael: Phillip Clayton
Charles: Jason R. Purdie
Cauchon: Slate Holmgren
Warwick: Jason R. Purdie
Historians: Luke Rebarchik, Moronai Kanekoa,
Slate Holmgren, Jason R. Purdie

CREW

Director: David Morgan
Dramaturgs: Shelley T. Graham, Jennie Pardoe, Katie Renville
Scenic Design: Ward L. Wright
Lighting Design: Michael G. Handley
Sound Design: Joseph Craven
Costume Design: Shiloh Cheney
Make-up/Hair Design: Emily Canady
Stage Manager: Brian Ramos
Assistant Stage Manager: Joyce Lim
Fight Choreographer: Matthew Carlin

> "My Lord has a book in which no scholar has read,
> how perfect soever he be in scholarship." — Joan the Maid

For Maxine Kirkham Larson, my grandmother

CHARACTERS

(three women, five men)

HISTORIANS.

CATHERINE.

MICHAEL, the Archangel.

MARGARET.

JOAN.

CHARLES, the Dauphin.

COURTIERS.

FRENCH SOLDIERS.

RICHARD BEAUCHAMP, Earl of Warwick (pronounced War-ick).

PIERRE CAUCHON, Bishop of Beauvais.

ENGLISH GUARDS.

NOTES

This piece might be played in a number of ways, though it should be clear that it is primarily Catherine's play. Joan is an essential presence, as it is her history being told; however the focus should be on Catherine experiencing that history along with Joan. This is a story about choice and faith rather than foreordination, and Catherine and Margaret are not perfect people; they are not angels or saints in the traditional sense, though they are working their way to that level. This play embraces the ideology that life continues after death, and that perfection—what some might term as "sainthood"— does not necessarily accompany martyrdom at the precise end of mortal existence.

A key theatricality relies on Catherine and Margaret being seen, heard, and touched by Joan, and by no one else in the mortal sphere unless specifically noted in the text.

With the exception of Michael, the male roles are meant to be doubled and can be divided among an ensemble of two to four, depending on the director's needs. The historians, courtiers, and soldiers' lines have been numbered to suggest a flow and rhythm, but their actual assignment is left to the director's discretion.

Costumes for the mortals should be era-specific. However, Catherine, Margaret, and Michael are otherworldly, and their appearance should not reflect Joan's France;

they shouldn't necessarily be relegated to halos and wings, either. The set should be minimal and suggestive, allowing for fluid changes between scenes that are driven by light.

Prologue

Lights rise slowly to reveal only a glimpse of something vast and all-encompassing: a library that goes on, literally, forever. In the space is a font, waist or perhaps chest high, filled with pure, white sand. Light reveals the HISTORIANS, *who care for the library's books.*

HISTORIAN 1. History.

HISTORIAN 2. Time.

HISTORIAN 3. Space.

HISTORIAN 4. Books.

HISTORIAN 1. Volumes filled with pages,

HISTORIAN 2. Lined with ink.

HISTORIAN 3. Some printed,

HISTORIAN 4. Others kept painstakingly by hand.

HISTORIAN 1. Illuminated,

HISTORIAN 2. Illustrated,

HISTORIAN 3. Immense.

HISTORIAN 4. Immortal.

HISTORIAN 1. Brimming with life,

HISTORIAN 2. Soul,

HISTORIAN 3. Being.

HISTORIAN 4. For every life lived,

HISTORIAN 1. For every circle of the earth,

HISTORIAN 2. And every round of the moon,

HISTORIAN 3. For every tiny grain of time that slips from one hour to the next,

HISTORIAN 4. There is a record kept.

HISTORIAN 1. It is our task to keep it.

HISTORIAN 2. We are the historians.

HISTORIAN 3. We are not makers,

HISTORIAN 4. Nor followers,

HISTORIAN 1. Nor prophets.

HISTORIAN 2. We are recorders.

HISTORIAN 3. We have a story to tell.

HISTORIAN 4. It's a story you might think you know.

HISTORIAN 1. A story of faith.

HISTORIAN 2. Of courage.

HISTORIAN 3. Of a girl who would change the world.

HISTORIAN 4. Joan of Arc.

HISTORIAN 1. Peasant.

HISTORIAN 2. Warrior.

HISTORIAN 3. Saint.

HISTORIAN 4. As a child, she was visited by spirits:

HISTORIAN 1. Messengers from on high.

HISTORIAN 2. She never denied hearing their voices.

HISTORIAN 3. The voices of Catherine

HISTORIAN 4. And Margaret,

HISTORIAN 1. Her counsel in all things.

HISTORIAN 2. Yet this core to her faith,

HISTORIAN 3. To her legend,

HISTORIAN 4. What this humble girl saw and heard,

HISTORIAN 1. Is somehow the one truth in her history most often overlooked.

HISTORIAN 2. To understand Joan, you must understand her inspiration.

> HISTORIAN 3 *takes down a book: its leather binding is plain, yet resplendent in its simplicity.*

HISTORIAN 3. The book is here.

HISTORIAN 4. We will open it.

HISTORIAN 1. For you.

HISTORIAN 2. The Book of Catherine.

HISTORIAN 3. Catherine of Alexandria, as she is sometimes called.

HISTORIAN 4. A woman who embraced the Church of Christ when Rome—

HISTORIAN 1. Cruel, brutal, pagan Rome—

HISTORIAN 2. Soaked the face of the known world in the bitter blood of persecution.

HISTORIAN 3. Maxentius, the Roman governor of Alexandria, victimized Christians.

HISTORIAN 4. Murder in the streets passed for entertainment.

HISTORIAN 1. And yet those of the Christian faith grew in numbers.

HISTORIAN 2. Among the flock in Alexandria was Catherine.

HISTORIAN 3. The daughter of a scholar,

HISTORIAN 4. Versed in poetry and educated in politics,

HISTORIAN 1. She renounced the mythos of Olympus for the bread of life.

HISTORIAN 2. One fateful day, Catherine came face to face with Maxentius.

HISTORIAN 3. She told him boldly that he had no right to persecute God's people.

HISTORIAN 4. The governor was amused by this girl,

HISTORIAN 1. This child of nineteen, who dared to question the whims of Rome.

HISTORIAN 2. He was so amused that he offered to execute his own wife if Catherine would take her place.

HISTORIAN 3. But Catherine would have none of it,

HISTORIAN 4. Of him.

HISTORIAN 1. Affronted,

HISTORIAN 2. Enraged,

HISTORIAN 3. Maxentius threw Catherine in prison,

HISTORIAN 4. Meaning to beat the faith out of her with a wheel.

HISTORIAN 1. A great wooden wheel built not for travel,

HISTORIAN 2. Not to haul rocks or till soil,

HISTORIAN 3. But to cause anguish.

HISTORIAN 4. Unendurable pain.

HISTORIAN 1. Though left to suffer in darkness,

HISTORIAN 2. Catherine did not yield.

HISTORIAN 3. That darkness is where we begin.

HISTORIAN 4. The darkness that must come

HISTORIAN 1. Before light can be appreciated.

HISTORIAN 2. We will tell you a story of faith.

HISTORIAN 3. The story . . .

HISTORIAN 4. Of a girl.

SCENE 1: DARKNESS

> MICHAEL *stands beside the font. As the lights come up, he is sifting the sand gently between his fingers.* CATHERINE, *on her hands and knees, stumbles blindly in the dark.* MICHAEL *watches her, though she is unaware of his presence.*

CATHERINE. My soul doth magnify the Lord, and my spirit hath rejoiced in God my Savior. For with God nothing shall be impossible. My soul . . . Margaret? Are you—Is someone there?

MICHAEL. Catherine.

CATHERINE. Who's there?

MICHAEL. I am.

CATHERINE. Who are you?

MICHAEL. I've been sent to meet you.

CATHERINE. You don't frighten me, whoever you are. And you can tell your master so. I've had enough of his meetings. He won't have me. He won't—

MICHAEL. He already does.

CATHERINE. No! Never—

MICHAEL. Catherine—

CATHERINE. Keep your distance.

MICHAEL. Of course. There is nothing for you to fear here.

CATHERINE. I can't . . . I can't see.

MICHAEL. Your eyes are accustomed to the dimness of prison. Your sight will return, I promise.

> *He raises a hand; the lights rise with it, gently. Gradually.*

CATHERINE. Who are you, really?

MICHAEL. You think I was sent to you by Maxentius.

CATHERINE. If not Maxentius, then who?

MICHAEL. No one in my charge will do you any harm. How do you feel?

> *She tries to gauge where he is.*

CATHERINE. What do you care? If you won't tell me who you are.

MICHAEL. My name is Michael.

CATHERINE. That's not a Roman name. It's Hebrew. It means "he who is like God."

MICHAEL. Yes.

CATHERINE. . . . I don't know how I feel. I don't really feel much of anything. A short while ago I would have said I was tired. Exhausted beyond belief. But now I feel . . .

MICHAEL. Rested.

CATHERINE. Nearly.

MICHAEL. Understand, I'm only here to help you.

CATHERINE. And Maxentius?

MICHAEL. You needn't worry on him anymore.

CATHERINE. How do you know that?

He bends down beside her; she recoils at his nearness. Nonplussed, he passes a hand over her eyes. She blinks at the light and looks at him: her sight has been restored.

MICHAEL. I prefer to stay informed.

CATHERINE. How did you—Thank you.

MICHAEL. I can't take credit for your faith.

CATHERINE. What is this place?

MICHAEL. What does it look like?

CATHERINE. A library, I think. But these books are strange to me. And I know books; I grew up surrounded by them. But these . . . How lovely. . . . I haven't even held a book in months.

She strokes the spine of a volume lovingly.

CATHERINE. The governor burned them all. At least, said he did.

MICHAEL. Maxentius.

CATHERINE. When I refused his advances, he took everything I had. Father's collection was very fine. The finest in our quarter. *(She takes down a book. Opens it, inhales its scent, almost reverently.)* He wouldn't burn them. He couldn't. They're too valuable. A common man could work his entire life and not be able to afford a single volume. But then, the governor was a madman. He burned men for my sake. Why not books? *(She closes the book, returns it to its shelf.)* It's just a book, after all. Just a thing, hardly important. Why am I here? If Maxentius is gone, why can't I go home?

MICHAEL. You are home.

CATHERINE. Perhaps I'm not being clear. How did I come to be here? If you have so much more power than Maxentius, then there are hundreds of people you could save. Should save. Why me?

MICHAEL. You were not saved from the Romans.

CATHERINE. Then I . . . Have I . . . ? Oh . . .

MICHAEL. Things likely appear strange to you, now that your eyes are clear.

CATHERINE. Michael. "He who is like . . . " You're—you're—

MICHAEL. Yes.

CATHERINE. Forgive me. I didn't—I didn't know—

MICHAEL. Catherine, the Father cares deeply for you, and has brought you here for a reason. This place, this is where much of His work begins.

CATHERINE. In a library?

MICHAEL. This is not just any library. Here you will find every book ever written and many that are not.

CATHERINE. There must be books that are singular. We had Greek texts that were unique in the world. Josephus and—

MICHAEL. However many copies are on earth, be it one or one thousand, a copy resides here. Every book, every letter, every life.

CATHERINE. Every book ever written? . . . Um. I wish I could say I was tired.

MICHAEL. A familiar face might ease your crossing.

Enter MARGARET.

CATHERINE. Margaret. You know Margaret?

MICHAEL. When first you met, it was I who sent her to you.

MARGARET. Praise God. (*Hugging* CATHERINE *fiercely.*) I'm sorry, I can't help it—Look at you. Well and whole and full of light—I knew that madman wouldn't have you in the end. I knew you were too strong for him. And here you are.

CATHERINE. You'll tell me what's happening, won't you? Where are we, really?

MARGARET. The simplest way to say it is that we are in between. We are near to the earth, but not in a way that mortals understand. Heaven is still beyond, as there is work to be done.

MICHAEL. Catherine, God has chosen you for your valiancy. There is a task at hand; you have been called to complete it. Will you accept this calling?

CATHERINE. Why me?

MARGARET. Because you have lived through more in a span of months than most will experience in their lifetimes. What the Romans did . . . It would have saved you great pain to tell Maxentius yes. But you did not.

CATHERINE. What kind of work is it?

MARGARET. There will be a girl, a child born in a country called France. France has been at war for generations with a nearby kingdom, England, over the succession to the French throne. The French have no king; they have a prince, the Dauphin, who lives in exile. The people have nothing to believe in; their churchmen are corrupt, and mercenaries randomly roam the countryside, burning it as they go.

CATHERINE. And this girl? What has she to do with all of this?

MARGARET. She will fight, and she will win, and France will be its own nation again, which will set in motion a number of events necessary to human progression.

CATHERINE. And I'm supposed to help her.

MARGARET. Yes.

CATHERINE. So the outcome of a war and the well-being of a nation are to rest on the shoulders of a child.

MARGARET. And on us.

CATHERINE. It makes no sense that so much would come to rest on one tiny thing. One tiny person in all the world. Why this girl? Why France?

MARGARET. We'll be told what we need to know; otherwise, we're meant to learn as we go along. All will be made clear, someday. This is how things work. How God works.

CATHERINE. I won't know what to do.

MARGARET. You'll know. I'll help you.

MICHAEL. It's time. You will talk with her, but not yet. For now, just look.

He goes to the font, takes a fingerful of sand and flicks it. JOAN, *thirteen, enters, setting down a basket. She takes linens from the basket and folds them.*

CATHERINE. She's so young. Such innocence . . .

Blithe and carefree, JOAN *sings a nonsensical song, adapting her work to fit its meter. She's only a girl. She has no education, no background.*

MARGARET. Not all education depends upon books.

JOAN *pauses in her work, as if she can hear the conversation but cannot fully make it out.*

CATHERINE. Can she . . . ?

MICHAEL. She senses your presence, but not in a way she can conceive.

JOAN *shakes her head and returns to her work.* MICHAEL *approaches her, whispering in her ear. A pillowcase falls from her nerveless fingers, floating back into the basket. She drops to her knees, crossing herself.*

MICHAEL. Joan. Behold the messenger of the Father.

JOAN *raises her head. Slowly, ever so slowly, she turns to look at* MICHAEL. *A light grows behind and then about him: brighter . . . Brighter . . . Brighter.*

JOAN. Father, have mercy.

MICHAEL. You shall have His mercy. Be a good girl and always go to church; I'll be watching, and will report all to your Father in Heaven. Remember what I have told you, and wait for my return.

The light fades and MICHAEL *disappears from* JOAN's *vision.*

MICHAEL. Out of the small comes the great. It's the law she will live her life by. She is already separate from her playmates in matters of the Spirit. Look.

JOAN, *still on the ground, is in tears.*

MARGARET. Joy.

CATHERINE. Yes. Such happiness that your soul aches with the force of it.

MARGARET *presses* CATHERINE's *hand.*

MARGARET. Then you do know why you're here. I'm so glad it's you.

MICHAEL. I will visit her as she grows. When the time is right, you will appear to her, and put the rest in motion.

CATHERINE *is beside* JOAN, *at her eye level. She raises a hand to touch the girl when:*

MICHAEL. Not yet.

CATHERINE. But she needs to be held.

MARGARET. She still has a mother to hold her.

JOAN *looks up, not quite at* CATHERINE, *but through her.*

CATHERINE. There is no need for you to be good. You are good. Such eyes, such a soul, I've never seen.

MICHAEL. You want to help her now, don't you?

CATHERINE. Yes.

MICHAEL. Good, then. Let's carry on.

He flicks a fingerful of sand and time passes. She is seventeen. She is teased for her piety, and is often left alone to her thoughts because her goodness troubles those around her. JOAN *looks to* CATHERINE *and* MARGARET, *seeing them for the first time; she does not see* MICHAEL.

JOAN. Good morning.

MARGARET *nudges* CATHERINE.

CATHERINE. . . . Good morning.

JOAN. Is there someone you're looking for?

Bewildered, CATHERINE *looks to her companion, who doesn't falter.*

MARGARET. You are Joan, are you not? Joan, daughter of Jacques and Isabelle?

JOAN *looks from one to the other, puzzled.*

JOAN. Most here call me—

MARGARET. Jeannette.

JOAN. ... Yes.

MARGARET. We are not, as you have likely guessed, from here. You are the one we were sent to find.

JOAN. What could you possibly want with me?

MARGARET. All that you might give God.

JOAN. Are you pilgrims?

    MARGARET *pokes* CATHERINE.

CATHERINE. ... Of a sort.

JOAN. *(With an infectious enthusiasm:)* You dress as I only dream a nun might dress. I've never seen a holy sister, but Maman speaks often of a convent she saw as a girl. It was part of a great cathedral, and the nuns did not speak outside of the convent, nor much inside, except in very low voices, and they wore but black, she said. I always thought a nun should wear white. ... Or the cream of fresh milk. ... Or the blue of a cloudless sky. ... Black seems so solemn for a bride of Christ.

MARGARET. Shouldn't a bride of Christ be solemn?

JOAN. One can be solemn without dressing darkly, can't one? And I can't imagine Heaven to be a dark and solemn place, else why should we want to go there?

MARGARET. *(Gently:)* Because God is there.

JOAN. Oh, yes, of course. I mean no disrespect, Sister. I only wonder ...

CATHERINE. What do you wonder?

JOAN. God is the creator of all things. There is beauty on earth; why should there be none in Heaven?

MARGARET. There is something we must tell you.

JOAN. Something to tell me? No one ever has anything to tell me, except those who say I spend too much time at prayer. Did Pierre send you to mock me?

MARGARET. Your brother has nothing to do with the matter. We have been sent to present you with a mission. You have been chosen—

JOAN. How did you know that Pierre is my brother? I never called him such.

MARGARET. There is a good deal about you that we know.

JOAN. But how? You are not from here. You don't know me. You can't. Please, no more. I don't know what you're trying to do, but—

CATHERINE. She's only a girl.

MARGARET. Catherine—

JOAN. I'll be eighteen with the new year—Catherine?

CATHERINE. What's the good in it? Margaret, she—

JOAN. Margaret. Saints. Why are you here? You bear the names of saints, and you speak of missions—Father won't be pleased when he hears I've wasted the morning listening to your foolishness. We have no bread nor room to spare. You must go. Please. I have chores—

CATHERINE. That sounds so nice.

JOAN. What?

CATHERINE. Chores. So wonderfully ordinary. *(Abruptly, to* MARGARET:*)* I don't understand why it must be this way.

JOAN moves to leave when MICHAEL appears in her path.

MICHAEL. *(Gently:)* Child of Lorraine, would you deny the will of God?

JOAN. I deny only my own worthiness.

He bends down to her; she shrinks away, terrified.

MICHAEL. Don't be afraid. The Father is with you. He has graven you upon the palms of His hands.

He offers his hand to her, palm up; she looks at it —at him —for a long moment. Tentatively she places her hand in his. Something in his touch galvanizes her. MICHAEL *motions with a hand, and all three disappear from* JOAN's *vision;* JOAN *is a little dazed, to say the least.* MARGARET *turns to* CATHERINE.

MARGARET. This is important—

CATHERINE. To us, or to her? I said I would help her, but is this too much to ask?

MARGARET. She must embrace her place and fulfill her duty, as you must yours.

CATHERINE. The only duty this girl has is to live righteously, and she is doing that. Why must we impose this fate on her? If she stays home, God will not love her any less. And this not-even-king, he doesn't know who she is. He doesn't care. We shouldn't risk her life for someone who doesn't know her name.

MICHAEL. *(Simply:)* God knows her name.

He goes to the font, takes a pinch of sand and flicks it off his finger: JOAN *is again aware of* CATHERINE *and* MARGARET's *presence.*

JOAN. Not you again.

Frustrated, she turns to go.

CATHERINE. Jeannette. We won't hurt you.

JOAN. Why can't you leave me be?

CATHERINE. You're not the only one who's been called.

JOAN. . . . You've been called?

MARGARET. We're to guide you to glory in the Father's name.

JOAN. I know my place in this world, and I don't mind that glory is far beyond it.

CATHERINE. But you are Joan, the Maid, child of God.

MARGARET. You have been chosen to rally France to her true king, Charles. That is your place in this world.

JOAN. The Dauphin? He is in exile, in Chinon. Hundreds of miles away.

MARGARET. He is waiting for you.

JOAN. Why should he?

MARGARET. You will lead his army, and you will save France.

JOAN suppresses a laugh.

JOAN. Save France? I can't but burn supper, and you want me to save France? It can't be me. It can't.

MARGARET. God chose you.

JOAN. What would I do, anyway? Walk to the Dauphin and tell him God has sent me to liberate his country?

MARGARET. Well—yes.

JOAN. This is madness. I'm telling you, I can't! I won't. Choose someone else. It can't be me. I won't do it.

JOAN again moves to leave, but stops at:

CATHERINE. I'll do it, if you will. This thing, this calling. I'll make you a promise if you'll do the same for me.

JOAN. What kind of promise?

CATHERINE. I don't understand it, and I don't expect you to. But I'll be honest with you, and I'll do all I can to protect you.

JOAN. . . . I don't—But what if I don't—What am I supposed to do?

CATHERINE. We'll work it out together.

MARGARET. You have a destiny; now meet it gladly, as your time is short.

JOAN. . . . I don't know why saints would come to me.

CATHERINE. We're not saints. I don't talk to God; I've yet to sit at his feet.

JOAN. But you gave your life for the faith. I've grown up worshipping you, adoring you. How can that be wrong?

CATHERINE. I'm not perfect. I don't deserve your worship, your adoration. I'm just like you: a woman who knows the truth, and who would tell the world. That is what a saint is: a follower, a believer. Like you, I follow Jesus Christ because I love him, because I know He is the Son of God. If you must call me saint, then know that you are as much a saint as I.

JOAN. But I'm just me. Only me. A girl with no sense other than chickens and spinning and—How will I know what to do?

CATHERINE. Faith. It's faith that quickens your heart and stills your soul. You do have faith.

JOAN. Yes.

CATHERINE. This is a work none of us can comprehend. We only know it's been asked of us, and of you.

CATHERINE. *(With a glance toward* MARGARET:*)* This is how things work. How God works.

JOAN. . . . You'll be here, with me. You won't leave me alone? Do you swear it?

CATHERINE. Yes.

JOAN. All the way to Chinon and the Dauphin?

CATHERINE. To the gates of hell and back again. *(*JOAN *moves to go.)* Jeannette—

JOAN. I will take Maman today's milk, as it is the last I can bring her for some time.

SCENE 2: ALONG THE ROAD TO CHINON

CATHERINE *and* MARGARET *instruct* JOAN:

CATHERINE. Shortly you will see the Dauphin. What will you say to him?

JOAN. I will tell him that God has sent me to see him crowned and anointed king at Reims. But how will I do that?

MARGARET. There will be great victories, battles that send the English running away. And you'll be there, you'll see them run. You'll be there, on the field, as the English retreat.

JOAN. But I'm no soldier. I know nothing of riding or warfare. How can you want me to go into battle?

MARGARET. It's expected. This war has been going on for decades and these men are too deep in it to go back. You must approach them in a way they will understand.

JOAN. I don't think I could kill anyone.

MARGARET. Well, if—

CATHERINE. You needn't kill anyone.

MARGARET. But should you—

CATHERINE. We need to think practically about long hours on horseback and heavy armor. You can't go as a woman.

MARGARET. Catherine—Slowly, please. Let's not be rash.

CATHERINE. We need to think of her safety as she rides through enemy territory. I've given it some thought, and it will be safer for you to dress like a man.

JOAN AND MARGARET. What?

CATHERINE. Who knows what will happen if you ride all the way from Lorraine to Chinon, through English and Burgundian patrols, as you are. Some villain will surely find you a pretty target.

Lights shift to the HISTORIANS, *who dress themselves as members of the French court.*

HISTORIAN 1. So Joan left home, and everything she had ever known or understood, to follow her voices across hundreds of miles of enemy territory.

HISTORIAN 2. Dressed in the apparel of a man, she called out for the restoration of the French king,

HISTORIAN 3. Winning followers wherever she went—

HISTORIAN 4. Soldiers and governors and statesmen—

HISTORIAN 1. As she made her way to Chinon.

And we are in Chinon.

HISTORIAN 2. Chinon. The adopted court of Joan's true and beloved Dauphin,

HISTORIAN 3. True heir to the French throne,

HISTORIAN 4. Charles.

One of the HISTORIANS *becomes* CHARLES *and the others become his* COURTIERS.

COURTIER 1. Your Majesty should send her packing.

COURTIER 2. She is only a peasant, after all.

CHARLES. So now that she has traveled all this way through Burgundy, you think I should send her back.

COURTIER 3. Naturally Your Majesty is all generosity and kindness.

COURTIER 1. But she has no right to expect any different.

COURTIER 2. Peasant that she is.

CHARLES. And if she is not?

COURTIER 3. Majesty?

CHARLES. What if she merely seems a peasant? What if she is God's anointed?

COURTIER 1. With all due respect, Majesty ...

COURTIER 2. You are God's anointed.

CHARLES. Yes, yes, yes. That's what I meant.

COURTIER 3. Forgive us our—simplemindedness, Sire.

COURTIER 1. And our impertinence.

COURTIER 2. Please do grace us with a fuller understanding.

CHARLES. There has to be a way.

COURTIER 3. A way?

CHARLES. To prove—

COURTIER 1. Or disprove.

CHARLES. If she is who she says she is.

COURTIER 2. A brilliant suggestion, my lord.

CHARLES. Yes, I know. Take my hat. *(He trades hats with* COURTIER 3.*)* And my cloak as well. She must believe you are the Dauphin. Can you do that? Make her believe you're me?

COURTIER 3. I—I will do what I can, Majesty.

CHARLES. And the rest of you, treat him as you would me. If this Maid is anyone for us to think on . . .

COURTIER 1. . . . Then she will know the difference?

CHARLES. Precisely.

COURTIER 2. An excellent plan, Sire.

CHARLES. Not me, you idiot. Him.

He indicates COURTIER 3, *who needs a moment to catch up.*

COURTIER 3. . . . Oh, yes. Um . . . Bring her in. Bring her in!

COURTIER 1 *bows and goes out.*

CHARLES. Well, we'll see what happens, won't we?

COURTIER 1 *re-enters, leading* JOAN; *she is dressed in men's clothing.* CATHERINE *and* MARGARET *enter opposite, watching.*

COURTIER 1. Presenting Joan d'Arc, the Maid of Lorraine. She would speak with Your Majesty.

COURTIER 2. Oh, how very—quaint.

CHARLES *and his* COURTIERS *bow low to* COURTIER 3. CATHERINE *looks over the scene, suspicious; she watches* CHARLES, *who doesn't quite fit in.*

CATHERINE. What are they playing at?

COURTIER 3 *looks* JOAN *over. Holds out his hand to her to kiss.* JOAN *is about to do so—*

CATHERINE. No, wait.

MARGARET. Catherine—

COURTIER 3. Won't you bow to your Dauphin?

COURTIER 1. To your King?

COURTIER 2. Have you no respect?

JOAN. Yes! Of course I do. But—

COURTIER 3. I don't have time for such things.

COURTIER 1. Send her home with a good whipping.

COURTIER 2. Or some time in the dungeon.

COURTIER 3. Silence. I shall decide what must be done here. After all, God has made me just.

COURTIER 1. What has he made you?

JOAN. I am—

CATHERINE. Jeannette, don't. It's not him.

MARGARET. Hush!

CATHERINE. And let her be jailed for their amusement? Absolutely not. *(To* JOAN, *indicating* CHARLES:*)* The quiet one. He is the Dauphin.

JOAN goes to CHARLES.

JOAN. Forgive me, sweet Dauphin, for my momentary confusion. My voices have told me you are the chosen King of France. And I never doubt what my saints tell me.

The COURTIERS *scoff:*

COURTIER 2. Voices?

COURTIER 3. Saints?

CHARLES. . . . I am not who you take me for.

JOAN. You are Charles, are you not? You are he the English robbed of his proper birthright. I bring you news from God, that our Lord will give you back your kingdom, bringing you to be crowned at Reims and hounding out your enemies. Set me bravely to work, and I will break off the siege at Orléans.

CHARLES. . . . You speak most convincingly.

JOAN. But Your Majesty is not convinced.

COURTIER 1. Ha!

COURTIER 2. No.

COURTIER 3. Uh-uh.

JOAN *looks to* CATHERINE *for help.*

CATHERINE. Send the others out and show him a sign.

MARGARET. A sign? What do you mean, a sign?

CATHERINE. If Charles doesn't believe, no one else will. And what will she be then? A fugitive? Not if I can help it.

JOAN. If I might speak with you alone, Majesty, I will prove to you that I am God's messenger, sent to make war on the English.

COURTIER 1. Ridiculous.

COURTIER 2. That is enough.

COURTIER 3. Be gone with you.

COURTIER 1. Don't insult His Majesty further.

CHARLES. I will settle this, friends. Excuse yourselves. *(The* COURTIERS *express their distaste for this idea: "She can't be—", "But—", etc. They are instantly silenced at:)* Go! Get out before you are removed.

The COURTIERS *exit in a huff.*

MARGARET. What have you done?

CATHERINE. I just want to help her. If he believes her, he will give her soldiers. An armed escort. We can't let her run across the countryside, alone and powerless—

MARGARET. So you'll show him a sign. What sign is that?

CATHERINE *chews on a fingernail, sheepish.*

CATHERINE. I haven't planned quite that far.

CHARLES. Now, Joan, is it?

JOAN. Yes, my Dauphin.

CHARLES. Let's be frank and open, shall we?

JOAN. Whatever pleases you.

CHARLES. It would please us very much to understand why you are here.

JOAN. God sent me, my Dauphin.

CHARLES. Mm-hmm. To do what, exactly?

JOAN. To liberate your kingdom and see you crowned.

CHARLES. You? You would liberate our kingdom?

Her answer is automatic, sincere. Clear as day.

JOAN. Yes.

CHARLES. But—How is such a thing possible?

JOAN. I dare not ask how, my Dauphin. I only do as I am told.

CATHERINE. We have to do something. Besides, miracles come to the faithful.

MARGARET. All right, all right. I know what to do.

She whispers to CATHERINE, *then moves to stand behind* CHARLES. CATHERINE *goes to the font. Drizzles sand from her fingers.*

CHARLES. We like you. That goes without saying. You do not possess the guile of the high-born. We believe you are honest enough. But we don't know that it is wise to take to heart everything you say you are. Forgive us if we are—wary of such notions. There are days when a prince can do naught but look over his shoulder.

JOAN. If my Dauphin should look over his shoulder, he shall see angels who will carry him to Reims.

CHARLES *turns to see* MARGARET *standing behind him.* CATHERINE *pulls a simple gold crown from the font; she sets the circlet on* JOAN's *open palms.* CHARLES *turns back to* JOAN, *and it seems to him that the crown has appeared from nowhere; stunned, he drops to his knees before* JOAN.

JOAN. Does my Dauphin believe now that I am in God's charge and will see only good done in His name?

CHARLES. Yes.

JOAN. Then it begins.

She crowns him.

JOAN. God give you life, gentle King.

CATHERINE *turns to* MARGARET, *thrilled.*

CATHERINE. Marvelous! Did you see his eyes? He can't doubt who she is now.

MARGARET. We can't just go throwing miracles about. It's not our place.

CATHERINE. But it is. I've realized something, Margaret. This girl is a force to be reckoned with. As are we.

SCENE 3: THE HISTORIANS

HISTORIAN 1. Charles gave Joan the strength of his army,

HISTORIAN 2. Leaving rumor to float like mist about this peculiar girl,

HISTORIAN 3. This girl who had won the Dauphin's trust with some secret miracle.

HISTORIAN 4. In spite of the Prince's blessing, there was dissension in the ranks.

HISTORIAN 1. Has she bewitched him?

HISTORIAN 2. There was murmuring among the generals who thought they were doing well enough without a peasant to tell them their business.

HISTORIAN 3. Who is she, anyway?

HISTORIAN 4. What right has she to speak on military matters?

HISTORIAN 1. But Joan paid the faithless no heed.

HISTORIAN 2. Her mind was set, her mission sure.

HISTORIAN 3. She would take back Orléans, that poor besieged city on the stolen road to Paris.

HISTORIAN 4. And along the way,

HISTORIAN 1. In a humble, ancient church in Fierbois,

HISTORIAN 2. Joan the Maid stopped to pray.

The HISTORIANS become FRENCH SOLDIERS at supper. Praying, JOAN kneels in a church apse. CATHERINE listens as the SOLDIERS complain.

SOLDIER 3. Three weeks on the road, and for this.

SOLDIER 4. To follow a girl who says she talks with saints.

SOLDIER 1. My mother would beat me for my impertinence.

SOLDIER 2. If she was my daughter, I wouldn't let her out of the house.

CATHERINE. Surely her own men should believe in her.

She whispers in JOAN's ear.

SOLDIER 3. A girl doesn't belong at the head of an army.

SOLDIER 4. A girl doesn't belong *in* the army.

SOLDIER 1. She'll get herself killed.

SOLDIER 2. Worse, she'll get us killed.

JOAN turns on the SOLDIERS, catching them off guard.

JOAN. Do you think God cannot hear your murmuring? For he can, and he does, and his wrath will be kindled against France if you do not curb your tongues, what with your dissent and your foul language. God does not abide cursing, and neither shall I.

The SOLDIERS laugh and scoff.

CATHERINE. It's all right. I have an idea.

CATHERINE whispers in JOAN's ear. As JOAN instructs the men, CATHERINE goes to the font, takes a pinch of sand, and throws it at the altar.

JOAN. This is the church of St. Catherine at Fierbois. You, and you, dig behind the altar. You will find a sword buried there. Bring it back to me. Go! Now!

The MEN go to the spot where CATHERINE tossed the sand and search. MARGARET approaches CATHERINE.

MARGARET. What is this?

CATHERINE. Proof.

MARGARET. Of what?

CATHERINE. Our Jeannette's divinity.

MARGARET. Divinity? What are you thinking? We aren't supposed to make her a god.

CATHERINE. But if the army thinks she is, why not use it to our advantage? Relics demand respect. People will give their lives to save hers.

MARGARET. Are their lives any less important?

CATHERINE. These men are simple people. There must be something for them to hold on to. We need only show them that they already believe, and the rest will fall into place.

MARGARET. Simple people, like Joan herself, they are the most faithful. All they need hold to is their faith—

> CATHERINE *turns away from* MARGARET. *The* MEN *reverently present* JOAN *with a wrapped object.* JOAN *can only stare at it.*

CATHERINE. Go on, love. Take it.

> JOAN *takes the object and unwraps the cloth swaddling it; within is a sword shining as if it has only been tempered moments before. The* SOLDIERS *are in awe, genuflecting and crossing themselves.*

MARGARET. What are you doing?

CATHERINE. What I'm supposed to.

MARGARET. Give signs? Act in God's behalf? Catherine, I thought you above this.

CATHERINE. These people need to circle around her. They need to have faith—

MARGARET. You can't hand faith to them anymore than—than you can sell indulgences.

CATHERINE. Would you prefer to beat it into them? Because faith is all about terror and pain, isn't it, as it was for us? Would you have her believe God has no mercy for the meek?

MARGARET. You can't just smooth her road with miracles. She won't learn if you stifle her experience.

CATHERINE. Experience means pain, and I've had more than my share. You witnessed it. You, who stood by and told me it would end. That I would awake safe and loved in the arms of Jesus. That hasn't happened yet.

MARGARET. Catherine, I—

CATHERINE. Neither of our histories ended happily. We should spare her that misery. I won't lie to her, and I won't stand by if something happens. I'll make certain she survives.

Lights shift to the HISTORIANS.

HISTORIAN 3. Now accepted and beloved by her men as a messenger of God, Joan arrives at Orléans,

HISTORIAN 4. Only to be ignored by General Dunois and mocked by the English forces.

HISTORIAN 1. The English were hearing stories of the Maid from Lorraine,

HISTORIAN 2. That she was a witch the French had employed to solicit the devil in their unholy cause.

HISTORIAN 3. And the French didn't know who this person was, now among them so unexpectedly,

HISTORIAN 4. This girl who had the blessing of the Dauphin—

HISTORIAN 1. And the ear of angels.

HISTORIAN 2. It was time to put an end to the rumors;

HISTORIAN 3. It was time for Joan to make her presence known.

Lights shift to CATHERINE *and* JOAN.

CATHERINE. These men, they must be inspired. And the English will fear you as they've never feared anything before.

JOAN. Why should the English listen to me?

CATHERINE. They want to go home as much as you. If we can avoid—

She catches herself. Tries another tack.

CATHERINE. Without you there is no cause. There is no victory.

JOAN. Do you believe that?

CATHERINE. I know it.

JOAN. Can't it be later? Tomorrow, perhaps, when we've had time to—

CATHERINE. The English are on the parapet, watching you. It must be now. You must show them you're unwilling to retreat, show them who's right and who's not. Let your faith shine through, let the fire of your words bite at their ears. They don't know what to make of you; let their imaginations run with terror, and they will go before blood is spilled. Now, love. Go on.

She turns JOAN *to face the unseen English forces;* JOAN *is struck with an immediate case of stage fright. All nerves herself,* CATHERINE *paces behind* JOAN; *but whenever* JOAN *looks back,* CATHERINE *is the very picture of support.*

JOAN. . . . Um, King of England? And you, Duke of Bedford, who call yourself Regent of the kingdom of France . . . (*She turns to go but* CATHERINE *stops her, turning her back to face the English.*) Do justice to the King of Heaven; surrender to me, the

Maid, who is sent here from God, King of Heaven, the keys of all the good towns you have taken and violated in France. I am come from God to uphold the blood royal.

CATHERINE. Good, good.

JOAN. King of England, know that I am sent here from God to put you, hand to hand, out of all France. In whatever place in France I come upon your men, I will make them leave it, will they or nil they.

CATHERINE. Yes. Ha!

JOAN is in the spirit now.

JOAN. And think not otherwise: for so God wills it; and so it has been revealed by the Maid, and King Charles, the true heir, shall enter Paris with a fair company. I, Joan the Maid, do pray and beseech you not to bring on your own destruction. Expect to hear news of me, who will shortly come to see you, to your very great damage. If you will not believe this news from God and the Maid, wherever we find you, there we shall strike; and we shall raise such a battle-cry as there has not been in France in a thousand years. Know surely that the King of Heaven will send more strength to the Maid than you can bring against me and my good soldiers in any assault. And when the blows begin, it shall be seen whose right is the better before the God of Heaven!

CATHERINE nearly bursts with pride. A SOLDIER offers a letter to JOAN; she does not take it.

CATHERINE. Will it work? Will they surrender?

JOAN. What does it say? Read it to me.

SOLDIER. They will not yield. They say they will not give the day to a French whore.

He exits.

JOAN. . . . They would call me whore?

CATHERINE. It doesn't mean anything.

JOAN. But it does! I have kept myself for God. I am not what they say.

MARGARET. Which is why they say it. There is always someone who will spend their time crushing the hopes of another. Put them out of mind, or they'll find satisfaction in your distress. What matters now is that they have denied your suit for peace.

JOAN. Then we must fight. But men will die.

MARGARET. People die for all great causes. It's how we know that what we do is great.

CATHERINE. Expectations differ from person to person.

MARGARET. Don't assume that yours is the only way. The right way.

CATHERINE. I'm not assuming anything—

JOAN. I would rather no one died.

The two stop and look at her. After a moment:

MARGARET. It's a lesson men must learn, that dying is sometimes the only answer.

CATHERINE. Spoken like a true martyr.

JOAN. You're not talking about me? Me, dying?

MARGARET. You've been given time, a window, to do this thing. Then . . .

JOAN. I can go home?

CATHERINE. Yes.

JOAN. How much time?

MARGARET. . . . A year, perhaps a little more.

JOAN. Then we must think to do good work in that year. I would so like to go home.

CATHERINE. You will, I promise.

MARGARET. There is still much to do.

JOAN. I'll do it, if I may return home afterward.

She exits.

MARGARET. You promised her she could go home. Who are we to make such a promise?

CATHERINE. Why not make it? After all of this is done, after we march on Orléans and the English armies tremble at the very sight of her, what else will there be for her to do? She can't be expected to give her whole life to this.

MARGARET. That's not our decision to make.

CATHERINE. We can keep our promise, Margaret. There's no reason—

MARGARET. It's your promise, and it's a reckless promise! I want to help her as much as you, but we need to be careful. It may seem that hers is the only soul we're protecting, but there are thousands that—

CATHERINE. We need to simplify things, focus on the one soul we know we can save.

MARGARET. We can't save her soul; she must do that herself.

CATHERINE. I will save her. I will keep her intact. Whole, spiritual, intact. Ready for . . .

MARGARET. For?

CATHERINE. For anything.

SCENE 4: ORLÉANS

JOAN sleeps, her head in CATHERINE's lap.

HISTORIAN 1. Imagine: the once great city of Orléans,

HISTORIAN 2. In all its faded pomp,

HISTORIAN 3. Slowly crumbling under the burden of an enemy siege.

HISTORIAN 4. Across the river, General Dunois and his men await a miracle,

HISTORIAN 1. Unaware that one sleeps among them.

HISTORIAN 2. And when much-needed reinforcements arrive,

HISTORIAN 3. Dunois does not rouse the Maid.

Somewhere distant, a trumpet sounds.

HISTORIAN 4. His army storms across what was once a meadow,

HISTORIAN 1. In what was once France.

MARGARET enters, going to CATHERINE.

MARGARET. She's still sleeping?

CATHERINE. It's a miracle she fell asleep at all. Besides, we must wait for reinforcements.

MARGARET. Reinforcements are here.

CATHERINE. But Dunois said—

MARGARET. Dunois did not do as he said.

The sounds of battle rise to a dull roar in the background. CATHERINE shakes JOAN awake.

CATHERINE. Jeannette, Jeannette.

JOAN. What? What's happening?

CATHERINE. Quickly, dear. General Dunois has already started the day.

JOAN. He would not dare. He knows—

MARGARET. He knows but what we've told him, and that doesn't mean he believes. You must go and join him at the front. They will lose the day if they go long without you. You must show them why you've been called.

CATHERINE. Not at the front.

MARGARET. Where else but at the front?

JOAN. It's true. I must be seen.

CATHERINE. To actually charge the field— She's not a soldier.

MARGARET. No soldiering is necessary. Men have already heard of your miraculous beginnings. They will rally to you.

JOAN. What shall I say?

MARGARET. The truth. Speak but the truth.

JOAN. My Lord has sent me to succor this good town of Orléans.

CATHERINE. There will be terrible things happening. Men bleeding, dying, everywhere. Don't look at them if you can help it. Concentrate on getting through. Should something hap—

MARGARET hands JOAN her sword.

MARGARET. Make certain that the men see you. Speak surely. Your fight is God's fight.

CATHERINE. Be safe, Jeannette. We are close by.

JOAN. In God's name, let us go on bravely!

The battle noise fades to silence with JOAN's exit.

CATHERINE. I prayed this day would never come.

MARGARET. Why are we here, if not for this day?

CATHERINE. You expect her to die.

MARGARET. It's a possibility we can't ignore. I wish her no harm; I love her as much as you. But we need to be ready for any eventuality. We can't say how things will end.

CATHERINE. But we may influence it. We have the power to choose, as does Joan, and we can affect her destiny. I see no fault in—

A scream is heard off. JOAN enters, helped by two SOLDIERS; an arrow protrudes from her shoulder.

SOLDIER 1. Gently, man, gently.

CATHERINE. Jeannette? Can you hear me?

JOAN. You seem very far away.

CATHERINE. We're right here, with you.

JOAN. Did I do all right?

MARGARET. Yes. Yes, you did very well. Of course you did.

SOLDIER 2. What are you talking about?

SOLDIER 1. She's lost blood. She doesn't know what she's saying.

CATHERINE. Jeannette—

JOAN. I must get back. The men, they won't fight without me. I must—

CATHERINE. Oh, no. I'm not letting you go back there.

SOLDIER 2. You can't go back. Listen to reason—

JOAN. Who are you to tell me what I can't do when I know what I must do?

CATHERINE. You're not making sense—

SOLDIER 1. You've an arrow in your shoulder.

SOLDIER 2. It doesn't look good. It'll have to come out.

SOLDIER 1. Perhaps we should put a charm on it, to speed the healing.

JOAN. No, no. That's blasphemy. I would rather die than do what I know is sin.

SOLDIER 2. Then we'll wait for the surgeon.

JOAN. No. Pull it out.

SOLDIER 1. What?

JOAN. The arrow. Pull it out.

SOLDIER 2. We've sent for a surgeon. He'll—

JOAN. I must get back. Pull out the arrow so I may go.

SOLDIER 1. I can't.

JOAN. Then my saints will guide my hand, and I'll do it myself. Stand clear. Stand clear!

> JOAN *looks up at* CATHERINE *expectantly, but* CATHERINE *can't do it.* MARGARET *kneels behind* JOAN, *supporting her, though to the mortal eye it appears that the* SOLDIERS *are holding her up.* MARGARET *wraps* JOAN'S *hand about the arrow, holds it there.*

MARGARET. Ready?

> JOAN *nods, takes a deep breath. They pull out the arrow, and* JOAN *faints. The* SOLDIERS *exit.*

MARGARET. Wasn't that something? She did it, all by herself. She didn't even think to ask us if it was right. She only knew it must happen.

CATHERINE. Look at this, at her. A bloody mess. Did you hear her scream? You wanted this—

MARGARET. I want nothing of the sort. Do you think it's easy for me to stand by? I can't take up a sword and defend her as you wish you could. Neither of us can. Do you think I enjoyed watching Maxentius torture you? That's what this is about, isn't it? I could have worked harder to help you. You think you can prove that by saving her. Oh, Catherine . . . Never for an instant did I wish harm to befall you. If I could have stepped in, if I could have taken your place, God knows I would have. But it's not how things work. It's not—

> *She stops herself. Looks away.*

CATHERINE. *(Apologetic:)* Margaret—

MARGARET. Don't assume that I feel nothing because I don't express it as you do.

> JOAN *stirs.*

JOAN. Dunois, we must take the bridge—Dunois? They left me here.

MARGARET. They're expecting you, when you're ready.

JOAN. Where is my sword?

CATHERINE. You must have dropped it where you were shot. You're not well enough to—

JOAN. Does it matter? We're about to take the city.

CATHERINE. Jeannette, you must take care—

JOAN. I'll be fine. The men need me. I must go.

> JOAN *gets to her feet and exits unaided. . . .* CATHERINE *looks back to* MARGARET.

CATHERINE. I'm sorry.

MARGARET. Never mind.

CATHERINE. To see her hurt—

MARGARET. I know.

CATHERINE. I don't know if I can take much more of this.

MARGARET. We will go to Reims and see the Dauphin crowned.

CATHERINE. Then Jeannette can go home, as she has always asked.

SCENE 5: REIMS

> JOAN *prays in one of the cathedral's chapels, bathed in the light of a rose window.* CHARLES *enters, newly crowned. Crossing himself, he joins* JOAN *at the altar.*

CHARLES. Ah, here you are. I've been looking for you everywhere.

JOAN. Why is it my King must look for me himself? Where are your servants, your lords?

CHARLES. Oh, they're all drinking. *(Off her look:)* It's celebration, not a sin. Leave them be. I needed but a bit of time away, that's all. I'm only a man, when it comes down to it, king or no. And this mantle . . . it weighs down like a guilty conscience.

JOAN. Allow me.

> *She removes his cloak.*

CHARLES. Bless you. You've saved me once again. And yet I've done nothing to show my appreciation. We are friends, and I'd be very happy to give you whatever you ask.

JOAN. I have everything I could ask, sweet King.

CHARLES. I doubt that. Come now, speak plainly. There must be something you want for yourself, perhaps for your family.

JOAN. I want to fight again.

CHARLES. No, we're done with that. You're done with that. Do you see this, this crown of mine? It was hard won, but it was won.

JOAN. I've only begun. I will win you the rest of France.

CHARLES. Oh, Jeannette . . .

JOAN. Paris is where you should rule, and it is overrun by your enemies. Let me take it back for you.

CHARLES. The Duke of Burgundy promised to give me Paris when the time was right.

JOAN. And as he speaks his treachery, thousands of English arrive to reinforce his position. Burgundy has no honor, no—

CHARLES. I will have a proclamation written up for your village. Domrémy, yes? No family living in Domrémy shall ever bear the burden of taxes. How's that?

JOAN. We must assure that the English are driven off. Not just to Calais, but back to their island, across the channel. The men will follow me, Majesty. They will flock to God's banner and we—

CHARLES. Stop it! I've spoken on the matter. Does that not satisfy you? How is a king to function when his subjects disregard him so?

JOAN. Forgive me, Majesty. I meant no offense.

CHARLES. Of course you didn't. You are one of the few I know to speak sincerely here. You have finished, and wonderfully. I enjoy your company, your frankness of opinion. You should stay here with me and enjoy the fruits of court life.

JOAN. What, gossip and playing for favor?

CHARLES. Your tone, Jeannette.

JOAN. I can't stay here. I'm not meant for this life, for the trappings of nobility. My year is not yet up; don't let it lie fallow.

CHARLES. We will create you a noble, and your family shall never want for anything. There, that should satisfy you.

JOAN. I won Orléans back for you. I won at Beaugency, at Patay. I will win again.

CHARLES. You tax my patience.

JOAN. God has sent me to you; use me. Please.

CHARLES. I've a headache. From all this dressing up and proceeding about. A man, I'm just a man. No one will let me be, not for two moments together. Such a headache. Go to Paris. *(Thrilled, she embraces him.)* Go to England —I don't care. Take your army and go before I change my mind.

He goes, and JOAN *returns to her knees.* CATHERINE *and* MARGARET *enter, as if in answer to her prayer.*

CATHERINE. Well, then, it's done.

MARGARET. Where is your family? I didn't think you'd be separated from them once they arrived.

CATHERINE. Now that you can go home with them—

JOAN. I'm not going home. Not yet.

CATHERINE. What are you talking about?

JOAN. I'm going to win back Paris. Won't it be wonderful? The anointed king will reclaim his capital.

CATHERINE. What have you done?

MARGARET. You should have consulted us first.

JOAN. You told me I had a year. There is still much to do.

CATHERINE. I don't believe it. I don't.

JOAN. I thought you'd be proud. The King has given us another task. Let's embrace it.

MARGARET. We don't answer to your king! You risk too much.

JOAN. The English are afraid. They know God is on our—

CATHERINE. How could you do this? How, after everything we've been through? I kept my promise. I kept you safe. Now, on the day you should be returning home, you do this? How could you be so foolish? Another battle—

JOAN. The king has already given his consent. Given me an army.

CATHERINE. And what of our consent? What if we can't protect you?

JOAN. I'm not a coward. I thought at first I might be, but I've learned that I can be brave. I will be brave.

MARGARET. We aren't doubting your courage. But we aren't prepared to go back to the front. And you are no soldier.

JOAN. I am now.

CATHERINE. What if Paris isn't supposed to be won? What if from now until the apocalypse French kings rule from Reims? Who are you to say it should be different?

JOAN. I am Joan the Maid, messenger of God. I will do what I must, and then I will go home.

CATHERINE. Go home now. Please.

    MICHAEL *enters, carrying* JOAN's *lost sword.*

MICHAEL. Go to Paris.

CATHERINE. What?

MICHAEL. She has made her choice. You must support her in it. *(To* JOAN:*)* As you say, you are no coward. But what lies ahead—

JOAN. I will see it through.

CATHERINE. And if something happens, if you're hurt or killed? What then?

MICHAEL. There is no going back. Your way lies with Joan until she releases you from it. *(Handing* JOAN *her sword:)* Go on.

JOAN. By my staff, we are enough. I shall see my good friends in Compiégne.

She exits.

MARGARET. I thought it would end with Reims.

CATHERINE. She's done what she was called to do, hasn't she? Isn't that enough?

MICHAEL. That decision isn't yours to make.

CATHERINE. What can we do if she won't listen? It should end here.

MICHAEL. The longest battle she will wage is only beginning.

He goes to the font and sifts sand through his fingers. Lights shift to JOAN, *at the head of her army, on the field of battle. As the battle progresses* JOAN *is separated from her army, surrounded by* ENGLISH SOLDIERS, *and captured.*

Blackout.

SCENE 6: ROUEN

During the following narration, two of the HISTORIANS *become the* EARL OF WARWICK *and* BISHOP PIERRE CAUCHON, *respectively.*

HISTORIAN 1. After the failed attempt to take Paris,

HISTORIAN 2. Joan was taken prisoner by the Duke of Burgundy,

HISTORIAN 3. A powerful lord who could play friend or rival to both England and France,

HISTORIAN 4. Dependent on who paid him best.

HISTORIAN 1. When his men captured Joan, Burgundy had allied himself with the English and,

HISTORIAN 2. Looking to further his own interests in France,

HISTORIAN 3. Sold the captive Maid into the hands of Richard Beauchamp, Earl of Warwick,

HISTORIAN 4. A personal advisor to Henry VI.

HISTORIAN 1. Now that they had their prize, the English weren't sure what to do with her.

HISTORIAN 2. So young King Henry's counselors called on Bishop Pierre Cauchon

HISTORIAN 3. To discover what evidence should condemn the Maid of Orléans.

WARWICK and CAUCHON confer in a prison hallway.

CAUCHON. She is devout, if nothing else. Her choice of apparel is a problem, certainly, but not impossibly so. With some re-education she might—

WARWICK. That would take some time, wouldn't it?

CAUCHON. My lord?

WARWICK. Re-education.

CAUCHON. Well, if it is required, then we must—

WARWICK. I will tell you what I require. That girl is a heretic and you will pronounce her so. His Majesty's soldiers, they are—frightened of the girl and her unnatural habits. To overcome that fear we must prove that she is from Satan.

CAUCHON. But if she is not—

WARWICK. She's not perfect. No one is. Find a way. Get her to say what you need her to say and she'll light her own pyre.

CAUCHON. Understand, I am on God's errand here, not yours.

WARWICK. God Himself would assure they are one and the same. I don't have time for a spiritual awakening, Bishop, and neither do you.

CAUCHON. We must at least put on the appearance of justice, don't you think?

A GUARD brings JOAN down the hall.

WARWICK. Try her, then, if you feel the need so keenly. But I'm not a patient man, and she does me no good alive. The Church isn't as insulated as once it was. Should you cross me, you'll regret it.

CAUCHON meets JOAN's eye; the exchange is brief but disconcerting.

CAUCHON. *(To WARWICK:)* "For yet a little while, and the wicked shall not be . . ."

The GUARD deposits JOAN in a cell, a tiny island of gray light in a sea of darkness.

JOAN. O God, where art thou? And where is the pavilion that covereth thy hiding place? Preserve me, O God:

CATHERINE appears at the edge of the light.

CATHERINE AND JOAN. For in thee do I put my trust.

CATHERINE. My soul doth magnify the Lord, and my spirit hath rejoiced in God my Savior. *(She goes to JOAN. Embraces her, comforts her.)* For with God nothing shall be impossible. He raiseth up the poor out of the dust, to set them among princes, and to make them inherit the throne of glory: for the pillars of the earth are the Lord's, and he hath set the world upon them. He will keep the feet of his saints, and the wicked shall be silent in darkness. Be of good courage, and he shall strengthen your heart, all ye that hope in the Lord.

CATHERINE AND JOAN. My soul doth magnify the Lord,

JOAN. And my spirit hath rejoiced in God my Savior. My soul doth magnify the Lord. My soul . . .

JOAN sleeps, her head in CATHERINE's *lap.* CATHERINE *looks heavenward.*

CATHERINE. Please, Father. Please . . .

— INTERVAL —

SCENE 7: A NIGHTMARE

JOAN sits in her prison cell, completely alone. CHARLES *enters, wearing his crown.*

JOAN. My gentle King!

CHARLES. Hello. Did you miss me?

JOAN. Very much. I was afraid that you wouldn't come for me.

CHARLES. They are demanding a ransom.

JOAN. I'm sorry that my freedom will cost you so.

CHARLES. Don't worry, Jeannette. Friend. Sister. Your freedom won't cost me anything.

JOAN. Your Majesty has always been most kind.

CHARLES. How can I not be? Without you, I would not be who I am. King. Look at me. I'm king. *(He takes off his crown, holds it up unceremoniously.)* Isn't it pretty? Don't you think it pretty? Don't you?

JOAN. I . . . Yes, of course.

CHARLES. Good, good. You always knew the right thing to say.

JOAN. My voices tell me what to—

CHARLES. Your voices? What voices?

JOAN. Catherine and Margaret. They—

CHARLES. Where are they?

JOAN. I don't—

CHARLES. Are they with you now?

JOAN. No. I—

CHARLES. That's too bad. Maybe they were bored. They probably don't have a pretty thing like this to play with. Catch! *(He tosses the crown at her as if it were a toy; it bounces out of her grasp and rolls to the floor.)* Oh, Joan, why did you have to go and do a thing like that?

JOAN. I didn't mean to—

CHARLES. That's right. You didn't mean to lose Paris. You didn't mean to be taken by the enemy.

JOAN. No, of course not—

CHARLES. And now the English have the audacity to say they will sell you back to me for the middling sum of a hundred thousand crowns. The thing is, I have only one, and I rather like it.

JOAN. I'm sorry. I'd hoped it would not be nearly so much—

CHARLES. Well, it is. But the ransom is not the issue. Joan, Joan, little Jeannette. Are you crying for me? Why?

JOAN. I never dreamt of causing you such distress.

CHARLES. As I said before, there is no distress. The gold is not the issue. I want to see you safely home.

TWO SOLDIERS come up behind JOAN on either side, grabbing her. A HOODED MAN enters.

JOAN. Your Majesty—

A SOLDIER claps a hand over her mouth.

CHARLES. *(To the HOODED MAN:)* I found a little something for you, Bishop. To remember me by.

The MAN drops his hood: it is CAUCHON.

CAUCHON. I've never been one for souvenirs.

CHARLES. Your type prefers relics? It's the thought that counts, anyway.

CAUCHON. All of this has been going on for too long as it is. Throw her in the fire. Like you, I've no further use for her.

CHARLES looks to JOAN and shrugs.

CHARLES. That's the best thing I've heard all day.

SOLDIER 1 brings a chair to JOAN.

JOAN. You must help me escape this place—

SOLDIER 1. Please, sit. Everything will be as it should.

He guides her into the chair.

SOLDIER 2. We're in for some good fishing this year, don't you think?

JOAN. I don't know what you're talking about.

SOLDIER 2 *brings over an armful of firewood.*

JOAN. You must help me! The king is mad. They're all mad—

SOLDIER 2 *begins to whistle.*

SOLDIER 1. That's a sprightly tune.

SOLDIER 2. Eh, it's a good day to die.

JOAN. What is wrong with you? *(She tries to stand, but cannot: it's as if she is fixed to the chair.)* I can't—Someone, help me, please—

SOLDIER 1 *pulls a string from his pocket and sets up a cat's cradle, offering it to* SOLDIER 2, *who joins in the game.*

CHARLES. *(To* CAUCHON:*)* Have you taken dinner?

CAUCHON. After the whore is dead.

CHARLES. Good man. I also like to work up an appetite. I know just the thing.

CAUCHON. It is a bit chilly in here, don't you think?

The SOLDIERS *pile wood around* JOAN's *chair.*

JOAN. Charles, please—

CHARLES. Don't speak to me as if you know me. You are a heretic and a whore, and I shan't worry over you anymore. Mother says it's not polite, not when company's coming—tonight.

CAUCHON. Um, excuse me, Charlie, but clever as you are, I think you might have forgotten something.

CHARLES. Drat, you're right. I should probably invite Henry. Do you think he cares for marmalade? With his dinner?

CAUCHON. I'm sure I don't know. He is just a child, after all.

CHARLES. Do Englishmen even like dinner? What about my hair? Will he like my hair? *(To* JOAN:*)* Do you like my hair?

JOAN. Majesty—

CHARLES. Oh, what do you know? Peasants are never good for anything. Someone get rid of her already.

CAUCHON. It will be a pleasure.

CATHERINE *and* MARGARET *enter, oblivious that anything may be out of the ordinary.*

JOAN. Thank heaven! You know I've done nothing save what you told me. What God told me—

MARGARET. God didn't tell you anything.

CAUCHON. He doesn't care for the likes of you.

CHARLES. Why would he speak to one so worthless?

JOAN. He hasn't . . .

CAUCHON. Exactly. *(In her ear:)* He's going to let you die.

CATHERINE. *(Going to* JOAN:*)* Are you all right? You seem a bit upset.

JOAN. Please, can we leave this place?

CATHERINE. Ssh, ssh. It's not quite that simple.

JOAN. What do you mean?

MARGARET. Well, in the end, Charles won't be there to burn you.

JOAN. What?

CATHERINE. We will.

All but JOAN *erupt into merry laughter —Black.* MICHAEL, *barely visible, stands at the font, sand dripping from his fingers. Lights slowly reveal* JOAN *sleeping fitfully, her head in* CATHERINE'S *lap.* MARGARET *sits nearby, reading. Another moment, and* JOAN *sits up, terrified.*

CATHERINE. . . . Ssh . . . It's all right. It was only a dream.

MARGARET. Yes, only a dream. A nightmare.

JOAN. The king. King Charles gave me to the English.

CATHERINE. Jeannette—

JOAN. Don't call me that. My friends call me that and my family. You are neither.

MARGARET. Be reasonable—

JOAN. It's perfectly reasonable to want to live. Don't tell me I'm being unreasonable.

CATHERINE. Please—

JOAN. Get away from me. You are not from God.

MARGARET. Oh, Joan. After everything you've done—Don't blaspheme.

JOAN. I don't care. I won't follow you any longer. Your road leads to doom and death and failure. I don't want to die! I'm young yet. I'm not past marriage. I should have children clinging to my skirts. Skirts! I haven't worn a dress in months, in more than a year. I'm a woman, aren't I? I want to be a woman. To raise children and know the love of a man. And the bishops, so many bishops, tell me that dressing as I do is a sin. Offensive to God.

MARGARET. That's nonsense.

JOAN. These are God's men on Earth, are they not? Are they so wrong in telling me I have sinned? I'm not perfect, I'm not above sin. What fault can there be in admitting so, in saying what they want me to say if it means I might go home?

CATHERINE. You don't mean that.

JOAN. I do mean it. I will speak for myself for once. I don't want this, and I don't want you. Guard! Send for the Bishop!

MARGARET. Ssh. You don't want—

JOAN. Don't tell me what I want! Only I know what I want, and I want to live! I want to see my mother. *(The memory is overwhelming:)* Mother. Even if it means a smack for being late to supper. I want to lose myself in the woods, in the meadows, in the folds of a dress. Here . . . There is nothing here but stone . . . Iron . . . Dank, stale air. A person can't live like this. Go away. I don't want you here.

CATHERINE. I know you're upset, you're afraid. But without us—

JOAN. You promised I could go home. But that's all it was, wasn't it? Just an empty promise, to drive me to finish the mission. The mission matters more.

CATHERINE. Don't say that. Don't even think it.

JOAN. Leave me alone. If there is any chance to reclaim the life I had before . . . Just go.

MICHAEL *throws down a line of sand, separating* JOAN *from* CATHERINE *and* MARGARET.

CATHERINE. She can't mean it.

MARGARET. We can't force her. She's made her choice.

CATHERINE. There must be some way . . . Jeannette. *(But* JOAN *can no longer see or hear* CATHERINE *and* MARGARET.*)* Joan? Joan!

MICHAEL. She has expelled you.

MARGARET. She will be alone, for the trial. She won't know what to say.

MICHAEL. Won't she?

CATHERINE. You can put it back as it was.

MICHAEL. I can't.

CATHERINE. What do you mean, you can't? You're Michael. General of the armies of heaven. Can't you do it, or won't you?

MICHAEL. I can only do it should she ask for it.

He goes. JOAN, *realizing she is completely alone, curls up on the floor in an attempt to sleep.*

CATHERINE. What do we do now? If it should all end now, like this, then what was the good in it? In everything we've done, in everything Joan's done? Is there any good in it?

MARGARET. There must be. It can't all be for nothing. There must be some purpose we need to better understand—

CATHERINE. Don't. Don't turn this into a lesson for our betterment. She is alone now, and the English will treat her as they would any heretic. Why couldn't she just go home? What difference would it have made if she left this place untouched and unhurt? She would be in the fields above Domrémy, reveling in God's sky, celebrating God's earth. She would be home, and safe, and loved. Not here, not like this. I can see her thirty years from now, on a shady lawn, covered in grandchildren. We've stolen something from them. From Joan.

Silence.

MARGARET. Do you recall the first time we met?

CATHERINE. Of course. What does it matter?

MARGARET. Tell me what you remember. Please.

CATHERINE. I couldn't sleep. Something inside me was stirring, and—It wasn't quite dawn, so I went to the roof to watch the sun rise. I looked down to the street and you were there, leading sheep. *(She smiles despite herself.)* You met my eye and smiled and I—I felt as if I already knew you. Then suddenly you were beside me, and you said,

MARGARET. Know ye that the Lord he is God: he that hath made us, and not we ourselves:

CATHERINE. We are his people, and the sheep of his pasture.

MARGARET. Yes, sheep. Do you ever think about sheep? They don't have the urgency people have, they don't have our cares of conscience. They simply trust that their shepherd will guide them home. When I was Joan's age, I met a shepherdess. It was apparent in the way she carried herself, in every step, in every motion, that she knew God. I heard it in her voice, the glad song of conviction. I longed to hear that song whole and clear, to have it echo in the halls of my heart forever. So I departed the comfort of home for the company of—sheep. I could have stayed at home, and my end would have been different, no doubt. But I would have had to deny the truth I had already embraced, and I couldn't do that. If I had, any joy thereafter would have been—hollow. It's the same for you. For Joan. She could return to her home, yes. But she'll have lost something far too dear to describe, let alone replace.

Silence.

CATHERINE. I can still save her. I have to try. I've never wanted anything more than to raze these walls and let her walk through the streets free, whole, triumphant. Think how beautiful that would be. Yes! If I could pull down these stones with my own hands, and bring down all the thunder of Heaven, so that she could leave this world in glory. . . . If only for my own selfishness, for my own sanity—I can't just sit by and watch.

MARGARET. What you and I want is irrelevant now. She must want it. She must choose it. As we both did.

SCENE 8

The HISTORIANS *set a table and chairs, forming a courtroom.*

HISTORIAN 1. Joan was in prison for nearly eight months,

HISTORIAN 2. Moved from chilly castle towers

HISTORIAN 3. To dank dungeons all over English territory.

HISTORIAN 4. King Charles made no move to ransom the girl who had won him his crown,

HISTORIAN 1. And Joan found herself completely alone in the world,

HISTORIAN 2. But for bloodthirsty enemies who tried her on charges of sorcery and heresy.

HISTORIAN 3. Under the authority of the Holy Inquisition,

HISTORIAN 4. And with the approval of the Earl of Warwick,

HISTORIAN 1. Bishop Cauchon commenced with Joan's trial in the city of Rouen.

One of the HISTORIANS *moves behind the table and becomes* BISHOP PIERRE CAUCHON. *A* GUARD *brings* JOAN *in and stands her before the table.* CAUCHON *and* JOAN *regard each other as old adversaries might: This isn't the first day of questioning.* CATHERINE, MARGARET, *and* MICHAEL *observe.*

CAUCHON. These revelations of yours, these voices you say you hear. Tell me about them. What do they say to you?

JOAN. Upon my faith, you ask me things that I won't tell you.

CAUCHON. Is that because they are not true?

JOAN. I've sworn not to tell. Consider well your saying you are my judge, and take thought over what you're doing. For truly, I am sent from God, and you're putting yourself in great danger.

CAUCHON. I am acting in God's name—

JOAN. I've been sent by God. I have no business here. I pray you, send me back to God from whom I am come.

CAUCHON. When did you last hear the voices? What did they say to you?

JOAN. They told me I should answer bravely and that God would help me.

CATHERINE. Good girl.

CAUCHON. What did your voices say to you concerning your king?

JOAN. Nothing you are fit to hear.

CAUCHON. Do you think it displeasing to God to have the truth told?

JOAN. I have certain things to tell the king, not you! The things my voices have told me are many and to my king's good, and I'd happily drink no wine till Easter to have him know them now. He'd sit down to his dinner with a lighter heart.

CAUCHON. Have your voices told you that you'll escape from prison?

JOAN. Am I supposed to tell you that?

CAUCHON. Do you know that you are in God's grace?

JOAN. If I am not, God put me there, and if I am, God keep me there. I should be the saddest creature in all the world if I knew I weren't in God's grace.

CAUCHON. Did you, in your girlhood, have a strong inclination to harm the English?

JOAN. I had a strong desire for my king to have his kingdom.

CAUCHON. Should you like to be given a woman's dress?

JOAN. Give me one: I'll take it and go! Otherwise I won't take it. I'm content with this attire, since it pleases God that I should wear it.

CAUCHON. Do you believe that you would have failed in your duty or committed a mortal sin if you had put on women's clothing?

JOAN. Give me a dress to go home to my mother in, and I'll take it.

CAUCHON. Did God command you to put on men's clothing?

JOAN. My clothing is a small matter, one of the least. But I didn't put on this clothing, nor do anything else, except at the bidding of God and the angels.

CAUCHON. Let us speak again of these angels. Which of them appeared to you first?

JOAN. I didn't recognize them as soon as that. I have told you often enough that they are St. Catherine and St. Margaret. Believe me if you like.

CAUCHON. In what form was St. Michael when he appeared to you?

JOAN. I saw no crown upon him. I know nothing of his garments.

CAUCHON. Was he naked?

JOAN. Do you think God cannot clothe him?

CAUCHON. When you saw St. Michael coming to you, was there any light?

JOAN. There was light all about, and so there should be. All light does not come to you.

CAUCHON *motions at the* GUARD, *who take* JOAN *out.* CAUCHON *follows.*

CATHERINE. What are they doing? Are they taking her somewhere?

MICHAEL. It's no longer your concern.

CATHERINE. If they kill her—

MARGARET. You don't know that they—

CATHERINE. They will.

MICHAEL. Did you ever think that perhaps they should?

MARGARET. You can't mean that.

MICHAEL. And you can't presume to fully understand the mystery of on high. What good would faith be then?

He takes a handful of sand and drops it back in the font, and the following scene is suddenly heard, projected from another space:

JOAN. *(From off.)* What is this place? Why have you brought me here?

CAUCHON. *(From off.)* I weary of your heresy.

JOAN. *(From off.)* I am a good Christian.

CAUCHON. *(From off.)* Then why has Jesus failed to save you?

JOAN. *(From off.)* That Jesus has failed me I deny.

CAUCHON. *(From off.)* I'm hoping that you will heed some temporal reasoning, so that I may save your soul.

JOAN. *(From off.)* Souls aren't saved here; lives are broken here.

CAUCHON. *(From off.)* The two can't be separated; the body must be broken in order to free the soul.

CATHERINE. Oh, no. No.

JOAN. *(From off.)* The Church would do this thing to me?

CAUCHON. *(From off.)* If it will see you redeemed before justice, and God. You there, go on with it.

MARGARET. Catherine . . .

CATHERINE. It can't be. They won't— *(Wood creaks: heavy, terrible, ruthless.)* Oh, no . . . They have a wheel. They're turning a wheel.

MARGARET. Dearest—

CATHERINE *attacks* MICHAEL *in a fury.*

CATHERINE. Are they doing it? Do they have her on a wheel? Tell me! I know that you know. Tell me!

MICHAEL *easily stops her, holds her.*

MICHAEL. Listen.

The wheel rasps to a stop.

JOAN. *(From off)* . . . Jesus have mercy.

CAUCHON. *(From off)* Would you care for a closer look?

JOAN. *(From off)* Do you think such threats will cause me to lie?

CAUCHON. *(From off)* They will cause you to tell the truth.

JOAN. *(From off)* I've done nothing else! Truly, if you were to have me torn limb from limb and send my soul out of my body, I would say nothing else. And if I did say anything, afterwards I should always say that you had made me do it by force.

CAUCHON. *(From off)* You are almost as foolish as you are hopeless.

JOAN. *(From off)* As long as I am not faithless.

SCENE 9: THE MARKETPLACE AT ROUEN

CATHERINE *and* MARGARET *are nearby as* CAUCHON *paces. Paperwork and a quill pen sit on the table; beside them lies a folded dress of plain homespun.* WARWICK *bursts into the square.*

WARWICK. You arrogant fool!

CAUCHON. My Lord Warwick—

WARWICK. I'm trying to win a war, and you—I had no idea you were so soft. Since when does the Inquisition merely threaten anyone? Put her on the wheel and be done with it.

CAUCHON. If she confesses, you cannot burn her. She will find her respite in the forgiving arms of the Church and—

WARWICK. I see. She's bewitched you as well. You think you can save her.

CAUCHON. We must consider her soul—

WARWICK. I don't give a whit for her soul. I bought her, Bishop, and I want what I paid for. I will have a burning tomorrow, so help me, whether it's her or you. And if it's you —Well, then, I'll burn her anyway.

He goes. CAUCHON *must steady himself. A* GUARD *brings* JOAN *out. She blinks at the daylight, the first she has seen in some time.*

JOAN. . . . Such a lovely day . . .

CAUCHON. What was that?

JOAN. I do so love the spring.

CAUCHON. Green things take longer to burn.

JOAN. Can you think of nothing else?

CAUCHON. I have sworn an oath not to rest until you have returned to the Lord's Church.

JOAN. I told you, I've never left it.

CAUCHON. Do you see that man in black, Joan? Standing beside the stake, there in the center? I need only give the word and—

JOAN. Then give it; you have more to give than I.

CAUCHON. You must know all I want is to save you. That's all any father wants for any of his children.

As if aiming a weapon, her eyes meet his.

JOAN. You are not my father.

He nearly loses the little that's left of his composure.

CAUCHON. This is tiresome! A panel of respectable churchmen have found you guilty of heresy, and this paper tells me I am to excommunicate and burn you.

CATHERINE. God forgive me . . .

She goes to JOAN.

MARGARET. It won't matter. She can't hear you. Catherine—

CAUCHON. It goes on for some time, outlining your crimes against man and your sins against God. It states that you are a useless, wily, dishonored woman and that you serve a king who is himself a heretic.

JOAN. Speak not against my king. He is the noblest Christian of all.

CAUCHON. I will hear none of your seditious fables. I will finish this today, whether by your signature or by your death. You give me little choice. And since you will not sign, light the torches! We haven't all day.

JOAN. *(Trying to laugh it off)* You can't mean now. Not now, not this very minute.

CAUCHON. This very instant. You stink of hell; I will do my duty and return you there.

JOAN. Please, my lord, I . . . (*She has seen the dress.* CAUCHON *watches as she tentatively fingers the fabric. She picks up the dress with shaking hands, holding it up before her.*) . . . Oh . . .

She feels the cloth, buries her face in it.

CAUCHON. It was for you. But it would pain me to see such a fine thing lost in a fire.

JOAN *is numb. Exhausted. Resigned.* CATHERINE *looks furtively into the girl's eyes, but* JOAN *is oblivious to her presence.*

JOAN. If I—

CAUCHON. Speak up.

JOAN. I will live if I sign.

CAUCHON. Yes.

JOAN. And all I need do is sign?

CAUCHON. You will sign, you will take on the apparel appropriate to your sex, and your confession will be real. Not merely words to save yourself.

JOAN. Might I have the Sacrament?

CAUCHON. . . . I don't see why not.

CATHERINE. Please, dearest. Consider—

JOAN. I will sign.

CAUCHON. You will.

JOAN. So very tired . . . I am content to do what you would have me. I would rather sign than—I will sign.

CAUCHON. You've come to your senses.

JOAN. I want to live. That is sensible, is it not?

CAUCHON. Then you will live, I promise you. Come, let it be done.

JOAN. . . . I don't know how.

He studies her for a moment.

CAUCHON. You can't read. And yet you quote scripture. Never mind. Here, I'll help you. (*He pulls* JOAN *away from* CATHERINE. *He guides her hand to the paper, helping her sign. It should take a moment.*) There. The Lord is always happy to bring his lost sheep back into the fold.

JOAN *stares at the document in wonder.*

JOAN. That's my name.

CAUCHON. Yes. Your soul again belongs to God.

SCENE 10: THE HISTORIANS

HISTORIAN 1. The deed was done. Joan had acquitted herself in the ways the bishop required,

HISTORIAN 2. And was assured the limited comfort and security of a church prison

HISTORIAN 3. Where she might spend her days in quiet contemplation of the weaknesses of humankind.

HISTORIAN 4. But such an end was only one man's promise.

And we are in a nondescript room lit only by moonlight. WARWICK *waits, hidden in the darkness. A* GUARD *shoves* JOAN *in; she wears the dress. She looks about her, confused, at first thinking she is alone. Then . . .*

WARWICK. So you're the slip of a girl who has everyone running about like fools. But you're so young, so afraid. What are you afraid of? *(He steps into the light, a bundle under his arm. Looks her over.)* The bishop, perhaps? Ah, but he's been trying all these months to save your cursed soul. No, my girl, Cauchon is not your enemy. I am.

JOAN. What do you want?

WARWICK. What any Englishman wants. That which is fair, that which is earned. The good bishop will see things my way, if you do your part.

He tosses his bundle at her feet: men's clothing.

JOAN. I can't. I gave my word. I signed a pledge that I would not—

He strikes her, hard, knocking her to the floor.

WARWICK. Whether or not you're from whatever God doesn't concern me. You could play your little games of divinity anywhere else, and I wouldn't blink. But you made the mistake of crossing my path.

She tries to move away but he grabs her. Pins her down.

JOAN. Don't. Please—

WARWICK. We should be sure you are a woman, after all.

Blackout.

SCENE 11: JOAN'S CELL

CATHERINE. All this waiting. I can't abide waiting. Margaret . . . Was it like this, for you? When I—

MARGARET. Don't trouble yourself.

CATHERINE. At least it's over this time. Really. They'll let Joan go home.

MICHAEL. Soon enough we will have her with us.

CATHERINE. Then Cauchon . . .

MARGARET. He believes he's done his office, but the English—

CATHERINE. As long as she's alive, she's a threat. They will push her to recant. They won't be satisfied with a confession. With imprisonment. What should we do?

MARGARET. Stay with her; she trusts you. Now that her mother cannot hold her, it's good she has you. Catherine, I—I have to go. I've been called elsewhere.

CATHERINE. I don't understand.

MARGARET. You'll know what to do. You're meant for this. And I . . .

CATHERINE. You'll be watching.

MARGARET. Always.

She leaves before she can change her mind.

CATHERINE. Margaret, I— *(But* MARGARET *is gone.)* Must it always be this hard?

She nearly weeps with frustration; MICHAEL *goes to her.*

MICHAEL. We only know joy by first knowing sorrow. If we don't act, if we don't struggle . . . *(He leads her to the font, drizzling a bit of sand into her hand and folding her fingers about it. He clasps his hands around hers momentarily, never breaking eye contact with her.)* The reward in store . . . *(He removes his hands and she opens her fingers, revealing a large pearl sitting in her open palm.)* Will have no value.

A GUARD *throws* JOAN *into her cell. Bruised and beaten, she crumples in a heap. She is again dressed in men's clothes.*

JOAN. "My soul doth magnify the Lord. My soul . . ." *(She can take no more.)* Catherine, please . . .

MICHAEL. Go. She won't see me again until her eyes are clear.

With his gesture the invisible barrier is lifted, and CATHERINE *goes to* JOAN.

JOAN. You shouldn't be here.

CATHERINE. If you want me to go, I'll go.

JOAN. No! No. But I don't deserve to have you here. What I said, I said for fear of the fire.

CATHERINE. You've said nothing to be ashamed of. You've spoken like no mortal I've seen or heard.

JOAN. I recanted, I said yes, I begged for mercy. I damned myself to save my life. It's worth nothing. *(She looks down at herself, at her clothing.)* There will be no church prison, will there? No sisters to look after me, not even priests. Only wicked Englishmen with wandering hands and—It's not worth it, to live like this.

CATHERINE. Whatever you decide, I'll be with you.

JOAN. God will not cast me out for perjuring myself as I have?

CATHERINE. He prizes you too highly. When I found Christ, it was as if the very vault of the sky cracked open just for me, and all of the stars pressed so close, shining as only the truth can. I knew the old ways were wrong. I simply knew, like I knew the taste of dates, my father's voice, my own name. I knew the truth, and I knew those stars would always be close. In those days, the Romans enjoyed tormenting Christians. It was a pastime, a terrible game. And one day in the marketplace . . . It was a foolish thing to do. Maxentius was the governor; I was just a girl, and a Christian at that. Rashly I told him that he was in the wrong. That he should let the Lord's people worship as they choose. I came to know a room like this one, and such pain as I cannot—There were moments when I wondered if I shouldn't give him what he wanted, to make it all stop. To make them all go away. Moments staring at unkind walls, willing myself not to flinch, not to scream, thinking I would be quite happy if I could be alone in some distant country and see no other human again. I couldn't help it. I couldn't help thinking it would be different if I had said yes.

JOAN. But you said no.

CATHERINE. As you can.

CAUCHON *and* WARWICK, *in mid-conversation, enter:*

CAUCHON. —I've spoken with the Archbishop, and I will write to the Pope himself if I must—*(He stops, staring at* JOAN.*)* Why are you dressed like that? Why? Do you know what this means? What you're doing to yourself, to your eternal soul?

JOAN. This is not living. You promised me my life.

CAUCHON. When you gave up your blasphemy. But this—Why won't you let me save your soul?

JOAN. My soul is not the one in need of saving.

CAUCHON *is in utter disbelief.*

CAUCHON. Then here it ends. I've done all I can.

WARWICK. Good, fine. We'll do it today.

JOAN. I glory in plainness; I glory in truth; I glory in my Jesus, for he hath redeemed my soul from hell. *(She turns to* CATHERINE:*)* The very vault of the sky?

CATHERINE. The very same.

CAUCHON. Who are you talking to? What are— (*He turns and sees* CATHERINE *standing beside* JOAN, *light streaming about them both. He stumbles back as* CATHERINE *levels her gaze at him.*) . . . Oh, God . . .

WARWICK. Get up. What's wrong with you?

CAUCHON. Devil—This is of the devil—

CATHERINE *looks straight at* CAUCHON. *She smiles wanly.*

CATHERINE. You know the devil better than I.

CAUCHON *can only stare at her.*

WARWICK. Pull yourself together! Another half an hour, and it's done.

CAUCHON. But—but—

> WARWICK *shakes him, hard.*

WARWICK. Listen to me—Listen! It's better her than you.

> *He goes.* CAUCHON *looks to* JOAN, *to* CATHERINE, *as if he might—* No. *He exits, and the vision fades away.*

JOAN. I thought I could finish it and go home quietly. That no one would take notice if the Maid went back to being—a maid. What's wrong with that?

CATHERINE. Nothing. But—

JOAN. This is the way it's supposed to be.

CATHERINE. Can you believe that?

JOAN. I know it. Once when I was a child, Maman was baking. She warned me not to touch the oven, but I was fascinated. The colors were so tempting, so warm and friendly-like. . . . I thought it was like a lamb, that I could pet it or something equally foolish. Of course, I only burned myself terribly; it was as if I screamed for days. You can still see the scars, though only faintly . . . Now I won't be able to pull my hand away. *(Suddenly:)*

You'll stay with me.

CATHERINE. Of course.

> JOAN *wanders to the window.*

JOAN. I can smell it—the pitch—already. They won't even let me have what's left of the day. I suppose sooner is better than later, isn't it? Look at all those people. . . . Look at the smoke . . .

CATHERINE. Dearest—

JOAN. I'm trembling.

> *Two* GUARDS *enter.*

CATHERINE. Oh, love, it's time.

JOAN. I don't want to think about what it will be like.

> CATHERINE *holds* JOAN's *hands in her own. Wipes away the tears.*

CATHERINE. Preserve me, O God:

CATHERINE AND JOAN. For in thee do I put my trust.

> *The* GUARDS *put* JOAN *on her knees and chain her to the stake.*

JOAN. My soul doth magnify the Lord, and my spirit hath rejoiced in God my Savior.

> *The pyre is lit.*

CATHERINE. The Lord bless thee, and keep thee: the Lord make his face shine upon thee and give thee peace—

JOAN. Catherine! *(As* CATHERINE *goes to* JOAN, *all darkens about them; it's difficult to make anything out.* JOAN *is hysterical: crying, screaming. Burning.* CATHERINE *remains beside her throughout.)* I can't—I can't bear it. Make it go away. My hair is burning, Catherine. Make it stop, please—

CATHERINE. Think of Domrémy, Jeannette.

JOAN. Not now . . . I can't . . .

CATHERINE. The fields are green as far as one can see. The wheat is touched with gold, and the brook the clearest anywhere. The brook. Think on the brook. It's so cool against your face, like your mother's hands when you're sick in bed. Cool, right, good . . .

JOAN. Maman! Maman, I'm sorry. I won't let her kick over the bucket. I know we need all the milk. I'm so sorry . . . *(Stillness . . . Silence. After a long moment the lights shift and, invisible to* CATHERINE, JOAN *stirs.)* I can't . . . I can't feel it anymore. I can't see anything. Show me the sun, Catherine. I can't see through the smoke. Where is the sun? *(A white light settles upon her, and she is struck with a vision and the force of a sudden, inexplicable joy:)* Jesus?

Blackout.

EPILOGUE: THE LIBRARY

CATHERINE *is alone. Disconsolate. After a moment,* MARGARET *enters. She goes directly to* CATHERINE *and holds her. Several long moments pass.* JOAN *enters the library on her hands and knees, as Catherine did at the start of the first scene.* MICHAEL *is there to meet her.*

MARGARET. Catherine, look.

JOAN. My soul doth magnify the Lord, and my spirit hath rejoiced in God my Savior. For with God nothing shall be impossible. My soul . . . Catherine? Are you—Is someone there?

MICHAEL *approaches* JOAN.

MICHAEL. Joan.

JOAN. Who's there?

MICHAEL. I am.

JOAN. I—I can't— (MICHAEL *passes a hand over her eyes: she can see.)* . . . Oh.

MARGARET. *(To* CATHERINE:*)* Go on.

CATHERINE *moves beside* MICHAEL, *into* JOAN's *line of vision.*

JOAN. Catherine.

CATHERINE *rushes to* JOAN, *embracing her.*

CATHERINE. Look at you. Thank God. I didn't mean to doubt. I thought if I could keep you from what I went through, then—But you knew better.

JOAN. I feel so distanced from everything. Separated. New. Here. Where is here, exactly?

CATHERINE. This is the library. We're . . . *(Stealing a glance at* MARGARET:*)*Between. Between the mortal and the, well—the heavenly.

JOAN *is a bit bewildered. Overwhelmed.*

JOAN. . . . Oh. Um . . .

CATHERINE. Don't worry, it will all make sense soon enough. We all have things to learn. You see, knowledge is the one thing we take with us from place to place.

JOAN. Then why me? Knowledge has never been a strength of mine.

CATHERINE. Are you sure of that?

She leads JOAN *to a shelf of books.*

JOAN. How beautiful.

Instinctively JOAN *reaches out to touch a book but stops herself.*

CATHERINE. It's all right. Choose one if you like. *(*JOAN *selects a book.)* Go on, open it. What does it say?

JOAN *opens the book and, without a second thought, reads from it:*

JOAN. "Be not forgetful to entertain strangers: for thereby some have entertained angels unawares." . . . I don't believe it. I can read.

CATHERINE. Of course you can. You'll be surprised, I think, at what you can do. I still am.

JOAN. What happens now?

CATHERINE. Well, you'll be called. To do something, to help someone.

JOAN. As you helped me.

CATHERINE. And as Margaret did for me. *(*MARGARET *joins them.)* There is a chain of servants, of workers if you will, that goes on from the beginning of time until—who knows?

At the font, MICHAEL *lets sand fall from between his first two fingers and thumb. A slip of paper falls from between the pages of Joan's book. She picks it up and reads from it.*

JOAN. A priest is troubled by his conscience. His name is Luther.

CATHERINE. You'll do very well with him, I'm sure. Inspire him as you have so many others.

JOAN. But . . .

CATHERINE. What?

JOAN. Shouldn't I start somewhere—smaller? Something less, I don't know, important? What am I supposed to say?

CATHERINE. You'll know. I'll help you. This is how things work. How—

JOAN. How God works.

CATHERINE. Yes.

> *One of the* HISTORIANS *carries an open book—the same from the prologue. He moves to close the book and return it to its shelf but stops when* MICHAEL *raises a hand. The* HISTORIAN *lays the book on the table, its pages open. Light pools around* CATHERINE, MARGARET, *and* JOAN.

BLACKOUT

I Am Jane

Margaret Blair Young

About the Playwright

Until recently, Margaret Blair Young was known chiefly for her novels and short stories. She has been a well-established and well-respected force in the Mormon literary community for decades. Her novels *Salvador, House without Walls,* and *Heresies of Nature*; as well as her collections of short stories, *Love Chains,* and *Elegies and Love Song,* have been lauded by critics and lay readers alike. She is also a professor of creative writing at Brigham Young University and became the president of the Association for Mormon Letters is 2009, in which capacity she still currently serves. Her list of awards is impressively long and extensive.

Two threads in her life began subtly but have since created beautiful, complex tapestries. The first is her involvement in the dramatic arts, especially playwriting. The second, and likely the more prominent and important work, has been her advocacy for African American Mormons, whose relationship with the LDS Church has been historically complicated and heart-wrenching. Both of these threads, theatre and African American studies in the Mormon context, converge in her beautiful and important play, *I Am Jane.*

Young's relationship with the Mormon theatrical community started early in her life, as she was an actress in the original production of Thomas Rogers's ground-breaking play *Huebener* at BYU. Although she had acted in many other shows, that great Mormon play stuck with her. "The play Tom had created—the play that had, for a couple of weeks, resurrected Helmuth Huebener—has stayed with me more than any play I have ever worked in," she says. "But how I wish Huebener could be honored here as he is in his homeland. Honored, even, by the Church he loved."[1]

Young would continue working in the Mormon theatrical tradition, even as she went on in her literary career. Once again, she would fuse together two of her loves as she wrote a play called *Dear Stone* based on her novel *Heresies of Nature.* Telling the tale of a family's struggle to cope with the mother's corrosive battle with multiple schlerosis, *Dear Stone* premiered at BYU's Margett's Theatre May 14, 1997, having previously won the 1996 BYU Studies Playwriting Competition.

In his review for the Association for Mormon Letters, Scott Parkin had high praise for the play:

---

1 Margaret Blair Young, "Doing Huebener," *Dialogue: A Journal of Mormon Thought* 21, no. 4 (Winter 1988): 131–32. For more on *Huebener* and Young's involvement with it, see also "Thomas F. Rogers: About the Playwright," in this volume.

The story was complex and interesting, and explored issues of love, manipulation, family stress, debilitating illness, strength of spirit, forgiveness, personal discovery, and faith. It touches on the little cruelties we inflict on each other, and the enormous difficulties faced by the family of someone suffering debilitating sickness. And while the story ends with positive resolution, it does so fairly, after its characters have struggled and suffered and raged, so that the successful resolution is earned and feels right. These characters found resolution with effort and pain, contrition and faith and real desire, and that makes all the difference.[2]

Her next theatrical endeavor, however, would be closely tied to her research of African Americans' relationship with the LDS faith. Young has been at the center of several projects about black Mormons over the years. She and her co-author, African American Mormon writer, filmmaker, and speaker Darius Gray, have created a trilogy of novels based on African American Mormon pioneers titled *Standing on the Promises*;[3] two documentaries: *Nobody Knows: The Untold Story of Black Mormons* and *Jane Manning James: Your Sister in the Gospel*; and has given countless lectures and papers on the subject of black Mormons. Then, of course, there is her play in this volume, *I Am Jane*.

The sense of mission is not lost on one who explores this interconnected body of material that Young has produced. She is obviously passionate about telling these stories with historic honesty and skill, striving to improve the relationship between African Americans and the Church. Yet the irony of a white Mormon woman writing stories about African Americans was not lost on Young:

> Why was I so presumptuous as to think I could write a book about black Mormon pioneers? I am so white I can't even tan. Yet it was more than the idea that "This book would sell" which led me to begin a historical novel on black pioneers. There was a need in me to approach this subject and all the problems it raised for a Mormon author—which problems had beset me from my youth. I was aware that I had been raised in a racist world, by a very good family, but one which subtly included racism in its traditions. There were little things—the licorice figures my grandmother called "nigger babies," the casual mentioning that someone had married "a Negro" which everyone simply understood was wrong. As a Mormon, I had been raised to accept the notion that God did not intend black men to hold the priesthood—at least not until 1978 [when President Spencer W. Kimball received the revelation that repealed the policy that had banned African American men from priesthood

---

2   Scott Parkin, "YOUNG: *Dear Stone* (drama)," *Association for Mormon Letters Review Archive*, http://www.aml-online.org/Reviews/Review.aspx?id=3065 (accessed April 17, 2012).

3   This trilogy includes: *One More River to Cross*, *Bound for Canaan*, and *The Last Mile of the Way*, originally published by Deseret Book, with new revised versions of the novels coming soon from Zarahemla Books.

ordination]. Even when I was a teenager, the policy troubled me deeply. So I came to my subject with curiosity, some urgency, and a sense of guilt that I, with my red-hair and white, untannable skin, should presume to tell the story of black folks whose culture I did not know except through literature.[4]

As if in answer to a prayer, help in understanding the African American culture came Young's way. First, in 1998, as she began her research, Young established a strong friendship with Susie Thomas, an African American woman who moved into her ward. Then, soon after, she came across the man who would become her constant collaborator, Darius Gray:

> I was scheduled . . . to give a presentation at a conference, a retrospective of the twenty years since the priesthood policy change. I included a small piece of the novel I was working on—a bit about Elijah Abel. As I took my seat at the session's beginning, a mostly white-haired, black man approached Gene England and me and introduced himself: "Hello. I'm Darius Gray."
> The tape I had played for my June Relief Society presentation was still in my purse. I fished it out and showed it to him. "I've got you on this tape!" I said. He looked at the title: "Alike unto God" and nodded, then took his seat. I wanted desperately to talk to him after the session. Again, it was something like the feeling I had had with Susie: This man was to be my friend. I exchanged comments with those who had attended the session but kept my eye on Darius. I didn't want him to leave before we had had a chance to talk. When I went up to him, he put his arm around me and said, "I don't know how to say this—I don't want to cry—but it feels so good to hear someone who's GOT it." I understood what he meant—not that I was anything special, but that I had understood the fundamental message of Christianity: that God is no respecter of persons and that any excuse we make for dividing ourselves from our brothers and sisters will also divide us from God. . . . One of the last things he said to me [that day] was, "Let's write a book."[5]

And write a book they did—three, in fact. Gray became an invaluable ally in Young's pursuit. One thing that Young hadn't yet been able to capture was the black voice. "I did not know 'black vernacular English'—but it was the language of [Darius's] childhood. There were aspects of black culture which were simply part of his life, but quite foreign to me. It became clear that we were intended to be partners in this project, even that we had been uniquely prepared."[6]

---

4   Margaret Blair Young, "Black and White, Male and Female: The Teamwork for *Standing on the Promises*," *Meridian Magazine*, August 7, 2001, http://ldsmag.net/books/010419bw.html (accessed April 19, 2012); capitalization and punctuation standardized.
5   Ibid.
6   Ibid.

Gray also was very well versed in black Mormon history and genealogy, as well as being very well connected with LDS historians and Church leaders. His educated input and the resources he had available to him were priceless, as he became a co-author of the series.[7]

Young also immersed herself in black literature, music, and films, drinking deep of the rich artistic heritage beginning in America with the Harlem Renaissance and other time periods, learning the works of Langston Hughes, Zora Neale Hurston, W. E. B. Dubois, and Spike Lee, as well as beautiful music that included jazz and gospel spirituals. All of these beautiful, black stories, images, and sounds have remained with her: "It is a passion in me," she reflects. "That tends to be where I gravitate. Even though I love all of the literature that I teach, I tend to gravitate toward black literature. It still holds me."[8]

The immersion in black literature and culture appears to have worked. The dialogue and culture of Young's African American characters in her stories is one of Young's strong suits, as one critic noted about *I Am Jane*:

> The . . . African American characters' dialects and dialogue is authentic, natural, specific to type and culture, and filled with genuine pathos, as well as humor. It was more like hearing the wonderful dialogue of an August Wilson play, rather than the white, culturally Mormon woman that I know that Margaret Blair Young is. The African American characters are fully developed, powerful and dynamic, especially Jane. Young seems to "get" this culture, even perhaps more than her own, which I think is very interesting. She has been working for a long time within the African American, Mormon community and it really shows by her passionate advocacy for the community's causes.[9]

This fixation upon the black culture, this mission to support it within the Church, did not end with the publication of her novels *Standing on the Promises*. Many of the same historical, African American Mormons who figured so predominantly in the series—such as Jane Manning and Elijah Abel—would soon be adapted to another beloved medium of Young's: theatre.

> We had our premiere performance in an LDS chapel for the Genesis Group[10] meeting. We turned the sacrament table into a deathbed and the

---

7   Ibid.
8   Ben Crowder, "Margaret Blair Young and Darius Gray," *Mormon Artist*, Issue 1 (September 2008): 3–4.
9   Mahonri Stewart, "Margaret Blair Young's *I Am Jane*: A Truly Important Play," *A Motley Vision*, June 3, 2010, http://www.motleyvision.org/2010/margaret-blair-youngs-_i-am-jane_-a-truly-important-play/ (accessed May 10, 2012).
10 An official branch and congregation of the LDS Church in Salt Lake City, organized as an outreach group for its black members in 1971. Darius Gray was the branch president of the

choir seats into a pioneer camp. It was a sweet evening. Nothing professional about it, but very sweet—probably because we did have some good actors, and certainly because we were depicting the compelling, inspiring story of Jane Elizabeth Manning James, a black Mormon pioneer. For black Mormons, her story often provides a link to Utah's Pioneer Day celebrations. As one of the actresses said, "I used to hate Pioneer Day. I'd think, 'Yeah, you had pioneer ancestors—but they CHOSE to come. My ancestors had no choice.'" Jane's story was a bridge builder.[11]

After this first amateur production, a number of professional productions followed. BYU showed an interest in staging *I Am Jane* for Black History Month. However, controversy about the script began to brew, as members of BYU's administration and Religion Department began to have issues with the historical honesty with which the play was written and the tough questions that subsequently rose from such honesty. A memo summarizing the concerns among the faculty was inadvertently copied to Young. She understood but rejected the perspective it conveyed:

> Perhaps the most telling line in the memo was this: "Jane always saw the good in people." That sentence began a paragraph indicating that perhaps Jane herself wouldn't want us to depict the more painful parts of her journey, in which Mormon people had not behaved as we might wish. Wouldn't it be better to tell the story of Jane which focused only on her courageous pioneer trek and skipped those parts wherein she met "much rebuff" in Nauvoo (the words she uses in her life story), or when a black man was lynched in Salt Lake City "in the shadow of the temple," as one appalled observer put it, or when, after many petitions, she was denied entrance to the temple? If Jane "always saw the good in people," wouldn't she prefer a niced-over (dare I say WHITE-WASHED?) play?[12]

Young did some minor revisions of the play, while keeping her key messages intact, and it was eventually performed at BYU. However, Young had some major reservations about the attitudes of those individuals who were so reticent to tell Jane's Manning's journey undiluted:

> Anyone writing about a real historical character will immediately wrestle with stereotype and expectation—and with the temptation to portray a character who fits a particular agenda. . . . In language that sounds quite flattering,

---

Genesis Group from 1997 to 2003.

11   Margaret Blair Young, "*I Am Jane* (with a Little Levinas)," *Dawning of a Brighter Day: Mormon Literature in the 21st Century*, June 6, 2010, http://latest.mormonletters.org/post/2010/06/06/I-Am-Jane-%28with-a-little-Levinas%29.aspx (accessed July 9, 2010).

12   Ibid.

we can presume to know another person rather than the version of them which we ourselves have created. Often, we are writing for our own satisfaction and even our vindication. I've found over and over that white descendants of slave-holding Mormon families have much different stories than do the black descendants of the enslaved.[13]

However, it is perhaps the issues of which some find the deepest reasons to fear that others have found to be the most moving and powerful moments in the play. One critic, for example, found the issue of Elijah Abel having the priesthood bestowed upon him by Joseph Smith himself, while having his temple blessings denied by Brigham Young and subsequent leaders, to be one of the most noteworthy pieces of information in the play:

> This is one of the most fascinating, if not uncomfortably tragic, issues the play brings up. In Nauvoo, under Joseph Smith, African Americans seemed not only to have had a better time in the Church, but seemed to have been welcomed with open arms, especially by Joseph Smith. . . .
>
> But things change drastically after Joseph Smith's martyrdom. . . . So the set up is quite a poignant, painful juxtaposition of what could have been. Under Joseph Smith, we see a tolerant, joyful acceptance of people of all races. In Utah, things become dark regarding racial progress, and we find policies changing and injustices served, and we see the prejudices inherited from the American culture of the time seeping in among the Saints and even affecting the leadership of the Church.[14]

Since the BYU production, another version of the play was performed at the Grand Theatre in Salt Lake City and at the Covey Center for the Arts in Provo, Utah. The play has also been performed in Chicago, California, and other areas. It has received a good deal of press and has been able to spread its message further and further as time goes on. However, there are "miles to go" before Young sleeps, as there is much work yet to be done in healing the wounds caused by the previous "Negro policy." Despite the huge strides made in race relations in the Church since the 1978 revelation, Young is still both concerned and hopeful. Gray and Young recently wrote:

> We believe that there must and will be a significant future for those of African descent in the Church, and far greater prominence in the leadership than we see today. But it won't come without full acknowledgment of the complexities that always attend race issues, and some bold approaches to the challenges before us. . . .

---

13   *Ibid.*
14   Stewart, "Margaret Blair Young's *I Am Jane*."

When we Mormons view our past, we tend to see ourselves as victims of mob violence, weeping over the dead at Haun's Mill, or running from Boggs's Extermination Order in Missouri, and from persecutors in Illinois. We dislike seeing ourselves as the ones doing the persecuting. Though Jane James never characterized the pioneers with whom she associated as "persecutors," she did endure prejudice, as did every black pioneer of her time. At some point, that part of our shared history will need to be acknowledged and fully told. Ultimately, it will edify and inspire all who hear it.

True equality is the work that Margaret Blair Young is pioneering in the Church, with the help of other dedicated Mormons such as Darius Gray. That mission is granted special power by the tenacity and passion with which she pursues it. Focusing less and less on her own individually crafted, literary characters through the years, Young has instead focused in on telling the stories of Jane Manning, Elijah Abel, and other important black Mormons across many genres and mediums. With a sense of divine purpose, Young strides forward with the Book of Mormon's injunction ringing in her ears and burning within her heart: "For none of these iniquities come of the Lord; for he doeth that which is good among the children of men . . . and he inviteth them all to come unto him and partake of his goodness; and he denieth none that come unto him, black and white, bond and free, male and female; and he remembereth the heathen; and all are alike unto God, both Jew and Gentile" (2 Ne. 26:33).

About *I Am Jane*

I Am Jane was first produced at the Genesis Chapel in Salt Lake City. It had subsequent productions at Brigham Young University, the Grand Theatre in Salt Lake City, and the Covey Center for the Arts in Provo, Utah. It also had productions in Chicago, California and other areas. The original production at the Genesis Chapel ran on May 7, 2000, with the following company:

CAST

Elijah Abel: James Sheppard
Jane Manning James: Denise Cutliff
Isaac James: Keith N. Hamilton
Phyllis Treadwell: Dot Todman
Young Sylvester: J. Stormy Sheppard
Sylvester James (older): Walter D. Wright
Sarah Stebbins: Tamu Smith
Anthony Stebbins: Randy Cutliff
Lucinda Manning: Natalie P. Sheppard
Angeline Manning: Lyn Dudley
Anna Amanning: Karyn Dudley
Isaac Lewis Manning: Marvin Perkins
Mary Ann Abel: Fiona Smith
Hark Lay: Abe Mills
Malvina: Lyn Dudley
Sheriff: Dell Blair
Emma Smith: Becky Brock
Samuel Smith: Andy Wilson
Angus Cannon/Orson Spenser: Kent W. Jones
Eliza Lyman/Young Eliza Lyman: Jennifer Groberg
Joseph Smith: Paul Sorensen
Agnes Thomas: Cassandra Fulton
Tom Thomas: Doug Stone
Priscenda: Kaila Fox
Lucy Mack Smith: Margaret Young
Zina D. H. Young: Katie Jensen
Soloists: Elizabeth Scott, Lita Giddins, Kevin Giddins

CREW

Director: Margaret Blair Young
Costumer: Jen Blair Lamber

CHARACTERS

(thirteen actors cover nineteen roles)

ELIJAH ABEL. Elijah also functions as stage manager.

JANE MANNING JAMES. Jane begins the play as a young woman, but must age to at least eighty. She is always bold, dignified, and full of indomitable faith.

ISAAC JAMES, Jane's husband/ex-husband. Near Jane's age, he is fun-loving and sometimes pretentious, but also ambitious and easily troubled. He has a temper, as does his wife.

PHYLLIS MANNING TREADWELL, Jane's mother. She is a dignified woman. If desired, her death can be suggested when Jane sings "Sometimes I Feel like a Motherless Child." The death should not be over-dramatized, merely an exit.

SARAH STEBBINS, Jane's sister. A little fiesty, pregnant. Also plays MARY ANN ABEL, Elijah's shy wife.

ANGELINE MANNING, Jane's sister—also lively and sassy. Also plays MALVINA, Jane's great-grand-daughter.

ISAAC LEWIS [LEW] MANNING, Jane's brother.

ANTHONY STEBBINS, Sarah's husband. Also plays SYLVESTER, Jane's angry son.

LUCINDA MANNING, Lew's wife.

EMMA SMITH. Also plays AGNES THOMAS.

SHERIFF. Also plays ANGUS CANNON.

ELIZA LYMAN. Also plays YOUNG ELIZA LYMAN.

JOSEPH SMITH.

NOTES ON PRODUCTION

This play can be performed with minimal staging. Benches and stools can become beds. Trellises can become orchards, covered wagons, or cabins—or the audience can simply imagine them through lighting. Props may be used or pantomimed. Costumes can be suggested by shawls and bonnets, though there must be distinguishing props or costume pieces (beards, caps, glasses, etc.) which help the audience identify separate characters being played by the same actor. Costumes may be kept in an onstage trunk, which actors access whenever they're changing or assuming roles, though this device is not essential.

In a fully costumed, full-setting production, the stage has two tiers, the upper tier representing heaven—full of trees—and the lower tier representing earth. As the play opens, lights come on slowly like sunrise—pink and orange—and soon angels are distinguishable in the trees, their gowns sparkling with the growing light. These angels will comprise the choir and will otherwise observe the happenings on Earth, except when they're called on to bring someone from mortality into immortality.

Act One

SCENE 1

Either the angels begin singing, or actors enter (preferably up aisles) singing:

SINGERS. Amen, amen, amen, amen, amen.

> Amen, amen, amen, amen, amen
>
> This little light of mine,
>
> I'm gonna let it shine;
>
> This little light of mine
>
> I'm gonna let it shine;
>
> This little light of mine
>
> I'm gonna let it shine
>
> Let it shine, let it shine, let it shine.
>
> Amen, amen, amen, amen, amen . . .

ELIJAH ABEL. *(Climbing onto the stage.)* You-all ready for some play acting? You'll have to use your imagination some, but this ought to be a good time. Good story, too. You all get to take part, if you want—even if it's just singin' or clappin'. *(He puts on a pioneer hat.)* I'm Elijah Abel. I'm the welding link between the past and the present, the black and the white. Right now, you all just let your minds settle into the past, and listen.

JANE. *(Stepping forward.)* I am Jane Elizabeth Manning James. One year after I was baptized, I started for Nauvoo with my mother and brothers and sisters. There were nine of us, including my son, Sylvester. We started from Wilton, Connecticut, and traveled by canal to Buffalo, New York. We were to go to Columbus, Ohio, before our fares were to be collected, but they insisted on having the money at Buffalo and would not take us farther. So we left the boat, and started on foot to travel a distance of over eight hundred miles. *(Her family joins her. Angelic chorus hums "Amazing Grace.")* We walked until our shoes were worn out, and our feet became sore and cracked open and bled until you could see the whole print of our feet with blood on the ground. We knelt and prayed. *(JANE kneels.)* We asked God the eternal Father to heal our feet, and our prayers were answered forthwith.

SARAH. Jane, would you get up?

JANE. *(Combing her hair.)* Wait just a minute.

SARAH. "Wait just a minute!" I've heard that so many times from you. You always have to look perfect even if you slogging through the mud. What—you combing your hair so it look good when the branches grab it?

JANE. *(Fingering her hair.)* I do what I can.

SARAH. Well, this here is your baby, and he's getting too heavy for me. I'd say it's your turn to tote him.

    JANE *takes* SYL *on her hip.*

ANGELINE. I'd give up all my hair for a good pair of shoe or leggin'.

ANTHONY. We ain't need no shoe. Our feets done turn leather.

ANGELINE. I'd rather use cow leather than Angeline leather. I'm tired to death!

JANE. And all you carryin' is yourself. You want to try carrying Sylvester? Might make you appreciate your lot.

ANGELINE. Thank you, no. I wish Lew had treated that steamship porter better.

LEW. You think if I done my role different, we'd be steamin' down the Mississipp 'stead of walking barefoot?

ANGELINE. Who say?

LEW. You blamin' me?

ANGELINE. Who say?

LEW. Ain't my fault!

JANE. 'Course 'tain't!

LEW. This whole trip was Jane's idea anyways.

JANE. This whole trip was the Lord's idea! I just let you all in on the information out of the goodness of my heart.

LEW. Well, thank you so much. I might've liked it more if the Lord had provided you a map and a boat along with his idea.

JANE. Lew, don't you go wonderin' about your tribulations. Whoever the Lord love best, He give that person the most trials.

LEW. Oh then. He must love me lots.

JANE. And don't you get saucy towards the Lord, Mr. Manning.

LEW. Oh no. Thank you, Lord, for these good signs of how much you love me. And I won't be needing no more signs, Lord.

    Enter SHERIFF.

SHERIFF. Stop right there. Show me your free papers. You heard me.

LEW. Lord, I swear you proved your point!

JANE. Sir, we ain't never been slaves. We Connecticut Negroes.

PHYLLIS. I once been a slave. Up Connecticut, all us been freed some time back. My children, they never know the bond.

JANE. (*Handing over the Church certificate of membership.*) These the only free paper we got. Our membership records for the Church of Jesus Christ of Latter-day Saints.

SHERIFF. Mormons! Worse still. Lawless, thieving, rifle-toting, cannibalizing Mormons. Good luck, girl. The last Negroes went to Nauvoo was never heard from again. Mormons look for black flesh so's they can boil it in oil, clean it off the bones. I could be the last soul you see who wants to do you some good.

JANE. (*Innocently.*) By putting us in jail?

SHERIFF. You might wish I'da done it, once they light a blaze under you.

JANE. Ain't no cannibals among the Mormon folk, sir. Which way Nauvoo?

SHERIFF. You don't believe a word I've said, do you?

JANE. No, sir.

SHERIFF. Straight ahead, about a hundred mile.

> SHERIFF *exits.*

PHYLLIS. (*To* SARAH.) Set your mind at ease, Sarah.

SARAH. That was too close.

PHYLLIS. You ain't no slave, you never been a slave, and you never will be one. And you ain't goin' to jail. You free! I doubt you know the full meaning of that word. But I know it.

> Oh Freedom! Oh freedom!
>
> Oh freedom over me!
>
> And before I'll be a slave,
>
> I'll be buried in my grave
>
> And go home to my Lord
>
> and be free!
>
> (*Others join her—tempo picks up, and by the end of the song, tambourines and full choir are involved.*)
>
> No mo' weepin . . .
>
> There'll be singin' . . .

ANGELINE. That song make me feel like I could skip all the way to Nauvoo! Sarah—what's troubling you? You look set to bust open and cry!

SARAH. Well, what if that sheriff be right?

ANGELINE. That Mormons be cannibals?

JANE. And what if yo' eyeballs fall out this second because you believe such rabbit droppings as that?

SARAH. My eyeballs ain't fallin' out.

JANE. They lookin' unstable to me. Lookin' unstable to you, Anthony?

ANTHONY. A little wobbly, yes, indeed.

JANE. Wobbly and bulgy, I say. Oh, they goin' pop certain. We goin' be walking our path, and Sarah's eyes goin' pop out like eggs.

SARAH. *(Touching her eyes.)* My eyeballs is fine! Anthony, you support my sister in making a mock of me, I's liable to do something drastic at you.

ANTHONY. You just too fun to tease, that's all.

SARAH. Resist temptation! What we know about the Mormons—really?

JANE. You a cannibal, Sarah?

SARAH. Oh now! Stop it!

JANE. Cause I know you be Mormon. I seen you come out the waters myself. You come out hankerin' after human flesh?

SARAH. Not at first. Only recent.

JANE. When?

SARAH. A minute ago. I's lookin' at you, Jane, and I's thinkin'—my, my, you'd make fine eatin'. A little cucumber and you taste just right. Don' you think so, Anthony?

ANTHONY. Cucumber? Naw. Peppers. Make the spice to match the flesh.

SARAH. You right. Cucumber way too cool for Mizz Jane flesh.

JANE. Sarah, you think I'd lead you to trouble? What would I do if something bad happen to you?

SARAH. I guess then you'd marry my Anthony.

JANE. Hah! You don't suppose I can do better than him?

SARAH. And what's so wrong about my Anthony?

JANE. Girl, he a southern Negro. He a used-ta-be slave!

SARAH. Not no more. He mine now. I laid claim on him.

JANE. Looks to me like he the one laid claim on you.

SARAH. Jane!

PHYLLIS. *(Sings under the dialogue to pacify her children.)* Children!

> PHYLLIS *begins singing "Walk with Me, Jesus," but* ANGELINE *and* LEW *start fighting. Song continues quietly under dialogue until Phyllis kneels in prayer.*

ANGELINE. You the one brought on this trek anyways, Lew—with your mean mouth.

LEW. I coulda been a lot meaner than I was.

ANGELINE. If the devil was helpin', you coulda been meaner. Maybe.

LUCINDA. Husband, treat your sister right.

LEW. What's this? You ain't got no words for her? You hear what she—

LUCINDA. I ain't married to her.

LEW. Now, how am I supposed to answer that?

JANE. *(Kneeling.)* Thank you, Lord, for making our feet hard as mule hooves!

ANTHONY. Thank you, Lord, for giving that sheriff such bad spit aim so's none of us got it in the eye!

SARAH. Thank you, Lord, for waking us up with that icy water, lest we fall asleep on the path!

ANGELINE. Thank you, Lord, for inspiring Lew's rude tongue so's we could all enjoy this good family togetherness.

LEW. Thank you, Lord, for giving me such fine control over my emotions that I ain't kill Angeline to this day and will probably make it to nightfall with clean hands.

LUCINDA. Thank you, Lord, for rosebuds.

LEW. *(After a stunned moment.)* Rosebuds? Where you seein' rosebuds?

LUCINDA. In my memory. Pink ones.

PHYLLIS. *(Kneeling, with tremendous dignity. There is an important pause while she prepares to speak.)* Thank you, Lord, for keeping us safe in your shadow, for bringing us peace in every moment of our trial, just like You always done, Lord, in all Your tender mercy.

SCENE 2

ELIJAH. You'll have to imagine the Nauvoo Temple. If we was to be realistic, we wouldn't have room for a audience. Picture it—a big, white building, soon to have a gold angel for a weathervane! And right over here, you'll have to imagine Joseph and Emma Smith's Mansion House.

The MANNINGS approach the Mansion House.

EMMA. *(Taking in the sight.)* Oh my! Walk in! Come in!

JANE. Ma'am?

EMMA. All of you!

JANE. Oh, ma'am! We awful dirty.

JOSEPH SMITH. *(From upstairs.)* The world looks on the outward appearance, but God sees the heart.

    JOSEPH *enters. The* MANNINGS *step inside.*

JANE. *(To* LEW.*)* That's Joseph Smith!

LEW. How you know that?

JANE. I told you! I seen him in a dream back in Connecticut!

JOSEPH. My, my, what have we here? Hello, I'm Joseph Smith.

JANE. I'm Jane Manning. This my family.

EMMA. Let me get them blankets. And let me feed them something.

JOSEPH. My wife always thinks of the important things. Yes, set on soup, Emma. In the meantime, I want to hear about their journey.

    They all enter the parlor.

JANE. We awful wet, sir.

JOSEPH. Please, call me "Brother Joseph."

JANE. *(Curtsying.)* We come thirty miles in the rain.

JOSEPH. Thirty miles? I had thought it was a longer journey than that.

    EMMA *appears with blankets for all.*

JANE. Thirty miles from La Harpe. From beginning to end, we come, oh—

ANTHONY. Eight hundred mile, sir.

JOSEPH. And you are?

ANTHONY. Anthony Stebbins, sir.

JOSEPH. Anthony. Eight hundred miles! On foot?

JANE. Yessir. And we awful wet.

JOSEPH. *(To* JANE.*)* You've been the head of this little band, haven't you?

JANE. Yes, sir, Brother Joseph.

JOSEPH. God bless you. Now tell me all about your trials.

JANE. Oh, not much to tell.

ANGELINE. Not much to tell!? Where you been?

JOSEPH. I suspect there may be some stories here.

ANGELINE. We was set to go to Columbus, Ohio, before our fares was to get collected, but they wanted the money right there at Buffalo. And then Lew was so rude to the steamship porter—

LEW. Pardon me, sir. My sister tends to exaggerate. You see, it's somewhat difficult for colored folk to find passage from one place to the other. The porter up and decided not take us. So we left the boat, and started on foot.

JOSEPH. To travel eight hundred miles. Bless you.

ANGELINE. Then Lew decided he'd take the lead.

JANE. Angeline, you don't have to give him every detail.

JOSEPH. Please. I want to hear it all.

ANGELINE. So he led us straight to a river with no bridge.

LEW. I didn't plan it havin' no bridge.

ANGELINE. So he says if it has no bridge, it must be shallow, follow him, and we walked right on in. If you want details, Brother Joseph, I tell you the water was up to our necks and near drowned us.

JANE. But, praise the Lord, we got safely across.

Singer[s] begin "Precious Lord" softly, under dialogue.

SINGERS. Precious Lord, take my hand

   Lead me on, help me stand

   I am tired, I am weak, I am worn

   In the storm, thru the night,

   Lead me on to the light

   Take my hand, Precious Lord,

   Lead me home.

JOSEPH. Praise the Lord indeed.

SARAH. Next day, we walked a considerable distance. We stayed that night in a forest, out in the open air. The frost fell on us so heavy that it was like a light fall of snow.

JANE. Oh it was beautiful, sir. Sparkly as crystal dust.

ANGELINE. Cold enough to freeze our toes and noses off! And Lew—

LEW. I swear, one more—

LUCINDA. Husband?

SARAH. We rose early, and started on our way walking through that frost with our bare feet, until the sun rose and melted it away.

JANE. But we went on our way rejoicing, singing hymns—

SARAH. *(Under JANE's words.)* Yes, we did.

JANE. —and thanking God for his goodness and mercy, in blessing us the way he had.

JOSEPH. *(Emotionally to EMMA.)* What do you think of that, Emma? Is that faith?

EMMA. Oh, Joseph, if it were me, I fear I'd have backed out and returned to my home.

JOSEPH. *(To all the* MANNINGS.*)* Well. You are among friends now.

SCENE 3

Enter ISAAC, *accompanied by* ANGUS CANNON. *Isaac is clearly aware that other blacks have come to Nauvoo. He goes to the* MANSION HOUSE *and peeks in a window.*

ANGUS CANNON. What did I tell you! A whole pack of them. And black as you!

ISAAC. What do I say?

ANGUS. Oh, come out with it. "Hello ladies! Anyone want a husband?"

ISAAC. You must think I be stupid. I ain't saying no such thing.

ANGUS. Then how about, "Ladies, this Nauvoo moonlight is worth a view! Come on outside and take a gander!"

JOSEPH SMITH *opens the door.*

ISAAC. *(To* JOSEPH SMITH.*)* Why Brother Joseph! Oh my! I didn't know you had company!

JOSEPH. Why, Brother Isaac, I didn't know you were so good at telling a lie.

ISAAC. Now, Brother—

JOSEPH. Telling a good lie is like wearing a lightning rod on your head—to test God's aim.

ISAAC. *(Stepping inside.)* I mean, I heard you had company. But I didn't know they was such good-lookin' company. Too bad you-all can't see the moon from in here. It's a good moon tonight. Makes the branches all silver. I wonder—anyone want to take a look at the moon?

LEW. *(Rising.)* Why yes. That sounds pleasant. If you ladies will excuse me.

ISAAC. *(Taken aback—having expected one of the women to join him—leading* LEW *outside.)* Well, there it is behind those clouds.

LEW. Yep. That's one good moon.

ISAAC. Pretty good one. My name's Isaac James.

LEW. Well, that's my name, too!

ISAAC. *(Not about to be fooled.)* No, it ain't.

LEW. The Isaac part. I'm Isaac Lewis Manning. Call me Lew.

ISAAC. So, Lew, which one of them women is your wife? Or is it all of them together?

LEW. All of them together? Lawd, what sort of crime you think I been committing to get that kind of punishment? Most of them's my sisters!

ISAAC. Some of 'em pretty young.

LEW. And some of 'em's married already. Like the one what's married to me. You after a wife?

ISAAC. Me? No! But any you might recommend?

LEW. Well, you'd be doing me a favor taking Angeline. Naw, you seem like a nice fellow. I couldn't do that to you. I'd recommend Jane. She's got her a child already, but no husband. And she the best of the lot. Providin' you treat her right.

ISAAC. I treat everything right! Go tell Jane come on out here. I teach her how to braid hats.

LEW. *(Calling inside.)* Janey! There's a man out here wants to teach you to braid cats.

ISAAC. Hats! I said hats!

JANE. *(From window.)* Thank you, but I won't be meetin' anyone until I'm dried off and cleaned up.

ISAAC. Tell her I'll come back later then.

LEW. *(Yelling.)* He'll come back later then.

ISAAC. Pleased to make your acquaintance, Lew.

LEW. Thanks for showin' me the moon, Mr. James. That's one nice moon.

SCENE 4

JANE. *(Sings.)* Sometimes I feel like a motherless child . . .

    A long ways from home . . .

    Sometimes I feel like I'm almost gone . . .

    A long ways from home . . .

ELIJAH. Didn't take long for most the Mannings to find places and work. But Jane didn't have her a place for a while. Stretch your imagination some, and let this be Jane's bed in the Mansion House.

    JANE *collapses on her bed.*

JOSEPH. Why, not crying?

JANE. Only a little, sir. The folks have all gone and got themselves homes and I have got none.

JOSEPH. You have a home right here, if you want it. Now, you mustn't cry. We dry up all tears here. Emma? Come in here, would you? *(EMMA enters.)* Here's a girl says she has no home. Haven't you a home for her?

EMMA. Why, yes, if she wants one.

JOSEPH. I believe she does.

JOSEPH pats Jane's shoulder and exits.

EMMA. We're quite accustomed to opening this place up to all sorts of folks. And we're glad to do it. Well, Jane, what can you do?

JANE. *(Standing.)* Ma'am, I can iron. Laundry. I been a household servant since my sixth year.

EMMA. I should warn you—living with us might not be the safest choice. Mobs of late have been—

JANE. I know. I heard the mobs.

EMMA. When you're rested, you may do the wash.

JANE. Ain't tired. Not one bit.

EMMA. Why don't you commence your work in the morning. To be truthful, I'm too tired to supervise you just now. Meanwhile, let's send Eliza Partridge to buy you a bolt of cloth and do you up some dresses.

SCENE 5

Enter LEW—downstage—dancing as the singers sing. Song should be done entirely, with as much energy as possible, involving the audience in clapping.

SINGERS. I'm going to lay down my burdens

    Down by the river side;

    Down by the river side;

    Down by the river side;

    Goin' to lay down my burdens,

    Down by the river side

    Ain't goin' to study war no mo';

    Ain't goin' to study war no mo';

    Study war no mo', study war no mo',

    Ain't goin' to study war no mo';

Study war no mo', study war no mo'.

JANE *joins* LEW *downstage.*

LEW. Guess what work I got, Janey!

JANE. With them fast feet—Lew, is you the Official Cockroach Smasher of Nauvoo? Congratulations!

LEW. I's the official Dance TEACHER—in the Masonic Hall. And I'm the Smith family cook too! Life turned pretty for me, didn't it!

JANE. Pretty scary, if you ask me. You hear the noise them mobs be makin' at night-time?

LEW. Aw, they just playing.

JANE. With blood, they be playin'. Or wantin' to.

Enter EMMA.

EMMA. Hello, Lew.

LEW. Ma'am.

EMMA. Jane, I'm glad you're here. Joseph wanted me to ask you a question. *(*LEW *leans in to hear. To* LEW, *awkwardly.)* I'm sure he'll have questions for you, too, in the future, Brother Manning. This one is for Jane, though. Would you excuse us?

LEW *straightens up, embarrassed.*

LEW. *(Regaining his dignity.)* Oh. If you'll pardon me, I got something in the oven for Brother Joseph.

He exits.

EMMA. *(Leading* JANE *inside.)* It feels natural to have you here, Jane. It's just like you're one of the family.

JANE. I feel I am.

EMMA. I'm so glad.

JANE. So what is it Brother Joseph be wantin' to ask of me?

EMMA. He and I both want to ask it. We've adopted many dear souls into our family over the years. We wonder if you would you like to be adopted to us, too.

JANE. Adopted? But I got me a mama. A daddy, too, though he's dead.

EMMA. This is somewhat different, Jane. Wouldn't you like to be part of our family in the eternities?

JANE. Oh. That's a long time, ain't it? That's a lot of laundry.

EMMA. Not adopted as our servant, Jane. As our child.

JANE. Eternity. That sure is a long time.

EMMA. Actually, I believe it's no time at all. There are no clocks or calendars in the eternities. You consider our question. I'll ask you again later.

JANE. *(Quickly.)* No, I don't think I want it. I'm not sure. I— *(LEW appears, moving past the door holding a small cake on a plate. JANE takes the opportunity to change the subject.)* Lew! What you doin' sneakin' around here with sugar cake?

LEW. Ain't for me. I told you I had something in the oven for Brother Joseph. I hope I ain't interruptin' you two in your conversation.

JOSEPH SMITH *calls.*

JOSEPH. *(Offstage.)* What's this I hear about sugar cake for Brother Joseph?

LEW. Ain't much. Just a morsel.

JOSEPH. *(Entering.)* Why, it's a sure answer to prayer. I was feeling worn out with all the noise. *(He takes a bite.)* Now I feel renewed.

LEW. That's the eggs in it. Only, if you tired, Brother Joseph, sir, you oughta sleep.

JOSEPH. Frankly, I am so inclined.

JANE. Mobs been keeping you up, too?

LEW. Then you sleep!

JOSEPH. If I napped now, this cake would certainly send me sweet dreams. Would anyone else care for some?

EMMA. Sweet dreams? Yes, I'll take that offer. A year's worth, if you please.

JOSEPH. *(Smiling.)* My dear, I wish I could dispense sugared dreams the way Lew dispenses sugar cake. Would you care for some of this cake, Emma?

EMMA. No, I'm fine. You go ahead.

LEW. I'm sorry I only made that small one, Brother Joseph. I made it for you alone because I wanted to do something to say—sir? I been listening at the door where you do law-making, if you forgive me. Couldn't help myself. I think you one great law man. Or lawyer, whatever the name be.

JOSEPH. You know what my brother Hyrum says about lawyers? "Lawyers were created in gizzard making time, when it was cheaper to get gizzards than souls. If a soul cost five dollars, a gizzard would cost nothing."

LEW. You ain't one of those sort. You one of the great ones. I heard that man brought up for whipping his slave. Heard you say—

SINGERS *begin humming "Oh Freedom."*

JOSEPH. "Lynch law will not do here!" And I believe it with all my heart. Those who engage in it must expect to be visited by the wrath of an indignant people—not according to the rule of Judge Lynch, but according to law and equity!

LEW. Like I say, you a great lawyer. But I do apologize for not making more of that cake.

EMMA. You needn't feel bad. Joseph is a great man. He might become president of the

United States.

JANE. President?!

EMMA. Why, Joseph, it appears these folks don't know your plans.

JOSEPH. I thought the whole world knew. Why, when I get hold of one of those papers and see how popular I am, I'm afraid myself I'll actually be elected!

LEW. Well, what if you get it? What would you do—

JANE. About slavery, sir.

JOSEPH. *(Very seriously.)* You should know I don't believe in shackles for any human soul. My platform calls on these United States to give liberty to the captive, to break off the shackles from the poor black man.

SINGERS. *(Under the dialogue.)* And before I'll be a slave

> I'll be buried in my grave
>
> And go home to my Lord
>
> And be free!

LEW. I knew it!

JOSEPH. Freedom has always been God's will. And many will suffer if we don't do His will in this. Wars worse than have ever visited this land. Brother against brother, father against son.

JANE. *(To JOSEPH.)* Sir, we still safe here, ain't we?

JOSEPH. I wish I could promise that.

JANE. Last night, I heard the mobs outside my window, squealing and shouting like the devil's babies.

JOSEPH. Jane, if you feel unsafe—

JANE. What if I moved to Burlington with Angeline?

JOSEPH. You go with my blessing, Jane. And remember your faith in the everlasting gospel.

JANE. I wouldn't want to—

JOSEPH. The Lord will bless you. The Lord *will* bless you.

SCENE 6

ELIJAH. There was all sorts of mobbin' at this time in Nauvoo. Eventually, for safety's sake, Jane did move to Burlington. And Isaac James started his courtship like one serious—no, one desperate man!

JANE irons. ISAAC knocks.

ISAAC. Can I come in?

JANE. Ain't locked.

ISAAC. *(Carrying a kerchief full of dripping blackberries.)* Guess what I got in here!

JANE. Don't tell me. You been to Lima.

ISAAC. Blackberry capital of the world! Y' ever taste Lima berries?

JANE. A bit early in the season, ain't it? These lookin' more pinkish than blackish.

ISAAC. Maybe a little pink, but—go on, taste one.

He holds a berry to her mouth. She takes it in her fingers.

JANE. I been able to feed myself many a year, Mr. James.

ISAAC. Sometimes, you ought to let a man do for you, Mizz.

JANE. *(Puckering.)* Sour! Wouldn't set right in a pie without five cups of sugar.

ISAAC. Which I would love.

JANE. Well, you just might at that.

ISAAC. *(Awkward, trying for conversation.)* You one lucky lady being in Burlington 'stead of Nauvoo just now.

JANE. Oh, I miss Nauvoo.

ISAAC. Gettin' scary there, Mizz. Not just the mobs. They's a mess of death threats against Brother Joseph. He's declare martial law.

JANE. What's that mean? "March Law"?

ISAAC. Oh—It refer to that marsh around Nauvoo. Marsh Law say anyone comin' across it looking meanly is like to get shot at. *(Pause.)* You so pretty when you smile, Mizz Jane.

JANE. And you touched in the head.

ISAAC. You know what I like about you? I hardly ever sees you dirty. Of course, when you first come to Nauvoo, you looked like something the dog drag in off the street.

JANE. Thank you kindly.

ISAAC. I don't mean no disrespect. Wasn't your fault. You couldn't look bright and new after such a journey. But since that day, you sure keep yourself clean.

JANE. I do what I can.

ISAAC. You clean as a new-shaved lamb. 'Cept for that bit of berry juice on your apron—

JANE. Your fault—

ISAAC. And I full accepts the blame—

JANE. I just washed the apron!

ISAAC. You clean as a newborn pig!

JANE. *(Stops ironing.)* Now is that really the best you can do, Isaac?

ISAAC. No. How's this? Marry me, Jane.

JANE. *(Stunned, then amused.)* That's pretty bold. Well, right this moment, I'm a bit busy and a bit sweaty to be a bride.

ISAAC. Now you know I don't mean right this moment.

JANE. No, I guess I should wash my apron first.

ISAAC. So. That be a "yes" or a "no," or a "let's us wait and see"?

JANE. One of 'em, sure 'nuff.

ISAAC. I keep bringin' berries til you gets your answer, then. I make you one good husband. Never had me a wife. Kept the Mormon faith many years now. Me and Elijah Abel, we was like brothers!

JANE. You and who? Abel?

ISAAC. Elijah Abel—one of the first Negro Mormons in this world! Sheesh, woman, ain't you never heard of him? He held the Melchizedek Priesthood, ordained by Brother Joseph himself! Got washed and anointed in the Kirtland Temple, and served a mission, too. And we was like brothers!

JANE. Sound like maybe he's the one I ought to be meetin' up with.

ISAAC. Except he's moved to Cincinnati. Sorry. But I'm still here. And you might want to face facts.

JANE. What facts you be referrin' to?

ISAAC. Mizz Jane, I jus' don't think you'll do better than me.

JANE. Because I got me a son without his having a proper daddy?

ISAAC. His daddy white, ain't he?

JANE. Good and white. A minister.

ISAAC. Oh. Best kind o' white. If that's what you want.

JANE. Wasn't what I wanted. I got took. But Sylvester Manning is surely my boy, and I won't have you bad-mouth him.

ISAAC. What you gettin' your jaws so tight about? Ain't you seen me with Sylvester? We friends!

JANE. Well that's good, then. Now, this Law of Marshes—

ISAAC. *(Relieved at the subject change.)* I seed it myself, Mizz Jane. Brother Joseph, he all dressed up in his finest. Lieutenant General of the Nauvoo Legion! Then he lift his sword high and he say, "I calls God and angels to witness"—and other words like them. Saying we goin' stay free.

JANE. We colored folk?

ISAAC. We Latter-day Saint folk.

JANE. Wish I'da seen it.

ISAAC. 'Course, you must know things is bad for Brother Joseph now. He's in hidin'. Last I hear, they taking him to Carthage jail. I don't know if he goin' be wearing them shirts you pressin'. Some folk say he won't be coming back to us alive.

JANE. Stop that! God wouldn't let his prophet get killed!

ISAAC. Them 'postates is sayin' he's a fell-down prophet. They callin' for his blood.

JANE. *(Looking at her stained apron.)* Brother Joseph's blood?

ISAAC. Aw, marry me, Jane.

JANE. I'll make you my answer later. You just gave me a lot to think on. I need me some good time.

ISAAC. Well, I need me some good times, too! *(Pause.)* Next time I come, the berries be black as night, ripe and sweet as you please. I hope your answer be that ripe, too.

JANE. Whatever that answer, Mr. James, it's sure to be a good, ripe one.

ISAAC *exits.* JANE *freezes.*

SCENE 7

Offstage song—male solo as LEW *does some chore onstage. He stops to listen, sensing something amiss.*

MALE SINGER. A poor wayfaring man of grief

   Hath often crossed me on his way

   Who sued so humbly for relief

   That I could never answer nay . . .

   I had not power to ask his name,

   whereto he went, or whence he came

   Yet there was something in his eye

   That won my love, I know not why.

ANGUS CANNON. *(Entering.)* We could use some help.

LEW. *(Suddenly fully aware of what's happened.)* Brother Joseph dead, ain't he?

ANGUS CANNON. Yes.

LEW. Hyrum, too?

ANGUS CANNON. Yes. We're heading to Carthage for the bodies. We could use some help.

LEW. I'da laid down my own life for him, sir. If I coulda.

ANGUS CANNON. I know that. So would I.

SCENE 8

Lights up on JANE *and* ISAAC.

JANE. *(Sitting, weary.)* How could God let his prophet get shot dead? I'd like to die myself!

ISAAC. Now you got you a son to take care of. And you shouldn't want to die just 'cause Brother Joseph did. We all gots to live and do every good thing we can.

JANE. I could just lay down and die like—

ISAAC. And one of the best things we can do is—

JANE. *(Quickly.)* Now, Isaac—

ISAAC. *(Taking her arms.)* Start families!

JANE. Even at a sad time like this, you ain't goin' give up on this matter, is you?

ISAAC. No, ma'am. I think Brother Joseph would approve of my not giving up on it.

JANE. He say something to you about that?

ISAAC. Not exactly. There was just a look in his eye. I think he knew—you and me is the best we got.

JANE. With such a compliment as that, a woman might not know how to respond.

ISAAC. Jane Manning, I love you.

JANE. *(Undoing herself from his arms.)* Mr. James, don't you be sayin' me lies.

ISAAC. Anyone ever tell you you're somewhat difficult? You ask me for a compliment and when I give it to you, you say to quit lyin'!

JANE. Go on then. Keep talkin'.

ISAAC. You want to see how much deeper I can dig my foot into this trap, do you? All right then. I don't exactly love you—yet—but you looks to me like a woman who could bring forth a good many children. And I be a man who know something about harvest. And God say we was meant to multiply and punish this earth.

JANE. *(Concealing a smile.)* How you plan on punishing this earth?

ISAAC. Don't you know about me? I'm one of the best farmers in Nauvoo! I punish this earth like it never been punished before!

JANE. Them the best courtin' words you can find?

ISAAC. Ain't used to courtin' women much. I court the fruit of the vine, and it don't usually answer back.

JANE. Maybe because you punish it too much.

ISAAC. But that's what God say to do! That's his will! So I figure if I can grow fat, juicy grapes, I can grow fat, juicy babies.

JANE. The word, Mr. James, is "replenish." "Multiply and replenish."

ISAAC. Listen to you! You so good with words! I ain't. Ain't much for this courtin' business either.

JANE. You doin' fine with this courtin' business. Problem is, I'm still mourning Brother Joseph. I ain't ready to think on getting multiplied and punished.

ISAAC. Well, will you let me know when you is ready?

JANE. You will be the very first to know, Mr. James. I promise.

SCENE 9

SINGERS. Come, come, ye Saints

> No toil or labor fear
>
> But with joy, wend your way
>
> Though hard to you
>
> This journey shall appear
>
> Grace shall be as your day . . .

Lights up on LEW *and* ANGELINE *as* JANE *hums the rest of the song.*

ANGELINE. No sir, I ain't goin'—even if Jane is. Over the Rockies? No sir! I got me a good life selling palm hats to steamships. Singin' for 'em, too.

LEW. Don't know what more you could ask than that.

ANGELINE. And I got me a beau. One that toot the ship's horn like God makin' thunder.

LEW. Sound like about the right man for you, Angeline. Someone who can drown out your words by just pulling a rope.

ANGELINE. I know you thinks you funny, but you ain't.

ANGELINE *and* LEW *exit.*

SCENE 10

ISAAC is gathering grapes. JANE approaches him, carrying a tray with a glass of water.

JANE. Thought you might be thirsty, Brother Isaac.

ISAAC. *(Very loudly.)* Well, will you lookee here!

JANE. Ow! You one noisy man! Maybe you'd best watch your mouth and quiet it down some.

ISAAC. There's another mouth I prefer to watch. That'd be your mouth. I'd prefer to watch it all day and all night long.

JANE. What you better watch is your whole self, Mr. James. Don't you try to spark with me.

ISAAC. Did I imagine it, or was it you brung me this water and cornbread?

JANE. Don't take it for more than it is. I'm just doin' my Christian duty, that's all.

ISAAC. You know what the Good Book say about Christian duty. "Better to marry than to burn." My, my, it is hot today, ain't it!

JANE. Do you believe in the Church?

ISAAC. Do I—. Would I be in Nauvoo if I didn't?

JANE. Maybe you just lookin' for a place where you don't get hurt. Well? Do you believe?

ISAAC. Nobody ever asked me so straight before. I believe in God. Pretty sure I do. And I's content to follow this people wherever they go to find Him.

JANE. Now tell me true, how do you feel about my son?

ISAAC. I told you, we great friends. I'd be pleased to be his daddy. And he needs a daddy.

JANE. You have a point there, Mr. James.

ISAAC. Mr. James?

JANE. You prefer "Brother Isaac"?

ISAAC. What I prefers is "honey doll" and "sugar pie."

JANE. Then you'd best check out a sweets market.

ISAAC. Wherever you be, Jane, there's enough sweets for me, honey.

JANE. I warn you, Brother Isaac—you'd best watch yourself.

ISAAC. I's watching myself in your pretty little eyes. And I think your eyes is getting 'customed to me. Maybe to like me a little?

JANE. You'd likely get the same impression from a lookin' glass, Isaac.

ISAAC. Aw, say me that again.

JANE. I say you likely get—

ISAAC. My name. Say me my name. I want to watch your mouth say me my name. Come on, now, honey. Say it.

JANE. Isaac.

ISAAC. Good. Now you just set down that tray. Let's make us a bargain and seal it up like we ought to.

She sets the tray down. ISAAC *kisses her.* ELIJAH *comes onstage.*

ELIJAH. It wasn't a fancy wedding, but it was a nice one, on a peaceful day. And since Nauvoo days were getting less peaceful all the time, everyone was happy for a reason to celebrate something. But the peace didn't last, of course. These Mormons in Nauvoo were bound to leave their beautiful city and head west.

SCENE 11

JANE. *(Sadly as her brother approaches.)* Hello, Lew.

LEW. Hello.

JANE. I heard you ain't going West with us. I knew the others wouldn't. Mama's too old, and the rest got other lives. But I thought you'd come!

LEW. I thought I would, too. For a while. My heart got buried with Brother Joseph. I ain't goin' far. Maybe back Missouri ways.

JANE. Slave state? Where they treat you like—.

LEW. Ain't ready for another journey.

JANE. Don't you know? This people is the only ones treat you right!

LEW. They ain't always treat me right.

JANE. But they *will*. We just at the start of Zion. Lew, it's like dawn. The sun don't get itself up in two seconds! First a leaf get lit up, then a branch, then a tree, then part of a hill. It's gradual, but it happen every morning.

LEW. Wish I had your faith. I don't, though. Leastways, not enough to set out across the prairie again. Jane, you sure you goin' find God over the Rockies?

JANE. Ain't sure where I'll find Him. Only sure He's callin' me.

LEW. It's like to be another hard journey.

JANE. I just take it a step at a time. How many good-byes you figure we said to each other in our life?

LEW. A hundred?

JANE. You was jus' a baby the first time—when I went to work for the Fitches. Now look at you. My, my, you one oak of a man!

LEW. A skinny oak.

JANE. So many good-byes, you'd think I'd be 'customed. Why ain't I?

LEW. Ain't you? Come to think on it, me neither.

JANE. I can't help wonder if this time, I might never—.

LEW. You got you a good man. I trust him to look after you same as I would. And if he don't, you find some way to get me word. I'll come 'cross the prairie and beat the tar outta him.

JANE. Aw, you couldn't beat the tar out of nothin' but a blackbird—less you dance a fellow to death.

LEW. *(Embracing her.)* That much trust! Don't let nothin' happen to you, Janey. We meet again. I feel that in my soul.

    ANGELINE, SARAH, *and* ANTHONY *enter.*

ANTHONY. I don't know why you so fixed on another trek, Janey!

JANE. Must be all them good memories from the first one.

ANGELINE. I made this special for you. Keep the sun from your eyes.

    She presents a palm hat.

JANE. Thank you, Angeline. I keep it forever.

SARAH. *(Kissing* JANE.*)* Go with God, Sis.

JANE. You, too.

ISAAC. *(Carrying* SYLVESTER *as the Nauvoo Bell sounds.)* That's the Nauvoo Bell. We ready, folks.

JANE. Pray for us.

LEW. Every day!

    Lights fade briefly. Singing—"The Gospel Train."

ELIJAH. This is Winter Quarters now, where the Mormon pioneers first stopped. And Jane just had her a baby boy.

    Enter AGNES THOMAS.

AGNES. Hello, there. I heard there was a new little nigger baby here. Can I see it?

ISAAC. My wife's in the wagon with our baby, but he was born real recent. I don't—

AGNES. *(Ignoring Isaac and calling into the wagon.)* Hello in there! You got company!

JANE. *(Peeking out of the wagon, straightening her hair.)* My, I did not expect visitors. I'm afraid I'm not at my best.

AGNES. You must be Black Jane. Of course, I'da knowed that first sight. You mind I look at the pickaninny?

JANE. My baby's name is Silas. He's sleepin over there.

AGNES. *(Peeking inside. She becomes mournfully nostalgic.)* Oh look! Cutest little nigger baby I ever did see! I owned me a pickaninny once. Four years old and black as a crow. I inherited it for my sixteenth birthday, but my husband made me give it up once we joined the Saints. I supported him in his decision, of course, did my duty— but it was hard. So when I heard you'd had you one, why, I came right over to see! Oh, just looking makes me miss my own. I left so much behind—my good clock, all my china, my pickaninny, and a fine silk dress. My husband asked me to, and I obeyed. Well, are you recovering all right, Black Jane?

JANE. A little tired yet. The birth wasn't easy.

AGNES. Childbirth—that's a pleasure I'm still waiting on. I've only took my husband eight months ago. Why, I hardly know how to—

JANE. *(Interrupting fast.)* I'm glad you could visit.

AGNES. When it's not sleeping, I want to hold it. Would you mind?

JANE. I don't—.

AGNES. I guess I'd better get back to my own wagon. I'll come back later. Bye now!

　　AGNES *exits.*

ISAAC. Thank you for callin'!

JANE. Yes, indeed! Excuse my appearance!

ELIJAH. Now, you'll just have to imagine the weeks and months of walking that come next. We wouldn't finish this story until next year if we showed you every trial they suffered—buffalo stampedes, folks dying of pneumonia or black canker. But mostly just the walkin, day after day. Long journey. Longer than you understand.

JANE. Isaac, I am so weary.

ISAAC. I know.

JANE. And I'm in the family way again.

ISAAC. Aw, Janey!

JANE. And you know when.

ISAAC. *(Remembering fondly.)* That night when the stars was so pretty and the moon—. So you jus' barely in that way, then.

JANE. Mister James, you either there or you not there. Ain't no in between, no barely, no mostly. You is or you isn't. And I is.

ISAAC. I guess I's payin' for the starlight, then. Yes, indeed, starlight's come collectin'!

JANE. It is pretty starlight, ain't it? I wish I could enjoy it more. Wish I didn't feel so sick.

ISAAC. That's the sickness God give you to make the baby a better reward because you went through so much to have it.

JANE. If you was a woman, your words might hold a bit more weight.

ISAAC. Can't nobody full understand nobody else's pain. You just keep on. We'll find the place.

SCENE 12

ELIJAH *comes forward.*

ELIJAH. *(Gesturing to set pieces.)* And they did find it, of course. These is cabins now. Poor, small cabins—but they home to these folk. Jane birthed a daughter, just after they arrived in the Salt Lake Valley. They all got along fine. Until grasshoppers and crickets come carrying destruction wherever they hop to. Some folks started starving.

ISAAC. *(To* JANE.*)* Where you goin' with that flour?

JANE. We don't have much, but we do have more than the Lymans. I'm taking this portion to Eliza Partridge Lyman. She's been my friend longer than you have, Isaac.

ISAAC. Well, she didn't marry you!

JANE *goes to Eliza's house.* ELIZA *appears.*

ELIZA. Why, Jane! What's this?

JANE. Not much. Two pounds of flour, that's all.

ELIZA. *(Hardly able to speak.)* You'd do this for me? You know—there is good in this poverty.

JANE. Ma'am?

ELIZA. For example, I do not think our enemies need envy us this locality, do you?

JANE. Oh, no, ma'am!

ELIZA. I do not think they'll disturb us here.

JANE. Not unless they stupid.

ELIZA. Like us?

JANE. Now, we ain't stupid. We devoted. We see past the uglies to the possibilities of this place.

ELIZA. As do the crickets.

JANE. With them bugly eyes, I expect so.

ELIZA. I think we're safe from human harm here. Well, how is your son?

JANE. Which one?

ELIZA. You and I both gave birth to healthy sons in Winter Quarters—within a few weeks of each other. My precious baby. I named him Don Carlos.

JANE. Yes, I remember. My Silas is a handful by now! Runs faster than I can.

ELIZA. Don Carlos died at five months.

JANE. I heard about that, ma'am. I wept over you something fierce and prayed for you with my whole soul.

ELIZA. I thought I'd die myself. Took the childbed fever after his birth. Lost all my hair.

JANE. I know. But it's growed back fine!

ELIZA. And I have another son now. Platte.

JANE. God gives and—.

ELIZA. Jane, were you surprised?

JANE. Ma'am?

ELIZA. By the barrenness here! When I first saw it, I thought, "If this is God's reward for our faith, I don't care to see His punishment!" After that journey! All we suffered! Then we get a desert, crickets, poverty. I have not said this to anyone but you. Oh Jane, I expected better! Weren't you surprised?

JANE. Why, there's surprises at every turn, ma'am. Good and bad.

ELIZA. *(Looking long at the flour.)* This flour might save our lives, you know. I have nothing.

JANE. *(Beginning to leave.)* I'm pleased to help out.

ELIZA. *(Calling her back.)* Jane? I never imagined a colored woman would be bringing me her own flour to keep me from starving.

JANE. Me, I never imagined such crickets.

ELIZA. That's how this life goes, isn't it. Surprises at every turn.

Lights down on ELIZA *and* JANE.

END ACT ONE

Act Two

SCENE 1

Song: "O Happy Day!" Sung in its entirety.

ELIJAH. *(Stepping forward.)* Well, now it's my turn to be one of them surprises! The year is 1852. Me and my wife, Mary Ann—we set to enter the valley.

ISAAC. *(Running onstage.)* He's here! Jane, Elijah Abel is here! Oh, things is goin' get good for us now!

ELIJAH. Why, Isaac James! And who might this be?

ISAAC. The wife, Brother Elijah. This is Jane.

ELIJAH. And this is Mary Ann.

MARY ANN. *(Nervously to* ELIJAH.*)* Elijah, I don't know these folks. I feel timid! Pardon me. I must look a sight.

ELIJAH. We brought three little ones across the plains from Cincinatti.

ISAAC. Well, we brought three, too—only one of 'em, we kept in Jane's belly until we got to the valley. And guess what we named her? Mary Ann! Same name as the wife you got!

ELIJAH. Ain't that something! You gave my wife a namesake before you even met her!

JANE. Sister Abel, you come on inside with me. Rest your bones a spell.

MARY ANN. Elijah?

ELIJAH. You go on inside with Jane. Make friends, honey.

MARY ANN. You know how I am!

ELIJAH. That's why I'm tellin' you to go inside and make friends!

JANE. I'm so happy to see you, Sister Abel. Please don't be shy.

   JANE *and* MARY ANN *go inside.*

ELIJAH. So how's things, Brother Isaac?

ISAAC. Good. I been workin' for Brother Brigham. Coachman.

ELIJAH. And how is Brigham Young?

ISAAC. Well, he's got him a good many women to keep him company and spread his reputation.

ELIJAH. Oh yes, I heard about that. Whole world heard.

ISAAC. He quite a leader, ain't he?

ELIJAH. Hard to imagine most anyone else gettin' all these folks to follow them to this here desert—and then to set up housekeepin'! He is a leader, that's for sure.

ISAAC. Speaks his mind no matter who's listenin'. Only sometimes he say—

ELIJAH. Don't think I'm going to be surprised by what Brigham Young say. That's a man with a strong will and a strong tongue. He say whatever come to mind even if someone's takin' notes!

ISAAC. You know, he say things about colored folk. About us being cursed because of Cain and Ham and whatever else they put in that recipe.

ELIJAH. Ain't nothin' new in that. No matter if it's Brigham Young or someone else halfway 'cross the world sayin' it. Why, you've heard that lineage talk before! Most every religion preaches some version of that. Even folk what don't got no 'ligion at all talk that talk. All us heard it before. Ain't you?

ISAAC. Yes, but I didn't think I'd hear it quite so much out here. Thought there'd be better turns to conversation. Thought we'd be—

ELIJAH. You poor?

ISAAC. We got along splendid for a time—had horses, cows, oxen, sheep, chickens—you name it.

ELIJAH. You poor now?

ISAAC. No! . . . Shoot, Elijah. You give me them eyes and I know you seein' straight through me.

ELIJAH. How poor?

ISAAC. Not intolerable. And things is lookin' up, now you're here! You was always the link between us and them. You was one of Joseph Smith's most best friends in the world.

ELIJAH. That is a fact. I'll see what I can do for you.

ISAAC. How about I see what I can do for you first? Like fill your gullet full of johnny cakes and potato soup!

ELIJAH. Now that sounds like a fine beginning! *(ISAAC goes inside, and ELIJAH begins to follow, then faces the audience, chuckling.)* I have to laugh remembering how big a fool I was back then. As though I could do a thing for Isaac! Oh, times had changed. I may have been one of Joseph Smith's best friends, but Brother Brigham hardly knew me! And when I asked if I could be sealed to my wife Mormon style, Brigham Young said such was a privilege he could not grant. Oh, he tried to comfort me. He told me the time would come when us blacks would have all the blessings we desired. He got me and other colored folks front seats in general conference. I thought that was considerate of him. But still, we could not partake of opportunities white folks had. I'd watch them go into the Endowment House, stepping inside the door like it was the easiest thing on God's green earth. I watched some of them take it all for granted, and it pained me to my marrow. Then other events began.

JANE *and* ISAAC *enter.* ELIJAH *observes.*

SCENE 2

ISAAC. Tom Colbourn's dead. Throat slit. And he got a nice, big sign stuck on his body. "Warning to all niggers: Stay Away from White Women."

JANE. Oh, Isaac! That's terrible, awful news. I hope it wasn't a Mormon done it. The Book of Mormon say—

ISAAC. Now don't you go quoting me scripture, Mizz! Between you and Brigham Young, I heard so much scripture I can't spit without dropping Bible words on the ground.

JANE. "All are alike unto God!"

ISAAC. I told you, no scriptures! All my Mormon days, I waited for things to turn better. Ain't happened. Fact is, things is turning the other direction. I don't see—

JANE. Stop it. I don't want to hear this. Been through enough today.

ISAAC. You still alive. That's more than Tom Colbourn can say. I've heard some of the folks around here talk about us like we was—

JANE. That's enough!

ISAAC. Animals!

JANE. Isaac, I said—

ISAAC. *(Exiting.)* Fine. Then I'll go talk to the trees. I expect they know what it's like to get chopped up and burned. What it's like to have a knife cut through their flesh. Hello, trees! You want to hear the latest? Let your leaves turn to ears, and take a listen! Hello, trees!

ELIJAH *approaches* JANE.

ELIJAH. Problems, sister?

JANE. Just the common ones. Husband goin' crazy, is all.

ELIJAH. Oh. Well, 'long as it ain't nothing serious.

JANE. Brother Elijah, now you tell me straight. I heard so much about curses: Cain, Canaan, black skin. But I've felt Jesus touch my heart and soul. I never have felt cursed by Him, only loved so deep seemed my bones might melt. Still, folks say—

ELIJAH. I took that question to God one time.

JANE. Did He answer?

ELIJAH. He might have. I feel, Sister Jane, that ours is: (BACKGROUND SONG—*under* ELIJAH's *words—hummed as the poem is recited, then sung afterwards*):

> "Were You There When they Crucified my Lord?"
>
> Were you there when they crucified my Lord?
>
> Were you there when they crucified my Lord?
>
> Oh, sometimes it causes me to tremble, tremble, tremble.
>
> Were you there when then crucified my Lord?
>
> Were you there when they laid him in the grave?
>
> Were you there when they laid him in the grave?
>
> Oh, sometimes it causes me to tremble, tremble, tremble.
>
> Were you there when they laid Him in the tomb?

> Not a curse but a gift t'us,
>
> The best path we could seek
>
> A place where God can lift us
>
> We kneel; our knees is weak.

> And when one of us is kneelin',
>
> We understand his fears.
>
> We know what all us is feelin'
>
> We cry each other's tears.

> That's just what Jesus done
>
> For all us human folk.
>
> He agreed to come get born
>
> To feel ever' pain and poke.

> So's he could understand us,
>
> What it is to be a slave.
>
> So's he could get beneath us
>
> And push us outa the grave.

Would you rather be the massa

Or the Roman with his whip?

Would you rather nail the Savior—

Put vinegar to his lip?

Or learn the lessons of sufferin'—

How we nothin' without grace.

Jesus, He give us a callin'

He gifted us our race.

JANE. I like that answer, Brother. At least better than other answers I get. I wish my husband could get a good answer, too.

JANE *exits.*

SCENE 3

ELIJAH. *(Going for a small, wood box.)* I'm a carpenter. Just like Jesus was. I consider that an honor. In Nauvoo, I was one of the first undertakers. Carpenters always did make the prettiest coffins. Joseph Smith himself gave me the calling to make the best death boxes the world would see. I did my utmost. I could carve grapevines around a coffin so good they'd look like they'd bear fruit once they got planted underground! But it's a sad job, making death-boxes. This here box is for Jane's and Isaac's baby. Stillborn.

ISAAC. *(Entering where Jane lies.)* How you doin'?

JANE. Did you see him?

ISAAC. Yes.

JANE. I knew he'd be born dead.

ISAAC. You didn't say nothin' about knowin' that.

JANE. Didn't want to trouble you. I stopped feeling life weeks ago. I waited. I hoped. That's why I didn't say anything.

ISAAC. You should've spoke up.

JANE. You'd think the Lord would let the goin' down pains ease up when the baby won't even be movin'. I screamed so hard, my voice is near gone, and I am aching everywhere down my soul.

ISAAC. Aw, don' cry, Janey. I know you done the best you could, and I want our baby to carry my name, just like we talked about.

JANE. Isaac, he never even took air!

ISAAC. Honey, listen to me. Now, I don't mean for you to pity me, not when you—. Only I can't keep my own feelin' inside no longer. You let that dead baby out—that little Isaac—and every dead part of me is begging to get out, too.

JANE. *(Sitting up.)* What you sayin'?

ISAAC. You know.

JANE. Today of all days, you talkin' about—?

ISAAC. California, Jane. You—our whole family—we all go together.

JANE. No! I told God I would let Him guide me, plant my feet where He wanted them. This is where God chose!

ISAAC. Don't be no fool! Losin' this baby is just the latest ripple in a whole river of sorry luck. Nothin' will change here. Folks got their hearts set.

JANE. I got my heart set, too. And my feet. And my house. And now the first grave our property has knowed. Here!

ISAAC. Then you be doin' exactly what they want! Oh, they'll come fawnin' over you now because you be grief-struck. But these folks WANT you set and planted like clover, so's they can walk on you. Every time you look like you goin' become something important, I swear they will mow you down.

JANE. Well, every time you look like you goin' become something important, you turn heel and run!

ISAAC. *(Quieter.)* Janey—honey—calm down. You shouldn't start a fight when you don't even got a voice to finish it.

JANE. I didn't start it.

ISAAC. Well then, you shouldn't encourage me.

JANE. You never cared about this people or this place!

ISAAC. *(Losing temper.)* I cared too long and too much—and you know it! They tell you there's some sort of reward waitin' for you just beyond them clouds. You know why they say such things? So you won't make a fuss if they step on your head on their way to California!

JANE. Isaac, stop it!

ISAAC. I'm sorry. Oh Janey, I didn't mean to upset you. Not today. I would never want to hurt you. But you got to know—there is nothing for me here. Nor for you either. Let's try California.

JANE. *(Falling back, exhausted.)* If you goin' try California, you goin' try it alone.

ISAAC. Aw, this ain't the time for a fight. I'll go get the box for little Isaac.

JANE. And then you'll leave us?

ISAAC. I didn't say that.

JANE. You think I don't know what you plannin'?

ISAAC. *(Realizing how well she knows him.)* Honey, I'll be back. Probably before Christmas.

JANE. *(Weakly, weeping.)* I have never begged you for anything in my life, but I am begging you now. Please don't go.

ISAAC. You watch for me. I'll be the one driving a gold surrey.

JANE. So this is how you comfort me after I birth a gone baby?

ISAAC. You're forgettin' something. It was my baby, too. Jane, it was me! *(ISAAC exits, murmuring:)* I love you.

> JANE *stands, puts a shawl on and ages herself to imply the passage of years. Her shoulders slope. Either* ELIJAH *or* PHYLLIS *(as an angel descending from Heaven) comes to her and paints white streaks in her hair.* JANE, *aged now, sings, or the angelic chorus sings for her:*

JANE OR SINGERS. Nobody knows the troubles I've seen

> Nobody knows but Jesus.
>
> Nobody knows the trouble I've seen,
>
> Glory hallelujah!
>
> Sometimes I'm up; sometimes I'm down
>
> Oh yes, Lord;
>
> Sometimes I'm almost to the ground
>
> Oh yes, Lord;
>
> Nobody knows the troubles I've seen
>
> Nobody knows but Jesus.

SCENE 4

> JANE *picks up a letter.* MARY ANN ABEL *joins her husband, who is standing near* JANE, *observing.*

ELIJAH. You go see if you can offer that woman some comfort. Husband's left her three years back. And now her children dyin' off. I ain't seen her in a while, and I get worried.

MARY ANN. Elijah, you know how I am! I never know what to say in these times. I can come off such a fool!

ELIJAH. Do your Christian duty anyway.

MARY ANN. Can't you come with me?

ELIJAH. No. This is women talk.

    ELIJAH *waits as* MARY ANN *approaches* JANE.

MARY ANN. Sister James? Hello?

JANE. *(Squeezing her blankets tightly.)* Hello, Mary Ann.

MARY ANN. You doin' all right?

JANE. I got news yesterday that my daughter, Miriam, died. In childbirth.

MARY ANN. Oh! Did she? I remember Miriam. She was a pretty one.

JANE. My prettiest. And sweetest. She took after me.

MARY ANN. That's three of your children gone in two years. My! And you bearin' it all alone.

JANE. Not alone. I don't have me a husband no more, but I ain't alone.

MARY ANN. Can I do anything for you?

JANE. Only Jesus can do anything for me.

MARY ANN. I can pray alongside you, maybe. You feel to pray?

JANE. *(Falling to her knees at once, weeping.)* Oh Jesus, please don't take no more of my children! Please, Lord! I know you got a reward of some sort waitin' for me, but my children was all my joy in this life. Let me keep the ones I got left!

MARY ANN. *(Awkwardly.)* Um—Amen. You feel better?

JANE. *(Returning to her chair.)* No.

MARY ANN. Would—would chicken soup help?

JANE. *(Smiling grimly.)* I would prefer the resurrection, sister.

MARY ANN. Well . . . how about corn bread, then! Fresh from the oven!

JANE. *(Relenting.)* Corn bread sounds fine. You're a good woman, Sister Mary Ann. You've had to wait on your own blessings, just like me. You set the example. I want to be like you.

MARY ANN. *(Tearing up.)* Oh no, ma'am! Oh, Jane! You the bravest woman I know! If I could just get behind your wings when you be made a angel, I think my feet will fly!

    ELIJAH *enters.*

ELIJAH. You ladies doin' all right?

JANE. Just planning how to arrange things when we be made angels.

ELIJAH. I always do admire you women for plannin' ahead.

MARY ANN. We prayed together, Elijah. I felt we should.

JANE. Not a prayer which was likely to get heard. We should pray for something easy. For good luck to come knockin' on the door.

There's a knock at the door. JANE, MARY ANN *and* ELIJAH *answer.* AGNES *stands in the portal.*

AGNES. Hello, Jane.

JANE. *(Quickly regaining herself.)* Why, Mizz Agnes Thomas. I hope there wasn't no problem with the laundry. Come in!

AGNES. No, I don't need to enter your house. And I didn't realize you had company.

ELIJAH. We was just leavin'. Pleasure!

ELIJAH *and* MARY ANN *exit.*

AGNES. The laundry is fine, Jane. I'm here because—

JANE. I know you don't like your collars over-starched. But nobody likes to feel like they wearing a piece of bark either. Is—

AGNES. The collars are fine. You are the most gifted washerwoman in the valley. I hope that doesn't arouse your pride.

JANE. Mizz Agnes, sometimes my pride could use a little wakin' up. I thank you for those kind words. I was fearful you'd—

AGNES. But I'm afraid what I must say today will not make you proud in any degree.

JANE. No, I didn't think you'd come all the way out here to talk about the wash, ma'am.

AGNES. My husband claims your son—Sylvester—has been making eyes at our daughter.

JANE. No. Syl's got a woman. A colored one. Miss Mary Ann Perkins.

AGNES. But you know as well as I, the ways of your—. You know—

JANE. Ma'am, I know my son.

AGNES. *(Fidgeting.)* Of course, it could be my husband was mistaken. No, he would not concoct such a tale. You must talk to your boy.

JANE. Of course, I will.

AGNES. I'll look for you on Thursday, then. May I wish you a fine morning?

JANE. Yes, ma'am, you may.

AGNES *exits as* SYLVESTER *enters.*

AGNES. *(Exiting.)* That's the one!

SYLVESTER. They makin' up all sorts of excuses for not givin' me work, Mama. How can I support a family if I can't work? And I would tell you what one particular Mormon man said to me, but I know you don't wanna hear me say such words.

JANE. If he said something mean, then he wasn't a GOOD Mormon.

SYLVESTER. You show me a GOOD Mormon, then!

JANE. *(Slapping him.)* Stop it now.

SYLVESTER. Mama, I'm a grown man. I don't want you touchin' my face with a open hand anymore.

JANE. I'm sorry you didn't find work, but you have got to face up to being colored.

SYLVESTER. *(Sullenly.)* Half-colored.

JANE. You the onlyest one talkin' percentage. Don't you make no danger. And don't you dare be makin' eyes at any white girl.

SYLVESTER. What?

JANE. *(Calmer.)* Sit down. Honey, you must understand things. I have worked—Lawd, how I've worked!—to keep us fed and housed. All on my own. And now you could go ruin it all. Not on purpose. But you make eyes at a white girl and—innocent as your eyes be—

SYLVESTER. *(Angry.)* I don't have to listen to this. Been through enough today.

JANE. Sylvester, now don't you dare—

> SYLVESTER *exits angrily.* JANE *looks around desperate, then kneels again. Song in background: "Give Me Jesus."*

JANE. All right, Lord—it's me again. Prayin' to you, because I ain't got nobody else to talk to this moment, and I need to talk! We've had us more conversation this day than we had all last week. Lord, I felt your Spirit when I was a child and so many times since. Brother Joseph said—the last words I ever heard him say—that I'd be blessed. And you know, Lord, I have tried to keep my feet where you set them. But I am so alone and so poor. And sometimes, I wonder. What is it you want from me? I am banging on the walls of Jericho and they still standing. And Lord, it is one thing for these folks to keep me outside their gates—I can live with that. But my children! Lord, I am losing my children! Mary Ann. Silas. And now Miriam. And my Sylvester, he either walkin' straight up to trouble, or trouble knockin' on his door. Now I know I shouldn't have slapped him. I didn't mean to. I didn't even get a chance to tell him his sister's dead. Lord, Lord!

> *Lights dim on* JANE.

SCENE 5

> *Lights up on* ELIJAH, *who picks up a rope.*

ELIJAH. This is a rope. I'll just bet you could've guessed that. Many uses for a rope. Out west, folks can lasso unruly calves and even wild stallions. But some folks think they ought to use ropes for other means. Never expected the likes of them here. *(ELIJAH drops the rope. Lights up on SYLVESTER.)* My, my—look at Sylvester! He appears almost drunk, don't he? But he ain't. I'll need to help him now. He's a grown and married man, but I think he needs his mama at this moment.

ELIJAH *helps him, takes him to JANE's house.*

JANE. *(Coming to the door.)* Brother Elijah! Wha—what's wrong with my boy?

ELIJAH. He seen something.

SYLVESTER. *(Clutching his stomach.)* Oh I'm goin' be sick. Let me catch my breath.

ELIJAH. *(Seating SYLVESTER.)* Sister Jane, Judge Lynch has arrived in Utah.

JANE. Judge—Someone—No! Who got lynched?

SYLVESTER. *(Fighting tears.)* That ex-soldier—one of us—Sam Joe Harvey. I brought him here two months ago. You gave him supper.

JANE. *(Sitting down hard.)* Lynched? No, no! How'd this happen?

SYLVESTER. The Grices promised him a job. Then Sam Joe learned that job was twelve miles outside the city. He got a temper, and he went to cuss Grice, and—oh, Mama—

ELIJAH. Take your time, son.

SYLVESTER. A ruckus broke out.

JANE. Lord Jesus, have mercy.

SYLVESTER. Mrs. Grice, she call Marshall Burt.

JANE. Andrew Burt?

SYLVESTER. Then everything—it got dizzy. Shots fired off and—before the smoke even cleared—Sam Joe aimed his gun right at Andrew Burt and—

JANE. Andrew Burt got killed?

SYLVESTER. Shot through the heart.

JANE. Sweet Lord, take pity!

SYLVESTER. Blood everywhere. Brother Abel was there. He wrestled the gun from Harvey's hands.

ELIJAH. Old as I be, I was strong enough for that. Just not soon enough.

SYLVESTER. Then Harvey got carted off to jail—lookin' at Brother Elijah and me the whole time, like we could do somethin' for him. Then others start lookin' our direction, too—the devil in their eyes.

ELIJAH. Take it easy, son.

SYLVESTER. Didn't you see the devil in their eyes, Elder Abel?

ELIJAH. *(Bowing his head painfully.)* Yes, I did.

SYLVESTER. Then the mob start yelling for the guard to "Let him out! Let him out!"

ELIJAH. And the guard let him out. I did not think—did not imagine—

SYLVESTER. The guard steps out with his gun in his hand, and he tells the people, "Back off!" Then Sam Joe gets pushed outside, and in two seconds he's getting stomped and kicked like a dog. Then the rope, it gets passed forward, hand over hand.

ELIJAH. Where I was standin', it got drawn over my arm. I felt it. My whole body shivered.

SYLVESTER. It gets noosed around Sam Joe's neck and a bunch of folks, must've been a thousand—folks we know!—they hoist him up. They throw the rope over a beam and they hoist him, yellin' the whole time: "Get him up there! Stretch his neck!" His hands was free. He try to get the rope off his neck and—oh Mama—two boys climb some benches and hit his arms until he lose his grip.

JANE. Lord, NO!

SYLVESTER. Then he struggle some, and then he just swingin' there, eyes stuck up in his head like they lookin' for God. They takes him down, then the whole mob drag his body through the streets, cheering all the way. Oh, my stomach's comin' up.

ELIJAH. Sister Jane, where's your bucket?

JANE. There. In the corner.

SYLVESTER. Cheerin' the whole way. Like Fourth of July. I don't need no bucket.

JANE. If Lynch Law is touchin' Utah, Syl, you stay here.

AGNES *knocks. A tense moment.*

JANE. *(Very nervous.)* Who is it?

AGNES. Jane, it's Sister Agnes Thomas.

JANE. You alone?

AGNES. By all that's holy, I know and swear I am completely alone. Oh—I did not realize you had company. Pardon me.

JANE. *(Opening the door part way, then wider.)* This is my son and Brother Elijah Abel. I believe you know—

AGNES. *(Staying at the door, curtsying.)* I hope I'm not interrupting.

JANE. Won't you step inside? You come all this ways on such a hot afternoon.

AGNES. Thank you, no. Jane, because of what happened—

JANE. I know you had nothin' to do with that.

AGNES. I don't want you to think my husband is a bad man. He's not bad, and I would never wish to criticize him. Only I wanted to say something, and I didn't know where else I could say it. I suppose you know Tom was with that mob.

ELIJAH. Yes, we know.

SYLVESTER. *(Quietly to* JANE.*)* Tom was leadin' it.

AGNES. Myself, I think the mob was on par with that murderer! I cannot imagine Tom would have participated in any way except for the mob fever. But it hasn't benefited Andrew Burt or his family to do this—this thing. And for it to happen in our city—in the shadow of the temple—it don't show a Christian feeling.

JANE. I agree with you, ma'am.

AGNES. Every man should have the recourse of law.

JANE. Mizz Agnes, it's so hot outside. Won't you come in? I'd be honored to pour you a glass of water.

AGNES. I'm sorry, but I can't enter your home or partake of your hospitality. I appreciate the offer. Now I must pick up my laundry. I'm hoping you've had a chance to finish it.

JANE. I was fixing to take it to you tomorrow, Mizz Agnes.

AGNES. I'm afraid—Jane, you understand. I can't accept your services as our laundress any longer. Tom won't allow it. Now, I haven't changed my mind about your talent and I doubt I'll find your match anywhere in the valley, but Tom will not permit a Nigra—

JANE. *(Smiling the best she can.)* No need to explain things. I only wish I'da knowed you was comin'. I'da ironed everything.

AGNES. I'll find someone else to finish it. Tom has someone in mind already. I have my buggy set to take the load now. Maybe, since you won't be washin' our clothes now, you'll have more time to do things you've been wanting to. Maybe you could write poetry. Wouldn't that be something?

JANE. Let me get the basket.

AGNES. We'd have you and Sister Eliza Snow both. Two kinds of Mormon poets.

JANE. *(Getting the baske.t)* I'm afraid I never got schoolin' in how to write.

AGNES. Why I could teach you! *(She stops herself.)* Not yet, of course. The mood around here must change first. I know you understand that . . .

JANE. Of course. I thank you for the privilege of doing your wash these many years, Mizz Agnes.

AGNES. *(Breaking down.)* This isn't what I wanted.

JANE. Mizz Agnes, why you cryin'?

AGNES. Times will get back to normal. I just know it!

ELIJAH. Let me take that basket to your buggy, Sister Thomas.

AGNES. I'd be obliged. Good-bye, Jane.

JANE *watches* AGNES *and* ELIJAH *leave.*

SYLVESTER. Mama, you so scared. You too timid around them. Always tryin' to show your good side. They don't care about your good side or your bad one. All they see is "Black Jane."

ELIJAH. *(Re-entering.)* Boy, don't you go diminishin' your mama. Now, you saw a terrible thing this mornin'—a thing with the devil in it. But you got to understand that your mama got a life worth of experience, and you honor that! Your mama and me been and done four times in our lives what you ain't done even once. Hear me?

SYLVESTER. I didn't mean no disrespect.

JANE. Go on home to your wife, Syl. She got to be worried about where you are.

SYLVESTER. Yes, ma'am.

He exits. Lights dim.

SCENE 6

ELIJAH. *(Picking up the rope again and looking at it.)* Well, no surprise that Tom Thomas got acquitted for his part in bringing about Sam Joe Harvey's demise. That's jus' the way things was in these times, all over America. Lynch law was everywhere. Night riders was fearsome, and the devil was ridin' his chariot so fast and so loud you could almost hear the wheels rattle. That's how it was. Wasn't no state in this union escaped that ugly long chain of Judge Lynch. And I'm sad to say that Sylvester James got excommunicated. I don't know the reasons, but I know he was bitter. As for me, well Mary Ann had passed on by this time, and—

JANE *enters.*

JANE. Elder Abel? How are you going to answer Judge Lynch?

ELIJAH. The only way to answer mob violence is through preaching the gospel of peace. I'd say it's time for me to be a missionary.

JANE. Here?

ELIJAH. Back east, maybe.

JANE. Good time to get away.

ELIJAH. No, ma'am. I ain't runnin'.

JANE. This be your third mission for the Church.

ELIJAH. That's right.

JANE. You know, everybody colored thinks of you like the best we got.

ELIJAH. That's sad news indeed.

JANE. I think you might be our best. If you undertake another mission, I know it's out of true desire, not just to prove yourself.

ELIJAH. The Lord will prove me. Now before I leave, I must ask you: Do you understand your position?

JANE. Pardon me?

ELIJAH. You and me, Jane James, we the only colored folks in this whole valley who knowed Brother Joseph Smith.

JANE. Best man I ever knew. That lovely hand—he'd reach it out to me just like I was his child.

ELIJAH. We the only colored folks here who got us patriarchal blessin's from the Smiths themselves. Father Smith blessed me, and said I was like his own son.

JANE. Joseph's brother—Hyrum—blessed me.

ELIJAH. We the only colored folks here with such memories and such position. We got a little voice. Now, you know I've asked time and again for my blessin's in the temple. I doubt I'll even be alive to see the temple when it's finished, but you likely will be. Ask for your blessings, sister. Don't let the petitions stop just because I'm gone. Go visit President Taylor, and keep askin'.

JANE. I will do that. Elder Abel, you'll be missed. Wherever your mission takes you, I hope you find yourself among friends.

ELIJAH. I hope the same for you. I been prayin' for you since all your troubles began.

JANE. My troubles began before you ever met me.

ELIJAH. But the worst ones, they come late in life, ain't that so? I prayed many a prayer for you.

JANE. It may surprise you to know it, but I have always been aware of your prayers. There was days I felt your prayers right in my house. Days I heard your voice, the very words you was speakin', though you was miles away. There was days when I was most alone that the angels carried your blessin's to me. And I thank you. I ask the good Lord to bless you.

    ELIJAH *steps back as* JANE *exits.*

MARY ANN. *(Entering in angelic robes as chorus sings.)* Swing low, sweet chariot,

    Coming for to carry me home.

    Swing low, sweet chariot,

    Coming for to carry me home. *(Humming continues.)*

ELIJAH. It's Christmas morning, ain't it?

MARY ANN. Hello, my dear.

ELIJAH. Suddenly, I am sick as a dog.

MARY ANN. Oh Elijah, I ain't accustomed to this.

ELIJAH. To what? You never see me sick, or you never took to hauntin' your own husband?

MARY ANN. Never took to hauntin' nobody.

ELIJAH. You doin' fine! And Lawd, Lawd, I'm seeing my first angel! Hope I ain't dreamin'.

MARY ANN. No, sir, you ain't dreamin'. You dyin'.

ELIJAH. Oh. That was a pretty bold message.

MARY ANN. Too bold? I'm never sure what to say.

ELIJAH. No, not too bold. Just the right amount of bold for a hauntin' angel such as yourself. So I'm dyin'. You know, I never thought those words would sound so good! Hold my hand, would you? Just lead me home. *(Looking back towards* JANE.*)* Now, Jane, you take care of yourself! It's time! Get up your courage, woman! There's work for you to do yet—and you promised me you'd do it!

JANE *stands resolutely.*

SCENE 7

Lights up on AGNES THOMAS *at a table.*

JANE. *(Crossing to* AGNES.*)* Sister Agnes?

AGNES. *(Rushes to her and embraces her like a true friend.)* Oh Jane! I can't tell you how good it is to see you. I must say, the laundress Tom found is nothing like you. Look at my dress!

JANE. It could use a bit more scrubbing on the washboard.

AGNES. Nothing's been the same since you left us.

JANE. Well, ma'am, if you recall, it wasn't entirely my desire—

AGNES. *(Near tears and surprised at her own joy.)* I feel so happy to see you. I've missed you, Jane! Now tell me why you're here.

JANE. It's what you said before about teaching me to write. Or maybe you could write something for me. You see, I need to send a letter of great import. To the president of the church.

AGNES. To President Taylor? Oh my. *(She takes out a quill and paper.)* Go on, then. You say the words and I'll write them. That's the least one friend can do for another.

JANE. *(Pacing.)* What I want to say is:

Dear Brother—

SINGERS *begin "Balm in Gilead" under dialogue.*

SINGERS. There is a balm in Gilead
    To make the wounded whole.
    There is a balm in Gilead
    To heal the sin-sick soul.
    Sometimes I feel discouraged,
    And think my work's in vain,
    But then the Holy Spirit
    Revives my soul again.

JANE. I called at your house last Thursday to have conversation with you concerning my future salvation. I did not explain my feelings or wishes to you. I realize my race and color and can't expect my endowments as others who are white. (ANGUS CANNON *comes on stage as* AGNES *continues writing.*) My race was handed down through the flood. And God promised Abraham that in his seed all the nations of the earth should be blessed. As this is the fullness of all dispensations—is there no blessing for me? I, with my father's family, came from Connecticut 42 years ago. I am the only one of my father's family that kept the faith. You know my history! According to the best of my ability, I have lived to all the requirements of the gospel.

Lights fade out on AGNES *and focus in two spots on* JANE JAMES *and* ANGUS CANNON.

ANGUS CANNON. *(Tenderly.)* Sister Jane, you must be content with what you have!

JANE. Emma Smith came to me and asked me how I would like to be adopted to them as a child. I was so green I did not give her a decided answer, and then Joseph died. If I could be adopted to him as a child, my soul would be satisfied!

ANGUS CANNON. I am your servant and brother in the gospel.

JANE. Please excuse me taking the liberty of writing to you—but be a brother! Show me kindness! I think you are somewhat acquainted with me. I lived in the Prophet's family!

ANGUS CANNON. I enclose you your recommend properly signed, which will entitle you to enter the temple to be baptized and confirmed for your dead kindred. You must be content with this privilege, awaiting further instructions from the Lord to his servants. Angus M. Cannon—Stake President, speaking for John Taylor.

JANE. *(Taking the recommend with joy, then becoming more serious.)* I remain your sister in the gospel—Jane E. James. I am colored.

ELIJAH ABEL—*in angelic robes—enters.*

ELIJAH. Good effort, sister. I didn't think you'd get everything you wanted, but you got something, didn't you! Don't give up, now. Keep up that petition!

JANE. Excuse me, sir?

ELIJAH. Oh, I haven't even introduced myself. I'm just a messenger. Come to tell you, you got company.

SCENE 8

ISAAC *comes onstage, aged and hunched down.*

JANE. Do I know you—Isaac! Is that really you?

ISAAC. *(Looking himself over.)* I'm pretty sure it is.

JANE. Y' ain't lookin' so good.

ISAAC. Ain't feelin' so good either. And I know I don't deserve a thing.

JANE. I might have to agree with you there. Now you come inside. You need to warm up and clean up. Let me draw you some warm water for a bath. Stove's already hot. I got me a good stove. It has a water bin.

ISAAC. *(Entering.)* I'm glad you got a good stove. *(Awkward pause.)* So, how's the children?

JANE. Well, they growed up.

ISAAC. Oh. I guess that makes sense.

JANE. Where's that gold surrey you told me you'd be drivin'?

ISAAC. I lost it. Janey, I been wanderin' in the wilderness. Decided it was my time to die.

JANE. You decided?

ISAAC. Been persuaded. I think God's infected my body with something or other goin' kill me.

JANE. Sorry to hear that. You in a lot of pain, then?

ISAAC. Quite a bit. I decided I didn't want to die alone.

JANE. You claimin' company for that trip?

ISAAC. Jane, you all I got in this world.

JANE. Are you askin' me to take you back, Mr. James?

ISAAC. Askin' for your mercy is all. You always had a strong tongue and a soft heart. I told myself you was probably like that still. You'd give me a sermon first, but maybe a bed afterwards.

JANE. Not my bed! We divorced, sir!

ISAAC. I ain't strong enough to take you on in bed anyway, Janey Liz—even if we was married. Just a place by the fire'd suit me fine. I only—I want to be with you before I pass.

JANE. We didn't part on the best terms.

ISAAC. I been movin' from moment to moment and dream to dream—like a ship that's tossed and driven.

    SINGERS *quietly under dialogue.*

SINGERS. Like a ship that's tossed and driven . . .

    Battered by an angry sea

    When the storms of life are raging

    And their fury falls on me.

    I wonder what I have done

    That makes this race so hard to run.

    Then I say to my soul, "Take courage—

    The Lord will make a way somehow."

    The Lord will make a way somehow

    When beneath the cross I bow.

    He will take away each sorrow

    Let him have your burdens now.

    When the load bears down so heavy,

    The weight is shown upon my brow,

    There's a sweet relief in knowing—

    The Lord will make a way somehow.

JANE. I am sorry for you, Isaac.

ISAAC. I don't imagine you can ever forgive me.

JANE. It does seem a tall order. But there's a way for most everything.

ISAAC. Why Janey, you done got old.

JANE. Well, with such a compliment as that, a woman may not know how to respond.

ISAAC. And you are beautiful with them wrinkles.

JANE. Glad you think so. You brought on a good many of them.

ISAAC. I did fine work, then. I see all our years together. They etched right there into your forehead. And here you are—spry and fiesty!

JANE. And here you are.

ISAAC. After I left you—oh, Janey, how have you survived?

JANE. I don't know. I just keep putting one foot in front of the other. My feet get to bleeding sometimes, Jesus heals them sometimes, and sometimes He lets them build scars. Most times, He just helps me endure. He has blessed me in ways I can't even explain. If I listed everything I've suffered, you'd think God was keeping his distance out of spite. But He's here. I feel Him here.

ISAAC. Me, too. Maybe because I'm with you again. Jane, I tell you with all the truth one sinful old man can muster: I love you more than I have ever loved another human being. I know I've hurt you—

JANE. Hush, now. I don't believe I'd like to dwell on sorrow. Let me draw you that bath, and when you're clean and rested, I can feed you some cornbread and water.

ANGUS CANNON *comes onstage as* ISAAC *exits.*

JANE. *(Stepping forward.)* Excuse me for bothering you. I had the privilege of being baptized for my dead in October last, yet I must ask again: Could I get adopted to Brother Joseph and Sister Emma as their child? And could my dear husband, Isaac James, get adopted, too?

ANGUS CANNON. *(Tenderly.)* You have been told before to be content with what you've already been given.

JANE. I am anxious for my welfare for the future!

ANGUS CANNON. *(Firmly but compassionately.)* Jane James, you must wait.

ANGUS *exits.* JANE *goes inside.* ELIJAH *knocks.*

SCENE 9

ELIJAH. I've come for Isaac.

JANE. Pardon me?

ELIJAH. He's been here long enough. His time's up now.

JANE. May I tell him who's calling?

ELIJAH. He knows.

JANE. Isaac, you have a caller.

ISAAC *appears.*

ELIJAH. Just up these stairs, Brother James. You'll be feeling better presently. *(*ISAAC *exits.)* So you ready for another visitor, sister?

JANE. I do know you, don't I?

ELIJAH. If you'll look down the street, you'll see your brother.

    ELIJAH *and* ISAAC *go up the stairs.* JANE *sees* LEW.

LEW. *(As* JANE *embraces him.)* Careful, woman! You must think I'm one oak of a man!

JANE. Lew! I knew you'd come to me!

LEW. Thought you could use some help.

JANE. I certainly could! I've been meaning to take up dance all these years and I never did get the chance.

SCENE 10

ELIJAH. *(Carrying two doilies.)* Now, I didn't embroider these myself. Wish I had, though. Ain't they pretty? This represents the seat in the tabernacle where Lew and Jane sat every Sunday for the next many years. Jane embroidered the seat covers. Her sight failed her after a while. Old age does bring its difficulties. She called that the hardest trial she had ever been called to bear. *(*JANE'*s bed set up. She is lying down, Lew and two young women sit near her.)* So, since Jane could no longer read, young women came to her home and read to her—scriptures mostly. Now this particular young woman *(he gestures to* YOUNG ELIZA.*)* is a descendant of Eliza Partridge Lyman, who you've met before. The other is Jane's own great-grand-daughter, Malvina. Jane's already requested the story of Joseph and the coat of many colors for today's reading.

ELIZA. *(Reading;* MALVINA *looks bored.)* "For indeed I was stolen away out of the land of my fathers, and here also have I done nothing that they should put me into the dungeon."

LEW. *(Always loud—apparently deaf.)* I know this part. The baker forgets Old Joseph entire.

JANE. Don't yell, Lew. Just because you can't hear your own self don't mean you ain't shoutin'.

LEW. *(To* ELIZA.*)* Speak up, would you?

ELIZA. *(Quite loudly.)* "Yet did not the chief butler remember Joseph, but forgat him."

MALVINA. Ain't that just the way?

LEW. What did I tell you? That dumb baker forgets Old Joseph entire—after all Joseph done for him!

JANE. Hush, Lew! *(To* ELIZA.*)* Read when Joseph reveals himself to his brothers. I love that.

LEW. There's Joseph all dressed up Egyptian, speaking Egyptian too, pretending—and his brothers, they got no idea, no idea at all!

JANE. Lew!

MALVINA. Haven't we been here long enough?

ELIZA. *(Handing* MALVINA *the Bible.)* Malvina, would you like to read it?

MALVINA. *(Bitter—but taking the book.)* I would not!

ELIZA. Here, I'll read.

MALVINA. No. I can do it. *(She struggles.)* "And there stood no man with him . . ."

ELIJAH. *(Standing over her shoulder, whispering the words—*MALVINA *is somehow aware of him.)* "While Joseph made himself known unto his brethren."

ELIZA. *(Condescending.)* You read that just fine!

JANE. Eliza, your voice is so much like your grandmother's. I wonder if you look like her too. I can't see you well.

ELIZA. I'm told I do resemble her.

JANE. Then you're lucky. Lew, does Malvina look like me?

LEW. No. She's lots prettier than you was.

JANE. Your memory is abandoning you, Mr. Manning.

LEW. And your imagination is gettin' better by the minute.

JANE. My descendant and Eliza Lyman's—right here with me! What if I hadn't taken Sister Lyman my flour that day, and her baby had died. Perhaps the baby who grew up to be your papa, Eliza! Then you wouldn't be here reading me scriptures!

ELIZA. You took my great-grandmother flour?

JANE. She was starving.

ELIJAH. And so was her baby. No food nor any way to get it.

JANE. *(Looking at* ELIJAH.*)* I do know you!

MALVINA *looks up at* ELIJAH—*apparently seeing him.*

ELIZA. *(Startled—to* LEW.*)* Who's she talking to?

LEW. Oh, she just having visions. She gets 'em. I'm used to it. She spoke in tongues once. 'Bout scared me out of my skin.

ELIJAH. Of course, you know me!

SARAH *and* ANGELINE *appear. If the two-tier stage is set up, they descend from the upper tier.*

JANE. Sarah? Angeline?

SARAH. You know what you should do, Jane? Let go of that old body!

ANGELINE. Hardly worth a thing by now! Honey, let it go!

    PHYLLIS *enters. Song behind dialogue: "Precious Lord" (second verse—"When my way grows drear")*

JANE. *(Seeing* PHYLLIS.*)* Is that Mama?

SARAH. 'Course it's Mama! You think she'd miss your arrival?

JANE. Why Mama, you younger than I am! My, my—how beautiful you are!

ANGELINE. Well what you expect? Them's the Manning good looks!

JANE. *(To* ELIZA *and* MALVINA.*)* I'm over eighty years old.

LEW. *(Also to* ELIZA *and* MALVINA.*)* You ain't read her what she wanted yet!

JANE. Not the first time I didn't get what I wanted. But I wait. Still waiting.

SARAH. We waitin', too!

JANE. Well, wait just a minute more!

SARAH. I heard that so many times! You always had to look perfect before you'd leave the house. Honey, you can't wear your velvet hat up here. Ain't nobody wearin' velvet.

JANE. Now that's a shame.

LEW. Read her what she wanted. Let her have her wish.

JANE. Oh, yes! Lord Jesus, let me have my wish!

MALVINA. *(Reading.* ELIJAH *prompts her.)* "And there stood no man with him, while Joseph made himself known unto his brethren—"

ELIJAH AND MALVINA. *(Together.)* "And he wept aloud, and the Egyptians and the house of Pharaoh heard. And Joseph said unto his brethren—"

JANE. *(With all her strength.)* "Brothers, I am Joseph, whom you cast into a pit and sold as a slave."

ELIJAH. That's right.

JANE. I know who you are.

ELIJAH. I am Elijah.

JANE. And I am Jane. Come near to me—both of you young women. Listen. God sent me before you to preserve you. I want to say something and I want you all to hear it: My faith in the gospel of Jesus Christ of Latter-day Saints is as strong today—nay, it is, if possible, stronger than it was the day I was first baptized. I pay my tithes and offerings, keep the Word of Wisdom, I go to bed early and rise early. I try in my feeble way to set a good example to all.

SARAH. Come on now, Jane. It's your time.

    JANE *sits up, stretching her hands to the girls.*

JANE. Receive my gift.

SARAH. You've waited long enough, sister.

JANE *rises and joins her family—including* ISAAC.

ELIJAH. Now you all know that many things have changed for us since the days of this story. There's still struggles, don't get me wrong. But I haven't wearied of the struggles. Have you, Jane?

JANE. Wearied? Why, I'm stronger than I been in years! Besides which, I can see like my eyes was new! All these folks are remembering me—I feel near resurrected!

ELIJAH. Me too. In fact— *(Singing.)*

> I don't feel no ways tired
>
> I've come too far
>
> From where I started from.
>
> Nobody told me that the road would be easy.
>
> I don't believe He bought me this far
>
> To leave me.
>
> I don't feel no ways tired. *(Repeat.)*

CHORUS AND FULL CAST. *(Finale:)* I don't believe he brought me this far

> I don't believe he brought me this far
>
> I don't believe he brought me this far . . .
>
> Just to leave me.

Curtain.

THE END

For parties interested in obtaining performance rights for any of the plays contained in this volume, do not contact Zarahemla Books. Rather, rights can be obtained by contacting and negotiating with the playwrights individually through the following channels:

James Arrington, *J. Golden* — blueskyerone@yahoo.com

J. Scott Bronson, *Stones* — oldfatandtired@gmail.com

Thom Duncan, *Matters of the Heart* — thomduncan@gmail.com

Robert Elliott, *Fires of the Mind* — relliott@ku.edu
Department of English
Wescoe Hall
1445 Jayhawk Blvd., Room 3001
Lawrence, KS 66045-7594

Susan Howe, *Burdens of Earth* — susan_howe@byu.edu
English Department, 4133 JFSB
Brigham Young University
Provo, UT 84602

Melissa Leilani Larson, *Martyrs' Crossing* — mel_leilani@me.com

Thomas Rogers, *Huebener* — thomasfrogers@gmail.com

Tim Slover, *Hancock County* — slover31@comcast.net

Eric Samuelsen, *Gadianton* — ericsamuelsen@gmail.com

Mahonri Stewart, *Farewell to Eden* — mahonristewart@gmail.com

Margaret Blair Young, *I Am Jane* — margaret_young@byu.edu

www.ingramcontent.com/pod-product-compliance
Lightning Source LLC
Chambersburg PA
CBHW032221230426
43666CB00033B/270